Web Coding & Development

ALL-IN-ONE

2nd Edition

by Paul McFedries

A Wiley Brand

Web Coding & Development All-in-One For Dummies®, 2nd Edition

Published by: **John Wiley & Sons, Inc.**, 111 River Street, Hoboken, NJ 07030-5774, www.wiley.com

Copyright © 2024 by John Wiley & Sons, Inc., Hoboken, New Jersey

Media and software compilation copyright © 2024 by John Wiley & Sons, Inc. All rights reserved.

Published simultaneously in Canada

No part of this publication may be reproduced, stored in a retrieval system or transmitted in any form or by any means, electronic, mechanical, photocopying, recording, scanning or otherwise, except as permitted under Sections 107 or 108 of the 1976 United States Copyright Act, without the prior written permission of the Publisher. Requests to the Publisher for permission should be addressed to the Permissions Department, John Wiley & Sons, Inc., 111 River Street, Hoboken, NJ 07030, (201) 748-6011, fax (201) 748-6008, or online at http://www.wiley.com/go/permissions.

Trademarks: Wiley, For Dummies, the Dummies Man logo, Dummies.com, Making Everything Easier, and related trade dress are trademarks or registered trademarks of John Wiley & Sons, Inc. and may not be used without written permission. All other trademarks are the property of their respective owners. John Wiley & Sons, Inc. is not associated with any product or vendor mentioned in this book.

For general information on our other products and services, please contact our Customer Care Department within the U.S. at 877-762-2974, outside the U.S. at 317-572-3993, or fax 317-572-4002. For technical support, please visit https://hub.wiley.com/community/support/dummies.

Wiley publishes in a variety of print and electronic formats and by print-on-demand. Some material included with standard print versions of this book may not be included in e-books or in print-on-demand. If this book refers to media such as a CD or DVD that is not included in the version you purchased, you may download this material at http://booksupport.wiley.com. For more information about Wiley products, visit www.wiley.com.

Library of Congress Control Number: 2023951076

ISBN 978-1-394-19702-6 (pbk); ISBN 978-1-394-19704-0 (ebk); ISBN 978-1-394-19703-3 (ebk)

SKY10062921_121823

Contents at a Glance

Table of Contents

Introduction

When the web first came to the attention of the world's non-geeks back in the mid-1990s, the vastness and variety of its treasures were a wonder to behold. However, it didn't take long before a few courageous and intrepid souls dug a little deeper into this phenomenon and discovered something truly phenomenal: *They* could make web pages, too!

Why was that so amazing? Well, think back to (or, if you're not old enough, *imagine*) those old days and consider, in particular, what it meant to create what we now call *content*. Consider television shows, radio programs, magazines, newspapers, books, and the other media of the time. The one thing they all had in common was that their creation was a decidedly *un*common thing. It required a team of professionals, a massive distribution system, and a lot of money. In short, it wasn't something that your average Okie from Muskogee would have any hope of duplicating.

The web appeared to change all that because learning HTML was within the grasp of all of us who could feed ourselves, it had a built-in massive distribution system (the internet, natch), and it required little or no money. For the first time in history, content was democratized and was no longer defined as the sole province of governments and mega-corporations.

Then reality set in.

People soon realized that merely building a website wasn't enough to attract "eyeballs," as the marketers say. A site had to have interesting, useful, or fun content, or people would stay away in droves. Not only that, but this good content had to be combined with a solid site design, which meant that web designers needed a thorough knowledge of HTML and CSS.

But, alas, eventually even all that was not enough. To make their websites dynamic and interesting, to make their sites easy to navigate, and to give their sites those extra bells and whistles that surfers had come to expect, people needed something more than content, HTML, and CSS.

That missing link was *code*.

What we've all learned the hard way over the past few years is that you simply can't put together a world-class website unless you have some coding prowess in your site design toolkit. You need to know how to program your way out of the basic problems that afflict most sites; how to use scripting to go beyond the inherent limitations of HTML and CSS; and how to use code to send and receive data from a web server. And it isn't enough just to copy the generic scripts available on the web and paste them into your pages. Most of those scripts are poorly written, and they invariably need some customization to work properly on your site.

About This Book

In this book, I give you a complete education on web coding and development. You learn how to set up the tools you need, how to use HTML and CSS to design and build your site, how to use JavaScript to program your pages, and how to use PHP and MySQL to program your web server. I show you that these technologies aren't hard to learn, and that even the greenest rookie programmers can learn how to put together web pages that will amaze their family and friends (and themselves).

If you're looking for lots of programming history, computer science theory, and long-winded explanations of concepts, you won't find them here. My philosophy throughout this book comes from Linus Torvalds, the creator of the Linux operating system: "Talk is cheap. Show me the code." I explain what needs to be explained and then I move on without further ado (or, most of the time, without any ado at all) to examples and scripts that do more to illuminate a concept that any verbose explanations I could muster (and believe me, I can muster verbosity with the best of them).

How you approach this book depends on your current level of web coding expertise (or lack thereof):

>> If you're just starting out, begin at the beginning with Book 1 and work at your own pace sequentially through to Books 2 and 3. This approach will give you all the knowledge you need to pick and choose what you want to learn throughout the rest of the book.

>> If you know HTML and CSS, you can probably get away with taking a fast look at Book 2 and then settling in with Book 3 and beyond.

>> If you've done some JavaScript coding, I suggest working quickly through the material in Book 3, and then digging into the first two chapters of Book 5 to bring your debugging skills up to snuff. You'll then be ready to branch out and explore the rest of the book as you see fit.

>> If you're a relatively experienced JavaScript programmer, use Books 3 and 5 as a refresher, and then tackle Book 4 to learn how to code the back end. I have a few tricks in there that you might find interesting. After that, feel free to consider the rest of the book as a kind of coding smorgasbord that you can sample as your web development taste buds dictate.

As I began updating this edition of the book, the world was awash in posts and talk and endless speculation about artificial intelligence, to the point where it seemed we'd soon be welcoming our new AI overlords. That's not likely to happen anytime soon, but AI is here to stay and has already established itself as a significant part of many people's workaday routines.

I've been as enamored of ChatGPT and its ilk as the biggest AI boosters. I use AI for entertainment and curiosity, but I don't use it for work. That is to say, not one word of the text, code, or examples used in this book has been generated by AI. Everything you read here is, for good or ill, the product of my warped-from-birth brain.

Foolish Assumptions

This book is not a primer on the internet or using the World Wide Web. It's a coding and development book, pure and simple, where I assume the following:

>> You know how to operate a basic text editor and how to get around the operating system and file system on your computer.

>> You have an internet connection.

>> You know how to use your web browser.

Yep, that's it.

If you've never done a stitch of computer programming before, even if you're not quite sure what programming really is, don't worry about it for a second because I had you in mind when I wrote this book. For too many years, programming has been the property of hackers and other technowizards. That made some sense because the programming languages they were using — with bizarre names such as C++ and Perl — were exceedingly difficult to learn and even harder to master.

This book's main coding technologies — HTML, CSS, JavaScript, PHP, and MySQL — are different. They're nowhere near as hard to learn as those for-nerds-only languages. I honestly believe that *anyone* can become a savvy and successful web coder, and this book is, I hope, the proof of that assertion. If you just follow along, examine my code carefully (particularly in the first few chapters), and practice what you learn, you *will* master web coding and development.

What if you've done some programming in the past? For example, you might have dipped a toe or two in the JavaScript waters already, or you might have dabbled with HTML and CSS. Will this book be too basic for you? No, not at all. In this book, I provide you with a ton of truly useful examples that you can customize and incorporate into your own site. The book's first few chapters start slowly to avoid scaring off those new to this programming business. But once you get past the basics, I introduce you to lots of great techniques and tricks that will take your web coding skills to a higher level.

Icons Used in This Book

REMEMBER

This icon points out juicy tidbits that are likely to be repeatedly useful to you — so please don't forget them.

TIP

Think of these icons as the fodder of advice columns. They offer (I hope) wise advice or a bit more information about a topic under discussion.

WARNING

Look out! In this book, you see this icon when I'm trying to help you avoid mistakes that can cost you time, money, or embarrassment.

TECHNICAL STUFF

When you see this icon, you've come across material that isn't critical to understand but will satisfy the curious. Think "inquiring minds want to know" when you see this icon.

Beyond the Book

Some extra content for this book is available on the web. Go online to find the following:

>> **The examples used in the book:** You can find these on my website:

```
https://paulmcfedries.com/books/web-coding-dev-aio-fd-2e/
```

Alternatively, the examples are also available via the book's GitHub repository:

```
https://github.com/paulmcfe/web-coding-and-dev-fd-2e
```

The examples are organized by book and then by chapter within each book. For each example, you can view the code, copy it to your computer's clipboard, and run the code in the browser.

» **The WebDev Workshop:** To view a few web coding tools and tutorials, as well as try your own code and see instant results, fire up the following site:

```
https://webdevworkshop.io
```

You won't break anything, so feel free to use the site to run some experiments and play around with HTML, CSS, and JavaScript.

1

Getting Ready to Code for the Web

Contents at a Glance

IN THIS CHAPTER

» **Learning how the web works**

» **Understanding the front-end technologies of HTML and CSS**

» **Understanding the back-end technologies of MySQL and PHP**

» **Figuring out how JavaScript fits into all of this**

» **Learning about dynamic web pages, web apps, and mobile web apps**

Chapter **1**

How Web Coding and Development Work

More than mere consumers of technology, we are makers, *adapting technology to our needs and integrating it into our lives.*

— DALE DOUGHERTY

The 1950s were a hobbyist's paradise with magazines such as *Mechanix Illustrated* and *Popular Science* showing the do-it-yourselfer how to build a go-kart for the kids and how to soup up a lawnmower with an actual motor! Seventy years later, we're now firmly entrenched in the age of do-it-yourself tech, where folks indulge their inner geek to engage in various forms of digital tinkering and hacking. The personification of this high-tech hobbyist renaissance is the *maker,* a modern artisan who lives to create things rather than merely consume them. Today's makers exhibit a wide range of talents, but the skill most sought-after not only by would-be makers themselves but by the people who hire them is web coding and development.

Have you ever visited a website and thought, "Hey, I can do better than that!"? Have you found yourself growing tired of merely reading text and viewing images that someone else has put on the web? Is there something creative in you — stories, images, expertise, opinions — that you want to share with the world? If you answered a resounding "Yes!" to any of these questions, congratulations: You have everything you need to get started with web coding and development. You have, in short, the makings of a maker.

The Nuts and Bolts of Web Coding and Development

If, as the King said very gravely in Lewis Carroll's *Alice in Wonderland*, it's best to "begin at the beginning," you've come to the right place. My goal here is to get you off on the right foot by showing you what web coding and web development are.

How the web works

Before you can understand web coding and development, you need to take a step back and understand a bit about how the web itself works. In particular, you need to know what happens behind the scenes when you click a link or type a web page address into your browser. Fortunately, you don't need to be a network engineer to understand this stuff, because I can explain the basics without much in the way of jargon. Here's a high-level (and not at all serious) blow-by-blow account of what happens:

1. **You tell the web browser the web page you want to visit.**

   You do that either by clicking a link to the page or by typing the location — known as the *uniform resource locator* or *URL* (usually pronounced "you-are-ell," but also sometimes "earl") — into the browser's address bar (see Figure 1-1).

FIGURE 1-1: One way to get to a web page is to type the URL in the browser's address bar.

New Tab

https://webdevworkshop.io/code/index.html

2. The browser decodes the URL.

Decoding the URL means two things. First, the browser sees what type of resource you're requesting by checking the prefix of the URL; this is usually `http://` or `https://`, both of which indicate that the resource is a web page. Second, it gets the URL's domain name — the `something.com` or `whatever.org` part — and asks the *domain name system* (DNS) to translate this into a unique location — called the IP (Internet Protocol) address — for the web server that hosts the page (see Figure 1-2).

FIGURE 1-2: The browser extracts the prefix, domain, and the server address from the URL.

Decoding https://webdevworkshop.io/code/index.html...

Results:

Prefix: `https://`
Domain name: `webdevworkshop.io`
Web server IP address: `172.64.80.1`

3. The browser contacts the web server and requests the web page.

With the web server's unique IP address in hand, the web browser sets up a communications channel with the server and then uses that channel to send along a request for the web page (see Figure 1-3).

FIGURE 1-3: The browser asks the web server for the web page.

Dear 172.64.80.1:

At your earliest convenience, please send me the webdevworkshop.io web page located at code/index.html.

Sincerely,
W. Browser

4. The web server decodes the page request.

Decoding the page request involves a number of steps. First, if the web server is shared between multiple user accounts, the server begins by locating the user account that owns the requested page. The server then uses the page address to find the directory that holds the page and the file in which the page code is stored (see Figure 1-4).

Decoding https://webdevworkshop.io/code/index.html...

Results:

User account: `paulmcfedries`
Directory: `code`
Filename: `index.html`

FIGURE 1-4: The server uses the page request to get the account, directory, and filename.

5. **The web server sends the web page file to the web browser (see Figure 1-5).**

```
Dear W. Browser:

Thank you for contacting us. Here is
the file you requested. Let us know
if you need anything else.

Best,
webdevworkshop.io Web Server
```

FIGURE 1-5: The web server sends the requested web page file to the browser.

6. **The web browser decodes the web page file.**

   Decoding the page file means looking for text to display, instructions on how to display that text, and other resources required by the page, such as images and fonts (see Figure 1-6).

Decoding https://webdevworkshop.io/code/index.html...

Results:

Text: Received
Formatting: Request `styles.css`
Images: Request `logo.png`
Audio: None
Video: None
Data: Request metadata for code tutorials

FIGURE 1-6: The web browser scours the page file to see if it needs anything else from the server.

7. **If the web page requires more resources, the web browser asks the server to pass along those resources (see Figure 1-7).**
8. **For each of the requested resources, the web server locates the associated file and sends it to the browser (see Figure 1-8).**
9. **The web browser gathers all the text, images, and other resources and displays the page in all its digital splendor in the browser's content window (see Figure 1-9).**

FIGURE 1-7:
The web browser
goes back to the
server to ask for
the other data
needed to display
the web page.

Dear 172.64.80.1:

Thank you for the page file. If it's not too
much trouble, could you please also send
along the following items:

styles.css
logo.png
Code tutorials metadata from the database

W. Browser

FIGURE 1-8:
The web server
sends the
browser the rest
of the requested
files.

```
Dear W. Browser:

You're very welcome. We're here to serve!
We're gathering your order and will send
along the extra data you requested shortly.

Best,
webdevworkshop.io Web Server
```

FIGURE 1-9:
At long last, the
web browser
displays the
web page.

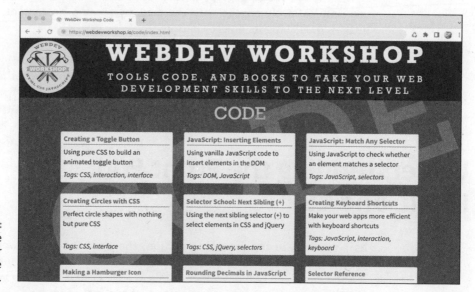

How the web works, take two

Another way to look at this process is to think of the web as a giant mall or shopping center, where each website is a storefront in that mall. When you request a web page from a particular site, the browser takes you into that site's store and asks the clerk for the web page. The clerk goes into the back of the store, locates the page, and hands it to the browser. The browser checks the page and asks for any other needed files, which the clerk retrieves from the back. This process is repeated until the browser has everything it needs, and it then puts all the page pieces together for you, right there in the front of the store.

This metaphor might seem a bit silly, but it serves to introduce yet another metaphor, which itself illustrates one of the most important concepts in web development. In the same way that our website store has a front and a back, so, too, is web development separated into a front end and a back end:

>> **Front end:** That part of the web page that the web browser displays in the browser window. That is, the front end is the page stuff you see and interact with.

>> **Back end:** That part of the web page that resides on the web server. That is, the back end is the page stuff that the server gathers based on the requests it receives from the browser.

As a consumer of web pages, you only ever deal with the front end, and even then you only passively engage with the page by reading its content, looking at its images, or clicking its links or buttons.

However, as a maker of web pages — that is, as a web developer — your job entails dealing with both the front end and the back end. Moreover, that job includes coding what others see on the front end, coding how the server gathers its data on the back end, and coding the intermediate tasks that tie the two together.

Understanding the Front End: HTML and CSS

As I mention in the preceding section, the *front end* of the web development process involves what users see and interact with in the web browser window. It's the job of the web developer to take a page design — which you might come up with yourself but is more often something cooked up by a creative type who specializes in web design — and make it web-ready. Getting a design ready for the web means translating the design into the code required for the browser to display the page somewhat faithfully. (I added the hedge word *somewhat* there because it's not always easy to take a design that looks great in Photoshop or Illustrator and make it look just as good on the web. However, with the techniques you learn in this book, you'll almost always be able to come pretty close.)

You need code to create the front end of a web page because without it your page will be quite dull. For example, consider the following text (found in bk01ch01/example01.html in this book's example files):

> There once was a boy named Flibbertigibbet. No, his parents most certainly did not give him that name when he was born. That would have been cruel, and they were really quite nice people. They actually named him Filbert. Yes, they named him after a nut. They were nice people, but they were also silly people who often didn't think things through.
>
> One day, when Filbert was about a year old, his mother was bouncing him on her knee when, mid-dandle, he smiled and said "Momma!" Oh, his mother was overjoyed that not only had Filbert said his first word but that word had been "Momma." She called her husband over and Filbert looked right at him and said "Dadda!" Amazing! They began pointing at him and repeating "Filbert!, Filbert!" to get him to say his own name. After a while, Filbert creased his brow as though concentrating ever so seriously, and then said "Flibbertigibbet!"
>
> Their jaws dropped. How could a boy so young know such a word? Ah, therein lies a tale. Unbeknownst to his parents, Filbert's maternal grandmother had been secretly whispering "You're my little Flibbertigibbet" in her grandson's ear over and over since the day he was born. By the time he was a year old, the boy didn't know many things, but there was one thing he knew with unshakeable conviction: His name was Flibbertigibbet!

If you plop that text onto the web, you get the result shown in Figure 1-10. As you can see, the text is very plain, and the browser didn't even bother to include the paragraph breaks.

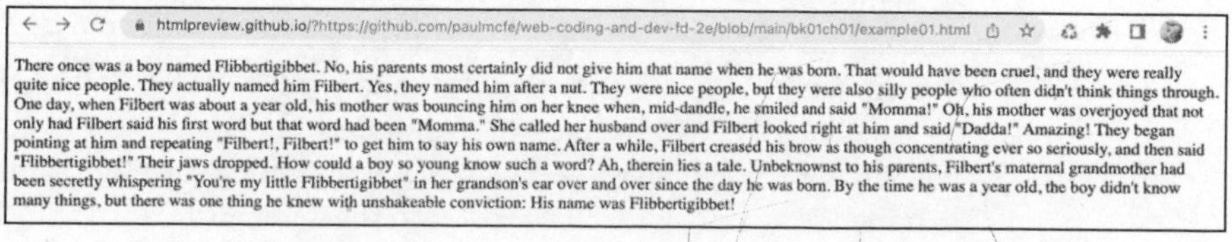

FIGURE 1-10: Text-only web pages are dishwater-dull.

So, if you can't just throw naked text onto the web, what's a would-be web developer to do? Ah, that's where you start earning your web scout merit badges by adding code that tells the browser how you want the text displayed. That code comes in two flavors: structure and formatting.

Adding structure: HTML

The first thing you usually do to code a web page is give it some structure. This means breaking up the text into paragraphs, adding special sections such as a header and footer, organizing text into bulleted or numbered lists, dividing the page into columns, and much more. The web coding technology that governs these and other web page structures is called (deep breath) *Hypertext Markup Language*, or *HTML*, for short.

HTML is a collection of special symbols called *tags* that you sprinkle strategically throughout the page. For example, if you want to tell the web browser that a particular chunk of text is a separate paragraph, you place the `<p>` tag (the p here is short for paragraph) before the text and the `</p>` tag after the text.

In the code that follows (check out bk01ch01/example02.html), I've added these paragraph tags to the plain text that I show earlier. As shown in Figure 1-11, the web browser displays the text as three separate paragraphs, no questions asked.

```
<p>
There once was a boy named Flibbertigibbet. No, his parents most
    certainly did not give him that name when he was born. That
    would have been cruel, and they were really quite nice people.
    They actually named him Filbert. Yes, they named him after a
    nut. They were nice people, but they were also silly people
    who often didn't think things through.
</p>
<p>
One day, when Filbert was about a year old, his mother was
    bouncing him on her knee when, mid-dandle, he smiled and
    said "Momma!" Oh, his mother was overjoyed that not only had
    Filbert said his first word but that word had been "Momma."
    She called her husband over and Filbert looked right at him
    and said "Dadda!" Amazing! They began pointing at him and
    repeating "Filbert!, Filbert!" to get him to say his own
    name. After a while, Filbert creased his brow as though
    concentrating ever so seriously, and then said
    "Flibbertigibbet!"
</p>
```

```
<p>
Their jaws dropped. How could a boy so young know such a word?
  Ah, therein lies a tale. Unbeknownst to his parents, Filbert's
maternal grandmother had been secretly whispering "You're my
little Flibbertigibbet" in her grandson's ear over and over
since the day he was born. By the time he was a year old, the
boy didn't know many things, but there was one thing he knew
with unshakeable conviction: His name was Flibbertigibbet!
</p>
```

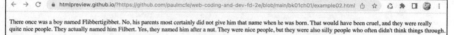

FIGURE 1-11:
Adding paragraph
tags to the text
separates the
text into three
paragraphs.

There once was a boy named Flibbertigibbet. No, his parents most certainly did not give him that name when he was born. That would have been cruel, and they were really quite nice people. They actually named him Filbert. Yes, they named him after a nut. They were nice people, but they were also silly people who often didn't think things through.

One day, when Filbert was about a year old, his mother was bouncing him on her knee when, mid-dandle, he smiled and said "Momma!" Oh, his mother was overjoyed that not only had Filbert said his first word but that word had been "Momma." She called her husband over and Filbert looked right at him and said "Dadda!" Amazing! They began pointing at him and repeating "Filbert!, Filbert!" to get him to say his own name. After a while, Filbert creased his brow as though concentrating ever so seriously, and then said "Flibbertigibbet!"

Their jaws dropped. How could a boy so young know such a word? Ah, therein lies a tale. Unbeknownst to his parents, Filbert's maternal grandmother had been secretly whispering "You're my little Flibbertigibbet" in her grandson's ear over and over since the day he was born. By the time he was a year old, the boy didn't know many things, but there was one thing he knew with unshakeable conviction: His name was Flibbertigibbet!

REMEMBER

HTML is one of the fundamental topics of web development, and you learn all about it in Book 2, Chapter 1.

Adding style: CSS

HTML takes care of the structure of the page, but if you want to change the formatting of the page, you need to turn to a second front-end technology: *cascading style sheets*, known almost universally as just *CSS*. With CSS in hand, you can play around with the page colors and fonts, you can add margins and borders around things, and you can mess with the position and size of page elements.

CSS consists of a large number of *properties* that enable you to customize many aspects of the page to make it look the way you want. For example, the width property lets you specify how wide a page element should be; the font-family property enables you to specify a typeface for an element; and the font-size property lets you dictate the type size of an element's text. Here's some CSS code that applies all three of these properties to every p element (that is, every <p> tag) that appears in a page (note that px is short for pixels):

```
p {
    width: 700px;
    font-family: sans-serif;
    font-size: 24px;
}
```

When used with the sample text from the previous two sections, you get the much nicer-looking text shown in Figure 1-12. (Also check out bk01ch01/example03.html.)

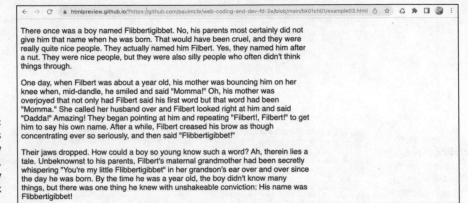

FIGURE 1-12: With the judicious use of a few CSS properties, you can greatly improve the look of a page.

REMEMBER

CSS is a cornerstone of web development. You learn much more about it in Book 2, Chapters 2, 3, and 4.

REMEMBER

You learn quite a bit of CSS in this book, but if you really want to dive deep into this crucial web development technology, see my book *HTML, CSS & JavaScript All-in-One For Dummies* (2023).

Understanding the Back End: PHP and MySQL

Many web pages are all about the front end. That is, they consist of nothing but text that has been structured by HTML tags and styled by CSS properties, plus a few extra files such as images and fonts. Sure, all these files are transferred from the web server to the browser, but that's the extent of the back end's involvement.

These simple pages are ideal when you have content that doesn't change very often, if ever. With these so-called *static* pages, you plop in your text, add some HTML and CSS, perhaps point to an image or two, and you're done. Static pages are awesome, by the way, which is why I talk about them in some detail in Book 6.

But another class of page has content that changes frequently. The content could be posts added once or twice a day, or sports or weather updates added once or twice an hour. With these so-called *dynamic* pages, you might have some text,

HTML, CSS, and other content that's static, but you almost certainly don't want to be updating the changing content by hand.

Rather than making constant manual changes to such pages, you can convince the back end to do it for you. You do that by taking advantage of two popular back-end technologies: MySQL and PHP.

Storing data on the server: MySQL

MySQL is a relational database management system that runs on the server. You use it to store the data you want to use as the source for some (or perhaps even all) of the data you want to display on your web page. Using a tool called Structured Query Language (SQL, pronounced "ess-kew-ell," or sometimes "sequel"), you can specify which subset of your data you want to use.

REMEMBER

If phrases such as "relational database management system" and "Structured Query Language" have you furrowing your brow, don't sweat it: I explain all in Book 4, Chapter 2.

Accessing data on the server: PHP

PHP is a programming language used on the server. It's a very powerful and full-featured language, but for the purposes of this book, you use PHP mostly to interact with MySQL databases. You can use PHP to extract from MySQL the subset of data you want to display, manipulate that data into a form that's readable by the front end, and then send the data to the browser.

REMEMBER

You learn about the PHP language in Book 4, Chapter 1, and you learn how to use PHP to access MySQL data in Book 4, Chapter 3.

How It All Fits Together: JavaScript

Okay, so now you have a front end consisting of HTML structure and CSS styling, and a back end consisting of MySQL data and PHP code. How do these two seemingly disparate worlds meet to create a full web page experience?

In the website-as-store metaphor that I introduce earlier in this chapter, I use the image of a store clerk taking an order from the web browser and then going into the back of the store to fulfill that order. That clerk is the obvious link between the front end and the back end, so what technology does that clerk represent? That would be JavaScript.

JavaScript is the secret sauce that brings the front end and the back end together to create the vast majority of the web pages you see today. JavaScript is a programming language and is the default language used for coding websites today. JavaScript is, first and foremost, a front-end web development language. That is, JavaScript runs inside the web browser and has access to everything on the page: the text, the images, the HTML tags, the CSS properties, and more. Having access to all the page stuff means that you can use code to manipulate, modify, and even add and delete web page elements.

But although JavaScript runs in the browser, it's also capable of reaching out to the server to access back-end stuff. For example, with JavaScript you can send data to the server to store that data in a MySQL database. Similarly, with JavaScript you can request data from the server and then use code to display that data on the web page.

REMEMBER

JavaScript is very powerful, very useful, and very cool, so Book 3 takes 11 full chapters to help you learn it well. Also, you learn how JavaScript acts as a bridge between the front end and the back end in Book 6, Chapter 1.

How Dynamic Web Pages Work

It's one thing to know about HTML and CSS and PHP and all the rest, but it's quite another to actually do something useful with these technologies. That, really, is the goal of this book, and to that end the book spends several chapters covering how to create wonderful things called dynamic web pages. A *dynamic web page* is one that includes content that, rather than being hard-wired into the page, is generated on-the-fly from the web server. This means the page content can change based on a request by the user, by data being added to or modified on the server, or in response to some event, such as the clicking of a button or link.

It likely sounds a bit like voodoo to you now, so perhaps a bit more detail is in order. For example, suppose you want to use a web page to display some data that resides on the server. Here's a general look at the steps involved in that process:

1. **JavaScript determines the data that it needs from the server.**

    JavaScript has various ways it can do this, such as extracting the information from the URL, reading an item the user has selected from a list, or responding to a click from the user.

2. **JavaScript sends a request for that data to the server.**

    In most cases, and certainly in every case you see in this book, JavaScript sends this request by calling a PHP script on the server.

3. **The PHP script receives the request and passes it along to MySQL.**

The PHP script uses the information obtained from JavaScript to create an SQL command that MySQL can understand.

4. **MySQL uses the SQL command to extract the required information from the database and then return that data to the PHP script.**

5. **The PHP script manipulates the returned MySQL data into a form that JavaScript can use.**

JavaScript can't read raw MySQL data, so one of PHP's most important tasks is to convert that data into a format called JavaScript Object Notation (JSON, for short, and pronounced like the name "Jason"), which JavaScript is on friendly terms with (see Book 6, Chapter 1 for more about this process).

6. **PHP sends the JSON data back to JavaScript.**

7. **JavaScript displays the data on the web page.**

One of the joys of JavaScript is that you get tremendous control over how you display the data to the user. Through existing HTML and CSS, and by manipulating these and other web page elements using JavaScript, you can show your data in the best possible light.

REMEMBER

To expand on these steps and learn how to create your own dynamic web pages, check out the first three chapters in Book 6.

What Is a Web App?

You no doubt have a bunch of apps residing on your smartphone. If you use Windows on your PC, you have the pre-installed apps such as Mail and Calendar and possibly one or more apps downloaded from the Windows Store. If the Mac is more your style, you're probably quite familiar with apps such as Music and Messages, and you might have installed a few others from the App Store. We live in a world full of apps that, in the context of your phone or computer, are software programs dedicated to a single topic or task.

So what then is a web app? It's very similar to an app on a device or PC. That is, it's a website, built using web technologies such as HTML, CSS, and JavaScript, that has two main characteristics:

>> The web app is focused on a single topic or task.

>> The web app offers some sort of interface that enables the user to operate the app in one or more ways.

In short, a *web app* is a website that looks and acts like an app on a device or a computer. (Gmail is an example of a web app.) This is opposed to a regular website, which usually tackles several topics or tasks and has an interface that for the most part only enables users to navigate the site.

REMEMBER

To get the scoop on building your very own web apps, head over to the four chapters in Book 7.

Understanding the Difference between Web Coding and Web Development

After all this talk of HTML, CSS, MySQL, and JavaScript, after the bird's-eye view of static sites, dynamic sites, and web apps, you might be wondering when the heck I'm going to answer the most pressing question: What in the name of Sir Tim Berners-Lee (inventor of the web) is the difference between web coding and web development?

I'm glad you asked! Some people would probably answer that question by saying there's no real difference because web coding and web development are two ways of referring to the same thing: creating web pages using programming tools.

Hey, it's a free country, but to my mind I think there's a useful distinction to be made between web coding and web development:

>> *Web coding* is the pure programming part of creating a web page, particularly using JavaScript on the front end and PHP on the back end.

>> *Web development* is the complete web page creation package, from building a page with HTML tags, to formatting the page with CSS, to storing data on the back end with MySQL, to accessing that data with PHP, to bridging the front and back ends using JavaScript.

However you look at the two terms, this book teaches you everything you need to know to become both a web coder and a web developer.

IN THIS CHAPTER

» **Understanding the need for a web development environment**

» **Gathering the tools you need for a local development setup**

» **Installing a local web development environment on a Windows PC**

» **Installing a local web development environment on a Mac**

» **Learning what to look for in a good text editor**

Chapter **2**

Setting Up Your Web Development Home

He is happiest, be he king or peasant, who finds peace in his home.

— JOHANN WOLFGANG VON GOETHE

One of the truly amazing things about web development is that, with just a few exceptions — such as images, media files, and server databases — all you ever work with are basic text files. But surely all the structure you add with HTML tags requires some obscure and complex file type? No way, José: It's text all the way down. What about all that formatting stuff associated with CSS? Nope: nothing but text. PHP and JavaScript? Text and, again, text.

What this text-only landscape means is that you don't need any highfalutin, high-priced software to develop for the web. A humble text editor is all you require to dip a toe or two in the web coding waters.

But what if you want to get more than your feet wet in web coding? What if you want to dive in, swim around, perhaps do a little snorkeling? Ah, then you need to take things up a notch or three and set up a proper web development environment on your computer. Doing so will give you everything you need to build, test, and refine your web development projects. In this chapter, you get your web coding adventure off to a rousing start by exploring how to set up a complete web development environment on your Windows PC or Mac.

What Is a Local Web Development Environment?

In programming circles, an *integrated development environment* (IDE) is a collection of software programs that make it easy and efficient to write code. Most development environments are tailored to a particular programming language and come with tools for editing, testing, and compiling code (that is, converting the code to its final form as an application).

In the web coding game, we don't have IDEs, per se, but we do have a similar beast called a *local web development environment*, which is also a collection of software. It usually includes the following:

>> A web server

>> A relational database management system (RDBMS) to run on the web server

>> A server-side programming language

>> An interface for controlling (starting, stopping, and so on) the web server

>> An interface for accessing and manipulating the RDBMS

The key point to grok here is that this is a "local" web development environment, which means it gets installed on your PC or Mac. This enables you to build and test your web development projects right on your computer. You don't need a web hosting service or even an internet connection. Everything runs conveniently on your computer, so you can concentrate on coding and leave the deployment of the site until you're ready.

Do You Need a Local Web Development Environment?

Okay, if it's possible to use a simple text editor to develop web pages, why not do just that? After all, every Windows PC and Mac in existence comes with a pre-installed text editor, and lots of free third-party text editors are ripe for downloading, so why bother installing the software for a local web development environment?

To be perfectly honest, I'm not going to stand here and tell you that a local web development setup is a must. Certainly, if all you're doing for now is getting started with a few static web pages built using HTML, CSS, and JavaScript, you don't yet need access to the back end. Similarly, if you are building websites and web apps for your own use and already have a web host that gives you access to MySQL and PHP, you can definitely get away with using just your trusty text editor.

However, two major exceptions pretty much require you to build your web stuff locally:

>> You're building a website or app for someone else and you don't have access to their web server.

>> You're building a new version of an existing website or app, which means you don't want to mess with the production code while tinkering (and therefore making mistakes) with the new code.

That said, there's also something undeniably cool about having a big-time web server purring away in your computer's background. So, even if you don't think you'll need a full-blown web development environment in the short term, think about installing one anyway, if only so you can say you're "running Apache 2.4 locally" at your next cocktail party.

Setting Up the XAMPP for Windows Development Environment

If you're running Windows, I highly recommend the web development environment XAMPP for Windows, which in its most recent version (at least as I write this in late-2023) requires Windows Vista or later. XAMPP for Windows is loaded with dozens of features, but for our needs the following are the most important:

>> **Apache:** An open-source web server that runs about half of all the websites on Earth

>> **MariaDB:** An open-source server database that is fully compatible with MySQL (discussed in Book 1, Chapter 1)

>> **PHP:** The server-side programming language that I talk about briefly in Book 1, Chapter 1

>> **phpMyAdmin:** An interface that enables you to access and manipulate MariaDB databases

So, all this high-end software requires big bucks, right? Nope. XAMPP for Windows is free.

To get started, head to the Apache Friends website at `www.apachefriends.org` and download XAMPP for Windows. Be sure to get the most recent version.

Installing XAMPP for Windows

Once the download is complete, follow these steps to install XAMPP for Windows:

1. Open the Downloads folder and then launch the installation file that you downloaded.

The download is an executable file, so you can double-click it to get the installation off the ground.

2. Enter your User Account Control (UAC) credentials to allow the install.

If you're the administrator of your PC, click Yes. Otherwise, you need to enter the username and password of the PC's administrator account.

3. When XAMPP displays a warning about installing with UAC activated, click OK.

This oddly worded warning means that if you install XAMPP in the default folder (usually `C:\Program Files`), it might have problems running normally because UAC imposes restrictions on that folder. You can ignore this because, in Step 6, I show you how to install XAMPP in a different folder that doesn't suffer from this problem.

4. When the XAMPP Setup Wizard appears, click Next.

5. **In the Select Components dialog box, shown in Figure 2-1, deselect the check box beside any component you don't want installed, and then click Next.**

For a basic install, you only need Apache, MySQL, PHP, and phpMyAdmin. If your PC is running low on disk space, consider not installing the other components. If you're rich in disk space, go ahead and install everything because, hey, after all of this you might be inspired to learn Perl (which is another server-side programming language).

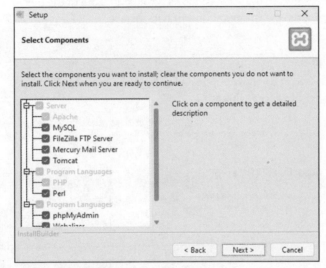

FIGURE 2-1: Use this Setup Wizard dialog box to deselect the check box beside any component you don't want installed.

6. **In the Installation Folder dialog box, type the location where you want XAMPP installed, then click Next.**

Be sure to avoid the folders `C:\Program Files` and `C:\Program Files (x86)`, for the reason I describe in Step 3. Most folks create a `xampp` folder in `C:\` and install everything there (as shown in Figure 2-2).

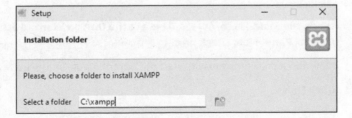

FIGURE 2-2: To install XAMPP, use a subfolder in the main C:\ folder (such as `C:\xampp`).

7. When the Setup Wizard asks what language you want to use, choose a language and then click Next.

8. Click Next to begin the installation.

9. If you encounter a Windows Security dialog box, click Show More. Select the Private Networks check box and deselect the Public Networks check box, as shown in Figure 2-3, and then click Allow.

REMEMBER

However, just because you select the Private Networks check box, it doesn't mean that people on your network can access (much less mess with) your local web server. XAMPP for Windows is configured out of the box to be accessible only from the computer on which it's installed.

Windows Security

Do you want to allow public and private networks to access this app?

Windows Firewall has blocked some features of Apache HTTP Server on all public and private networks.

Apache HTTP Server

Publisher	Apache Software Foundation
Path	C:\xampp\apache\bin\httpd.exe

Allow access to these types of networks

☐ Public networks

☑ Private networks

Learn more

Show less

Allow	Cancel

FIGURE 2-3: If the Windows Security dialog box shows up, be sure to allow Apache to communicate on your private network but not on any public networks.

10. When the install is complete, deselect the Do You Want to Start the Control Panel Now check box.

I talk about the correct way to start the Control Panel in the next section.

11. Click Finish.

Running the XAMPP for Windows Control Panel

The XAMPP Control Panel enables you to start, stop, and configure the XAMPP apps, particularly the Apache web server and the MySQL database system. For best results, you should start the program with administrator privileges, which you can do by following these steps:

1. **Click Start.**

2. **In the All Apps list, find and open the XAMPP folder.**

   Depending on your version of Windows, you might have to click All Apps to get to the All Apps list.

3. **Right-click XAMPP Control Panel, click More, and then click Run as Administrator.**

   Depending on your version of Windows, you might not have to click More to get to the Run as Administrator command.

   The User Account Control dialog appears.

4. **If you're the administrator of your PC, click Yes. Otherwise, you need to enter the username and password of the PC's administrator account.**

   The XAMPP Control Panel appears, as shown in Figure 2-4.

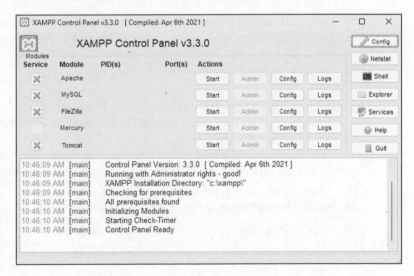

FIGURE 2-4: You use the XAMPP Control Panel to control and configure apps such as Apache and MySQL.

To start an app, click the corresponding Start button. That button name changes to Stop, meaning you can later stop the service by clicking its Stop button.

TIP

You'll always want the Apache and MySQL apps running, so you can save a bit of time by having the XAMPP Control Panel launch these two apps automatically when you open the program. Click the Config button near the upper-right corner of the XAMPP Control Panel window, select the Apache and MySQL check boxes, and then click Save.

REMEMBER

If when you start an app you run into a Windows Security Alert dialog box similar to the one shown earlier in Figure 2-3, click Show More, select the Private Networks check box, deselect the Public Networks check box, and then click Allow Access.

Accessing your local web server

With XAMPP for Windows installed and Apache up and running, congratulations are in order: You have a web server running on your PC! That's great, but how do you access your shiny, new web server? There are two ways, depending on what you want to do:

>> **Add files and folders to the web server:** Place the files and folders in the htdocs subfolder of your main XAMPP install folder. For example, if you installed XAMPP to C:\xampp, your web server's root folder will be C:\xampp\htdocs.

>> **View the files and folders on the server:** Open your favorite web browser and navigate to the http://localhost address (or to 127.0.0.1, which gets you to the same place). If you have the XAMPP Control Panel open, you can also click the Apache app's Admin button.

By default, your local website is configured to automatically redirect http://localhost to http://localhost/dashboard/, shown in Figure 2-5, which gives you access to several XAMPP tools.

You can use the following links, which appear in the page header:

>> **Apache Friends:** Returns you to the main Dashboard page.

>> **FAQs:** Displays a list of XAMPP frequently asked questions.

>> **How-To Guides:** Displays a list of links to step-by-step guides for a number of XAMPP for Windows tasks.

>> **PHPInfo:** Displays a for-geeks-only page of information about the version of PHP that you have installed.

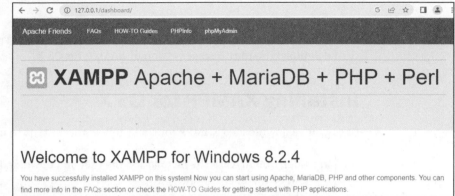

FIGURE 2-5:
The `http://`
`localhost/`
`dashboard/`
address gives you
access to a few
XAMPP tools.

>> **phpMyAdmin:** Opens the phpMyAdmin tool, which lets you create and
manipulate MariaDB/MySQL databases. You can open phpMyAdmin also by
navigating directly to `http://localhost/phpmyadmin/`, or in the XAMPP
Control Panel, by clicking the MySQL app's Admin button. However you get
there, just be sure to have the MySQL app running before you open
phpMyAdmin.

Setting Up the XAMPP for OS X Development Environment

If you'll be doing your web work on a Mac, I recommend the web development
environment XAMPP for OS X (yep, the name uses *OS X* instead of *macOS*), which
in its most recent version (at least as I write this in mid-2023) requires OS X Snow
Leopard (10.6) or later. XAMPP for OS X is packed with programs and features, but
you'll probably only concern yourself with the following:

>> **Apache:** An open-source web server that runs about half of all the
websites on Earth

>> **MariaDB:** An open-source server database fully compatible with MySQL
(discussed in Book 1, Chapter 1)

>> **PHP:** The server-side programming language that I mention in Book 1,
Chapter 1

>> **phpMyAdmin:** An interface that enables you to access and work with
MariaDB databases

The best news of all is XAMPP for OS X is completely free. Nice! To get the show on the road, surf to the Apache Friends website at www.apachefriends.org, and then download the most recent version of XAMPP for OS X.

Installing XAMPP for OS X

Once you've downloaded XAMPP for OS X, follow these steps to install it:

1. **In Finder, double-click the installation file that you downloaded to open the XAMPP installer window.**

2. **Double-click the XAMPP icon.**

3. **If macOS displays a warning that "the developer cannot be verified," you need to do the following to get back on track:**

   a. *Click Cancel.*

   b. *Open System Settings and click Privacy & Security.*

   c. *Click the Open Anyway button.*

   d. *Enter your Mac administrator credentials, and then click the Modify Settings button.*

   e. *In Finder, double-click the XAMPP icon you downloaded earlier to restart the installer.*

   f. *When macOS warns you once again that "the developer cannot be verified," say "It's cool, bro" and click Open.*

4. **Enter your macOS administrator password and then click OK.**

5. **When the XAMPP Setup Wizard appears, click Next.**

6. **In the Select Components dialog, deselect the XAMPP Developer Files check box, as shown in Figure 2-6, and then click Next.**

   The developer files might sound like they're right up your alley, but they're for people who want to add to or modify the code for XAMPP itself.

7. **In the Installation Directory dialog, click Next.**

8. **Click Next to launch the installation.**

9. **If macOS asks whether you want the application "httpd" (that would be the Apache web server) to accept incoming network connections, be sure to click Allow.**

   Otherwise, your web server won't work.

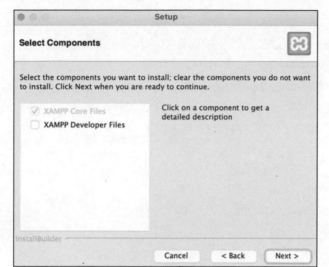

FIGURE 2-6:
In the Setup
wizard dialog,
deselect the
check box beside
XAMPP Developer
Files.

10. **When the install is complete, click Finish.**

   If you want to head right into XAMPP Manager, leave the Launch XAMPP check box selected.

REMEMBER

What about the security of your local web server? Fortunately, that's not an issue because people on your network can't access your web server. XAMPP is configured by default to be accessible only from the Mac on which it's installed.

Running XAMPP Application Manager

XAMPP Application Manager enables you to start, stop, and configure the XAMPP servers, particularly the Apache web server and the MySQL database system. To launch XAMPP Application Manager, you have two choices:

>> If you still have the final Setup wizard dialog onscreen, leave the Launch XAMPP check box selected and click Finish.

>> In Finder, open the Applications folder, open the XAMPP folder, and then double-click Manager-OSX.

XAMPP Application Manager appears. To work with the XAMPP servers, click the Manage Servers tab, shown in Figure 2-7.

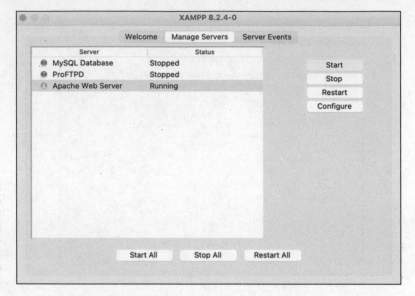

FIGURE 2-7:
You use the
XAMPP control
panel to control
and configure
services such
as Apache and
MySQL.

In the Manage Servers tab, you can perform the following actions:

>> **Start a server.** Click the server and then click Start.

>> **Start all the servers.** Click Start All.

>> **Restart a server.** Click the server and then click Restart.

>> **Restart all the servers.** Click Restart All.

>> **Stop a server.** Click the server and then click Stop.

>> **Stop all the servers.** Click Stop All.

Accessing your local web server

With XAMPP for OS X installed and Apache up and running, it's time for high-fives all around because you have a web server running on your Mac! That's awesome, but how do you access your web server? There are two ways, depending on what you want to do:

>> **Add files and folders to the web server:** Place the files and folders in the htdocs subfolder of your main XAMPP install folder. To get there, open Applications, open XAMPP, and then double-click htdocs. Alternatively, if you have XAMPP Application Manager open, you can click the Welcome tab, click Open Application Folder, and then open htdocs.

>> **View the files and folders on the server:** Open your favorite web browser and navigate to the `http://localhost` address (or to `http://127.0.0.1`, which gets you to the same place). Alternatively, if you have XAMPP Application Manager running, you can click the Welcome tab and then click Go To Application.

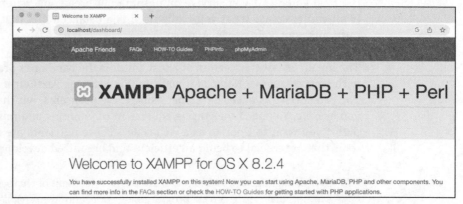

FIGURE 2-8:
The `http://localhost/dashboard/` address gives you access to a few XAMPP for OS X features.

By default, your local website is configured to automatically redirect `http://localhost` to `http://localhost/dashboard/`, shown in Figure 2-8, which gives you access to several XAMPP tools.

You can use the following links in the page header:

>> **Apache Friends:** Returns you to the main Dashboard page.

>> **FAQs:** Displays a list of XAMPP frequently asked questions.

>> **How-To Guides:** Displays a list of links to step-by-step guides for a number of XAMPP for OS X tasks.

>> **PHPInfo:** Displays a for-geeks-only page of information about the version of PHP that you have installed.

>> **phpMyAdmin:** Opens the phpMyAdmin tool, which lets you create and manipulate MariaDB/MySQL databases. You can also open phpMyAdmin by navigating directly to `http://localhost/phpmyadmin/`. Either way, make sure you have the MySQL Database server running before you open phpMyAdmin.

Choosing Your Text Editor

I mention at the beginning of this chapter that all you need to develop web pages is a text editor. However, saying that all you need to code is a text editor is like saying that all you need to live is food: It's certainly true, but more than a little short on specifics. After all, to a large extent, the quality of your life depends on the food you eat. If you survive on nothing but bread and water, well, surviving is all you're doing. What you really need is a balanced diet that supplies all the nutrients your body needs. And pie.

The bread-and-water version of a text editor is the barebones program that came with your computer: Notepad if you run Windows, or TextEdit if you have a Mac. You can survive as a web developer using these programs, but that's not living, if you ask me. You need the editing equivalent of vitamins and minerals (and, yes, pie) if you want to flourish as a web coder. These nutrients are the features and tools that are crucial to being an efficient and organized developer:

>> **Syntax highlighting:** *Syntax* refers to the arrangement of characters and symbols that create correct programming code, and *syntax highlighting* is an editing feature that color-codes certain syntax elements for easier reading. For example, while regular text might appear black, all HTML tags might be shown in blue and CSS properties might appear red. The best text editors let you choose the syntax colors, either by offering prefab themes or by letting you apply custom colors.

>> **Line numbers:** It might seem like a small thing, but having a text editor that numbers each line, as shown in Figure 2-9, can be a major timesaver. When the web browser alerts you to an error in your code (refer to Book 5, Chapter 2), it gives you an error message and, crucially, the line number of the error. This enables you to quickly locate the culprit and (fingers crossed) fix the problem pronto.

>> **Code previews:** A good text editor will let you view a preview of how your code will look in a web browser. The preview might appear in the same window as your code or in a separate window, and it should update automatically as you modify and save your code.

>> **Code completion:** When you start typing something, this handy feature displays a list of possible code items that complete your typing. You can then select the one you want and press Tab or Enter to add it to your code without having to type the whole thing.

>> **Spell checking:** You always want to put your best web foot forward, which in part means posting pages that don't contain typos or misspellings. A good text editor has a built-in spell checker that will catch your gaffes before you put your pages on the web.

```
1   <!DOCTYPE html>
2   <html lang="en">
3       <head>
4           <meta charset="utf-8">
5           <meta name="viewport" content="width=device-width, initial-scale=1.0">
6           <title>Adding Padding</title>
7           <style>
8               * {
9                   box-sizing: border-box;
10              }
11
12              body {
13                  margin: 2rem;
14                  width: 30rem;
15                  text-align: justify;
16              }
17
18              aside {
19                  border: 1px solid ■black;
20                  margin: 1.5rem;
21              }
22
23              .padded {
24                  padding: 1rem;
25              }
26          </style>
27      </head>
28      <body>
29          <aside class="padded">
30              <b>Note:</b> Creating a new word by chopping off the initial letter or syllable of an existing word
31              is called <i>aphaeresis</i> (which means "to take away"). This not-as-uncommon-as-you-might-think
32              process was the source of words such as <i>mend</i> (a shortening of <i>amend</i>), <i>spy</i> (from
33              <i>espy</i>), <i>cute</i> (from <i>acute</i>), and <i>squire</i> (from <i>esquire</i>).
34          </aside>
35      </body>
36  </html>
```

FIGURE 2-9:
Line numbers,
such as the ones
shown here down
the left side of
the window,
are a crucial text
editor feature.

>> **Text processing:** The best text editors offer a selection of text processing
features, such as automatic indentation of code blocks, converting tabs to
spaces and vice versa, shifting chunks of code right or left, removing
unneeded spaces at the end of lines, and hiding blocks of code.

The good news is that there's no shortage of text editors that support all these
features and many more. That's also the bad news because it means you have a
huge range of programs to choose from. To help you get started, here, in alphabetical order, are a few editors to take for test drives:

>> **Brackets** (`https://brackets.io/`): Available for Windows and Mac.
Also free!

>> **Notepad++** (`https://notepad-plus-plus.org/`): Available for Windows
only. Another freebie.

>> **Nova** (`https://nova.app`): Available for Mac only. $99, but a free trial is
available.

>> **Sublime Text** (`www.sublimetext.com`): Available for both Windows and Mac.
$99, but a free trial is available.

>> **Visual Studio Code** (`https://code.visualstudio.com/`): Available for
Windows and Mac. Why, yes, this one is free, as well.

IN THIS CHAPTER

» **Understanding web hosting providers**

» **Examining the various choices for hosting your site**

» **Choosing the host that's right for you**

» **Getting comfortable with your new web home**

» **Getting your site files to your web host**

Chapter **3**

Finding and Setting Up a Web Host

You will end up with better software by releasing as early as practically possible, and then spending the rest of your time iterating rapidly based on real-world feedback. So trust me on this one: Even if version 1 sucks, ship it anyway.

— JEFF ATTWOOD

You build your web pages from the comfort of your Mac or PC, and if you have a local development environment running (as I describe in Book 1, Chapter 2), you can even use your computer to preview how your web pages appear before you put them online.

That's fine and dandy, but I think you'll agree that the whole point of building a web page is to, you know, put it on the web! First, you need to subject your code to the wilds of the wider web to make sure it works out there. Even if it seems to be running like a champ on your local server, you can't give it the seal of approval until you've proven that it runs champlike on a remote server. Second, once your code is ready, the only way the public can appreciate your handiwork is for you to get it out where they can access it.

Whether you're testing or shipping your code, you need somewhere to put it, and that's what this chapter is about. Here you explore the wide and sometimes wacky world of web hosts. You delve into what they offer, investigate ways to choose a good one, and then take a tour of your web home away from home.

Understanding Web Hosting Providers

A common question posed by web development newcomers is "Where the heck do I put my web page when it's done?" If you've asked that question, you're doing okay because it means you're clued in to something crucial: Just because you've created a web page and you have an internet connection doesn't mean your site is automatically part of the web.

After all, people on the web have no way of getting to your computer. Even if you're working with a local web development environment (which I discuss in Book 1, Chapter 2), you're working in splendid isolation because no one either on your network or on the internet can access that environment.

In other words, your computer isn't set up to hand out documents (such as web pages) to remote visitors who ask for them. Computers that can do this are called *servers* (because they serve stuff out to the web), and computers that specialize in distributing web pages are called *web servers*. So, your web page isn't on the web until you store it on a remote web server. Because this computer is, in effect, playing host to your pages, such machines are also called *web hosts*. Companies that run these web hosts are called *web hosting providers*.

Now, just how do you go about finding a web host? Well, the answer to that depends on a bunch of factors, including the type of site you have, how you get connected to the internet in the first place, and how much money (if any) you're willing to fork out for the privilege. In the end, you have three choices:

>> Your existing internet provider

>> A free hosting provider

>> A commercial hosting provider

REMEMBER

In the rest of this chapter, I assume that you want a web host that enables you not only to store HTML, CSS, and JavaScript files but also to work with MySQL data and PHP scripts on the server. If you'll be creating a static site that doesn't require a full-fledged server, you should consider some excellent (and free!) hosting alternatives. See Book 6, Chapter 4 to learn how to create and deploy static web pages.

Using your existing internet provider

If you access the internet via a corporate or educational network, your institution might have its own web server you can use. If you get online via an internet service provider (ISP), surf to the ISP's support pages, which should tell you whether the company has a web server available. Almost all ISPs provide space so their customers can put up personal pages free of charge.

Finding a free hosting provider

If cash is in short supply, a few hosting providers will bring your website in from the cold out of the goodness of their hearts. In some cases, these services are open only to specific groups such as students, artists, and nonprofit organizations. However, plenty of providers put up personal sites free of charge.

What's the catch? Well, there are almost always restrictions both on how much data you can store and on the type of data you can store (no ads, no dirty pictures, and so on). You might also be required to display some kind of banner advertisement for the hosting provider on your pages.

Signing up with a commercial hosting provider

For personal and business-related websites, many web artisans end up renting a chunk of a web server from a commercial hosting provider. You normally hand over a setup fee to get your account going and then pay a monthly fee.

Why shell out all that cash when so many free sites are lying around? Because, as with most things in life, you get what you pay for. By paying for your host, you generally get more features, better service, and fewer annoyances (such as the ads that some free sites have you display).

A Buyer's Guide to Web Hosting

Unfortunately, choosing a web host isn't as straightforward as you might like it to be. For one thing, hundreds of hosts are clamoring for your business; for another, the pitches and come-ons your average web host employs are strewn with jargon and technical terms. I can't reduce the number of web hosts, but I can help you understand what those hosts are yammering about. Here's a list of the terms you're most likely to come across when researching web hosts:

>> **Storage space:** This term refers to the amount of room allotted to you on the host's web server to store your files. The amount of acreage you get determines the amount of data you can store. For example, if you get a 1MB (1 megabyte) limit, you can't store more than 1MB worth of files on the server. HTML files don't take up much real estate, but large graphics sure do, so you need to watch your limit. For example, you could probably store about 200 pages in 1MB of storage (assuming about 5KB per page), but only about 20 images (assuming about 50KB per image). Generally, the more you pay for a host, the more storage space you get.

>> **Bandwidth:** The bandwidth is a measure of how much of your data the server serves. For example, suppose the HTML file for your page is 1KB (1 kilobyte) and the graphics associated with the page consume 9KB. If someone accesses your page, the server ships out a total of 10KB; if ten people access the page (either at the same time or over a period of time), the total bandwidth is 100KB. Most hosts give you a bandwidth limit (or cap), which is most often a certain number of megabytes or gigabytes per month. (A gigabyte is equal to about 1,000 megabytes.) Again, the more you pay, the greater the bandwidth you get.

WARNING

If you exceed your bandwidth limit, users will usually still be able to get to your pages (although some hosts shut down access to an offending site). However, almost all web hosts charge you an extra fee for exceeding your bandwidth, so check this out before signing up. The usual penalty is a set fee per every megabyte or gigabyte over your cap.

>> **Domain name:** The domain name is a general internet address, such as wiley.com or whitehouse.gov. A domain name tends to be easier to remember than the long-winded addresses most web hosts supply you by default, so they're a popular feature. Two types of domain names are available:

- A regular domain name (such as *yourdomain*.com or *yourdomain*.org)

- A subdomain name (such as *yourdomain*.*webhostdomain*.com)

To get a regular domain, you either need to use one of the many domain registration services such as GoDaddy (www.godaddy.com) or Register.com (www.register.com). A more convenient route is to choose a web hosting provider that will do this for you. Either way, it will usually cost you $35 per year (although some hosts offer cheap domains as a loss leader and recoup their costs with hosting fees; also, discount domain registrars such as GoDaddy offer domains for as little as $9.99 per year (although that price might only apply to the first year, so buyer beware). If you go the direct route, almost all web hosts will host your domain, which means that people who use your domain name will get directed to your website on the host's web server. For this to work, you must tweak the domain settings on the registrar. This task usually involves changing the DNS servers associated with the domain so that they point to the web host's domain name servers. Your web host will give you instructions on how to do this.

With a subdomain name, *webhostdomain*.com is the domain name of the web hosting company, and it simply tacks on whatever name you want at the beginning. Many web hosts will provide you with this type of domain, often for free.

» **Email addresses:** Most hosts offer you one or more email addresses along with your web space. The more you pay, the more mailboxes you get. Some hosts offer *email forwarding,* which enables you to have messages sent to your web host address rerouted to some other email address.

» **Shared server:** If the host offers a *shared server* (or *virtual server*), you'll be sharing the server with other websites — dozens or even hundreds of them. The web host takes care of all the highly technical server management chores, so all you have to do is maintain your site. This option is by far the best (and cheapest) choice for individuals or small business types.

» **Dedicated server:** With a dedicated server, you get your own server computer on the host. That may sound like a good thing, but it's usually up to you to manage the server, which can be a dauntingly technical task. Also, dedicated servers are much more expensive than shared servers.

» **Operating system:** You usually have two choices for the operating system on the web server, Unix (or Linux) and Windows Server. Unix systems have the reputation of being very reliable and fast, even under heavy traffic loads, so they're usually the best choice for a shared server. Windows systems are a better choice for dedicated servers because they're easier to administer than their Unix cousins. Note, too, that Unix servers are case sensitive in terms of file and directory names, while Windows servers are not.

» **Databases:** This term refers to the number and type of databases you may create with your account. Unix systems usually offer MySQL databases, whereas Windows servers offer SQL Server databases.

» **Administration interface:** This is the host app that you use to perform tasks on the server, such as uploading files or creating users. Many hosts offer the excellent cPanel interface, and most Unix-based systems offer the phpMyAdmin app for managing your MySQL data.

» **Ad requirements:** A few free web hosts require you to display some type of advertising on your pages, such as a banner ad across the top of the page, a pop-up ad that appears each time a person accesses your pages, or a watermark ad, usually a semitransparent logo that hovers over your page. Fortunately, free hosts that insist on ads are rare these days, so you can usually find a host without this requirement (your visitors will thank you!).

>> **Uptime:** Uptime refers to the percentage of time the host's server is up and serving. There's no such thing as 100 percent uptime because all servers require maintenance and upgrades at some point. However, the best hosts have uptime numbers over 99 percent. (If a host doesn't advertise its uptime, it's probably because it's very low. Be sure to ask before committing yourself.)

>> **Tech support:** If you have problems setting up or accessing your site, you want to know that help — in the form of *tech support* — is just around the corner. The best hosts offer 24/7 tech support, which means you can contact the company — by chat, phone, or email — 24 hours a day, 7 days a week.

>> **FTP support:** You usually use the internet's *FTP service* to transfer your files from your computer to the web host. If a host offers *FTP access* (some hosts have their own method for transferring files), be sure you can use it any time you want and there are no restrictions on the amount of data you can transfer at one time.

>> **Website statistics:** Website statistics will tell you things such as how many people have visited your site, which pages are the most popular, how much bandwidth your site is consuming, and which browsers and browser versions surfers are using. Most decent hosts offer a ready-made stats package, but the best ones also give you access to the raw log files so you can play with the data yourself.

>> **Ecommerce:** Some hosts offer a service that lets you set up a web store so you can sell stuff on your site. This service usually includes a shopping script, access to credit card authorization and other payment systems, and the capability to set up a secure connection. You usually get this feature in only the more expensive hosting packages, and you'll most often have to pay a setup fee to get your store built.

>> **Scalability:** This term refers to the host's capability to modify your site's features as required. For example, if your site becomes popular, you might need to increase your bandwidth limit. If the host is scalable, it can easily change your limit (or any other feature of your site).

Finding a Web Host

Okay, you're ready to start researching the hosts to find one that suits your web style. As I mention earlier, there are hundreds, perhaps even thousands, of hosts, so how is a body supposed to whittle them down to some kind of short list? Here are some ideas:

>> **Ask your friends and colleagues.** The best way to find a good host is that old standby, word of mouth. If someone you trust says a host is good, chances are you won't be disappointed — assuming you and your pal have similar hosting needs. If you want a full-blown ecommerce site, don't solicit recommendations from someone who has only a humble home page.

>> **Solicit host reviews from experts.** Ask existing webmasters and other people "in the know" about which hosts they recommend or have heard good things about. A good place to find such experts is Web Hosting Talk (www. webhostingtalk.com), a collection of forums related to web hosting.

>> **Contact web host customers.** Visit sites that use a particular web host and send an email message to the webmaster asking what they think of the host's service.

>> **Peruse the lists of web hosts.** A number of sites track and compare web hosts, so they're an easy way to get in a lot of research. Careful, though, because a lot of sketchy lists are only trying to make a buck by getting you to click ads. Here are some reputable places to start:

- **CNET Web Hosting Solutions:** www.cnet.com/web-hosting

- **PC Magazine Web Site Hosting Services Reviews:** www.pcmag.com/reviews/web-hosting-services

- **Review Hell:** www.reviewhell.com

- **Review Signal Web Hosting Reviews:** https://reviewsignal.com/webhosting

Finding Your Way around Your New Web Home

After you sign up with a web hosting provider and your account is established, the web administrator creates two things for you: a directory on the server that you can use to store your website files, and your very own web address. (This is true also if you're using a web server associated with your corporate or school network.) The directory — which is known in the biz as your *root directory* — usually takes one of the following forms:

```
/yourname/
/home/yourname/
/yourname/public_html/
```

In each case, *yourname* is the login name (or username) the provider assigns to you, or it may be your domain name (with or without the .com part). Remember, your root directory is a slice of the host's web server, and this slice is yours to mess around with however you like. Usually, you can do all or most of the following to the root:

>> Add files to the directory.

>> Add subdirectories to the directory.

>> Move or copy files from one directory to another.

>> Rename files or directories.

>> Delete files from the directory.

Your web address normally takes one of the following shapes:

```
https://provider/yourname/
https://yourname.provider/
https://www.yourname.com/
```

Here, *provider* is the host name of your provider (for example, www.hostcompany.com or just hostcompany.com), and *yourname* is your login name or domain name. Here are some examples:

```
https://www.hostcompany.com/mywebsite/
https://mywebsite.hostcompany.com/
https://www.mywebsite.com/
```

Your directory and your web address

A direct and important relationship exists between your server directory and your address. That is, your address points to your directory and enables other people to view the files you store in that directory. For example, suppose I decide to store a file named thingamajig.html in my directory and my main address is https://mywebsite.hostcompany.com/. This means someone else can view that page by typing the following URL into a web browser:

```
https://mywebsite.hostcompany.com/thingamajig.html
```

Similarly, suppose I create a subdirectory named `stuff` and use it to store a file named `index.html`. A surfer can view that file by convincing a web browser to head for the following URL:

```
https://mywebsite.hostcompany.com/stuff/index.html
```

In other words, folks can surf to your files and directories by strategically tacking on the appropriate filenames and directory names after your main web address.

REMEMBER

For most web servers, the default file in each directory is `index.html`, where *default* means it's the file that gets served if no filename is specified. For example, the following addresses will both display the `index.html` file:

```
https://mywebsite.hostcompany.com/stuff/index.html
https://mywebsite.hostcompany.com/stuff/
```

Making your hard disk mirror your web home

As a web developer, one of the key ways to keep your projects organized is to set up your directories on your computer, and then mirror those directories on your web host. Believe me, this will make your testing and uploading duties immeasurably easier.

REMEMBER

Copying a file from your computer to a remote location (such as your web host's server) is known in the file transfer trade as *uploading.*

This process begins at the root. On the web host, you already have a root directory assigned to you by the hosting provider, so now you need to designate a folder on your computer to be the root mirror. If you're using the XAMPP web development environment (refer to Book 1, Chapter 2), the XAMPP installation's `htdocs` subfolder is perfect as your local root. Otherwise, choose or create a folder on your computer to use as the local root.

What you do from here depends on the number of web development projects you're going to build, and the number of files in each project:

>> **A single web development project consisting of just a few files:** In this case, just put all the files into the root directory.

>> **A single web development project consisting of many files:** The more likely scenario for a typical web development project is to have multiple HTML, CSS, JavaScript, and PHP files, plus lots of ancillary files such as images and fonts. Although it's okay to place all your HTML files in the root directory, do yourself a favor and organize all your other files into subfolders by file type: a css subfolder for CSS files, a js subfolder for JavaScript files, and so on.

>> **Multiple web development projects:** As a web developer, you'll almost certainly create tons of web projects, so it's crucial to organize them. The ideal way to do this is to create a separate root subdirectory for each project. Then within each of these subdirectories, create sub-subdirectories for file types such as CSS, JavaScript, images, and so on.

To help you understand why mirroring your local and remote directory structures is so useful, suppose you set up a subfolder on your computer named graphics that you use to store your image files. To insert into your page a file named mydog.jpg from that folder, you'd use the following reference:

```
graphics/mydog.jpg
```

When you send your HTML file to the server and then display the file in a browser, it looks for mydog.jpg in the graphics subdirectory. If you don't have such a subdirectory — either you didn't create it or you used a different name, such as images — the browser won't find mydog.jpg and your image won't appear. However, if you match the subdirectories on your web server with the subfolders on your computer, your page will work properly without modifications both at home and on the web.

One common faux pas beginning web developers make is to include the local drive and all the folder names when referencing a file. Here's an example:

```
C:\xampp\htdocs\graphics\mydog.jpg
```

This image will show up just fine when it's viewed from your computer. But it will fail miserably when you upload it to the server and view it on the web because the C:\xampp\htdocs\ part exists only on your computer.

The Unix (or Linux) computers that play host to the vast majority of web servers are downright finicky when it comes to uppercase and lowercase letters in file and directory names. It's crucial that you check the file references in your code to be sure the file and directory names you use match the combination of uppercase and lowercase letters used on your server. For example, suppose you have a CSS file on your server that's named styles.css. If your HTML references that file as, say, STYLES.CSS, the server won't find the file and your styles won't get applied.

Uploading your site files

Once your web page or site is ready for its debut, it's time to get your files to your host's web server. If the server is on your company or school network, you send the files over the network to the directory set up by your system administrator. Otherwise, you upload the files to the root directory created for you on the hosting provider's web server.

How you go about uploading your site files depends on the web host, but here are the four most common scenarios:

>> **Use an FTP program.** It's a rare web host that doesn't offer support for the File Transfer Protocol (FTP, for short), which is the internet's most popular method for transferring files from here to there. To use FTP, you usually need to get a piece of software called an *FTP client,* which enables you to connect to your web host's FTP server (your host can provide you with instructions for this) and offers an interface for standard file tasks, such as navigating and creating folders, uploading the files, and deleting and renaming files. Popular Windows clients are CuteFTP (www.globalscape.com/cuteftp) and Cyberduck (https://cyberduck.io). For the Mac, try Transmit (https://panic.com/transmit) or FileZilla (https://filezilla-project.org).

>> **Use your text editor's file upload feature.** Some text editors come with an FTP client built-in, so you can edit a file and then immediately upload it with a single command. The Nova text editor (https://nova.app) supports this too-handy-for-words feature.

>> **Use the File Manager feature of cPanel.** I mention earlier that lots of web hosts offer an administration tool called cPanel that offers an interface for hosting tasks such as email and domain management. cPanel also offers a file manager feature that you can use to upload files and perform other file management chores.

>> **Use the web host's proprietary upload tool.** For some reason, a few web hosts offer only their own proprietary interface for uploading and messing around with files and directories. Refer to your host's Help or Support page for instructions.

Making changes to your web files

What happens if you send a web development file to your web host and then realize you've made a typing gaffe or spy a coding mistake? Or what if you have more information to add to one of your web pages? How do you make changes to the files you've already sent?

Well, here's the short answer: You don't. That's right, after you've sent your files, you never have to bother with them again. That doesn't mean you can never update your site, however. Instead, you make your changes to the files that reside on your computer and then send these revised files to your web host. These files replace the old files, and your site is updated just like that.

WARNING

Be sure you send the updated file to the correct directory on the server. Otherwise, you may overwrite a file that happens to have the same name in some other directory.

2

Coding the Front End, Part 1: HTML and CSS

Contents at a Glance

IN THIS CHAPTER

» **Getting comfy with HTML**

» **Figuring out HTML tags and attributes**

» **Understanding the basic blueprint for all web pages**

» **Adding text, images, and links to your page**

» **Building bulleted and numbered lists**

Chapter **1**

Structuring the Page with HTML

I am always fascinated by the structure of things; why do things work this way and not that way.

— URSUS WEHRLI

When it comes to web development, it's no exaggeration to say that the one indispensable thing, the *sine qua non* for those of you who studied Latin in school, is HTML. Absolutely everything else you make as a web developer — your CSS rules, your JavaScript code, even your PHP scripts — can't hang its hat anywhere but on some HTML. These other web development technologies don't even make sense outside of an HTML context.

So, in a sense, this chapter is the most important for you as a web coder because all the rest of the book depends to a greater or lesser degree on the HTML know-how found in the following pages. If that sounds intimidating, not to worry: One of the great things about HTML is that it's not a huge topic, so you can get up to full HTML speed without a massive investment of time and effort.

Because HTML is so important, you'll be happy to know that I don't rush things. You'll get a thorough grounding in all things HTML, and when you're done you'll be more than ready to tackle the rest of your web development education.

Getting the Hang of HTML

Building a web page from scratch may seem like a daunting task. It doesn't help that the codes you use to set up, configure, and format a web page are called the Hypertext Markup Language (HTML for short), a name that could only warm the cockles of a geek's heart. Here's a mercifully brief review of each term:

>> **Hypertext:** An oblique reference to the links that are the defining characteristic of web pages. In prehistoric times — that is, the 1980s — tall-forehead types referred to any text that, when selected, takes you to a different document, as *hypertext*.

>> **Markup:** Instructions that specify how the content of a web page should be displayed in the web browser.

>> **Language:** The set of codes that make up all the markup possibilities for a page.

But even though the name HTML is intimidating, the codes used by HTML aren't even close to being hard to learn. There are only a few of them, and in many cases they even make sense!

At its most basic, HTML is nothing more than a collection of markup codes — called *tags* — that specify the structure of your web page. In HTML, *structure* is a rubbery concept that can refer to anything from the entire page all the way down to a single word or even just a character or two.

You can think of a tag as a kind of container. What types of things can it contain? Mostly text, although lots of tags contain things like chunks of the web page and even other tags.

Most tags use the following generic format:

```
<tag>content</tag>
```

What you have here are a couple of codes (the `<tag>` and `</tag>` placeholders, above) that define a container. Most of these codes are one- or two-letter abbreviations, but sometimes they're entire words. You always surround these codes with angle brackets, `<>`, which tell the web browser that it's dealing with a chunk of HTML and not just some random text.

The first of these codes — represented by the ⟨*tag*⟩ placeholder — is called the *start tag* and marks the opening of the container; the second of the codes — represented by the ⟨/*tag*⟩ placeholder — is called the *end tag* and marks the closing of the container. (Note the extra slash (/) that appears in the end tag.)

In between you have *content*, which refers to whatever is contained in the tag. For example, here's a simple sentence that might appear in a web page (check out bk02ch01/example01.html in this book's example files):

```
In this book, you learn that HTML is awesome.
```

Figure 1-1 shows how this might appear in a web browser.

FIGURE 1-1:
The sample sentence as it appears in a web browser.

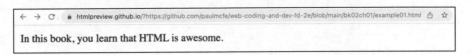

← → C 🔒 htmlpreview.github.io/?https://github.com/paulmcfe/web-coding-and-dev-fd-2e/blob/main/bk02ch01/example01.html ⬒ ☆

In this book, you learn that HTML is awesome.

Ho hum, right? Suppose you want to punch this up a bit by emphasizing *awesome*. In HTML, the tag for emphasis is ⟨em⟩, so you'd modify your sentence like so:

```
In this book, you learn that HTML is <em>awesome</em>.
```

Note how I've surrounded the word awesome with ⟨em⟩ and ⟨/em⟩? The first ⟨em⟩ is the start tag and it says to the browser, "Yo, Browser Boy! You know the text that comes after this? Be a good fellow and treat it as emphasized text." This continues until the browser reaches the end tag ⟨/em⟩, which lets the browser know it's supposed to stop what it's doing. So the ⟨/em⟩ tells the browser, "Okay, okay, that's enough with the emphasis already!"

All web browsers display emphasized text in italics, so that's how the word now appears, as shown in Figure 1-2 (check out bk02ch01/example02.html).

FIGURE 1-2:
The sentence revised to italicize the word *awesome*.

← → C 🔒 htmlpreview.github.io/?https://github.com/paulmcfe/web-coding-and-dev-fd-2e/blob/main/bk02ch01/example02.ht... ⬒ ☆

In this book, you learn that HTML is *awesome*.

There are tags for lots of other structures, including important text, paragraphs, headings, page titles, links, and lists. HTML is just the collection of all these tags.

Structuring the Page with HTML

WARNING

One of the most common mistakes rookie web weavers make is to forget the slash (/) that identifies an end tag. If your page appears wrong when you view it in a browser, check for a missing slash. Also check for a backslash (\) instead of a slash, which is another common error.

Understanding Tag Attributes

You'll often use tags straight up, but all tags are capable of being modified in various ways. This change might be as simple as supplying a unique identifier to the tag for use in a script or a style, or it might be a way to change how the tag operates. Either way, you modify a tag by adding one or more *attributes* to the start tag. Most attributes use the following generic syntax:

```
<tag attribute="value">
```

Here, you replace `attribute` with the name of the attribute you want to apply to the tag, and you replace `value` with the value you want to assign the attribute.

For example, the `<a>` tag marks up text as a link. A link to what, you ask? To whatever address you specify as the value of the `href` attribute (which I explain in more detail later in the "Linking basics" section), as demonstrated in the following example (bk02ch01/example03.html):

```
Be sure to stop by my <a href="https://paulmcfedries.com/">home
    page</a>.
```

As shown in Figure 1-3, the web browser converts the `home page` text into a link that points to the address `https://paulmcfedries.com/`. (Refer to the section "Creating Links," later in this chapter, for more info on the `<a>` tag.)

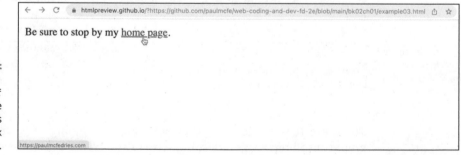

FIGURE 1-3: For the `<a>` tag, the `href` attribute specifies the link destination.

Learning the Fundamental Structure of a Web Page

In this section, I show you the tags that serve as the basic blueprint you'll use for all your web pages.

Your HTML files will always lead with the following tag:

```
<!DOCTYPE html>
```

This tag (it has no end tag) is the so-called *doctype declaration,* and it has an eye-glazingly abstruse technical meaning that, happily, you can safely ignore. All I'll say about it is that you have to include this tag at the top of all your HTML files to make sure your pages render properly. (Also, I tend to write DOCTYPE in upper-case letters out of habit, but writing it as doctype is perfectly legal.)

Next up you add the `<html lang="en">` tag. This tag tells any web browser that tries to read the file that it's dealing with a file that contains HTML doodads. It also uses the lang attribute to specify the document's language, which in this case is English.

Similarly, the last line in your document will always be the corresponding end tag: `</html>`. You can think of this tag as the HTML equivalent for "The End." So, each of your web pages will include this on the second line:

```
<html lang="en">
```

and this on the last line:

```
</html>
```

The next items serve to divide the page into two sections: the head and the body. The head section is like an introduction to the page. Web browsers use the head to glean various types of information about the page. A number of items can appear in the head section, but the only one that makes sense at this early stage is the title of the page, which I talk about in the next section, "Giving your page a title."

To define the head, add `<head>` and `</head>` tags immediately below the `<html>` tag you typed earlier. So your web page should now appear like this:

```
<!DOCTYPE html>
<html lang="en">
    <head>
    </head>
</html>
```

REMEMBER

Although technically it makes no difference if you enter your tag names in upper-case or lowercase letters, the HTML powers-that-be recommend HTML tags in lowercase letters, so that's the style I use in this book, and I encourage you to do the same.

REMEMBER

Note that I indented the `<head>` and `</head>` tags a bit (by four spaces). This indentation is good practice when HTML tags reside within another HTML container because it makes your code easier to read and easier to troubleshoot.

While you're in the head section, here's an added head-scratcher:

```
<meta charset="utf-8">
```

You place this element between the `<head>` and `</head>` tags (indented another four spaces for easier reading). It tells the web browser that your web page uses the UTF-8 character set, which you can mostly ignore except to know that UTF-8 contains almost every character (domestic and foreign), punctuation mark, and symbol known to humankind.

The body section is where you enter the text and other fun stuff that the browser will display. To define the body, place `<body>` and `</body>` tags after the head section (that is, below the `</head>` tag):

```
<!DOCTYPE html>
<html lang="en">
    <head>
        <meta charset="utf-8">
    </head>
    <body>
    </body>
</html>
```

WARNING

A common page error is to include two or more copies of these basic tags, particularly the `<body>` tag. For best results, be sure you use each of the four basic structural tags — `<!DOCTYPE>`, `<html>`, `<head>`, and `<body>` — only one time on each page.

Giving your page a title

When you surf the web, you've probably noticed that your browser displays some text in the current tab. That tab text is the web page title, which is usually a short phrase that gives the page a name. You can give your own web page a name by adding the `<title>` tag to the page's head section.

To define a title, surround the title text with the `<title>` and `</title>` tags. For example, if you want the title of your page to be "My Humble Home Page," enter it as follows:

```
<title>My Humble Home Page</title>
```

Note that you always place the title inside the head section, so your basic HTML document now appears like this (bk02ch01/example04.html):

```
<!DOCTYPE html>
<html lang="en">
    <head>
        <meta charset="utf-8">
        <title>My Humble Home Page</title>
    </head>
    <body>
    </body>
</html>
```

Figure 1-4 shows this HTML file loaded into a web browser. Notice how the title appears in the browser's tab bar.

FIGURE 1-4:
The text you insert into the `<title>` tag shows up in the browser tab.

Structuring the Page with HTML

Here are a few things to keep in mind when thinking of a title for your page:

>> Be sure your title describes what the page is all about.

>> Don't make your title longer than 50 or 60 characters. Otherwise, the browser might chop off the end because the tab doesn't have enough room to display it.

>> Use a title that makes sense when someone views it out of context. For example, if someone really likes your page, that person might add it to their list of favorites or bookmarks. The browser displays the page title in the Favorites list, so it's important that the title makes sense when the person accesses their bookmarks later.

>> Don't use cryptic or vague titles. Titling a page "Link #42" or "My Web Page" might make sense to you, but your visitors will almost certainly be scratching their heads.

Adding some text

Now it's time to put some flesh on your web page's bones by entering the text you want to appear in the body of the page. For the most part, you can type the text between the <body> and </body> tags, like this (bk02ch01/example05.html):

```
<!DOCTYPE html>
<html lang="en">
    <head>
        <meta charset="utf-8">
        <title>My Humble Home Page</title>
    </head>
    <body>
        Hello HTML World!
    </body>
</html>
```

Figure 1-5 shows how a web browser displays this HTML.

FIGURE 1-5:
Text you add to the page body appears in the browser's content window.

Before you start typing willy-nilly, however, you should know the following:

>> You might think you can line things up and create some interesting effects by stringing together two or more spaces. Ha! Web browsers chew up all those extra spaces and spit them out into the nether regions of cyberspace. Why? Well, the philosophy of the web is that you can use only HTML tags to lay out a document. So a run of multiple spaces (or *whitespace,* as it's called) is ignored.

>> Tabs also fall under the rubric of whitespace. You can enter tabs all day long, but the browser ignores them.

>> Browsers also like to ignore the carriage return. It might sound reasonable to the likes of you and me that pressing Enter (or Return on a Mac) starts a new paragraph, but that's not so in the HTML world.

>> If you want to separate two chunks of text, you have multiple ways to go, but here are the two easiest:

  • *For no space between the texts:* Place a
 (for line break) tag between the two bits of text.

  • *For some breathing room between the texts:* Surround each chunk of text with the <p> and </p> (for paragraph) tags.

>> If HTML documents are just plain text, does that mean you're out of luck if you need to use characters such as © and €? Luckily, no. For the most part, you can just add these characters to your file. However, HTML also has special codes for these kinds of characters. I talk about them a bit later in this chapter in the "Inserting Special Characters" section.

>> If, for some reason, you're using a word processor instead of a text editor, know that it won't help to format your text using the program's built-in commands. The browser cheerfully ignores even the most elaborate formatting jobs because browsers understand only HTML (and CSS and JavaScript). And besides, a document with formatting is, by definition, not a pure text file, so a browser might bite the dust trying to load it.

Some Notes on Structure versus Style

One of the key points of front-end web development is to separate the structure of the web page from its styling. This makes the page faster to build, easier to maintain, and more predictable across a range of browsers and operating systems. HTML provides the structure side, while CSS handles the styling.

That's fine as far as it goes, but HTML performs its structural duties with a couple of quirks you need to understand:

>> **This isn't your father's idea of structure.** That is, when you think of the structure of a document, you probably think of larger chunks such as articles, sections, and paragraphs. HTML does all that, but it also deals with structure at the level of sentences, words, and even characters.

>> **HTML's structures often come with some styling attached.** Or, I should say, all web browsers come with predefined styling that they use when they render some HTML tags. Yes, I know I just said that it's best to separate structure and style. Think of it this way: When you build a new deck using cedar, your completed deck has a natural cedar appearance to it, but you're free to apply a coat of varnish or paint. HTML is the cedar, whereas CSS is the paint.

I mention these quirks because they can help answer some questions that might arise as you work with HTML tags.

REMEMBER

Another key to understanding why HTML does what it does is that much of HTML has been set up so that a web page is understandable to an extent by software that analyzes the page. One important example is a screen reader used by surfers with low vision. If a screen reader can easily figure out the entire structure of the page from its HTML tags, it can present the page properly to the user. Similarly, software that seeks to index, read, or otherwise analyze the page will be able to do its task successfully only if the page's HTML tags are a faithful representation of the page's intended structure.

Applying the Basic Text Tags

HTML has a few tags that enable you to add structure to text. Many web developers use these tags only for the built-in browser formatting that comes with them, but you really should try to use the tags *semantically*, as the geeks say, which means to use them based on the meaning you want the text to convey.

Emphasizing text

One of the most common meanings you can attach to text is emphasis. By putting a little extra oomph on a word or phrase, you tell the reader to add stress to that text, which can subtly alter the meaning of your words. For example, consider the following sentence:

```
You'll never fit in there with that ridiculous thing on your
    head!
```

Now consider the same sentence with emphasis added to one word:

```
You'll never fit in there with that ridiculous thing on your
    head!
```

You emphasize text on a web page by surrounding that text with the `<em>` and `</em>` tags (bk02ch01/example06.html)):

```
You'll <em>never</em> fit in there with that ridiculous thing on
    your head!
```

All web browsers render the emphasized text in italics, as shown in Figure 1-6.

FIGURE 1-6:
The web
browser renders
emphasized text
using italics.

← → C 🔒 htmlpreview.github.io/?https://github.com/paulmcfe/web-coding-and-dev-fd-2e/blob/main/bk02ch01/example06.html ⬚ ☆

You'll *never* fit in there with that ridiculous thing on your head!

HTML has a closely related tag: `<i>`. The `<i>` tag's job is to mark up *alternative text*, which refers to any text that you want treated with a different mood or role than regular text. Common examples include book titles, technical terms, foreign words, or a person's thoughts. All web browsers render text between `<i>` and `</i>` in italics.

Marking important text

One common meaning that you'll often want your text to convey is importance. It might be some significant step in a procedure, a vital prerequisite or condition for something, or a crucial passage within a longer text block. In each case, you're dealing with text that you don't want your readers to miss, so it needs to stand out from the regular prose that surrounds it.

In HTML, you mark text as important by surrounding it with the `<strong>` and `</strong>` tags, as in this example (bk02ch01/example07.html):

```
As you enter the building, you'll see on the wall to your
right a large, red button that says, "DO NOT PRESS!" You
will be sorely tempted to press that button. The desire
```

```
to press that button will be well-nigh irresistible.
However, I urge you in the strongest possible terms:
<strong>Do not press that button!</strong>
```

All web browsers render text marked up with the <strong> tag in bold, as shown in Figure 1-7.

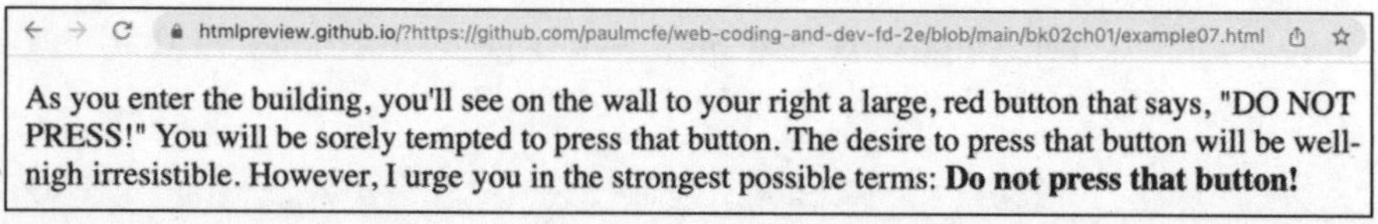

FIGURE 1-7:
The browser
renders
important text
using bold.

> ← → C   🔒 htmlpreview.github.io/?https://github.com/paulmcfe/web-coding-and-dev-fd-2e/blob/main/bk02ch01/example07.html 📋 ☆
>
> As you enter the building, you'll see on the wall to your right a large, red button that says, "DO NOT PRESS!" You will be sorely tempted to press that button. The desire to press that button will be well-nigh irresistible. However, I urge you in the strongest possible terms: **Do not press that button!**

Just to keep us all on our web development toes, HTML also offers a close cousin of the <strong> tag: the <b> tag. You use the <b> tag to mark up keywords in the text. A *keyword* is a term that you want to draw attention to because it plays a different role than the regular text. It could be a company name or a person's name (think of those bold faced names that are the staple of celebrity gossip columns). The browser renders text between the <b> and </b> tags in a bold font.

Nesting tags

It's perfectly legal — and often necessary — to combine multiple tag types by nesting one inside the other. For example, check out this code (bk02ch01/example08.html):

```
As you enter the building, you'll see on the wall to your
right a large, red button that says, "DO NOT PRESS!" You
will be sorely tempted to press that button. The desire
to press that button will be well-nigh irresistible.
However, I urge you in the strongest possible terms:
<strong>Do <em>not</em> press that button!</strong>
```

Did you notice what I did there? In the text between the <strong> and </strong> tags, I marked up the word not with the <em> and </em> tags. The result? You got it: bold, italic text, as shown in Figure 1-8.

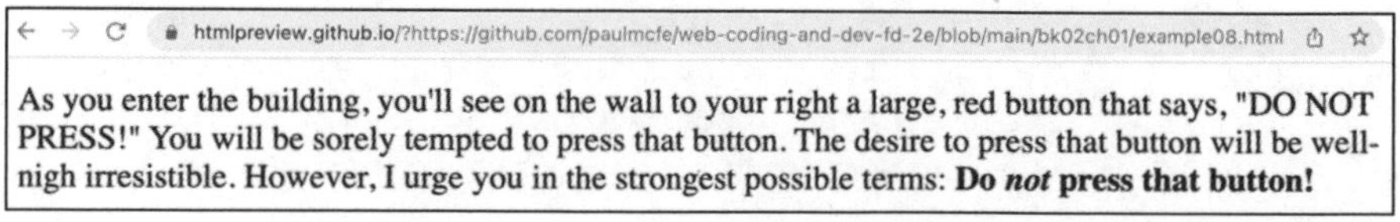

FIGURE 1-8:
The browser
usually combines
nested tags, such
as the bold, italic
text shown here.

> ← → C   🔒 htmlpreview.github.io/?https://github.com/paulmcfe/web-coding-and-dev-fd-2e/blob/main/bk02ch01/example08.html 📋 ☆
>
> As you enter the building, you'll see on the wall to your right a large, red button that says, "DO NOT PRESS!" You will be sorely tempted to press that button. The desire to press that button will be well-nigh irresistible. However, I urge you in the strongest possible terms: **Do *not* press that button!**

Adding headings

Earlier you saw that you can give your web page a title using the aptly named `<title>` tag. However, that title appears only in the browser's tab. What if you want to add a title that appears in the body of the page? That's almost easier done than said because HTML comes with a few tags that enable you to define *headings,* which are bits of text that appear in a separate paragraph and usually stick out from the surrounding text by being bigger, appearing in a bold typeface, and so on.

There are six heading tags, ranging from `<h1>`, which uses the largest type size, down to `<h6>`, which uses the smallest size. Here's some web page code (bk02ch01/example09.html) that demonstrates the six heading tags, and Figure 1-9 shows how they appear in a web browser:

```
<h1>This is Heading 1</h1>
<h2>This is Heading 2</h2>
<h3>This is Heading 3</h3>
<h4>This is Heading 4</h4>
<h5>This is Heading 5</h5>
<h6>This is Heading 6</h6>
For comparison, here's some regular text.
```

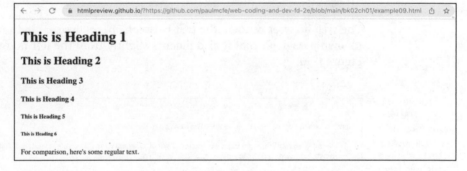

FIGURE 1-9:
The six HTML heading tags.

What's up with all the different headings? The idea is that you use them to create a kind of outline for your web page. How you do this depends on the page, but here's one possibility:

>> Use `<h1>` for the overall page title.

>> Use `<h2>` for the page subtitle.

>> Use <h3> for the titles of the main sections of your page.

>> Use <h4> for the titles of the subsections of your page.

Adding quotations

You might have noticed that each chapter of this book begins with a short, apt quotation. Hey, who doesn't love a good quote, right? The readers of your web pages will be quote-appreciators, too, I'm sure, so why not sprinkle your text with a few words from the wise?

In HTML, you designate a passage of text as a quotation by using the <block-quote> tag. Here's an example (bk02ch01/example10.html):

```
Here's what the Scottish biographer James Boswell had to say
    about puns:
<blockquote>
    For my own part I think no innocent species of wit
    or pleasantry should be suppressed: and that a good
    pun may be admitted among the smaller excellencies
    of lively conversation.
</blockquote>
I couldn't agree more!
```

The web browser renders the text between <blockquote> and </blockquote> in its own paragraph that it also indents slightly from the left margin, as shown in Figure 1-10.

FIGURE 1-10:
The web browser renders <blockquote> text indented slighted from the left.

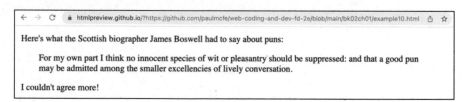

Creating Links

When all is said and done (actually, long before that), your website will consist of anywhere from 2 to 102 pages (or even more, if you've got lots to say). Here's the thing, though: If you manage to cajole someone onto your home page, how do you get that person to your other pages? That really is what the web is all about, isn't it, getting folks from one page to another? And of course, you already know the answer to the question. You get visitors from your home page to your other pages by creating links that take people from here to there. In this section, you learn how to build your own links and how to finally put the *hypertext* into HTML.

Linking basics

The HTML tags that do the link thing are `<a>` and `</a>`. Here's how the `<a>` tag works:

```
<a href="address">
```

Here, `href` stands for *hypertext reference*, which is just a fancy-schmancy way of saying "address" or "URL." Your job is to replace *address* with the address of the web page you want to use for the link. And yes, you have to enclose the address in quotation marks.

The form of `address` value you use depends on where the web page is located with respect to the page that has the link. There are three possibilities:

>> **Local web page in the same directory:** Refers to a web page that's part of your website and is stored in the same directory as the HTML file that has the link. In this case, the `<a>` tag's `href` value is the filename of the page. Here's an example:

```
<a href="kumquats.html">
```

>> **Local web page in a different directory:** Refers to a web page that's part of your website and is stored in a directory other than the one used by the HTML file that has the link. In this case, the `<a>` tag's `href` value is a backslash (/), followed by the directory name, another backslash, and then the filename of the page. Here's an example:

```
<a href="/wordplay/puns.html">
```

>> **Remote web page:** Refers to a web page that's not part of your website. In this case, the `<a>` tag's `href` value is the full URL of the page. Here's an example:

```
<a href="https://webdevworkshop.io/wb">
```

You're not done yet, though, not by a long shot (insert groan of disappointment here). What are you missing? Right: You have to give the reader some descriptive link text to click. That's pretty straightforward because all you do is insert the text between the ⟨a⟩ and ⟨/a⟩ tags, like this:

```
<a href="address">Link text</a>
```

Need an example? You got it (bk02ch01/example11.html):

```
For web coding fun, check out the
<a href="https://webdevworkshop.io/">
Web Dev Workshop</a>!
```

Figure 1-11 shows how it appears in a web browser. Note how the browser colors and underlines the link text, and when I point my mouse at the link, the address I specified in the ⟨a⟩ tag appears in the lower-left corner of the browser window.

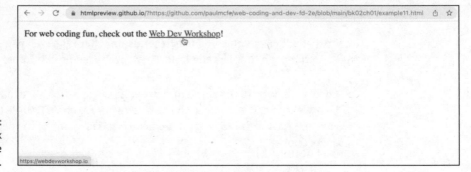

FIGURE 1-11:
How the link appears in the web browser.

Anchors aweigh: Internal links

When a surfer clicks a standard link, the page loads and the browser displays the top part of the page. However, it's possible to set up a special kind of link that will force the browser to initially display some other part of the page, such as a section in the middle of the page. For these special links, I use the term *internal links* because they take the reader directly to some inner part of the page.

When would you ever use an internal link? Most of your HTML pages will probably be short and sweet, and the web surfers who drop by will have no trouble navigating their way around. But if, like me, you suffer from a bad case of terminal verbosity combined with bouts of extreme long-windedness, you'll end up with web pages that are lengthy, to say the least. Rather than force your readers to scroll through your tomelike creations, you can set up links to various sections of the document. You can then assemble these links at the top of the page to form a sort of "hypertable of contents," as an example.

Internal links link to a specially marked element — called an *anchor* — that you've inserted somewhere on the same page. To understand how anchors work, think of how you might mark a spot in a book you're reading. You might dog-ear the page, attach a note, or place something between the pages, such as a bookmark or your cat's tail.

An anchor performs the same function: It marks a particular spot in a web page, and you can then use a regular ‹a› tag to link to that spot. Here's the general format for an anchor tag:

```
<element id="name">
```

An anchor tag appears a lot like a regular tag, except that it also includes the id attribute, which is set to the name you want to give the anchor. Here's an example:

```
<section id="section1">
```

REMEMBER

You can use whatever you want for the name, but it must begin with a letter and can include any combination of letters, numbers, underscores (_), and hyphens (–). Also, id values are case-sensitive; for example, the browser treats the id value section1 differently than the id value Section1.

To set up the anchor link, you create a regular ‹a› tag, but the href value becomes the name of the anchor, preceded by a hash symbol (#):

```
<a href="#name">
```

Here's an example that links to the anchor I showed earlier:

```
<a href="#section1">
```

TECHNICAL STUFF

Have you been wondering why the tag to create a link is ‹a› and not something more intuitive, such as ‹link› (which is used for something completely different)? The *a* in the ‹a› tag comes from the word *anchor*. Confusingly, this isn't the same *anchor* as in an anchor tag or an anchor link. Instead, in the early days of HTML, the link text that you clicked was called *anchor text,* and that text was created by surrounding it with the ‹a› and ‹/a› tags. The phrase *anchor text* is no longer used, but the ‹a› tag is here to stay.

Although you'll mostly use anchors to link to sections of the same web page, there's no law against using them to link to specific sections of other pages.

Simply add the appropriate anchor to the other page and then link to it by adding the anchor's name (preceded, as usual, by #) to the end of the page's filename. Here's an example:

```
<a href="chapter57.html#section1">
```

Building Bulleted and Numbered Lists

For some reason, people love lists: Best (and Worst) Dressed lists, Top Ten lists, My All-Time Favorite *X* lists, where *X* is whatever you want it to be: movies, songs, books, *I Love Lucy* episodes — you name it. People like lists, for whatever reasons.

Okay, so let's make some lists. Easy, right? Well, sure, any website jockey can just plop a Best Tootsie Roll Flavors Ever list on a page by typing each item, one after the other. Perhaps our list maker even gets a bit clever and inserts the <br> tag between each item, which displays them on separate lines. Ooooh.

Yes, you can make a list that way, and it works well enough, I suppose, but there's a better way. HTML has a few tags designed to give you much more control over your list-building chores. For example, you can create a bulleted list that actually has those little bullets out front of each item. Nice! Want a Top Ten list instead? HTML has your back by offering special tags for numbered lists, too.

Making your point with bulleted lists

A no-frills,
-separated list isn't very useful or readable because it doesn't come with any visual indicators that help differentiate one item from the next. An official, HTML-approved bulleted list solves that problem by leading off each item with a bullet — a cute little black dot.

Bulleted lists use two types of tags:

>> The entire list is surrounded by the <ul> and </ul> tags. Why *ul*? Well, what the rest of the world calls a bulleted list, the HTML pooh-bahs call an *unordered list.*

>> Each item in the list is preceded by the <li> (list item) tag and is closed with the </li> end tag.

Here's the general setup:

```
<ul>
    <li>Bullet text goes here</li>
    <li>And here</li>
    <li>Yes, here as well</li>
    <li>You get the idea...</li>
</ul>
```

Note that I've indented the list items by four spaces, which makes it easier to get that they're part of a `<ul></ul>` container. Here's an example to chew on (bk02ch01/example12.html):

```
<h3>My All-Time Favorite Oxymorons</h3>
<ul>
    <li>Pretty ugly</li>
    <li>Awfully good</li>
    <li>Jumbo shrimp</li>
    <li>Original copy</li>
    <li>Random order</li>
    <li>Act naturally</li>
    <li>Tight slacks</li>
    <li>Freezer burn</li>
    <li>Sight unseen</li>
    <li>Crash landing</li>
</ul>
```

Figure 1-12 shows how the web browser renders this code, cute little bullets and all.

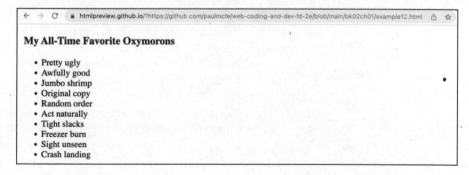

FIGURE 1-12:
A typical
bulleted list.

Numbered lists: Easy as one, two, three

If you want to include a numbered list of items — it could be a Top Ten list, bowling league standings, steps to follow, or any kind of ranking — don't bother adding the numbers yourself. Instead, you can use a *numbered list* to make the web browser generate the numbers for you.

Like bulleted lists, numbered lists use two types of tags:

>> The entire list is surrounded by the <ol> and </ol> tags. The *ol* here is short for *ordered list* because those HTML nerds just have to be different, don't they?

>> Each item in the list is surrounded by <li> and </li>.

Here's the general structure to use:

```
<ol>
    <li>First item</li>
    <li>Second item</li>
    <li>Third item</li>
    <li>You got this...</li>
</ol>
```

I've indented the list items by four spaces to make it easier to see that they're inside an <ol></ol> container. Here's an example (bk02ch01/example13.html):

```
<h3>My Ten Favorite U.S. College Nicknames</h3>
<ol>
    <li>U.C. Santa Cruz Banana Slugs</li>
    <li>Delta State Fighting Okra</li>
    <li>Kent State Golden Flashes</li>
    <li>Evergreen State College Geoducks</li>
    <li>New Mexico Tech Pygmies</li>
    <li>South Carolina Fighting Gamecocks</li>
    <li>Southern Illinois Salukis</li>
    <li>Whittier Poets</li>
    <li>Western Illinois Leathernecks</li>
    <li>Delaware Fightin' Blue Hens</li>
</ol>
```

Note that I didn't include a number before each list item. However, when I display this document in a browser (check out Figure 1-13), the numbers are automatically inserted. Pretty slick, huh?

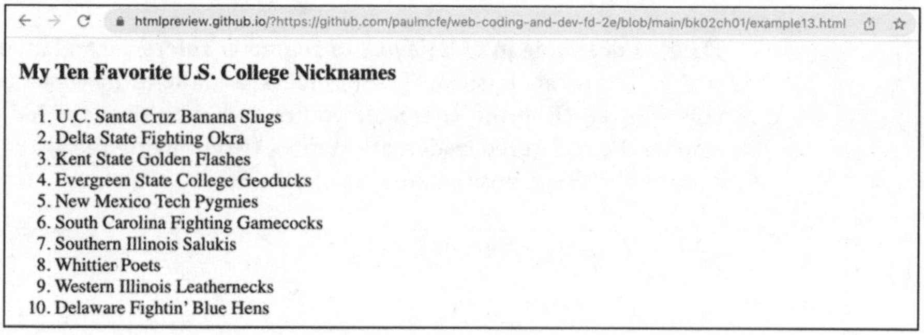
htmlpreview.github.io/?https://github.com/paulmcfe/web-coding-and-dev-fd-2e/blob/main/bk02ch01/example13.html
My Ten Favorite U.S. College Nicknames
1. U.C. Santa Cruz Banana Slugs
2. Delta State Fighting Okra
3. Kent State Golden Flashes
4. Evergreen State College Geoducks
5. New Mexico Tech Pygmies
6. South Carolina Fighting Gamecocks
7. Southern Illinois Salukis
8. Whittier Poets
9. Western Illinois Leathernecks
10. Delaware Fightin' Blue Hens

FIGURE 1-13: When the web browser renders the ordered list, it's kind enough to add the numbers for you automatically.

Inserting Special Characters

Earlier in this chapter, I talk briefly about a special `<meta>` tag that goes into the head section:

```
<meta charset="utf-8">
```

That tag, which on the surface appears to be nothing but gibberish, actually adds a bit of magic to your web page. The voodoo is that now you can add special characters such as © and ™ directly to your web page text and the web browser will display them without complaint.

The trick is how you add these characters directly to your text, and that depends on your operating system. First, if you're using Windows, you have two choices:

- Hold down the Alt key and then press the character's four-digit ASCII code using your keyboard's numeric keypad. For example, you type an em dash (—) by pressing Alt+0151.
- Paste the character from the Character Map application that comes with Windows.

If you're a Mac user, you also have two choices:

- Type the character's special keyboard shortcut. For example, you type an em dash (—) by pressing Option+Shift+- (hyphen).
- Paste the character from the Symbols Viewer that comes with macOS.

However, there's another way to add special characters to a page. The web wizards who created HTML came up with special codes called *character entities* (which is surely a name only a true geek would love) that represent these oddball symbols.

These codes come in two flavors: a character reference and an entity name. *Character references* are basically just numbers, and the *entity names* are friendlier symbols that describe the character you're trying to display. For example, you can display the registered trademark symbol (®) by using the ® character reference or the ® entity name, as shown here:

```
Print-On-Non-Demand&174;
```

or

```
Print-On-Non-Demand&reg;
```

Note that both character references and entity names begin with an ampersand (&) and end with a semicolon (;). Don't forget either character when using special characters in your own pages.

REMEMBER

One common use of character references is to display HTML tags without the web browser rendering them as tags. To do this, replace the tag's less-than sign (<) with < (or <) and the tag's greater-than sign (>) with > (or >).

Inserting Images

Whether you want to tell stories, give instructions, pontificate, or just plain rant about something, you can do all of that and more by adding text to your page. But to make it more interesting for your readers, add a bit of eye candy every now and then. To that end, you can uses an HTML tag to add one or more images to your page.

However, before we get too far into this picture business, I should tell you that, unfortunately, you can't use just any old image on a web page. Browsers are limited in the types of images they can display. You can use four main types of image formats:

>> **GIF:** The original web graphics format (it's short for Graphics Interchange Format). GIF (it's pronounced "giff" or "jiff") is limited to 256 colors, so it's best for simple images like line art, clip art, and text. GIFs are also useful for creating simple animations.

>> **JPEG:** Gets its name from the Joint Photographic Experts Group that invented it. JPEG (it's pronounced "jay-peg") supports complex images that have many millions of colors. The main advantage of JPEG files is that, given the same image, they're smaller than PNGs, so they take less time to download. Careful,

though: JPEG uses *lossy* compression, which means it makes the image smaller by discarding redundant pixels. The greater the compression, the more pixels that are discarded and the less sharp the image will appear. That said, if you have a photo or similarly complex image, JPEG is almost always the best choice because it gives the smallest file size.

>> **PNG:** The Portable Network Graphics format supports millions of colors. PNG (pronounced "p-n-g" or "ping") is a compressed format, but unlike JPEGs, PNGs use *lossless* compression. This means images retain sharpness, but the file sizes can get quite big. If you have an illustration or icon that uses solid colors or a photo that contains large areas of near-solid color, PNG is a good choice. PNG also supports transparency.

>> **SVG:** With the Scalable Vector Graphics (SVG) format, images are generated using *vectors* (mathematical formulas based on points and shapes on a grid) rather than pixels. Surprisingly, these vectors reside as a set of instructions in a special text-based format, which means you can edit the image using a text editor! SVG is a good choice for illustrations, particularly if you have software that supports the SVG format, such as Inkscape or Adobe Illustrator.

Okay, enough of all that. Time to start squeezing some images onto your web page. As I mention earlier, an HTML code tells a browser to display an image. It's the `<img>` tag, and here's how it works:

```
<img src="filename" alt="description">
```

Here, `src` is short for source, `filename` is the name of the graphics file you want to display, and `description` is a short description of the image (which is read by screen readers or revealed when users aren't displaying images or when the image fails to load). Note that there's no end tag to add here.

Here's an example. Suppose you have an image named `logo.png`. To add it to your page, you use the following line:

```
<img src="logo.png" alt="The Logophilia Ltd. company logo">
```

In effect, this tag says to the browser, "Excuse me? Would you be so kind as to go out and grab the image file named `logo.png` and insert it in the page right here where the `<img>` tag is?" Dutifully, the browser loads the image and displays it in the page.

For this simple example to work, bear in mind that your HTML file and your graphics file need to be sitting in the same directory. Many webmasters create a subdirectory just for images, which keeps things neat and tidy. If you plan on doing this, be sure to study my instructions for using directories and subdirectories in Book 1, Chapter 3.

Here's an example (bk02ch01/example14.html), with Figure 1-14 showing how things appear in a web browser:

```
To see a World in a Grain of Sand<br>
And a Heaven in a Wild Flower<br>
<img src="images/flower-and-ant.jpg"
     alt="Macro photo showing an ant exploring a flower">
```

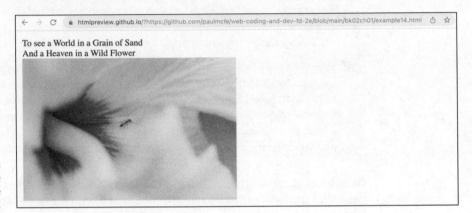

FIGURE 1-14:
A web page
with an image
thrown in.

Carving Up the Page

Adding a bit of text, some links, and maybe a list or three to the body of the page is a good start, but any web page worth posting will require much more than that. For starters, all your web pages require a high-level structure. Why? Well, think about the high-level structure of this book, which includes the front and back covers, the table of contents, an index, and seven mini-books, each of which contains several chapters, which in turn consist of many sections and paragraphs within those sections. It's all nice and neat and well-organized, if I do say so myself.

Now imagine, instead, that this entire book was just page after page of undifferentiated text: no mini-books, no chapters, no sections, no paragraphs, plus no table of contents or index. I've just described a book-reader's worst nightmare, and I'm sure I couldn't even pay you to read such a thing.

Your web pages will suffer the same fate unless you add some structure to the body section, and for that you need to turn to HTML's high-level structure tags.

The first thing to understand about these tags is that they're designed to infuse meaning — that is, semantics — into your page structures. You'll learn what this means as I introduce each tag, but for now get a load of the abstract page shown in Figure 1-15.

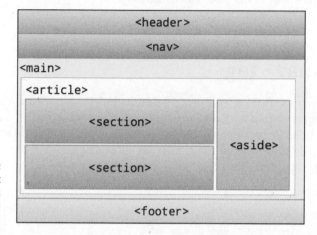

FIGURE 1-15: An abstract view of HTML5's semantic page structure tags.

I next discuss each of the tags shown in Figure 1-15.

The <header> tag

You use the ‹header› tag to create a *page header*, which is usually a strip across the top of the page that includes elements such as the site or page title and a logo. (Don't confuse the page header with the page's head section that appears between the ‹head› and ‹/head› tags.)

Since the header almost always appears at the top of the page, the ‹header› tag is usually placed right after the ‹body› tag, as shown in the following example and in Figure 1-16 (refer to bk02ch01/example15.html):

```
<body>
    <header>
        <img src="images/wdw-logo.png" alt="Web Dev Workshop
    logo">
        <h1>Welcome to Web Dev Workshop</h1>
        <hr>
    </header>
    ...
</body>
```

CHAPTER 1 **Structuring the Page with HTML** 77

FIGURE 1-16:
A page header with a logo, title, and horizontal rule.

Welcome to Web Dev Workshop

The <nav> tag

The <nav> tag defines a page section that includes a few elements that help visitors navigate your site. These elements could be links to the main sections of the site, links to recently posted content, or a search feature. The <nav> section typically appears after the header, as shown here and in Figure 1-17 (refer to bk02ch01/example16.html):

```
<body>
    <header>
        <img src="images/wdw-logo.png" alt="Web Dev Workshop
logo">
        <h1>Welcome to Web Dev Workshoph1>
        <hr>
    </header>
    <nav>
        <a href="/">Home</a>
        <a href="tools.html">Tools</a>
        <a href="code.html">Code</a>
        <a href="books.html">Books</a>
    </nav>
    ...
</body>
```

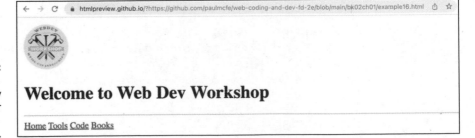

FIGURE 1-17:
The <nav> section usually appears just after the <header> section.

Welcome to Web Dev Workshop

Home Tools Code Books

The <main> tag

The `<main>` tag sets up a section to hold the content that is, in a sense, the point of the page. For example, if you're creating the page to tell everyone all that you know about Siamese Fighting Fish, your Siamese Fighting Fish text, images, links, and so on would go into the `<main>` section.

The `<main>` section usually comes right after the `<head>` and `<nav>` sections:

```
<body>
    <header>
        ...
    </header>
    <nav>
        ...
    </nav>
    <main>
        Main content goes here
    </main>
    ...
</body>
```

The <article> tag

You use the `<article>` tag to create a page section that contains a complete composition of some sort: a blog post, an essay, a poem, a review, a diatribe, or a jeremiad.

In most cases, you'll have a single `<article>` tag nested inside your page's `<main>` section:

```
<body>
    <header>
        ...
    </header>
    <nav>
        ...
    </nav>
    <main>
        <article>
            Article content goes here
        </article>
    </main>
    ...
</body>
```

However, it isn't a hard-and-fast rule that your page can have only one <arti-cle> tag. In fact, it isn't a rule at all. If you want to have two or more compositions in your page — and thus two or more <article> sections within your <main> tag — be my guest.

The <section> tag

The <section> tag indicates a major part of the page: usually a heading tag followed by some text. How do you know whether a chunk of the page is major or not? The easiest way is to imagine if your page had a table of contents. If you'd want a particular part of your page to be included in that table of contents, it's major enough to merit the <section> tag.

Most of the time, your <section> tags will appear within an <article> tag:

```
<main>
    <article>
        <section>
            Section 1 heading goes here
            Section 1 text goes here
        </section>
        <section>
            Section 2 heading goes here
            Section 2 text goes here
        </section>
        ...
    </article>
</main>
```

The <aside> tag

You use the <aside> tag to cordon off a bit of the page for content that, although important or relevant for the site as a whole, is at best tangentially related to the page's <main> content. The <aside> is often a sidebar that includes site news or links to recent content, but it might also include links to other site pages related to the current page.

The <aside> tag most often appears within the <main> area but after the <article> content:

```
<body>
    <header>
        ...
    </header>
    <nav>
        ...
    </nav>
    <main>
        <article>
            ...
        </article>
        <aside>
            Aside content goes here
        </aside>
    </main>
    ...
</body>
```

The <footer> tag

You use the ⟨footer⟩ tag to create a *page footer,* which is typically a strip across the bottom of the page that includes elements such as a copyright notice, contact info, and social media links.

Since the footer almost always appears at the bottom of the page, the ⟨footer⟩ tag is usually positioned right before the ⟨/body⟩ tag, as shown here:

```
<body>
    <header>
        ...
    </header>
    <nav>
        ...
    </nav>
    <main>
        <article>
            ...
        </article>
        <aside>
            ...
        </aside>
    </main>
```

```
        <footer>
            Footer content goes here
        </footer>
    </body>
```

Handling non-semantic content with <div>

The ‹header›, ‹nav›, ‹main›, ‹article›, ‹section›, ‹aside›, and ‹footer› tags create meaningful structures within your page, which is why HTML nerds call these *semantic* elements. Even the humble ‹p› tag, which I introduced earlier in this chapter, is semantic in that it represents a single paragraph, usually within a ‹section› tags.

But what are would-be web weavers to do when they want to add a chunk of content that just doesn't fit any of the standard semantic tags? That situation happens a lot, and the solution is to slap that content inside a div (for *division*) element. The ‹div› tag is a generic container that doesn't represent anything meaningful, so it's the perfect place for any non-semantic stuff that needs a home:

```
<div>
    Non-semantic content goes right here
</div>
```

Here's an example (bk02ch01/example17.html)):

```
<div>
    Requisite social media links:
</div>
<div>
    <a href="https://facebook.com/">Facebook</a>
    <a href="https://X.com/">X</a>
    <a href="https://instagram.com/">Instagram</a>
    <a href="https://hbo.com/silicon-valley">Hooli</a>
</div>
```

Note in Figure 1-18 that the browser renders the two ‹div› elements on separate lines.

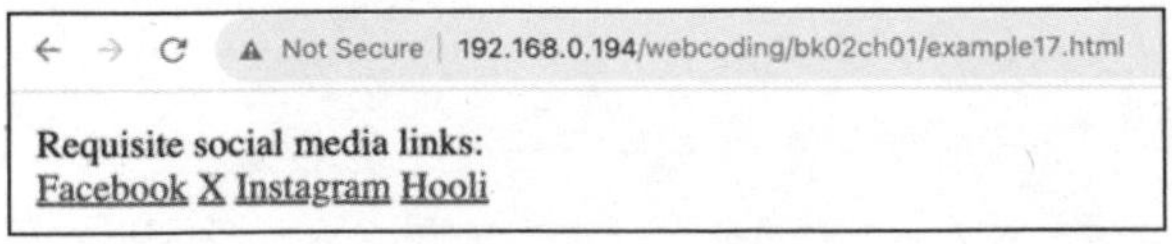

FIGURE 1-18:
The browser renders each ‹div› element on a new line.

```
← → C   🔒 Not Secure | 192.168.0.194/webcoding/bk02ch01/example17.html
```
Requisite social media links:
Facebook X Instagram Hooli

Handling words and characters with <span>

If you might want to do something with a small chunk of a larger piece of text, such as a phrase, a word, or even a character or three, you need to turn to a so-called *inline element,* which creates a container that exists within some larger element and flows along with the rest of the content in that larger element.

The most common inline element to use is span, which creates a container around a bit of text (bk02ch01/example18.html):

```
<p>
Notice how an <span style="font-variant: small-caps">
inline element</span> flows right along with the
rest of the text.
</p>
```

What's happening here is that the <span> tag is applying a style called *small caps* to the text between <span> and </span>. As shown in Figure 1-19, the <span> text flows along with the rest of the paragraph.

FIGURE 1-19:
Using <span>
makes the
container
flow with the
surrounding text.

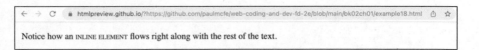

Commenting Your HTML Code

One way you can help to make your code more readable and understandable — particularly if someone else is going to be examining your code or if you want to give yourself a hand when you return to the code several months from now — is to add a generous helping of comments to the code. In an HTML file, a *comment* is a bit of text that the web browser ignores when it renders the page. That might sound useless to you, but rest assured that comments have quite a few uses:

» To add text that explains why a particular chunk of HTML is written the way it is

» To help differentiate parts of the HTML code that use similar tag structures

» To mark sections of the HTML file that you or someone else needs to start or complete

To mark some text as a comment, precede the text with ‹!-- and follow the text with --›. Here's an example (bk02ch01/example19.html):

```html
<div>
    Requisite social media links:
</div>
<!--
    Each of the following links needs to be updated with the
    full address of our corresponding social media page.
    Thanks!
-->
<div>
    <a href="https://facebook.com/">Facebook</a>
    <a href="https://X.com/">X</a>
    <a href="https://instagram.com/">Instagram</a>
    <a href="https://hbo.com/silicon-valley">Hooli</a>
</div>
```

IN THIS CHAPTER

» **Understanding cascading style sheets**

» **Learning the three methods you can use to add a style sheet**

» **Applying styles to web page elements**

» **Working with fonts and colors**

» **Taking advantage of selectors and other style sheet timesavers**

Chapter **2**

Styling the Page with CSS

HTML elements enable Web-page designers to mark up a document's structure, but beyond trust and hope, you don't have any control over your text's appearance. CSS changes that. CSS puts the designer in the driver's seat.

— HÅKON WIUM LIE, THE "FATHER" OF CSS

One of the things that makes web coding with HTML so addictive is that you can slap up a page using a few basic tags and, when you examine the result in the browser, it usually works pretty good. A work of art it's not, but it won't make your eyes sore. That basic functionality and appearance are baked-in courtesy of the default formatting that all web browsers apply to various HTML elements. For example, <strong> text appears in a bold font, there's a bit of vertical space between <p> tags, and <h1> text shows up quite a bit larger than regular text.

The browsers' default formatting means that even a basic page appears reasonable, but I'm betting you're reading this book because you want to shoot for something more than reasonable. In this chapter, you discover that the secret to creating beautiful pages is to override the default browser formatting with your own. You explore custom styling and dig into specific styles for essentials such as fonts, alignment, and colors.

Figuring Out Cascading Style Sheets

If you want to control the appearance of your web pages, the royal road to that goal is a web development technology called *cascading style sheets,* or *CSS.* As I mention in Book 2, Chapter 1, your design goal should always be to separate structure and formatting when you build any web project. HTML's job is to take care of the structure part, but to handle the formatting of the page you must turn to CSS. Before getting to the specifics, I answer three simple questions: What's a style? What's a sheet? What's a cascade?

Styles: Bundles of formatting options

If you've ever used a fancy-schmancy word processor such as Microsoft Word, Google Docs, or Apple Pages, you've probably stumbled over a style or two in your travels. In a nutshell, a *style* is a combination of two or more formatting options rolled into one nice, neat package. For example, you might have a Title style that combines four formatting options: bold, centered, 24-point type size, and a Verdana typeface. You can then apply this style to any text, and the program dutifully formats the text with all four options. If you change your mind later and decide your titles should use, say, an 18-point font, all you have to do is redefine the Title style. The program automatically trudges through the entire document and updates each bit of text that uses the Title style.

In a web page, a style performs a similar function. That is, it enables you to define a series of formatting options for a given page knickknack, such as a tag like ‹div› or ‹h1›. Like word processor styles, web page styles offer two main advantages:

» They save time because you create the definition of the style's formatting once, and the browser applies that formatting each time you use the corresponding page element.

» They make your pages easier to modify because all you need to do is edit the style definition — all the places where the style is used within the page are updated automatically.

For example, Figure 2-1 shows some ‹h1› text as it appears with the web browser's default formatting (check out bk02ch02/example01.html in this book's example files). Figure 2-2 shows the same ‹h1› text, but now I've souped up the text with several styles, including a border, a font size of 72 pixels, the Verdana typeface, and page centering (check out bk02ch02/example02.html).

FIGURE 2-1:
An <h1> heading that appears with the web browser's default formatting.

FIGURE 2-2:
The same text from Figure 2-1, now with added styles.

Sheets: Collections of styles

So far so good, but what the heck is a sheet? The term *style sheet* harkens back to the days of yore when old-timey publishing firms would keep track of their preferences for things such as typefaces, type sizes, and margins. All these so-called house styles were stored in a manual known as a *style sheet.* On the web, a style sheet is similar: It's a collection styles that you can apply to a web page.

Cascading: How styles propagate

The *cascading* part of the name *cascading style sheets* is a bit technical; it refers to a mechanism built into CSS for propagating styles between elements. For example, suppose you want all your page text to be blue instead of the default black. Does that mean you have to create a "display as blue" CSS instruction for every single text-related tag on your page? No, thank goodness! Instead, you apply it just once, to, say, the <body> tag, and CSS makes sure that every text tag in the <body> tag gets displayed as blue. This is called *cascading* a style. I go into this cascading business in a bit more detail later in the chapter (in the section titled "Revisiting the Cascade"), but before you get there, you need to learn more about how CSS works.

Getting the Hang of CSS Rules and Declarations

Before I show you how to use CSS in your web pages, I want to take a second to give you an overview of how a style is structured.

The simplest case is where a single formatting option is applied to an element. The general syntax is

```
selector {
    property: value;
}
```

Here, `selector` is a reference to the web page doodad to which you want the style applied. This reference (known in the CSS trade as a *selector* because it selects what you want to format) is often an HTML element name (such as h1 or div), but CSS has a powerful toolbox of ways you can reference things, which I discuss later in this chapter.

The `property` part is the name of the CSS property you want to apply. CSS offers a large collection of properties, each of which is a short, alphabetic keyword, such as font-family for the typeface, color for the text color, and border-width for the thickness of a border. The property name is followed by a colon (:), a space for readability, the `value` you want to assign to the property, and then a semicolon (;). This combination — property name, colon, space, and value — is known in the trade as a *CSS declaration* (although the moniker *property-value pair* is common, as well).

REMEMBER

Always enter the `property` name using lowercase letters. If the `value` includes any characters other than letters or a hyphen, you need to surround the value with quotation marks.

Note, too, that the declaration is surrounded by braces ({ and }). All the previous code — from the selector down to the closing brace (}) is called a *style rule.*

For example, the following rule applies a 72-pixel (indicated by the px unit) font size to the <h1> tag:

```
h1 {
    font-size: 72px;
}
```

Your style rules aren't restricted to just a single declaration: You're free to add as many as you need. The following example shows the rule I used to style the h1 element as shown earlier in Figure 2-2 (again, check out bk02ch02/example02.html):

```
h1 {
    border-color: black;
    border-style: solid;
```

```
    border-width: 1px;
    font-family: Verdana;
    font-size: 72px;
    text-align: center;
}
```

REMEMBER

Note that the *declaration block* — that is, the part of the rule within the braces ({ and }) — is most easily read if you indent the declarations with a tab or with either two or four spaces. The order of the declarations isn't crucial; some developers use alphabetical order, whereas others group related properties.

Besides applying multiple styles to a single selector, it's also possible to apply a single style to multiple selectors. You set up the style in the usual way, but instead of a single selector at the beginning of the rule, you list all the selectors that you want to style, separated by commas. In the following example, a yellow background color is applied to the ‹header›, ‹aside›, and ‹footer› tags:

```
header,
aside,
footer {
    background-color: yellow;
}
```

Adding Styles to a Page

With HTML tags, you just plop the tag where you want it to appear on the page, but styles aren't quite so straightforward. In fact, you can style your web page in three main ways: inline styles, internal style sheets, and external style sheets.

Inserting inline styles

An *inline style* is a style rule that you insert directly into whatever tag you want to format. Here's the general syntax to use:

```
<element style="property1: value1; property2: value2; ...">
```

That is, you add the style attribute to your tag, and then set it equal to one or more declarations, separated by semicolons.

For example, to apply 72-pixel type to an ‹h1› heading, you'd add an inline style that uses the font-size CSS property:

```
<h1 style="font-size: 72px;">
```

REMEMBER

Note that an inline style gets applied only to the tag within which it appears. Consider the following code (bk02ch02/example03.html):

```
<h1 style="font-size: 72px;">The Big Kahuna</h1>
<h1>Kahunas: Always Big?</h1>
<h1>Wait, What the Heck Is a Kahuna?</h1>
```

As shown in Figure 2-3, the larger type size only gets applied to the first ‹h1› tag, whereas the other two h1 elements appear in the browser's default size.

```
←  →  C    🔒 htmlpreview.github.io/?https://github.com/paulmcfe/web-coding-and-dev-fd-2e/blob/main/bk02ch02/example03.html    🔲  ☆
```

The Big Kahuna

Kahunas: Always Big?

Wait, What the Heck Is a Kahuna?

FIGURE 2-3:
Only the top ‹h1›
tag has the inline
style, so only its
text is styled
at 72 pixels.

Embedding an internal style sheet

Inline styles are a useful tool, but because they get shoehorned inside tags they end up scattered all over the page's HTML code and tend to be difficult to maintain. Also, an inline style applies to just a single element, but you're more likely to want a particular style rule applied to multiple page elements.

For easier maintenance of your styles, and to take advantage of the many ways that CSS offers to apply a single style rule to multiple page elements, you need to turn to style sheets, which can be either internal (as I discuss here) or external (as I discuss in the next section).

An *internal style sheet* is a style sheet that resides within the same file as the page's HTML code. Specifically, the style sheet is embedded between the ‹style› and ‹/style› tags in the page's head section, like so:

```
<!DOCTYPE html>
<html lang="en">
```

```
        <head>
            <meta charset="utf-8">
            <title>Page title</title>
            <style>
                Your style rules go here
            </style>
        </head>
        <body>
...
```

Here's the general syntax to use:

```
<style>
    selectorA {
        propertyA1: valueA1;
        propertyA2: valueA2;
        ...
    }
    selectorB {
        propertyB1: valueB1;
        propertyB2: valueB2;
        ...
    }
    ...
</style>
```

An internal style sheet consists of one or more style rules embedded within a <style> tag, which is why an internal style sheet is also sometimes called an *embedded style sheet*.

In the following code (bk02ch02/example04.html), I apply border styles to the h1 and h2 elements: solid and dotted, respectively. Figure 2-4 shows the result.

HTML:

```
<h1>Whither Solid Colors?</h1>
<h2>In Praise of Polka Dots</h2>
<h2>What's Dot and What's Not</h2>
<h2>What Dot to Wear</h2>
```

CSS:

```
<style>
    h1 {
        border-color: black;
```

```
        border-style: solid;
        border-width: 2px;
    }
    h2 {
        border-color: black;
        border-style: dotted;
        border-width: 2px;
    }
</style>
```

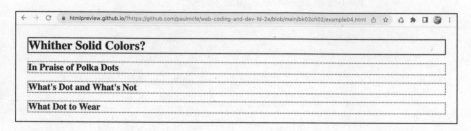

FIGURE 2-4:
An internal style
sheet that applies
different border
styles to the
h1 (top) and h2
elements.

Note, in particular, that my single style rule for the h2 element gets applied to all the <h2> tags in the web page. That's the power of an internal style sheet: You need only a single rule to apply one or more styles to every instance of a particular element.

The internal style sheet method is best when you want to apply a particular set of style rules to just a single web page. If you have rules that you want applied to multiple pages, you need to go the external style sheet route.

Linking to an external style sheet

Style sheets get insanely powerful when you use an *external style sheet*, which is a separate file that contains your style rules. To use these rules within any web page, you add a special <link> tag inside the page head. This tag specifies the name and location of the external style sheet file, and the browser then uses that file to grab the style rules.

Here are the steps you need to follow to set up an external style sheet:

1. **Use your favorite text editor to create a shiny new text file.**

2. **Add your style rules to this file.**

   Note that you don't need the <style> tag or any other HTML tags.

3. Save the file.

It's traditional to save external style sheet files using a `.css` extension (for example, `styles.css`), which helps you remember down the road that this is a style sheet file. You can either save the file in the same folder as your HTML file or create a subfolder (named, say, `css` or `styles`).

4. For every page in which you want to use the styles, add a `<link>` tag inside the page's head section.

Here's the general format to use (where *filename*`.css` is the name of your external style sheet file):

```
<link rel="stylesheet" href="filename.css">
```

If you created a subfolder for your CSS files, be sure to add the subfolder to the `href` value (for example, `href="styles/filename.css"`).

For example, suppose you create a style sheet file named `styles.css`, and that file includes the following style rules (bk02ch02/styles.css):

```
h1 {
    color: red;
}
p {
    font-size: 20px;
}
```

You then refer to that file by using the `<link>` tag, as shown here (bk02ch02/example05.html):

```
<!DOCTYPE html>
<html lang="en">
    <head>
        <meta charset="utf-8">
        <title>Page title</title>
        <link rel="stylesheet" href="styles.css">
    </head>
    <body>
        <h1>This Heading Will Appear Red</h1>
        <p>This text will be displayed in a 20-pixel font</p>
    </body>
</html>
```

Why is having an external style sheet so powerful? You can add the same `<link>` tag to any number of web pages, and they'll all use the same style rules. This one-sheet-to-style-them-all approach makes it a breeze to create a consistent look and feel for your site. And if you decide that your <h1> text should be, say, green instead, all you have to do is edit the style sheet file (styles.css). Automatically, every single one of your pages that link to this file will be updated with the new style!

Styling Page Text

You'll spend the bulk of your CSS development time applying styles to your web page text. CSS offers a huge number of text properties, but those I show in Table 2-1 are the most common. I discuss each of these properties in more detail in the sections that follow.

TABLE 2-1 ## Some Common CSS Text Properties

Property	Example	Description
font-size	font-size: 20px;	Sets the size of the text
font-family	font-family: serif;	Sets the typeface of the text
font-weight	font-weight: bold;	Sets whether the text uses a bold font
font-style	font-style: italic;	Sets whether the text uses an italic font
text-decoration	text-decoration: underline;	Applies (or removes) underline or strikethrough styles
text-align	text-align: center;	Aligns paragraph text horizontally
text-indent	text-indent: 8px;	Sets the size of the indent for the first line of a paragraph

Setting the type size

When it comes to the size of your page text, the CSS tool to pull out of the box is font-size:

```
font-size: value;
```

Here, value is the size you want to apply to your element, which means a number followed by the unit you want to use. I discuss the units you can use in the next section, but for now we can stick with one of the most common units: pixels. The pixels unit is represented by the letters px, and a single pixel is equivalent to

1/96 of an inch. All browsers set a default size for regular text, and that default is usually 16px. However, if you prefer that, say, all your paragraph (`<p>`) text get displayed at the 20-pixel size, you'd include the following rule in your style sheet:

```
p {
    font-size: 20px;
}
```

Getting comfy with CSS measurement units

CSS offers a few measurement units that you need to know. You use these units not only for setting type sizes but also for setting the size of padding, borders, margins, shadows, and many other CSS properties. Table 2-2 lists the most common CSS measurement units.

TABLE 2-2   **Some CSS Measurement Units**

Unit	Name	Type	Equals
px	pixel	Absolute	1/96 of an inch
pt	point	Absolute	1/72 of an inch
em	em	Relative	The element's default, inherited, or defined font size
rem	root em	Relative	The font size of the root element of the web page
vw	viewport width	Relative	1/100 of the current width of the browser's content area
vh	viewport height	Relative	1/100 of the current height of the browser's content area

Here are some notes about these units that I hope will decrease that furrow in your brow:

>> An *absolute* measurement unit is one that has a fixed size: either 1/96 of an inch in the case of a pixel or 1/72 of an inch in the case of a point.

>> A *relative* unit is one that doesn't have a fixed size. Instead, the size depends on whatever size is supplied to the element. For example, suppose the browser's default text size is 16px, which is equivalent then to 1em. If your page consists of a single `<article>` tag and you set the `article` element's `font-size` property to 1.5em, the browser will display text within the `<article>` tag at 24px (since 16 times 1.5 equals 24). If, however, the browser user has configured their default text size to 20px, they'll get your `article` text displayed at 30px (20 times 1.5 equals 30).

» The em unit can sometimes be a head-scratcher because it takes its value from whatever element it's contained within. For example, if your page has an `<article>` tag and you set the article element's `font-size` property to 1.5em, the browser will display text within the `<article>` tag at 24px (assuming a 16px default size). However, if within the `<article>` tag you have a `<section>` tag and you set the section element's `font-size` property to 1.25em, the browser will display text within the `<section>` tag at 30px (since 24 times 1.25 equals 30).

» If you want more consistency in your text sizes, use rem instead of em, because rem is always based on the default font size defined by either the web browser or the user. For example, if your page uses a 16px default size and has an `<article>` tag with the `font-size` property set to 1.5rem, the browser will display text within the `<article>` tag at 24px. If within the `<article>` tag you have a `<section>` tag and you set the section element's `font-size` property to 1.25rem, the browser will display text within the `<section>` tag at 20px (since 16 times 1.25 equals 20).

Applying a font family

You can make a huge difference in the overall appeal of your web pages by paying attention to the typefaces you apply to your headings and body text. A *typeface* is a particular design applied to all letters, numbers, symbols, and other characters. CSS types prefer the term *font family*, hence the property you use to set text in a specific typeface is named `font-family`:

```
font-family: value;
```

Here, *value* is the name of the typeface, which needs to be surrounded by quotation marks if the name contains spaces, numbers, or punctuation marks other than a hyphen (–). Feel free to list multiple typefaces, as long as you separate each with a comma. When you list two or more font families, the browser reads the list from left to right, and uses the first font that's available either on the user's system or in the browser itself.

When it comes to specifying font families, you have three choices:

» **Use a generic font.** This font is implemented by the browser itself and set by using one of the following five keywords: serif (offers small cross strokes at the ends of many characters), sans-serif (doesn't use the cross strokes), cursive (similar to handwriting), fantasy (a decorative font), or monospace (gives equal space to each character). Figure 2-5 shows each of these generic fonts in action (for the code, check out bk02ch02/example06.html).

FIGURE 2-5:
Generic fonts
are implemented
by all web
browsers and
come in five
flavors: `serif`,
`sans-serif`,
`cursive`,
`fantasy`, and
`monospace`.

htmlpreview.github.io/?https://github.com/paulmcfe/web-coding-and-dev-fd-2e/blob/main/bk02ch02/example06.html

Generic font family: serif

Generic font family: sans-serif

Generic font family: cursive

Generic font family: fantasy

`Generic font family: monospace`

>> **Use a system font.** This typeface is installed on the user's computer. How can
you possibly know that? You don't. Instead, you have two choices. One
possibility is to use a system font that's installed universally. Examples include
Georgia and Times New Roman (serifs), Verdana and Tahoma (sans serifs),
and Courier New (monospace). The other way to go is to list several system
fonts, knowing that the browser will use the first one that's implemented on
the user's PC. Here's a sans-serif example:

```
font-family: "Gill Sans", Calibri, Verdana, sans-serif;
```

TIP

One useful system font is `system-ui`, which tells the web browser to use the
default typeface of the user's operating system. This font can give your web
pages a familiar feel. (For an example, check out bk02ch02/example07.html,
mentioned in the next section.)

>> **Use a Google font.** Google Fonts offers access to hundreds of free and
well-crafted fonts that you can use on your site. Go to `https://fonts.`
`google.com`, click a font you like, and then click the plus sign (+) beside styles
such as bold and italic. In the Use On the Web section of the right sidebar,
copy the `<link>` tags and then paste them in your HTML file, somewhere in
the `<head>` section (before your `<style>` tag if you're using an internal style
sheet, or before your CSS `<link>` tag if you're using an external style sheet).
Go back to the Use On the Web section, copy the `font-family` declaration,
and then paste that into each CSS rule where you want to use the font.

Changing the font weight

In Book 2, Chapter 1, I talk about how the `<strong>` and `<b>` tags have semantic
definitions (important text and keywords, respectively). But what if you want text
to appear bold, but that text isn't important or a keyword? In that case, you can
style the text the CSS way with the `font-weight` property:

```
font-weight: value;
```

Here, *value* is either the word `bold`, or one of the numbers `100`, `200`, `300`, `400`, `500`, `600`, `700` (this is the same as using `bold`), `800`, and `900`, where the higher numbers give bolder text and the lower numbers give lighter text (check out bk02ch02/example07.html and Figure 2-6); `400` is regular text, which you can also specify using the word `normal`. Note, however, that depending on the typeface you're using, not all of these values will give you bolder or lighter text.

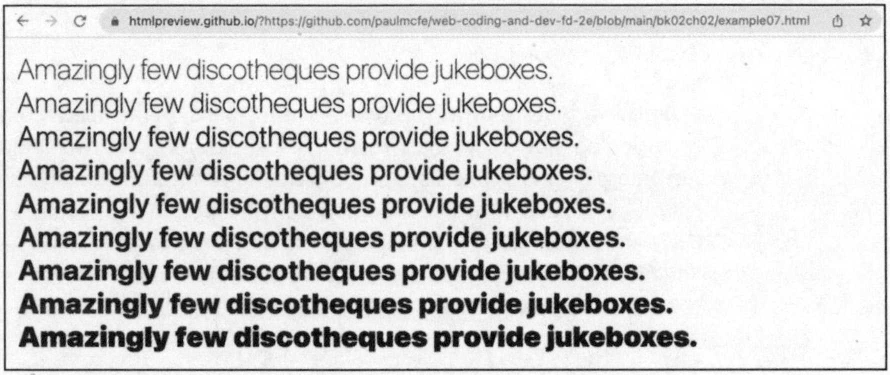

FIGURE 2-6: These sentences demonstrate font-weight values from 100 (top) to 900 (bottom).

Styling text with italics

In Book 2, Chapter 1, I mention that the `<em>` and `<i>` tags have semantic significance (emphasis and alternative text, respectively). But what if you have text that should get rendered in italics but not with emphasis or as alternative text? No problem: Get CSS on the job by adding the `font-style` property to your rule (bk02ch02/example08.html):

```
font-style: italic;
```

Styling links

When you add a link to the page, the web browser displays the link text in a different color (usually blue) and underlined. This might not fit with the rest of your page design, so go ahead and adjust the link styling as needed.

You can apply any text style to a link, including changing the font size, typeface, and color (which I discuss later in this chapter), and adding bold or italics.

One common question web coders ask is "Links: underline or not?" Not everyone is a fan of underlined text, and if you fall into that camp, you can use the following rule to remove the underline from your links:

```
a {
    text-decoration: none;
}
```

WARNING

Creating a custom style for links is standard operating procedure for web developers, but a bit of caution is in order because a mistake made by many new web designers it to style links too much like regular text (particularly when they've removed underlining from their links). Your site visitors should be able to recognize a link from ten paces, so be sure to make your links stick out from the regular text in some way.

TIP

If you style, say, an `aside` element with various text properties (such as `color` and `font-size`) and then include a link within that `aside`, the web browser will stubbornly refuse to apply the `aside` element's styles to the link! Cue the frustration! The reason is technical, but the solution is to use either the descendant combinator or the child combinator, both of which I discuss later in this chapter (in the "Getting to Know the Web Page Family" section).

Aligning text horizontally

By default, your web page text lines up nice and neat along the left margin of the page. Nothing wrong with that, but what if you want things to align along the right margin, instead? Or perhaps you want to center something on the page. Wouldn't that be nice? You can do all that and more by pulling out the `text-align` property (check out bk02ch02/example09.html and Figure 2-7):

```
text-align: left|center|right|justify;
```

The `justify` value tells the web browser to align the element's text on both the left and right margin.

FIGURE 2-7:
The `left`, `center`, `right`, and `justify` alignment options in action (from left to right).

Indenting a paragraph's first line

You can signal the reader that a new paragraph is being launched by indenting the first line a bit from the left margin. This is easier done than said with CSS by applying the `text-indent` property:

```
text-indent: value;
```

Here, `value` is a number followed by any of the CSS measurement units I mention earlier in this chapter. For example, a common indent value is `1em`, which I've applied here to the `p` element:

```
p {
    text-indent: 1em;
}
```

Working with Colors

When rendering the page using their default styles, browsers don't do much with colors, other than showing link text a default and familiar blue. But CSS offers some powerful color tools, so there's no reason not to show the world your true colors.

Specifying a color

I begin by showing you the three main ways that CSS provides for specifying the color you want:

» **Use a color keyword.** CSS defines more than 140 color keywords. Some of these are straightforward, such as `red`, `yellow`, and `purple`, while others are, well, a bit whimsical (and hunger-inducing): `lemonchiffon`, `papayawhip`, and `peachpuff`. My Web Dev Workshop (`https://webdevworkshop.io/tools/css-color-keywords/`) lists them all, as shown in Figure 2-8.

» **Use the `rgb()` function.** `rgb()` is a built-in CSS function that takes three values: one for red, one for green, and one for blue (separated by spaces). Each of these can be a value between 0 and 255, and these combinations can produce any of the 16 million or so colors on the spectrum. For example, the following function produces a nice red:

```
rgb(255 99 71)
```

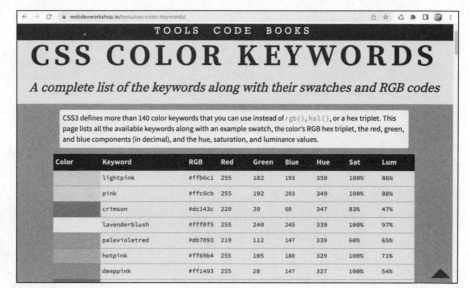

CSS3 defines more than 140 color keywords that you can use instead of rgb(), hsl(), or a hex triplet. This page lists all the available keywords along with an example swatch, the color's RGB hex triplet, the red, green, and blue components (in decimal), and the hue, saturation, and luminance values.

Color	Keyword	RGB	Red	Green	Blue	Hue	Sat	Lum
	lightpink	#ffb6c1	255	182	193	350	100%	86%
	pink	#ffc0cb	255	192	203	349	100%	88%
	crimson	#dc143c	220	20	60	347	83%	47%
	lavenderblush	#fff0f5	255	240	245	339	100%	97%
	palevioletred	#db7093	219	112	147	339	60%	65%
	hotpink	#ff69b4	255	105	180	329	100%	71%
	deeppink	#ff1493	255	20	147	327	100%	54%

FIGURE 2-8: Go to the Web Dev Workshop to access a full list of the CSS color keywords.

» **Use an RGB code.** An *RGB code* is a six-digit value that takes the form #*rrggbb*, where *rr* is a two-digit value that specifies the red component of the color, *gg* is a two-digit value that specifies the green component, and *bb* is a two-digit value that specifies the blue component. Alas, these two-digit values are hexadecimal — base 16 — numbers, which run from 0 to 9 and then *a* to *f*. As two-digit values, the decimal values 0 through 255 are represented as 00 through *ff* in hexadecimal. For example, the following RGB code produces the same red as in the previous example:

```
#ff6347
```

Coloring text

To apply a CSS color to some text, you use the color property:

```
color: value;
```

Here, *value* can be a color keyword, an rgb() function, or an RGB code. The following three rules produce the same color text:

```
color: tomato;
color: rgb(255 99 71);
color: #ff6347;
```

Coloring the background

For some extra page pizazz, try adding a color to the background of either the entire page or a particular element. You do this in CSS by using the `background-color` property:

```
background-color: value;
```

Here, `value` can be a color keyword, an `rgb()` function, or an RGB code. The following example displays the page with white text on a black background:

```
body {
    color: rgb(255 255 255);
    background-color: rgb(0 0 0);
}
```

WARNING

When you're messing around with text and background colors, make sure you leave enough contrast between the text and background to ensure that your page visitors can still read the text without shaking their fists at you. But too much contrast isn't conducive to easy reading, either. For example, using pure white for text and pure black for the background (as I did in the preceding code, tsk, tsk) isn't great because there's too much contrast. Darkening the text a shade and lightening the background a notch makes all the difference:

```
body {
    color: rgb(222 222 222);
    background-color: rgb(32 32 32);
}
```

Getting to Know the Web Page Family

One of the prerequisites for becoming a web developer is understanding both the structure of a typical web page and the odd (at least at first) lingo associated with that structure. As an example, I'm going to refer to the semantic HTML elements that I demonstrate in Book 2, Chapter 1 (in Figure 1-16, in particular). Figure 2-9 shows that semantic structure as a tree diagram:

The tree has the ‹html› tag at the top. The second level consists of the ‹head› tag and the ‹body› tag, and the ‹head› tag leads to a third level that consists of the ‹title› and ‹style› tags. For the ‹body› tag, the third level contains four tags: ‹header›, ‹nav›, ‹main›, and ‹footer›. The ‹main› tag leads to the ‹article› tag, which contains two ‹section› tags and an ‹aside› tag.

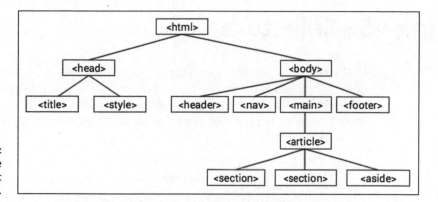

FIGURE 2-9:
The structure
of a semantic
HTML web page.

Okay, I can see the "So what?" thought bubble over your head, so I'll get to the heart of the matter. With this structure in mind, you can now identify and define five useful members of the web page family tree:

» **Parent:** An element that contains one or more other elements in the level below it. For example, in Figure 2-9, the ‹html› tag is the parent of the ‹head› and ‹body› tags, whereas the ‹head› tag is the parent of the ‹title› and ‹style› tags.

» **Child:** An element that is contained within another element that sits one level above it in the tree. (Which is another way of saying that the element has a parent.) In Figure 2-9 the ‹header›, ‹nav›, ‹main›, and ‹footer› tags are children of the ‹body› tag, whereas the two ‹section› tags and the ‹aside› tag are children of the ‹article› tag.

» **Siblings:** Two or more elements that share the same parent element. In Figure 2-9 the ‹header›, ‹nav›, ‹main›, and ‹footer› tags are siblings because they share the ‹body› tag as a parent element.

» **Ancestor:** An element that contains one or more levels of elements. In Figure 2-9, the ‹body› tag is an ancestor of the ‹aside› tag, whereas the ‹html› tag is an ancestor of everything on the page.

» **Descendant:** An element that is contained within another element that sits one or more levels above it in the tree. In Figure 2-9, the ‹section› tags are descendants of the ‹main› tag, whereas the ‹article› tag is a descendant of the ‹body› tag.

This no doubt seems far removed from web development, but these ideas play a crucial role in CSS (and also in JavaScript; refer to Book 3) because they enable your code to target page elements powerfully and succinctly. That targeting is done with special codes called selectors, which I discuss next.

Using CSS Selectors

When you add a CSS rule to an internal or external style sheet, you assemble your declarations into a declaration block (that is, you surround them with the { and } thingies) and then assign that block to a selector that specifies the page item (or items) you want to style. For example, the following rule throws a few properties at the page's ‹h1› tags:

```
h1 {
    font-size: 72px;
    font-family: Verdana;
    text-align: center;
}
```

But the selector you assign to the declaration block doesn't have to be an HTML tag name. In fact, CSS has a huge number of ways to specify a selector to define what parts of the page you want to style. When you use a tag name, for example, you're specifying a *type selector*. However, there are many more selectors — a few dozen, in fact — but lucky for you, the ones I discuss in the sections that follow should cover most of your web development needs.

The class selector (.)

If you master just one CSS selector, make it the class selector because you'll use it time and again in your web projects. A *class selector* is one that targets its styles at a particular web page class. So, what's a class? I'm glad you asked. A *class* is an attribute assigned to one or more page tags that enables you to create a kind of grouping for those tags. Here's the syntax for adding a class to an element:

```
‹element class="class-name"›
```

Replace `element` with the name of the element and replace `class-name` with the name you want to assign. The name must begin with a letter and the rest can be any combination of letters, numbers, hyphens (-), and underscores (_). Here's an example:

```
‹div class="caption"›
```

With your classes assigned to your tags as needed, you're ready to start selecting those classes using CSS. You do that by preceding the class name with a dot (.) in your style rule:

```
.class-name {
    property1: value1;
    property2: value2;
    ...
}
```

For example, here's a rule for the caption class (bk02ch02/example10.html):

```
.caption {
    font-size: .75rem;
    font-style: italic;
}
```

The advantage here is that you can assign the caption class to any tag on the page, and CSS will apply the same style rule to each of those elements.

The id selector (#)

In Book 2, Chapter 1, I talk about creating an anchor by adding a unique id attribute to a tag, which enables you to create a link that targets the anchor:

```
<element id="id-name">
```

Here's an example:

```
<h2 id="subtitle">
```

You can also use the id attribute as a CSS selector, which enables you to target a particular element with extreme precision. You set this up by preceding the id value with a hashtag symbol (#) in your CSS rule:

```
#id-name {
    property1: value1;
    property2: value2;
    ...
}
```

For example, here's a rule for the subtitle id (bk02ch02/example11.html):

```
#subtitle {
    color: gray;
    font-size: 1.75rem;
    font-style: italic;
}
```

This isn't as useful as the class selector because it can only target a single element, which is why web developers use id selectors only rarely.

The descendant combinator

Rather than targeting specific tags, classes, or ids, you might need to target every instance of a particular element that is contained within another element. As I explain earlier (refer to "Getting to Know the Web Page Family"), those contained elements are called *descendants,* and CSS offers the *descendant combinator* for applying styles to them. To set up a descendant selector, you include in your rule the ancestor selector and the descendant selector you want to style, separated by a space:

```
ancestor descendant {
    property1: value1;
    property2: value2;
    ...
}
```

For example, here's a rule that applies a few styles to every <a> tag that's contained with an <aside> tag (bk02ch02/example12.html):

```
aside a {
    color: red;
    font-style: italic;
    text-decoration: none;
}
```

The child combinator (>)

The descendant combinator that I discuss in the preceding section is one of the most powerful in the CSS kingdom because it targets all the descendants of a particular selector that reside within an ancestor, no matter how many levels down the page hierarchy those descendants live. However, it's often more suitable and more manageable to target only those descendants that reside one level down: in short, the children of some parent element.

To aim some styles at the child elements of a parent, you use the CSS *child combinator,* where you separate the parent and child selectors with a greater-than sign (>):

```
parent > child {
    property1: value1;
```

```
        property2: value2;
        ...
}
```

For example, here's a rule that targets the links that are the immediate children of an ⟨aside⟩ tag (bk02ch02/example13.html):

```
aside > a {
    color: green;
    font-style: bold;
    text-decoration: none;
}
```

The subsequent-sibling combinator (~)

One common CSS task is to apply a style rule to a particular subject that meets the following criteria:

» The target element appears in the HTML after a specified element, which is known as the *reference* element.

» The target element and the reference element are siblings.

To apply some styles to such a subject, you use the *subsequent-sibling combinator*, where you separate the reference and target selectors with a tilde (~):

```
reference ~ target {
    property1: value1;
    property2: value2;
    ...
}
```

For example, here's a rule that targets any ul element that's a subsequent sibling of an h3 element (bk02ch02/example14.html):

```
h3 ~ ul {
    background: lightpink;
    border: 5px outset crimson;
    list-style-type: square;
    padding: 8px 20px;
}
```

The next-sibling combinator (+)

Rather than target all the siblings that come after some reference element, as does the subsequent-sibling combinator that I discuss in the preceding section, you might need to target only the *next* sibling that comes after the reference element.

For example, suppose you have a page full of h2 elements, each of which is followed by multiple p elements, where the first p element is some text that summarizes the p elements that follow. In this case, it makes sense to style those first p elements differently, perhaps by italicizing the text.

To apply a style rule to just the next sibling that comes after some reference element, you use the *next-sibling combinator*, where you separate the reference and target selectors with a plus sign (+):

```
reference + target {
    property1: value1;
    property2: value2;
    ...
}
```

For example, here's a rule that targets any p element that's the next sibling of an h2 element (bk02ch02/example15.html):

```
h2 + p {
    font-style: italic;
}
```

A review of some pseudo-classes

A class selector targets elements assigned a particular class. However, in many cases, instead of having a class in common, the elements you want to target have a particular condition in common. For example, consider each page element that's a first child of its parent. All such page elements have the condition of first-child-ness in common. How can you target such elements? By using a *pseudo-class*, which is a CSS selector that acts like a class by generically targeting elements that meet some condition (such as first-child-ness).

All pseudo-classes begin with a colon (:), followed by one or more dash-separated words. You can use a pseudo-class on its own or modified by an element. Here's the general on-its-own syntax:

```
:pseudo-class {
    property1: value1;
    property2: value2;
    ...
}
```

Using a pseudo-class on its own means your rule matches every element that meets the pseudo-class's underlying condition.

To style every element that's a first child of its parent element, you use the :first-child pseudo-class:

```
:first-child {
    font-style: italic;
}
```

However, you're more likely to want to apply your rule to first children of a specific element type. You do that by putting the element name before the pseudo-class, like so:

```
element:pseudo-class {
    property1: value1;
    property2: value2;
    ...
}
```

For example, the following rule applies a style to every p element that's a first child of its parent:

```
p:first-child {
    font-style: italic;
}
```

You can combine pseudo-classes with other selectors, particularly the combinators. For example, the following rule applies a style to every p element that's a first child of an article element:

```
article > p:first-child {
    font-style: italic;
}
```

Another common way to combine pseudo-classes and selectors is to modify the element name with a class, like so:

```
element.class:pseudo-class {
    property1: value1;
    property2: value2;
    ...
}
```

For example, the following rule applies a style to every p element that uses the intro class and is a first child of its parent:

```
p.intro:first-child {
    font-style: italic;
}
```

CSS offers several dozen pseudo-classes. Yep, several *dozen*. If that sounds like an alarming amount, don't worry: Many — perhaps even the majority of — pseudo-classes are obscure and used only occasionally at best, even by professionals. In Table 2-3, I list the most useful pseudo-classes.

TABLE 2-3   ## Some Common Pseudo-Classes

Pseudo-Class	Selects	Example

element:
first-child
	Any child element that is the first of a parent element's children.	p:first-child {
		    text-indent: 0;
		}
		Refer to bk02ch02/example16.html.

element:
last-child
	Any child element that is the last of a parent element's children.	p:last-child {
		    margin-bottom: 1.5rem;
		}
		Refer to bk02ch02/example17.html.

Pseudo-Class	Selects	Example
| *element*:<br>nth-child(*n*) | One or more elements based on their position in a parent element's collection of children. For *n*, you can use any of the following:<br><br>• An integer. For example, nth-child(2) selects the second child of the parent.<br><br>• An integer multiple. For example, nth-child(3n) selects every third child of the parent.<br><br>• An integer multiple plus an integer offset. For example, p:nth-child(3n+2) selects any p element that's in the second (n=0), fifth (n=1), eighth (n=2), and so on position of a parent's child elements.<br><br>• The keyword even. For example, nth-child(even) selects the even-numbered children of the parent.<br><br>• The keyword odd. For example, nth-child(odd) selects the odd-numbered children of the parent. | ```css
tr:nth-child(even) {

    background-color:
lightgray;

}
```<br>Refer to bk02ch02/example18.html. |
| *element*:<br>first-of-type | Any child element that's the first of its type in a parent element's children. | ```css
aside:first-of-type {

    border: 5px
double black;

}
```<br>Refer to bk02ch02/example19.html. |
| *element*:<br>last-of-type | Any child element that's the last of its type in a parent element's children. | ```css
p:last-of-type {

    margin-bottom: 1.5rem;

}
```<br>Refer to bk02ch02/example20.html. |
| *element*:<br>nth-of-type(*n*) | One or more elements of a specified type based on their position in a parent element's collection of children. You specify *n* using the same methods I outline earlier for the :nth-child() pseudo-class. | ```css
p:nth-of-type(3n) {

    background-color: gray;

}
```<br>Refer to bk02ch02/example21.html. |

(continued)

TABLE 2-3 *(continued)*

Pseudo-Class	Selects	Example
element:focus	The element that has the focus (that is, the element currently selected on the page, usually by tabbing to the element, but also by clicking within an element such as a text box).	```input:focus { background-color: lightsteelblue; }``` Refer to bk02ch02/example22.html.
element:hover	The element over which the user is hovering the mouse pointer.	```button:hover { box-shadow: 10px 5px 5px grey; }``` Refer to bk02ch02/example23.html.
element:is(*selector-list*)	Any of the selectors in the specified selector list.	```:is(h1, h2, h3) { margin: 20px 16px; }``` Refer to bk02ch02/example24.html.
element:not(*selector-list*)	Every element that doesn't match any of the selectors in the specified selector list.	```:not(.decorative) { font-family: Georgia, serif; }``` Refer to bk02ch02/example25.html.
element:where(*selector-list*)	Any of the selectors in the specified selector list.	```:where(h1, h2, h3) { margin: 20px 16px; }``` Refer to bk02ch02/example26.html.
element:has(*selector-list*)	Any element that's a parent of any item in a selector list of child elements. You can also use :has() to match an ancestor, a previous sibling, or a later sibling; see the example file.	```nav:has(> a) { background: lightgrey; border: 4px double darkgrey; }``` Refer to bk02ch02/example27.html.

TECHNICAL STUFF

The :is() and :where() pseudo-classes sure look identical, don't they? The difference is that while the specificity of :is() is the highest specificity of whatever's in the selector list, the specificity of :where() is always zero. Refer to "Revisiting the Cascade," later in this chapter, to learn about specificity.

A few pseudo-elements you need to know

As your CSS career progresses, sooner or later (almost always sooner) you'll bump up against two conundrums that have bedeviled web page designers since Day One:

» How can I insert and style content on the fly based on the current state of an element?

» How can I style a specific chunk of an element, such as its first line?

The common thread that runs through both problems is that you want to style something that's not part of the original page's HTML. In the first case, you want to add new content; in the second case, you want to style a chunk that doesn't have an HTML equivalent. In other words, you want to work with page items that are not quite elements, which are known as *pseudo-elements* in the land of CSS.

All pseudo-elements begin with two colons (::), followed by a keyword. Here's the general syntax:

```
element::pseudo-element {
    property1: value1;
    property2: value2;
    ...
}
```

where:

» *element* is the name of the element type you want to target.

» *pseudo-element* is the name of the pseudo-element.

Table 2-4 lists the four most useful pseudo-elements: `::after` and `::before`, which you use to add content on the fly — known as *generated content* — and `::first-letter` and `::first-line`, which you use to style chunks of an element.

TABLE 2-4   ## Some Common Pseudo-Elements

Pseudo-Class	Description	Example

`parent::after {`
   `content: 'content';`
   `property1: value1;`
   `property2: value2;`
   `...`
`}`
	Generates a new last child element for the specified target parent element	`:is(h2, h3)::after {`
		   `content: '¶';`
		   `color: #333;`
		   `font-size: 1rem;`
		   `margin-left: 0.25rem;`
		`}`
		Refer to bk02ch02/example28.html.

`parent::before {`
   `content: 'content';`
   `property1: value1;`
   `property2: value2;`
   `...`
`}`
	Generates a new first child element for the specified target parent element	`.tip::before {`
		   `content: 'TIP';`
		   `display: block;`
		   `color: green;`
		   `font-size: 12px;`
		`}`
		Refer to bk02ch02/example29.html.

`element::first-letter {`
   `property1: value1;`
   `property2: value2;`
   `...`
`}`
	Targets the first letter of a specified block-level element	`h2 + p::first-letter {`
		   `color: crimson;`
		   `font-size: 32px;`
		`}`
		Refer to bk02ch02/example30.html.

`element::first-line {`
   `property1: value1;`
   `property2: value2;`
   `...`
`}`
	Targets the first line of text in a specified block element	`h2 + p::first-line {`
		   `text-transform: uppercase;`
		`}`
		Refer to bk02ch02/example31.html.

Revisiting the Cascade

TECHNICAL STUFF

I close this first CSS chapter with a quick review of the cascade concept, which you need to drill into your brain if you want to write good CSS and troubleshoot the inevitable CSS problems that will crop up in your web development career.

At its heart, the *cascade* is a sorting algorithm for property declarations. For each element (or pseudo-element) on the page, the cascade begins by looking through all the page's CSS sources for every property declaration with a selector that matches the element.

If a given property declaration occurs only once for the element, the cascade applies that declaration to the element, no questions asked. However, often a property has multiple declarations for the same element and two or more of those declared property values are different. When multiple possible values can apply to an element property, the algorithm must figure out which declaration to use. To decide which declaration gets applied, the cascade assigns a *weight* — a measure of relevance — to each declaration and then styles the element using the declaration that has the greatest weight.

To figure out the declaration with the greatest weight, the cascade algorithm works through one or more tiebreaking criteria in the following order:

>> The declaration type

>> The origin type

>> Specificity

>> Source code order

The next few sections flesh out the specifics of these tiebreakers.

Understanding declaration types

CSS includes a kind of Get Out of Jail Free card that enables a property declaration to climb to the top (or close to the top) of the cascade's relevance hierarchy. That miraculous mechanism is the !important annotation, which you add to a declaration just after the end of the property value:

```
color: navy !important;
```

A declaration that includes the !important annotation is said to be using the *important* declaration type, whereas all other declarations are said to be using the *normal* declaration type.

WARNING

It's tempting to trot out the `!important` annotation any time you have a problem getting the cascade to do what you want. Every now and then you may have a good reason to go this route. However, it's almost always better to understand why the cascade is doing what it's doing and come up with a solution — for example, a more relevant selector — before launching the nuclear option of the `!important` annotation.

Understanding origin types

The source of a particular CSS declaration is known as its *origin*. The origin is important because the cascade algorithm takes the origin into account when it decides which declarations to use when rendering the page. Here's a quick summary of the major *origin types:*

>> **User agent style sheet:** The list of default styles that the web browser applies to certain HTML tags.

>> **User style sheet:** The styles that the web browser user has configured, such as a new default type size.

>> **Author style sheets:** The styles that you create or that a third-party developer has created. Author style sheets come in three varieties:

  • **External style sheets:** The style rules that reside in separate `.css` files.

  • **Internal style sheets:** The style rules you add between the `<style>` and `</style>` tags in the head section of the HTML file.

  • **Inline styles:** The style declarations you add to a tag's `style` attribute.

What do the origin types have to do with the cascade algorithm, exactly? Friend, it's all about weight.

Declaration type, origin type, and weight

The two declaration types (normal and important) combine with the different origin types to define a built-in hierarchy of weight. That is, for a given declaration, the cascade assigns a weight based on the declaration's type and origin. When two or more declarations for the same property are competing to be applied to an element, the cascade first uses the declaration type/origin type hierarchy in Table 2-5 (listed from lowest weight to highest weight) to decide which declaration gets applied.

TABLE 2-5

Declaration Type/Origin Type Weight Hierarchy

Weight Ranking (lowest to highest)	Origin Type	Declaration Type
1	User agent stylesheet	Normal
2	User stylesheet	Normal
3	Author stylesheets: Internal or external	Normal
4	Author stylesheets: Inline	Normal
5	Author stylesheets: Internal or external	Important
6	Author stylesheets: Inline	Important
7	User stylesheet	Important
8	User agent stylesheet	Important

So, for example, a normal property declaration in any author stylesheet (weight ranking 3 or 4 in Table 2-5) always overrides the same normal property declaration in the user agent stylesheet (weight ranking 1 in Table 2-5) because author stylesheets are given more weight. Similarly, an inline normal property declaration (weight ranking 4) overrides the same normal property declaration in an external or internal stylesheet (weight ranking 3) because inline styles are given more weight.

Figuring out specificity

What happens when two or more property declarations with the same declaration type and the same origin type target the same element? The declarations will have the same weight ranking from Table 2-5, so you have to turn to the cascade's next tiebreaking mechanism: specificity.

One of the jobs of the cascade is to differentiate between two kinds of selector:

>> **Broad:** A selector that targets a large range of elements. For example, the following rule targets every element in the body of the page:

```
body {
    color: slateblue;
}
```

>> **Narrow:** A selector that targets a small range of elements. For example, the following rule targets just the element that has the id value of subtitle:

```
#subtitle {
    color: dodgerblue;
}
```

Most crucially for your purposes here is the CSS concept called *specificity*, which is a measure of whether a particular selector is broad, narrow, or something in between. That is, a selector that targets a broad range of elements is said to have *low specificity*, whereas a selector that targets a narrow range of elements is said to have *high specificity*.

The general idea is that, from the cascade's point of view, the more narrowly a selector targets an element, the more likely it is that the CSS developer's intention was to have the rule apply to the element. Therefore, the more specific a selector, the higher its specificity score and the more weight the cascade gives to the selector's declaration block.

Let me stress here that the preceding is from the point of view of the *cascade*, which gives preference to selectors with the highest specificity. That doesn't mean that *you* must always prefer high-specificity selectors. Sometimes a broad selector will get the job done; sometimes a narrow selector will do. *You* get to decide the specificity of your selectors, but you must choose your selectors knowing that, for a given property declaration, the cascade will give preference to the selector with the highest specificity.

Specificity is calculated as a kind of score that examines the components of a given selector and plops them into one of the following three buckets, which for easy memorization I've labeled I, C, and E:

>> **I:** Score one point for each ID selector (that is, a selector that begins with #).

>> **C:** Score one point for each class or pseudo-class selector.

>> **E:** Score one point for each element (type) or pseudo-element selector.

You then take the total for each category — each *ICE bucket*, as I like to say — and arrange the scores in the following general way:

I-C-E

For example, if a selector has one ID selector, two class selectors, and four element selectors, the specificity is as follows:

1-2-4

Similarly, a selector with no ID selectors, three class selectors, and two element selectors would have the following specificity:

0-3-2

How does the cascade decide which of these has the higher specificity? It compares each bucket, reading them from left to right:

1. Compare the I (ID) buckets of selector A and selector B:

   - If one selector has a higher I score, that selector has the higher specificity, so skip the rest of the steps.

   - If both selectors have the same score, continue with Step 2.

2. Compare the C (class, pseudo-class) buckets of selector A and selector B:

   - If one selector has a higher C score, that selector has the higher specificity, so skip the rest of the steps.

   - If both selectors have the same C score, continue with Step 3.

3. Compare the E (element, pseudo-element) buckets of selector A and selector B:

   - If one selector has a higher E score, that selector has the higher specificity.

   - If both selectors have the same E score, it means the selectors have the same specificity, so the cascade moves on to the next tiebreaker (which is source code order; head to the next section "The ultimate tiebreaker: source code order").

So, in the preceding specificity scores, 1-2-4 has a higher specificity than 0-3-2.

To help you get a feel for converting selectors into specificity scores, the following table offers a few examples.

Selector	I Bucket	C Bucket	E Bucket	Specificity (I-C-E)
`#title`	`#title`			1-0-0
`#title > h2`	`#title`		h2	1-0-1
`.warning`		`.warning`		0-1-0

Selector	I Bucket	C Bucket	E Bucket	Specificity (I-C-E)
`section`			`section`	0-0-1
`header > nav > a:hover`		`:hover`	`header, nav, a`	0-1-3
`p.intro + aside`		`.intro`	`p, aside`	0-1-2
`footer > div.social::before`		`.social`	`footer, div, ::before`	0-1-3
`#nav-header li.external > span`	`#nav`	`.external`	`p, li, span`	1-1-3

In practice, you can use specificity to figure out why a particular element has styles that don't seem right. Quite often, the problem is that the browser is applying some other style rule that has a selector with a higher specificity.

TIP

Rather than calculate the specificity yourself, you can let one of several online calculators handle that chore for you. Here's a good one: `https://polypane.app/css-specificity-calculator/`.

The ultimate tiebreaker: Source code order

If two or more property declarations have the same declaration type, the same origin type weight ranking, and the same selector specificity, the cascade has one last tiebreaking strategy it can fall back on: source code order. That is, given multiple property declarations with equal weight, the declaration that appears latest in the source code is declared the winner.

Just to be clear (because this tiebreaker is crucial to figuring out what the cascade is doing and to solving cascade problems), here's what I mean by *latest* in the source code:

>> If the declarations all reside in the same internal or external stylesheet, *latest* means the declaration that's closest to the bottom of the stylesheet. Consider the following code:

```
p {
    color: darkorchid;
}
...
div, aside, p {
    color: indigo;
}
```

Text in the p element will be colored indigo because that declaration appears later in the source code than the darkorchid declaration.

» If the declarations reside in different external stylesheets, *latest* means the external stylesheet <link> tag that's closest to the bottom of the HTML file head section. Consider the following:

```
<head>
    <meta charset="utf-8">
    <title>Remember MySpace?</title>
    <link rel="stylesheet" href="yourstyles.css">
    <link rel="stylesheet" href="mystyles.css">
</head>
```

If both external stylesheets have a property declaration with equal weight, the declaration in the mystyles.css files will be the one the browser applies.

Putting it all together: The cascade algorithm

Okay, now I can combine all the stuff about declaration types, origin types, specificity, and source code order to explain just how the cascade goes about choosing which property declarations to apply to an element.

The cascade calculates declaration weights by running through the following steps:

1. Sort the property declarations based on the declaration type/origin type weight ranking, from highest (most weight) to lowest.

2. Check for the property declaration that has the highest ranking. One of two things can happen here:

   - If just one declaration has the top ranking, apply that declaration and then skip the rest of the steps.

   - If two or more declarations are tied at the top of the ranking, discard all the other declarations and proceed to Step 3.

3. For the property declarations tied with the highest declaration type/origin type weight ranking, calculate the specificity of each of the declarations' selectors and sort the declarations from highest specificity to lowest.

4. Check for the property declaration with the highest specificity. Again, one of two things can happen now:

- If one declaration has the highest specificity, apply that declaration and then skip the rest of the steps.

- If two or more declarations are tied with the highest specificity, discard all the other declarations and proceed to Step 5.

5. For the declarations tied with the highest specificity, sort the declarations by their order of appearance in the CSS source code.

6. Apply whichever property declaration appears latest in the code.

IN THIS CHAPTER

» Wrapping your head around the CSS box model

» Setting the sizes of page elements

» Encrusting elements with padding, borders, and margins

» Letting elements float where they may

» Positioning elements exactly where you want them

Chapter **3**

Sizing and Positioning Page Elements

Every element in web design is a rectangular box. This was my ah-ha moment that helped me really start to understand CSS-based web design and accomplish the layouts I wanted to accomplish.

— CHRIS COYIER

'm not going to lie to you: When you're just getting started with CSS, the elements on the page will sometimes seem to defy your every command. Like surly teenagers, they ignore your best advice and refuse to understand that you are — or you are supposed to be — the boss of them. Okay, I did lie to you a little: That can happen to even the most experienced web coders. Why the attitude? Because although web browsers are fine pieces of software for getting around the web, by default they're not adept at laying out a web page. Like overly permissive grandparents, they just let the page elements do whatever they like. Your job as a parent, er, I mean, a web developer, is to introduce some discipline to the page.

Fortunately, CSS comes with a huge number of tools and techniques that you can wield to make stubborn page elements behave themselves. In this chapter, you discover many of these tools and explore how best to use them to gain mastery over anything you care to add to a web page. You delve into styles that cover properties such as dimensions (the height and width of things), padding and margins (the amount of space around things), borders (lines around things), and position (where things appear on the page).

Learning about the CSS Box Model

Everything in this chapter is based on something called the CSS *box model*. So I begin by discussing what this box model thing is all about and why it's important.

Every web page consists of a series of HTML tags, and each of those tags represents an element on the page. In the strange and geeky world known as Style Sheet Land, each of these elements is considered to have an invisible box around it (okay, it's a very strange world). You might be tempted to think that this invisible box surrounds only block-level elements, which are the tags that start new sections of text: ⟨p⟩, ⟨blockquote⟩, ⟨h1⟩ through ⟨h6⟩, ⟨div⟩, all the page layout semantic tags, such as ⟨header⟩, ⟨article⟩, and ⟨section⟩. That makes sense, but in fact every single tag, even inline tags such as ⟨a⟩ and ⟨span⟩, have a box around them.

This box has the following components:

>> **Content:** The stuff inside the box (the text, the images, or whatever)

>> **Padding:** The space around the content

>> **Border:** A line that surrounds the box padding

>> **Margin:** The space outside of the border separating the box from other boxes to the left and right, as well as above and below

>> **Dimensions:** The height and width of the box

>> **Position:** The location of the box within the page

Of these, the first four — the content, padding, border, and margin — make up the box model. Figure 3-1 shows what the aforementioned invisible box looks like in the abstract, and Figure 3-2 points out the box model components using an actual page element (the code for which you can find in bk02ch03/example01.html in this book's example files).

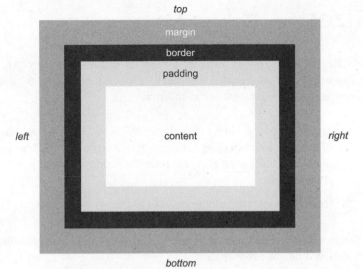

FIGURE 3-1:
The components
of the CSS
box model.

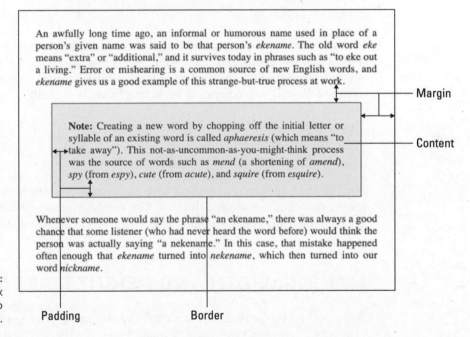

FIGURE 3-2:
The CSS box
model applied to
a page element.

Styling Sizes

When the web browser renders a page, it examines each element and sets the dimensions of that element. For block-level elements such as `header` and `div`, the browser sets the dimensions as follows:

» **Width:** Set to the width of the element's parent. Because by default the width of the body element is set to the width of the browser's content area, in practice all block-level elements have their widths set to the width of the content area.

» **Height:** Set just high enough to hold all the element's content.

You can (and should) run roughshod over these defaults by styling the element's width and height properties:

```
width: value;
height: value;
```

In both cases, you replace `value` with a number and one of the CSS measurement units I talk about in Book 2, Chapter 2: `px`, `em`, `rem`, `vw`, or `vh`. For example, if you want your page to take up only half the width of the browser's content area, you'd use the following rule (check out bk02ch03/example02.html):

```
body {
    width: 50vw;
}
```

Most of the time you'll only mess with an element's width because getting the height correct is notoriously difficult. The height depends on too many factors: the content, the browser's window size, the user's default font size, and more.

MAKING WIDTH AND HEIGHT MAKE SENSE

Width and height seem like such straightforward concepts, but you might as well learn now that CSS has a knack for turning the straightforward into the crooked-sideways. A block element's dimensions are a case in point, because you'd think the size of a block element would be the size of its box out to the border: that is, the content, plus the padding, plus the border itself. Nope. By default, the size of a block element's box is just the content part of the box.

That may not sound like a cause for alarm, but it does mean that when you're working with an element's dimensions, you have to take into account its padding widths and border sizes if you want to get things right. Believe me, doing so is no picnic. Fortunately, help is just around the corner. You can avoid all those extra calculations by forcing the web browser to be sensible and define an element's size to include not just the content but the padding and border, as well. A CSS property called `box-sizing` is the superhero here:

```
element {
    box-sizing: border-box;
}
```

The declaration `box-sizing: border-box` tells the browser to set the element's height and width to include the content, padding, and border. You could add this declaration to all your block-level element rules, but that's way too much work. Instead, you can use a trick where you use an asterisk (`*`) "element," which is a shorthand way of referencing every element on the page:

```
* {
    box-sizing: border-box;
}
```

Put this at the top of your style sheet, and then you never have to worry about it again.

**TECHNICAL
STUFF**

Height and width apply only to block-level elements such as `article`, `div`, and `p`, and not to inline elements such as `span` and `a`. However, it's possible to convert inline elements into blocks. CSS offers two methods for this inline-to-block makeover:

>> **Make it an inline block.** If you want to set an inline element's width, height, or other block-related properties but still allow the element to flow along with the surrounding text, add the following to the element's CSS rule:

```
display: inline-block;
```

>> **Make it a true block.** If you want to set an inline element's block-related properties and you no longer want the element to flow with the surrounding text, turn it into an honest-to-goodness block-level element by adding the following to the element's CSS rule:

```
display: block;
```

Adding Padding

In the CSS box model, the *padding* is the space that surrounds the content out to the border, if the box has one. Your web pages should always have lots of *whitespace* (that is, blank, content-free chunks of the page), and one way to do that is to give each element generous padding to ensure that the element's content isn't crowded either by its border or by surrounding elements.

The padding has four sections — above, to the right of, below, and to the left of the content — so CSS offers four corresponding properties for adding padding to an element:

```
element {
    padding-top: top-value;
    padding-right: right-value;
    padding-bottom: bottom-value;
    padding-left: left-value;
}
```

Each value is a number followed by a CSS measurement unit: px, em, rem, vw, or vh. Here's an example:

```
.margin-note {
    padding-top: 1rem;
    padding-right: 1.5rem;
    padding-bottom: .5rem;
    padding-left: 1.25rem;
}
```

CSS also offers a shorthand syntax that uses the padding property. You can use four different syntaxes with the padding property, and they're all listed in Table 3-1.

TABLE 3-1   **The padding Shorthand Property**

Syntax	Description
padding: *value1*;	Applies *value1* to all four sides
padding: *value1 value2*;	Applies *value1* to the top and bottom and *value2* to the right and left
padding: *value1 value2 value3*;	Applies *value1* to the top, *value2* to the right and left, and *value3* to the bottom
padding: value1 value2 value3 value4;	Applies *value1* to the top, *value2* to the right, *value3* to the bottom, and *value4* to the left

To help you remember the four-value syntax, note that the values start at the top of the element's box and proceed clockwise around the box.

Here's how you'd rewrite the previous example using the padding shorthand:

```
.margin-note {
    padding: 1rem 1.5rem .5rem 1.25rem;
}
```

To illustrate what a difference padding can make in your page designs, take a peek at Figure 3-3 (and bk02ch03/example03.html). Here you have two `<aside>` elements, where the one on top looks cramped and uninviting, whereas the one on the bottom offers ample room for reading. These two elements are styled identically, except the one on the bottom has its padding set with the following declaration:

```
padding: 1rem;
```

FIGURE 3-3: Without padding (top), your text can look uncomfortably crowded by its border, but when you add padding (bottom), the same text has room to breathe.

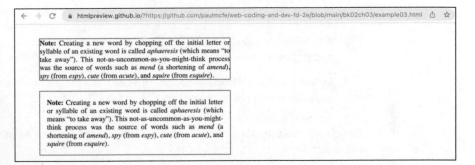

Building Borders

Modern web design eschews vertical and horizontal lines as a means of separating content, preferring, instead, to let copious amounts of whitespace do the job. However, that doesn't mean you should never use lines, particularly borders, in your designs. An element's *border* is the set of lines that enclose the element's content and padding. These lines are invisible by default, but you can use CSS not only to display the borders but also to format them to suit your design needs. Borders are an often useful way to make it clear that an element is separate from the surrounding elements in the page.

Four lines are associated with an element's border — above, to the right of, below, and to the left of the padding — so CSS offers four properties for adding borders to an element:

```
element {
    border-top: top-width top-style top-color;
    border-right: right-width right-style right-color;
    border-bottom: bottom-width bottom-style bottom-color;
    border-left: left-width left-style left-color;
}
```

Each border requires three values:

>> **Width:** The thickness of the border line, which you specify using a number followed by a CSS measurement unit: px, em, rem, vw, or vh. Note, however, that most border widths are measured in pixels, often 1px. You can also specify one of the following keywords: thin, medium, or thick.

>> **Style:** The type of border line, which must be one of the following keywords: dotted, dashed, solid, double, groove, ridge, inset, or outset. Note that the effects of styles such as double, groove, ridge, inset, or outset appear only when you use a relatively wide border (between at least 3px and 8px, depending on the style).

>> **Color:** The color of the border line. You can use a color keyword, an rgb( ) function, or an RGB code, as I describe in Book 2, Chapter 2.

Here's an example that adds a 1-pixel, dashed, red bottom border to the header element:

```
header {
    border-bottom: 1px dashed red;
}
```

If you want to add a full border around an element and you want all four sides to use the same width, style, and color, CSS mercifully offers a shorthand version that uses the border property:

```
border: width style color;
```

Here's the declaration I used to add the borders around the elements in Figure 3-2 (bk02ch03/example03.html):

```
border: 1px solid black;
```

Making Margins

The final component of the CSS box model is the *margin*, which is the space around the border of the box. Margins are an important detail in web design because they prevent elements from rubbing up against the edges of the browser content area, ensure that two elements don't overlap each other, and create separation between elements.

As with padding, the margin has four sections — above, to the right of, below, and to the left of the border — so CSS offers four corresponding properties for adding margins to an element:

```
element {
    margin-top: top-value;
    margin-right: right-value;
    margin-bottom: bottom-value;
    margin-left: left-value;
}
```

Each value is a number followed by one of the standard CSS measurement units: px, em, rem, vw, or vh. Here's an example:

```
aside {
    margin-top: 1rem;
    margin-right: .5rem;
    margin-bottom: 2rem;
    margin-left: 1.5rem;
}
```

Like padding, CSS also offers a shorthand syntax that uses the margin property. Table 3-2 lists the four syntaxes you can use with the margin property.

To help you remember the four-value syntax, note that the values start at the top of the element's box and proceed clockwise around the box.

Here's the shorthand version of the previous example:

```
aside {
    margin: 1rem .5rem 2rem 1.5rem;
}
```

TABLE 3-2　　**The `margin` Shorthand Property**

Syntax	Description
margin: *value1*;	Applies *value1* to all four sides
margin: *value1 value2*;	Applies *value1* to the top and bottom and *value2* to the right and left
margin: *value1 value2 value3*;	Applies *value1* to the top, *value2* to the right and left, and *value3* to the bottom
margin: value1 value2 value3 value4;	Applies value1 to the top, value2 to the right, value3 to the bottom, and value4 to the left

Resetting the margin

If you notice a web developer pulling their hair or gnashing their teeth, it's a good bet that they're battling the web browser's default styles for margins. These defaults are one of the biggest sources of frustration for web coders because they force you to relinquish control over one of the most important aspects of web design: the whitespace on the page.

Most modern web developers have learned not to fight against these defaults but to eliminate them entirely. They simply reset everything to zero by adding the following rule to the top of every style sheet they build:

```
* {
    margin: 0;
}
```

The downside is that you must now specify the margins for all your page elements, but that extra work is a blessing in disguise because now you have complete control over the whitespace in your page.

Collapsing margins ahead!

CSS has no shortage of eccentricities, and you'll come across most of them in your web development career. In this section you look at one of the odder things that CSS does. First, here's some HTML and CSS code to chew over (bk02ch03/example04.html):

HTML:

```
<header>
    <img src="images/notw.png" alt="News of the Word logo">
```

```
    <h1>News of the Word</h1>
    <p class="subtitle">Language news you won't find anywhere
  else (for good reason!)</p>
</header>
<nav>
    <a href="#">Home</a>
    <a href="#">What's New</a>
    <a href="#">What's Old</a>
    <a href="#">What's What</a>
</nav>
```

CSS:

```
nav {
    margin-top: .5rem;
    padding: .75rem;
    border: 1px solid black;
}
```

I'd like to draw your attention in particular to the `margin-top: .5rem` declaration in the `nav` element's CSS rule. As Figure 3-4 shows, the browser has rendered a small margin above the `nav` element.

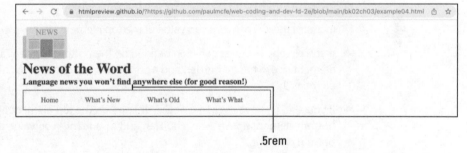

FIGURE 3-4:
The nav element
(with the border)
has a .5rem top
border.

Suppose now I decide that I want a bit more space between the `header` and the `nav` elements, so I add a bottom margin to the `header` (bk02ch03/example05.html):

```
header {
    margin-bottom: .5rem;
}
```

Figure 3-5 shows the result.

CHAPTER 3 **Sizing and Positioning Page Elements** 133

News of the Word
Language news you won't find anywhere else (for good reason!)

Home   What's New   What's Old   What's What

.5rem (still!)

No, you're not hallucinating: The space between the header and nav elements didn't change one iota! Welcome to the wacky world of CSS! In this case, the wackiness comes courtesy of a CSS "feature" called *collapsing margins*. When one element's bottom margin butts up against another element's top margin, common sense would dictate that the web browser would add the two margin values together. Hah, you wish! Instead, the browser uses the larger of the two margin values and throws out the smaller value. That is, it collapses the two margin values into a single value.

So, does that mean you're stuck? Not at all. To get some extra vertical space between two elements, you have four choices:

>> Increase the margin-top value of the bottom element.

>> Increase the margin-bottom value of the top element.

>> If you already have margin-top defined on the bottom element and the top element doesn't use a border, add a padding-bottom value to the top element.

>> If you already have margin-bottom defined on the top element and the bottom element doesn't use a border, add a padding-top value to the bottom element.

In the last two bullets, combining a top or bottom margin on one element with a bottom or top padding on the other element works because the browser doesn't collapse a margin-and-padding combo.

Getting a Grip on Page Flow

When a web browser renders a web page, one of the boring things it does is lay out the tags by applying the following rules to each element type:

» **Inline elements:** Rendered from left to right within each element's parent container

» **Block-level elements:** Stacked on top of each other, with the first element at the top of the page, the second element below the first, and so on

This way of laying out inline and block-level elements is called the *page flow*. For example, consider the following HTML code (bk02ch03/example06.html):

```
<header>
    The page header goes here.
</header>
<nav>
    The navigation doodads go here.
</nav>
<section>
    This is the first section of the page.
</section>
<section>
    This is—you got it—the second section of the page.
</section>
<aside>
    This is the witty or oh-so-interesting aside.
</aside>
<footer>
    The page footer goes here.
</footer>
```

This code is a collection of six block-level elements — a header, a nav, two section tags, an aside, and a footer. Figure 3-6 shows how the web browser renders them as a stack of boxes.

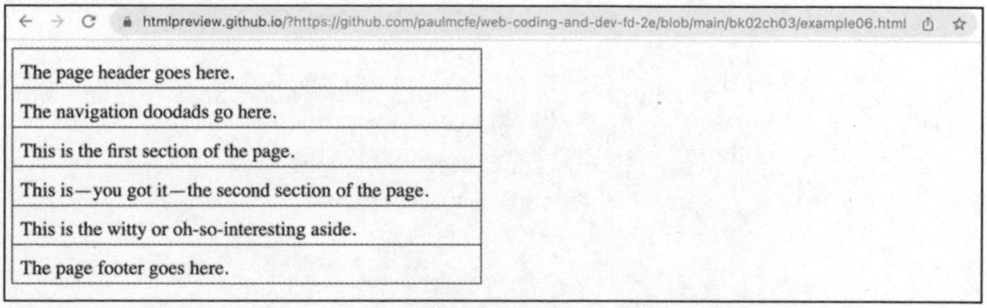

← → C 🔒 htmlpreview.github.io/?https://github.com/paulmcfe/web-coding-and-dev-fd-2e/blob/main/bk02ch03/example06.html ⬆ ☆
The page header goes here.
The navigation doodads go here.
This is the first section of the page.
This is—you got it—the second section of the page.
This is the witty or oh-so-interesting aside.
The page footer goes here.

FIGURE 3-6: The web browser renders the block-level elements as a stack of boxes.

Nothing is inherently wrong with the default page flow, but having your web page render as a stack of boxes lacks a certain flair. Fortunately for your creative spirit, you're not married to the default, one-box-piled-on-another flow. CSS gives you many useful methods for breaking out of the normal page flow. In the rest of this chapter, I talk about two ways of giving your pages some out-of-the-flow piz-zazz: floating and positioning. (For more ways to break out of the default page flow, refer to Book 2, Chapter 4.)

Floating Elements

When you *float* an element, the web browser takes the element out of the default page flow. Where the element ends up on the page depends on whether you float it to the left or to the right:

>> **Float left:** The browser places the element as far to the left and as high as possible within the element's parent container.

>> **Float right:** The browser places the element as far to the right and as high as possible within the element's parent container.

In both cases, the non-floated elements flow around the floated element.

You convince the web browser to float an element by adding the float property:

```
element {
    float: left|right|none;
}
```

For example, consider the following code (bk02ch03/example07.html) and its rendering in Figure 3-7:

```
<header>
    <img src="images/notw.png" alt="News of the Word logo">
    <h1>News of the Word</h1>
    <p class="subtitle">Language news you won't find anywhere
  else (for good reason!)</p>
</header>
<nav>
    <a href="#">Home</a>
    <a href="#">What's New</a>
    <a href="#">What's Old</a>
    <a href="#">What's What</a>
</nav>
```

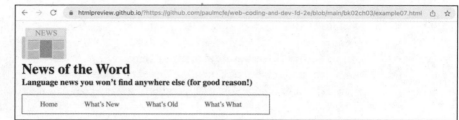

FIGURE 3-7:
As usual, the browser displays the block-level elements as a stack of boxes.

As shown in Figure 3-7, the web browser is up to its usual page flow tricks: stacking all the block-level elements on top of each other. However, I think this page would look better if the title (the ‹h1› tag) and the subtitle (the ‹p› tag) appeared to the right of the logo. To do that, I can float the ‹img› tag to the left (bk02ch03/example08.html):

```
header img {
    float: left;
    margin-right: 2em;
}
```

Figure 3-8 shows the results. With the logo floated to the left, the rest of the content — particularly the ‹h1› tag and the ‹p› tag — now flows around the ‹img› tag.

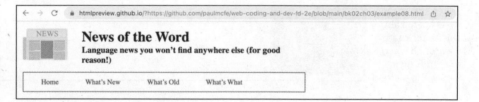

FIGURE 3-8:
When the logo gets floated left, the rest of the content flows around it.

Clearing your floats

The default behavior for non-floated stuff is to wrap around anything that's floated, which is often exactly what you want. However, there will be times when you want to avoid having an element wrap around your floats. For example, consider the following code (bk02ch03/example09.html) and how it gets rendered, as shown in Figure 3-9.

```
<header>
    <h1>Can't You Read the Sign?</h1>
</header>
```

```
<nav>
    <a href="/">Home</a>
    <a href="semantics.html">Signs</a>
    <a href="contact.html">Contact Us</a>
    <a href="about.html">Suggest a Sign</a>
</nav>
<article>
    <img src="images/keep-off-the-grass.jpg"
        alt="A sign that reads 'Keep off the grass' with a
        well-worn dirt path beside it.">
</article>
<footer>
    &copy; Can't You Read?, Inc.
</footer>
```

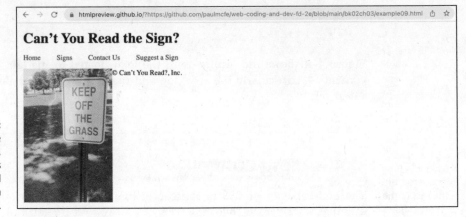

FIGURE 3-9:
When the image is floated left, the footer wraps around it and ends up in a weird place.

With the `<img>` tag floated to the left, the rest of the content flows around it, including the content of the `<footer>` tag, which now appears by the top of the image.

You want your footer to appear at the bottom of the page, naturally, so how can you fix this? By telling the web browser to position the `footer` element so that it *clears* the floated image, which means that it appears after the image in the page flow. You clear an element by adding the `clear` property:

```
element {
    clear: left|right|both|none;
}
```

Use clear: left to clear all left-floated elements, clear: right to clear all right-floated elements, or clear: both to clear everything. When I add clear: left to the footer element (bk02ch03/example10.html), Figure 3-10 shows that the footer content now appears at the bottom of the page.

```
footer {
    clear: left;
}
```

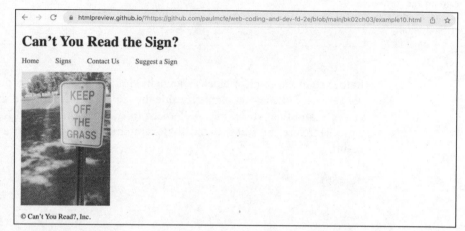

FIGURE 3-10:
Adding clear:
left to the
footer element
causes the footer
to clear the left-
floated image
and appear
at the bottom
of the page.

Collapsing containers ahead!

The odd behavior of CSS is apparently limitless, and floats offer yet another example. Consider the following HTML (bk02ch03/example11.html) and its result in Figure 3-11:

```
<article>
    <section>
        New words are often created...
    </section>
    <aside>
        <b>Note:</b> The Oxford English Dictionary...
    </aside>
</article>
```

Note, in particular, that I've styled the article element with a border.

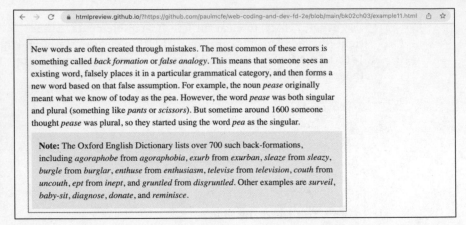

New words are often created through mistakes. The most common of these errors is something called *back formation* or *false analogy*. This means that someone sees an existing word, falsely places it in a particular grammatical category, and then forms a new word based on that false assumption. For example, the noun *pease* originally meant what we know of today as the pea. However, the word *pease* was both singular and plural (something like *pants* or *scissors*). But sometime around 1600 someone thought *pease* was plural, so they started using the word *pea* as the singular.

Note: The Oxford English Dictionary lists over 700 such back-formations, including *agoraphobe* from *agoraphobia*, *exurb* from *exurban*, *sleaze* from *sleazy*, *burgle* from *burglar*, *enthuse* from *enthusiasm*, *televise* from *television*, *couth* from *uncouth*, *ept* from *inept*, and *gruntled* from *disgruntled*. Other examples are *surveil*, *baby-sit*, *diagnose*, *donate*, and *reminisce*.

FIGURE 3-11:
An <article>
tag containing a
<section> tag
and an <aside>
tag, rendered
using the default
page flow.

Rather than the stack of blocks shown in Figure 3-11, you might prefer to have the `section` and the `aside` elements side-by-side. Great idea! Add `width` properties to each, and float the `section` element to the left and the `aside` element to the right. Here are the rules (bk02ch03/example12.html), and Figure 3-12 shows the result.

```
section {
    float: left;
    width: 28rem;
}
aside {
    float: right;
    width: 20rem;
}
```

The <article> tag has collapsed!

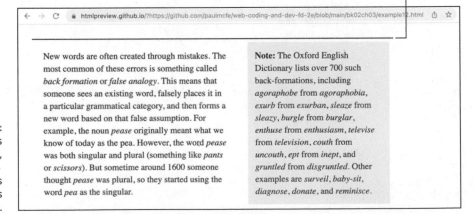

New words are often created through mistakes. The most common of these errors is something called *back formation* or *false analogy*. This means that someone sees an existing word, falsely places it in a particular grammatical category, and then forms a new word based on that false assumption. For example, the noun *pease* originally meant what we know of today as the pea. However, the word *pease* was both singular and plural (something like *pants* or *scissors*). But sometime around 1600 someone thought *pease* was plural, so they started using the word *pea* as the singular.

Note: The Oxford English Dictionary lists over 700 such back-formations, including *agoraphobe* from *agoraphobia*, *exurb* from *exurban*, *sleaze* from *sleazy*, *burgle* from *burglar*, *enthuse* from *enthusiasm*, *televise* from *television*, *couth* from *uncouth*, *ept* from *inept*, and *gruntled* from *disgruntled*. Other examples are *surveil*, *baby-sit*, *diagnose*, *donate*, and *reminisce*.

FIGURE 3-12:
With its
content floated,
the <article>
element collapses
down to just its
border.

Well, that's weird! The line across the top is what's left of the article element. What happened? Because I floated both the section and the aside elements, the browser removed them from the page flow, which made the article element behave as though it had no content at all. The result? A CSS bugaboo known as *container collapse*.

To fix this, you have to give the parent container some content that forces the parent to clear its own children (bk02ch03/example 13.html):

HTML:

```
<article class="self-clear">
```

CSS:

```
.self-clear::after {
    content: "";
    display: block;
    clear: both;
}
```

The ::after pseudo-element (refer to Book 2, Chapter 2) tells the browser to create an element and add it as the last child of whatever element gets the class. What's being added here is an empty string (since you don't want to add anything substantial to the page), and that empty string is displayed as a block that uses clear: both to clear the container's children. Since the container now has some (empty) content, it no longer collapses, as shown in Figure 3-13.

The full <article> tag now appears

FIGURE 3-13: With the self-clear class added to the <article> tag, the article element now has content that clears its own children, so the element is no longer collapsed.

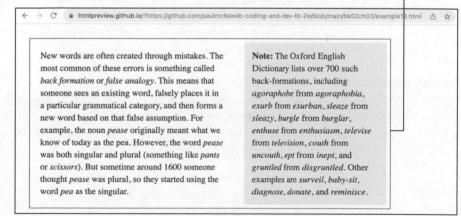

New words are often created through mistakes. The most common of these errors is something called *back formation* or *false analogy*. This means that someone sees an existing word, falsely places it in a particular grammatical category, and then forms a new word based on that false assumption. For example, the noun *pease* originally meant what we know of today as the pea. However, the word *pease* was both singular and plural (something like *pants* or *scissors*). But sometime around 1600 someone thought *pease* was plural, so they started using the word *pea* as the singular.

Note: The Oxford English Dictionary lists over 700 such back-formations, including *agoraphobe* from *agoraphobia*, *exurb* from *exurban*, *sleaze* from *sleazy*, *burgle* from *burglar*, *enthuse* from *enthusiasm*, *televise* from *television*, *couth* from *uncouth*, *ept* from *inept*, and *gruntled* from *disgruntled*. Other examples are *surveil*, *baby-sit*, *diagnose*, *donate*, and *reminisce*.

Positioning Elements

A second method for breaking out of the web browser's default stacked boxes page flow is to position an element yourself using CSS properties. For example, you could tell the browser to place an image in the top-left corner of the window, no matter where that element's `<img>` tag appears in the page's HTML code. This method is known as *positioning* in the CSS world, and it's a powerful tool, so much so that most web developers use positioning only sparingly.

The first bit of positioning wizardry you need to know is, appropriately, the `position` property:

```
element {
    position: static|relative|absolute|fixed|sticky;
}
```

where:

>> `static` places the element in its default position in the page flow.

>> `relative` offsets the element from its default position with respect to its parent container while keeping the element in the page flow.

>> `absolute` offsets the element from its default position with respect to its parent (or sometimes an earlier ancestor) container while removing the element from the page flow.

>> `fixed` offsets the element from its default position with respect to the browser window while removing the element from the page flow.

>> `sticky` starts the element with relative positioning until the element's parent crosses a specified offset with respect to the browser viewport (usually because the user is scrolling the page), at which point the element switches to fixed positioning. If the opposite boundary of the element's parent block then scrolls to where the element is stuck, the element reverts to relative positioning and scrolls with the parent.

Because `static` positioning is what the browser does by default, I won't say anything more about it. For the other four positioning values — `relative`, `absolute`, `fixed`, and `sticky` — note that each one offsets the element. Where do these offsets come from? From the following CSS properties:

```
element {
    top: top-value;
    right: right-value;
```

```
        bottom: bottom-value;
        left: left-value;
    }
```

where `top` shifts the element down, `right` shifts the element from the right, bottom shifts the element up, and `left` shifts the element from the left.

In each case, the value you supply is either a number followed by one of the CSS measurement units (px, em, rem, vw, or vh) or a percentage.

Using relative positioning

Relative positioning is a bit weird because not only does it offset an element relative to its parent container, but it still keeps the element's default space in the page flow intact.

Here's an example (bk02ch03/example14.html):

HTML:

```
<h1>
    keyhole path
</h1>
<div>
    <i>n.</i> A straight footpath with overhanging trees
    that create a tunnel effect.
</div>
<img src="images/keyholepath1.jpg"
    alt="Photo of a keyhole path">
<img src="images/keyholepath2.jpg"
    alt="Photo of a keyhole path" class="offset-image">
<img src="images/keyholepath3.jpg"
    alt="Photo of a keyhole path">
```

CSS:

```
.offset-image {
    position: relative;
    left: 300px;
}
```

The CSS code defines a rule for a class named `offset-image`, which applies relative positioning and offsets the element from the left by `300px`. In the HTML code, the `offset-image` class is applied to the middle image. As shown in Figure 3-14, not only is the middle image shifted from the left, but the space in the page flow where it would have appeared by default remains intact, so the third image's place in the page flow doesn't change. As far as that third image is concerned, the middle image is still right above it.

The image's original position in the page flow   The offset image

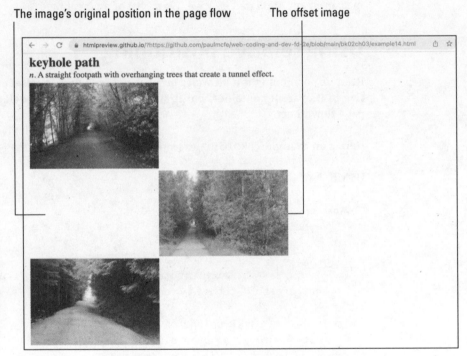

FIGURE 3-14: The middle image uses relative positioning to shift from the left, but its place in the page flow remains.

Giving absolute positioning a whirl

Absolute positioning not only offsets the element from its default position, but it also removes the element from the page flow. Sounds useful, but if the element is no longer part of the page flow, from what element is it offset? Good question, and here's the short answer: the closest ancestor element that uses non-static positioning.

If that has you furrowing your brow, I have a longer answer that should help. To determine which ancestor element is used for the offset of the absolutely positioned element, the browser goes through a procedure similar to this:

1. Move one level up the page hierarchy to the previous ancestor.

2. Check the `position` property of that ancestor element.

3. If the `position` value of the ancestor is `static`, go back to Step 1 and repeat the process for the next level up the hierarchy; otherwise (that is, if the `position` value of the parent is anything other than `static`), offset the original element with respect to the ancestor.

4. If, after going through Steps 1 to 3 repeatedly, you end up at the top of the page hierarchy — that is, at the `<html>` tag — use that to offset the element, which means in practice that the element is offset with respect to the browser's content area.

I mention in the preceding section that relative positioning is weird because it keeps the element's default position in the page flow intact. However, now that weirdness turns to goodness because if you want a child element to use absolute positioning, you add `position: relative` to the parent element's style rule. Because you don't also supply an offset to the parent, it stays put in the page flow, but now you have what CSS nerds called a *positioning context* for the child element.

I think an example would be welcome right about now (bk02ch03/example15. html):

HTML:

```
<section>
    <img src="images/new.png"
        alt="Starburst with the text 'New'">
    <h2>
        holloway
    </h2>
    <div>
        <i>n.</i> A sunken footpath or road; a path that is
enclosed by high embankments on both sides.
    </div>
    <div>
        There are two main methods that create holloways: By
years (decades, centuries) of constant foot traffic that wears
down the path (a process usually accelerated somewhat by water
erosion); or by digging out a path between two properties and
piling up the dirt on either side.
    </div>
</section>
```

CSS:

```
section {
    position: relative;
    border: 1px double black;
}
img {
    position: absolute;
    top: 0;
    right: 0;
}
```

In the CSS, the section element is styled with the position: relative declaration, and the img element is styled with position: absolute and top and right offsets set to 0. In the HTML code, note that the <section> tag is the parent of the <img> tag, so the latter's absolute positioning will be with respect to the former. With top and right offsets set to 0, the image will now appear in the top-right corner of the section element and, indeed, it does, as shown in Figure 3-15.

The absolutely positioned image

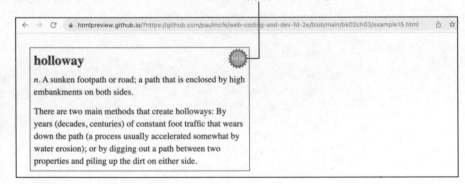

FIGURE 3-15:
The img element uses absolute positioning to send it to the top right corner of the section element.

Trying out fixed positioning

With *fixed positioning,* the element is taken out of the normal page flow and is then offset with respect to the browser's content area, which means the element doesn't move, not even a little, when you scroll the page (that is, the element is fixed in its new position).

One of the most common uses of fixed positioning is to plop a header at the top of the page and make it stay there while the user scrolls the rest of the content. Here's an example that shows you how to create such a header (bk02ch03/example16.html):

HTML:

```
<header>
    <img src="images/holloway3.jpg">
    <h2>
        holloway
    </h2>
</header>
<main>
...
</main>
```

CSS:

```
header {
    position: fixed;
    top: 0;
    left: 0;
    width: 100%;
    height: 4rem;
    border: 1px double black;
    background-color: rgb(147, 196, 125);
}
main {
    margin-top: 4rem;
}
```

The HTML code includes a header element with an image and a heading, followed by a longish main section that I don't include here for simplicity's sake. In the CSS code, the header element is styled with position: fixed, and the offsets top and left set to 0. These offsets fix the header to the top left of the browser's content area. I also added width: 100% to give the header the entire width of the window. Note, too, that I set the header height to 64px. To make sure the main section begins below the header, I styled the main element with margin-top: 4rem. Figure 3-16 shows the results.

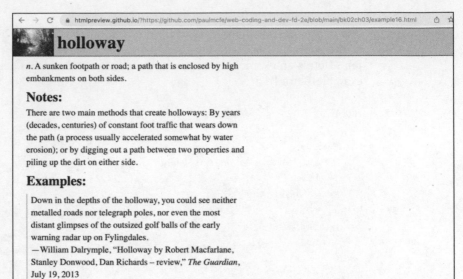

FIGURE 3-16:
A page with the
header element
fixed to the top of
the screen. When
you scroll the rest
of the page, the
header remains
where it is.

Making elements stick (temporarily)

Sticky positioning is a kind of combination of relative and fixed. That is, the element starts off with relative positioning until the element's containing block crosses a specified threshold (usually because the user is scrolling the page), at which point the element switches to fixed positioning. If the opposite edge of the element's containing block then scrolls to where the element is stuck, the element reverts to relative positioning and resumes scrolling with the containing block.

For example, suppose your page has a `section` element, and inside that `section` is an `h2` element that you've positioned as sticky. Here's an abbreviated version of the code (check out bk02ch03/example17.html for the complete version):

HTML:

```
<section>
    <h2>Cat ipsum</h2>
    <p><a href="http://www.catipsum.com/">http://www.catipsum.
com/</a></p>
    <p>Sample:</p>
    <p class="sample-text">
        Cat ipsum dolor sit amet, prance along on top of the
garden fence, annoy the neighbor's dog and make it bark stuff
and things intrigued by the shower. Please stop looking at
```

```
    your phone and pet me sleep everywhere, but not in my bed get
    my claw stuck in the dog's ear and adventure always but drool
    yet roll over and sun my belly. Ooh, are those your $250
    dollar sandals?
    </p>
</section>
```

CSS:

```
h2 {
    position: sticky;
    top: 0;
}
```

In the CSS code, notice that for the h2 element, I set position: sticky. To specify
the threshold at which the element sticks, I set top: 0, which means this element
will stick in place when the top edge of the section element hits the top of the
viewport, as shown in Figure 3-17.

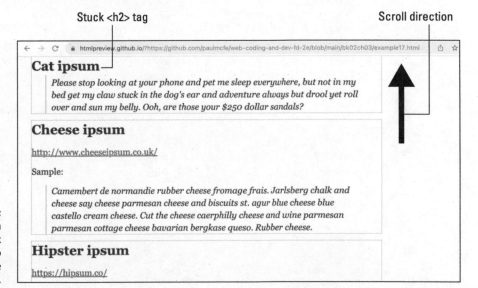

Stuck <h2> tag

Scroll direction

FIGURE 3-17:
A page with an
h2 element stuck
(temporarily) to
the top of the
screen.

Chapter 4

Creating the Page Layout

Flexbox is essentially for laying out items in a single dimension — in a row OR a column. Grid is for layout of items in two dimensions — rows AND columns.

— RACHEL ANDREWS

Why are some web pages immediately appealing, while others put the "Ugh" in "ugly"? There are lots of possible reasons: colors, typography, image quality, the density of exclamation points. For my money, however, the number one reason why some pages soar while others are eyesores is the overall look and feel of the page. We've all visited enough websites to have developed a kind of sixth sense that tells us immediately whether a page is worth checking out. Sure, colors and fonts play a part in that intuition, but we all respond viscerally to the big picture that a page presents.

That big picture refers to the overall layout of the page, and that's the subject you explore in this chapter. Here you discover what page layout is all about, and you investigate two CSS-based methods for making your web pages behave the way you want them to. By the time you're done mastering the nitty-gritty of page layout, you'll be in a position to design and build beautiful and functional pages that'll have them screaming for more.

What Is Page Layout?

The *page layout* is the arrangement of the page elements within the browser's content area, including not only what appears when you first open the page but also the rest of the page that comes into view as you scroll down. The page layout acts as a kind of blueprint for the page, and like any good blueprint, the page layout details how a page looks at two levels:

>> **The macro level:** Refers to the overall layout of the page, which determines how the major sections of the page — header, nav, main, footer, and so on — fit together as a whole.

>> **The micro level:** Refers to the layout within a section or subsection of the page. For example, the page's header element might have one layout, whereas the page's article section might have another.

CSS offers two main layout techniques, each of which you can apply at either the macro level or the micro level:

>> **CSS Flexible Box (Flexbox):** Arranges elements either vertically or horizontally within flexible boxes.

>> **CSS Grid:** Arranges the elements in a row-and-column structure.

The rest of this chapter discusses each of these techniques.

Making Flexible Layouts with Flexbox

For many years, the go-to layout technique for most CSS pros was either floating elements or inline blocks (that is, setting a block element's display property to inline-block so that the element behaves, layout-wise, as an inline element). Both techniques offered numerous banana peels in the path that tripped up many a developer, including forgetting to clear your floats and having containers collapse (check out Book 2, Chapter 3 to learn more about these pitfalls).

However, beyond these mere annoyances, float-based or inline-block-based layouts had trouble with a few more important things, making it very hard to get

>> An element's content centered vertically within the element's container

>> Elements evenly spaced horizontally across the full width (or vertically across the full height) of their parent container

>> A footer element to appear at the bottom of the browser's content area

Fortunately, these troubles vanish if you use a CSS technology called Flexible Box Layout Module, or *Flexbox*, for short. The key here is the *flex* part of the name. As opposed to the default page flow and layouts that use floats and inline blocks, all of which render content using rigid blocks, Flexbox renders content using containers that can grow and shrink — I'm talking both width and height here — in response to changing content or browser window size. But Flexbox also offers powerful properties that make it a breeze to lay out, align, distribute, and size the child elements of a parent container.

The first thing you need to know is that Flexbox divides its world into two categories:

>> **Flex container:** A block-level element that acts as a parent to the flexible elements inside it

>> **Flex items:** The elements that reside within the flex container

Setting up the flex container

To designate an element as a flex container, you set its display property to flex:

```
container {
    display: flex;
}
```

With that done, the element's children automatically become flex items.

Flexbox is a one-dimensional layout tool, which means the flex items are arranged within their flex container either horizontally — that is, in a row — or vertically — that is, in a column. This direction is called the *primary axis* and you specify it using the flex-direction property:

```
element {
    display: flex;
    flex-direction: row|row-reverse|column|column-reverse;
}
```

where:

>> row is the primary axis is horizontal and the flex items are arranged from left to right. This is the default value.

>> row-reverse is the primary axis is horizontal and the flex items are arranged from right to left.

>> `column` is the primary axis is vertical and the flex items are arranged from top to bottom.

>> `column-reverse` is the primary axis is vertical and the flex items are arranged from bottom to top.

The axis that is perpendicular to the primary axis is called the *secondary axis*.

As an example, here's some CSS and HTML code (check out bk02ch04/example01. html in this book's example files). Figure 4-1 shows how it looks if you let the browser lay it out:

HTML:

```html
<div class="container">
    <div class="item item1">1</div>
    <div class="item item2">2</div>
    <div class="item item3">3</div>
    <div class="item item4">4</div>
    <div class="item item5">5</div>
</div>
```

CSS:

```css
.container {
    border: 5px double black;
}
.item {
    border: 1px solid black;
    padding: .1rem;
    font-family: "Verdana", sans-serif;
    font-size: 5rem;
    text-align: center;
}
.item1 {
    background-color: rgb(240, 240, 240);
}
.item2 {
    background-color: rgb(224, 224, 224);
}
.item3 {
    background-color: rgb(208, 208, 208);
}
```

```
.item4 {
    background-color: rgb(192, 192, 192);
}
.item5 {
    background-color: rgb(176, 176, 176);
}
```

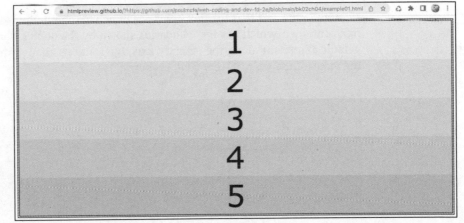

FIGURE 4-1:
If you let the
browser lay out
the elements, you
get the default
stack of blocks.

The browser does its default thing where it stacks the `div` blocks on top of each other and makes each one take up the full width of its parent `div` (the one with the `container` class), which has its boundaries marked by the double border in Figure 4-1.

Now configure the parent `div` — again, the one with the `container` class — as a flex container with a horizontal primary axis (check out bk02ch04/example02. html):

```
.container {
    display: flex;
    flex-direction: row;
    border: 5px double black;
}
```

This automatically configures the child `div` elements — the ones with the `item` class — as flex items. As shown in Figure 4-2, the flex items are now aligned horizontally and only take up as much horizontal space as their content requires.

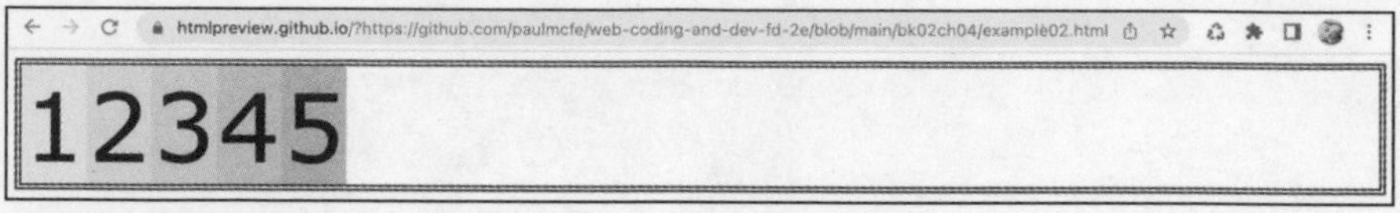

FIGURE 4-2:
With their
parent as a flex
container, the
child elements
become
flex items.

With their parent as a flex container, the child elements become flex items.

Aligning flex items along the primary axis

Note in Figure 4-2 that the flex items are bunched together on the left side of the flex container (which has its boundaries shown by the double border). This is the default alignment along the primary axis, but you can change that by modifying the value of the justify-content property:

```
container {
    display: flex;
    justify-content: flex-start|flex-end|center|space-around
    |space-between|space-evenly;
}
```

where:

>> flex-start aligns all the flex items with the start of the flex container (where *start* means left if flex-direction is row; right if flex-direction is row-reverse; top if flex-direction is column; or bottom if flex-direction is column-reverse). This value is the default, so you can leave out the justify-content property if flex-start is the alignment you want.

>> flex-end aligns all the flex items with the end of the flex container (where *end* means right if flex-direction is row; left if flex-direction is row-reverse; bottom if flex-direction is column; or top if flex-direction is column-reverse).

>> center aligns all the flex items with the middle of the flex container.

>> space-around assigns equal amounts of space before and after each flex item. Note that this distribution doesn't result in even spacing along the primary axis because the inner flex items (2, 3, and 4 in Figure 4-3) have two units of space between them, whereas the starting and ending flex items (1 and 5, respectively, in Figure 4-3) have only one unit of space to the outside (that is, to the left of item 1 and to the right of item 5).

>> space-between places the first flex item at the start of the flex container, the last flex item at the end of the flex container, and then distributes the rest of the flex items evenly in between.

» space-evenly assigns equal amounts of space before and after each flex item, where the amount of space is calculated to get the flex items distributed evenly along the primary axis.

Figure 4-3 (bk02ch04/example03.html) demonstrates each of the possible values of the justify-content property when the flex-direction property is set to row.

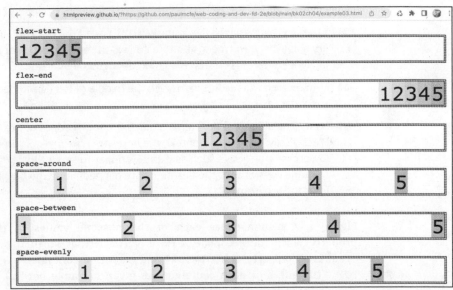

FIGURE 4-3: How the justify-content values align flex items when the primary axis is horizontal (flex-direction: row).

Aligning flex items along the secondary axis

Besides aligning the flex items along the primary axis, you can also align them along the secondary axis. For example, if you've set flex-direction to row, which gives you a horizontal primary axis, the secondary axis is vertical, which means you can also align the flex items vertically. By default, the flex items always take up the entire height of the flex container, but you can get a different secondary axis alignment by changing the value of the align-items property:

```
container {
    display: flex;
    align-items: stretch|flex-start|flex-end|center|baseline;
}
```

where:

>> stretch expands each flex item in the secondary axis direction until it fills the entire height (if the secondary axis is vertical) or width (if the secondary axis is horizontal) of the flex container. This alignment is the default, so you can leave out the align-items property if stretch is the alignment you want.

>> flex-start aligns all the flex items with the start of the flex container's secondary axis (where *start* means top if flex-direction is row or row-reverse; or left if flex-direction is column or column-reverse).

>> flex-end aligns all the flex items with the end of the flex container's secondary axis (where *end* means bottom if flex-direction is row or row-reverse; or right if flex-direction is column or column-reverse).

>> center aligns all the flex items with the middle of the flex container's secondary axis.

>> baseline aligns the flex items along the bottom edges of the item text. (Technically, given a line of text, the *baseline* is the invisible line upon which lowercase characters such as *o* and *x* appear to sit.) If the flex items contain multiple lines of text, the flex items are aligned along the baseline of the first lines in each item.

Figure 4-4 demonstrates each of the possible values of the align-items property when the secondary axis is vertical (that is, in this case, the flex-direction property is set to row) and each flex container is given a height of 30vh (the edges of each container are given a double border). (Also check out bk05ch02/example04.html.) To make the baseline example useful, I added random amounts of top and bottom padding to each flex item.

Centering an element horizontally and vertically

In the olden days of CSS, centering an element both horizontally and vertically within its parent was notoriously difficult. Style wizards stayed up until late at night coming up with ways to achieve this feat. They succeeded, but their techniques were obscure and convoluted. Then Flexbox came along and changed everything by making it almost ridiculously easy to plop something smack dab in the middle of the page:

```
container {
    display: flex;
    justify-content: center;
    align-items: center;
}
```

FIGURE 4-4:
How the align–
items values
align flex items
when the second-
ary axis is vertical.

Yes, that's all there is to it. Here's an example (bk02ch04/example05.html):

HTML:

```html
<div class="container">
    <div class="item">Look, ma, I'm centered!</div>
</div>
```

CSS:

```css
.container {
    display: flex;
    justify-content: center;
    align-items: center;
    height: 25vh;
    border: 5px double black;
}
.item {
    font-family: "Georgia", serif;
    font-size: 2rem;
}
```

As shown in Figure 4-5, the flex item sits right in the middle of its flex container.

FIGURE 4-5:
To center an item, set the container's justify-content and align-items properties to center.

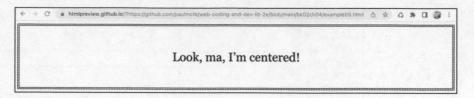

Laying out a navigation bar with Flexbox

One common web page component is a navigation bar that has several links arranged horizontally within a nav element. You could use either floats or inline blocks (refer to Book 2, Chapter 3) to lay out the navigation bar, but you'll end up resorting to finicky finagling of vertical and horizontal padding to get the links nicely positioned within the nav element.

With Flexbox, however, you don't need to resort to such time-consuming tweaking to gets things lined up nice and neat. Here's a Flexbox version of a navigation bar (bk02ch04/example06.html). Figure 4-6 shows how it looks in the browser:

HTML:

```html
<nav>
    <ul>
        <li><a href="#">Home</a></li>
        <li><a href="#">Blog</a></li>
        <li><a href="#">Store</a></li>
        <li><a href="#">About</a></li>
        <li><a href="#">Contact</a></li>
    </ul>
</nav>
<main>
    Main content goes here...
</main>
```

CSS:

```css
nav {
    background-color: #ccc;
}
nav ul {
    display: flex;
    justify-content: space-around;
    align-items: center;
```

```
        height: 2.5rem;
        list-style-type: none;
    }
    main {
        margin-top: 1rem;
    }
```

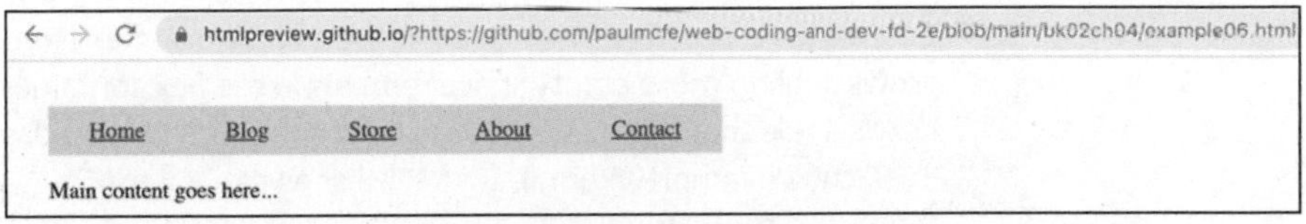

FIGURE 4-6:
Using Flexbox,
you can modify
flex container
properties for
nicely spaced
links.

Note that I made the ul element the flex container. By setting justify-content to space-around and align-items to center, you get the flex items — that is, the navigation links — perfectly spaced within the navigation bar.

Allowing flex items to grow

By default, when you set the justify-content property to flex-start, flex-end, or center, the flex items take up only as much room along the primary axis as they need for their content, as shown earlier in Figures 4-2 and 4-3. This is admirably egalitarian, but it does often leave a bunch of empty space in the flex container. Interestingly, one of the meanings behind the *flex* in Flexbox is that you can make one or more flex items grow to fill that empty space.

You configure a flex item to grow by setting the flex-grow property on the item:

```
item {
    flex-grow: value;
}
```

Here, value is a number greater than or equal to 0. The default value is 0, which tells the browser not to grow the flex items. That usually results in empty space in the flex container, as shown in Figure 4-7 (bk02ch04/example07.html).

FIGURE 4-7:
By default, all
flex items have a
flex-grow value
of 0, which often
results in empty
space.

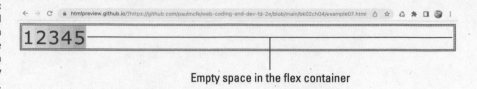

Empty space in the flex container

For positive values of flex-grow, there are three scenarios to consider:

>> **You assign a positive flex-grow value to just one flex item.** The flex item grows until no more empty space remains in the flex container. For example, here's a rule that sets flex-grow to 1 for the element with class item1 (bk02ch04/example08.html). Figure 4-8 shows that item 1 has grown until there is no more empty space in the flex container:

```css
.item1 {
    flex-grow: 1;
}
```

FIGURE 4-8:
With flex-
grow: 1, an item
grows until
the container
has no more
empty space.

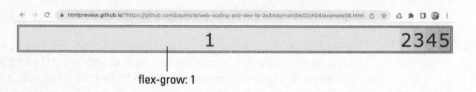

flex-grow: 1

>> **You assign the same positive flex-grow value to two or more flex items.** The flex items grow equally until no more empty space remains in the flex container. For example, here's a rule that sets flex-grow to 1 for the elements with the classes item1, item2, and item3 (bk02ch04/example09. html). Figure 4-9 shows that items 1, 2, and 3 have grown until there is no more empty space in the flex container:

```css
.item1,
.item2,
.item3 {
    flex-grow: 1;
}
```

FIGURE 4-9:
When items 1, 2,
and 3 are styled
with flex-grow:
1, the items grow
equally.

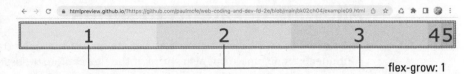

» **You assign a different positive flex-grow value to two or more flex items.** The flex items grow proportionally based on the flex-grow values until no more empty space remains in the flex container. For example, if you give one item a flex-grow value of 1, a second item a flex-grow value of 2, and a third item a flex-grow value of 1, the proportion of the empty space given to each will be, respectively, 25 percent, 50 percent, and 25 percent. Here's some CSS code that supplies these proportions to the elements with the classes item1, item2, and item3 (bk02ch04/example10.html). Figure 4-10 shows the results:

```
.item1 {
    flex-grow: 1;
}
.item2 {
    flex-grow: 2;
}
.item3 {
    flex-grow: 1;
}
```

TECHNICAL STUFF

To calculate what proportion of the flex container's empty space is assigned to each flex item, add up the flex-grow values, and then divide the individual flex-grow values by that total. For example, values of 1, 2, and 1 add up to 4, so the percentages are 25 percent (1/4), 50 percent (2/4), and 25 percent (1/4), respectively.

FIGURE 4-10:
Items 1 and 3 get
25 percent of the
container's empty
space, whereas
item 2 gets
50 percent.

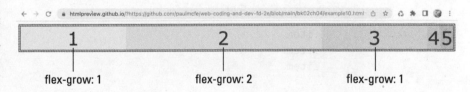

Creating the Page Layout

Allowing flex items to shrink

The flexibility of Flexbox means that flex items can not only grow to fill a flex container's empty space but also shrink if the flex container doesn't have enough space to fit the items. Shrinking flex items to fit inside their container is the default Flexbox behavior, but you gain a measure of control over which items shrink and by how much by using the flex-shrink property on a flex item:

```
item {
    flex-shrink: value;
}
```

Here, value is a number greater than or equal to 0. The default value is 1, which tells the browser to shrink all the flex items equally to get them to fit inside the flex container.

For example, consider the following code (bk02ch04/example11.html):

HTML:

```
<div class="container">
    <div class="item item1">1</div>
    <div class="item item2">2</div>
    <div class="item item3">3</div>
    <div class="item item4">4</div>
    <div class="item item5">5</div>
</div>
```

CSS:

```
.container {
    display: flex;
    width: 500px;
    border: 5px double black;
}
.item {
    width: 200px;
}
```

The flex container (the container class) is 500px wide, but each flex item (the item class) is 200px wide. To get everything to fit, the browser shrinks each item equally, and the result is shown in Figure 4-11.

FIGURE 4-11:
By default, the
browser shrinks
the items equally
along the primary
axis until they fit.

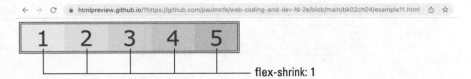

flex-shrink: 1

**TECHNICAL
STUFF**

The browser shrinks each flex item truly equally (that is, by the same amount) only when each item has the same size along the primary axis (for example, the same width when the primary axis is horizontal). If the flex items have different sizes, the browser shrinks each item roughly in proportion to its size: Larger items shrink more, whereas smaller items shrink less. I use the word *roughly* here because in fact the calculations the browser uses to determine the shrinkage factor are brain-numbingly complex. If you want to learn more (don't say I didn't warn you!), check out `https://madebymike.com.au/writing/understanding-flexbox`.

For positive values of `flex-shrink`, you have three ways to control the shrinkage of a flex item:

>> **Assign the item a `flex-shrink` value between 0 and 1.** The browser shrinks the item less than the other flex items. For example, here's a rule that sets `flex-shrink` to `.5` for the element with class `item1`, and Figure 4-12 shows that item 1 has shrunk less than the other items in the container:

```
.item1 {
    flex-shrink: .5;
}
```

FIGURE 4-12:
Styling item
1 with `flex-
shrink: .5`
shrinks it less
than the other
items.

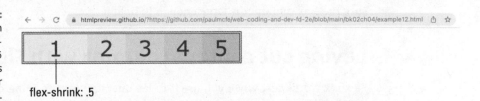

flex-shrink: .5

>> **Assign the item a `flex-shrink` value greater than 1.** The browser shrinks the item more than the other flex items. For example, the following rule sets `flex-shrink` to `2` for the element with class `item1`, and Figure 4-13 shows that item 1 has shrunk more than the other items in the container:

```
.item1 {
    flex-shrink: 2;
}
```

FIGURE 4-13:
Styling item
1 with flex-
shrink: 2
shrinks the item
more than the
others.

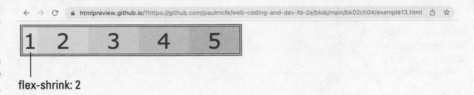

flex-shrink: 2

>> **Assign the item a `flex-shrink` value of 0.** The browser doesn't shrink the item. The following rule sets `flex-shrink` to 0 for the element with class `item1`, and Figure 4-14 shows that the browser doesn't shrink item 1:

```
.item1 {
    flex-shrink: 0;
}
```

FIGURE 4-14:
Styling item
1 with flex-
shrink: 0
doesn't shrink the
item.

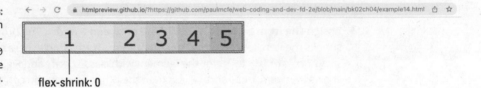

flex-shrink: 0

WARNING

If a flex item is larger along the primary axis than its flex container, and you set `flex-shrink: 0` on that item, ugliness ensues. That is, the flex item breaks out of the container and, depending on where it sits within the container, might take one or more other items with it. If you don't want a flex item to shrink, make sure the flex container is large enough to hold it.

Laying out content columns with Flexbox

Flexbox works best when you use it to lay out components along one dimension, but that doesn't mean you can't use it to lay out an entire page. As long as the page structure is relatively simple, Flexbox works great for laying out elements both horizontally and vertically.

A good example is the classic page layout that has a header and navigation bar across the top of the page, a main section with an article and a sidebar beside it, and a footer across the bottom of the page. Here's some Flexbox code (bk02ch04/example15.html) that creates this layout, which is shown in Figure 4-15:

HTML:

```html
<body>
    <header>
        Header
    </header>
    <nav>
        Navigation
    </nav>
    <main>
        <article>
            Article
        </article>
        <aside>
            Aside
        </aside>
    </main>
    <footer>
        Footer
    </footer>
</body>
```

CSS:

```css
html {
    height: 100%;
}
body {
    display: flex;
    flex-direction: column;
    gap: 1rem;
    justify-content: flex-start;
    align-items: stretch;
    font-size: 2rem;
    height: 100%;
    margin-left: 1rem;
    width: 75vw;
}
header,
nav,
article,
aside,
```

```
footer {
    border: 1px solid black;
    padding: 0.5rem;
}
main {
    flex-grow: 1;
    display: flex;
    flex-direction: row;
    gap: 1rem;
    justify-content: flex-start;
    align-items: stretch;
}
article {
    flex-grow: 1;
}
aside {
    flex-grow: 0;
    flex-shrink: 0;
    flex-basis: 10rem;
}
```

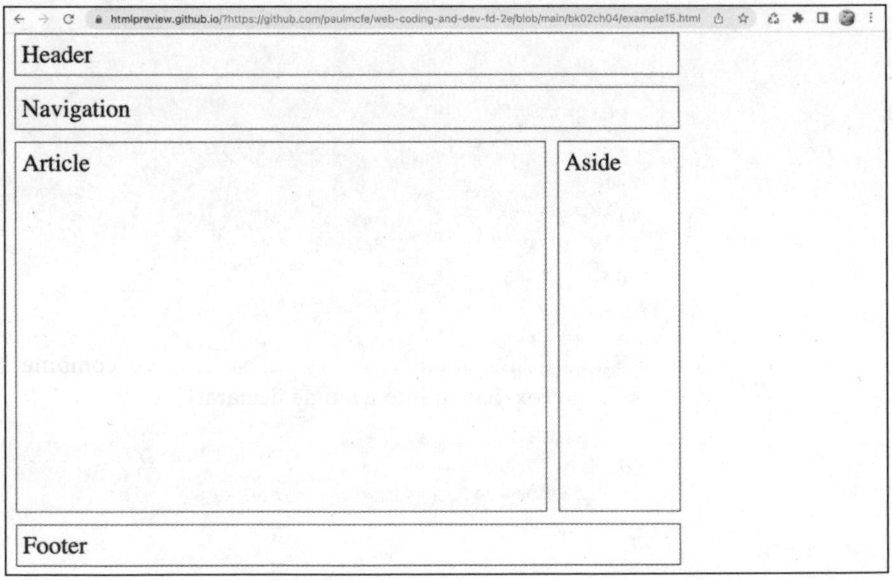

FIGURE 4-15:
A classic
page layout,
Flexbox-style.

Here's a closer look at what's happening in this code:

>> The ‹body› tag is set up as a flex container, and that container is styled with flex-direction: column to create a vertical primary axis for the page as a whole.

>> The body element has its height property set to 100%, which makes the flex container always take up the entire height of the browser's content area. Note that setting height: 100% on the body element only works because earlier I added the same declaration to the html element.

>> The body element also declares gap: 1rem to create a 1rem space between each flex item.

>> All the content elements — header, nav, article, aside, and footer elements are given a border and some padding.

>> The main element is styled with flex-grow: 1, which tells the browser to grow the main element vertically until it uses up the empty space in the flex container. This also ensures that the footer element appears at the bottom of the content area even if there isn't enough content to fill the main element.

>> The main element is also a flex container styled with flex-direction: row to create a horizontal primary axis. Note, as well, the use of the gap property to set a 1rem horizontal gap between each flex item.

>> Inside the main flex container, the article element is given flex-grow: 1, so it grows as needed to take up the remaining width of the main element (that is, after the width of the aside element is taken into account).

>> To get a fixed-width sidebar, the aside element's rule has both flex-grow and flex-shrink set to 0, and it also includes the declaration flex-basis: 10rem. The flex-basis property provides the browser with a suggested starting point for the size of the element. In this case, with both flex-grow and flex-shrink set to 0, the flex-basis value acts like a fixed width.

TIP

You can use a shorthand property called flex to combine flex-grow, flex-shrink, and flex-basis into a single declaration:

```
item {
    flex: grow-value shrink-value basis-value;
}
```

For example, I could rewrite the `aside` element's rule in the preceding example as follows:

```
aside {
    flex: 0 0 10rem;
}
```

Shaping the Overall Page Layout with CSS Grid

One of the most exciting and anticipated developments in recent CSS history is the advent of a technology called CSS Grid. The Grid specification gives you a straightforward way to divide a container into one or more rows and one or more columns — that is, as a *grid* — and then optionally assign the container's elements to specific sections of the grid. With CSS Grid, you can give the web browser instructions such as the following:

>> Set up the <body> tag as a grid with four rows and three columns.

>> Place the header element in the first row and make it span all three columns.

>> Place the nav element in the second row and make it span all three columns.

>> Place the article element in the third row, columns one and two.

>> Place the aside element in the third row, column three.

>> Place the footer element in the fourth row and make it span all three columns.

Before you learn how to do all of this and more, you need to know that a Grid uses two categories of elements:

>> **Grid container:** A block-level element that acts as a parent to the elements inside it and that you configure with a set number of rows and columns

>> **Grid items:** The elements that reside within the grid container and that you assign (or the browser assigns automatically) to specific parts of the grid

Setting up the grid container

To designate an element as a grid container, you set its `display` property to `grid`:

```
container {
    display: grid;
}
```

With that first step complete, the element's children automatically become grid items.

Specifying the grid rows and columns

Your grid container doesn't do much on its own. To make it useful, you need to create a *grid template*, which specifies the number of rows and columns you want in your grid. You set up your template by adding the `grid-template-columns` and `grid-template-rows` properties to your grid container:

```
container {
    display: grid;
    grid-template-columns: column-values;
    grid-template-rows: row-values
}
```

The *column-values* and *row-values* are space-separated lists of the sizes you want to use for each column and row in your grid. The sizes can be numbers expressed in any of the standard CSS measurement units (px, em, rem, vw, or vh), a percentage, or the keyword `auto`, which tells the browser to automatically set the size based on the other values you specify.

Here's an example (bk02ch04/example 16.html), and Figure 4-16 shows the result:

HTML:

```
<div class="container">
    <div class="item item1">1</div>
    <div class="item item2">2</div>
    <div class="item item3">3</div>
    <div class="item item4">4</div>
    <div class="item item5">5</div>
    <div class="item item6">6</div>
</div>
```

Creating the Page
Layout

CSS:

```
.container {
    display: grid;
    grid-template-columns: 100px 300px 200px;
    grid-template-rows: 100px 200px;
}
```

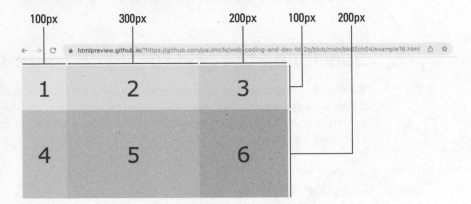

FIGURE 4-16:
A basic grid
created by
setting just three
properties:
display, grid-
template-
columns,
and grid-
template-rows.

TECHNICAL STUFF

You can also specify a column or row size using a unit called fr, which is specific to Grid and represents a fraction of the free space available in the grid container, either horizontally (for columns) or vertically (for rows). For example, if you assign one column 1fr of space and another column 2fr, the browser gives one third of the horizontal free space to the first column and two thirds of the horizontal free space to the second column.

TIP

If you leave out the grid-template-rows property, the browser automatically configures the row heights based on the height of the tallest element in each row.

Creating grid gaps

By default, the browser doesn't include any horizontal space between each column or any vertical space between each row. If you'd prefer some daylight between your grid items, you can add the column-gap and row-gap properties to your grid container:

```
container {
    display: grid;
    column-gap: column-gap-value;
    row-gap: row-gap-value
}
```

In both properties, the value is a number expressed in any of the standard CSS measurement units (px, em, rem, vw, or vh). Here's an example (bk02ch04/example17.html):

```
.container {
    display: grid;
    grid-template-columns: 100px 300px 200px;
    grid-template-rows: 100px 200px;
    column-gap: 10px;
    row-gap: 15px;
}
```

TIP

You can use a shorthand property called gap to combine column-gap and row-gap into a single declaration:

```
container {
    display: grid;
    gap: row-gap-value [column-gap-value];
}
```

REMEMBER

When you use the gap shorthand property, if you specify only *row-gap-value*, Grid applies the value to both rows and columns.

Assigning grid items to rows and columns

Rather than letting the web browser populate the grid automatically, you can take control of the process and assign your grid items to specific rows and columns. For each grid item, you specify four values:

```
item {
    grid-column-start: column-start-value;
    grid-column-end: column-end-value;
    grid-row-start: row-start-value;
    grid-row-end: row-end-value;
}
```

where:

>> grid-column-start is a number that specifies the column where the item begins.

» `grid-column-end` is a number that specifies the column before which the item ends. For example, if `grid-column-end` is set to 4, the grid item ends in column 3. Some notes:

- If you omit this property, the item uses only the starting column.

- If you use the keyword end, the item runs from its starting column through to the last column in the grid.

- You can use the keyword span followed by a space and then a number that specifies the number of columns you want the item to span across the grid. For example, the following two sets of declarations are equivalent:

```
grid-column-start: 1;
grid-column-end: 4;
grid-column-start: 1;
grid-column-end: span 3;
```

» `grid-row-start` is a number that specifies the row where the item begins.

» `grid-row-end` is a number that specifies the row before which the item ends. For example, if `grid-row-end` is set to 3, the grid item ends in row 2. Some notes:

- If you omit this property, the item uses only the starting row.

- If you use the keyword end, then the item runs from its starting row through to the last row in the grid.

- You can use the keyword span followed by a space and then a number that specifies the number of rows you want the item to span down the grid. For example, the following two sets of declarations are equivalent:

```
grid-row-start: 2;
grid-row-end: 4;
grid-row-start: 2;
grid-row-end: span 2;
```

Here's an example (bk02ch04/example18.html), and the results are shown in Figure 4-17:

HTML:

```
<div class="container">
    <div class="item item1">1</div>
    <div class="item item2">2</div>
    <div class="item item3">3</div>
    <div class="item item4">4</div>
    <div class="item item5">5</div>
```

```
        <div class="item item6">6</div>
</div>
```

CSS:

```css
.container {
    display: grid;
    grid-template-columns: repeat(5, 100px);
    grid-template-rows: repeat(3, 150px);
}
.item1 {
    grid-column-start: 1;
    grid-column-end: 3;
    grid-row-start: 1;
    grid-row-end: 1;
}
.item2 {
    grid-column-start: 3;
    grid-column-end: span 3;
    grid-row-start: 1;
    grid-row-end: 1;
}
.item3 {
    grid-column-start: 1;
    grid-column-end: 1;
    grid-row-start: 2;
    grid-row-end: end;
}
.item4 {
    grid-column-start: 2;
    grid-column-end: 4;
    grid-row-start: 2;
    grid-row-end: end;
}
.item5 {
    grid-column-start: 4;
    grid-column-end: span 2;
    grid-row-start: 2;
    grid-row-end: 2;
}
.item6 {
    grid-column-start: 4;
    grid-column-end: span 2;
    grid-row-start: 3;
    grid-row-end: 3;
}
```

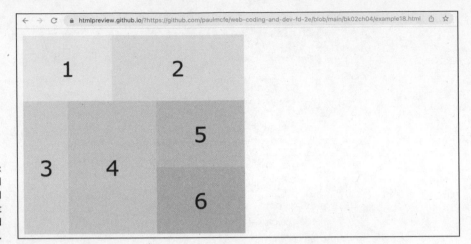

FIGURE 4-17:
Some grid items assigned to different columns and rows in the grid.

TIP

In the example, note that I use a function named repeat to specify multiple columns and rows that are the same size. Here's the syntax to use:

```
repeat(number, size)
```

Replace *number* with the number of columns or rows you want to create, and replace *size* with the size you want to use for each of those columns or rows. For example, the following two declarations are equivalent:

```
grid-template-rows: 150px 150px 150px;
grid-template-rows: repeat(3, 150px);
```

TIP

CSS also offers two shorthand properties that you can use to make the process of assigning items to columns and rows a bit more streamlined:

```
item {
    grid-column: column-start-value / column-end-value;
    grid-row: row-start-value / row-end-value;
}
```

Aligning grid items

CSS Grid offers several properties that you can use to align stuff in your grid. Grid's alignment properties fall into two general categories:

» **Direction:** Refers to the axis along which the alignment is performed:

- **Justify:** Sets the alignment along the grid container's inline axis.
- **Align:** Sets the alignment along the grid container's block axis.

>> **Target:** Refers to the part of the grid to which the alignment is applied:

- **Content:** Sets the alignment on all the columns or all the rows in the grid.

- **Items:** Sets the alignment on individual grid items within their assigned grid areas.

Given the preceding categories, CSS Grid defines four alignment properties:

>> justify-content: Sets the alignment along the inline axis of all grid's columns. Here's the syntax:

```
container {
    justify-content:
    start|center|end|stretch|space-around|space-between|
    space-evenly;
}
```

>> align-content: Sets the alignment along the block axis of all grid's rows. Here's the syntax:

```
container {
    align-content: start|center|end|stretch|space-around|
    space-between|space-evenly|baseline;
}
```

REMEMBER

For align-content (or align-items, coming up) to work, you need to set a height on the grid container — specifically, a height greater than the combined natural height of all the rows. Without that custom height, the browser will set the container height just tall enough to fit the rows, so there's no extra space for align-content (or align-items) to do its thing.

>> justify-items: Sets the alignment along the inline axis of each grid item within its grid area. Here's the syntax:

```
container {
    justify-items: start|center|end|stretch;
}
```

>> align-items: Sets the alignment along the block axis of each grid item within its grid area. Here's the syntax:

```
container {
    align-items: start|center|end|stretch|baseline;
}
```

Laying out content columns with Grid

As a two-dimensional layout system, Grid is perfect for laying out an entire page. This includes the classic page layout that I talk about earlier: a header and navigation bar across the top of the page, an article with a sidebar beside it, and a footer across the bottom of the page. Here's some Grid code (bk02ch04/example19.html) that creates this layout, which is shown in Figure 4-18:

HTML:

```
<body>
    <header>
        Header
    </header>
    <nav>
        Navigation
    </nav>
    <article>
        Article
    </article>
    <aside>
        Aside
    </aside>
    <footer>
        Footer
    </footer>
</body>
```

CSS:

```
html {
    height: 100%;
}
body {
    display: grid;
    grid-template-columns: 1fr 10rem;
    grid-template-rows: 2.5rem 2.5rem 1fr 2.5rem;
    gap: 1rem 1rem;
    font-size: 2rem;
    height: 100%;
    margin-left: 1rem;
    width: 75vw;
}
header {
    grid-column: 1 / end;
```

```
        grid-row: 1;
        border: 1px solid black;
    }
    nav {
        grid-column: 1 / end;
        grid-row: 2;
        border: 1px solid black;
    }
    article {
        grid-column: 1;
        grid-row: 3;
        border: 1px solid black;
    }
    aside {
        grid-column: 2 / end;
        grid-row: 3;
        border: 1px solid black;
    }
    footer {
        grid-column: 1 / end;
        grid-row: 4;
        border: 1px solid black;
    }
```

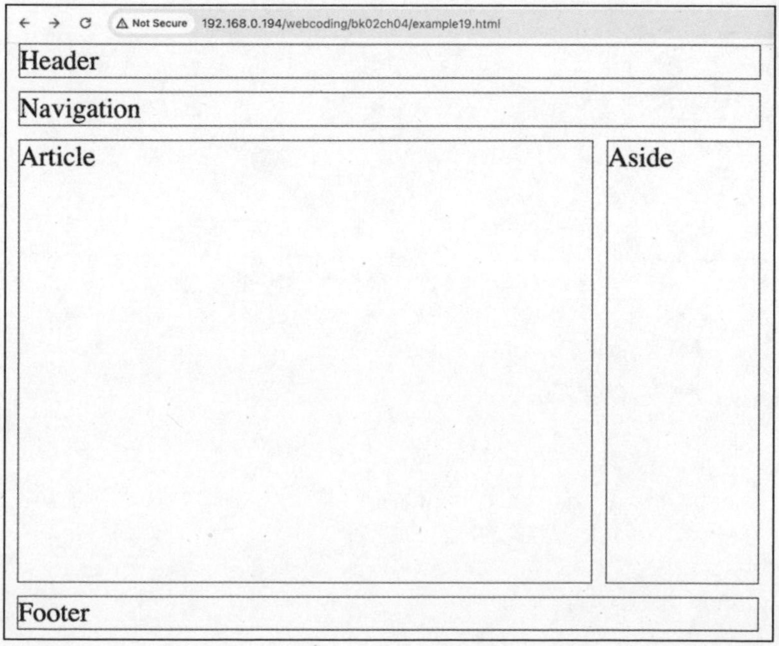

FIGURE 4-18:
The classic page
layout, Grid-style.

Here's a detailed look at what the code does:

>> The `<body>` tag is set up as a grid container, and that container is styled with two columns and four rows.

>> The `body` element has its `height` property set to `100%`, which makes the grid container always take up the entire height of the browser's content area. Note that setting `height: 100%` on the `body` element works only because earlier I added the same declaration to the `html` element.

```
html {
    height: 100%;
}
```

>> All `header`, `nav`, and `footer` elements span from the first column to the end of the grid, and they're assigned rows 1, 2, and 4, respectively.

>> The `article` element uses only column 1 and row 3, both of which were defined with the size `1fr`, which allows the `article` element to take up the free space in the grid.

>> The `aside` element uses column 2, which was assigned a width of `10rem`, so its width is fixed.

3

Coding the Front End, Part 2: JavaScript

Contents at a Glance

IN THIS CHAPTER

» Understanding programming in general and JavaScript in particular

» Getting a taste of what you can (and can't) do with JavaScript

» Learning the tools you need to get coding

» Adding JavaScript code to a web page

» Getting acquainted with the all-important console

Chapter **1**

An Overview of JavaScript

What's in your hands, I think and hope, is intelligence: the ability to see the machine as more than when you were first led up to it, that you can make it more.

— ALAN PERLIS

When we talk about web coding, what we're really talking about is JavaScript. Yep, you need HTML and CSS to create a web page, and you need tools such as PHP and MySQL to convince a web server to give your page some data, but the glue — and sometimes the duct tape — that binds all these technologies is JavaScript. The result is that JavaScript is now (and has been for a while) the default programming language for web development. If you want to control a page using code (and I know you do), you must use JavaScript to do it.

It also means that JavaScript is (and has been for a while) universal on the web. Sure, there are plenty of barebones home pages out there that are nothing but HTML and a sprinkling of CSS, but everything else — from humble personal blogs to fancy-pants designer portfolios to bigtime corporate ecommerce operations — relies on JavaScript to make things look good and work the way they're supposed to (most of the time, anyway).

So when it comes to the care and feeding of your web development education, JavaScript is one of the most important — arguably *the* most important — of all the topics you need to learn. Are you excited to start exploring JavaScript? I *knew* it!

JavaScript: Controlling the Machine

When a web browser is confronted with an HTML file, it goes through a simple but tedious process: It reads the file one line at a time, starting from (usually) the `<html>` tag at the top and finishing with the `</html>` tag at the bottom. Along the way, it might have to break out of this line-by-line monotony to perform some action based on what it has read. For example, if it stumbles over the `<img>` tag, the browser will immediately ask the web server to ship out a copy of the graphics file specified in the `src` attribute (refer to Book 2, Chapter 1).

The point here is that, at its core, a web browser is just a page-reading machine that doesn't know how to do much of anything else besides follow the instructions (the markup) in an HTML file. (For convenience, I'm ignoring the browser's other capabilities, such as saving bookmarks.)

One of the reasons that many folks get hooked on creating web pages is that they realize from the beginning that they have control over this page-reading machine. Slap some text between a `<b>` tag and its corresponding `</b>` end tag and the browser dutifully displays the text as bold. Create a CSS Grid structure (check out Book 2, Chapter 4) and the browser displays your formerly haphazard text in nice, neat rows and columns, no questions asked. These two examples show that, instead of just viewing pages from the outside, you now have a key to get *inside* the machine and start working its controls. *That* is the hook that grabs people and gets them seriously interested in web page design.

Imagine if you could take this idea of controlling the page-reading machine to the next level. Imagine if, instead of ordering the machine to process mere tags and text, you could issue much more sophisticated commands that could control the inner workings of the page-reading machine. Who wouldn't want that?

Well, that's the premise behind JavaScript. It's essentially just a collection of commands that you can wield to control the browser. Like HTML tags, JavaScript commands are inserted directly into the web page file. When the browser does its line-by-line reading of the file and it comes across a JavaScript command, it executes that command, just like that.

However, the key here is that the amount of control JavaScript gives you over the page-reading machine is much greater than what you get with HTML tags. The reason is that JavaScript is a full-fledged *programming language.* Although the *L* in HTML stands for *language,* there isn't even the tiniest hint of a programming language associated with HTML. JavaScript, though, is the real programming deal.

What Is a Programming Language?

So what does it mean to call something a "programming language"? To understand this term, you need look no further than the language you use to speak and write. At its most fundamental level, human language is composed of two things — words and rules:

>> The words are collections of letters that have a common meaning among all the people who speak the same language. For example, the word *book* denotes a type of object, the word *heavy* denotes a quality, and the word *read* denotes an action.

>> The rules are the ways in which words can be combined to create coherent and understandable concepts. If you want to be understood by other speakers of the language, you have only a limited number of ways to throw two or more words together. *I read a heavy book* is an instantly comprehensible sentence, but *book a I read heavy* is gibberish.

The key goal of human language is being understood by someone else who is listening to you or reading something you wrote. If you use the proper words to refer to things and actions, and if you combine words according to the rules, the other person will understand you.

A programming language works in more or less the same way. That is, it, too, has words and rules:

>> The words are a set of terms that refer to the specific things that your program works with (such as the browser window) or the specific ways in which those things can be manipulated (such as sending the browser to a specified address). They're known as *reserved words* or *keywords.*

>> The rules are the ways in which the words can be combined to produce the desired effect. In the programming world, these rules are known as the language's *syntax*.

In JavaScript, many of the words you work with are straightforward. Some refer to aspects of the browser, some refer to parts of the web page, and some are used internally by JavaScript. For example, in JavaScript, the word `document` refers to a specific object (the web page as a whole), and the word `write()` refers to a specific action (writing data to the page).

The crucial concept here is that just as the fundamental purpose of human language is to be understood by another person, the fundamental purpose of a programming language is to be understood by whatever machine is processing the language. With JavaScript, that machine is the page-reading machine: the web browser.

You can make yourself understood by the page-reading machine by using the proper JavaScript words and by combining them using the proper JavaScript syntax. For example, JavaScript's syntax rules tell you that you can combine the words `document` and `write()` like so: `document.write()`. If you use `write().document` or `document write()` or any other combination, the page-reading machine won't understand you.

The key, however, is that being "understood" by the page-reading machine really means being able to *control* the machine. That is, your JavaScript "sentences" are commands that you want the machine to carry out. For example, if you want to add the text "Hello World!" to a web page using JavaScript, you include the following statement in your code:

```
document.write("Hello World!");
```

When the page-reading machine trudges through the HTML file and comes upon this statement, it will go right ahead and insert the text between the quotation marks into the page.

Is JavaScript Hard to Learn?

I think there's a second reason why many folks get jazzed about creating web pages: It's not that hard. HTML sounds like it's a hard thing, and certainly if you look at the source code of a typical web page without knowing anything about HTML, the code appears about as intimidating as anything you can imagine.

However, I've found that anyone can learn HTML as long as they start with the basic tags, examine lots of examples of how they work, and slowly work their way up to more complex pages. It's just a matter of creating a solid foundation and then building on it.

I'm convinced that JavaScript can be approached in much the same way. I'm certainly not going to tell you that JavaScript is as easy to learn as HTML. That would be a bald-faced lie. However, I will tell you that there is nothing inherently difficult about JavaScript. Using our language analogy, it just has a few more words to know and a few more rules to learn. But I believe that if you begin with the basic words and rules, study tons of examples to learn how they work, and then slowly build up to more complex scripts, you can learn JavaScript programming. I predict here and now that by the time you finish this book, you'll even be a little bit amazed at yourself and at what you can do.

What You Can Do with JavaScript

The people I've taught to create web pages are a friendly bunch who enjoy writing to me to tell me how their pages are coming along. In many cases, they tell me they've hit the web page equivalent of a roadblock. That is, there's a certain thing they want to do, but they don't know how to do it in HTML. So, I end up getting lots of questions like these:

>> How do I display one of those pop-up boxes?

>> How do I add content to the page on-the-fly?

>> How can I make something happen when a user clicks a button?

>> How can I make an image change when the mouse hovers over it?

>> How can I calculate the total for my order form?

For each question, the start of the answer is always this: "Sorry, but you can't do that using HTML; you have to use JavaScript instead." I then supply them with a bit of code that they can cut and paste into their web pages and then get on with their lives.

If you're just getting started with JavaScript, my goal in this book is to help you to move from cut-and-paste to code-and-load. That is, you'll end up being able to create your own scripts to solve your own unique HTML and web page problems.

I hope to show you that learning JavaScript is worthwhile because you can do many other things with it:

>> Ask a web server for data and then display that data on your page.

>> Add, modify, or remove page text, HTML tags, and even CSS properties.

>> Display messages to the user and ask the user for info.

>> "Listen" for and then perform actions based on events such as a visitor clicking their mouse or pressing a key.

>> Send the user's browser to another page.

>> Validate the values in a form before submitting it to the server. For example, you can make sure that certain fields are filled in.

>> Collect, save, and retrieve data for each of your users, such as site customizations.

In this book, you learn how to do all these things and many more.

What You Can't Do with JavaScript

JavaScript is good, but it's not that good. JavaScript can do many things, but there's a long list of things that it simply can't do. Here's a sampling of what falls outside the scope of browser-based JavaScript:

>> Write data permanently to an existing file. For example, you can't take the data from a guest book and add it to a file that stores the messages.

>> Access files on the server.

>> Glean any information about the user, including email or IP addresses.

>> Submit credit-card–based purchases for authorization and payment.

>> Create multiplayer games.

>> Get data directly from a server database.

>> Handle file uploads.

JavaScript can't do most of these things because it's what is known in the trade as a *client-side* programming language, which means that it runs on the user's browser (which programming types like to call a *client*).

Server-side JavaScript tools can do some of these things, but they're super-sophisticated and therefore beyond the scope here. The good news is that many of the items in the preceding list are doable using PHP and MySQL, which I discuss later on (starting in Book 4). For now, though, just know that there are so many things that client-side JavaScript can do that you'll have no trouble being as busy as you want to be.

What You Need to Get Started

One of the nicest things about HTML and CSS is that the hurdles you have to leap to get started are not only low, but few in number. In fact, you really need only two things, both of which are free: a text editor to enter the text, tags, and properties; and a browser to view the results. (You'll also need a web server to host the finished pages, but the server isn't necessary when you're creating the pages.) Yes, there are high-end HTML editors and fancy graphics programs, but these fall into the bells and whistles category; you can create perfectly respectable web pages without them.

The basic requirements for JavaScript programming are the same as for HTML: a text editor and a browser. Again, programs are available to help you write and test your scripts, but you don't need them.

To learn more about text editors and using web browsers to test your code, check out Book 1, Chapter 2.

Basic Script Construction

Okay, that's more than enough theory. It's time to roll up your sleeves, crack your knuckles, and start coding. This section describes the standard procedure for constructing and testing a script. You'll see a working example that you can try out, and later you'll move on to other examples that illustrate some JavaScript techniques that you'll use throughout this book.

The <script> tag

The basic container for a script is, naturally enough, the HTML <script> tag and its associated </script> end tag:

```
<script>
    JavaScript statements go here
</script>
```

TECHNICAL STUFF

In HTML5, you can use <script> without any attributes. Before HTML5, the tag would look like this:

```
<script type="text/javascript">
```

The type attribute told the browser the programming language being used in the script, but JavaScript is the default now, so you no longer need it. You still come across the <script> tag with the type attribute used on a ton of pages, so I thought I'd better let you know what it means.

Where do you put the <script> tag?

With certain exceptions, it doesn't matter a great deal where you put your <script> tag. Some people place the tag between the page's </head> and <body> tags. The HTML standard recommends placing the <script> tag within the page header (that is, between <head> and </head>), so that's the style I use in this book:

```
<!DOCTYPE html>
<html lang="en">
    <head>
        <meta charset="utf-8">
        <title>Where do you put the script tag?</title>
        <script>
            JavaScript statements go here
        </script>
    </head>
    <body>
    </body>
</html>
```

Here are the exceptions to the put-your-script-anywhere technique:

>> If your script is designed to write data to the page, the <script> tag must be positioned within the page body (that is, between the <body> and </body> tags) in the exact position where you want the text to appear.

>> If your script refers to an item on the page (such as a form object), the script must be placed *after* that item. In most cases where the script refers to one or more page objects, coders plop the <script> tag at the bottom of the page body (that is, just above the </body> tag).

>> With many HTML tags, you can add one or more JavaScript statements as attributes directly within the tag.

REMEMBER

It's perfectly acceptable to insert multiple <script> tags within a single page, as long as each one has a corresponding </script> end tag, and as long as you don't put one <script> block within another one.

Example #1: Displaying a message to the user

You're now ready to construct and try out your first script. This example shows you the simplest of all JavaScript actions: displaying a simple message to the user. The following code shows the script within an HTML file (check out bk03ch01/example01.html in this book's example files):

```
<!DOCTYPE html>
<html lang="en">
    <head>
        <meta charset="utf-8">
        <title>Displaying a Message to the User</title>
        <script>
            alert("Hello Web Coding World!");
        </script>
    </head>
    <body>
    </body>
</html>
```

As shown here, place the script within the header of a page, save the file, and then open the HTML file within your browser.

This script consists of just a single line:

```
alert("Hello Web Coding World!");
```

This is called a *statement,* and each statement is designed to perform a single JavaScript task. You might be wondering about the semicolon (;) that appears at the end of the statement. Good eye. You use the semicolon to mark the end of each of your JavaScript statements.

Your scripts will range from simple programs with just a few statements to huge projects consisting of hundreds of statements. In the example, the statement runs the JavaScript alert() method, which displays to the user whatever message is enclosed by quotation marks within the parentheses (which could be a welcome message, an announcement of new features on your site, an advertisement for a promotion, and so on). Figure 1-1 shows the message that appears when you open the file.

FIGURE 1-1:
This alert message appears when you open the HTML file containing the example script.

TECHNICAL STUFF

A *method* is a special kind of JavaScript feature. I discuss methods in detail in Book 3, Chapter 6. For now, however, think of a method as a kind of action you want your code to perform.

How did the browser know to run the JavaScript statement? When a browser processes (*parses*, in the vernacular) a page, it basically starts at the beginning of the HTML file and works its way down, one line at a time, as I mention earlier. If it trips over a ‹script› tag, it knows one or more JavaScript statements are coming, and it automatically executes those statements, in order, as soon as it reads them. The exception is when JavaScript statements are enclosed within a *function*, which I explain in Book 3, Chapter 5.

WARNING

One of the cardinal rules of JavaScript programming is "one statement, one line." That is, each statement must appear on only a single line, and there should be no more than one statement on each line. I said "should" in the second part of the preceding sentence because it's possible to put multiple statements on a single line, as long as you separate each statement with a semicolon (;). There are rare times when it's necessary to have two or more statements on one line, but you should avoid it for the bulk of your programming because multiple-statement lines are difficult to read and to troubleshoot.

Example #2: Writing text to the page

One of JavaScript's most powerful features is the capability to write text and even HTML tags and CSS properties to the web page on-the-fly. That is, the text (or whatever) gets inserted into the page when a web browser loads the page.

What good is that? For one thing, it's ideal for time-sensitive data. For example, you might want to display the date and time that a web page was last modified so that visitors know how old (or new) the page is. Here's some code that shows just such a script (check out bk03ch01/example02.html):

```html
<!DOCTYPE html>
<html lang="en">
    <head>
        <meta charset="utf-8">
        <title>Writing Data to the Page</title>
    </head>
    <body>
        This is a regular line of text.<br>
        <script>
            document.write("Last modified: " + document.
    lastModified);
        </script>
        <br>This is another line of regular text.
    </body>
</html>
```

Note how the script appears within the body of the HTML document, which is necessary whenever you want to write data to the page. Figure 1-2 shows the result.

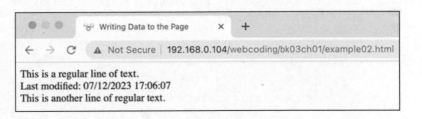

FIGURE 1-2: When you open the file, the text displays the date and time the file was last modified.

This script makes use of the document object, which is a built-in JavaScript construct that refers to whatever HTML file (document) the script resides in (refer to Book 3, Chapter 6 for more about the document object). The document.write() statement tells the browser to insert into the web page whatever text is between the quotation marks within the parentheses. The document.lastModified portion returns the date and time the web page file was last changed and saved.

A Quick Introduction to the Console

Every major web browser comes with an extensive suit of developer tools that enable you to monitor, edit, and troubleshoot your HTML, CSS, and JavaScript code. These tools are so important that I devote an entire book to them: Check out Book 5.

Arguably the most important of these developer tools is the *console,* which is an interactive window that enables you to display messages, run JavaScript code on the fly, and look for script error messages. You learn all about the console in Book 5, Chapter 2. However, over the rest of the chapters here in Book 3, I use the console in many of the examples, so here I present a brief introduction to this vital tool.

The first thing you need to know is that your JavaScript code can use the `console.log()` method to output a message to the console. As you learn in Book 5, Chapter 2, displaying messages to the console is one of the most common techniques that developers use when writing and troubleshooting their code. The simplest method for sending a message to the console is to invoke `console.log` with some text:

```
console.log("message")
```

Replace *message* with the text you want to appear in the console. The following example (bk03ch01/example03.html) sends the message Hello Web Coding World! to the console:

```
<!DOCTYPE html>
<html lang="en">
    <head>
        <meta charset="utf-8">
        <title>Sending a Message to the Console</title>
        <script>
            console.log("Hello Web Coding World!");
        </script>
    </head>
    <body>
    </body>
</html>
```

To display the console in most web browsers, right-click the web page, click Inspect (or press Ctrl+Shift+I in Windows or Option+⌘+I in macOS), and then click the Console tab. Figure 1-3 shows Chrome's Console tab with the `Hello Web Coding World!` message displayed.

Dealing with a Couple of Exceptional Cases

In this book, I make a couple of JavaScript assumptions related to the people who'll be visiting the pages you post to the web:

>> They have JavaScript enabled in their web browser.

>> They are using a relatively up-to-date version of a modern web browser, such as Chrome, Edge, Safari, or Firefox.

These are pretty safe assumptions, but it pays to be a bit paranoid and wonder how you may handle the teensy percentage of people who don't pass one or both tests.

Handling browsers with JavaScript turned off

You don't have to worry about web browsers not being able to handle JavaScript because all modern browsers have supported JavaScript for a very long time. You may, however, want to worry about people who have turned off their browser's JavaScript functionality. Why would someone do such a thing? Many people disable JavaScript because they're concerned about security, they don't want cookies written to their hard drives, and so on.

To handle these iconoclasts, place the `<noscript>` tag within the body of the page:

```
<noscript>
    <p>
        Hey, your browser has JavaScript turned off!
    </p>
    <p>
        Okay, cool, but remember that some site features
        require JavaScript, so a few things may not work
        properly or at all.
    </p>
</noscript>
```

If the browser has JavaScript enabled, the browser doesn't display any of the text within the `<noscript>` tag. However, if JavaScript is disabled, the browser displays the text and tags in the `<noscript>` tag to the user.

To test your site with JavaScript turned off, here are the techniques to use in some popular browsers:

>> **Chrome (desktop):** Open Settings, click Privacy and Security, click Site Settings, click JavaScript, and then select the Don't Allow Sites to Use JavaScript option, as shown in Figure 1-4.

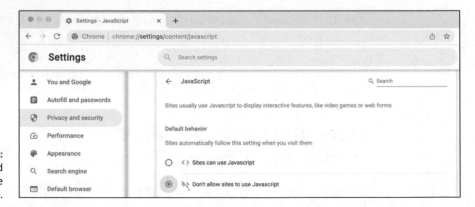

FIGURE 1-4:
JavaScript turned off in Google Chrome.

>> **Chrome (Android):** Open Settings, tap Site Settings, tap JavaScript, and then tap the JavaScript switch off.

>> **Edge:** Open Settings, click the Settings menu, click Cookies and Site Permissions, click JavaScript, and then click the Allowed switch off.

>> **Safari (macOS):** Open Settings, click the Advanced tab, select the Show Develop Menu in Menu Bar, and then close Settings. Choose Develop ⇨ Disable JavaScript.

>> **Safari (iOS or iPadOS):** Open Settings, tap Safari, tap Advanced, and then tap the JavaScript switch off.

>> **Firefox (desktop):** In the address bar, type **about:config** and press Enter or Return. If Firefox displays a warning page, click Accept the Risk and Continue to display the Advanced Preferences page. In the Search Preference Name box, type **javascript**. In the search results, look for the `javascript.enabled` preference. On the far right of that preference, click the Toggle button to turn the value of the preference from `true` to `false`, as shown in Figure 1-5.

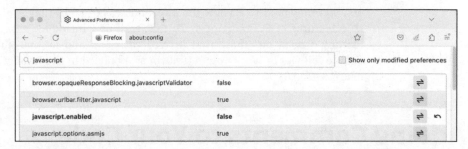

FIGURE 1-5:
JavaScript turned off in Firefox.

Handling very old browsers

In this book, you learn the version of JavaScript called ECMAScript 2015, also known as ECMAScript 6, or just ES6. Why this version, in particular, and not any of the later versions? Two reasons:

>> ES6 has excellent browser support, with more than 98 percent of all current browsers supporting the features released in ES 6. Later versions of JavaScript have less support.

>> ES6 has everything you need to add all kinds of useful and fun dynamic features to your pages. Unless you're a professional programmer, the features released in subsequent versions of JavaScript are way beyond what you need.

Okay, so what about that few percent of browsers that don't support ES6?

First, know that the number of browsers that choke on ES6 features is getting smaller every day. Sure, it's 2 percent now (about 1.7 percent, actually), but it will be 1 percent in six months, a .5 percent in a year, and so on until the numbers just get too small to measure.

Second, the percentage of browsers that don't support ES6 varies by region (it's higher in many countries in Africa, for example) and by environment. Most of the people running browsers that don't fully support ES6 are using Internet Explorer 11, and most of those people are in situations in which they can't upgrade (some corporate environments, for example).

If luck has it that your web pages draw an inordinate share of these older browsers, you may need to eschew the awesomeness of ES6 in favor of the tried-and-true features of ECMAScript 5. To that end, as I introduce each new JavaScript feature, I point out those that arrived with ES6 and let you know if there's a simple fallback or workaround (known as a polyfill in the JavaScript trade) if you need to use ES5.

Adding Comments to Your Code

A script that consists of just a few lines is usually easy to read and understand. However, your scripts won't stay that simple for long, and these longer and more complex creations will be correspondingly more difficult to read. (This difficulty will be particularly acute if you're looking at the code a few weeks or months after you first wrote it.) To help you decipher your code, it's good programming practice to make liberal use of comments throughout the script. A *comment* is text that describes or explains a statement or group of statements. Comments are ignored by the browser, so you can add as many as you deem necessary.

For short, single-line comments, use the double-slash (//). Put the // at the beginning of the line, and then type in your comment after it. Here's an example:

```
// Display the date and time the page was last modified
document.write("Last modified: " + document.lastModified);
```

You can also use // comments for two or three lines of text. If you have more than that, however, you're better off using multiple-line comments that begin with the /* symbol and end with the */ symbol. Here's an example:

```
/*
This script demonstrates JavaScript's ability
to write text to the web page by using the
document.write() method to display the date and time
the web page file was last modified.
This script is Copyright 2024 Paul McFedries.
*/
```

WARNING

Although it's fine to add quite a few comments when you're just starting out, you don't have to add a comment to everything. If a statement is trivial or its purpose is glaringly obvious, forget the comment and move on. If you're not sure whether to comment some code, go ahead and add the comment, particularly while you're building a script. Adding copious comments to your new code is a great way to organize your thoughts and keep your code readable. Later, you can always go back and delete comments that you no longer need.

Creating External JavaScript Files

Putting a script inside the page header or body isn't a problem if the script is relatively short. However, if your script (or scripts) take up dozens or hundreds of lines, your HTML code can look cluttered. Another problem you might run into is needing to use the same code on multiple pages. Sure, you can just copy the code into each page that requires it, but if you make changes down the road, you need to update every page that uses the code.

The solution to both problems is to move the code out of the HTML file and into an external JavaScript file. Moving the code reduces the JavaScript presence in the HTML file to a single line (as you'll learn shortly) and means that you can update the code by editing only the external file.

Here are some things to note about using an external JavaScript file:

» The file must use a plain text format.

» Use the .js extension when you name the file.

» Don't use the <script> tag within the file. Just enter your statements exactly as you would in an HTML file.

>> The rules for when the browser executes statements within an external file are identical to those used for statements in an HTML file. That is, statements outside functions are executed automatically when the browser comes across your file reference, and statements within a function aren't executed until the function is called.

To let the browser know that an external JavaScript file exists, add the src attribute to the <script> tag. For example, if the external file is named myscripts.js, your <script> tag is set up as follows:

```
<script src="myscripts.js">
```

This example assumes that the myscripts.js file is in the same directory as the HTML file. If the file resides in a different directory, adjust the src value accordingly. For example, if the myscripts.js file is in a subdirectory named scripts, you use this:

```
<script src="scripts/myscripts.js">
```

You can even specify a file from another site (presumably your own!) by specifying a full URL as the src value:

```
<script src="http://www.host.com/myscripts.js">
```

As an example, the following code shows a one-line external JavaScript file named footer.js:

```
document.write("Copyright " + new Date().getFullYear());
```

This statement writes the text *Copyright* followed by the current year. (I know: This code looks like gobbledygook right now. Don't sweat it, because you learn exactly what's going on here when I discuss the JavaScript Date object in Book 3, Chapter 9.)

The following code shows an HTML file that includes a reference for the external JavaScript file (bk03ch01/example03.html):

```
<!DOCTYPE html>
<html lang="en">
    <head>
        <meta charset="utf-8">
        <title>Using an External JS File</title>
```

```
    </head>
    <body>
        <hr>
        <footer>
            <script src="footer.js">
            </script>
        </footer>
    </body>
</html>
```

When you load the page, the browser runs through the HTML line by line. When it gets to the `<footer>` tag, it notices the external JavaScript file referenced by the `<script>` tag. The browser loads that file and then runs the code in the file, which writes the *Copyright* message to the page, as shown in Figure 1-6.

FIGURE 1-6: This page uses an external JavaScript file to display a footer message.

IN THIS CHAPTER

» Getting your head around variables

» Assigning names to variables

» Introducing JavaScript data types

» Figuring out numbers

» Stringing strings together

Chapter **2**

Understanding Variables

You should imagine variables as tentacles, rather than boxes. They do not contain values; they grasp them.

—MARIJN HAVERBEKE

You may have heard about — or perhaps even know — someone who, through mishap or misfortune, has lost the ability to retain short-term memories. If you introduce yourself to one of these folks, they'll be asking you your name again five minutes later. They live in a perpetual present, seeing the world anew every minute of every day.

What, I'm sure you're asking yourself by now, can any of this possibly have to do with coding? Just that, by default, your JavaScript programs also live a life without short-term memory. The web browser executes your code one statement at a time, until no more statements are left to process. It all happens in the perpetual present. Ah, but notice that I refer to this lack of short-term memory as the *default* state of your scripts. You have the power to give your scripts the gift of short-term memory, by using handy little chunks of code called variables. In this chapter, you delve into variables, which is a fundamental and crucial programming topic. You investigate what variables are, what you can do with them, and how to wield them in your JavaScript code.

Understanding Variables

Why would a script need short-term memory? Because one of the most common concepts that crops up when coding is the need to store a temporary value for use later on. In most cases, you want to use that value a bit later in the same script. However, you may also need to use it in some other script, to populate an HTML form, or as part of a larger or more complex calculation.

For example, your page may have a button that toggles the page text between a larger font size and the regular font size, so you need some way to remember that choice. Similarly, if your script performs calculations, you may need to set aside one or more calculated values to use later. For example, if you're constructing a shopping cart script, you may need to calculate taxes on the order. To do that, you must first calculate the total value of the order, store that value, and then later take a percentage of it to work out the tax.

In programming, the way you save a value for later use is by storing it in a variable. A *variable* is a small chunk of computer memory set aside for holding program data. The good news is that the specifics of how the data is stored and retrieved from memory happen well behind the scenes, so it isn't something you ever have to worry about. As a coder, working with variables involves just three things:

>> Creating (or *declaring*) variables

>> Assigning values to those variables

>> Including the variables in other statements in your code

The next three sections fill in the details.

Declaring a variable with let

The process of creating a variable is called *declaring* in programming terms. All declaring really means is that you're supplying the variable with a name and tell-ing the browser to set aside a bit of room in memory to hold whatever value you end up storing in the variable. To declare a variable in JavaScript, you use the let keyword, followed by a space, the name of the variable, and the usual line-ending semicolon. For example, to declare a variable named interestRate, you'd use the following statement:

```
let interestRate;
```

REMEMBER

Here are a few things to bear in mind when you're declaring variables in your scripts:

>> **Declare a variable only once.** Although you're free to use a variable as many times as you need to in a script, you declare the variable only once. Trying to declare a variable more than once will cause an error.

>> **Use a comment to describe each variable.** Variables tend to proliferate to the point where it often becomes hard to remember what each variable represents. You can make the purpose of each variable clear by adding a comment right after the variable declaration, like so:

```
let interestRate; // Annual interest rate for the loan
    calculation
```

>> **Declare each variable before you use it.** If you use a variable before you declare it, you'll get an error.

REMEMBER

When I say that you'll "get an error," I don't mean that an error message will pop up on the screen. The only thing you'll notice is that your script doesn't run. To read the error message, you need to access your browser's console, as I describe in Book 3, Chapter 1. For details on JavaScript errors and how to troubleshoot them, refer to Book 5, Chapter 2.

>> **Declare each variable right before you first use it.** You'll make your programming and debugging (refer to Book 5, Chapter 2) life much easier if you follow this one simple rule: Declare each variable just before (or as close as possible to) the first use of the variable.

TECHNICAL STUFF

The let keyword was introduced in ECMAScript 2015 (ES6). If you need to support really old browsers — I'm looking at *you* Internet Explorer 11 and earlier —use the var keyword, instead.

Storing a value in a variable

After your variable is declared, your next task is to give it a value. You use the assignment operator — the equals (=) sign — to store a value in a variable, as in this general statement:

```
variableName = value;
```

Here's an example that assigns the value 0.06 to a variable named interestRate:

```
interestRate = 0.06;
```

Note, too, that if you know the initial value of the variable in advance, you can combine the declaration and initial assignment into a single statement, like this:

```
let interestRate = 0.06;
interestRate = 0.06 / 12;
```

As a final note about using variable assignment, check out a variation that often causes some confusion among new programmers. Specifically, you can set up a statement that assigns a new value to a variable by changing its existing value. Here's an example:

```
interestRate = interestRate / 12;
```

If you've never come across this kind of statement before, it probably looks a bit illogical. How can something equal itself divided by 12? The secret to understanding such a statement is to remember that the browser always evaluates the right side of the statement — that is, the expression to the right of the equals sign (=) — first. In other words, it takes the current value of interestRate, which is 0.06, and divides it by 12. The resulting value is what's stored in interestRate when all is said and done. For a more in-depth discussion of operators and expressions, head over to Book 3, Chapter 3.

REMEMBER

Because of this evaluate-the-expression-and-*then*-store-the-result behavior, JavaScript assignment statements shouldn't be read as "variable *equals* expression" or "variable *is the same as* expression." Instead, it makes more sense to read them as "variable *is set to* expression" or "variable *assumes the value given by* expression." Reading assignment statements this way helps to reinforce the important concept that the expression result is being stored in the variable.

Declaring a variable another way: const

The word *variable* implies that the value assigned to a variable is allowed to *vary*, which is the case for most variables you declare. Most, but not all. Sometimes your scripts will need to use a value that remains constant. For example, suppose you're building a calculator that converts miles to kilometers. The conversion factor is 1.60934, and that value will remain constant throughout your script.

It's good programming practice to store such values in a variable for easier reading. However, if you use let for this declaration, you run the risk of accidentally changing the value somewhere in your code because variables declared with let can change.

To avoid accidentally changing a value that you want to remain constant, you can declare the variable using the const (short for *constant*) keyword instead. Here's the general syntax:

```
const variableName = value;
```

Note that, unlike with let, you must assign a value to the variable when you declare it with const. Here's an example that declares a variable named miles ToKilometers and assigns it the value 1.60934:

```
const milesToKilometers = 1.60934;
```

REMEMBER

Most JavaScript programmers refer to any variable declared with const as a *constant*, despite the oxymoronic undertow of the phrase *constant variable*.

REMEMBER

Are there any real benefits to using const over let in cases where a variable's value must never change? Yep, there are two pretty good ones:

>> Using the const keyword is a reminder that you're dealing with a non-changing value, which helps you to remember not to assign the variable a new value.

>> If you do try to change the value of a variable declared with const, you'll generate an error, which is another way to remind you that the variable's value is not to be messed with.

TIP

Given these advantages, many JavaScript programmers use const by default and use let only for variables that they know will change. As your code progresses, if you find that a const variable needs to change, you can go back and change const to let.

Using variables in statements

With your variable declared and assigned a value, you can then use that variable in other statements. When the browser comes across the variable, it goes to the computer's memory, retrieves the current value of the variable, and then substitutes that value into the statement. The following code presents an example (check out bk03ch02/example01.html in this book's example files):

```
let interestRate = 0.06;
interestRate = interestRate / 12;
console.log(interestRate);
```

This code declares a variable named interestRate with the value 0.06; it then divides that value by 12 and stores the result in the variable. The console.log() statement then displays the current value of the variable, as shown in Figure 2-1.

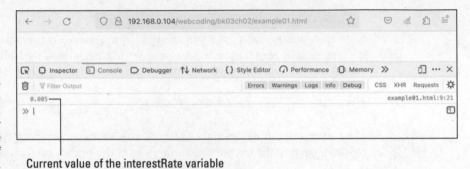

FIGURE 2-1:
When you use a variable in a statement, the browser substitutes the current value of that variable.

Current value of the interestRate variable

To display the console in most web browsers, right-click the web page, click Inspect (or press Ctrl+Shift+I in Windows or Option+⌘+I in macOS), and then click the Console tab.

TIP

Naming Variables: Rules and Best Practices

If you want to write clear, easy-to-follow, and easy-to-debug scripts (and who doesn't?), you can go a long way toward that goal by giving careful thought to the names you use for your variables. This section helps by running through the rules you need to follow and by giving you some tips and guidelines for creating good variable names.

Rules for naming variables

JavaScript has only a few rules for variable names:

>> The first character must be a letter or an underscore (_). You can't use a number as the first character.

>> The rest of the variable name can include any letter, any number, or the underscore. You can't use any other characters, including spaces, symbols, and punctuation marks.

» As with the rest of JavaScript, variable names are case sensitive. That is, a variable named `InterestRate` is treated as a different variable than one named `interestRate`.

» There's no limit to the length of the variable name.

» You can't use one of JavaScript's *reserved words* as a variable name (such as `let`, `const`, or `var`). All programming languages have a supply of words that are used internally by the language and that can't be used for variable names, because doing so would cause confusion (or worse). Check out "JavaScript Reserved Words," later in this chapter, for a complete list.

Ideas for good variable names

The process of declaring a variable doesn't take much thought, but that doesn't mean you should just type any old variable name that comes to mind. Take a few extra seconds to come up with a good name by following these guidelines:

» **Make your names descriptive.** Sure, using names that are just a few characters long makes them easier to type, but I guarantee that you won't remember what the variables represent when you look at the script down the road. For example, if you want a variable to represent an account number, use `accountNumber` or `accountNum` instead of, say, `acnm` or `accnum`.

REMEMBER

» **Mostly avoid single-letter names.** Although it's best to avoid single-letter variable names, such short names are accepted in some places, such as when constructing loops, as described in Book 3, Chapter 4.

» **Use multiple words with no spaces.** The best way to create a descriptive variable name is to use multiple words. However, because JavaScript doesn't take kindly to spaces in names, you need some way of separating the words to keep the name readable. The two standard conventions for using multi-word variable names are *camelCase,* where you cram the words together and capitalize all but the first word (for example, `lastName`), or separating each word with an underscore (for example, `last_name`). I prefer the former style, so I use it throughout this book.

» **Use separate naming conventions.** Use one naming convention for JavaScript variables and a different one for HTML identifiers and CSS classes. For example, if you use camelCase for JavaScript variables, use dashes for `id` values and class names.

» **Differentiate your variable names from JavaScript keywords.** Try to make your variable names look as different from JavaScript's keywords and other built-in terms (such as `alert`) as possible. Differentiating variable names helps avoid the confusion that can arise when you look at a term and can't remember if it's a variable or a JavaScript word.

» **Don't make your names too long.** Although short, cryptic variable names are to be shunned in favor of longer, descriptive names, that doesn't mean you should be using entire sentences. Extremely long names are inefficient because they take so long to type, and they're dangerous because the longer the name, the more likely you are to make a typo. Names of 2 to 4 words and 8 to 20 characters should be all you need.

Understanding Literal Data Types

In programming, a variable's *data type* specifies what kind of data is stored in the variable. The data type is a crucial idea because it determines not only how two or more variables are combined (for example, mathematically) but also whether they can be combined at all. *Literals* are a special class of data type, and they cover those values that are fixed (even if only temporarily). For example, consider the following variable assignment statement:

```
let todaysQuestion = "What color is your parachute?";
```

Here, the text What color is your parachute? is a literal string value. JavaScript supports three kinds of literal data types: numeric, string, and Boolean. The next three sections discuss each type.

Working with numeric literals

Unlike many other programming languages, JavaScript treats all numbers the same, so you don't have to do anything special when working with the two basic numeric literals, which are integers and floating-point numbers:

» **Integers:** These are numbers that don't have a fractional or decimal part. So, you represent an integer using a sequence of one or more digits, as in these examples:

```
0
42
2001
-20
```

» **Floating-point numbers:** These are numbers that do have a fractional or decimal part. Therefore, you represent a floating-point number by first writing the integer part, followed by a decimal point, followed by the fractional or decimal part, as in these examples:

```
0.07
3.14159
-16.6666667
7.6543e+21
1.234567E-89
```

Exponential notation

The last two floating-point examples require a bit more explanation. These two use *exponential notation*, which is an efficient way to represent really large or really small floating-point numbers. Exponential notation uses an e (or E) followed by the *exponent*, which is a number preceded by a plus sign (+) or a minus sign (–).

You multiply the first part of the number (that is, the part before the e or E) by 10 to the power of the exponent. Here's an example:

```
9.87654e+5;
```

The exponent is 5, and 10 to the power of 5 is 100,000. So multiplying 9.87654 by 100,000 results in the value 987,654.

Here's another example:

```
3.4567e-4;
```

The exponent is –4, and 10 to the power of –4 is 0.0001. So, multiplying 3.4567 by 0.0001 results in the value .00034567.

JavaScript has a ton of built-in features for performing mathematical calculations. To get the details on these, head for Book 3, Chapter 9.

**TECHNICAL
STUFF**

Earlier, I mention that JavaScript treats all numeric literals the same. But what I really meant was that JavaScript treats the numeric literals as floating-point values. This is fine (after all, there's no practical difference between 2 and 2.0), but it does put a limit on the maximum and minimum integer values that you can work with safely. The maximum is 9007199254740992 and the minimum is –9007199254740992. If you use numbers outside this range (unlikely, but you never know), JavaScript won't be able to maintain accuracy. One solution is to use

BigInt values, either by appending n to the end of a large integer value or by using BigInt(*value*), where *value* is a variable containing a large integer value.

Hexadecimal integer values

You'll likely deal with the usual decimal (base-10) number system throughout most of your JavaScript career. However, just in case you have cause to work with hexadecimal (base-16) numbers, this section shows you how JavaScript deals with them.

The hexadecimal number system uses the digits 0 through 9 and the letters *A* through *F* (or *a* through f), where these letters represent the decimal numbers 10 through 15. So, what in the decimal system would be 16 is actually 10 in hexadecimal. To specify a hexadecimal number in JavaScript, begin the number with a 0x (or 0X), as shown in the following examples:

```
0x23;
0xff;
0X10ce;
```

Working with string literals

A *string literal* is a sequence of one or more letters, numbers, or punctuation marks, enclosed either in double quotation marks (") or single quotation marks ('). Here are some examples:

```
"Web Coding and Development";
'August 23, 2024';
"";
"What's the good word?";
```

The string "" (or ' ' — two consecutive single quotation marks) is called a *null string* or an *empty string*. It represents a string that doesn't contain any characters.

Using quotation marks within strings

The final example in the preceding section shows that it's okay to insert one or more instances of one of the quotation marks (such as ') inside a string that's enclosed by the other quotation mark (such as "). Being able to nest quotation marks comes in handy when you need to embed one string inside another, which is common (particularly when using bits of JavaScript in HTML tags). Here's an example:

```
onsubmit="processForm('testing')";
```

However, it's illegal to insert in a string one or more instances of the same quotation mark that encloses the string, as in this example:

```
"This is "illegal" in JavaScript.";
```

Understanding escape sequences

What if you must include, say, a double quotation mark within a string that's enclosed by double quotation marks? Having to nest the same type of quotation mark is rare, but it is possible if you precede the double quotation mark with a backslash (\), like this:

```
"The double quotation mark (\") encloses this string.";
```

The \" combination is called an *escape sequence.* You can combine the backslash with a number of other characters to form other escape sequences, and each one enables the browser to represent a character that, by itself, would be illegal or not representable otherwise. Table 2-1 lists the most commonly used escape sequences.

TABLE 2-1

Common JavaScript Escape Sequences

Escape Sequence	Character It Represents
\'	Single quotation mark
\"	Double quotation mark
\b	Backspace
\f	Form feed
\n	New line
\r	Carriage return
\t	Tab
\\	Backslash

The following code shows an example script that uses the \n escape sequence to display text on multiple lines with an alert box.

```
console.log("This is line 1.\nSo what. This is line 2.");
```

Figure 2-2 shows the result.

FIGURE 2-2:
Using the \n
escape sequence
enables you to
format text so
that it displays on
different lines.

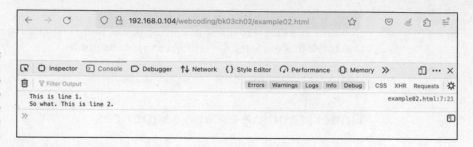

To learn how to combine two or more string literals, check out Book 3, Chapter 3. Also, JavaScript has a nice collection of string manipulation features, which I discuss in Book 3, Chapter 9.

Working with Boolean literals

Booleans are the simplest of all the literal data types because they can assume only one of two values: true or false. That simplicity may make it seem as though Booleans aren't particularly useful, but the capability to test whether a particular variable or condition is true or false is invaluable in JavaScript programming.

You can assign Boolean literals directly to a variable, like this:

```
taskCompleted = true;
```

Alternatively, you can work with Boolean values implicitly using expressions:

```
currentMonth === "August"
```

The comparison expression currentMonth === "August" asks the following: Does the value of the currentMonth variable equal the string "August"? If it does, the expression evaluates to the Boolean value true; if it doesn't, the expression evaluates to false. I discuss much more about comparison expressions in Book 3, Chapter 3.

JavaScript Reserved Words

As I mention earlier, JavaScript has a bunch of reserved words that you need to avoid when naming your variables. Table 2-2 presents a list of the JavaScript reserved words. It's illegal to use any of these words as variable or function names.

TABLE 2-2   JavaScript's Reserved Words

abstract	arguments	await	boolean
break	byte	case	catch
char	class	const	continue
debugger	default	delete	do
double	else	enum	eval
export	extends	false	final
finally	float	for	function
goto	if	implements	import
in	instanceof	int	interface
let	long	native	new
null	package	private	protected
public	return	short	static
super	switch	synchronized	this
throw	throws	transient	true
try	typeof	var	void
volatile	while	with	yield

JavaScript Keywords

Table 2-3 presents the complete list of keywords used in JavaScript and HTML that you should avoid using for variable and function names. It's not illegal to use these words, but using them outside their natural habitat could cause confusion.

TABLE 2-3   JavaScript and HTML Keywords

alert	all	anchor	anchors
area	Array	assign	blur
button	checkbox	clearInterval	clearTimeout
clientInformation	close	closed	confirm

(continued)

TABLE 2-3 *(continued)*

constructor	crypto	Date	decodeURI
decodeURIComponent	defaultStatus	document	element
elements	embed	embeds	encodeURI
encodeURIComponent	escape	eval	event
fileUpload	focus	form	forms
frame	frameRate	frames	function
hasOwnProperty	hidden	history	image
images	Infinity	innerHeight	innerWidth
isFinite	isNaN	isPrototypeOf	layer
layers	length	link	location
Math	mimeTypes	name	NaN
navigate	navigator	Number	Object
offscreenBuffering	onblur	onclick	onerror
onfocus	onkeydown	onkeypress	onkeyup
onload	onmousedown	onmouseover	onmouseup
onsubmit	open	opener	option
outerHeight	outerWidth	packages	pageXOffset
pageYOffset	parent	parseFloat	parseInt
password	pkcs11	plugin	prompt
propertyIsEnum	prototype	radio	reset
screenX	screenY	scroll	secure
select	self	setInterval	setTimeout
status	String	submit	taint
text	textarea	top	toString
undefined	unescape	untaint	valueOf
window			

IN THIS CHAPTER

» **Understanding what expressions are**

» **Figuring out numeric expressions**

» **Tying up string expressions**

» **Getting the hang of comparison expressions**

» **Learning about logical expressions**

Chapter **3**

Building Expressions

It's not at all important to get it right the first time. It's vitally important to get it right the last time.

—DAVID THOMAS

The JavaScript variables described in the preceding chapter can't do all that much by themselves. They don't become useful members of your web code community until you give them something productive to do. For example, you can assign values to them, use them to assign values to other variables, use them in calculations, and so on.

This productive side of variables in particular, and JavaScript-based web code in general, is brought to you by a JavaScript feature known as the expression. When coding in JavaScript, you use expressions constantly, so it's vital to understand what they are and to get comfortable with the types of expressions available to you. Every JavaScript coder is different, but I can say without fear of contradiction that every *good* JavaScript coder is fluent in expressions.

This chapter takes you through everything you need to know about expressions. You discover some expression basics and then you explore a number of techniques for building powerful expressions using numbers, strings, and Boolean values.

Understanding Expression Structure

To be as vague as I can be, an *expression* is a collection of symbols, words, and numbers that performs a calculation and produces a result. That's a nebulous definition, I know, so I'll make it more concrete.

When your check arrives after a restaurant meal, one of the first things you probably do is take out your smartphone and use the calculator to figure out the tip amount. The service and food were good, so you're thinking 20 percent is appropriate. With phone in hand, you tap in the bill total, tap the multiplication button, tap 20%, and then tap Equals. Voilà! The tip amount appears on the screen and you're good to go.

A JavaScript expression is something like this kind of procedure because it takes one or more inputs, such as a bill total and a tip percentage, and combines them in some way — for example, by using multiplication. In expression lingo, the inputs are called *operands*, and they're combined by using special symbols called *operators*:

>> **operand:** An input value for an expression. It is, in other words, the raw data that the expression manipulates to produce its result. It could be a number, a string, a variable, a function result (refer to Book 3, Chapter 5), or an object property (refer to Book 3, Chapter 6).

>> **operator:** A symbol that represents a particular action performed on one or more operands. For example, the * operator represents multiplication, and the + operator represents addition. I discuss the various JavaScript operators throughout this chapter.

Here's an expression that calculates a tip amount and assigns the result to a variable:

```
tipAmount = billTotal * tipPercentage;
```

The expression is everything to the right of the equals sign (=). Here, `billTotal` and `tipPercentage` are the operands, and the multiplication sign (*) is the operator.

TECHNICAL STUFF

Expression results always have a particular data type — numeric, string, or Boolean. So, when you're working with expressions, always keep in mind what type of result you need and then choose the appropriate operands and operators accordingly.

REMEMBER

Another analogy I like to use for operands and operators is a grammatical one — that is, if you consider an expression to be a sentence, the operands are the nouns (the things) of the sentence, and the operators are the verbs (the actions) of the sentence.

Building Numeric Expressions

Calculating a tip amount on a restaurant bill is a mathematical calculation, so you may be thinking that JavaScript expressions are going to be mostly mathematical. If I were standing in front of you and happened to have a box of gold stars on me, I'd certainly give you one because, yes, math-based expressions are probably the most common type you'll come across.

In JavaScript, a mathematical calculation is called a *numeric expression*, and it combines numeric operands and arithmetic operators to produce a numeric result. This section discusses all the JavaScript arithmetic operators and shows you how best to use them to build useful and handy numeric expressions.

A quick look at the arithmetic operators

JavaScript's basic arithmetic operators are more or less the same as those found in your smartphone's calculator app or on the numeric keypad of your computer's keyboard, plus a couple of extra operators for more advanced work. Table 3-1 lists the basic arithmetic operators you can use in your JavaScript expressions. (In subsequent sections I discuss each one in more detail.)

TABLE 3-1 JavaScript Arithmetic Operators

Operator	Name	Example	Result
+	Addition	10 + 4	14
++	Increment	10++	11
–	Subtraction	10 – 4	6
–	Negation	–10	–10
--	Decrement	10--	9
*	Multiplication	10 * 4	40
/	Division	10 / 4	2.5
%	Modulus	10 % 4	2

JavaScript also comes with a few extra operators that combine some of the arithmetic operators and the assignment operator, which is the humble equals sign (=) that assigns a value to a variable. Table 3-2 lists these *arithmetic assignment* operators.

TABLE 3-2   ## JavaScript Arithmetic Assignment Operators

Operator	Example	Equivalent
+=	x += y	x = x + y
-=	x -= y	x = x - y
*=	x *= y	x = x * y
/=	x /= y	x = x / y
^=	x ^= y	x = x ^ y
%=	x %= y	x = x % y

Using the addition (+) operator

You use the addition operator (+) to calculate the sum of two operands. The operands are usually of the numeric data type, which means they can be numeric literals, variables that store numeric values, or methods or functions that return numeric values. Here's an example (check out bk03ch03/example01.html in this book's example files):

```
widthMax = widthContent + widthSidebar + 100;
```

You could use such an expression in a web app when you need to know the maximum width to assign to the app's container. In this case, you take the width of the app's content (represented by the widthContent variable), add the width of the app's sidebar (the widthSidebar variable), and then add the literal value 100 (which may be a value in pixels).

Using the increment (++) operator

One of the most common programming operations involves adding 1 to an existing value, such as a variable. This operation is called *incrementing* the value, and the standard way to write such a statement is as follows:

```
someVariable = someVariable + 1;
```

However, JavaScript offers a much more compact alternative that uses the increment operator (++), which you place immediately after the variable name (check out bk03ch03/example02.html):

```
let someVariable = 0;
someVariable++;
```

After these two statements are executed, the value of someVariable will be 1.

WARNING

It is now considered bad programming practice to use the increment operator. Why? Most of the reasons are fairly technical, but the main reason is that this operator is a tad cryptic and makes code hard to read. Almost all modern code gurus recommend using the addition assignment operator (+=), instead of the increment operator (refer to "Using the arithmetic assignment operators," later in this chapter).

That is, instead of this:

```
someVariable++;
```

use this:

```
someVariable += 1;
```

THE PRE- AND POST-INCREMENT OPERATORS

TECHNICAL STUFF

JavaScript coders often use the ++ operator as part of an expression that assigns a value to another variable. Again, I don't recommend using this method, but I thought you should know about it just in case you come across it in someone else's code.

The first alternative use of ++ is to increment a variable and then assign this new value to another variable, using the following form:

```
someVariable = ++anotherVariable;
```

This gives the same result as the following two statements:

```
anotherVariable = anotherVariable + 1;
someVariable = anotherVariable;
```

(continued)

(continued)

Because the ++ appears before the variable, it is often called the *pre-increment operator*.

The second alternative use of ++ is called the *post-increment operator*:

```
someVariable = anotherVariable++;
```

In this case, the ++ operator appears after the variable. Big whoop, right? Actually, there is a subtle but crucial difference. The following two statements do the same thing as the post-increment operator:

```
someVariable = anotherVariable;
anotherVariable = anotherVariable + 1;
```

As you can see, the first variable is set equal to the second variable and then the second variable is incremented.

Using the subtraction and negation (-) operators

The subtraction operator (–) subtracts the numeric value to the right of the operator from the numeric value to the left of the operator. For example, consider the following statements (bk03ch03/example03.html):

```
const targetYear = 2025;
const birthYear = 1985;
const yearsDifference = targetYear - birthYear;
```

The third statement subtracts 1985 from 2025 and the result — 40 — is stored in the yearsDifference variable.

The negation operator (–) is the same symbol, but it works in a totally different way. You use it as a kind of prefix by appending it to the front of an operand. The result is a new value that has the opposite sign of the original value. In other words, applying the negation operator to an operand is the same as multiplying the operand by -1. This means that the following two statements are identical:

```
negatedValue = -originalValue;
negatedValue = originalValue * -1;
```

Using the decrement (--) operator

Another common programming operation is subtracting 1 from an existing variable or other operand. This operation is called *decrementing* the value, and the usual way to go about this is with a statement like this one:

```
thisVariable = thisVariable - 1;
```

However (you just knew there was going to be a *however*), JavaScript offers a much more svelte alternative that takes advantage of the decrement operator (--), which you place immediately after the variable name (bk03ch03/example04. html):

```
let thisVariable = 1;
thisVariable--;
```

WARNING

As with the increment operator, using the decrement operator is frowned upon these days. Instead, your code will read better if you use the subtraction assignment operator (-=) instead of the decrement operator (refer to "Using the arithmetic assignment operators," later in this chapter).

That is, instead of this:

```
thisVariable--;
```

use this:

```
thisVariable -= 1;
```

**TECHNICAL
STUFF**

THE PRE- AND POST-DECREMENT OPERATORS

JavaScript programmers often use the -- operator as part of an expression that assigns a value to another variable. I don't recommend using this method, but you should know about it just in case you trip over it in someone else's code.

The first alternative use of -- is to decrement a variable and then assign this new value to another variable, which is called the *pre-decrement* form:

```
thisVariable = --thatVariable;
```

(continued)

(continued)

This has the same effect as the following two statements:

```
thatVariable = thatVariable - 1;
thisVariable = thatVariable;
```

The second alternative use of –– is to assign the value of a variable to another variable and then decrement the first variable, which is called the *post-decrement* form:

```
thisVariable = thatVariable--;
```

Again, the following two statements do the same thing:

```
thisVariable = thatVariable;
thatVariable = thatVariable - 1;
```

As you can see, the first variable is set equal to the second variable and then the second variable is decremented.

Using the multiplication (*) operator

The multiplication operator (∗) multiplies two operands. Here's an example (bk03ch03/example05.html):

```
const columns = 8;
const columnWidth = 100;
const totalWidth = columns * columnWidth;
```

You might use this code when you want to calculate the width taken up by a web page layout that uses multiple columns. This code assigns literal numeric values to the variables columns and columnWidth. It then uses a numeric expression to multiply these two values and assign the result to the totalWidth variable.

Using the division (/) operator

The division operator (/) divides one numeric value by another. You can show off at parties by remembering that the number to the left of the slash (/) is called the *dividend*, and the number to the right of the / is called the *divisor*:

```
dividend / divisor
```

Here's an example (bk03ch03/example06.html):

```
const contentWidth = 600;
const windowWidth = 1200;
const contentRatio = contentWidth / windowWidth;
```

You can use this code to calculate the portion of the browser's window width that the page content is currently using. In this code, the contentWidth and windowWidth variables are assigned literal numeric values, and then a numeric expression divides the first of the values by the second, the result of which is stored in the contentRatio variable.

WARNING

Whenever you use the division operator, you must guard against cases where the divisor is 0. If that happens, your script will produce an Infinity result, which is almost certain to wreak havoc on your calculations. Before performing any division, your script should use an if() statement (refer to see Book 3, Chapter 4) to check whether the divisor is 0 and, if it is, to cancel the division or perform some kind of workaround.

Using the modulus (%) operator

The modulus operator (%) divides one number by another and then returns the remainder as the result:

```
dividend % divisor
```

For example, the following code stores the value 1 in the myRemainder variable because 5 (the myDivisor value; also known as the *modulus*) divides into 16 (the myDividend value) three times and leaves a remainder of 1 (bk03ch03/example07.html):

```
const myDividend = 16;
const myDivisor = 5;
const myRemainder = myDividend % myDivisor;
```

On a more practical level, suppose that you are trying to come up with a web-page color scheme and want to use two colors that are complements of each other. Complementary means that the two hues are on the opposite side of the color wheel, so one way to calculate the second color is by adding 180 to the first color's hue value. That approach works when the hue of the first color is between 0 and 179, which gives second color hue values between 180 and 359. However, an initial hue of 180, 181, and so on produces a second hue of 360, 361, and so on, which are illegal values. You can work around that issue by using a modulus expression like this (bk03ch03/example07.html):

```
complementaryColor = (originalColor + 180) % 360;
```

This statement adds 180 to the original color, but then uses % 360 to return the remainder when divided by 360 to avoid illegal values.

Using the arithmetic assignment operators

Your web coding scripts will often update the value of a variable by adding to it the value of some other operand. Here's an example:

```
totalInterestPaid = totalInterestPaid + monthlyInterestPaid
```

Coders are an efficiency-loving bunch, so the fact that the totalInterestPaid variable appears twice in that statement is like chewing tin foil to your average programmer. The JavaScript brain trust hates that kind of thing, too, so they came up with the addition assignment operator (+=), which you use like so (bk03ch03/example08.html):

```
totalInterestPaid += monthlyInterestPaid
```

Yep, this statement does exactly the same thing as the first one, but it does it with 19 fewer characters. Sweet!

If you need to subtract one operand from another, again you can do it the old-fashioned way:

```
principalOwing = principalOwing - monthlyPrincipalPaid
```

To avoid other coders laughing behind your back at your inefficiency, use the subtraction assignment operator (-=), which works like this (bk03ch03/example08.html):

```
principalOwing -= monthlyPrincipalPaid
```

REMEMBER

Like the increment and decrement operators, the arithmetic assignment operators are designed to save wear and tear on your typing fingers and to reduce the size of your scripts, particularly if you use long variable names.

Building String Expressions

A *string expression* is one where at least one of the operands is a string, and the result of the expression is another string. String expressions are straightforward in the sense that there is only one operator to deal with: *concatenation* (+). You use this operator to combine (or *concatenate*) strings within an expression. For example, the expression `"Java"` + `"Script"` returns the string `"JavaScript"`. Note, however, that you can also use strings with the comparison operators discussed in the next section.

It's unfortunate that the concatenation operator is identical to the addition operator because this similarity can lead to some confusion. For example, the expression `2` + `2` returns the numeric value 4 because the operands are numeric. However, the expression `"2"` + `"2"` returns the string value 22 because the two operands are strings.

To further complicate matters, JavaScript will often convert numbers into strings depending on the context:

>> If the first operand in an expression is a string, JavaScript converts any number in the expression to a string. For example, the following expression returns the string 222:

```
"2" + 2 + 2
```

TIP

BREAKING UP LONG STATEMENTS

Each of your JavaScript statements should appear on a single line (refer to Book 4, Chapter 1). An exception to this rule is any statement that contains a long expression, which you can break into multiple lines as long as the break occurs immediately before or after an operator. For example, you can write a string expression in multiple lines as long as the break occurs immediately before or after the + operator, as in the following examples:

```
const message1 = "How did the fool and his money " +
                 "get together in the first place?";
const message2 = "Never put off until tomorrow that which you "
               + "can put off until the day after tomorrow.";
```

>> If the first two or more operands in an expression are numbers and the rest of the expression contains a string, JavaScript handles the numeric part of the expression first and then converts the result into a string. For example, the following expression returns the string 42 because the result of 2 + 2 is 4, which is then concatenated as a string to "2":

```
2 + 2 + "2"
```

As an example of how this conversion can be a problem, consider the script in the following code (bk03ch03/example09.html):

```
const preTipTotal = 10.00;
const tipAmount = preTipTotal * 0.15;
const message1 = "Your tip is ";
const message2 = "<br>Your total bill is ";
document.write(message1 + tipAmount + message2 + preTipTotal +
    tipAmount);
```

The preTipTotal variable stores a total for a restaurant bill, and the tipAmount variable stores 15 percent of the total. The variables message1 and message2 are initialized with strings, and then the results are written to the page. In particular, the expression preTipTotal + tipAmount is included in the document.write() method to display the total bill. However, as shown in Figure 3-1, the "total" displayed is 101.5 instead of 11.5 (10 plus 1.5 for the tip).

FIGURE 3-1: Concatenating instead of adding the preTipTotal and tipAmount values.

← → C   ○ 🔒 192.168.0.104/webcoding/bk03ch03/example09.html   ☆

Your tip is 1.5
Your total bill is 101.5

Because the first part of the expression in the document.write() method was a string, JavaScript converted the preTipTotal and tipAmount values to strings and concatenated them instead of adding them.

To fix this problem, you could perform the addition in a separate statement and then use only this sum in the document.write() expression. The following code demonstrates this approach (bk03ch03/example10.html):

```
const preTipTotal = 10.00;
const tipAmount = preTipTotal * 0.15;
const totalBill = preTipTotal + tipAmount;
const message1 = "Your tip is ";
```

```
const message2 = "<br>Your total bill is ";
document.write(message1 + tipAmount + message2 + totalBill);
```

A new variable named `totalBill` is declared and is used to store the `preTipTotal` + `tipAmount` sum. `totalBill` is then used to display the sum in the `document.write()` expression, which, as shown in Figure 3-2, now displays the correct answer.

FIGURE 3-2:
Calculating
`preTipTotal`
and `tipAmount`
separately fixes
the problem.

Your tip is 1.5
Your total bill is 11.5

Building Comparison Expressions

You use *comparison expressions* to compare the value of two or more numbers, strings, variables, properties, or function results. If the expression is true, the expression result is set to the Boolean value `true`; if the expression is false, the expression result is set to the Boolean value `false`. You'll use comparisons with alarming frequency in your JavaScript code, so it's important to understand what they are and how you use them.

The comparison operators

Table 3-3 summarizes JavaScript's comparison operators.

TABLE 3-3   JavaScript Comparison Operators

Operator	Name	Example	Result
==	Equality	10 == 4	false
!=	Inequality	10 != 4	true
>	Greater than	10 > 4	true
<	Less than	10 < 4	false
>=	Greater than or equal	10 >= 4	true
<=	Less than or equal	10 <= 4	false
===	Strict equality	"10" === 10	false
!==	Strict inequality	"10" !== 10	true

Using the equality (==) operator

You use the equality operator (==) (often also called the equals operator) to compare the values of two operands. If both have the same value, the comparison returns true; if the operands have different values, the comparison returns false.

For example, in the following statements the variables booksRead and weeksPassed contain the same value, so the expression booksRead == weeksPassed returns true (check out Figure 3-3 and bk03ch03/example11.html):

```
const booksRead = 48;
const weeksPassed = 48;
const bookAWeek = booksRead == weeksPassed;
document.write("Me: I'm averaging a book a week, amirite?<br>");
document.write("JavaScript: " + bookAWeek);
```

FIGURE 3-3:
The expression
booksRead ==
weeksPassed
returns true.

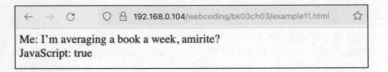

← → C   ○ 🔒 192.168.0.104/webcoding/bk03ch03/example11.html   ☆

Me: I'm averaging a book a week, amirite?
JavaScript: true

WARNING

One of the most common mistakes made by beginning and experienced JavaScript programmers alike is to use = instead of == in a comparison expression. If your script isn't working properly or is generating errors, one of the first things you should check is that your equality operator has two equal signs.

REMEMBER

It's important to understand here that the equality operator returns true when the two operands have the same value *even if* the two operands have different data types. (For an explanation of why this happens, check out "The comparison operators and data conversion," later in this chapter.) For example, in the following code, the bookAWeek variable still winds up with the value true:

```
const booksRead = 48;
const weeksPassed = "48";
const bookAWeek = booksRead == weeksPassed;
```

This might be what you want, but you're more likely to want the comparison to return false. For that you need to use the strict equality operator (===), discussed later in this section.

Using the inequality (!=) operator

You use the inequality operator (!=) to compare the values of two operands, but in the opposite sense of the equality operator. That is, if the operands have different values, the comparison returns true; if both operands have the same value, the comparison returns false.

In the following statements, for example, the variables currentFontSize and defaultFontSize contain different values, so the expression currentFontSize!= defaultFontSize returns true (bk03ch03/example12.html):

```
const currentFontSize = 19;
const defaultFontSize = 16;
const usingCustomFontSize = currentFontSize != defaultFontSize;
```

REMEMBER

The inequality operator returns false (meaning the two operands have the same value) *even if* the two operands have different data types. This might be what you want, but you're more likely to want the comparison to return true. For that you need to use the strict inequality operator (!==), discussed later in this section.

Using the greater than (>) operator

You use the greater than operator (>) to compare two operands to determine whether the operand to the left of > has a greater value than the operand to the right of >. If it does, the expression returns true; otherwise, it returns false.

In the following statements, the value of the contentWidth variable is more than that of the windowWidth variable, so the expression contentWidth > windowWidth returns true (bk03ch03/example13.html):

```
const contentWidth = 1000;
const windowWidth = 800;
const tooBig = contentWidth > windowWidth;
```

Using the less than (<) operator

You use the less than operator (<) to compare two operands to determine whether the operand to the left of < has a lesser value than the operand to the right of <. If it does, the expression returns true; otherwise, it returns false.

For example, in the statements that follow, the values of the kumquatsInStock and kumquatsSold variables are the same, so the expression kumquatsInStock < kumquatsSold returns false (check out Figure 3-4 and bk03ch03/example14. html):

```
const kumquatsInStock = 3;
const kumquatsSold = 3;
const backordered = kumquatsInStock < kumquatsSold;
document.write("Are kumquats on back order? " + backordered);
```

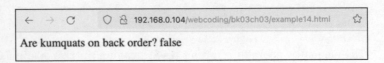

Using the greater than or equal (>=) operator

You use the greater than or equal operator (>=) to compare two operands to determine whether the operand to the left of >= has a greater value than or an equal value to the operand to the right of >=. If either or both of those comparisons get a thumbs up, the expression returns true; otherwise, it returns false.

In the following statements, for example, the value of the score variable is more than that of the prize1Minimum variable and is equal to that of the prize2Minimum variable. Therefore, both the expressions score >= prize1Minimum and score >= prize2Minimum return true (bk03ch03/example15.html):

```
const score = 90;
const prize1Minimum = 80;
const prize2Minimum = 90;
const getsPrize1 = score >= prize1Minimum;
const getsPrize2 = score >= prize2Minimum;
```

Using the less than or equal (<=) operator

You use the less than or equal operator (<=) to compare two operands to determine whether the operand to the left of <= has a lesser value than or an equal value to the operand to the right of <=. If either or both of those comparisons get a nod of approval, the expression returns true; otherwise, it returns false.

For example, in the following statements, the value of the defects variable is less than that of the defectsMaximumA variable and is equal to that of the defects MaximumB variable. Therefore, both the expressions defects <= defectsMaximumA and defects <= defectsMaximumB return true (bk03ch03/example16.html):

```
const defects = 5
const defectsMaximumA = 10
const defectsMaximumB = 5
const getsBonus = defects <= defectsMaximumA
const getsRaise = defects <= defectsMaximumB
```

The comparison operators and data conversion

In the examples in the previous sections, I use only numbers to demonstrate the various comparison operators. However, you can also use strings and Boolean values. These comparisons are straightforward if your expressions include only operands of the same data type; that is, if you compare two strings or two Booleans. (However, refer to my discussion in the section "Using strings in comparison expressions," a bit later in this chapter.)

TECHNICAL STUFF

Things become less straightforward if you mix data types in a single comparison expression. In this case, you need to remember that JavaScript always attempts to convert each operand into a number before running the comparison. Here's how it works:

>> If one operand is a string and the other is a number, JavaScript attempts to convert the string into a number. For example, in the following statements the string "5" gets converted to the number 5, so the comparison value1 == value2 returns true:

```
const value1 = "5";
const value2 = 5;
const result = value1 == value2;
```

If the string can't be converted to a number (for example, the string "rutabaga"), the comparison always returns false.

The null string ("") gets converted to 0.

REMEMBER

>> If one operand is a Boolean and the other is a number, JavaScript converts the Boolean to a number as follows:

- true — This value is converted to 1.

- false — This value is converted to 0.

For example, in the following statements, the Boolean `true` gets converted to the number 1, so the comparison `value1 == value2` returns true:

```
const value1 = true;
const value2 = 1;
const result = value1 == value2;
```

» If one operand is a Boolean and the other is a string, JavaScript converts the Boolean to a number as in the preceding item, and attempts to convert the string into a number. For example, in the following statements, the Boolean `false` is converted to the number 0 and the string `"0"` is converted to the number 0, so the comparison `value1 == value2` returns true:

```
const value1 = false;
const value2 = "0";
const result = value1 == value2;
```

If the string can't be converted to a number, the comparison always returns false.

Using the strict equality (===) operator

The strict equality operator (===) checks whether two operands are identical, which means that it checks not only that the operands' values are equal but also that the operands are of the same data type. (This is why the strict equality operator is sometimes called the *identity operator*.)

For example, in the following statements, the `albumName` variable contains a string and the `albumReleaseDate` variable contains a number. These values are of different data types, so the expression `albumName === albumReleaseDate` returns false (bk03ch03/example17.html):

```
const albumName = "1984";
const albumReleaseDate = 1984;
const result = albumName === albumReleaseDate;
```

By comparison, if instead you used the equality operator (==), which doesn't check the operand data types, the expression `albumName == albumReleaseDate` would return true.

REMEMBER

So, when should you use equality (==) and when should you use strict equality (===)? Many pro JavaScript coders ignore this question and just use the strict equality operator all the time. You should, too.

Using the strict inequality (!==) operator

The strict inequality operator (!==) performs (sort of) the opposite function of the strict equality operator. That is, it checks to see not only whether the values of two operands are different but also whether the operands are of different data types. (This is why the strict inequality operator is sometimes called the *non-identity operator*.)

In the following statements, the hasBugs variable contains the Boolean value true and the totalBugs variable contains a number. These values are of different data types, so the expression hasBugs !== totalBugs returns true (bk03ch03/example18.html):

```
const hasBugs = true;
const totalBugs = 1;
const result = hasBugs !== totalBugs;
```

Using strings in comparison expressions

Comparison expressions involving only numbers hold few surprises, but comparisons involving only strings can sometimes raise an eyebrow or two. The comparison is based on alphabetical order, as you may expect, so *A* comes before *B* and *a* comes before *b*. Ah, but this isn't your father's alphabetical order. In JavaScript's world, all the uppercase letters come before all the lowercase letters, which means that, for example, *B* comes before *a*, so the following expression would return false:

```
"a" < "B"
```

Another thing to keep in mind is that most string comparisons involve multiple-letter operands. In these situations, JavaScript compares each string letter-by-letter. For example, consider the following expression:

```
"Smith" < "Smyth"
```

The first two letters in each string are the same, but the third letters are different. The internal value of the i in Smith is less than the internal value of the y in Smyth, so the preceding comparison would return true. (Note, too, that after a point of difference is found, JavaScript ignores the rest of the letters in each string.)

UNICODE STRING VALUES (OR, WHY *a* ISN'T LESS THAN *B*)

In the "a" ‹ "B" returning `false` example, what does it mean to say that all the uppercase letters "come before" all the lowercase letters? The story here is that a technology called Unicode keeps track of (give or take) every possible character, nearly 150,000 of them as I write this. Each of those characters is given a unique numeric value. For example, the asterisk (*) has the value 42, whereas the digit *5* has the value 53.

For some reason, Unicode lists the uppercase Latin letters before the lowercase letters. The letter *A* is given the value 65, *B* is 66, and so on to *Z*, which has the value 90. The lowercase Latin letters start with *a*, which is given the value 97, *b* has 98, and so on up to *z*, which has the value 122.

When you use a comparison operator to compare two letters, what JavaScript is comparing are the letters' Unicode values. That's why the string "a" (value 97) is greater than the string "B" (value 66).

Also, a space is a legitimate character for comparison purposes, and its internal value comes before all other letters and printable symbols. (If you read the "Unicode string values (or, why *a* isn't less than *B*)" sidebar, you'll understand what I mean when I say that the Unicode value for the space character is 32.) Consider, then, the following comparison:

```
"Marge Simpson" > "Margerine"
```

The expression returns `false` because the sixth "letter" of the left operand is a space, whereas the sixth letter of "Margerine" is r.

Using the ternary (?:) operator

Knowing the comparison operators also enables you to use one of my favorite expression tools, a complex but oh-so-handy item called the *ternary operator* (?:). Here's the basic syntax for using the ternary operator in an expression:

```
expression ? result_if_true : result_if_false
```

The *expression* is a comparison expression that results in a `true` or `false` value. You can use any variable, function result, or property that has a `true` or `false`

Boolean value. The *result_if_true* is the value that the expression returns if the *expression* evaluates to true; the *result_if_false* is the value that the expression returns if the *expression* evaluates to false.

TIP

In JavaScript, by definition, the following values are the equivalent of false:

» 0 (the number zero)

» "" (the empty string)

» null

» undefined (which is, say, the "value" of an uninitialized variable)

Everything else is the equivalent of true.

Here's an example (bk03ch03/example19.html):

```
const screenWidth = 768;
const maxTabletWidth = 1024;
const screenType = screenWidth > maxTabletWidth ? "Desktop!" :
    "Tablet!";
```

The screenWidth variable is initialized to 768, the maxTabletWidth variable is initialized to 1024, and the screenType variable stores the value returned by the conditional expression. For the latter, screenWidth > maxTabletWidth is the comparison expression, "Desktop!" is the string returned with a true result, and "Tablet!" is the string returned with a false result. Because screenWidth is less than maxTabletWidth, the comparison will be false, so "Tablet!" will be the result.

Building Logical Expressions

You use *logical expressions* to combine or manipulate Boolean values, particularly comparison expressions. For example, if your code needs to test whether two different comparison expressions are both true before proceeding, you can do that with a logical expression.

The logical operators

Table 3-4 lists JavaScript's logical operators.

TABLE 3-4   ### JavaScript Logical Operators

Operator	Name	General Syntax	Returned Value
&&	AND	*expr1* && *expr2*	true if both *expr1* and *expr2* are true; false otherwise
||	OR	*expr1* || *expr2*	true if one or both of *expr1* and *expr2* are true; false otherwise
!	NOT	!*expr*	true if *expr* is false; false if *expr* is true

Using the AND (&&) operator

You use the AND operator (&&) when you want to test two Boolean operands to determine whether they're both true. For example, consider the following statements (bk03ch03/example20.html):

```
const finishedDinner = true;
const clearedTable = true;
const getsDessert = finishedDinner && clearedTable;
```

Because both finishedDinner and clearedTable are true, the logical expression finishedDinner && clearedTable evaluates to true.

On the other hand, consider these statements:

```
const haveWallet = true;
const haveKeys = false;
const canGoOut = haveWallet && haveKeys;
```

In this example, because haveKeys is false, the logical expression haveWallet && haveKeys evaluates to false. The logical expression would also return false if just haveWallet were false or if both haveWallet and haveKeys were false.

Table 3-5 lists the various operands you can enter and the results they generate (this is called a *truth table*).

TABLE 3-5   ### Truth Table for the AND (&&) Operator

left_operand	right_operand	left_operand && right_operand
true	true	true
true	false	false
false	true	false
false	false	false

Using the OR (||) operator

You use the OR (||) operator when you want to test two Boolean operands to determine whether at least one of them is true. For example, consider the following statements (bk03ch03/example21.html):

```
const hasFever = true;
const hasCough = false;
const missSchool = hasFever || hasCough;
```

Because hasFever is true, the logical expression hasFever || hasCough evaluates to true because only one of the operands needs to be true. You get the same result if only hasCough is true or if both operands are true.

On the other hand, consider these statements:

```
const salesOverBudget = false;
const expensesUnderBudget = false;
const getsBonus = salesOverBudget || expensesUnderBudget;
```

In this example, because both salesOverBudget and expensesUnderBudget are false, the logical expression salesOverBudget || expensesUnderBudget evaluates to false.

Table 3-6 displays the truth table for the various operands you can enter.

TABLE 3-6

Truth Table for the OR (||) Operator

left_operand	right_operand	left_operand || right_operand
true	true	true
true	false	true
false	true	true
false	false	false

Using the NOT (!) Operator

The NOT (!) operator is the logical equivalent of the negation operator (–) I cover earlier in the chapter. In this case, NOT returns the opposite Boolean value of

an operand. For example, consider the following statements (bk03ch03/
example22.html):

```
const dataLoaded = false;
const waitingForData = !dataLoaded;
```

dataLoaded is false, so !dataLoaded evaluates to true.

Table 3-7 displays the truth table for the various operands you can enter.

TABLE 3-7   **Truth Table for the NOT (!) Operator**

Operand	!Operand
true	false
false	true

Advanced notes on the && and || operators

TECHNICAL STUFF

I mention earlier that JavaScript defines various values that are the equivalent of false — including 0 and "" — and that all other values are the equivalent of true. These equivalences mean that you can use both the AND operator and the OR operator with non-Boolean values. However, if you plan on using non-Booleans, you need to be aware of exactly how JavaScript evaluates these expressions.

I'll begin with an AND expression:

1. Evaluate the operand to the left of the AND operator.

2. If the left operand's value is false or is equivalent to false, return that value and stop; otherwise, continue with Step 3.

3. If the left operand's value is true or is equivalent to true, evaluate the operand to the right of the AND operator.

4. Return the value of the right operand.

This behavior is quirky, indeed, and there are two crucial concepts you need to bear in mind:

>> If the left operand evaluates to false or its equivalent, the right operand is *never* evaluated.

>> The logical expression returns the result of either the left or right operand, which means the expression might *not* return `true` or `false`; instead, it might return a value equivalent to `true` or `false`.

To try out these concepts out, use the following code (bk03ch03/example23.html):

```
const v1 = true;
const v2 = 10;
const v3 = "testing";
const v4 = false;
const v5 = 0;
const v6 = "";
const leftOperand =
    eval(prompt("Enter the left operand (a value or
  expression):", true));
const rightOperand =
    eval(prompt("Enter the right operand (a value or
  expression):", true));
const result = leftOperand && rightOperand;
document.write(result);
```

The script begins by declaring and initializing six variables. The first three (v1, v2, and v3) are given values equivalent to `true` and the last three (v4, v5, and v6) are given values equivalent to `false`. The script then prompts for a left operand and a right operand, which are entered into an AND expression. The key here is that you can enter any value for each operand, or you can use the v1 through v6 variables to enter a comparison expression, such as v2 > v5. The use of `eval()` on the `prompt()` result ensures that JavaScript uses the expressions as they're entered.

The following table lists some sample inputs and the results they generate:

left_operand	right_operand	left_operand && right_operand
true	true	true
true	false	false
5	10	10
false	"Yo"	false
v2	v5	0
true	v3	testing
v5	v4	0
v2 > v5	v5 == v4	true

Like the AND operator, the logic of how JavaScript evaluates an OR expression is strange and needs to be understood, particularly if you'll be using operands that are true or false equivalents:

1. Evaluate the operand to the left of the OR operator.

2. If the left operand's value is true or is equivalent to true, return that value and stop; otherwise, continue with Step 3.

3. If the left operand's value is false or is equivalent to false, evaluate the operand to the right of the OR operator.

4. Return the value of the right operand.

Understanding Operator Precedence

Your JavaScript code will often use expressions that are blissfully simple: just one or two operands and a single operator. Alas, *often* here doesn't mean *mostly*, because many expressions you use will have a number of values and operators. In these more complex expressions, the order in which the calculations are performed becomes crucial. For example, consider the expression 3+5*2. If you calculate from left to right, the answer you get is 16 (3+5 equals 8, and 8*2 equals 16). However, if you perform the multiplication first and then the addition, the result is 13 (5*2 equals 10, and 3+10 equals 13). In other words, a single expression can produce multiple answers depending on the order in which you perform the calculations.

To control this ordering problem, JavaScript evaluates an expression according to a predefined *order of precedence*. This order of precedence lets JavaScript calculate an expression unambiguously by determining which part of the expression it calculates first, which part second, and so on.

The order of precedence

The order of precedence that JavaScript uses is determined by the various expression operators that I've covered so far in this chapter. Table 3-8 summarizes the complete order of precedence used by JavaScript.

For example, Table 3-8 tells you that JavaScript performs multiplication before addition. Therefore, the correct answer for the expression 3+5*2 (just discussed) is 13.

TABLE 3-8 **JavaScript Order of Precedence for Operators**

Operator	Operation	Order of Precedence	Order of Evaluation
++	Increment	First	R -> L
−−	Decrement	First	R -> L
−	Negation	First	R -> L
!	NOT	First	R -> L
*, /, %	Multiplication, division, modulus	Second	L -> R
+, −	Addition, subtraction	Third	L -> R
+	Concatenation	Third	L -> R
<, <=	Less than, less than, or equal	Fourth	L -> R
>, >=	Greater than, greater than, or equal	Fourth	L -> R
==	Equality	Fifth	L -> R
!=	Inequality	Fifth	L -> R
===	Strict equality	Fifth	L -> R
!==	Strict inequality	Fifth	L -> R
&&	AND	Sixth	L -> R
||	OR	Sixth	L -> R
?:	Ternary	Seventh	R -> L
=	Assignment	Eighth	R -> L
+=, −=, etc.	Arithmetic assignment	Eighth	R -> L

Note, as well, that some operators in Table 3-8 have the same order of precedence (for example, multiplication and division). Having the same precedence means that the order in which JavaScript evaluates these operators doesn't matter. For example, consider the expression 5*10/2. If you perform the multiplication first, the answer you get is 25 (5*10 equals 50, and 50/2 equals 25). If you perform the division first, you also get an answer of 25 (10/2 equals 5, and 5*5 equals 25).

However, JavaScript does have a predefined order for these kinds of expressions, which is what the Order of Evaluation column tells you. A value of L -> R means that operations with the same order of precedence are evaluated from left-to-right; R -> L means the operations are evaluated from right-to-left.

Controlling the order of precedence

Sometimes you want to take control of the situation and override the order of precedence. This might seem like a decidedly odd thing to do, so perhaps an example will help. As you probably know, you calculate the total cost of a retail item by multiplying the retail price by the tax rate, and then adding that result to the retail price:

```
Total Price = Retail Price + Retail Price * Tax Rate
```

However, what if you want to reverse this calculation? That is, suppose you know the final price of an item and, given the tax rate, you want to know the original (that is, pre-tax) price. Applying a bit of algebra to the preceding equation, it turns out that you can calculate the original price by dividing the total price by 1 plus the tax rate. So, if the total price is $11.00 and the tax rate is 10 percent, you divide 11 by 1.1 and get an answer of $10.00.

Okay, now I'll convert this calculation to JavaScript code. A first pass at the new equation might look something like this:

```
retailPrice = totalPrice / 1 + taxRate;
```

The following code implements this formula and Figure 3-5 shows the result (bk03ch03/example24.html):

```javascript
const totalPrice = 11.00;
const taxRate = .1;
const retailPrice = totalPrice / 1 + taxRate;
document.write("The pre-tax price is " + retailPrice);
```

FIGURE 3-5:
The result of our first stab at calculating the pre-tax cost of an item.

The pre-tax price is 11.1

`192.168.0.104/webcoding/bk03ch03/example24.html`

As you can see, the result is incorrect. What happened? Well, according to the rules of precedence, JavaScript performs division before addition, so the `totalPrice` value first is divided by 1 and then is added to the `taxRate` value, which isn't the correct order.

To get the correct answer, you have to override the order of precedence so that the addition 1 + taxRate is performed first. You override precedence by surrounding that part of the expression with parentheses, as shown in the following code. Using this revised script, you get the correct answer, as shown in Figure 3-6 (bk03ch03/example25.html):

```
const totalPrice = 11.00;
const taxRate = .1;
const retailPrice = totalPrice / (1 + taxRate);
document.write("The pre-tax price is " + retailPrice);
```

FIGURE 3-6:
The revised script calculates the pre-tax cost correctly.

192.168.0.104/webcoding/bk03ch03/example25.html

The pre-tax price is 10

WARNING

One of the most common mistakes when using parentheses in expressions is to forget to close a parenthetical term with a right parenthesis. Most modern code editors will automatically add a right parenthesis as soon as you type a left one. If your editor doesn't do this, you need to make sure you've closed each parenthetical term. One method you can use it to count all the left parentheses and count all the right parentheses. If these totals don't match, you know you've left out a parenthesis.

Terms inside parentheses are always calculated first, and terms outside parentheses are calculated sequentially (according to the order of precedence). To gain even more control over your expressions, you can place parentheses inside one another; this is called *nesting* parentheses, and JavaScript always evaluates the innermost set of parentheses first.

Using parentheses to determine the order of calculations allows you to gain full control over JavaScript expressions. This way, you can make sure that the answer given by an expression is the one you want.

IN THIS CHAPTER

» Understanding how you control the flow of JavaScript

» Setting up your code to make decisions

» Understanding code looping

» Setting up code loops

» Avoiding the dreaded infinite loop

Chapter 4

Controlling the Flow of JavaScript

A good programmer is someone who always looks both ways before crossing a one-way street.

— DOUG LINDER

When the web browser comes across a `<script>` tag, it puts on its JavaScript hat and starts processing the statements. Not surprisingly, the browser doesn't just leap randomly around the script, parsing the statements willy-nilly. That would be silly. No, the browser puts its head down and starts processing the statements one at a time: the first statement, the second statement, and so on until there's no more JavaScript left to parse.

That linear statement-by-statement progression through the code makes sense, but it doesn't fit every situation. Sometimes you want your code to test some condition and then run different chunks of code depending on the result of that test. Sometimes you want your code to repeat a collection of statements over and over again, with some subtle or significant change occurring with each repetition. Code that runs tests and code that repeats itself all fall under the rubric of controlling the flow of JavaScript. In this chapter, you dive into this fascinating and powerful subject.

Making True/False Decisions with if Statements

A smart script performs tests on its environment and then decides what to do next based on the results of each test. For example, suppose you've declared a variable that you later use as a divisor in an expression. You should test the variable before using it in the expression to make sure that the variable's value isn't 0.

The most basic test is the simple true/false decision (which could also be thought of as a yes/no or an on/off decision). In this case, your program looks at a certain condition, determines whether it's currently true or false, and acts accordingly. Comparison and logical expressions (covered in Book 3, Chapter 3) play a big part here because they always return a true or false result.

In JavaScript, simple true/false decisions are handled by the if statement. You can use either the *single-line* syntax:

```
if (expression) statement;
```

or the *block* syntax:

```
if (expression) {
    statement1;
    statement2;
    . . .
}
```

In both cases, *expression* is a comparison or logical expression that returns true or false, and *statement(s)* represent the JavaScript statement or statements to run if *expression* returns true. If *expression* returns false, JavaScript skips over the statements.

TIP

This is a good place to note that JavaScript defines the following values as the equivalent of false: 0, "" (that is, the empty string), null, and undefined. Everything else is the equivalent of true.

REMEMBER

This is the first time you've encountered JavaScript's braces ({ and }), so take a second to understand what they do because they come up a lot. The braces surround one or more statements that you want JavaScript to treat as a single entity. This entity is a kind of statement itself, so the whole caboodle — the braces and the code they enclose — is called a *block statement*. Also, any JavaScript construction that consists of a statement (such as if) followed by a block statement is called a *compound statement*. And, just to keep you on your toes, note that the lines that include the braces don't end with semicolons.

Whether you use the single-line or block syntax depends on the statements you want to run if the *expression* returns a true result. If you have only one statement, you can use either syntax. If you have multiple statements, use the block syntax.

Consider the following example (check out bk03ch04/example01.html in this book's example files):

```
if (totalSales != 0) {
    const grossMargin = (totalSales - totalExpenses) /
   totalSales;
}
```

Assume that earlier in the code, the script calculated the total sales and total expenses, which are stored in the totalSales and totalExpenses variables, respectively. The code now calculates the gross margin, which is defined as gross profit (that is, sales minus expenses) divided by sales. The code uses if to test whether the value of the totalSales variable is not equal to zero. If the totalSales != 0 expression returns true, the grossMargin calculation is executed; otherwise, nothing happens. The if test in this example is useful because it ensures that the divisor in the calculation — totalSales — is never zero.

TECHNICAL STUFF

A QUICK LOOK AT BLOCK SCOPE

Now that you've been introduced to JavaScript blocks, I'd like to take a brief foray in a concept called block scope. I get into this topic in much more detail in Book 3, Chapter 5, but for now just know that *scope* specifies where a variable is accessible to other statements in your code. When a variable has *block scope*, it means that the variable is accessible only to other statements within that block. When does a variable have block scope? When the variable is declared using let or const within a block statement.

For example, consider this section's example code once again, with an extra document. write statement tacked on:

```
if (totalSales != 0) {
    const grossMargin = (totalSales - totalExpenses) /
   totalSales;
}
document.write(grossMargin);
```

Here you see that the grossMargin variable is declared using const within the if statement's block. This means that grossMargin is *not* accessible outside the block. Therefore, the browser doesn't run the document.write statement because it doesn't know what to do with this "undefined" grossMargin variable.

Branching with if. . .else Statements

Using the `if` statement to make decisions adds a powerful new weapon to your JavaScript arsenal. However, the simple version of `if` suffers from an important limitation: A `false` result only bypasses one or more statements; it doesn't execute any of its own. This is fine in many cases, but there will be times when you need to run one group of statements if the condition returns `true` and a different group if the result is `false`. To handle these scenarios, you need to use an `if...else` statement:

```
if (expression) {
    statements-if-true
} else {
    statements-if-false
}
```

The *expression* is a comparison or logical expression that returns `true` or `false`. *statements-if-true* represents the block of statements you want JavaScript to run if *expression* returns `true`, and *statements-if-false* represents the block of statements you want executed if *expression* returns `false`.

As an example, consider the following code (check out bk03ch04/example02.html):

```
let discountRate;
if (currMonth === "December.") {
    discountRate = 0.2;
} else {
    discountRate = 0.1;
}
const discountedPrice = regularPrice * (1 - discountRate);
```

This code calculates a discounted price of an item, where the discount depends on whether the current month is December. Assume that earlier in the code, the script set the value of the current month (`currMonth`) and the item's regular price (`regularPrice`). After declaring the `discountRate` variable, an `if...else` statement checks whether `currMonth` equals December. If it does, `discount Rate` is set to 0.2; otherwise, `discountRate` is set to 0.1. Finally, the code uses the `discountRate` value to calculate `discountedPrice`.

TIP

if...else statements are much easier to read when you indent the statements within each block, as I did in my examples. This indentation lets you easily identify which block will run if there is a `true` result and which block will run if the result is `false`. I find that an indent of four spaces does the job, but many programmers prefer either two spaces or a tab.

The if...else statements are similar to the ternary operator (?:), which I discuss in Book 3, Chapter 3. In fact, for a specific subset of if...else statements, the two are identical.

The ?: operator evaluates a comparison expression and then returns one value if the expression is true or another value if it's false. For example, if you have a variable named currentHour that contains the hour part of the current time of day, consider the following statement:

```
const greeting = currentHour < 12 ? "Good morning!" :
    "Good day!";
```

If currentHour is less than 12, the string "Good morning!" is stored in the greeting variable; otherwise, the string "Good day!" is stored in the variable. This statement does the same thing as the following if...else statements:

```
let greeting;
if (currentHour < 12) {
    greeting = "Good morning!";
} else {
    greeting = "Good day!";
}
```

The ternary operator version is clearly more efficient, both in terms of total characters typed and total lines used. So, any time you find yourself testing a condition only to store something in a variable depending on the result, use a ternary operator statement instead of if...else.

Making Multiple Decisions

The if...else control structure makes only a single decision. The if part calculates a single logical result and performs one of two actions. However, plenty of situations require multiple decisions before you can decide which action to take.

For example, to calculate the pre-tax price of an item given its total price and its tax rate, you divide the total price by the tax rate plus 1. In real-world web coding, one of your jobs as a developer is to make sure you're dealing with numbers that make sense. What makes sense for a tax rate? Probably that it's greater than or equal to 0 and less than 1 (that is, 100 percent). That's two things to test about any tax rate value in your code, and JavaScript offers multiple ways to handle this kind of thing.

Using the AND (&&) and OR (||) operators

One solution to a multiple-decision problem is to combine multiple comparison expressions in a single if statement. As I discuss in Book 3, Chapter 3, you can combine comparison expressions by using JavaScript's AND (&&) and OR (||) operators.

The following code shows an example if statement that combines two comparison expressions using the && operator (bk03ch04/example03.html):

```
if (taxRate >= 0 && taxRate < 1) {
    const retailPrice = totalPrice / (1 + taxRate);
    document.write(retailPrice);
} else {
    document.write("Please enter a tax rate between 0 and 1.");
}
```

The key here is the if statement:

```
if (taxRate >= 0 && taxRate < 1);
```

This tells the browser that only if the taxRate value is greater than or equal to 0 and less than 1 should the statements in the true block be executed. If either one is false (or if both are false), the browser writes the message in the false block instead.

Stringing together multiple if statements

A third syntax for the if...else statement lets you string together as many logical tests as you need using a *multi-block statement* (so-called because it contains multiple if/else blocks):

```
if (expression1) {
   statements-if-expression1-true
} else if (expression2) {
   statements-if-expression2-true
}
etc.
else {
   statements-if-false
}
```

JavaScript first tests *expression1*. If *expression1* returns true, JavaScript runs the block represented by *statements-if-expression1-true* and skips over everything else. If *expression1* returns false, JavaScript then tests *expression2*. If *expression2* returns true, JavaScript runs the block represented by *statements-if-expression2-true* and skips over everything else. Otherwise, if all the if tests return false, JavaScript runs the block represented by *statements-if-false*.

The following code shows a script that strings together several if statements (bk03ch04/example04.html):

```
let greeting;
if (currentHour < 12) {
    greeting = "Good morning!";
} else if (currentHour < 18) {
    greeting = "Good afternoon!";
} else {
    greeting = "Good evening!";
}
document.write(greeting);
```

Assume that earlier in the script, the current hour value was stored in the currentHour variable. The first if checks whether currentHour is less than 12. If so, the string "Good morning!" is stored in the greeting variable; if not, the next if checks whether currentHour is less than 18 (that is, less than 6:00 p.m.). If so, greeting is assigned the string "Good afternoon!"; if not, greeting is assigned "Good evening", instead.

Using the switch statement

Performing multiple tests with if...else if is a handy technique — it's a JavaScript tool you'll reach for quite often. However, it quickly becomes unwieldy as the number of tests you need to make gets larger. It's okay for two or three tests, but any more than that makes the logic harder to follow.

When you need to make, say, four or more tests, JavaScript's switch statement is a better choice. The idea is that you provide an expression at the beginning and then list a series of possible values for that expression. For each possible result — called a *case* — you provide one or more JavaScript statements to execute should the case match the expression. Here's the syntax:

```
switch(expression) {
    case Case1:
        Case1 statements
        break;
```

```
    case Case2:
        Case2 statements
        break;
    etc.
    default:
        Default statements
}
```

The *expression* is evaluated at the beginning of the structure. It must return a value (numeric, string, or Boolean). *Case1*, *Case2*, and so on are possible values for *expression*. JavaScript examines each case value to determine whether one matches the result of *expression*. If *expression* returns the *Case1* value, the code represented by *Case1 statements* is executed, and the break statement tells JavaScript to stop processing the rest of the switch statement. Otherwise, if *expression* returns the *Case2* value, the code represented by *Case2 statements* is executed, and JavaScript stops processing the rest of the switch statement. Finally, the optional default statement is used to handle situations where none of the cases matches *expression*, so JavaScript executes the code represented by *Default statements*.

If you do much work with dates in JavaScript, your code is likely to eventually need to figure out how many days are in any month. No built-in JavaScript property or method tells you this, so you need to construct your own code, as shown here (bk03ch04/example05.html):

```javascript
let daysInMonth;
switch(monthName) {
    case "January":
        daysInMonth = 31;
        break;
    case "February":
        if (yearValue % 4 === 0) {
            daysInMonth = 29;
        }
        else {
            daysInMonth = 28;
        }
        break;
    case "March":
        daysInMonth = 31;
        break;
    case "April":
        daysInMonth = 30;
        break;
```

```
        case "May":
            daysInMonth = 31;
            break;
        case "June":
            daysInMonth = 30;
            break;
        case "July":
            daysInMonth = 31;
            break;
        case "August":
            daysInMonth = 31;
            break;
        case "September":
            daysInMonth = 30;
            break;
        case "October":
            daysInMonth = 31;
            break;
        case "November":
            daysInMonth = 30;
            break;
        case "December":
            daysInMonth = 31;
}
```

Assume that earlier in the code, the script set monthName as the name of the month you want to work with and yearValue as the year. (You need the latter to know when you're dealing with a leap year.) The switch is based on the name of the month:

```
switch(monthName)
```

Then case statements are set up for each month. For example:

```
case "January":
    daysInMonth = 31;
    break;
```

If monthName is "January", this case is true and the daysInMonth variable is set to 31. All the other months are set up the same, with the exception of February:

```
case "February":
    if (yearValue % 4 === 0) {
        daysInMonth = 29;
    }
```

```
    else {
        daysInMonth = 28;
    }
    break;
```

Here you need to know whether you're dealing with a leap year, so the modulus (%) operator checks to determine whether yearValue is divisible by 4. If so, it's a leap year, so daysInMonth is set to 29; otherwise, it's set to 28.

Time geeks will no doubt have their feathers ruffled by my assertion that a year is a leap year if it's divisible by 4. In fact, that works only for the years 1901 to 2099, which should take care of most people's needs. The formula doesn't work for 1900 and 2100 because, despite being divisible by 4, these years aren't leap years. The general rule is that a year is a leap year if it's divisible by 4 and it's not divisible by 100 unless it's also divisible by 400.

Understanding Code Looping

Some would say that the only real goal of the programmer should be to get the job done. As long as the code produces the correct result or performs the correct tasks in the correct order, everything else is superfluous. Perhaps, but *real* programmers know that the true goal of programming is not only to get the job done but to get it done *as efficiently as possible.* Efficient scripts run faster, take less time to code, and are usually (not always, but usually) easier to read and troubleshoot.

One of the best ways to introduce efficiency into your coding is to avoid reinventing too many wheels. For example, consider the following code fragment:

```
let sum = 0;
let num = prompt("Type a number:", 1);
sum += Number(num);
num = prompt("Type a number:", 1);
sum += Number(num);
num = prompt("Type a number:", 1);
sum += Number(num);
document.write("The total of your numbers is " + sum);
```

This code first declares a variable named sum. The code prompts the user for a number (using the prompt method with a default value of 1) that gets stored in the num variable, adds that value to sum, and then repeats this prompt-and-sum routine two more times. (Note my use of the Number function, which ensures that the value returned by prompt is treated as a number rather than a string.) Finally, the sum of the three numbers is displayed to the user.

Besides being a tad useless, this code reeks of inefficiency because most of the code consists of the following two lines appearing three times:

```
num = prompt("Type a number:", 1);
sum += Number(num);
```

Wouldn't it be more efficient if you put these two statements just once in the code and then somehow get JavaScript to repeat these statements as many times as necessary?

Why, yes, it would, and the good news is that not only is it possible to do this, but JavaScript also gives you a number of different methods to perform this looping. I spend the rest of this chapter investigating each of these methods.

Using while Loops

The most straightforward of the JavaScript loop constructions is the while loop, which uses the following syntax:

```
while (expression) {
    statements
}
```

Here, *expression* is a comparison or logical expression (that is, an expression that returns true or false) that, as long as it returns true, tells JavaScript to keep executing the *statements* within the block.

Essentially, JavaScript interprets a while loop as follows: "Okay, as long as *expression* remains true, I'll keep running through the loop statements, but as soon as *expression* becomes false, I'm out of there."

Here's a closer look at how a while loop works:

1. Evaluate the *expression* in the while statement.

2. If *expression* is true, continue with Step 3; if *expression* is false, skip to Step 5.

3. Execute each of the statements in the block.

4. Return to Step 1.

5. Exit the loop (that is, execute the next statement that occurs after the while block).

The following code demonstrates how to use `while` to rewrite the inefficient code I presented in the preceding section (bk03ch04/example06.html):

```
let sum = 0;
let counter = 1;
let num;
while (counter <= 3) {
    num = prompt("Type a number:", 1);
    sum += Number(num);
    counter += 1;
}
document.write("The total of your numbers is " + sum);
```

To control the loop, the code declares a variable named `counter` and initializes it to 1, which means the expression `counter <= 3` is true, so the code enters the block, does the prompt-and-sum thing, and then increments `counter`. This is repeated until the third time through the loop, when `counter` is incremented to 4, at which point the expression `counter <= 3` becomes `false` and the loop is done.

TIP

To make your loop code as readable as possible, always use a two- or four-space indent for each statement in the `while` block. The same applies to the `for` and `do...while` loops, which I talk about later in this chapter.

The `while` statement isn't the greatest loop choice when you know exactly how many times you want to run through the loop. For that, use the `for` statement, described in the next section. The best use of the `while` statement is when your script has some naturally occurring condition that you can turn into a comparison expression. A good example is when you're prompting the user for input values. You'll often want to keep prompting the user until they click the Cancel button. The easiest way to set this up is to include the prompt inside a `while` loop, as shown here (bk03ch04/example07.html):

```
let sum = 0;
let num = prompt("Type a number or click Cancel:", 1);
while (num != null) {
    sum += Number(num);
    num = prompt("Type a number or click Cancel:", 1);
}
document.write("The total of your numbers is " + sum);
```

The first `prompt` method displays a dialog box like the one shown in Figure 4-1 to get the initial value, and stores it in the `num` variable.

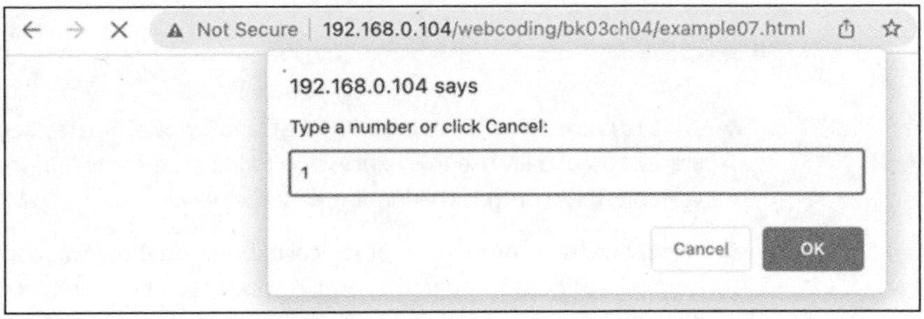

FIGURE 4-1:
Set up
your `while`
expression
so that the
prompting stops
when the user
clicks the Cancel
button.

Then the `while` statement checks the following expression:

```
num != null
```

Two things can happen here:

» If the user enters a number, this expression returns `true` and the loop continues. In this case, the value of `num` is added to the `sum` variable, and the user is prompted for the next number.

» If the user clicks Cancel, the value returned by `prompt` is `null`, so the expression becomes `false` and the looping stops.

Using for Loops

Although `while` is the most straightforward of the JavaScript loops, the most common type by far is the `for` loop. This is slightly surprising when you consider (as you will shortly) that the `for` loop's syntax is a bit more complex than that of the `while` loop. However, the `for` loop excels at one thing: looping when you know exactly how many times you want to repeat a group of statements. This is common in all types of programming, so it's no wonder `for` is so often used in scripts.

Here's the general syntax used with `for` loops:

```
for (initialization; condition; update) {
    statement(s)
}
```

where:

» *initialization* is an expression that JavaScript evaluates before the loop starts. You usually use this expression to initialize some feature (such as a variable) that controls the looping in some way.

» *condition* is a comparison or logical expression that JavaScript evaluates before each pass through the loop. If *condition* evaluates to true, JavaScript runs the *statement(s)*; if *condition* evaluates to false, JavaScript skips the *statement(s)* and terminates the loop.

» *update* is an expression that JavaScript evaluates at the end of each pass through the loop (and before the next evaluation of *condition*). In most cases, you use *update* to modify some aspect of whatever you initialized with the *initialization* expression (such as incrementing the variable).

» *statement(s)* are the statement or statements you want JavaScript to execute each time through the loop.

That syntax description is all a bit theoretical, I know, so let me bring everything down to earth. The happy news about for loops is that 99.9999 percent of them use a specific variation on the preceding general syntax. The structure of almost every for loop you'll ever see or code yourself looks like this:

```
for (let counter = start; counterExpression; counterUpdate) {
    statement(s)
}
```

There's a lot going on here, so I'll take it one bit at a time:

» *counter*: A numeric variable used as a *loop counter*. The loop counter is a number that counts how many times the procedure has gone through the loop. (Note that you need to include let only if this is the first time you've used the variable in the script.)

» *start*: The initial value of *counter*. This value is usually 1, but you can use whatever value makes sense for your script.

» *counterExpression*: A comparison or logical expression that determines the number of times through the loop. This expression usually compares the current value of *counter* to some maximum value.

» *counterUpdate*: An expression that changes the value of *counter*. Most of the time you'll increment the value of counter with the expression *counter* += 1.

When JavaScript stumbles upon a for statement that uses the counter syntax, it changes into its for-loop outfit and follows this seven-step process:

1. Set *counter* equal to *start*.

2. Evaluate the *counterExpression* in the for statement.

3. If *counterExpression* is true, continue with Step 4; if *counterExpression* is false, skip to Step 7.

4. Execute each of the statements in the block.

5. Use *counterUpdate* to increment (or whatever) *counter*.

6. Return to Step 2.

7. Exit the loop (that is, execute the next statement that occurs after the for block).

As an example, the following code shows how to use for to rewrite the inefficient code shown earlier in this chapter (bk03ch04/example08.html):

```
let sum = 0;
let num;
for (let counter = 1; counter <= 3; counter += 1) {
    num = prompt("Type a number:", 1);
    sum += Number(num);
}
document.write("The total of your numbers is " + sum);
```

This is the most efficient version yet because the declaring, initializing, and incrementing of the counter variable all take place in the for statement.

TECHNICAL STUFF

It's worth mentioning that every expression inside the for parentheses – the initialization, the condition, and the update — is optional. Wait, *what*? Yep:

» You can omit the initialization expression (*counter* = *start* in the earlier syntax) if you initialize the counter variable outside the loop:

```
let sum = 0;
let num;
let counter = 0;
for (; counter <= 3; counter += 1) {
    num = prompt("Type a number:", 1);
    sum += Number(num);
}
```

» You can omit the condition expression (*counterExpression* in the earlier syntax) by including a new condition inside the loop that runs a break statement (refer to "Exiting a loop using the break statement," later in this chapter) when the condition becomes `false`:

```
let sum = 0;
let num;
for (let counter = 1; ; counter += 1) {
    if (counter > 3) break;
    num = prompt("Type a number:", 1);
    sum += Number(num);
}
```

» You can omit the update expression (*counterUpdate* in the earlier syntax) if you move the update expression inside the loop:

```
let sum = 0;
let num;
for (let counter = 1; counter <= 3;) {
    num = prompt("Type a number:", 1);
    sum += Number(num);
    counter += 1;
}
```

» You can even omit all three expressions:

```
let sum = 0;
let num;
let counter = 0;
for (;;) {
    if (counter > 3) break;
    num = prompt("Type a number:", 1);
    sum += Number(num);
    counter += 1;
}
```

REMEMBER

To keep the number of variables declared in a script to a minimum, always try to use the same name in all your for loop counters. The letters i through n traditionally are used for counters in programming. For greater clarity, you may prefer full words such as count or counter.

TECHNICAL STUFF

It's not obvious, but any variable you declare in the for statement (particularly the counter variable) has scope only within the for block.

Here's a slightly more complex example (bk03ch04/example09.html):

```
let sum = 0;
for (let counter = 1; counter < 4; counter += 1) {
    let num;
    let ordinal;
    switch (counter) {
        case 1:
            ordinal = "first";
            break;
        case 2:
            ordinal = "second";
            break;
        case 3:
            ordinal = "third";
    }
    num = prompt("Enter the " + ordinal + " number:", 1);
    sum += Number(num);
}
document.write("The average is " + sum / 3);
```

The purpose of this script is to ask the user for three numbers and then to display the average of those values. The for statement is set up to loop three times. (Note that counter < 4 is the same as counter <= 3.) The first thing the loop block does is use switch to determine the value of the ordinal variable: If counter is 1, ordinal is set to "first"; if counter is 2, ordinal becomes "second"; and so on. These values enable the script to customize the prompt message with each pass through the loop (check out Figure 4-2). With each loop, the user enters a number, and that value is added to the sum variable. When the loop exits, the average is displayed.

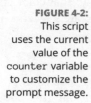

FIGURE 4-2:
This script uses the current value of the counter variable to customize the prompt message.

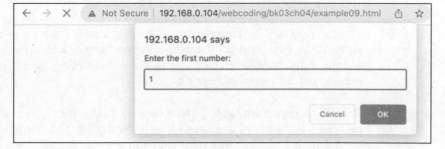

Not Secure | 192.168.0.104/webcoding/bk03ch04/example09.html

192.168.0.104 says

Enter the first number:

1

Cancel   OK

It's also possible to use for to count down. You do this by using the subtraction assignment operator instead of the addition assignment operator:

```
for (let counter = start; counterExpression; counter -= 1) {
    statements
}
```

In this case, you must initialize the *counter* variable to the maximum value you want to use for the loop counter, and use the *counterExpression* to compare the value of *counter* to the minimum value you want to use to end the loop.

In the following example (bk03ch04/example10.html), I use a decrementing counter to ask the user to rank, in reverse order, their top three CSS colors (refer to Book 3, Chapter 5 for the details on using colors):

```
for (let rank = 3; rank >= 1; rank -= 1) {
    let ordinal;
    let color;
    switch (rank) {
        case 1:
            ordinal = "first";
            break;
        case 2:
            ordinal = "second";
            break;
        case 3:
            ordinal = "third";
    }
    color = prompt("What is your " + ordinal + "-favorite CSS
color?", "");
    document.write(rank + ". " + color + "<br>");
}
```

The for loop runs by decrementing the rank variable from 3 down to 1. Each iteration of the loop prompts the user to type a favorite CSS color, and that color is written to the page, with the current value of rank being used to create a reverse-ordered list, as shown in Figure 4-3.

TIP

There's no reason why the for loop counter has to be only incremented or decremented. You're free to use any expression to adjust the value of the loop counter. For example, suppose you want the loop counter to run through only the odd numbers 1, 3, 5, 7, and 9. Here's a for statement that will do that:

```
for (let counter = 1; counter <= 9; counter += 2)
```

FIGURE 4-3:
The
decrementing
value of the rank
variable is used to
create a reverse-
ordered list.

```
← → C          ○ 🔒 192.168.0.104/webcoding/bk03ch04/example10.html

3. blanchedalmond
2. mintcream
1. papayawhip
```

The expression `counter += 2` uses the addition assignment operator to tell JavaScript to increase the `counter` variable by 2 each time through the loop.

Using do. . .while Loops

JavaScript has a third and final type of loop that I've left until the last because it isn't one that you'll use often. To understand when you might use it, consider this code snippet:

```
let sum = 0;
let num = prompt("Type a number or click Cancel:", 1);
while (num != null) {
    sum += Number(num);
    num = prompt("Type a number or click Cancel:", 1);
}
```

The code needs the first `prompt` statement so that the `while` loop's expression can be evaluated. The user may not feel like entering *any* numbers, and they can avoid it by clicking Cancel in the first prompt box so that the loop will be bypassed.

That seems reasonable enough, but what if your code requires that the user enter at least one value? The following presents one way to change the code to ensure that the loop is executed at least once:

```
let sum = 0;
let num = 0;
while (num !== null || sum === 0) {
    num = prompt("Type a number; when you're done, click
  Cancel:", 1);
    sum += Number(num);
}
document.write("The total of your numbers is " + sum);
```

The changes here are that the code initializes both `sum` and `num` as 0. Initial-izing both to 0 ensures that the `while` expression — `num !== null || sum`

=== 0 — returns true the first time through the loop, so the loop will definitely execute at least once. If the user clicks Cancel right away, sum will still be 0, so the while expression — num !== null || sum === 0 — still returns true and the loop repeats once again.

This approach works fine, but you can also turn to JavaScript's third loop type, which specializes in just this kind of situation. It's called a do...while loop, and its general syntax looks like this:

```
do {
    statements
}
while (expression);
```

Here, statements represents a block of statements to execute each time through the loop, and expression is a comparison or logical expression that, as long as it returns true, tells JavaScript to keep executing the statements within the loop.

This structure ensures that JavaScript executes the loop's statement block at least once. How? Take a closer look at how JavaScript processes a do...while loop:

1. Execute each of the statements in the block.

2. Evaluate the expression in the while statement.

3. If expression is true, return to Step 1; if expression is false, continue with Step 4.

4. Exit the loop.

For example, the following shows you how to use do...while to restructure the prompt-and-sum code I presented you earlier (bk03ch04/example11.html):

```
let sum = 0;
let num;
do {
    num = prompt("Type a number; when you're done, click
  Cancel:", 1);
    sum += Number(num);
}
while (num !== null || sum === 0);
document.write("The total of your numbers is " + sum);
```

This code is similar to the `while` code I showed earlier in this section. All that's really changed is that the `while` statement and its expression have been moved after the statement block so that the loop must be executed once before the expression is evaluated.

Controlling Loop Execution

Most loops run their natural course and then the procedure moves on. Sometimes, however, you may want to exit a loop prematurely or skip over some statements and continue with the next pass through the loop. You can handle each situation with, respectively, the `break` and `continue` statements.

Exiting a loop using the break statement

You use `break` when your loop comes across some value or condition that would prevent the rest of the statements from executing properly or that satisfies what the loop was trying to accomplish. The following code demonstrates `break` with a simple example (bk03ch04/example12.html):

```javascript
let sum = 0;
for (let counter = 1; counter <= 3; counter += 1) {
    let num = prompt("Type a positive number:", 1);
    if (num < 0) {
        sum = 0;
        break;
    }
    sum += Number(num);
}
if (sum > 0) {
    document.write("The average of your numbers is " + sum / 3);
}
```

This script sets up a `for` loop to prompt the user for positive numbers. For the purposes of this section, the key code is the `if` test:

```javascript
if (num < 0) {
    sum = 0;
    break;
}
```

If the user enters a negative number, the sum variable is reset to 0 (to prevent the message from being written to the page later in the script). Also, a break statement tells JavaScript to bail out of the loop altogether.

Here's a more complex example (bk03ch04/example13.html):

```javascript
const numberToGuess = Math.ceil(Math.random() * 10);
let promptMessage = "Guess a number between 1 and 10:";
let totalGuesses = 1;
do {
    const guess = Number(prompt(promptMessage, ""));
    if (guess === 0) {
        break;
    } else if (guess === numberToGuess) {
        document.write ("You guessed it in " + totalGuesses +
             (totalGuesses === 1 ? " try." : " tries."));
        break;
    } else if (guess < numberToGuess) {
        promptMessage = "Sorry, your guess was too low. Try
  again:";
    } else {
        promptMessage = "Sorry, your guess was too high. Try
  again:";
    }
    totalGuesses += 1;
}
while (true);
```

This script is a game in which a number between 1 and 10 is generated and the user has to try and guess what it is. The first four lines set up some variables. The head-scratcher here is the expression for the numberToGuess variable. This expression uses a couple of methods of the Math object, which I discuss in Book 3, Chapter 9. For now, suffice it to say that this expression generates a random integer between (and including) 1 and 10.

Then a do...while loop is set up with the following structure:

```javascript
do {
    statements
}
while (true);
```

This tells JavaScript to run the loop without bothering with a comparison expression. As you'll learn, the loop itself will take care of exiting the loop by using the break statement.

Next the user is prompted to enter a guess, which is stored in the guess variable. The script then checks whether guess equals 0, which would mean that the user clicked Cancel. (Clicking Cancel returns null, but the Number function converts null to 0.) If so, then break is used to stop the game by exiting the loop:

```
const guess = Number(prompt(promptMessage,""));
if (guess === 0) {
    break;
}
```

Otherwise, a series of if statements tests the guessed number against the actual number. The first one checks whether they're the same. If so, a message is written to the page and then another break statement exits the loop because the game is finished:

```
else if (guess === numberToGuess) {
    document.write("You guessed it in " + totalGuesses +
        (totalGuesses === 1 ? " try." : " tries."));
    break;
}
```

TIP

Note that the document.write statement contains a ternary operator expression:

```
totalGuesses === 1 ? " try." : " tries."
```

This illustrates an extremely common programming situation: You have to display a word to the user, but that word may be either singular or plural depending on the value of some variable or expression. In this case, if totalGuesses equals 1, you want to display the word try (as in 1 try); if totalGuesses is more than 1, you want to display the word tries (as in 2 tries). This is what the ternary operator does in the previous code.

The other two tests check whether the guess was lower or higher than the actual number, and a message to that effect is displayed, as shown in Figure 4-4.

FIGURE 4-4:
If you guess
wrong, the script
lets you know
if your guess
was too high or
too low.

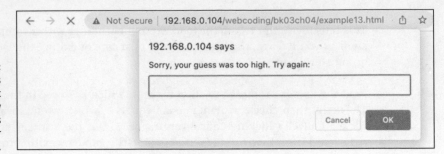

Bypassing loop statements using the continue statement

The continue statement is similar to break, but instead of exiting a loop entirely, continue tells JavaScript to bypass the rest of the statements in the loop block and begin a new iteration of the loop.

A good use for continue is when you want the user to enter one or more values no matter what. If they click Cancel in the prompt box, you want the script to keep on looping until the user enters the correct number of values. The following code shows one way to do this (bk03ch04/example14.html):

```
let counter = 0;
let sum = 0;
while (counter < 3) {
    const num = prompt("Type a number:", 1);
    if (num === null) {
        continue;
    }
    sum += Number(num);
    counter += 1;
}
document.write("The average of your numbers is " + sum / 3);
```

Because you don't know in advance how many times the code will have to run through the loop, a while loop is a better choice than a for loop. You need to count the number of values entered, however, so a variable named counter is initialized for that purpose. The script requires three numbers, so the while statement is set up to continue looping as long as counter is less than 3. The prompt result is stored in the num variable, which is then tested:

```
if (num === null) {
    continue;
}
```

If the user enters a number, the `if` expression returns `false` and the rest of the loop executes: sum is updated and `counter` is incremented.

However, if the user clicks Cancel, `num` equals `null`, so the `if` expression returns `true`. What you want here is to keep looping, but you don't want the rest of the loop statements to execute. That's exactly what the `continue` statement accomplishes.

Avoiding Infinite Loops

Whenever you use a `while`, `for`, or `do...while` loop, there's always the danger that the loop will never terminate. This is called an *infinite loop*, and it has been the bugbear of programmers for as long as people have been programming. Here are some notes to keep in mind to help you avoid infinite loops:

» The statements in the `for` block should never change the value of the loop counter variable. If they do, your loop may either terminate prematurely or end up in an infinite loop.

» In `while` and `do...while` loops, make sure you have at least one statement within the loop that changes the value of the comparison variable (that is, the variable you use in the loop's comparison statement). Otherwise, the statement might always return `true` and the loop will never end.

» In `while` and `do...while` loops, never rely on the user to enter a specific value to end the loop. They may cancel the prompt box or do something else that prevents the loop from terminating.

» If you have an infinite loop and you're not sure why, insert one or more debugger and `console.log` statements in the loop statement block to enable you to step through the script one statement at a time and display the current value of the counter or comparison variable. (Wondering what the heck *debugger* and *console.log* might be? I cover them in Book 5, Chapter 2.) This process enables you to learn what happens to the variable with each pass through the loop.

Chapter **5**

Harnessing the Power of Functions

To iterate is human, to recurse divine.

— L. PETER DEUTSCH

As I demonstrate throughout this book, JavaScript comes with a huge number of built-in features that perform specific tasks. For example, something called the Math object has a built-in method for calculating the square root of a number. Similarly, a feature called the String object has a ready-made method for converting a string value to all lowercase letters.

Hundreds of these ready-to-roll features perform tasks that range from the indispensable to the obscure. But JavaScript can't possibly do everything that you'd like or need it to do. What happens if your web development project requires a particular task or calculation that isn't part of the JavaScript language? Are you stuck? Not even close! The solution is to roll up your sleeves and then roll your own code that accomplishes the task or runs the calculation.

This chapter shows you how to create such do-it-yourself code. In the pages that follow, you explore the powerful and infinitely useful realm of custom functions, where you craft reusable code that performs tasks that out-of-the-box JavaScript can't do.

What Is a Function?

A *function* is a group of JavaScript statements that are separate from the rest of the script and that perform a designated task. (Technically, a function can perform any number of chores, but as a general rule it's best to have each function focus on a specific task.) When your script needs to perform that task, you tell it to run — or *execute*, in the vernacular — the function.

Functions are also useful for those times when you need to control exactly when a particular task occurs (if ever). If you just enter some statements between your web page's ‹script› and ‹/script› tags, the browser runs those statements automatically when the page loads. However, the statements within a function aren't executed by the browser automatically. (Later in the chapter, I mention some exceptions to that rule.) Instead, the function doesn't execute until either your code asks the function to run or some event occurs — such as the user clicking a button — and you've set up your page to run the function in response to that event.

The Structure of a Function

The basic structure of a function looks like this:

```
function functionName([arguments]) {
    JavaScript statements
}
```

where:

>> function identifies the block of code that follows it as a function.

>> *functionName* is a unique name for the function. The naming rules and guidelines that I outline for variables in Book 3, Chapter 2 also apply to function names.

>> *arguments* are one or more values that are passed to the function and act as variables within the function. Arguments (or *parameters,* as they're sometimes

called) are typically one or more values that the function uses as the raw materials for its tasks or calculations. You always enter arguments between parentheses after the function name, and you separate multiple arguments with commas. If you don't use arguments, you must still include the parentheses after the function name.

» *JavaScript statements* are the code that performs the function's tasks or calculations.

TIP

When I present the syntax of a function that includes one or more optional arguments, I surround those arguments with square brackets — [and] — to let you know.

TIP

Note how the *JavaScript statements* line in the example is indented slightly from the left margin. This is a standard and highly recommended programming practice because it makes your code easier to read. This example is indented four spaces, which is enough to do the job but isn't excessive. Some programmers use two spaces, and others indent using a single tab.

Note, too, the use of braces ({ and }). These are used to enclose the function's statements within a block, which tells you (and the browser) where the function's code begins and ends. There are only two rules for where these braces appear:

» The opening brace must appear after the function's parentheses and before the first function statement.

» The closing brace must appear after the last function statement.

No set-in-stone rule exists that specifies exactly where the braces appear. The positions used in the preceding function syntax are traditional, but you're free to try other positions, if you want. For example:

```
function functionName([arguments])
{
    JavaScript statements
}
```

Where Do You Put a Function?

For most applications, it doesn't matter where you put your functions, as long as they reside in a ‹script› block. However, one of the most common uses of functions is to handle events when they're triggered. It's possible that a particular event may fire when the page is loading, and if that happens before the browser has parsed the corresponding function, you could get strange results or an error. To prevent that, it's good practice to place the script containing all your functions in the page's header section (or in an external JavaScript file).

Note, as well, that you can add as many functions as you want in a single `<script>` block, but make sure that each function has a unique name. In fact, all the functions that exist in or are referenced by a page must have unique names.

Calling a Function

After your function is defined, you'll eventually need to tell the browser to execute – or *call* – the function. You can do this in three main ways:

>> When the browser parses the `<script>` tag

>> After the page is loaded

>> In response to an event, such as the user clicking a button

The next three sections cover each of these scenarios.

Calling a function when the `<script>` tag is parsed

The simplest way to call a function is to include in your script a statement consisting of only the function name, followed by parentheses (assuming for the moment that your function uses no arguments.) The following code (check out bk03ch05/example01.html in this book's example files) provides an example. (I listed the entire page to show you where the function and the statement that calls it appear in the page code.)

```
<!DOCTYPE html>
<html lang="en">
<head>
    <meta charset="utf-8">
    <title>Calling a function when the &lt;script&gt;
 tag is parsed</title>
    <script>
        function displayGreeting() {
            const currentHour = new Date().getHours();
```

```
        if (currentHour < 12) {
            console.log("Good morning!");
        } else {
            console.log("Good day!");
        }
    }
    displayGreeting();
    </script>
</head>
<body>
</body>
</html>
```

The `<script>` tag includes a function named displayGreeting, which determines the current hour of the day and then writes a greeting to the console (check out Figure 5-1) based on whether it's currently morning. The function is called by the displayGreeting statement that appears just after the function.

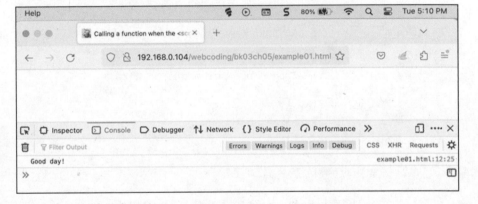

FIGURE 5-1: An example of calling a function when the `<script>` tag is parsed.

REMEMBER

The console is part of each web browser's developer tools. You use the console to display messages (as in this section's example), run JavaScript code on the fly, and look for script error messages. You learn all about the console in Book 5, Chapter 2.

TIP

To display the console in most web browsers, right-click the web page, click Inspect (or press Ctrl+Shift+I in Windows or Option+⌘+I in macOS), and then click the Console tab.

Calling a function after the page is loaded

If your function references a page element, calling the function from the page's head section won't work because when the browser parses the script, the rest of the page hasn't loaded yet, so your element reference will fail.

To work around this problem, place another <script> tag at the end of the body section, just before the closing </body> tag, as shown here (bk03ch05/example02.html):

```
<!DOCTYPE html>
<html lang="en">
<head>
    <meta charset="utf-8">
    <title>Calling a function after the page is loaded</title>
    <script>
        function makeBackgroundRed() {
            document.body.style.backgroundColor = "red";
            console.log("The background is now red.");
        }
    </script>
</head>
<body>
    <!-- Other body elements go here -->

    <script>
        makeBackgroundRed();
    </script>
</body>
</html>
```

The makeBackgroundRed function does two things: It uses document.body.style. backgroundColor to change the background color of the body element to red, and it uses console.log to write a message to that effect on the console.

In the function, document.body is a reference to the body element, which doesn't exist until the page is fully loaded. If you try to call the function with the initial script, you'll get an error. To execute the function properly, a second <script> tag appears at the bottom of the body element, and that script calls the function with the following statement:

```
makeBackgroundRed();
```

By the time the browser executes that statement, the body element exists, so the function runs without an error (check out Figure 5-2).

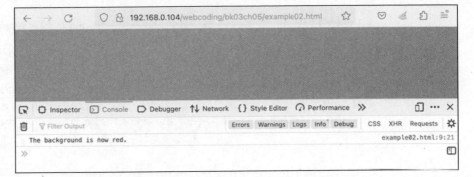

FIGURE 5-2:
An example of
calling a function
after the page
has loaded.

Calling a function in response to an event

One of the most common ways that JavaScript functions are called is in response to some event. Events are such an important topic that I devote an entire chapter to them later in the book (refer to Book 3, Chapter 7). For now, check out a relatively straightforward application: executing the function when the user clicks a button. The following code shows one way to do it (bk03ch05/example03.html):

```html
<!DOCTYPE html>
<html lang="en">
<head>
    <meta charset="utf-8">
    <title>Calling a function in response to an event</title>
    <script>
        function makeBackgroundRed() {
            document.body.style.backgroundColor= "red";
        }

        function makeBackgroundWhite() {
            document.body.style.backgroundColor= "white";
        }
    </script>
</head>
<body>
    <button onclick="makeBackgroundRed()">
        Make Background Red
    </button>
    <button onclick="makeBackgroundWhite()">
        Make Background White
    </button>
</body>
</html>
```

I placed two functions in the script: makeBackgroundRed changes the page background to red, as before, and makeBackgroundWhite changes the background color back to white.

The buttons are standard HTML button elements (check out Figure 5-3), each of which includes the onclick attribute. This attribute defines a *handler* — that is, the function to execute — for the event that occurs when the user clicks the button.

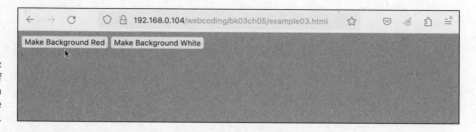

FIGURE 5-3:
An example of calling a function in response to an event.

For example, consider the first button:

```
<button onclick="makeBackgroundRed()">
```

The onclick attribute says, in effect, "When somebody clicks this button, call the function named makeBackgroundRed."

WARNING
The example I've used here is a tad old-fashioned in that it defines the event handler inside an HTML tag, which is now considered bad programming practice because it mixes HTML and JavaScript. The modern way is to keep the worlds of HTML and JavaScript apart by setting up an event listener using a separate script. I show you a revised version of this example that uses an event listener later in the chapter (in the "Getting Your Head around Anonymous Functions" section). I talk more about event listeners in Book 3, Chapter 7.

Passing Values to Functions

One of the main reasons to use functions is to gain control over when some chunk of JavaScript code gets executed. The preceding section, for example, discusses how easy it is to use functions to set things up so that code doesn't run until the user clicks a button.

However, another major reason to use functions is to avoid repeating code unnecessarily. To understand what I mean, consider the two functions from the preceding section:

```
function makeBackgroundRed() {
    document.body.style.backgroundColor= "red";
}
function makeBackgroundWhite() {
    document.body.style.backgroundColor= "white";
}
```

These functions perform the same task — changing the background color — and the only difference between them is one changes the color to red and the other changes it to white. When you end up with two or more functions that do essentially the same thing, you know your code is inefficient.

So how do you make the code more efficient? That's where the arguments mentioned earlier come into play. An *argument* is a value that is sent — or *passed*, in programming terms — to the function. The argument acts just like a variable, and it automatically stores whatever value is sent.

Passing a single value to a function

As an example, you can take the previous two functions, reduce them to a single function, and set up the color value as an argument. Here's a new function that does just that:

```
function changeBackgroundColor(newColor) {
    document.body.style.backgroundColor = newColor;
}
```

The argument is named newColor and is added between the parentheses that occur after the function name. JavaScript declares newColor as a variable automatically, so you don't need a separate let or const statement. The function then uses the newColor value to change the background color. So how do you pass a value to the function? The following code presents a sample file that does so (bk03ch05/example04.html):

```
<!DOCTYPE html>
<html lang="en">
<head>
    <meta charset="utf-8">
    <title>Passing a single value to a function</title>
```

```
    <script>
        function changeBackgroundColor(newColor) {
            document.body.style.backgroundColor = newColor;
        }
    </script>
</head>
<body>
    <button onclick="changeBackgroundColor('red')">
        Make Background Red
    </button>
    <button onclick="changeBackgroundColor('white')">
        Make Background White
    </button>
</body>
</html>
```

The key here is the `onclick` attribute that appears in both `<button>` tags. For example:

```
onclick="changeBackgroundColor('red')"
```

The string `'red'` is inserted into the parentheses after the function name, so that value is passed to the function itself. The other button passes the value `'white'`, and the function result changes accordingly.

WARNING

In the two `onclick` attributes in the example code, note that the values passed to the function are enclosed in single quotation marks (`'`). This is necessary because the `onclick` value as a whole is enclosed in double quotation marks (`"`).

Passing multiple values to a function

For more complex functions, you may need to use multiple arguments so that you can pass different kinds of values. If you use multiple arguments, separate each one with a comma, like this:

```
function changeColors(newBackColor, newForeColor) {
    document.body.style.backgroundColor = newBackColor;
    document.body.style.color = newForeColor;
}
```

In this function, the `document.body.style.color` statement changes the foreground color (that is, the color of the page text). The following code shows a revised page where the buttons pass two values to the function (bk03ch05/example05.html):

```
<!DOCTYPE html>
<html lang="en">
<head>
    <meta charset="utf-8">
    <title>Passing multiple values to a function</title>
    <script>
        function changeColors(newBackColor, newForeColor) {
            document.body.style.backgroundColor = newBackColor;
            document.body.style.color = newForeColor;
        }
    </script>
</head>
<body>
    <h1>Passing Multiple Values to a Function</h1>
    <button onclick="changeColors('red', 'white')">
        Red Background, White Text
    </button>
    <button onclick="changeColors('white', 'red')">
        White Background, Red Text
    </button>
</body>
</html>
```

If you define a function to have multiple arguments, you must always pass values for each of those arguments to the function. If you don't, the "value" undefined is passed instead, which can cause problems.

If you use a variable to pass data to a function, only the current value of that variable is sent, not the variable itself. Therefore, if you change the value of the argument within the function, the value of the original variable isn't changed. Here's an example:

```
let passThis = 10;
function sendMe(acceptThis) {
    acceptThis = 5;
}
sendMe(passThis);
console.log(passThis);
```

The passThis variable starts off with a value of 10. The sendMe function is defined to accept an argument named acceptThis and to change the value of that argument to 5. sendMe is called and the value of the passThis variable is passed to it. Then a console.log statement displays the value of passThis. If you run this code, the displayed value will be 10, the original value of passThis. In other words, changing the value of `acceptThis` in the function had no effect on the value of the `passThis` variable.

Making an argument optional

In most of your functions, arguments will be required and the function will fail in some way if it's called without including all arguments. However, making an argument optional is not unusual. Your function may still require some kind of value to produce the correct result, but you can specify a default value to use if the argument isn't included in the function call.

For example, the following function calculates a tip:

```
function calculateTip(preTip, tipPercent) {
    const tipResult = preTip * tipPercent;
    return tipResult;
}
```

And here's an example call:

```
calculateTip(100, 0.15);
```

If you usually tip 15 percent, it would be nice if you didn't have to always specify the `tipPercent` argument with each function call. You can set that up — that is, you can make the `tipPercent` argument optional — by setting the `tipPercent` argument to a default value:

```
function calculateTip(preTip, tipPercent = 0.15) {
    const tipResult = preTip * tipPercent;
    return tipResult;
}
```

Now you can call this function like so:

```
calculateTip(100);
```

JavaScript notices the missing `tipPercent` argument, so it uses the default value of `0.15` for the calculation.

TIP

If your function has multiple optional arguments, how do you skip one of the middle arguments when you call the function? Excellent question! Here's an example of such a function where the second and third arguments are optional:

```
function addEmUp(argA, argB = 10, argC = 15) {
    return argA + argB + argC;
}
```

How do you skip just the second argument in a function call? You pass the `undefined` value, like this:

```
addEmUp(100, undefined, 200);
```

REMEMBER

Specifying a default value to make a function argument optional is an ES6 (ECMAScript 2015) feature, so avoid it if you have to support way-past-their-prime browsers such as Internet Explorer 11.

Returning a Value from a Function

So far, I've outlined two major advantages of using functions. You can use them to:

>> Control when code is executed

>> Consolidate repetitive code into a single routine

The third major benefit that functions bring to the JavaScript table is that you can use them to perform calculations and then return the result. As an example, here's a function that calculates the tip on a restaurant bill (bk03ch05/example06.html):

```
function calculateTip(preTip, tipPercent) {
    const tipResult = preTip * tipPercent;
    return tipResult;
}
const preTipTotal = 100.00;
const tipPercentage = 0.15;
const tipCost = calculateTip(preTipTotal, tipPercentage);
const totalBill = preTipTotal + tipCost;
document.write("Your total bill is $" + totalBill);
```

The function named `calculateTip` takes two arguments: `preTip` is the total of the bill before the tip, and `tipPercent` is the percentage used to calculate the tip. The function then declares a variable named `tipResult` and uses it to store the calculation — `preTip` multiplied by `tipPercent`. The key for this example is the second line of the function:

```
return tipResult;
```

The return statement is JavaScript's way of sending a value *back* to the statement that called the function. That statement comes after the function:

```
tipCost = calculateTip(preTipTotal, tipPercentage);
```

This statement first passes the value of `preTipTotal` (initialized as `100.00` earlier in the script) and `tipPercentage` (initialized as `0.15` earlier) to the `calculateTip` function. When that function returns its result, the entire expression `calculateTip(preTipTotal, tipPercentage)` is replaced by that result, meaning that it gets stored in the `tipCost` variable. Then `preTipTotal` and `tipCost` are added together, the result is stored in `totalBill`, and a `document.write` statement displays the final calculation (check out Figure 5-4).

FIGURE 5-4:
The output includes the return value of the custom function calculation.

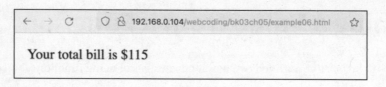

This variety of function syntax creates an *anonymous function* because — that's right — the function has no name.

Getting Your Head around Anonymous Functions

Here's another look at the function syntax from earlier in this chapter:

```
function functionName([arguments]) {
    JavaScript statements
}
```

This version of function syntax creates a *named function* because — you guessed it — the function has a name.

However, creating a function that doesn't have a name is also possible:

```
function ([arguments]) {
    JavaScript statements
}
```

This variety of function syntax creates an *anonymous function* because — that's right — the function has no name.

Why use anonymous functions? The main reason is to avoid creating a named object when you don't need to. Every large web project has a huge *namespace*, which refers to the full collection of identifiers you assign to things such as variables and functions. The larger the namespace, the greater the chance of a *namespace collision*, where you use the same identifier for two different things. Bad news!

Anonymous functions were introduced in ES6, so don't use them if you need to support very old browsers, such as Internet Explorer 11.

If you have a function that will be used only once in your project, it's considered good modern programming practice to make it an anonymous function so that you have one less identifier in your namespace.

Okay, I hear you thinking, earlier you said we invoke a function by using the function name. If an anonymous function has no name, how are we supposed to run it? Excellent question! There are two main methods to consider:

>> Assigning the function to a variable

>> Replacing a function call with the function itself

Assigning an anonymous function to a variable

Once again, here's the example code from the previous section:

```
const preTipTotal = 100.00;
const tipPercentage = 0.15;

function calculateTip(preTip, tipPercent) {
    const tipResult = preTip * tipPercent;
    return tipResult;
}

const tipCost = calculateTip(preTipTotal, tipPercentage);
const totalBill = preTipTotal + tipCost;
document.write("Your total bill is $" + totalBill);
```

This code defines the named function `calculateTip()` and later uses the `tipCost` variable to store the function result. This is a perfect example of when a named function is not needed because you use the named function only to calculate the `tipCost` value. Adding an identity to the namespace when you don't have to is called *polluting* the namespace, and it's a big no-no in modern JavaScript programming.

You can rewrite this code to use an anonymous function, instead (bk03ch05/example07.html):

```
const preTipTotal = 100.00;
const tipPercentage = 0.15;

// Declare tipCost using an anonymous function
const tipCost = function (preTip, tipPercent) {
    const tipResult = preTip * tipPercent;
    return tipResult;
};

const totalBill = preTipTotal + tipCost(preTipTotal,
    tipPercentage);
document.write("Your total bill is $" + totalBill);
```

The big change here is that now I declare the value of the `tipCost` variable to be an anonymous function. That anonymous function is the same as the `calculateTip()` named function from before, just without the name. In the second-last statement, I invoke the anonymous function by using `tipCost(preTipTotal, tipPercentage)`.

Replacing a function call with an anonymous function

One of the most common uses for anonymous functions is when you need to pass a function as an argument to another function. The passed function is known as a *callback function*.

First, let's look at an example that uses named functions (bk03ch05/example08.html):

```
<body>
    <button id="bgRed">
        Make Background Red
    </button>
    <button id="bgWhite">
        Make Background White
    </button>
```

```
<script>
    function makeBackgroundRed() {
        document.body.style.backgroundColor= 'red';
    }

    function makeBackgroundWhite() {
        document.body.style.backgroundColor= 'white';
    }
    document.getElementById('bgRed').addEventListener(
        'click',
        makeBackgroundRed
    );
    document.getElementById('bgWhite').addEventListener(
        'click',
        makeBackgroundWhite
    );
</script>
</body>
```

The script declares two named functions: makeBackgroundRed() and make
BackgroundWhite(). The code then creates two event listeners. One of them
listens for clicks on the button that has the id value bgRed and, when a click
is detected, runs the makeBackgroundRed() callback function. The other event
listener listens for clicks on the button that has the id value bgWhite and, when
a click is detected, runs the makeBackgroundWhite() callback function. Refer to
Book 3, Chapter 6 to get the details on the document object and the getElement
ById() and addEventListener() methods.

Again, we have two functions that don't need to be named, so we can remove them
from the namespace by replacing the callbacks with anonymous functions. Here's
the revised code (bk03ch05/example09.html):

```
<body>
    <button id="bgRed">
        Make Background Red
    </button>
    <button id="bgWhite">
        Make Background White
    </button>
    <script>
        document.getElementById('bgRed').addEventListener(
            'click',
```

```
                    function() {
                            document.body.style.backgroundColor= 'red';
                    }
            );
        document.getElementById('bgWhite').addEventListener(
            'click',
                function() {
                        document.body.style.backgroundColor= 'white';
                }
            );
    </script>
</body>
```

Moving to Arrow Functions

As you progress in JavaScript, you'll find yourself using anonymous functions constantly. When you get to that stage, you'll be happy to know that ES6 also offers a simpler anonymous function syntax. That is, instead of using this:

```
function ([arguments]) {
    JavaScript statements
}
```

you can use this:

```
([arguments]) => {
    JavaScript statements
}
```

All I did here is remove the function keyword and replace it with the characters = and › between the arguments and the opening brace. The characters => look like an arrow (JavaScripters call it a *fat arrow*), so this version of the syntax is known as an *arrow function*.

REMEMBER

Arrow functions are an ES6 invention, so don't use them if you need to support very old browsers, such as Internet Explorer 11.

REMEMBER

The argument parentheses aren't required if you're passing just one argument to the function:

```
argA => {
    console.log(argA);
}
```

For example, here's an anonymous function from a bit earlier (the "Assigning an anonymous function to a variable" section):

```
// Declare tipCost using an anonymous function
const tipCost = function (preTip, tipPercent) {
    const tipResult = preTip * tipPercent;
    return (tipResult);
};
```

You can rewrite this using an arrow function (bk03ch05/example10.html):

```
// Declare tipCost using an arrow function
const tipCost = (preTip, tipPercent) => {
    const tipResult = preTip * tipPercent;
    return (tipResult);
};
```

If your anonymous function consists of a single statement, you can take advantage of an arrow function feature called *implicit return:*

```
([arguments]) => statement;
```

Here, JavaScript assumes that a single-statement function means that the function returns right after executing the statement, so you can leave out the braces and the `return` keyword. Here's an example:

```
// Declare tipCost using an arrow function with implicit return
const tipCost = (preTip, tipPercent) => preTip * tipPercent;
```

Similarly, here's one of the anonymous callback functions from the previous section:

```
document.getElementById('bgRed').addEventListener(
    'click',
    function() {
        document.body.style.backgroundColor= 'red';
    }
);
```

You can rewrite this code as follows to use an arrow function with implicit return (bk03ch05/example11.html):

```
document.getElementById('bgRed').addEventListener(
    'click',
    () => document.body.style.backgroundColor= 'red'
);
```

Running Functions in the Future

In the scripts I've presented so far in this book, the code has executed in one of three ways:

>> Automatically when the page loads

>> When your script calls a function

>> In response to some event, such as the user clicking a button

JavaScript also offers a fourth execution method that's based on time. There are two possibilities:

>> Have some code run once after a specified number of milliseconds. This is called a *timeout*.

>> Have some code run after a specified number of milliseconds, and then repeat each time that number of milliseconds expires. This is called an *interval*.

The next couple of sections show you how to set up both procedures.

Using a timeout to perform a future action once

To set up a JavaScript timeout, use the setTimeout method:

```
setTimeout(function, delay, arg1, arg2, ...);
```

where:

>> *function* is the anonymous or named function that you want JavaScript to run when the timeout expires. Instead of a function, you can also use a JavaScript statement, surrounded by quotation marks.

>> *delay* is the number of milliseconds that JavaScript waits before executing *function*.

>> *arg1, arg2, . . .* are optional arguments to pass to *function*.

Note that setTimeout returns a value that uniquely identifies the timeout. You can store this value just in case you want to cancel the timeout (as described later in this section).

Here's some code that shows how setTimeout works (bk03ch05/example12.html):

```
// Create a message
const str = "Hello World!";

// Set the timeout
const timeoutId = setTimeout(function (msg) {
    document.write(msg);
}, 5000, str);
```

The script begins by creating a message string and storing it in the str variable. Then the setTimeout method tells JavaScript to run an anonymous function after five seconds (5,000 milliseconds) have elapsed, and to pass the str variable to that function. The anonymous function takes the msg argument and displays it on the page with document.write.

If you've set up a timeout and then decide that you don't want the code to execute after all for some reason, you can cancel the timeout by running the clear Timeout method:

```
clearTimeout(id)
```

where *id* is the name of the variable used to store the setTimeout method's return value.

For example, suppose you set a timeout with the following statement:

```
const timeoutId = setTimeout(function (msg) {
    document.write(msg);
}, 5000, str);
```

You could then cancel the timeout using the following statement:

```
clearTimeout(timeoutId);
```

Using an interval to perform a future action repeatedly

Running code once after a specified number of seconds is an occasionally useful procedure. A much more practical skill is being able to repeat code at a specified interval. Doing so enables you to set up countdowns, timers, animations, image slide shows, and more. To set up an interval, use the setInterval method:

```
setInterval(function, delay, arg1, arg2, ...);
```

where:

>> *function* is the anonymous or named function that you want JavaScript to run at the end of each interval. Instead of a function, you can also use a JavaScript statement, surrounded by quotation marks.

>> *delay* is the number of milliseconds in each interval, after which JavaScript executes *function*.

>> *arg1, arg2, ...* are the optional arguments to pass to *function*.

As with setTimeout, the setInterval method returns a value that uniquely identifies the interval. You could use that value to cancel the interval with the clearInterval method:

```
clearInterval(id);
```

where *id* is the name of the variable used to store the setInterval method's return value.

For example, suppose you set an interval with the following statement:

```
const intervalId = setInterval(countdown, 5000);
```

You'd then cancel the interval using the following statement:

```
clearInterval(intervalId);
```

Note that although the clearTimeout method is optional with setTimeout, you should always use clearInterval with setInterval. Otherwise, the interval will just keep executing.

The following code demonstrates both `setInterval` and `clearInterval` (bk03ch05/example13.html):

```
let counter = 10;

// Set the interval
const intervalId = setInterval(function () {

    // Display the countdown and then decrement the counter
    document.open();
    document.write(counter);
    counter -= 1;

    // Cancel the interval after we hit 0
    if (counter < -1) {
        clearInterval(intervalId);
        document.open();
        document.write("All done!");
    }
}, 1000);
```

The purpose of this script is to display a countdown from 10 to 0 on the page. The script begins by declaring a variable named `counter` and initializing it to `10`. Then the `setInterval` method sets up an anonymous function to run at intervals of one second (1,000 milliseconds). The anonymous function clears the page using `document.open`, displays the current value of `counter` on the page, and decrements `counter`. Then an `if` test checks the value of `counter`. If it's negative, it means that `counter` was just `0`, so it's done. The `clearInterval` method cancels the interval, and then a final message is written to the page.

Understanding Variable Scope

In programming, the *scope* of a variable defines where in the script a variable can be used and where it can't be used. To put it another way, a variable's scope determines which statements and functions can access and work with the variable. You need to be concerned with scope for two main reasons:

>> **You may want to use the same variable name in multiple functions.** If these variables are otherwise unrelated, you'll want to make sure that there is no confusion about which variable you're working with. In other words, you'll want to restrict the scope of each variable to the block or function in which it is declared.

>> **You may need to use the same variable in multiple blocks or functions.** For example, a function may use a variable to store the results of a calculation, and other functions may also need to use that result. In this case, you'll want to set up the scope of the variable so that it's accessible to multiple functions.

JavaScript lets you establish three types of scope for your variables:

>> Block scope

>> Function scope

>> Global scope

The next three sections describe each type in detail.

Working with block scope

When a variable has *block scope*, the variable was declared using let or const inside a statement block — that is, between a set of braces: { and } — and the only statements that can access the variable are the ones within that same block. Statements outside the block and statements in other blocks can't access the variable (bk03ch05/example14.html):

```
if (true) {
    const myMessage = "I'm in the scope!";
    console.log("Inside the if block: " + myMessage);
}
console.log("Outside the if block: " + myMessage);
```

This code uses an if construction to create a statement block. Inside that block, the code declares a variable named myMessage, sets its value to a text string, and uses JavaScript's console.log method to display the string in the console.

After the if block, another console.log statement attempts to display the myMessage variable. However, as shown in Figure 5-5, JavaScript generates an error that says myMessage is not defined. Why? Because the scope of the myMessage variable extends only to the if block. Statements outside that block can't "see" the myMessage variable, so it has nothing to display. In fact, after the if statement finishes executing, JavaScript removes the myMessage variable from memory, so that's why the myMessage variable referred to in the final line is undefined.

FIGURE 5-5:
Attempting
to display the
myMessage
variable outside
of the if block
results in an
error.

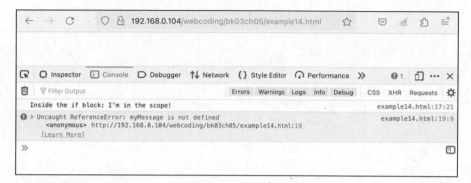

Working with function scope

When a variable has *function scope* (often also known as *local scope*), the variable was declared inside a function and the only statements that can access the variable are the ones in that same function. Statements outside the function and statements in other functions can't access the variable.

The following code demonstrates function scope (bk03ch05/example15.html):

```
function A() {
    const myMessage = "I'm in the scope!";
    console.log("Function A: " + myMessage);
}
function B() {
    console.log("Function B: " + myMessage);
}
A();
B();
```

There are two functions here, named A and B. Function A declares a variable named myMessage, sets its value to a text string, and uses JavaScript's console.log method to display the string in the console.

Function B also uses console.log to attempt to display the myMessage variable. As shown in Figure 5-6, JavaScript generates an error that says myMessage is not defined. Why? Because the scope of the myMessage variable extends only to function A; function B can't "see" the myMessage variable, which was removed from memory as soon as function A finished executing.

FIGURE 5-6:
Trying to use
the myMessage
variable in
function B
generates
an error.

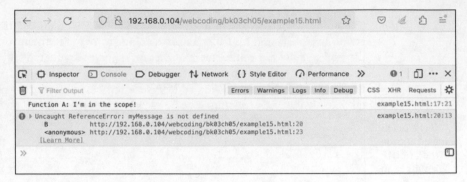

The same result occurs if you attempt to use the myMessage variable outside any function, as in the following code:

```javascript
function A() {
    const myMessage = "I'm in the scope!";
    console.log("Function A: " + myMessage);
}
A();
// The following statement generates an error:
console.log(myMessage);
```

Working with global scope

What if you want to use the same variable in multiple functions or even in multiple script blocks within the same page? In that case, you need to use *global scope*, which makes a variable accessible to any statement or function on a page. (That's why global scope is also called *page-level scope*.) To set up a variable with global scope, declare it outside any block or function. The following code gives this a whirl (bk03ch05/example16.html):

```javascript
const myMessage = "I've got global scope!";

if (true) {
    console.log("Inside the if block: " + myMessage);
}
function C() {
    console.log("Function C: " + myMessage);
}
C();
console.log("Outside any block or function: " + myMessage);
```

The script begins by declaring the myMessage variable and setting it equal to a string literal. Then an if block uses a console.log statement to attempt to display the myMessage value. Next, a function named C is created and displays a console message that attempts to display the value of myMessage. After the function is called, another console.log statement attempts to display the myMessage value outside any block or function. Figure 5-7 shows the results: All three console.log statements display the value of myMessage without a problem.

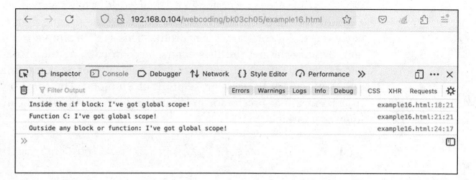

FIGURE 5-7:
When you declare
a global variable,
you can access its
value both inside
and outside any
block or function.

Using Recursive Functions

One of the stranger things you can do with a function is have it execute itself. That is, you place a statement within the function that calls the function. This is called *recursion*, and such a function is called a *recursive function.*

Before trying out a practical example, here's a simple script that demonstrates the basic procedure (bk03ch05/example17.html):

```
let counter = 0;
addOne();

function addOne() {
    counter += 1;
    if (confirm("counter is now " + counter + ". Add another
  one?")) {
        addOne();
    }
}

document.write("Counter ended up at " + counter);
```

The script begins by declaring a variable named counter and initializing it to 0. Then a function named addOne is called. This function increments the value of counter. It then displays the current value of counter and asks if you want to add another. If you click OK, the addOne function is called again, but this time it's called from within addOne itself! This just means that the whole thing repeats itself until you eventually click Cancel in the dialog box. After the function is exited for good, a document.write statement shows the final counter total.

What possible use is recursion in the real world? That's a good question. Consider a common business problem: calculating a profit-sharing plan contribution as a percentage of a company's net profits. This isn't a simple multiplication problem, because the net profit is determined, in part, by the profit-sharing figure. For example, suppose that a company has sales of $1,000,000 and expenses of $900,000, which leaves a gross profit of $100,000. The company also sets aside 10 percent of net profits for profit sharing. The net profit is calculated with the following formula:

```
Net Profit = Gross Profit - Profit Sharing Contribution;
```

That looks straightforward enough, but it's really not because the Profit Sharing Contribution value is derived with the following formula:

```
Profit Sharing Contribution = Net Profit * 10%;
```

In other words, the Net Profit value appears on both sides of the equation, which complicates things considerably.

One way to solve the Net Profit formula is to guess at an answer and calculate how close you come. For example, because profit sharing should be 10 percent of net profits, a good first guess may be 10 percent of *gross* profits, or $10,000. If you plugged this number into the Net Profit formula, you get a value of $90,000. This wouldn't be right, however, because you'd end up with a profit sharing value — 10 percent of $90,000 — of $9,000. Therefore, the original profit-sharing guess would be off by $1,000.

So, you can try again. This time, use $9,000 as the profit-sharing number. Plugging this new value into the Net Profit formula returns a value of $91,000. This number translates into a profit-sharing contribution of $9,100. This time you're off by only $100, so you're getting closer.

If you continue this process, your profit-sharing guesses will get closer to the calculated value. (This process is called *convergence.*) When the guesses are close enough (for example, within a dollar), you can stop and pat yourself on the back for finding the solution.

The process of calculating a formula and then continually recalculating it using different values is what recursion is all about.

TECHNICAL STUFF

AVOIDING INFINITE RECURSION

If you're trying to call a function recursively, you may get error messages such as Stack overflow or Too much recursion. These error messages indicate that you have no brakes on your recursive function so, if not for the errors, it would call itself forever. This is called *infinite recursion*. The maximum number of recursive calls depends on the browser and operating system and how much memory your device has installed.

In any case, it's important to build in some kind of test to ensure that the function will stop calling itself after a certain number of calls:

- The addOne function avoids infinite recursion by asking users if they want to continue or stop.

- The calculateProfitSharing function avoids infinite recursion by testing the sum of netProfit and profitSharing to determine if this sum is equal to grossProfit. (Although note that you may not know in advance whether the calculation converges, so some other way of limiting the recursion may be needed at first. For example, you could declare a global counter variable that is incremented with each recursive function call and is tested within the function to ensure that it doesn't exceed some maximum value.)

If you don't have a convenient or obvious method for stopping the recursion, you can set up a counter that tracks the number of function calls. When that number hits a predetermined maximum, the script should bail out of the recursion process. The following code presents such a script (bk03ch05/example19.html):

```
let currentCall = 1;
const maximumCalls = 3;

recursionTest();

function recursionTest() {
    if (currentCall <= maximumCalls) {
        console.log(currentCall);
        currentCall += 1;
        recursionTest();
    }
}
```

(continued)

(continued)

The currentCall variable is the counter, and the maximumCalls variable specifies the maximum number of times the recursive function can be called. In the function, the following statement compares the value of currentCall and maximumCalls:

```
if (currentCall <= maximumCalls)
```

If currentCall is less than or equal to maximumCalls, all is well and the script can continue. In this case, a console message displays the value of currentCall, that value is incremented, and the recursionTest function is called again. When currentCall becomes greater than maximumCalls, the function exits and the recursion is done.

Now it's time to show you how to go about writing a script that runs recursively. Check out the following code (bk03ch05/example18.html):

```javascript
const profitSharingPercent = 0.1;
const grossProfit = 100000;
let netProfit;

// Here's the initial guess
let profitSharing = grossProfit * profitSharingPercent;

calculateProfitSharing(profitSharing);

function calculateProfitSharing(guess) {

    // First, calculate the new net profit
    netProfit = grossProfit - guess;

    // Now use that to guess the profit-sharing value again
    profitSharing = Math.ceil(netProfit * profitSharingPercent);

    // Do we have a solution?
    if ((netProfit + profitSharing) != grossProfit) {
        // If not, plug it in again
        calculateProfitSharing(profitSharing);
    }
}
// Write the solution
document.write("Gross Profit: " + grossProfit +
    "<br>Net Profit: " + netProfit +
    "<br>Profit Sharing: " + profitSharing);
```

The grossProfit variable is initialized at 100000, the netProfit variable is declared, the profitSharingPercent variable is set to 0.1 (10 percent), and the profitSharing variable is set to the initial guess of 10 percent of gross profits. Then the calculateProfitSharing function is called, and the profitSharing guess is passed as the initial value of the guess argument.

The function first calculates the netProfit and then uses that value to calculate the new profitSharing number. Remember your goal here is to end up with the sum of netProfit and profitSharing equal to grossProfit. The if statement tests that, and if the sum is not equal to grossProfit, the calculateProfit Sharing function is called again (here's the recursion), and this time the new profitSharing value is passed. When the correct values are finally found, the function exits and displays the results, as shown in Figure 5-8.

FIGURE 5-8:
Using recursion to calculate a profit sharing value.

Gross Profit: 100000
Net Profit: 90909
Profit Sharing: 9091

REMEMBER

Note that all the variables in previous example are declared as globals. That's because if you declared them within the calculateProfitSharing function, they would get wiped out and reset with each call, which is not what you want when doing recursion.

IN THIS CHAPTER

» **Understanding objects**

» **Messing with object properties and methods**

» **Specifying elements by ID, tag, class, and selector**

» **Taking a deep dive into the Document Object Model**

» **Programming parents, children, siblings, and other family members**

Chapter **6**

Playing with the Document Object Model

The programmer, like the poet, works only slightly removed from pure thought-stuff. He builds his castles in the air, from air, creating by exertion of the imagination. Few media of creation are so flexible, so easy to polish and rework, so readily capable of realizing grand conceptual structures.

— FRED BROOKS

talk a lot of JavaScript in the past few chapters, but in a very real sense all that talk has been the programming equivalent of noshing on a few appetizers. Now it's time to sit down for the main course: programming the Document Object Model. I explain what that is shortly, but for now it's enough to know that it means taking control over every aspect of the web page. Want to change some web page text on the fly? JavaScript can do that. Want to add an element to the page? JavaScript's up to the task. Want to modify an element's CSS? JavaScript's all over that. Want to perform some action based on the user clicking something or pressing a key combination? JavaScript raises its hand and says, "Ooh, ooh, pick me, pick me!"

In this chapter, you explore the fascinating world of the Document Object Model. You learn lots of powerful coding techniques that enable you to make your web pages do almost anything you want them to do. You learn, too, that this is where web coding becomes fun and maybe just a little addictive (in a good way, I promise).

Working with Objects

Before I talk about the Document Object Model, you need to get familiar with what is arguably the most important word in that name: *object*. Over the next few pages, you learn what objects are, what you can do with them, and why they're important.

What is an object, anyway?

Only the simplest JavaScript programs do nothing but assign values to variables and calculate expressions. To go beyond these basic programming beginnings — that is, to write truly useful scripts — you have to do what JavaScript was designed to do from the start: manipulate the web page that it's displaying. That's what JavaScript is all about, and that manipulation can come in many different forms:

>> Add text and HTML attributes to an **element**.

>> Modify a CSS **property** of a class or other selector.

>> Store some data in the browser's internal **storage**.

>> Validate a **form's** data before submitting it.

The bold items in this list are examples of the "things" you can work with, and they're special for no other reason than they're programmable. In JavaScript parlance, these "programmable things" are called *objects*.

You can work with objects in JavaScript in any of the following three ways:

>> You can read and make changes to the object's *properties*.

>> You can make the object perform a task by activating a *method* associated with the object.

>> You can define a procedure that runs whenever a particular *event* happens to the object.

To help you understand objects and their properties, methods, and events, I'll put them in real-world terms. Specifically, consider your computer as though it were an object:

>> If you wanted to describe your computer as a whole, you'd mention things like the name of the manufacturer, the price, the size of the hard drive, and the amount of RAM. Each of these items is a *property* of the computer.

>> You also can use your computer to perform tasks such as writing letters, crunching numbers, and coding web pages. These are the *methods* associated with your computer.

>> A number of things happen to the computer that cause it to respond in predefined ways. For example, when the On button is pressed, the computer runs through its Power On Self-Test, initializes its components, and so on. The actions to which the computer responds automatically are its *events*.

These properties, methods, and events give you an overall description of your computer.

But your computer is also a collection of objects, each with its own properties, methods, and events. The hard drive, for example, has various properties, including its speed and data-transfer rate. The hard drive's methods are actions such as storing and retrieving data. A hard drive event may be a scheduled maintenance task, such as checking the drive for errors.

In the end, you have a complete description of the computer: its appearance (its properties), how you interact with it (its methods), and to what actions it responds (its events).

Manipulating object properties

All JavaScript objects have at least one property, and some of them have a couple dozen or more. What you do with these properties depends on the object, but you generally use them for the following tasks:

>> **Gathering information about an object's current settings:** With an element object (such as a `div` or `p` element), for example, you can use the `textContext` property to get whatever text is currently in the element.

>> **Changing an object's current settings:** For example, you can use the `document` object's `location` property to send the web browser to a different URL.

>> **Changing an object's appearance:** With an element's `style` object, for example, you can use the `fontSize` property to change the size of the element's text.

Referencing a property

Whatever the task, you refer to a property by using the syntax in the following generic expression:

```
object.property
```

where:

>> *object* is the object that has the property.

>> *property* is the name of the property you want to work with.

The dot (.) in between is called the *property access operator*.

For example, consider the following expression:

```
document.location
```

This expression refers to the document object's location property, which holds the address of the document (usually a web page) currently displayed in the browser window. (In conversation, you'd pronounce this expression as "document dot location.") The following code (check out bk03ch06/example01.html in this book's example files) shows a simple one-line script that displays this property in the console, as shown in Figure 6-1.

```
console.log(document.location);
```

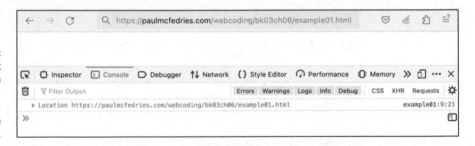

To display the console in most web browsers, right-click the web page, click Inspect (or press Ctrl+Shift+I in Windows or Option+⌘+I in macOS), and then click the Console tab.

Because the property always contains a value, you're free to use property expressions in just about any type of JavaScript statement and as an operand in a JavaScript expression. For example, the following statement assigns the current value of the document.location property to a variable named currentUrl:

```
const currentUrl = document.location;
```

Similarly, the following statement includes document.location as part of a string expression:

```
const message = "The current address is " + document.
  location + ".";
```

Realizing that some properties are objects

Just to keep you on your toes when you're working with objects, you'll constantly come across a common but mystifying notion: Some properties pull double-duty as full-fledged objects! This property/object double identity is one of the most confusing aspects of the relationship between objects and properties, but it's also one of the most important, so I'll dive into this a bit deeper to make sure you understand what's going on.

The basic idea is that the value returned by a property is usually a literal (which is programmer-speak for "it is what it is") such as a string or number, but sometimes it's an object. An example of the latter is the document object's location property, which actually returns a Location object. Because location is an object, it also has its own properties. For example, it has a hostname property that references just the host name part of the address (for example, paulmcfedries.com). To work with this property, you extend the expression syntax accordingly:

```
document.location.hostname
```

Changing the value of a property

Some properties are *read only*, which means your code can only read the current value and can't change it. However, many properties are *read/write*, which means you can also change their values. To change the value of a property, use the following generic syntax:

```
object.property = value
```

where:

>> *object* is the object that has the property.

>> *property* is the name of the property you want to change.

>> *value* is a literal value (such as a string or number) or an expression that returns the value to which you want to set the property.

Here's an example (bk03ch06/example02.html):

```
const newAddress = prompt("Enter the address you want
    to surf to:");
document.location = newAddress;
```

This script prompts the user for a web page address and stores the result in the newAddress variable. This value is then used to change the document.location property, which in this case tells the browser to open the specified address.

Working with object methods

Every JavaScript object has at least one or two methods that you can wield to make the object do something. These actions generally fall into the following categories:

>> **Simulate a user's action:** For example, the form object's submit() method submits a form to the server just as though the user clicked the form's submit button.

>> **Perform a calculation:** For example, the Math object's sqrt() method calculates the square root of a number.

>> **Manipulate an object:** For example, the String object's toLowerCase() method changes all of a string's letters to lowercase.

To run a method, begin with the simplest case, which is a method that takes no arguments:

```
object.method()
```

where:

>> *object* is the object that has the method you want to work with.

>> *method* is the name of the method you want to execute.

For example, consider the following statement:

```
history.back();
```

This runs the `history` object's `back()` method, which tells the browser to go back to the previously visited page. The following code shows this method at work (bk03ch06/example03.html):

```
const goBack = confirm("Do you want to go back?");
if (goBack === true) {
    history.back();
}
```

The user is first asked whether they want to go back. If the user clicks OK, the Boolean value `true` is stored in the `goBack` variable and the comparison expression `goBack === true` becomes `true`, so the `history.back()` method runs.

I mention in Book 3, Chapter 5 that you can define a function so that it accepts one or more arguments, and these arguments are then used as input values for whatever calculations or manipulations the function performs. Methods are similar in that they can take one or more arguments and use those values as raw data.

If a method requires arguments, you use the following generic syntax:

```
object.method (argument1, argument2, ...)
```

For example, consider the `confirm()` method, used in the following statement, which takes a single argument — a string that specifies the text to display to the user:

```
confirm("Do you want to go back?")
```

Finally, as with properties, if the method returns a value, you can assign that value to a variable (as I do with the `confirm()` method in the earlier example) or you can incorporate the method into an expression.

Rolling your own objects

Although you'll mostly deal with prefab objects such as those built in to JavaScript or exposed by a Web API (refer to the next section), you can also create objects. Why would you ever want to do that? There are lots of reasons, but for our purposes here the biggest reason is that a custom object enables you to store multiple, related values in a single data structure.

For example, suppose your script needs to work with the following user preferences for the styles that get applied to your page when the user visits: background color, text color, text size, and typeface. You could store these preferences in separate variables:

```
const userBgColor = "darkolivegreen";
const userTextColor = "antiquewhite";
const userTextSize = "1.25em";
const userTypeface = "Comic Sans";
```

This approach isn't terrible, but it feels a bit unwieldy, and it would *definitely* get unwieldy if you had to store this info for multiple users or if the number of preferences you had to store increased to 10 or 15 or more. Hey, it can happen!

A much easier and more flexible way to deal with such a collection of related data is to pour everything into a custom object using the following syntax:

```
const objectName = {
    propertyName1: value1,
    propertyName2: value2,
    ...
    propertyNameN: valueN
}
```

where:

» *objectName* is the variable name of the object.

» *propertyName1* through *propertyNameN* are the names of the object's properties.

» *value1* through *valueN* are the values assigned to the properties. Each value can be a literal value (such as a string, number, or Boolean), an array, a function result, a variable name (assuming the variable has already been declared and initialized), or even another object literal.

This data structure is called an *object literal*. Here's how you'd use an object literal to store the user preferences from earlier:

```
const userPrefs = {
    bgColor: "darkolivegreen",
    textColor: "antiquewhite",
    textSize: "1.25em",
    typeface: "Comic Sans"
};
```

You can then reference a property's value using the standard *property.value* syntax:

```
document.body.style.backgroundColor = userPrefs.bgColor;
```

You can also change a property value in the usual way:

```
userPrefs.textColor = "papayawhip";
```

REMEMBER

Wait, what!? I declared `userPrefs` with `const` and then I changed a property value? How is this possible? This common question strikes at the heart of what it means to declare a variable with `const`. In this case, `const` is binding `userPrefs` to a particular object, and you can't change that binding. However, you're free to change the *contents* of that object.

What about custom object methods? Yep, you can add them, as well:

```
const objectName = {
    propertyName1: value1,
    propertyName2: value2,
    ...
    propertyNameN: valueN,
    methodName: function([arguments]) {
        code
    }
};
```

where:

>> *methodName* is the name of the method.

>> *arguments* is an optional (comma-separated) list of the arguments taken by the method.

>> *code* is the JavaScript code to run when the method is invoked.

TIP

Instead of *methodName*: function(*arguments*), you can alternatively use *methodName*(*arguments*).

Here's an example (bk03ch06/example04.html):

```
const userPrefs = {
    bgColor: "darkolivegreen",
    textColor: "antiquewhite",
    textSize: "1.25em",
```

```
    typeface: "Comic Sans",
    resetDefaults: function() {
        document.body.style.backgroundColor = 'white';
        document.body.style.color = 'black';
        document.body.style.fontSize = '1em';
        document.body.style.fontFamily = 'initial';
    }
};
```

This code defines a resetDefaults() method that, when run, resets the background color, text color, text size, and typeface to their default values. Your code would invoke this method as follows:

```
userPrefs.resetDefaults();
```

Introducing the web APIs

JavaScript has its own set of built-in objects, including the String, Date, and Math objects, which are the subject of Book 3, Chapter 9. However, a huge collection of objects exists outside JavaScript, and these objects are available to your scripts. This collection consists of the web application programming interfaces, or web APIs, for short.

To understand how the web APIs work, consider your car (if you have one; if not, consider someone else's car). The engine inside the car is a monumentally complex piece of engineering, but you don't have to worry about any of that to start the car. Instead, all you have to do is insert the key (or fob, or whatever) into the ignition and turn (or push the button, or whatever). The complexity of the engine and its startup process is hidden from you and is reduced to putting the key (or fob or whatever) into the ignition.

From a programming point of view, the car engine is an object and the ignition is what's known as an *interface*: that is, a way of accessing the properties and methods of the object (such as the "method" of starting the engine).

In the simplest terms, an *application programming interface* (API) is a way for your JavaScript code to access a hidden (and presumably complex) object by exposing that object's properties and methods. Fortunately, many web APIs are built right into the web browser, so your JavaScript code can access many sophisticated objects right out of the box.

A good example is the Web Storage API, which enables your JavaScript code to store and retrieve data within the user's web browser. It's an extremely handy API, which is why I devote an entire chapter to it (refer to Book 3, Chapter 10).

Other web APIs enable you to access a device's battery state (Battery API), the clipboard (Clipboard API), server data (Fetch API), geolocation data (Geolocation API), audio (Web Audio API), and notifications (Web Notifications API).

However, for this chapter's purposes (and, indeed, for pretty much the rest of this book) the Big Kahuna API is the Document Object Model, which I turn to next.

Getting to Know the Document Object Model

Here's some source code for a simple web page:

```
<html lang="en">
    <head>
        <title>So Many Kale Recipes</title>
    </head>
    <body>
        <header>
            <h1>Above and Beyond the Kale of Duty</h1>
        </header>
        <main>
            <p>
                Do you love to cook with <a href="kale.
html">kale</a>?
            </p>
        </main>
    </body>
</html>
```

One way to examine this code is hierarchically. That is, the html element is the topmost element because every other element is contained within it. The next level down in the hierarchy contains the head and body elements. The head element contains a title element, which contains the text So Many Kale Recipes. Similarly, the body element contains a header element and a main element. The header element contains an h1 element with the text Above and Beyond the Kale of Duty, while the main element contains a p element with the text Do you love to cook with kale?.

Hierarchies are almost always more readily grasped in visual form, so Figure 6-2 graphs the page elements hierarchically.

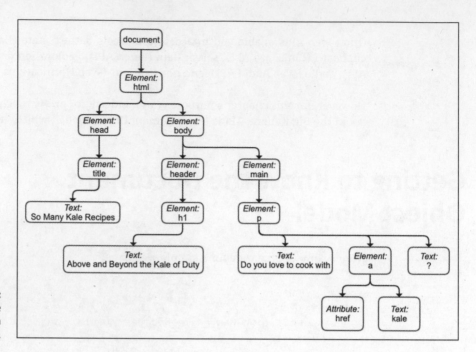

FIGURE 6-2:
The web page
code as a
hierarchy.

REMEMBER

When speaking of object hierarchies, if object P contains object C, object P is said to be the *parent* of object C, and object C is said to be the *child* of object P. In Figure 6-2, the arrows represent parent-to-child relationships. Also, elements on the same level — such as the header and main elements — are known as *siblings*.

You have several key points to consider here:

>> Every box in Figure 6-2 represents an object.

>> Every object in Figure 6-2 is one of three types: element, text, or attribute.

>> Every object in Figure 6-2, regardless of its type, is called a *node*.

>> The page as a whole is represented by the document object.

Therefore, this hierarchical object representation is known as the Document Object Model, or the DOM as it's usually called. The DOM is a web API that enables your JavaScript code to access the complete structure of an HTML document. This access is the source of one of JavaScript's most fundamental features: the capability it offers you as a web developer to read and change the elements of a web page, even after the page is loaded. To that end, this section presents a quick tour of some extremely useful and powerful JavaScript techniques for dealing with the DOM and the document object.

To get you started, Table 6-1 describes a few common properties of the document object.

TABLE 6-1   ## Useful Properties of the document Object

Property	What It Returns
activeElement	An object that represents the element that currently has the focus on the current web page
body	An object that represents the current web page's body element
childElementCount	The number of child elements in the current web page
children	A collection that contains all the current web page's elements
forms	A collection that contains all the current web page's form elements
head	An object that represents the current web page's head element
images	A collection that contains all the current web page's img elements
lastModified	The date and time the current web page was last changed
links	A collection that contains all the current web page's a elements
location	An object that represents the URL of the current web page
title	An object that represents the current web page's title element
URL	A string that contains the URL of the current web page

Specifying Elements

Elements represent the tags in a document, so you'll be using them constantly in your code. This section shows you several methods for referencing one or more elements.

Specifying an element by ID

If you want to work with a specific element in your script, you can reference the element directly by first assigning it an identifier using the id attribute:

```
<header id="page-banner">
```

With that done, you can then refer to the element in your code by using the document object's getElementById() method:

```
document.getElementById(id)
```

where *id* is a string representing the id attribute of the element you want to work with.

For example, the following statement (refer to bk03ch06/example05.html) returns a reference to the previous <div> tag (the one that has id=" kale-quotations"):

```
document.getElementById("page-banner")
```

When you're coding the document object, don't put your <script> tag in the web page's head section (that is, between the <head> and </head> tags). If you place your code there, the web browser will run the code before it has had a chance to create the document object, which means your code will fail, big time. Instead, place your <script> tag at the bottom of the web page, just before the </body> tag.

Specifying elements by tag name

Besides working with individual elements, you can work also with collections of elements. One such collection is the set of all elements in a page that use the same tag name. For example, you could reference all the <a> tags or all the <div> tags. This is a handy way to make large-scale changes to these tags (such as by changing all the target attributes in your links).

The mechanism for returning a collection of elements that have the same tag is the getElementsByTagName() method:

```
document.getElementsByTagName(tag)
```

where *tag* is a string representing the HTML name used by the tags you want to work with.

This method returns an array-like collection that contains all the elements in the document that use the specified tag. (Refer to Book 3, Chapter 8 to find out how arrays work. Also check out "Working with collections of elements," later in this chapter.) For example, to return a collection that includes all the p elements in the current page, you'd use the following statement (bk03ch06/example05.html):

```
const paragraphs = document.getElementsByTagName("p");
```

Specifying elements by class name

Another collection you can work with is the set of all elements in a page that use the same class. The JavaScript tool for returning all the elements that share a specific class name is the getElementsByClassName() method:

```
document.getElementsByClassName(class)
```

where *class* is a string representing the class name used by the elements you want to work with.

This method returns an array-like collection that contains all the elements in the document that use the specified class name. The collection order is the same as the order in which the elements appear in the document. Here's an example (bk03ch06/example06.html):

```
const keywords = document.getElementsByClassName("keyword");
```

Specifying elements by selector

In Book 2, Chapter 2, I discuss CSS selectors, including the id, tag, and class selectors, the descendant, child, and subsequent-sibling combinators, pseudo-classes, and pseudo-elements. You can use those same selectors in your JavaScript code to reference page elements by using the document object's querySelector() and querySelectorAll() methods:

```
document.querySelector(selector)
document.querySelectorAll(selector)
```

where *selector* is a string representing the selector for the element or elements you want to work with.

The difference between these methods is that querySelectorAll() returns a collection of all the elements that match your selector, whereas querySelector() returns only the first element that matches your selector.

For example, the following statement returns the collection of all p elements that are direct children of a main element (bk03ch06/example07.html):

```
const main_paragraphs = document.querySelectorAll("main > p");
```

REMEMBER

Rather than use three distinct document object methods to reference page elements by id, tag, and class — that is, getElementById(), getElementsByTagName(), and getElementsByClassName() — many web developers prefer the more generic approach offered by querySelector() and querySelectorAll().

Working with collections of elements

The getElementsByTagName(), getElementsByClassName(), and query SelectorAll() methods each return an array-like collection that contains all the elements in the document that use the specified tag, class, or selector, respectively. The collection order is the same as the order in which the elements appear in the document. For example, consider the following HTML code (bk03ch06/example08.html):

```
<div id="div1">
    This, of course, is div 1.
</div>
<div id="div2">
    Yeah, well <em>this</em> is div 2!
</div>
<div id="div3">
    Ignore those dudes. Welcome to div 3!
</div>
```

Now consider the following statement:

```
divs = document.getElementsByTagName("div");
```

In the resulting collection, the first item (divs[0]) will be the <div> element with id equal to div1; the second item (divs[1]) will be the <div> element with id equal to div2; and the third item (divs[2]) will be the <div> element with id equal to div3.

You can also refer to elements directly by using their id values. For example, the following statements are equivalent:

```
const firstDiv = divs[0];
const firstDiv = divs.div1;
```

To learn how many items are in a collection, use the length property:

```
const totalDivs = divs.length;
```

To perform one or more operations on each item in the collection, you can use a for...of loop to run through the collection one item at a time. In the JavaScript trade, this is known as *iterating* over the collection. Here's the syntax to use:

```
for (const item of collection) {
    statements
}
```

where:

» *item* is a variable that holds an item in the collection. The first time through the loop, *item* is set to the first element in the collection; the second time through the loop, *item* is set to the second element; and so on.

» *collection* is the collection of elements you want to iterate over.

» *statements* is the JavaScript code you want to use to manipulate (or view, or whatever) *item*.

For example, here's some code that iterates over the preceding div elements and displays each item's id value in the console (refer to Book 5, Chapter 2 for details on the console), as shown in Figure 6-3 (bk03ch06.example08.html):

```
divs = document.getElementsByTagName("div");
for (const d of divs) {
    console.log(d.id);
}
```

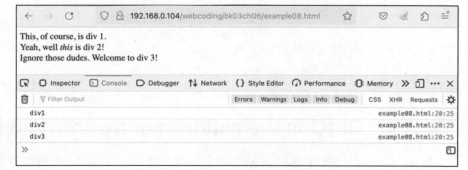

FIGURE 6-3:
The output of
the script that
iterates over the
div elements.

WARNING

The for...of loop is an ECMAScript 2015 (ES6) addition. If you need to support ancient browsers such as Internet Explorer 11, you can use a regular for loop, instead:

```
for (var i = 0; i < collection.length; i += 1) {
    statements
    // Use collection[i] to refer to each item
}
```

Traversing the DOM

One common task in JavaScript code is working with the children, parent, or siblings of some element in the page. This is known as *traversing the DOM* because you're using these techniques to move up, down, and along the DOM hierarchy.

In the sections that follow, I use the following HTML code for each example technique (bk03ch06/example09.html):

```html
<html lang="en">
    <head>
        <title>So Many Kale Recipes</title>
    </head>
    <body>
        <header id="page-banner">
            <h1>Above and Beyond the Kale of Duty</h1>
        </header>
        <main id="page-content">
            <p>
                Do you love to cook with <a href="kale.
    html">kale</a>?
            </p>
        </main>
    </body>
</html>
```

Getting the children of a parent element

When you're working with a particular element, it's common to want to perform one or more operations on that element's children. Every parent element offers several properties that enable you to work with all or just some of its child nodes:

» All the child nodes

» The first child node

» The last child node

Getting all the child nodes

To return a collection of all the child nodes of a parent element, use the `childNodes` property:

```
parent.childNodes
```

where *parent* is the parent element you're working with.

For example, the following statement stores all the child nodes of the body element in a variable:

```
const bodyChildren = document.body.childNodes;
```

The result is a NodeList object, which is a collection of nodes. If you were to use the console (refer to Book 5, Chapter 2) to display the value of bodyChildren, you'd get the output shown in Figure 6-4.

FIGURE 6-4:
The value of the bodyChildren variable displayed in the console.

TIP

If you need to iterate over a NodeList collection, you can use the for...of loop, which I talk about earlier in this chapter (head back to "Working with collections of elements").

Here's the output shown in the console:

```
NodeList(5) [ #text, header#page-banner, #text, main#page-
    content, #text ]
```

The (5) part tells you there are five items in the NodeList, and from the values within the square brackets you know that the nodes consist of the header and main elements, as expected, but also three text nodes. Where did those text nodes come from? They represent (in this example) the whitespace between the elements. For example, the first text node is the carriage return and eight spaces that appear between the end of the <body> tag and the start of the <header> tag. The other text nodes represent the whitespace between the </header> and <main> tags and between the </main> and </body> tags.

If what you really want is the collection of child nodes that are elements, you need to turn to a different property:

```
parent.children
```

where *parent* is the parent element.

For example, the following statement stores all the child element nodes of the body element in a variable:

```
const bodyChildElements = document.body.children;
```

The result is an HTMLCollection object, which is an array-like collection of element nodes. If you were to use the console (refer to Book 5, Chapter 2) to display the value of bodyChildElements, you'd get the output shown in Figure 6-5.

FIGURE 6-5:
The value of the bodyChild Elements variable displayed in the console.

Here's the output:

```
HTMLCollection { 0: header#page-banner, 1: main#page-content,
    length: 2 }
```

The numbers 0 and 1 are the index numbers of each child. For example, you could use bodyChildElements[0] to refer to the first element in the collection, which in this example is the header element.

Getting the first child node

If you use a parent element's childNodes or children property to return the parent's child nodes, as I describe in the preceding section, you can refer to the first item in the resulting collection by tacking [0] on to the collection's variable name. For example:

```
bodyChildren[0]
bodyChildElements[0]
```

However, the DOM offers a more direct route to the first child node:

```
parent.firstChild
```

where *parent* is the parent element.

For example, suppose you want to work with the first child node of the `main` element from the HTML example at the beginning of this section. Here's some code that'll do the job (bko3ch06/example10.html):

```
const content = document.getElementById("page-content");
const firstContentChildNode = content.firstChild;
```

In this example, the resulting node is a text node (the whitespace between the `<main>` and `<p>` tags. If you want the first child element node, use the `first ElementChild` property, instead:

```
parent.firstElementChild
```

where *parent* is the parent element.

To get the first child element node of the `main` element from the code at the beginning of this section, you'd do something like this (bko3ch06/example11.html):

```
const content = document.getElementById("page-content");
const firstContentChildElement = content.firstElementChild;
```

In this example, this code returns the `p` element.

Getting the last child node

If your code needs to work with the last child node, use the `lastChild` property of the parent element:

```
parent.lastChild
```

where *parent* is the parent element.

For example, suppose you want to work with the last child node of the p element from the HTML example at the beginning of this section. The following code will do the job (bk03ch06/example12.html):

```
const para = document.querySelector("main > p");
const lastParaChildNode = para.lastChild;
```

In this example, the resulting node is a text node representing the question mark (?) and the whitespace to the </p> tag. If you want the last child element node, use the lastElementChild property, instead:

```
parent.lastElementChild
```

where *parent* is the parent element.

To get the last child element node of the p element from the code at the beginning of this section, you could do this (bk03ch06/example13.html):

```
const para = document.querySelector("main > p");
const lastParaChildElement = para.lastElementChild;
```

In the example, this code returns the a element.

Getting the parent of a child element

If your code needs to work with the parent of a child element, use the child element's parentNode property:

```
child.parentNode
```

where *child* is the child element.

For example, suppose you want to work with the parent element of the h1 element from the HTML example at the beginning of this section. This code does the job (bk03ch06/example14.html):

```
const childElement = document.querySelector("h1");
const parentElement = childElement.parentNode;
```

Getting the siblings of an element

It's often important to work with an element's siblings in your code. Recall that an element's *siblings* are those elements in the DOM that share the same parent element.

A parent's child nodes appear in the DOM in the same order that they appear in the HTML code, which means the siblings also appear in the order they appear in the HTML code. Therefore, for a given child element, there are two sibling possibilities:

» **Previous sibling:** This is the sibling that appears in the DOM immediately before the child element you're working with. If the child element is the first sibling, it will have no previous sibling.

» **Next sibling:** This is the sibling that appears in the DOM immediately after the child element you're working with. If the child element is the last sibling, it will have no next sibling.

Getting the previous sibling

To return the previous sibling of a particular element, use the `previousElement Sibling` property:

```
element.previousElementSibling
```

where `element` is the element you're working with.

For example, the following statement stores the previous sibling of the `main` element in a variable (bk03ch06/example15.html):

```
const currElement = document.querySelector("main");
const prevSibs = currElement.previousElementSibling;
```

Getting the next sibling

To return the next sibling of a particular element, use the `nextElementSibling` property:

```
element.nextElementSibling
```

where `element` is the element you're working with.

For example, the following statement stores the next sibling of the `header` element in a variable (bk03ch06/example16.html):

```
const currElement = document.querySelector("header");
const nextSibs = currElement.nextElementSibling;
```

Manipulating Elements

Once you have a reference to one or more elements, you can use code to manipulate those elements in various ways, as shown in this section.

Adding an element to the page

One of the most common web development chores is to add elements to a web page on the fly. When you add an element, you always specify the parent element to which it will be added, and then you decide whether you want the new element added to the end or to the beginning of the parent's collection of children.

To add an element to the page, you follow three steps:

1. Create an object for the type of element you want to add.

2. Add the new object from Step 1 as a child element of an existing element.

3. Insert some text and tags into the new object from Step 1.

Step 1: Creating the element

For Step 1, you use the document object's createElement() method:

```
document.createElement(elementName)
```

where *elementName* is a string containing the HTML element name for the type of the element you want to create.

This method creates the element and then returns it, which means you can store the new element in a variable. Here's an example:

```
const newArticle = document.createElement("article");
```

Step 2: Adding the new element as a child

With your element created, Step 2 is to add it to an existing parent element. You have four choices:

>> **Append the new element to the end of the parent's collection of child elements:** Use the append() method:

```
parent.append(child)
```

where:

- *parent* is a reference to the parent element to which the new element will be appended.

- *child* is a reference to the child element you're appending. Note that you can append multiple elements at the same time by separating each element with a comma. The *child* parameter can also be a text string.

» **Prepend the new element to the beginning of the parent's collection of child elements:** Use the prepend() method:

```
parent.prepend(child)
```

where:

- *parent* is a reference to the parent element to which the new element will be prepended.

- *child* is a reference to the child element you're prepending. Note that you can prepend multiple elements at the same time by separating each element with a comma. The *child* parameter can also be a text string.

» **Insert the new element just after an existing child element of the parent:** Use the after() method:

```
child.after(sibling)
```

where:

- *child* is a reference to the child element after which the new element will be inserted.

- *sibling* is a reference to the new element you're inserting. Note that you can insert multiple elements at the same time by separating each element with a comma. The *sibling* parameter can also be a text string.

» **Insert the new element just before an existing child element of the parent:** Use the before() method:

```
child.before(sibling)
```

where:

- *child* is a reference to the child element before which the new element will be inserted.

- *sibling* is a reference to the new element you're inserting. Note that you can insert multiple elements at the same time by separating each element with a comma. The *sibling* parameter can also be a text string.

Here's an example that creates a new `article` element and then appends it to the `main` element (bk03ch06/example17.html):

```
const newArticle = document.createElement("article");
document.querySelector("main").append(newArticle);
```

Here's an example that creates a new `nav` element and then prepends it to the `main` element:

```
const newNav = document.createElement("nav");
document.querySelector("main").prepend(newNav);
```

Step 3: Adding text and tags to the new element

With your element created and appended or prepended to a parent, the final step is to add some text and tags using the `innerHTML` property:

```
element.innerHTML = text
```

where:

>> *element* is a reference to the new element within which you want to add the text and tags.

>> *text* is a string containing the text and HTML tags you want to insert.

WARNING

Whatever value you assign to the `innerHTML` property completely overwrites an element's existing text and tags, so use caution when wielding `innerHTML`. Check out the next section to learn how to insert text and tags rather than overwrite them.

In this example, the code creates a new `nav` element, prepends it to the `main` element, and then adds a heading (bk03ch06/example17.html):

```
const newNav = document.createElement("nav");
document.querySelector("main").prepend(newNav);
newNav.innerHTML = "<h2>Navigation</h2>";
```

Inserting text or HTML into an element

You can use an element's `innerHTML` property to overwrite that element's tags and text, as I describe in the preceding section. However, it's often the case that you want to keep the element's existing tags and text and insert new tags and text. Each element offers a couple of methods that enable you to do this:

» **To insert just text into an element:** Use the insertAdjacentText( )
method:

```
element.insertAdjacentText(location, text)
```

where:

- *element* is a reference to the element into which the new text will be inserted.

- *location* is a string specifying where you want the text inserted. I outline your choices for this argument below.

- *text* is a string containing the text you want to insert.

» **To insert tags and text into an element:** Use the insertAdjacentHTML( )
method:

```
element.insertAdjacentHTML(location, data)
```

where:

- *element* is a reference to the element into which the new tags and text will be inserted.

- *location* is a string specifying where you want the tags and text inserted. I outline your choices for this argument shortly.

- *data* is a string containing the tags and text you want to insert.

For both methods, you can use one of the following strings for the *location*
argument:

» "beforebegin": Inserts the data outside of and just before the element

» "afterbegin": Inserts the data inside the element, before the element's first child

» "beforeend": Inserts the data inside the element, after the element's last child

» "afterend": Inserts the data outside of and just after the element

For example, suppose your document has the following element:

```
<h2 id="nav-heading">Navigation</h2>
```

If you want to change the heading to Main Navigation, the following code will do
the job (bk03ch06/example18.html):

```
const navHeading = document.getElementById("nav-heading");
navHeading.insertAdjacentText("afterbegin", "Main ");
```

CHAPTER 6 **Playing with the Document Object Model** 331

Removing an element

If you no longer require an element on your page, you can use the element's remove() method to delete it from the DOM:

```
element.remove()
```

For example, the following statement removes the element with an id value of temp-div from the page:

```
document.getElementById("temp-div").remove();
```

Modifying CSS with JavaScript

Although you specify your CSS rules in a static stylesheet (.css) file, that doesn't mean the rules themselves have to be static. With JavaScript on the job, you can work with and modify an element's CSS in a number of ways. You can

>> Read the current value of a CSS property.

>> Change the value of a CSS property.

>> Add or remove a class.

>> Toggle a class on or off.

Why would you want to make these changes to your CSS? You already know that a big part of a well-designed web page is a strong CSS component that uses typography, colors, and spacing to create a page that's easily readable, sensibly navigable, and pleasing to the eye. But all that applies to the initial page displayed to the user. In the sorts of dynamic web apps that you're learning how to build, your page will change in response to some condition changing, such as the user clicking a button or pressing a key. This dynamic behavior needs to be matched with dynamic changes to the page, including changes to the CSS to highlight or reflect what's happening.

Changing an element's styles

Most HTML tags can have a style attribute that you use to set inline styles. Because standard attributes all have corresponding element object properties (as I explain a bit later in the "Tweaking HTML Attributes with JavaScript" section), you won't be surprised to learn that most elements also have a style property that enables you to get and modify a tag's styles. It works like this: The style property actually returns a style object that has properties for every CSS style. When referencing these style properties, you need to keep two things in mind:

>> For single-word CSS properties (such as color and visibility), use all-lowercase letters.

>> For multiple-word CSS properties, drop the hyphen and use uppercase for the first letter of the second word and for each subsequent word if the property has more than two. For example, the font-size and border-left-width CSS properties become the fontSize and borderLeftWidth style object properties, respectively.

Here's an example (bk03ch06/example19.html):

```
const pageTitle = document.querySelector("h1");
pageTitle.style.fontSize = "64px";
pageTitle.style.color = "maroon";
pageTitle.style.textAlign = "center";
pageTitle.style.border = "1px solid black";
```

This code gets a reference to the page's first <h1> element. With that reference in hand, the code then uses the style object to style four CSS properties of the heading: font-size, color, text-align, and border.

Adding a class to an element

If you have a class rule defined in your CSS, you can apply that rule to an element by adding the class attribute to the element's tag and setting the value of the class attribute equal to the name of your class rule. You can manipulate these classes using JavaScript.

First, you can get a list of an element's assigned classes by using the classList property:

```
element.classList
```

where element is the element you're working with.

The returned list of classes is an array-like object that includes an add() method that you can use to add a new class to the element's existing classes:

```
element.classList.add(class)
```

where:

>> *element* is the element you're working with.

>> *class* is a string representing the name of the class you want to add to *element*. You can add multiple classes by separating each class name with a comma.

Here's an example (bk03ch06/example20.html), and Figure 6-6 shows the result.

HTML:

```
<div id="my-div">
    Hello World!
</div>
```

CSS:

```
.my-class {
    display: flex;
    justify-content: center;
    align-items: center;
    border: 6px dotted black;
    font-family: Verdana, serif;
    font-size: 2rem;
    background-color: lightgray;
}
```

JavaScript:

```
document.getElementById('my-div').classList.add('my-class');
```

FIGURE 6-6:
This code uses the add() method to add the class named my-class to the <div> tag.

REMEMBER

If the class attribute doesn't exist in the element, the addClass() method inserts it into the tag. So, in the preceding example, after the code executes, the <div> tag would appears like this:

```
<div id="my-div" class="my-class">
```

Removing a class

To remove a class from an element's class attribute, the classList object offers the remove() method:

```
element.classList.remove(class)
```

where:

» *element* is the element you're working with.

» *class* is a string representing the name of the class you want to remove from *element*. You can remove multiple classes by separating each class name with a comma.

Here's an example:

```
document.getElementById('my-div').classList.remove('my-class');
```

Toggling a class

One common web development scenario is switching a web page element between two different states. For example, you may want to change an element's styles depending on whether a check box is selected or deselected, or you may want to alternate between showing and hiding an element's text when the user clicks the element's heading.

One way to handle switching between two states is to use the classList object's add() method to add a particular class when the element is in one state (for example, the user clicks the element's header for the first time) and then use the remove() method to remove that class when the element is in the other state (for example, the user clicks the element's header for a second time).

That approach would work, but your code would have to check the element's current state, using something like this pseudo-code:

```
if (the element has the class applied) {
    remove the class
```

```
} else {
    add the class
}
```

That's a lot of extra work, but fortunately it isn't work you have to worry about because your old friend the classList object has got your back on this one. The toggle() method does the testing for you. That is, it checks the element for the specified class. If the class is there, JavaScript removes it; if the class isn't there, JavaScript adds it. Sweet! Here's the syntax:

```
element.classList.toggle(class)
```

where:

>> *element* is the element you're working with.

>> *class* is a string representing the name of the class you want to toggle for *element*.

Here's an example:

```
document.getElementById('my-div').classList.toggle('my-class');
```

Tweaking HTML Attributes with JavaScript

One of the key features of the DOM is that each tag on the page becomes an element object. You may be wondering, do these element objects have any properties? Yep, they have tons. In particular, if the tag included one or more attributes, those attributes become properties of the element object.

For example, consider the following `<img>` tag:

```
<img id="header-image"
    src="mangosteen.png"
    alt="Drawing of a mangosteen">
```

This tag has three attributes: id, src, and alt. In the DOM's representation of the `<img>` tag, these attributes become properties of the img element object. Here's some JavaScript code that references the img element (bk03ch06/example21. html):

```
const headerImage = document.getElementById("header-image");
```

The headerImage variable holds the img element object, so your code could now reference the img element's attribute values with any of the following property references:

```
headerImage.id
headerImage.src
headerImage.alt
```

However, the DOM doesn't create properties either for custom attributes or for attributes added programmatically (as I describe in the preceding section). Fortunately, each element object also offers methods that enable you to read any attribute, as well as add, modify, or remove the element's attributes. The next few sections tell all.

Reading an attribute value

If you want to read the current value of an attribute for an element, use the element object's getAttribute() method:

```
element.getAttribute(attribute)
```

where:

>> *element* is the element you want to work with.

>> *attribute* is the name of the attribute you want to read.

Here's an example that gets the src attribute of the element with an id value of header-image:

```
const headerImage = document.getElementById("header-image");
const srcHeaderImage = headerImage.getAttribute("src");
```

Setting an attribute value

To set an attribute value on an element, use the element object's setAttribute() method:

```
element.setAttribute(attribute, value);
```

where:

>> *element* is the element you want to work with.

>> *attribute* is the name of the attribute you want to set.

>> *value* is the string value you want to assign to *attribute*.

If the attribute already exists, setAttribute overwrites the attribute's current value; if the attribute doesn't exist, setAttribute adds it to the element.

Here's an example that sets the alt attribute for the element with an id value of header-image:

```
const headerImage = document.getElementById("header-image");
headerImage.setAttribute("alt", "Lithograph of a mangosteen");
```

Removing an attribute

To remove an attribute from an element, use the element object's removeAttribute() method:

```
element.removeAttribute(attribute);
```

where:

>> *element* is the element you want to work with.

>> *attribute* is a string specifying the name of the attribute you want to remove from the element.

Here's an example:

```
const headerImage = document.getElementById("header-image");
headerImage.removeAttribute("id");
```

Chapter 7

Building Reactive Pages with Events

Handle your tools without mittens.

— BENJAMIN FRANKLIN

W hen you buy a car, no matter how much you paid for it or how technologically advanced it is, the car just sits there unless you do something. (If you're reading this in a future in which all cars are autonomous, my apologies.) Having a car just sitting there may be fine if it's a good-looking car, but you're likely to want the car to do something, anything. Here's a short list of actions you can take to achieve that goal:

>> Start the car.

>> Put the transmission into gear.

>> Press the accelerator.

>> Turn on the radio.

The common denominator for all these actions is that they set up a situation to which the car must respond in some way: turning on, engaging the gears, moving, playing sounds. Approached from this angle, the car is a machine that responds to external stimuli, or, in a word, events.

Somewhat surprisingly, a web page is also a machine that responds to external stimuli. Read on to discover what I mean.

What's an Event?

In web development, an *event* is an action that occurs in response to some external stimulus. A common type of external stimulus is when a user interacts with a web page. Here are some examples:

>> Surfing to or reloading the page

>> Clicking a button

>> Pressing a key

>> Scrolling the page

How can your web page possibly know when any of these actions occur? The secret is that JavaScript was built with events in mind. As the computer science professors would say, JavaScript is an *event-driven* language.

So why don't web pages respond to events automatically? Why do they just sit there? Because web pages are *static* by default, meaning they ignore the events firing all around them. Your job as a web developer is to change that behavior by making your web pages "listen" for particular events to occur. You do that by setting up special chunks of code called *event handlers* that say, in effect, "Be a dear and watch out for event X to occur, will you? When it does, be so kind as to execute the code I've placed here for you. Thanks so much." An event handler consists of two parts:

>> **Event listener:** An instruction to the web browser to watch out ("listen") for a particular event occurring on a particular element

>> **Callback function:** The code that the web browser executes when it detects that the event has occurred

In the rest of this chapter, I talk about how to use JavaScript to build your own event handlers and take your scripts to a more interactive level.

Understanding the Event Types

Your web page can respond to dozens of possible events, but lucky for you only a small subset of these events are needed in most day-to-day web development. I'll break these down into the following five categories:

>> **Document:** Events that fire in relation to the loading of the document object. The only event you need to worry about here is DOMContentLoaded, which fires when the document object has completed loading.

>> **Mouse:** Events that fire when the user does something with the mouse (or a similar device, such as a trackpad or touchscreen). The most important events in this category are click (the user clicks the mouse); dblclick (the user double-clicks the mouse); and mouseover (the user moves the mouse pointer over an element).

>> **Keyboard:** Events that fire when the user interacts with the keyboard. The main event in this category is keydown, which fires when a key is pressed, but not yet released, which is great for creating keyboard shortcuts (a technique I describe in Book 6, Chapter 2). (If you need to monitor when the user releases a pressed key, use the keyup event.)

>> **Form:** Events associated with web page forms. The important ones are focus (an element gains the focus, for example, when the user tabs to a form control); blur (an element loses the focus); change (the user changes the value of a form control); and submit (the user submits the form). Check out Book 6, Chapters 2 and 3 to learn about forms and form events.

>> **Browser window:** Events that fire when the user interacts with the browser window. The two main events here are scroll, which fires when the user scrolls the window vertically or horizontally, and resize, which fires when the user changes the window width or height.

Listening for an Event

You configure your code to listen for and react to an event by setting up an event handler using the element object's addEventListener() method. Here's the syntax:

```
element.addEventListener(event, callback)
```

where:

» *element* is the web page element to be monitored for the event. The event is said to be *bound* to the element.

» *event* is a string specifying the name of the event you want the browser to listen for. For the main events I mention in the preceding section, use one of the following, enclosed in quotation marks: DOMContentLoaded, click, dblclick, mouseover, keypress, focus, blur, change, submit, scroll, or resize.

» *callback* is the callback function that JavaScript executes when the event occurs. The callback can be an anonymous function or a reference to a named function.

Here's an example (bk03ch07/example01.html):

HTML:

```
<div id="my-div"></div>
<button id="my-button">Click to add some text, above</button>
```

JavaScript:

```
const myButton = document.getElementById('my-button');
myButton.addEventListener('click', function() {
    const myDiv = document.getElementById('my-div');
    myDiv.innerHTML = '<h1>Hello Click World!</h1>';
});
```

The HTML code sets up an empty div element and a button element. The JavaScript code attaches a click event listener to the button, and the callback function adds the HTML string <h1>Hello Click World!</h1> to the div. Figure 7-1 shows the resulting page after the button has been clicked.

FIGURE 7-1:
The click event callback function adds some HTML and text to the div element.

Getting Data about the Event

When an event fires, the DOM creates an Event object, the properties of which contain info about the event, including the following:

>> target: The web page element to which the event occurred. For example, if you set up a click handler for a div element, that div is the target of the click.

>> which: A numeric code that specifies the key that was pressed during a keypress event.

>> pageX: The distance (in pixels) of the mouse pointer from the left edge of the browser's content area when the event fired.

>> pageY: The distance (in pixels) of the mouse pointer from the top edge of the browser's content area when the event fired.

>> metaKey: A Boolean value that equals true if the user had the Windows key (⊞) or the Mac Command key (⌘) held down when the event fired.

>> shiftKey: A Boolean value that equals true if the user had the Shift key held down when the event fired.

To access these properties, you insert a name for the Event object as an argument in your event handler's callback function:

```
element.addEventListener(event, function(e) {
    This code runs when the event fires
});
```

where e is a name for the Event object that the DOM generates when the event fires. You can use whatever name you want, but most coders use e (although evt and event are also common).

For example, when handling the keydown event, you need access to the Event object's which property to find out the code for the key the user is pressing. Here's an example page that can help you determine which code value to check for (bk03ch07/example02.html):

HTML:

```
<div>
    Type a key:
</div>
<input id="key-input" type="text">
```

```
<div>
    Here's the code of the key you pressed:
</div>
<div id="key-output">
</div>
```

JavaScript:

```
const keyInput = document.getElementById('key-input');
keyInput.addEventListener('keydown', function(e) {
    const keyOutput = document.getElementById('key-output');
    keyOutput.innerHTML = e.which;
});
```

The HTML code sets up an `<input>` tag to accept a keystroke and a `<div>` tag with id="key-output" to use for the output. The JavaScript code adds a keydown event listener to the `input` element, and when the event fires, the callback function writes e.which to the output `div`. Figure 7-2 shows the page in action.

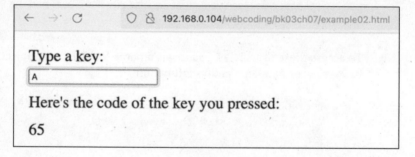

Preventing the Default Event Action

TIP

Some events come with default actions that they perform when the event fires. For example, a link's click event opens the target URL, whereas a form's submit event sends the form data to a script on the server. Most of the time, these default actions are exactly what you want, but that's not always the case. For example, you may want to intercept a link click to perform some custom action, such as displaying a menu. Similarly, rather than let the browser submit a form, you may prefer to massage the form data and then send the data via your script (as I demonstrate in Book 6, Chapter 2).

For these and many similar situations, you can tell the web browser not to per-form an event's default action by running the Event object's preventDefault() method:

```
event.preventDefault();
```

where *event* is a reference to the Event object that the DOM creates when an event fires.

For example, examine the following code (bk03ch07/example03.html):

HTML:

```
<a href="https://wiley.com/">Wiley</a><br>
<a href="https://262.ecma-international.org/6.0/">ECMAScript
    2015 Spec</a><br>
<a href="https://webdev.mcfedries.com/tools/workbench/">Web Dev
    Workbench</a>
<div id="output">
    Link URL:
</div>
```

JavaScript:

```
const links = document.getElementsByTagName('a')
for (const link of links) {
    link.addEventListener('click', function(e) {
        e.preventDefault();
        strURL = e.target.href;
        document.getElementById('output').innerHTML = 'Link
    URL: ' + strURL;
    })
}
```

The HTML code defines three links (styled as inline blocks, which I haven't shown here) and a div element. The JavaScript uses a for...of loop to set up a click event listener for all a elements, and the callback function does three things:

>> It uses the e.preventDefault() method to tell the browser not to navigate to the link address.

>> It uses e.target.href to get the URL of the link.

>> It displays that URL in the div element. Figure 7-3 shows an example.

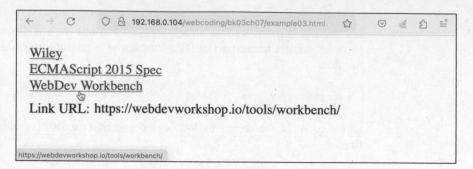

FIGURE 7-3:
You can use
`e.prevent
Default()` to
stop the browser
from navigating
to the link URL.

Example: The DOMContentLoaded Event

If you want to run some code after the web page document has loaded, add an event handler to the `document` object that listens for the `DOMContentLoaded` event. Here's an example (bk03ch07/example04.html):

```html
<head>
    <meta charset="utf-8">
    <title>Running code after the page is loaded</title>
    <script>
    document.addEventListener('DOMContentLoaded', function() {

        //Display a message in the console
        console.log('Yep, the DOM is now loaded!');

        // Access an element
        const output = document.getElementById('output');
        output.innerHTML = `Look, ma, I can access the DOM
                            from the <code>head</code>
                            element. <em>Awesome</em>!!!`;
    });
    </script>
</head>
<body>
    <div id="output"></div>
</body>
```

Figure 7-4 shows the result.

TIP

If your eyes are sharp, you might have noticed that the `innerHTML` value is a string surrounded by back ticks (`) instead of the usual quotation marks. This is a trick to enable multiline strings. I explain these string templates in Book 3, Chapter 9.

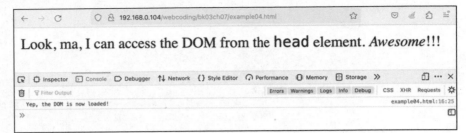

FIGURE 7-4:
The output of the DOMContent Loaded event handler.

In my coverage of the Document Object Model (DOM) in Book 3, Chapter 6, I mention that when your JavaScript code needs to reference a DOM object, you need to place your `<script>` tag near the bottom of the HTML file, just above the `</body>` tag. That way, you can be sure that the DOM object is loaded before your script tries to access it.

However, in the callback function for the `DOMContentLoaded` event listener, notice that even though the script resides in the head element, the code is still able to reference and work with DOM elements. JavaScript can access the DOM in this case because the `DOMContentLoaded` event fires only after the DOM has completed its loading chores.

Example: The dblclick Event

The `dblclick` event fires when the user double-clicks the primary button of a mouse or double-taps a pointing device such as a trackpad or a touchscreen.

Here's an example (bk03ch07/example05.html):

HTML:

```
<p>Double-click an image to expand/shrink it</p>
<div>
    <img src="image01.jpg" class="thumbnail" alt="">
</div>
<div>
    <img src="image02.jpg" class="thumbnail" alt="">
</div>
<div>
    <img src="image03.jpg" class="thumbnail" alt="">
</div>
```

CSS:

```css
.thumbnail {
    width: 100px;
    height: auto;
}
.full-size {
    width: 100%;
}
```

JavaScript:

```javascript
// Get all the img elements
const images = document.getElementsByTagName('img');

// Loop through the images
for (const image of images) {

    // Listen for the dblclick event on each image
    image.addEventListener('dblclick', function(e) {

        // Prevent the default action
        e.preventDefault();

        // Toggle the full-size class on the image
        image.classList.toggle('full-size');
    });
}
```

The HTML code sets up the page with three images, each of which is assigned the class thumbnail. In the CSS, that thumbnail class scales each image down to a width of 100px. The JavaScript first returns the collection of img elements on the page, and then loops through that collection to add a listener for the dblclick event to each image. The callback function prevents the default action and then toggles the full-size class, which sets the image width to 100%. In practice, double-clicking (or double-tapping) an image expands it to the width of the browser window; double-clicking (or double-tapping) the same image shrinks the image back to its thumbnail size.

IN THIS CHAPTER

» **Learning what arrays can do for you**

» **Declaring an array variable**

» **Populating an array with data**

» **Trying out multidimensional arrays**

» **Working with JavaScript's Array object**

Chapter **8**

Working with Arrays

I choose a lazy person to do a hard job. Because a lazy person will find an easy way to do it.

— BILL GATES

I talk quite a bit about efficient programming in this book because I believe (okay, I know) that efficient scripts run faster and take less time to program and debug. Efficiency in programming really means eliminating unnecessary repetition, whether it's consolidating statements into a loop that can be repeated as often as required (refer to Book 3, Chapter 4) or moving code into a function that can be called as often as you need (refer to Book 3, Chapter 5).

In this chapter, you take your coding efficiency to an even higher level by exploring one of JavaScript's most important concepts: the array. Arrays are important not only because they're extremely efficient and very powerful, but also because after you know how to use them, you'll think of a thousand and one uses for them. To make sure you're ready for your new array-filled life, this chapter explains what they are and why they're so darn useful, and then explores all the fantastic ways that arrays can make your coding life easier.

What Is an Array?

One common source of unnecessary code repetition involves variables. For example, consider the following declarations:

```
const dog1 = "dog-1";
const dog2 = "dog-2";
const dog3 = "dog-3";
const dog4 = "dog-4";
const dog5 = "dog-5";
```

These are string variables and they store the names of some dog photos.

This code may not seem outrageously inefficient, but what if instead of five images you had to take 10, 20, or even 100 images into account? I'm sure the idea of typing 100 const declarations isn't your idea of a good time.

To understand the solution to this problem, first understand that the variables dog1 through dog5 all contain related values. That is, each variable holds part of the filename of a dog photo, which in turn is part of the full URL for that image. In JavaScript (or, indeed, in just about any programming language), whenever you have a collection of variables with related data, you can group them into a single variable called an *array.* You can enter as many values as you want into the array, and JavaScript tracks each value using an *index number.* For example, the first value you add is given the index 0. (For obscure reasons, programmers since time immemorial have started numerical lists with 0 instead of 1.) The second value you put into the array is given the index 1; the third value gets 2; and so on. You can then access any value in the array by specifying the index number you want.

The next couple of sections flesh out this theory with the specifics of creating and populating an array.

Declaring an Array

Because an array is a type of variable, you need to declare it before using it. In fact, unlike regular numeric, string, or Boolean variables that don't need to be declared (but always should be), an array must be declared in advance. You use the const (or let) statement, but this time with a slightly different syntax. Actually, there are four syntaxes you can use. Here's the syntax that's the most informative:

```
const arrayName = new Array();
```

Here, *arrayName* is the name you want to use for the array variable.

In JavaScript, an array is an object, so what the new keyword is doing here is creating a new Array object. The Array() part of the statement is called a *constructor* because its job is to construct the object in memory. For example, to create an array named dogPhotos, you'd use the following statement:

```
const dogPhotos = new Array();
```

The second syntax is useful if you know in advance the number of values (or *elements*) you'll be putting into the array:

```
const arrayName = new Array(num);
```

where:

>> *arrayName* is the name you want to use for the array variable.

>> *num* is the number of values you'll be placing into the array.

For example, here's a statement that declares a new dogPhotos array with five elements:

```
const dogPhotos = new Array(5);
```

If you're not sure how many elements you need, don't worry because JavaScript is happy to let you add elements to and delete elements from the array as needed, and it will grow or shrink the array to compensate. I talk about the other two array declaration syntaxes in the next section.

Populating an Array with Data

After your array is declared, you can start populating it with the data values you want to store. Here's the general syntax:

```
arrayName[index] = value;
```

where:

>> *arrayName* is the name of the array variable.

>> *index* is the array index number where you want the value stored.

>> *value* is the value you're storing in the array.

JavaScript is willing to put just about any type of data inside an array, including numbers, strings, Boolean values, and even other arrays! You can even mix multiple data types within a single array.

TIP

You most commonly add new elements to the end of the array. Happily, the Array object has a special method for doing just that. It's called push( ), and I talk about it later in this chapter (specifically, the section "Adding elements to the end of an array: push()").

As an example, here are a few statements that declare a new array named dog Photos and then enter five string values into the array (check out bk03ch08/example01.html in this book's example files):

```
const dogPhotos = new Array(5);
dogPhotos[0] = "dog-1";
dogPhotos[1] = "dog-2";
dogPhotos[2] = "dog-3";
dogPhotos[3] = "dog-4";
dogPhotos[4] = "dog-5";
```

REMEMBER

When you declare an array using const, it just means that the variable name is bound to that particular array and that binding can't be changed. It doesn't mean you can't make changes to the contents of that array.

To reference an array value (say, to use it in an expression), you specify the appropriate index:

```
strURL + dogPhotos[3]
```

The following code offers a complete example (check out bk03ch08/example02.html):

HTML:

```
<div id="output">
</div>
```

JavaScript:

```
// Declare the array
const dogPhotos = new Array(5);

// Initialize the array values
dogPhotos[0] = "dog-1";
```

```
dogPhotos[1] = "dog-2";
dogPhotos[2] = "dog-3";
dogPhotos[3] = "dog-4";
dogPhotos[4] = "dog-5";

// Display an example
document.getElementById('output').innerHTML = '<img
    src="images/' + dogPhotos[0] + '.png" alt="">';
```

Declaring and populating an array at the same time

Earlier I mentioned that JavaScript has two other syntaxes for declaring an array. Both enable you to declare an array *and* populate it with values by using just a single statement.

The first method uses the Array() constructor in the following general format:

```
const arrayName = new Array(value1, value2, ...);
```

where:

➤ *arrayName* is the name you want to use for the array variable.

➤ *value1*, *value2*, ... are the initial values with which you want to populate the array.

Here's an example:

```
const dogPhotos = new Array("dog-1", "dog-2", "dog-3", "dog-4",
    "dog-5");
```

JavaScript also supports the creation of *array literals*, which are similar to string, numeric, and Boolean literals. In the same way that you create, say, a string literal by enclosing a value in quotation marks, you create an array literal by enclosing one or more values in square brackets. Here's the general format:

```
const arrayName = [value1, value2, ...];
```

where:

» *arrayName* is the name you want to use for the array variable.

» *value1*, *value2*, ... are the initial values with which you want to populate the array.

An example:

```
const dogPhotos= ["dog-1", "dog-2", "dog-3", "dog-4", "dog-5"];
```

Most JavaScript programmers prefer this syntax over using the `Array` constructor.

REMEMBER

Including values in the declaration of an array literal is optional, which means that you can declare an empty array using the following statement:

```
const arrayName = [];
```

Using a loop to populate an array

So far, you probably don't think arrays are all that much more efficient than using separate variables. That's because you haven't yet learned about the single most powerful aspect of working with arrays: using a loop and a counter variable to access an array's index number programmatically.

For example, here's a `for()` loop that replaces the six statements I used earlier to declare and initialize the `dogPhotos` array:

```
const dogPhotos = [];
for (let counter = 0; counter < 5; counter += 1) {
    dogPhotos[counter] = "dog-" + (counter + 1);
}
```

The statement inside the `for()` loop uses the `counter` variable as the array's index. For example, when `counter` is 0, the statement looks like this:

```
dogPhotos[0] = "dog-" + (0 + 1);
```

In this case, the expression to the right of the equals sign evaluates to `"dog-1"`, which is the correct value. The following code shows this loop technique at work (bk03ch08/example03.html):

HTML:

```html
<div id="output">
</div>
```

JavaScript:

```javascript
// Declare the array
const dogPhotos = [];

// Initialize the array values using a loop
for (let counter = 0; counter < 5; counter += 1) {
    dogPhotos[counter] = "dog-" + (counter + 1);
}

// Display an example
document.getElementById('output').innerHTML = '<img
    src="images/' + dogPhotos[0] + '.png" alt="">';
```

Using a loop to insert data into an array works best in two situations:

>> When the array values can be generated using an expression that changes with each pass through the loop

>> When you need to assign the same value to each element of the array

REMEMBER

If you declare your array with a specific number of elements, JavaScript doesn't mind at all if you end up populating the array with more than that number.

How Do I Iterate Thee? Let Me Count the Ways

The problem with using a large number of similar variables isn't so much declaring them but working with them in your code. Here's an example (bk03ch08/example01.html):

```javascript
const dog1 = "dog-1";
const dog2 = "dog-2";
const dog3 = "dog-3";
const dog4 = "dog-4";
const dog5 = "dog-5";
```

```
const promptNum = prompt("Enter the dog you want to see
    (1-5):", "");

if (promptNum !== "" && promptNum !== null) {
    const promptDog = "dog-" + promptNum;
    if (promptDog === dog1) {
        document.body.style.backgroundImage = "url('images/" +
dog1 + ".png')";
    } else if (promptDog === dog2) {
        document.body.style.backgroundImage = "url('images/" +
dog2 + ".png')";
    } else if (promptDog === dog3) {
        document.body.style.backgroundImage = "url('images/" +
dog3 + ".png')";
    } else if (promptDog === dog4) {
        document.body.style.backgroundImage = "url('images/" +
dog4 + ".png')";
    } else if (promptDog === dog5) {
        document.body.style.backgroundImage = "url('images/" +
dog5 + ".png')";
    }
}
```

In this example, the script has to use five separate if() tests to check the input value against all five variables.

Arrays can help make your code more efficient by enabling you to reduce these kinds of long-winded procedures to a much shorter routine that fits inside a function. These routines are iterative methods of the Array object, where *iterative* means that the method runs through the items in the array, and for each item, a function (known as a *callback*) performs some operation on or with the item.

The Array object has 14 iterative methods! I don't cover them all, but over the next few sections I talk about the most useful methods.

Iterating an array: forEach()

The Array object's forEach() method runs a callback function for each element in the array. That callback takes up to three arguments:

>> *value*: The value of the element

>> *index*: (Optional) The array index of the element

>> *array*: (Optional) The array being iterated

You can use any of the following syntaxes:

```
array.forEach(namedFunction);
array.forEach(function (value[, index][, array]) { code });
array.forEach((value[, index][, array]) => { code });
```

where:

» *array* is the Array object you want to iterate.

» *namedFunction* is the name of an existing function. This function should accept the *value* argument and can accept the optional *index* and *array* arguments.

» *code* is the statements to run during each iteration.

Here's an example (bk03ch08/example04.html):

```
// Declare the array
const dogPhotos= ["dog-1", "dog-2", "dog-3", "dog-4", "dog-5"];

// Iterate the array
dogPhotos.forEach((value, index) => {
    console.log("Element " + index + " has the value " + value);
});
```

After declaring the array, the code uses forEach() to iterate the array. During each iteration, console.log() (refer to Book 5, Chapter 2) displays a string that includes the index and value parameters. Figure 8-1 shows the results.

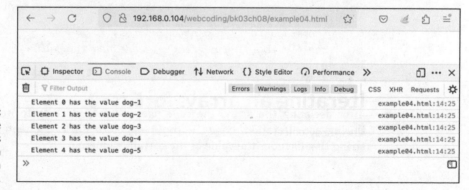

FIGURE 8-1:
The console messages displayed with each iteration using forEach().

To display the console in most web browsers, right-click the web page, click Inspect (or press Ctrl+Shift+I in Windows or Option+⌘+I in macOS), and then click the Console tab.

Iterating an array: for. . .of

Although you'll usually iterate an array with the `forEach()` method, you'll sometimes need to use a more traditional loop to run through each array element. That loop type is the `for...of` loop:

```
for (element of array) {
    code
}
```

where:

>> *array* is the Array object you want to iterate.

>> *element* it the current array element during each pass through the loop.

>> *code* is the statements to run during each iteration.

The `for...of` loop was introduced in ECMAScript 2015 (ES6), so don't use it if you need to support ancient browsers, such as Internet Explorer 11.

Here's an example (bk03ch08/example04a.html):

```
// Declare the array
const dogPhotos= ["dog-1", "dog-2", "dog-3", "dog-4", "dog-5"];

// Iterate the array
for (const currentPhoto of dogPhotos) {
    console.log("The current element has the value " +
  currentPhoto);
}
```

After declaring the array, the code uses a `for...of` loop to iterate the array. During each iteration, `console.log()` (refer to Book 5, Chapter 2) displays a string that includes the value of the current element.

Iterating to test an array's elements: every() and some()

One common array pattern is to check each array element value to determine whether some or all of the values pass some test. For example, if you have an array of interest rates as decimal values, you may want to test that they're all within a reasonable range (say, between 0.01 and 0.1). Similarly, suppose you have an array of numbers that at some point in your script will be used as divisors in a calculation. Before getting that far, you may want to determine if at least one of the numbers in the array is zero and, if so, whether your script would bypass the calculation.

Testing whether all elements pass a test: every()

To check whether all the elements in an array pass some test, use the Array object's every() method. There are three syntaxes you can use:

```
array.every(namedFunction);
array.every(function (value[, index][, array]) { code });
array.every((value[, index][, array]) => { code });
```

where:

>> *array* is the Array object with the values you want to test.

>> *namedFunction* is the name of an existing function that performs the test on each array value. This function should accept the *value* argument and can accept the optional *index* and *array* arguments.

>> *code* is the statements to run during each iteration to test each value.

In the *namedFunction* or *code*, use a return statement to send the result of the test back to the every() method. If all the array elements pass the test, every() returns true; otherwise, it returns false.

Here's an example (bk03ch08/example05.html):

```
// Declare an array of interest rates
const rates = [0.02, 0.025, 0.03, 0.035, 0.04, 0.045, 0.5];

// Test each rate
const legitRates = rates.every(currentValue => {
    return currentValue >= 0.01 && currentValue <= 0.1;
});

// Output the result
console.log(legitRates);
```

This code declares an array of interest rates (as decimal values). Then the `every()` method iterates the `rates` array and with each pass tests whether the current array element value (stored in the `currentValue` parameter) is between (or equal to) `0.01` and `0.1`. The final result is stored in the `legitRates` variable, the value of which is then displayed in the console, as shown in Figure 8-2. The result is `false` because the `rates` array includes the value `0.5`, which means that not every value is within the allowed range.

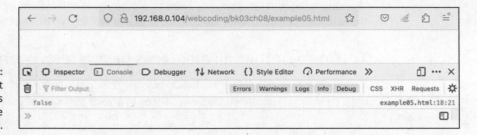

FIGURE 8-2:
The final result
(`false`, in this
case) of the
`every()` method.

REMEMBER

The `every()` method isn't a true iterative method because it stops iterating when it comes across the first array element value that doesn't pass the test.

Testing whether some elements pass a test: some()

To check whether at least one of the elements in an array passes some test, use the `Array` object's `some()` method. You can use three syntaxes:

```
array.some(namedFunction);
array.some(function (value[, index][, array]) { code });
array.some((value[, index][, array]) => { code });
```

where:

>> *array* is the `Array` object with the values you want to test.

>> *namedFunction* is the name of an existing function that performs the test on each array value. This function should accept the *value* argument and can accept the optional *index* and *array* arguments.

>> *code* is the statements to run during each iteration to test each value.

In the *namedFunction* or *code*, use a `return` statement to send the result of the test back to the `some()` method. If at least one array element passes the test, `some()` returns `true`; otherwise, it returns `false`.

Here's an example (bk03ch08/example06.html):

```
// Declare an array of divisors
const divisors = [27, 53, 6, 0, 17, 88, 32];

// Test each divisor
const zeroDivisors = divisors.some(currentValue => {
    return currentValue === 0;
});

// Output the result
console.log(zeroDivisors);
```

This code declares an array of divisors, and then the `some()` method iterates the `divisors` array and with each pass tests whether the current array element value (stored in the `currentValue` parameter) equals zero. The final result is stored in the `zeroDivisors` variable, the value of which is then displayed in the console, as shown in Figure 8-3. The result is `true` because the `divisors` array includes the value `0`, which means that at least one value passes the test.

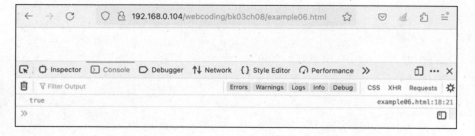

FIGURE 8-3:
The final result
(true, in this
case) of the
`some()` method.

REMEMBER

The `some()` method isn't a true iterative method because it stops iterating when it comes across the first array element value that passes the test.

Iterating to create a new array: map()

When you iterate an array, it's common to apply some operation to each element value. In some cases, however, you want to preserve the original array values and create another array that contains the updated values.

The easiest way to create an array that stores updated values of an existing array is to use the Array object's map() method. You can use three syntaxes:

```
array.map(namedFunction);
array.map(function (value[, index][, array]) { code });
array.map((value[, index][, array]) => { code });
```

where:

>> *array* is the Array object with the values you want to use.

>> *namedFunction* is the name of an existing function that performs the operation on each array value. This function should accept the *value* argument and can accept the optional *index* and *array* arguments.

>> *code* is the statements to run during each iteration to perform the operation on each value.

The map() method returns an Array object that contains the updated values, so be sure to store the result in a variable.

Here's an example (bk03ch08/example07.html):

```
// Declare an array of Fahrenheit temperatures
const tempsFahrenheit = [-40, 0, 32, 100, 212];

// Convert each array value to Celsius
const tempsCelsius = tempsFahrenheit.map(currentTemp => {
    return (currentTemp - 32) * 0.5556;
});

// Output the result
console.log(tempsCelsius);
```

This code declares an array of Fahrenheit temperatures, and then the map() method iterates the tempsFahrenheit array and with each pass converts the current Fahrenheit value (stored in the currentTemp parameter) to Celsius. The result is a new array named tempsCelsius, which is displayed in the console, as shown in Figure 8-4.

Iterating an array down to a value: reduce()

One common iteration pattern is to perform a cumulative operation on every element in an array to produce a value. For example, you may want to know the sum of all the values in the array.

FIGURE 8-4:
The map()
method creates
a new array
by applying an
operation to
each value in the
original array.

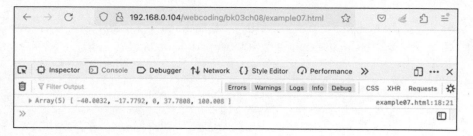

Iterating an array in this way to produce a value is the job of the Array object's reduce() method. You can use three syntaxes:

```
array.reduce(namedFunction, initialValue);
array.reduce(function (accumulator, value[, index][, array]) {
  code }, initialValue);
array.reduce((accumulator, value[, index][, array]) => { code },
  initialValue);
```

where:

>> *array* is the Array object with the values you want to reduce.

>> *namedFunction* is the name of an existing function that performs the reducing operation on each array value. This function should accept the *accumulator* and *value* arguments and can accept the optional *index* and *array* arguments.

>> *accumulator* is a parameter that stores the updated value of the reducing operation. With each iteration, *code* performs one or more operations that update the value of *accumulator*.

>> *code* is the statements to run during each iteration to perform the reducing operation on each value.

>> *initialValue* is the starting value of *accumulator*. If you omit *initialValue*, JavaScript uses the value of the first element in *array*.

Here's an example (bk03ch08/example08.html):

```
// Declare an array of product inventory
const unitsInStock = [547, 213, 156, 844, 449, 71, 313, 117];

// Get the total units in stock
const initialUnits = 0;
```

```
const totalUnits = unitsInStock.reduce((accumulatedUnits,
    currentInventoryValue) => {
    return accumulatedUnits + currentInventoryValue;
}, initialUnits);

// Output the result
console.log("Total units in stock: " + totalUnits);
```

This code declares an array of product inventory and declares `initialUnits` with a value of 0. Then the `reduce()` method (using `initialUnits` as the starting value of the accumulator) iterates the `unitsInStock` array and with each pass adds the current product inventory value (stored in the `currentInventoryValue` parameter) to the accumulator (stored in the `accumulatedUnits` parameter). The resulting total is stored in the `totalUnits` variable, which is then displayed in the console, as shown in Figure 8-5.

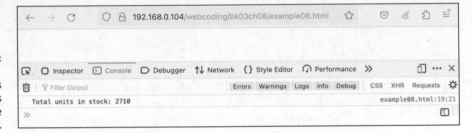

FIGURE 8-5:
The reduce()
method iterates
an array's values
down to a single
value.

Iterating to locate an element: find()

To search within an array for the first element that matches some condition, use the Array object's `find()` method. You can use three syntaxes:

```
array.find(namedFunction);
array.find(function (value[, index][, array]) { code });
array.find((value[, index][, array]) => { code });
```

where:

>> *array* is the Array object with the values in which you want to search.

>> *namedFunction* is the name of an existing function that applies the condition to each array value. This function should accept the *value* argument and can accept the optional *index* and *array* arguments.

>> *code* is the statements to run during each iteration to apply the condition to each value.

In the *namedFunction* or *code*, you set up a logical condition that tests each element in the array and use a `return` statement to send the result of the test back to the `find()` method. The final value returned by `find()` is the first element for which the test is `true`, or `undefined` if the test is `false` for all the array elements.

Here's an example (bk03ch08/example08a.html):

```javascript
// Declare an array of product objects
const products = [
    { name: 'doodad', units: 547 },
    { name: 'gizmo', units: 213 },
    { name: 'gimcrackery', units: 156 },
    { name: 'knickknack', units: 844 },
    { name: 'bric-a-brac', units: 449 },
    { name: 'thingamajig', units: 71 },
    { name: 'watchamacallit', units: 313 },
    { name: 'widget', units: 117 }
];

// Query the array
const strQuery = "gizmo";
const stock = products.find((currentProduct) => {
    return currentProduct.name === strQuery;
});

// Output the result
if (stock) {
    console.log("Product " + stock.name + " has " + stock.units
  + " units in stock.");
} else {
    console.log("Product " + strQuery + " not found.");
}
```

This code declares an array of object literals. Then the `find()` method iterates the `products` array and with each pass checks whether the `name` property of the current array element value (passed to the callback function using the `current Product` parameter) is equal to whatever value is stored in the `strQuery` variable. The result is stored in the `stock` variable. An `if` test checks the result: If `stock` is defined, the product name and inventory are displayed in the console; otherwise, a message saying the product was not found is displayed.

TIP

If you want to know the index number of the array item that matches the condition, use `findIndex()` instead of `find()`.

Creating Multidimensional Arrays

A *multidimensional array* is one where two or more values are stored in each array element. For example, if you want to create an array to store user data, you may need each element to store a first name, a last name, a username, a password, and more. The bad news is that JavaScript doesn't support multidimensional arrays. The good news is that you can use a trick to simulate a multidimensional array.

The trick is to populate your array in such a way that each element is itself an array. To understand how such an odd idea may work, first recall the general syntax for an array literal:

```
[value1, value2, ...]
```

Now recall the general syntax for assigning a value to an array element:

```
arrayName[index] = value;
```

In a one-dimensional array, the `value` is usually a string, number, or Boolean. Now imagine instead that `value` is an array literal. For a two-dimensional array, the general syntax for assigning an array literal to an array element looks like this:

```
arrayName[index] = [value1, value2];
```

As an example, say you want to store an array of background and foreground colors. Here's how you may declare and populate such an array:

```
const colorArray = [];
colorArray[0] = ['white', 'black'];
colorArray[1] = ['aliceblue', 'midnightblue'];
colorArray[2] = ['honeydew', 'darkgreen'];
```

Alternatively, you can declare and populate the array using only the array literal notation:

```
const colorArray = [
    ['white', 'black'],
    ['aliceblue', 'midnightblue'],
    ['honeydew', 'darkgreen']
];
```

Either way, you can then refer to individual elements using two sets of square brackets, as in these examples:

```
colorArray[0][0]; // Returns 'white'
colorArray[0][1]; // Returns 'black'
colorArray[1][0]; // Returns 'aliceblue'
colorArray[1][1]; // Returns 'midnightblue'
colorArray[2][0]; // Returns 'honeydew'
colorArray[2][1]; // Returns 'darkgreen'
```

The number in the left set of square brackets is the index of the overall array, and the number in the right set of square brackets is the index of the element array.

Manipulating Arrays

The Array object comes with a large collection of properties and methods that enable you to work with and manipulate arrays. The rest of this chapter takes a look at a few of the most useful of these properties and methods.

Working with the length property

The Array object has just a couple of properties, but the only one of these that you'll use frequently is the length property:

```
array.length
```

The length property returns the number of elements in the specified array. This is useful when looping through an array because it means you don't have to specify a literal as the maximum value of the loop counter. For example, consider the following for statement:

```
for (let counter = 0; counter < 5; counter += 1) {
    dogPhotos[counter] = "dog-" + (counter + 1);
}
```

This statement assumes that the dogPhotos array has five elements, which may not be the case. To enable the loop to work with any number of elements, replace 5 with dogPhotos.length:

```
for (let counter = 0; counter < dogPhotos.length; counter
  += 1) {
    dogPhotos[counter] = "dog-" + (counter + 1);
}
```

Note, too, that the loop runs while the counter variable is *less than* dogPhotos. length. That's because array indexes run from 0 to the array's length value minus 1. In other words, the preceding for loop example is equivalent to the following:

```
for (let counter = 0; counter <= dogPhotos.length - 1;
    counter += 1)
```

Concatenating to create an array: concat()

The concat() method takes the elements of one or more existing arrays and concatenates them to an existing array to create another array:

```
array.concat(array1, array2, ...)
```

where:

>> *array* is the name of the array you want to work with.

>> *array1*, *array2*, ... are the arrays you want to concatenate to *array*. These can also be values.

Note that the original array remains unchanged. The following code (bk03ch08/ example09.html) demonstrates using concat() to concatenate two arrays into a third array, each element of which is printed to the page, as shown in Figure 8-6.

```
// Declare the arrays
const array1 = ["One", "Two", "Three"];
const array2 = ["A", "B", "C"];

// Concatenate them
const array3 = array1.concat(array2);

// Display the concatenated array
console.log(array3);
```

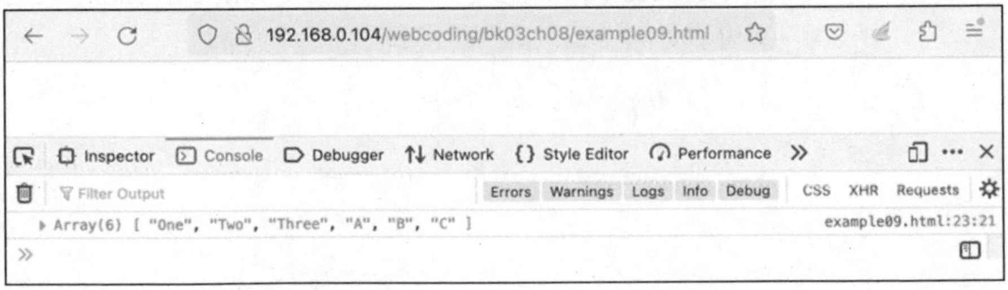

FIGURE 8-6:
Concatenating
array1 and
array2 produces
array3 with
the values
shown here.

Creating a string from an array's elements: join()

The `join()` method enables you to take the existing values in an array and concatenate them to form a string. Check out the syntax:

```
array.join([separator])
```

where:

>> *array* is the name of the array you want to work with.

>> *separator* is an optional character or string to insert between each array element when forming the string. If you omit this argument, a comma is inserted between each element.

In the following code (bk03ch08/example10.html), three arrays are created and then `join()` is applied to each array using a space as a separator in the first array, a null string ("") as a separator in the second, and no separator in the third. Figure 8-7 shows the resulting page output.

HTML:

```
<div id="output">
</div>
```

JavaScript:

```
// Declare the arrays
const array1 = ["Make", "this", "a", "sentence."];
const array2 = ["antid", "isest", "ablis", "hment", "arian",
   "ism"];
const array3 = ["John", "Paul", "George", "Ringo"];

//Join them to strings
const string1 = array1.join(" ");
const string2 = array2.join("");
const string3 = array3.join();

// Display the results
document.getElementById('output').innerHTML = string1 +
   '<br>' + string2 + '<br>' + string3;
```

FIGURE 8-7:
Joining the arrays
with a space, null
string (""), and
default comma.

> 192.168.0.104/webcoding/bk03ch08/example10.html

Make this a sentence.
antidisestablishmentarianism
John,Paul,George,Ringo

REMEMBER

The Array object's toString() method performs a similar function to the join() method. Using *array*.toString() takes the values in *array*, converts them all to strings, and then concatenates them into a single, comma-separated string. In other words, *array*.toString() is identical to *array*.join(","), or just *array*.join().

TIP

You can use the Array object's from() method to perform the opposite operation: create an array from a string, where the array elements are the individual string characters:

```
Array.from("Boo!") // Returns ["B", "o", "o", "!"]
```

Removing an array's last element: pop()

The pop() method removes the last element from an array and returns the value of that element. Here's the syntax:

```
array.pop()
```

For example, consider the following statements:

```
const myArray = ["First", "Second", "Third"];
const myString = myArray.pop();
```

The last element of myArray is "Third", so myArray.pop() removes that value from the array and stores it in the myString variable.

REMEMBER

After you run the pop() method, JavaScript reduces the value of the array's length property by one.

Adding elements to the end of an array: push()

The push() method is the opposite of pop(): It adds one or more elements to the end of an array. Here's the syntax to use:

```
array.push(value1, value2, ...)
```

where:

>> *array* is the name of the array you want to work with.

>> *value1*, *value2*, ... are the values you want to add to the end of *array*. A value can also be another array.

push() differs from the concat() method in that it doesn't return a new array. Instead, it changes the existing array by adding the new values to the end of the array. For example, consider the following statements:

```
const myArray = ["First", "Second", "Third"];
const pushArray = ["Fourth", "Fifth", "Sixth"];
for (let i = 0; i < pushArray.length; i += 1) {
    myArray.push(pushArray[i]);
}
```

After these statements, myArray contains six values: "First", "Second", "Third", "Fourth", "Fifth", and "Sixth". Why didn't I just add the entire pushArray in one fell swoop? That is, like so:

```
myArray.push(pushArray);
```

That's perfectly legal, but myArray would contain the following four elements: "First", "Second", "Third", and pushArray, which means you've created a kind of hybrid multidimensional array, which is probably not what you want in this situation.

REMEMBER

After you run the push() method, JavaScript increases the value of the array's length property by the number of new elements added.

Reversing the order of an array's elements: reverse()

The `reverse()` method takes the existing elements in an array and reverses their order: The first moves to the last, the last moves to the first, and so on. The syntax takes just a second to show:

```
array.reverse()
```

The following code (bk03ch08/example11.html) puts the `reverse()` method to work, and Figure 8-8 shows what happens.

```
const myArray = ["Show", "Place", "Win"];
myArray.reverse();
console.log(myArray);
```

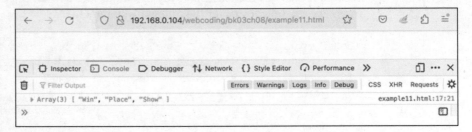

Removing an array's first element: shift()

The `shift()` method removes the first element from an array and returns the value of that element:

```
array.shift()
```

For example, consider the following statements:

```
const myArray = ["First", "Second", "Third"];
const myString = myArray.shift();
```

The first element of `myArray` is `"First"`, so `myArray.shift()` removes that value from the array and stores it in the `myString` variable.

After you run the `shift()` method, JavaScript reduces the value of the array's `length` property by one.

REMEMBER

Returning a subset of an array: slice()

The `slice()` method returns a new array that contains a subset of the elements in an existing array. Here's the syntax:

```
array.slice(start, [end]);
```

where:

>> *array* is the name of the array you want to work with.

>> *start* is a number that specifies the index of the first element in *array* that you want to include in the subset. If this number is negative, the subset starting point is counted from the end of *array* (for example, −1 is the last element of the array). If you leave out this value, JavaScript uses 0 (that is, the first element of the array).

>> *end* is an optional number that specifies the index of the element in *array* *before which* you want the subset to end. If you leave out this value, the subset includes all the elements in *array* from *start* to the last element. This value can be negative.

TIP

A quick way to make a copy of an array is to use `slice()` without any parameters:

```
const thisArray = ["alpha", "beta", "gamma"];
const thatArray = thisArray.slice();
// thatArray() is ["alpha", "beta", "gamma"];
```

TIP

You can also quickly copy an array by using the spread operator (...); as described in Book 3, Chapter 11:

```
const thisArray = ["alpha", "beta", "gamma"];
const thatArray = [...thisArray];
// thatArray() is ["alpha", "beta", "gamma"];
```

The following code (bk03ch08/example12.html) defines an array and then tries out various values for the `slice()` arguments. The results are shown in Figure 8-9.

HTML:

```
<div id="output">
</div>
```

JavaScript:

```
const myArray = ["A", "B", "C", "D", "E", "F"];
const array1 = myArray.slice(0, 4);
```

```
const array2 = myArray.slice(3);
const array3 = myArray.slice(-3, -1);
let str = "array1: " + array1 + "<br>";
str += "array2: " + array2 + "<br>";
str += "array3: " + array3;
document.getElementById('output').innerHTML = str;
```

```
←  →  C        ○  🔒  192.168.0.104/webcoding/bk03ch08/example12.html        ☆

array1: A,B,C,D
array2: D,E,F
array3: D,E
```

Ordering array elements: sort()

The sort() method is an easy way to handle a common programming problem: rearranging an array's elements to put them in alphabetical, numerical, or some other order. You can use four syntaxes:

```
array.sort()
array.sort(namedFunction)
array.sort(namedFunction (a, b) { code });
array.sort((a, b) => { code });
```

where:

» *array* is the name of the array you want to sort.

» *namedFunction* is the name of an existing function that performs the sorting operation by comparing the array items two at a time, where the first array item in the comparison is passed as argument *a* and the second array item in the comparison is passed as argument *b*.

» *code* is the statements to run during each iteration to perform the sorting operation on each value.

Using sort() without an argument gives you a straightforward alphabetical sort:

```
myArray.sort();
```

If you want to sort the array based on some other criterion, you need to create a function to define the sort order. Your function must be set up as follows:

> The function must accept two arguments that represent two array values to be compared so that they can be sorted relative to each other. For the purposes of this list, I'll call these arguments a and b.

> Using these arguments, the function must define an expression that returns a numeric value.

> For those cases where you want a sorted before b, the function must return a negative value.

> For those cases where you want a sorted after b, the function must return a positive value.

> For those cases where you want a and b to be treated equally, the function must return zero.

The following code (bk03ch08/example13.html) shows a function named numericSort that you can use if you want a numeric sort from lowest to highest. Figure 8-10 displays the original array and then the sorted array.

HTML:

```
<div id="output">
</div>
```

JavaScript:

```
// This function sorts numbers from highest to lowest
function numericSort(a, b) {
    return (b - a);
}

const myArray = [3, 5, 1, 6, 2, 4];

// Write the array before sorting it
let str = "myArray (before sorting): " + myArray + "<br>";

// Sort the array
myArray.sort(numericSort);

// Write the array after sorting it
str+= "myArray (after sorting): " + myArray;

document.getElementById('output').innerHTML = str;
```

FIGURE 8-10:
Using sort() and
a function to sort
items numerically
from highest to
lowest.

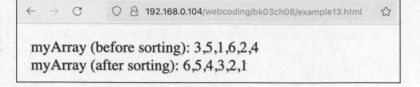

myArray (before sorting): 3,5,1,6,2,4
myArray (after sorting): 6,5,4,3,2,1

TIP

To get a numeric sort from lowest to highest, either use sort() without an argument or use the following return expression:

```
return a - b;
```

TIP

What if you want a reverse alphabetical sort? Just chain sort() with reverse():

```
myArray.sort().reverse();
```

Removing, replacing, and inserting elements: splice()

The splice() method is a complex function that comes in handy in all kinds of situations. First, here's the syntax:

```
array.splice(start, [elementsToDelete][, value1, value2, ... ])
```

where:

>> *array* is the name of the array you want to work with.

>> *start* is a number that specifies the index of the element where the splice takes place.

>> *elementsToDelete* is an optional number that specifies how many elements to delete from *array* beginning at the *start* position. If you don't include this argument, elements are deleted from *start* to the end of the array.

>> *value1, value2, ...* are the optional values to insert into *array* beginning at the *start* position.

With splice() at your side, you can perform one or more of the following tasks:

>> **Deletion:** If *elementsToDelete* is greater than zero or unspecified and no insertion values are included, splice() deletes elements beginning at the index *start*. The deleted elements are returned in a separate array.

- **Replacement:** If *elementsToDelete* is greater than zero or unspecified and one or more insertion values are included, splice() first deletes elements beginning at the index *start*. It then inserts the specified values at index *start*.

- **Insertion:** If *elementsToDelete* is 0, splice() inserts the specified values at index *start*.

The following code (bk03ch08/example14.html) demonstrates all three tasks, and the results are shown in Figure 8-11.

HTML:

```
<div id="output">
</div>
```

JavaScript:

```
const array1 = ["A", "B", "C", "D", "E", "F"];
const array2 = ["A", "B", "C", "D", "E", "F"];
const array3 = ["A", "B", "C", "D", "E", "F"];

// DELETION
// In array1, start at index 2 and delete to the end
// Return the deleted elements to the delete1 array
const delete1 = array1.splice(2);

// Write array1
let str = "array1: " + array1 + "<br>";

// Write delete1
str += "delete1: " + delete1 + "<br>";

// REPLACEMENT
// In array2, start at index 3 and delete 2 elements
// Insert 2 elements to replace them
// Return the deleted elements to the delete2 array
const delete2 = array2.splice(3, 2, "d", "e");

// Write array2
str += "array2: " + array2 + "<br>";

// Write delete2
str += "delete2: " + delete2 + "<br>";
```

```
// INSERTION
// In array3, start at index 1 and insert 3 elements
array3.splice(1, 0, "1", "2", "3")

// Write array3
str += "array3: " + array3;

document.getElementById('output').innerHTML = str;
```

← → C ○ 🔒 192.168.0.104/webcoding/bk03ch08/example14.html ☆

array1: A,B
delete1: C,D,E,F
array2: A,B,C,d,e,F
delete2: D,E
array3: A,1,2,3,B,C,D,E,F

Inserting elements at the beginning of an array: unshift()

The unshift() method is the opposite of the shift() method: It inserts one or more values at the beginning of an array. When it's done, unshift() returns the new length of the array. Here's the syntax:

```
array.unshift(value1, value2, ...)
```

where:

>> *array* is the name of the array you want to work with.

>> *value1, value2,* . . . are the values you want to add to the beginning of *array*.

For example, consider the following statements:

```
const myArray = ["First", "Second", "Third"];
const newLength = myArray.unshift("Fourth", "Fifth", "Sixth");
```

After these statements, myArray contains six values — "Fourth", "Fifth", and "Sixth", "First", "Second", and "Third" — and the value of newLength is 6.

Chapter **9**

Manipulating Strings, Dates, and Numbers

First learn computer science and all the theory. Next develop a programming style. Then forget all that and just hack.

— GEORGE CARRETTE

Although your JavaScript code will spend much of its time dealing with web page knickknacks such as HTML tags and CSS properties, it will also perform lots of behind-the-scenes chores that require manipulating strings, dealing with dates and times, and performing mathematical calculations. To help you through these tasks, in this chapter you explore three of JavaScript's built-in objects: the String object, the Date object, and the Math object. You investigate the most important properties of each object, master the most used methods, and encounter lots of useful examples along the way.

Manipulating Text with the String Object

I've used dozens of examples of strings so far in this book. These include not only string literals (such as "Web Coding and Development For Dummies") but also methods that return strings (such as the prompt() method). So it should be clear by now that strings play a major role in all JavaScript programming, and it will be a rare script that doesn't have to deal with strings in some fashion.

For this reason, it pays to become proficient at manipulating strings, which includes locating text within a string and extracting text from a string. You learn about all that and more in this section.

Any string you work with — whether it's a string literal or the result of a method or function that returns a string — is a `String` object. So, for example, the following two statements are equivalent:

```
const bookName = new String("Web Coding and Development For
    Dummies");
const bookName = "Web Coding and Development For Dummies";
```

This means you have quite a bit of flexibility when applying the properties and methods of `String` objects. For example, the `String` object has a `length` property that I describe a bit later (refer to "Determining the length of a string"). The following are all legal JavaScript expressions that use this property:

```
bookName.length;
"Web Coding and Development For Dummies".length;
prompt("Enter the book name:").length;
myFunction().length;
```

The last example assumes that `myFunction()` returns a string value.

Working with string templates

Before diving in to the properties and methods of the `String` object, take a second to examine a special type of string that's designed to solve three string-related problems that will come up again and again in your coding career:

>> **Handling internal quotation marks:** String literals are surrounded by quotation marks, but what do you do when you need the same type of quotation mark inside the string?

One solution is to use a different type of quotation mark to delimit the string. For example, this is illegal:

```
'There's got to be a better way to do this.'
```

But this is fine:

```
"There's got to be a better way to do this."
```

A second solution is to escape the internal quotation mark with a slash, like so:

```
'There\'s got to be a better way to do this.'
```

These solutions work fine, but *remembering* to use them is harder than you may think!

» **Incorporating variable values:** When you need to use the value of a variable inside a string, you usually end up with something ungainly such as the following:

```
const adjective = "better";
const lament = "There's got to be a " + adjective + " way
    to do this.";
```

» **Multiline strings:** It's often useful to define a string using multiple lines. However, if you try the following, you'll get a `string literal contains an unescaped line break` error:

```
const myHeader = '
    <nav class="banner">
        <h3 class="nav-heading">Navigation</h3>
        <ul class="nav-links">
            <li>Home</li>
            <li>Away</li>
            <li>In Between</li>
        </ul>
    </nav>'
```

You can solve all three problems by using a *string template* (also called a *template literal*), which is a kind of string literal where the delimiting quotation marks are replaced by back ticks (`` ` ``):

```
`Your string goes here`
```

REMEMBER

String templates were introduced as part of ECMAScript 2015 (ES6), so use them only if you don't need to support ancient web browsers such as Internet Explorer 11.

Here's how you can use a string template to solve each of the three problems just described:

» **Handling internal quotation marks:** You're free to plop any number of single or double quotation marks inside a string template:

```
`Ah, here's the better way to do this!`
```

CHAPTER 9 **Manipulating Strings, Dates, and Numbers** 381

>> **Incorporating variable values:** String templates support something called *variable interpolation,* which is a technique for referencing a variable value directly within a string. Here's an example:

```
const adjective = "better";
const paean = `Ah, here's the ${adjective} way to do this!`;
```

Within any string template, using ${*variable*} inserts the value of *variable*, no questions asked. Actually, you don't have to stick to just variables. String templates can also interpolate any JavaScript expression, including function results.

>> **Multiline strings:** String templates are happy to work error-free with strings that are spread over multiple lines:

```
const myHeader = `
    <nav class="banner">
        <h3 class="nav-heading">Navigation</h3>
        <ul class="nav-links">
            <li>Home</li>
            <li>Away</li>
            <li>In Between</li>
        </ul>
    </nav>`
```

Determining the length of a string

The only inherent property of a String object is its length, which tells you how many characters are in the string:

```
string.length
```

All characters within the string — including spaces and punctuation marks — are counted towards the length. The only exceptions are escape sequences (such as \n), which count as one character. The following code grabs the length property value for various String object types:

```
function myFunction() {
    return "filename.htm";
}
const bookName = "Web Coding and Development For Dummies";

length1 = myFunction().length; // Returns 12
length2 = bookName.length; // Returns 37
length3 = "123\n5678".length; // Returns 8
```

What the `String` object lacks in properties it more than makes up for in methods. There are dozens, and they enable your code to perform many useful tasks, from converting between uppercase and lowercase letters, to finding text in a string, to extracting parts of a string.

Searching for substrings

A *substring* is a portion of an existing string. For example, some substrings of the string "JavaScript" would be "Java", "Script", "vaSc", and "v". When working with strings in your scripts, you'll often have to determine whether a given string contains a given substring. For example, if you're validating a user's email address, you should check that it contains an @ symbol.

Table 9-1 lists the several `String` object methods that find substrings within a larger string.

TABLE 9-1 **String Object Methods for Searching for Substrings**

Method	What It Does
string.endsWith(*substring*, *position*)	Tests whether *substring* appears at the end of *string*
string.includes(*substring*, *position*)	Tests whether *substring* appears in *string*
string.indexOf(*substring*, *position*)	Searches *string* for the first instance of *substring*
string.lastIndexOf(*substring*, *position*)	Searches *string* for the last instance of *substring*
string.startsWith(*substring*, *position*)	Tests whether *substring* appears at the beginning of *string*

You'll use each of these methods quite often in your scripts, so I take a closer look at them in the sections that follow.

The startsWith(), includes(), and endsWith() methods

If you just want to know whether a particular substring exists within a larger string, use one of the following methods:

```
string.startsWith(substring[, position])
string.includes(substring[, position])
string.endsWith(substring[, position])
```

where:

>> *string* is the string in which you want to search.

>> *substring* is the substring that you want to search for in *string*.

>> *position* is an optional numeric value that defines either the starting character position for the search (for the startsWith() and includes() methods) or the ending character position for the search (for the endsWith() method). If you omit this argument, JavaScript starts the search from the beginning of the string (for the startsWith() and includes() methods) or the end of the string (for the endsWith() method).

The search is case sensitive. These methods return true if they find *substring* in *string*; otherwise, they return false. Here are some examples (check out bk03ch09/example01.html in this book's example files):

```
const bookName = "Web Coding and Development For Dummies";
console.log(bookName.startsWith("Web")); // Returns true
console.log(bookName.startsWith("Coding", 4)); // Returns true
console.log(bookName.includes("Development")); // Returns true
console.log(bookName.includes("And")); // Returns false
console.log(bookName.endsWith("Dummies")); // Returns true
console.log(bookName.endsWith("Coding", 10)); // Returns true
```

On a more practical note, the following code (check out bk03ch09/example02. html) presents a simple validation script that uses includes():

```
let emailAddress = "";
do {
    emailAddress = prompt("Enter a valid email address:");
    if (emailAddress === null) {
        break;
    }
}
while (!emailAddress.includes("@"));
```

The script prompts the user for a valid email address, which is stored in the emailAddress variable. Any valid address will contain the @ symbol, so the while() portion of a do...while() loop checks to determine whether the entered string contains @:

```
while (!emailAddress.includes("@"));
```

If not (that is, if emailAddress.includes("@") returns false), the loop continues and the user is prompted again. If the user clicks Cancel in the prompt box, then emailAddress === null returns true and the loop quits.

REMEMBER

The startsWith(), endsWith(), and includes() methods were introduced as part of ECMAScript 2015 (ES6), so use them only if you don't need to support ancient web browsers such as Internet Explorer 11.

The indexOf() and lastIndexOf() methods

When you want to find the first instance of a substring, or if all you want to know is whether a string contains a particular substring, use the indexOf() method; if you need to find the last instance of a substring, use the lastIndexOf() method:

```
string.indexOf(substring[, start])
string.lastIndexOf(substring[, start])
```

where:

>> *string* is the string in which you want to search.

>> *substring* is the substring that you want to search for in *string*.

>> *start* is an optional character position from which the search begins. If you omit this argument, JavaScript starts the search from the beginning of the string.

Here are some notes you should keep in mind when using indexOf() or lastIndexOf():

>> Each character in a string is given an index number, which is the same as the character's position in the string.

>> Strings, like arrays, are *zero-based*, which means that the first character has index 0, the second character has index 1, and so on.

>> Both methods are case-sensitive. For example, if you search for B, neither method will find any instances of b.

>> If either method finds *substring*, they return the index position of the first character of *substring*.

>> If either method doesn't find *substring*, they return −1.

The following code (bk03ch09/example03.html) tries out these methods in a few different situations:

HTML:

```
<pre>
Web Coding and Development For Dummies
012345678901234567890123456789012345 67
</pre>
<div id="output"></div>
```

JavaScript:

```
const bookName = "Web Coding and Development For Dummies";

let str = `
    "C\" is at index ${bookName.indexOf("C")}<br>
    "v" is at index ${bookName.indexOf("v")}<br>
    The first space is at index ${bookName.indexOf(" ")}<br>
    The first "D" is at index ${bookName.indexOf("D")}<br>
    The last "D" is at index ${bookName.lastIndexOf("D")}<br>
    The first "e" after index 2 is at index ${bookName.
  indexOf("e", 2)}<br>
    The substring "Develop" begins at index ${bookName.
  indexOf("Develop")}
`;

document.getElementById("output").innerHTML = str;
```

As shown in Figure 9-1, the numbers show you the index positions of each character in the script.

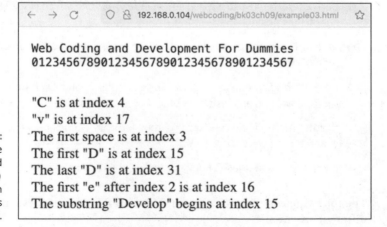

FIGURE 9-1:
The
indexOf() and
lastIndexOf()
methods search
for substrings
within a string.

Methods that extract substrings

Finding a substring is one thing, but you'll often have to extract a substring, as well. For example, if the user enters an email address, you may need to extract just the username (the part to the left of the @ sign) or the domain name (the part to the right of @). For these kinds of operations, JavaScript offers six methods, listed in Table 9-2.

TABLE 9-2   String Object Methods for Extracting Substrings

Method	What It Returns
string.charAt(*index*)	The character in *string* that's at the index position specified by *index*
string.charCodeAt(*index*)	The code of the character in *string* that's at the index position specified by *index*
string.slice(*start, end*)	The substring in *string* that starts at the index position specified by *start* and ends immediately before the index position specified by *end*
string.split(*separator, limit*)	An array where each item is a substring in *string*, where those substrings are separated by the *separator* character
string.substr(*start, length*)	The substring in *string* that starts at the index position specified by *start* and is *length* characters long
string.substring(start, end)	The substring in *string* that starts at the index position specified by *start* and ends immediately before the index position specified by *end*

The charAt() method

You use the charAt() method to return a single character that resides at a specified position in a string:

```
string.charAt(index)
```

where:

>> *string* is the string that contains the character.

>> *index* is the position in *string* of the character you want.

Here are some notes about this method:

>> To return the first character in *string*, use the following:

```
string.charAt(0)
```

>> To return the last character in *string*, use this:

```
string.charAt(string.length - 1)
```

>> If the *index* value is negative or is greater than or equal to *string*.length, JavaScript returns the empty string ("").

The following code presents an example (bk03ch09/example04.html):

HTML:

```
<div id="output"></div>
```

JavaScript:

```
// Set up an array of test strings
const stringArray = [];
stringArray[0] = "Not this one.";
stringArray[1] = "Not this one, either.";
stringArray[2] = "1. Step one.";
stringArray[3] = "Shouldn't get this far.";

// Loop through the array
for (const currentString of stringArray) {

    // Get the first character of the string
    const firstChar = currentString.charAt(0);

    // Is it a number?
    if (!isNaN(firstChar)) {

        // If so, display the string because that's the one we want
        document.getElementById("output").innerHTML = `Here's
the one: "${currentString}"`;

        // We're done here, so break out of the loop
        break;
    }
}
```

The idea here is to examine a collection of strings and find the one that starts with a number. The collection is stored in the `stringArray` array, and a `for...of` loop is set up to run through each item in the array. The `charAt()` method is applied to each array item (stored in the `currentString` variable) to return the first character, which is stored in the `firstChar` variable. In the `if` test, the logical expression `!isNaN(firstChar)` returns `true` if the `firstChar` value is a number (the `isNaN(value)` function returns `true` if *value* is not a number), at which point the correct string is displayed in the web page and the loop breaks.

TIP

Each character in a JavaScript string has an index number, where the first character is index 0, the second character is index 1, and so on. You specify a particular character using square bracket notation. For example, the expression `myString[5]` references the character at index 5 of whatever string is stored in the `myString` variable.

Therefore, an alternative to using `charAt()` is to reference the character you want by its index number. For example, the following two expressions reference the same character:

```
currentString.charAt(0)
currentString[0]
```

The slice() method

Use the `slice()` method to carve out a piece of a string:

```
string.slice(start[, end])
```

where:

>> *string* is the string you want to work with.

>> *start* is the position within *string* of the first character you want to extract.

>> *end* is an optional position in *string* immediately after the last character you want to extract. If you leave out this argument, JavaScript extracts the substring that runs from *start* to the end of the string. Also, this argument can be negative, in which case it specifies an offset from the end of the string.

To be clear, `slice()` extracts a substring that runs from the character at *start* up to, but not including, the character at *end*.

The following code (bk03ch09/example05.html) runs through a few examples (check out Figure 9-2):

HTML:

```
<pre>
Web Coding and Development For Dummies
012345678901234567890123456789012345567
</pre>
<div id="output"></div>
```

JavaScript:

```
const bookName = "Web Coding and Development For Dummies";

let str = `
    slice(0, 3) = ${bookName.slice(0, 3)}<br>
    slice(4, 10) = ${bookName.slice(4, 10)}<br>
    slice(15) = ${bookName.slice(15)}<br>
    slice(0, -12) = ${bookName.slice(0, -12)}
`;

document.getElementById("output").innerHTML = str;
```

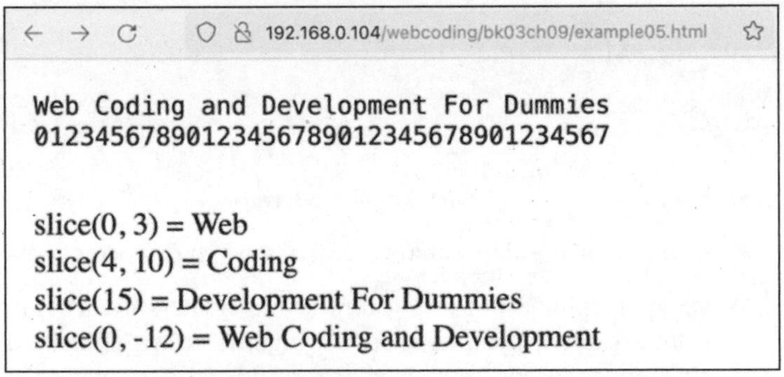

FIGURE 9-2:
Some examples
of the slice()
method in action.

Browser window content:
```
← → C    ○ 🔒 192.168.0.104/webcoding/bk03ch09/example05.html    ☆

Web Coding and Development For Dummies
012345678901234567890123456789012345567

slice(0, 3) = Web
slice(4, 10) = Coding
slice(15) = Development For Dummies
slice(0, -12) = Web Coding and Development
```

The split() method

The split() method breaks up a string and returns an array that stores the pieces:

```
string.split(separator[,limit])
```

where:

- *string* is the string you want to work with.

- *separator* is the character used to mark the positions at which *string* is split. For example, if *separator* is a comma, the splits will occur at each comma in *string*.

- *limit* is an optional value that sets the maximum number of items to store in the array. For example, if *limit* is 5, split() stores the first five pieces in the array and then ignores the rest of the string.

TIP

If you want each character in the string stored as an individual array item, use the empty string ("") as the *separator* value.

The split() method is useful for those times when you have a well-structured string. This means that the string contains a character that acts as a delimiter between each string piece that you want to set up as an array item. For example, it's common to have to deal with *comma-delimited* strings:

```
string1 = "Sunday,Monday,Tuesday,Wednesday,Thursday,Friday,
    Saturday";
```

Handily, each day in the string is separated by a comma, which makes using the split() method a no-brainer:

```
const string1Array = string1.split(",");
```

When you run this statement, string1Array[0] will contain "Sunday", string1Array[1] will contain "Monday", and so on. Note, too, that JavaScript sets up the array for you automatically. You don't have to declare the array using new Array().

The following code (bk03ch09/example06.html) tries out split() with a couple of example strings:

HTML:

```
<div id="output"></div>
```

JavaScript:

```
const string1 = "Sunday,Monday,Tuesday,Wednesday,Thursday,Friday,
    Saturday";
const string2 = "ABCDEF";
```

```
let str = "";

const string1Array = string1.split(",");
string1Array.forEach((value, index) => {
    str += `string1Array[${index}] = ${value}<br>`;
});

const string2Array = string2.split("", 4);
string2Array.forEach ((value, index) => {
    str += `string2Array[${index}] = ${value}<br>`;
});

document.getElementById("output").innerHTML = str;
```

After `string1` is split into `string1Array`, that array's `forEach()` method runs through the array and writes the items to the global `str` variable. For `string2`, the empty string is used as the separator and a limit of 4 is placed on the size of the `string2Array`. Again, that array's `forEach()` methods writes the array values to the `str` variable. The script closes by writing `str` to the page. Figure 9-3 shows what happens.

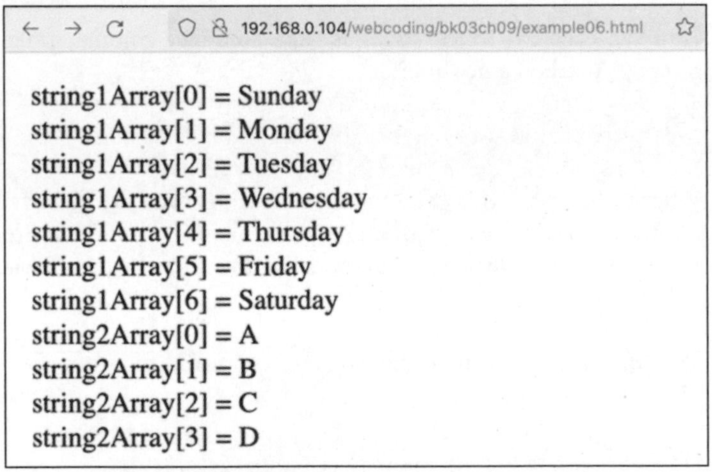

FIGURE 9-3:
Some examples
of the `split()`
method.

```
←  →  C      ○  🔒  192.168.0.104/webcoding/bk03ch09/example06.html    ☆

string1Array[0] = Sunday
string1Array[1] = Monday
string1Array[2] = Tuesday
string1Array[3] = Wednesday
string1Array[4] = Thursday
string1Array[5] = Friday
string1Array[6] = Saturday
string2Array[0] = A
string2Array[1] = B
string2Array[2] = C
string2Array[3] = D
```

The substr() method

If you want to extract a substring and you know how long you want that substring to be, the `substr()` method is often the best approach:

string.substr(*index, length*)

where:

>> *string* is the string you want to work with.

>> *index* is the position in *string* of the first character you want to extract.

>> *length* is an optional value that specifies the length of the substring. If you omit this argument, JavaScript extracts all the way to the end of the string.

The following code (bk03ch09/example07.html) runs `substr()` through some examples; the results appear in Figure 9-4.

HTML:

```
<pre>
Web Coding and Development For Dummies
01234567890123456789012345678901234567
</pre>
<div id="output"></div>
```

JavaScript:

```
const bookName = "Web Coding and Development For Dummies";

let str = `
    substr(0, 10) = ${bookName.substr(0, 10)}<br>
    substr(15, 11) = ${bookName.substr(15, 11)}<br>
    substr(27) = ${bookName.substr(27)}
`;

document.getElementById("output").innerHTML = str;
```

```
←  →  C      ○  ⟨  192.168.0.104/webcoding/bk03ch09/example07.html    ☆

Web Coding and Development For Dummies
01234567890123456789012345678901234567


substr(0, 10) = Web Coding
substr(15, 11) = Development
substr(27) = For Dummies
```

FIGURE 9-4:
Some examples of the `substr()` method.

The substring() method

Use the substring() method to extract a substring from a string:

string.substring(*start*[, *end*])

where:

- ❯❯ *string* is the string you want to work with.
- ❯❯ *start* is the position in *string* of the first character you want to extract.
- ❯❯ *end* is an optional value that specifies the position in *string* immediately after the last character you want to extract. If you don't include this argument, JavaScript extracts the substring that runs from *start* to the end of the string.

The following code (bk03ch09/example08.html) gives the substring() method a whirl, and the results are shown in Figure 9-5.

HTML:

```
<pre>
Web Coding and Development For Dummies
01234567890123456789012345678901234567
</pre>

<div id="output"></div>
```

JavaScript:

```
const bookName = "Web Coding and Development For Dummies";

let str = `
    substring(0, 10) = ${bookName.substring(0, 10)}<br>
    substring(11, 14) = ${bookName.substring(11, 14)}<br>
    substring(31) = ${bookName.substring(31)}
`;

document.getElementById("output").innerHTML = str;
```

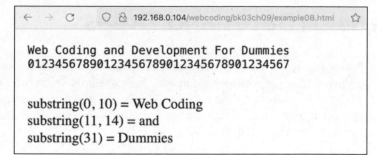

FIGURE 9-5:
Some examples of the substring() method.

```
Web Coding and Development For Dummies
01234567890123456789012345678901234567


substring(0, 10) = Web Coding
substring(11, 14) = and
substring(31) = Dummies
```

Understanding the differences between splice(), substr(), and substring()

The splice(), substr(), and substring() methods are similar and often confused by even experienced JavaScript programmers. Here are some notes to help you understand the differences between these three string extraction methods:

» The splice() and substring() methods perform the same task. The only difference is that splice() enables you to use a negative value for the *end* argument. This feature is handy if you want to leave out a certain number of characters from the end of the original string. For example, if you want to extract everything but the last three characters, you'd use this:

```
string.splice(0, -3)
```

» Use either splice() or substring() when you're not sure how long the extracted string will be. In this situation, usually you'll use the indexOf() and lastIndexOf() methods to find particular characters that mark the starting and ending points of the substring you want. You then use those values as the *start* and *end* arguments of splice() or substring(). For example, suppose you have a string of the form www.domain.com and you want to extract just the domain part. Here's a short routine that will do it:

```
const hostName = "www.domain.com";
const firstDot = hostName.indexOf(".");
const lastDot = hostName.lastIndexOf(".");
const domainName = hostName.substring(firstDot + 1, lastDot);
```

TIP

This technique for extracting the domain name is illustrative but woefully inefficient. Here's a one-liner that takes advantage of the split() method (which I discuss earlier in this chapter; check out "The split() method"):

```
const domainName = hostName.split('.')[1];
```

» On the other hand, if you know in advance how long the extracted string must be, use the substr() method.

Dealing with Dates and Times

Dates and times seem like the kind of things that ought to be straightforward programming propositions. After all, there are only 12 months in a year, 28 to 31 days in a month, 7 days in a week, 24 hours in a day, 60 minutes in an hour, and 60 seconds in a minute. Surely something so set in stone couldn't get even the least bit weird, could it?

You'd be surprised. Dates and times *can* get strange, but they are much easier to deal with if you remember three crucial points:

>> JavaScript time is measured in milliseconds, or thousandths of a second. More specifically, JavaScript measures time by counting the number of milliseconds that elapsed between January 1, 1970 and the date and time in question. So, for example, *you* may come across the date January 1, 2001 and think, "Ah, yes, the start of the new millennium." *JavaScript,* however, comes across that date and thinks "978307200000."

>> In the JavaScript world, time began on January 1, 1970, at midnight Greenwich Mean Time. Dates before that have *negative* values in milliseconds.

>> Since your JavaScript programs run inside a user's browser, dates and times are almost always the user's *local* dates and times. That is, the dates and times your scripts will manipulate will *not* be those of the server on which your page resides. This means you can never know what time the user is viewing your page.

Arguments used with the Date object

Before getting to the nitty-gritty of the Date object and its associated methods, I'll take a second to run through the various arguments that JavaScript requires for many date-related features. Doing so will save me from repeating these arguments tediously later. Table 9-3 has the details.

Working with the Date object

Whenever you work with dates and times in JavaScript, you work with an instance of the Date object. More to the point, when you deal with a Date object in JavaScript, you deal with a specific moment in time, down to the millisecond. A Date object can never be a block of time, and it's not a kind of clock that ticks along while your script runs. Instead, the Date object is a temporal snapshot that you use to extract the specifics of the time it was taken: the year, month, date, hour, and so on.

TABLE 9-3   **Arguments Associated with the Date Object**

Argument	What It Represents	Possible Values
date	A variable name	A Date object
yyyy	The year	Four-digit integers
yy	The year	Two-digit integers
month	The month	The full month name from "January" to "December"
mth	The month	Integers from 0 (January) to 11 (December)
dd	The day of the month	Integers from 1 to 31
hh	The hour of the day	Integers from 0 (midnight) to 23 (11:00 PM)
mm	The minute of the hour	Integers from 0 to 59
ss	The second of the minute	Integers from 0 to 59
ms	The milliseconds of the second	Integers from 0 to 999

Specifying the current date and time

The most common use of the Date object is to store the current date and time. You do that by invoking the Date() function, which is the constructor function for creating a new Date object. Here's the general format:

```
const dateToday = new Date();
```

Specifying any date and time

If you need to work with a specific date or time, you need to use the Date() function's arguments. There are five versions of the Date() function syntax (refer to the list of arguments near the beginning of this section):

```
const date = new Date("month dd, yyyy hh:mm:ss");
const date = new Date("month dd, yyyy");
const date = new Date(yyyy, mth, dd, hh, mm, ss);
const date = new Date(yyyy, mth, dd);
const date = new Date(ms);
```

The following statements give you an example for each syntax:

```
const myDate = new Date("August 23, 2024 3:02:01");
const myDate = new Date("August 23, 2024");
```

```
const myDate = new Date(2024, 8, 23, 3, 2, 1);
const myDate = new Date(2024, 8, 23);
const myDate = new Date(1727064000000);
```

Extracting information about a date

When your script just coughs up whatever Date object value you stored in the variable, the results aren't particularly appealing. If you want to display dates in a more attractive format, or if you want to perform arithmetic operations on a date, you need to dig a little deeper into the Date object to extract specific information such as the month, year, hour, and so on. You do that by using the Date object methods listed in Table 9-4.

TABLE 9-4 **Date Object Methods That Extract Date Values**

Method Syntax	What It Returns
date.getFullYear()	The year as a four-digit number (1999, 2000, and so on)
date.getMonth()	The month of the year; from 0 (January) to 11 (December)
date.getDate()	The date in the month; from 1 to 31
date.getDay()	The day of the week; from 0 (Sunday) to 6 (Saturday)
date.getHours()	The hour of the day; from 0 (midnight) to 23 (11:00 PM)
date.getMinutes()	The minute of the hour; from 0 to 59
date.getSeconds()	The second of the minute; from 0 to 59
date.getMilliseconds()	The milliseconds of the second; from 0 to 999
date.getTime()	The milliseconds since January 1, 1970 GMT

One of the ways you can take advantage of these methods is to display the time or date to the user using any format you want. Here's an example (bk03ch09/example09.html):

HTML:

```
<div id="output"></div>
```

JavaScript:

```javascript
const timeNow = new Date();
const hoursNow = timeNow.getHours();
const minutesNow = timeNow.getMinutes();
let message = "It's ";
let hoursText;

if (minutesNow <= 30) {
    message += minutesNow + (minutesNow === 1 ? " minute past "
  : " minutes past ");
    hoursText = hoursNow;
} else {
    message += (60 - minutesNow) + ((60 - minutesNow) === 1 ? "
  minute before " : " minutes before ");
    hoursText = hoursNow + 1;
}

if (hoursNow == 0 && minutesNow <= 30) {
    message += "midnight.";
} else if (hoursNow == 11 && minutesNow > 30) {
    message += "noon.";
} else if (hoursNow < 12) {
    message += hoursText + " in the morning.";
} else if (hoursNow == 12 && minutesNow <= 30) {
    message += "noon.";
} else if (hoursNow < 18) {
    message += parseInt(hoursText - 12) + " in the afternoon.";
} else if (hoursNow == 23 && minutesNow > 30) {
    message += "midnight.";
} else {
    message += parseInt(hoursText - 12) + " in the evening.";
}
document.getElementById("output").innerHTML = message;
```

This script begins by storing the user's local time in the timeNow variable. Then the current hour is extracted using getHours() and stored in the hoursNow variable, and the current minute is extracted using getMinutes() and stored in the minutesNow variable. A variable named message is initialized and will be used to store the message displayed in the web page. The hoursText variable will hold the nonmilitary hour (for example, 4 instead of 16).

Then the value of minutesNow is checked to determine whether it's less than or equal to 30 because this determines the first part of the message as well as the value of hoursText. Here are two examples of how the message will appear:

```
It's 20 minutes past 10 // minutesNow is less than or equal to
   30 (10:20)
It's 1 minute to 11 // minutesNow is greater than 30 (10:59)
```

Then the script checks the value of hoursNow:

>> If it equals 0 and minutesNow is less than or equal to 30, the string midnight is added to the message.

>> If it equals 11 and minutesNow is greater than 30, the string noon is added to the message.

>> If it's less than 12, the value of hoursText and the string in the morning are added to the message.

>> If it equals 12 and minutesNow is less than or equal to 30, the string noon is added to the message.

>> If it's less than 18 (6:00 PM), the result of hoursText – 12 and the string in the afternoon are added.

>> If it equals 23 and minutesNow is greater than 30, the string midnight is added to the message.

>> Otherwise, hoursText – 12 and the string in the evening are added.

Finally, the result is written to the page, as shown in Figure 9-6.

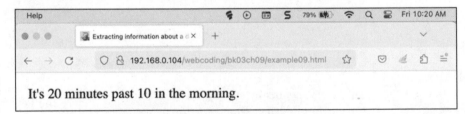

FIGURE 9-6:
The results of
the script.

It's 20 minutes past 10 in the morning.

Extracting the month name from a date

If you want to use the month in a nicer format than the standard Date object display, you have one problem. The getMonth() method returns a number instead of the name of the month: 0 for January, 1 for February, and so on. If you prefer to use the name, you need to extract the name from the Date object.

The easiest way to extract the month name from a date is to use the toLocaleDateString() method, which returns a string that corresponds to the portion (such as the month) of a specified date. Here's the syntax:

```
date.toLocaleDateString(locale, options)
```

where:

» *date* is the Date object from which you want to extract the month name.

» *locale* is a string specifying the language to use such as en-us. Use default for the current language.

» *options* is a JavaScript object that specifies the method output. The object can contain one or more key-value pairs, where the key can be the weekday, day, month, or year keyword and the value is a string that specifies the format of the property. For weekday and month, use the short or long strings; for day or year, use the numeric string. For example, to extract just the month name, use the { month: 'long' } object.

Here's an example (bk03ch09/example10.html):

HTML:

```
<div id="output"></div>
```

JavaScript:

```
const dateNow = new Date();
document.getElementById("output").innerHTML =
    `The date is ${dateNow}<br>
    The month name is ${dateNow.toLocaleDateString('default',
{ month: 'long' })}`;
```

TIP

To extract information about a time, use the toLocaleTimeString() method: *date*.toLocaleTimeString(*locale*, *options*). Again, *options* is a JavaScript object containing one or more key-value pairs, where the key can be the hour, minute, or second keyword and the value is the numeric string. For example, to extract just the hour, use the { hour: 'numeric' } object.

Extracting the day name from a date

You face a similar problem with getDay() as you do with getMonth(): converting the returned number into a friendly name, such as, in this case, Sunday for 0, Monday for 1, and so on. The solution, as you can imagine, is also similar: Use the `toLocaleDateString()` method, but this time specify the `{ weekday: 'long' }` object as the *options* parameter. Here's an example (bk03ch09/example11.html):

HTML:

```
<div id="output"></div>
```

JavaScript:

```
const dateNow = new Date();
document.getElementById("output").innerHTML =
    `The date is ${dateNow}<br>
    The day name is ${dateNow.toLocaleDateString('default',
  { weekday: 'long' })}`;
```

Setting the date

When you perform date arithmetic, you often have to change the value of an existing Date object. For example, an e-commerce script may have to calculate a date that is 90 days from the date that a sale occurs. It's usually easiest to create a Date object and then use an expression or literal value to change the year, month, or some other component of the date. You do that by using the Date object methods listed in Table 9-5.

TABLE 9-5   ## Date Object Methods That Set Date Values

Method Syntax	What It Sets
date.setFullYear(*yyyy*)	The year as a four-digit number (1999, 2000, and so on)
date.setMonth(*mth*)	The month of the year; from 0 (January) to 11 (December)
date.setDate(*dd*)	The date in the month; from 1 to 31
date.setHours(*hh*)	The hour of the day; from 0 (midnight) to 23 (11:00 PM)
date.setMinutes(*mm*)	The minute of the hour; from 0 to 59
date.setSeconds(*ss*)	The second of the minute; from 0 to 59
date.setMilliseconds(*ms*)	The millisecond of the second; from 0 to 999
date.setTime(*ms*)	The milliseconds since January 1, 1970 GMT

The following code (bk03ch09/example12.html) tries out some of these methods:

HTML:

```html
<div>
    <label for="user-year">Enter a year:</label>
    <input type="text" id="user-year" size="4" value="2024">
</div>
<div>
    <label for="user-month">Enter a month (1-12):</label>
    <input type="text" id="user-month" size="2" value="1">
</div>
<div>
    <label for="user-day">Enter a day (1-31):</label>
    <input type="text" id="user-day" size="2" value="1">
</div>
<div id="output"></div>
```

JavaScript:

```javascript
// Get the inputs
const inputs = document.querySelectorAll('input');

// Add a 'change' event listener to each input
inputs.forEach( input => {
    input.addEventListener('change', makeDate);
});

// Run this function each time an input changes
function makeDate() {

    // Get the year, month (minus 1), and day
    const userYear = document.querySelector('#user-year').value;
    const userMonth = document.querySelector('#user-month').
  value - 1;
    const userDay = document.querySelector('#user-day').value;

    // Create a new Date object
    const userDate = new Date();

    // Set the year, month, and date
    userDate.setFullYear(userYear);
    userDate.setMonth(userMonth);
    userDate.setDate(userDay);
```

```
    // Convert the date info to strings
    const dateString = userDate.toLocaleDateString('default',
 { month: 'long', day: 'numeric', year: 'numeric' });
    const dayName = userDate.toLocaleDateString('default',
 { weekday: 'long' });

    // Display the message
    document.getElementById("output").innerHTML =
        `The date entered is: ${dateString}<br>
        The day of the week is: ${dayName}`;
}

// Run the function as soon as the page loads
makeDate();
```

The HTML code defines three input elements that gather the year, month, and day of the month. The JavaScript stores the input elements in the inputs node list and then loops through the elements, adding a change event handler to each element, which defines makeDate as the callback function.

The makeDate() callback function stores the value of each input element in a variable. Note that the script subtracts 1 from the month value to get a proper month number for JavaScript to use.

The next four statements are the keys to this example. A new Date object is stored in the userDate variable. Then the script runs the setFullYear(), setMonth(), and setDate() methods.

At this point, the userDate variable contains a new date that corresponds to the supplied date. This means you can use the toLocaleDateString method to convert the date into whatever string you need. The script first defines string (dateString) for the full date and then defines a string (dayName) for just the weekday name. Then the script displays the date and the day of the week that it corresponds to (check out Figure 9-7).

REMEMBER

All the set methods also return values. Specifically, they return the number of milliseconds from January 1, 1970 GMT to whatever new date is the result of the method. Therefore, you can use the return value of a set method to create a new Date object:

```
newDate = new Date(userDate.setFullYear(userYear))
```

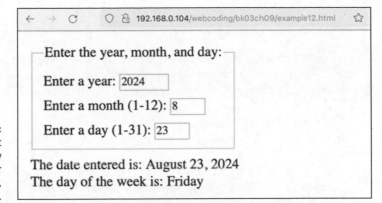

FIGURE 9-7:
The script displays the day of the week for a given year, month, and day.

The browser window shows:

Enter the year, month, and day:

Enter a year: 2024

Enter a month (1-12): 8

Enter a day (1-31): 23

The date entered is: August 23, 2024
The day of the week is: Friday

192.168.0.104/webcoding/bk03ch09/example12.html

Performing date calculations

Many of your date-related scripts will need to make arithmetic calculations. For example, you may need to figure out the number of days between two dates, or you may need to calculate the date that's six weeks from today. The methods you've learned so far, and the way JavaScript represents dates internally, serve to make most date calculations straightforward.

The simplest calculations are those that involve whole numbers of the basic JavaScript date and time units: years, months, days, hours, minutes, and seconds. For example, suppose you need to calculate a date that's five years from the current date. Here's a code snippet that will do it:

```
const myDate = new Date();
const myYear = myDate.getFullYear() + 5;
myDate.setFullYear(myYear);
```

You use `getFullYear()` to get the year, add 5 to it, and then use `setFullYear()` to change the date.

Determining a person's age

As a practical example, the following code presents a script that calculates a person's age (bk03ch09/example13.html):

HTML:

```
<label for="date-picker">Select your birth date:</label>
<input type="date" id="date-picker" value="2000-01-01">

<div id="output"></div>
```

JavaScript:

```javascript
// Add a 'change' event listener to the date picker
const datePicker = document.querySelector('#date-picker');
datePicker.addEventListener('change', calculateAge);

// Run this function when the date changes
function calculateAge() {

    // Create a new Date object from the date picker value
    const birthDate = new Date(datePicker.value);

    // Store the user's birth year
    const birthYear = birthDate.getFullYear();

    // Make a Date object and set it
    // to the user's birthday this year
    const birthdayDate = new Date();
    birthdayDate.setMonth(birthDate.getMonth());
    birthdayDate.setDate(birthDate.getDate());

    // Store the current date and current year
    const currentDate = new Date();
    const currentYear = currentDate.getFullYear();

    // Calculate the user's age
    let userAge = currentYear - birthYear;

    // Has the birthday occurred yet this year?
    if (currentDate < birthdayDate) {
        // If not, adjust the age down by one year
        userAge -= 1;
    }
    // Output the result
    document.getElementById("output").innerHTML =
        `You are ${userAge} years old.`;
}
```

The HTML code sets up a date picker to get the user's birth date. The JavaScript adds a change event listener to the date picker and runs the calculateAge() function each time the date picker changes. The calculateAge() function converts the date picker value to a Date object, and then extracts the birth year to the birthYear variable.

The script creates a new Date object and stores it in birthdayDate. The date is changed using setMonth(), which is set to birthDate.getMonth(), and setDate(), which is set to birthDate.getDate(), but *not* setFullYear(). This gives you the user's birthday for this year. Then the current date is stored in currentDate and the year is stored in currentYear.

Now the script calculates the user's age by subtracting birthYear from currentYear. However, that calculation won't be accurate if the user's birthday hasn't occurred yet this year, so the script compares currentDate and birthdayDate: If currentDate is less, the user's birthday hasn't happened, so the script subtracts 1 from the user's age.

Performing complex date calculations

Other date calculations are more complex. For example, you may need to calculate the number of days between two dates. For this kind of calculation, you need to take advantage of the fact that JavaScript stores dates internally as millisecond values. They're stored, in other words, as numbers, and once you're dealing with numeric values, you can use numeric expressions to perform calculations on those values.

The key here is converting the basic date units — seconds, minutes, hours, days, and weeks — into milliseconds. Here's some code that will help:

```
const ONESECOND = 1000;
const ONEMINUTE = ONESECOND * 60;
const ONEHOUR = ONEMINUTE * 60;
const ONEDAY = ONEHOUR * 24;
const ONEWEEK = ONEDAY * 7;
```

REMEMBER

In programming, whenever you have variables that are *constants* — that is, they have values that will never change throughout the script — it's traditional to write them entirely in uppercase letters (using underscores to separate "words") to help differentiate them from regular variables.

Because one second equals 1,000 milliseconds, the ONESECOND variable is given the value 1000; because one minute equals 60 seconds, the ONEMINUTE variable is given the value ONESECOND * 60, or 60,000 milliseconds. The other values are derived similarly.

Calculating the days between two dates

A common date calculation involves figuring out the number of days between any two dates. The following code presents a function that performs this calculation (bk03ch09/example14.html):

```
function daysBetween(date1, date2) {

    // Convert both dates to milliseconds
    const date1Ms = date1.getTime();
    const date2Ms = date2.getTime();

    // Calculate the difference in milliseconds
    const differenceMs = Math.abs(date1Ms - date2Ms);

    // The number of milliseconds in one day
    const ONEDAY = 1000 * 60 * 60 * 24;

    // Convert to days and return
    return Math.round(differenceMs/ONEDAY);
}
```

This function accepts two Date object arguments — date1 and date2. Note that it doesn't matter which date is earlier or later because this function calculates the absolute value of the difference between them. The ONEDAY constant stores the number of milliseconds in a day, and then the two dates are converted into milliseconds using the getTime() method. The results are stored in the date1Ms and date2Ms variables.

Next, the following statement calculates the absolute value, in milliseconds, of the difference between the two dates:

```
const differenceMs = Math.abs(date1Ms - date2Ms);
```

This difference is then converted into days by dividing it by the ONEDAY constant. Math.round() (which I discuss in the next section) ensures an integer result.

Working with Numbers: The Math Object

It's a rare JavaScript programmer who never has to deal with numbers. Most of us have to cobble together scripts that process order totals, generate sales taxes and shipping charges, calculate mortgage payments, and perform other number-crunching duties. JavaScript's numeric tools aren't the greatest in the programming world, but they have plenty of features to keep most scripters happy. This section tells you about those features, with special emphasis on the Math object.

The first thing to know is that JavaScript likes to keep things simple, particularly when it comes to numbers. For example, JavaScript is limited to dealing with just two numeric data types: *integers* — numbers without a fractional or decimal part, such as 1, 759, and –50 — and *floating-point numbers* — values that have a fractional or decimal part, such as 2.14, 0.01, and –25.3333.

Converting between strings and numbers

When you're working with numeric expressions in JavaScript, it's important to make sure that all your operands are numeric values. For example, if you prompt the user for a value, you need to check the result to make sure it's not a letter or undefined (the default prompt() value). If you try to use the latter, for example, JavaScript will report that its value is NaN (not a number).

Similarly, if you have a value that you know is a string representation of a number, you need some way of converting that string into its numerical equivalent.

For these situations, JavaScript offers several techniques to ensure that your operands are numeric.

The parseInt() function

I begin with the parseInt() function, which you use to convert a string into an integer:

```
parseInt(string[,base]);
```

where:

>> *string* is the string value you want to convert.

>> *base* is an optional base used by the number in *string*. If you omit this value, JavaScript uses base 10.

Note that if the *string* argument contains a string representation of a floating-point value, parseInt() returns only the integer portion. Also, if the string begins with a number followed by some text, parseInt() returns the number (or, at least, its integer portion). The following table shows you the parseInt() results for various *string* values.

string	*parseInt(*string*)*
"5"	5
"5.1"	5
"5.9"	5
"5 feet"	5
"take 5"	NaN
"five"	NaN

The parseFloat() function

The parseFloat() function is similar to parseInt(), but you use it to convert a string into a floating-point value:

```
parseFloat(string);
```

Note that if the *string* argument contains a string representation of an integer value, parseFloat() returns just an integer. Also, like parseInt(), if the string begins with a number followed by some text, parseFloat() returns the number. The following table shows you the parseFloat() results for some *string* values.

string	*parseFloat(*string*)*
"5"	5
"5.1"	5.1
"5.9"	5.9
"5.2 feet"	5.2
"take 5.0"	NaN
"five-point-one"	NaN

The + operator

For quick conversions from a string to a number, I most often use the + operator, which tells JavaScript to treat a string that contains a number as a true numeric value. For example, consider the following code:

```
const numOfShoes = '2';
const numOfSocks = 4;
const totalItems = +numOfShoes + numOfSocks;
```

By adding + in front of the numOfShoes variable, I force JavaScript to set that variable's value to the number 2, and the result of the addition will be 6.

The Math object's properties and methods

The Math object is a bit different than most of the other objects you come across in this book because you never create an instance of the Math object that gets stored in a variable. Instead, the Math object is a built-in JavaScript object that you use as is. The rest of this chapter explores some properties and methods associated with the Math object.

Properties of the Math object

The Math object's properties are all constants that are commonly used in mathematical operations. Table 9-6 lists all the available Math object properties.

TABLE 9-6 The Properties of the Math Object

Property Syntax	What It Represents	Approximate Value
Math.E	Euler's constant	2.718281828459045
Math.LN10	The natural logarithm of 10	2.302585092994046
Math.LN2	The natural logarithm of 2	0.6931471805599453
Math.LOG2E	Base 2 logarithm of E	1.4426950408889633
Math.LOG10E	Base 10 logarithm of E	0.4342944819032518
Math.PI	The constant pi	3.141592653589793
Math.SQRT1_2	The square root of 1/2	0.7071067811865476
Math.SQRT2	The square root of 2	1.4142135623730951

Methods of the Math object

The Math object's methods enable you to perform mathematical operations such as square roots, powers, rounding, and trigonometry. Many of the Math object's methods are summarized in Table 9-7.

TABLE 9-7   **Some Methods of the Math Object**

Method Syntax	What It Returns
`Math.abs(`*number*`)`	The absolute value of *number* (that is, the number without any sign)
`Math.cbrt(`*number*`)`	The cube root of *number*
`Math.ceil(`*number*`)`	The smallest integer greater than or equal to *number* (`ceil` is short for *ceiling*)
`Math.cos(`*number*`)`	The cosine of *number*; returned values range from −1 to 1 radians
`Math.exp(`*number*`)`	E raised to the power of *number*
`Math.floor(`*number*`)`	The largest integer that is less than or equal to *number*
`Math.log(`*number*`)`	The natural logarithm (base E) of *number*
`Math.max(`*number1*`, `*number2*`)`	The larger of *number1* and *number2*
`Math.min(`*number1*`, `*number2*`)`	The smaller of *number1* and *number2*
`Math.pow(`*number1*`, `*number2*`)`	*number1* raised to the power of *number2*
`Math.random()`	A random number between 0 and 1
`Math.round(`*number*`)`	The integer closest to *number*
`Math.sin(`*number*`)`	The sine of *number*; returned values range from −1 to 1 radians
`Math.sqrt(`*number*`)`	The square root of *number* (which must be greater than or equal to 0)
`Math.tan(`*number*`)`	The tangent of *number*, in radians
`Math.trunc(`*number*`)`	The integer portion of *number*

For example, to calculate the area of a circle, you use the formula πr^2, where π (pi) is the ratio of the circumference of a circle to its diameter and r is the radius of the circle. Here's a function that takes a radius value and returns the area of the circle (bk03ch11/example12.html):

```
function areaOfCircle(radius) {
    return Math.PI * Math.pow(radius, 2);
}
```

The code uses `Math.PI` to represent pi and `Math.pow(radius, 2)` to raise the `radius` value to the power of 2.

IN THIS CHAPTER

» **Getting the hang of the Web Storage API**

» **Taking your first look at JSON**

» **Adding stuff to storage**

» **Getting stuff from storage**

» **Removing stuff from storage**

Chapter **10**

Storing User Data in the Browser

Data is like garbage. You'd better know what you are going to do with it before you collect it.

—ANONYMOUS

O ne of the hallmarks of a bigtime website is that most of what you as a site visitor see is data that has been retrieved from a server. This data has been created and managed by a database specialist, and the code that asks for the required data and then returns that data to the web browser is created by a *back-end* web developer.

Programming the back end is the subject of Book 4, but not every web page that works with data needs back-end coding. For example, suppose your web page enables each user to set custom background and text colors. Setting up a complex back-end edifice to store those two pieces of data would be like building the Taj Mahal to store a few towels.

Fortunately, you don't have to embark on a major construction job to save small amounts of data for each user. Instead, you can take advantage of a technology called *web storage* that enables you to store data for each user right in that person's web browser. It's all very civilized, and you find out everything you need to know in this chapter.

Understanding Web Storage

Web storage is possible via a technology called the Web Storage API (application programming interface), which defines two properties of the `Window` object (the object that references the user's browser window):

» `localStorage`: A storage space created within the web browser for your domain (meaning that only your local code can access this storage). Data in this storage can't be larger than 5MB per domain. This data resides permanently in the browser until you delete it.

» `sessionStorage`: The same as `localStorage`, except that the data persists for only the current browser session. That is, the browser erases the data when the user closes the last browser tab or window in which a page from the domain is open.

WARNING

Users can also delete web storage data by using their browser's command for removing website data. If your web page really needs its user data to be permanent (or, at least, completely under your control), you need to store it on the server.

Both `localStorage` and `sessionStorage` do double duty as objects that implement several methods that your code can use to add, retrieve, and delete user data. Each data item is stored as a key-value pair as part of a JSON object. What on Earth is a "JSON object" you ask? Read on, dear reader, read on.

Introducing JSON

Long ago, someone with a tall forehead realized that the JavaScript world needed a straightforward way to move data to and from a script (from and to a web server, say, or from and to a web browser). The format needed to be pure text, have a relatively simple syntax, and be an open standard so that there would be no restrictions on its use.

The result was a data format called *JavaScript Object Notation*, or *JSON* (pronounced "Jason," like the name), for short. The *JavaScript* part of the name tells you that JSON is part of the JavaScript standard, which includes a JSON object for working with JSON strings. The *Object* part of the name tells you that (as I describe in the next section) JSON's syntax is very much like the syntax used by JavaScript objects.

Learning the JSON syntax

I talk about JavaScript object literals in several places in this book, and if you know about object literals, JSON objects will look familiar. Here's the general syntax:

```
{
    "property1": value1,
    "property2": value2,
    ...
    "propertyN": valueN
}
```

JSON data looks like an object, but it's really just text that consists of one or more property–value pairs with the following characteristics:

>> Each property name is surrounded by double quotation marks (").

>> Each value can be one of the following:

- A number

- A string (in which case the value must be surrounded by double quotation marks)

- A Boolean (true or false)

- null (that is, no value)

- A JavaScript array literal (comma-separated values surrounded by square brackets — [and])

- A JavaScript object literal (comma-separated *property*: *value* pairs surrounded by braces — { and })

>> The property-value pairs are separated by commas.

>> The block of property-value pairs is surrounded by braces ({ and}).

Here's an example:

```
{
    "account": 853,
    "name": "Alfreds Futterkiste",
    "supplier": false,
```

```
    "recentOrders": [28394,29539,30014],
    "contact": {
        "name": "Maria Anders",
        "phone": "030-0074321",
        "email": "m.anders@futterkiste.com"
    }
}
```

Declaring and using JSON variables

In the next section, I talk about how useful JSON is for getting data to and from web storage. However, you can also use JSON data in your non-web-storage code. You begin by declaring a JSON variable (check out bk03ch10/example01.html in this book's example files):

```
const customer = {
    "account": 853,
    "name": "Alfreds Futterkiste",
    "supplier": false,
    "recentOrders": [28394,29539,30014],
    "contact": {
        "name": "Maria Anders",
        "phone": "030-0074321",
        "email": "m.anders@futterkiste.com"
    }
}
```

You can then refer to any property in the JSON data by using the *variable.property* syntax. Here are some examples:

```
customer.account          // Returns 853
customer.name             // Returns "Alfreds Futterkiste"
customer.recentOrders[1]  // Returns 29539
customer.contact.email    // Returns "m.anders@futterkiste.com"
```

TIP

The JSON syntax can be a bit tricky, so it's a good idea to check that your data is valid before using it in your code. The easiest way to do that is to use the JSONLint (https://jsonlint.com) validation tool. Copy your JSON code, paste it into the JSONLint text area, and then click Validate JSON.

Converting a JavaScript object to JSON

Although you can use JSON data directly in your code, you're more likely to store your data in a JavaScript object. If you then need to convert that object to the JSON format, you can *stringify* the object by invoking the `stringify()` method of the JSON object. Here's the simplified syntax to use:

```
JSON.stringify(object, replacer[,spaces])
```

where:

> » *object* is the JavaScript object you want to convert to JSON format.

> » *replacer* is a function or array that modifies the stringification process in some way. This parameter is beyond the scope of this book, so in the examples I set this parameter to `null`.

> » *spaces* is an optional value that specifies the number of spaces you want your JSON string to be indented for readability. (If you won't ever look at the resulting JSON string, you can leave off the `null` and *spaces* arguments and use just the *object* argument.)

Here's an example (check out bk03ch10/example02.html):

HTML:

```
<pre id="output">
</pre>
```

JavaScript:

```
// Declare a JavaScript object
const userData = {
    bgColor: "darkolivegreen",
    textColor: "antiquewhite",
    textSize: "1.25em",
    typefaces: ["Georgia", "Verdana", "serif"],
    subscriber: true,
    subscriptionType: 3
};
```

```
// Stringify it
const userDataJSON = JSON.stringify(userData, null, "    ");

// Display the result
document.querySelector('#output').innerHTML = userDataJSON;
```

Figure 10-1 shows the output.

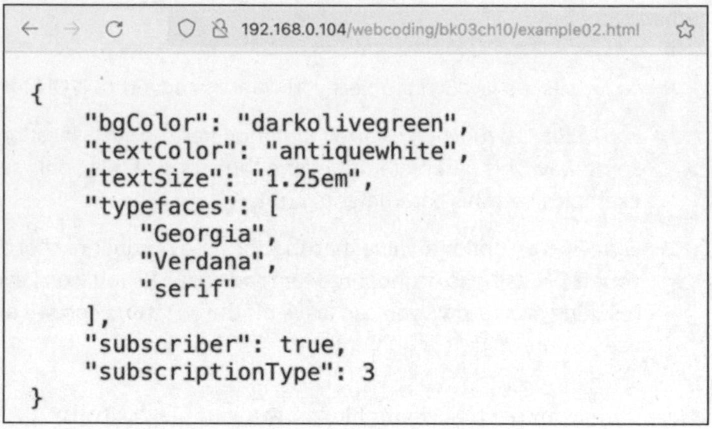

192.168.0.104/webcoding/bk03ch10/example02.html

```
{
    "bgColor": "darkolivegreen",
    "textColor": "antiquewhite",
    "textSize": "1.25em",
    "typefaces": [
        "Georgia",
        "Verdana",
        "serif"
    ],
    "subscriber": true,
    "subscriptionType": 3
}
```

FIGURE 10-1:
The JavaScript
object converted
to a JSON string.

Converting a JSON string to a JavaScript object

When your script receives a JSON string (from the server or, for the purposes of this chapter, from web storage), you'll usually want to convert that string to a good, old-fashioned JavaScript object. You make that conversion by invoking the parse() method of the JSON object:

```
JSON.parse(json)
```

where *json* is the JSON string you want to convert to a JavaScript object.

Here's an example (bk03ch10/example03.html):

```
// Declare a JSON string
const userDataJSON = `{
    "bgColor": "darkolivegreen",
    "textColor": "antiquewhite",
    "textSize": "1.25em",
```

```
    "typefaces": [
        "Georgia",
        "Verdana",
        "serif"
    ],
    "subscriber": true,
    "subscriptionType": 3
}`;

// Parse it
const userData = JSON.parse(userDataJSON);

// Display the result
console.log(userData);
```

Note the use of back tick (`) delimiters in the userDataJSON string, which enable me to display the JSON data on multiple lines for readability (as I describe in Book 3, Chapter 9). Figure 10-2 shows the output in the console (see Book 5, Chapter 2).

FIGURE 10-2:
The JSON string converted to a JavaScript object.

TIP

To display the console in most web browsers, right-click the web page, click Inspect (or press Ctrl+Shift+I in Windows or Option+⌘+I in macOS), and then click the Console tab.

Adding Data to Web Storage

When you want to store data beyond the current browser session with local Storage or just for the current browser session with sessionStorage, you add data to web storage by using the setItem() method:

```
localStorage.setItem(key, value)
```

or:

```
sessionStorage.setItem(key, value)
```

where:

>> *key* is a string that specifies the key for the web storage item.

>> *value* is the value associated with the web storage key. The value can be a
string, a number, a Boolean, or an object. Note, however, that web storage
can store only strings, so any value you specify will be converted to a string
when it's stored.

Here's an example:

```
localStorage.setItem('fave-color', '#ba55d3');
```

It's common to store a collection of related key-value pairs as a JSON string. For
example, suppose you collect your data into a JavaScript object:

```
// Declare a JavaScript object
const userData = {
    bgColor: "darkolivegreen",
    textColor: "antiquewhite",
    textSize: 20,
    typefaces: ["Georgia", "Verdana", "serif"],
    subscriber: true,
    subscriptionType: 3
}
```

Before you can add such an object to web storage, you have to stringify it using the
JSON.stringify() method (bk03ch10/example04.html):

```
localStorage.setItem('user-data', JSON.stringify(userData));
```

TIP

When you're testing your web page, you may want to check that your data is being
stored correctly. You can just try getting the data back from storage, as I describe
in the next section. Alternatively, you can open your browser's web development
tools (see Book 5, Chapter 1) and then display the Application tab (if you're using
Chrome or Edge) or the Storage tab (for Firefox or Safari). Check the tab's Local
Storage or Session Storage items to see whether your data was stored correctly
(refer to Figure 10-3).

FIGURE 10-3:
Viewing local
storage data
in the web
browser's
development
tools.

REMEMBER

When you store user data using web storage, that data is available only to the user in the same web browser running on the same device. For example, if you save data for a user running, say, Safari on an iPhone, when that user returns to your site using, say, Chrome on a desktop computer, that data will not be available to the user.

Getting Data from Web Storage

After you've stored some data, you can retrieve an item from web storage by using the `getItem()` method of either the `localStorage` or `sessionStorage` object (use the same storage object that you used to store the data in the first place):

```
localStorage.getItem(key)
```

or:

```
sessionStorage.getItem(key)
```

where *key* is a string that specifies the key for the storage item.

Here's an example:

```
const userFaveColor = localStorage.getItem('fave-color');
```

If you stored a JavaScript object as a JSON string, use `JSON.parse()` to restore the object (bk03ch10/example05.html):

```
const userData = JSON.parse(localStorage.getItem('user-data'));
```

Removing Data from Web Storage

Web storage is limited, so if you've stored some data you no longer need, it's best to remove it from either the localStorage or sessionStorage object (depending on where you stored the data originally).

To delete some data, use the removeItem() method:

```
localStorage.removeItem(key)
```

or:

```
sessionStorage.removeItem(key)
```

where *key* is a string that specifies the key for the storage item.

Here's an example:

```
localStorage.removeItem('fave-color');
```

If you want to start fresh and delete everything from web storage, use the clear() method:

```
localStorage.clear()
```

or:

```
sessionStorage.clear()
```

Chapter 11

More JavaScript Goodies

I'm an inveterate fox and not a hedgehog, so I always think you should try everything.

— CLIFFORD GEERTZ

There's an old saying that "A jack of all trades is a master of none" and it means that if you spend all your time learning a little about a lot of things, you'll never learn a lot about one thing. However, did you know that the full saying is "A jack of all trades is a master of none, but oftentimes better than a master of one"? This expanded version implies that having a broad base of skills can often be more useful than having a narrow expertise.

That expanded saying could serve as the unofficial motto for this book. Here you're learning not everything there is to know about HTML, CSS, JavaScript, PHP, or MySQL but everything you need to know about *all* of those topics. You're becoming a jack (or jill) of all these web development trades which, for all but the largest websites, makes you more useful than someone who has mastered just one of them.

The chapters in Book 3 provide you with just about everything you need to know about JavaScript. In this chapter, you complete your JavaScript education with an exploration of a few useful coding topics, including the spread operator, the rest parameter, and exporting and importing code. Note that all these topics are

ECMAScript 2015 (ES6) innovations, so don't use them if you have to support very old browsers, such as Internet Explorer 11.

Expanding Arrays and Objects with the Spread Operator

You can make many JavaScript statements easier to understand and faster to code by using the spread operator (sometimes called the *spread syntax*). The *spread operator* is three dots (...) appended to a reference to whatever item you want to apply it to. For example, if you have an array named myArray, you apply the spread operator like so:

```
...myArray
```

You can use the spread syntax with an array, a JavaScript object, or a string. In each case, the spread operator takes a reference to a single item (again, an array, an object, or a string) and expands (or "spreads out") that single item into its component items, as follows:

>> **Array:** The spread operator expands the array into the items stored in the array.

>> **Object:** The spread operator expands the object into the property-value pairs stored in the object.

>> **String:** The spread operator expands the string into the individual characters of the string.

None of this might strike you as the least bit useful at the moment, but I hope to convince you otherwise over the next few sections.

Using the spread operator with an array

The spread operator is most commonly used with arrays. Quite a few use cases demonstrate how the spread operator makes array code easier to understand and write; the next few sections take you through some of these cases.

REMEMBER

If you need to get up to speed on JavaScript arrays, Book 3, Chapter 8 is the place to go.

Copying an array

It's surprisingly hard to copy an array in JavaScript. For example, this looks like it works:

```
const thisArray = ["alpha", "beta", "gamma"];
const thatArray = thisArray;
console.log(thatArray); // ["alpha", "beta", "gamma"]
```

Suppose you then make a change to the original array:

```
thisArray[0] = "aleph";
console.log(thatArray); // ["aleph", "beta", "gamma"]
```

Whoa! You changed the value of the first item in `thisArray`, but the same change also propagated to `thatArray`. When you run `thatArray = thisArray`, all you're doing is pointing `thatArray` at the same memory object as the one `thisArray` points to. Change one and the other always changes along with it.

When you need a separate copy of an array, use the spread operator (check out bk03ch11/example01.html in this book's example files):

```
// Define the original array
const thisArray = ["alpha", "beta", "gamma"];

// Make a copy using the spread operator
const thatArray = [...thisArray];

// Confirm the copy
console.log(thatArray);

// Change something in the original array
thisArray[0] = "aleph";

// Confirm that the copy is unchanged
console.log(thatArray);
```

The workhorse here is the following line:

```
const thatArray = [...thisArray];
```

The `...thisArray` operand says to the browser, in effect, "Excuse me, but would you mind taking all the items in `thisArray` and inserting them here as separate items? Thanks ever so much!" In other words, the spread operator expands or "spreads out" the items in the specified array. Since, in this case, those items are expanded into an array literal, the result is a true copy of the original array.

Figure 11-1 shows that, indeed, the copied array remains unchanged after the original array was modified.

FIGURE 11-1:
The copied array remains the same after the original array was changed.

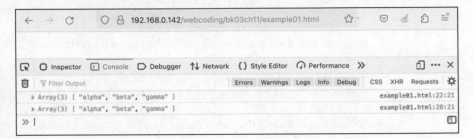

Concatenating arrays

In Book 3, Chapter 8, you learn that you can combine two or more arrays by using the concat() method. You can also concatenate an array by using the spread operator. Here's an example (check out bk03ch11/example02.html):

```javascript
// Declare the arrays
const electronics = ["Silent alarm clock", "Electric dog
    polisher", "Instant slow cooker"];
const recreation = ["Inflatable dartboard", "One ounce
    dumbbell", "Stringless tennis racket"];
const home = ["Banana peel welcome mat", "Sandpaper bathroom
    tissue", "Flame-retardant firewood"];

// Combine them with the spread operator
const featuredProducts = [...electronics, ...home];

// Display the concatenated array
console.log(featuredProducts);
```

Figure 11-2 shows the displayed concatenated array.

Inserting items into an array literal

Here's a JavaScript scenario that comes up more often than you might think. Consider the following array literal:

```javascript
const myArray = ["tigers", "bears"];
```

FIGURE 11-2:
The concatenated
array.

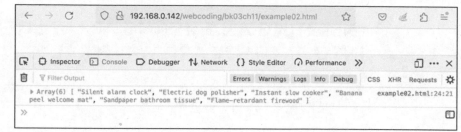

Suppose you want to create a new array literal that has the `"lions"` string as the first item, the items of `myArray` as the next two items, and then the `"oh my!"` string as the last item. Here's one way you could do it:

```
const myFullArray = ["lions"].concat(myArray).concat(["oh
    my!"]);
```

This code produces the following array:

```
["lions", "tigers", "bears", "oh my!"]
```

That's great, but the two calls of the `concat()` method make the code hard to read and unintuitive. You'd think that inserting an existing array literal into a new array literal would be straightforward!

Well, working with arrays in this way can be made easier and more intuitive using the spread operator, like so (bk03ch11/example03.html):

```
// Declare the initial array literal
const myArray = ["tigers", "bears"];

// Use the spread operator (...) to insert the
// array literal into a new array
const myFullArray = ["lions", ...myArray, "oh my!"];

// Display the result
console.log(myFullArray);
```

The statement that creates `myFullArray` is much easier to understand than the earlier code that uses all those `concat()` methods. And Figure 11-3 shows that it works.

INSERTING AN EXISTING ARRAY LITERAL INTO ANOTHER ARRAY LITERAL

A complex (but also quite common) scenario is when you have two array literals and you want to insert one inside the other:

```
const myArray1 = ["lions", "oh my!"];
const myArray2 = ["tigers", "bears"];
```

In regular JavaScript, to insert the second array inside the first array after the first item, you'd use the following code:

```
myArray1.splice.apply(myArray1, [1, 0].concat(myArray2));
```

Yuck! The underlying machinations behind this code are so abstruse and technical that I'm doing you a favor by skipping over them. Here, instead, is the equivalent code using the spread operator (bk03ch11/example04.html):

```
myArray1.splice(1, 0, ...myArray2);
```

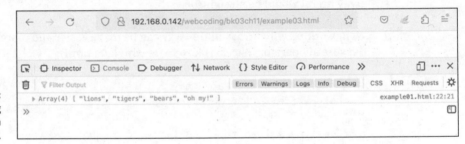

FIGURE 11-3:
The resulting array displayed in the console.

Passing an array's items as function arguments

The spread operator is also useful if you want to use an array's elements as the arguments for a function. Consider the following function (bk03ch11/example05.html):

```
function volumeOfPrism(length, width, height) {
    return length * width * height;
}
```

If you have an array that consists of a particular length, width, and height, you can apply the spread operator to use the array's individual elements as the function's arguments:

```
const myPrism = [5, 8, 10];
const myPrismVolume = volumeOfPrism(...myPrism);
```

Using the spread operator with an object

The spread operator also works with JavaScript objects and can make object-related code quicker to write and easier to understand. The next few sections take you through some example use cases.

REMEMBER

To learn about JavaScript objects, refer to Book 3, Chapter 6.

Copying an object

Copying an object isn't as straightforward as you might think. For example, this looks like a reasonable approach:

```
let currentProduct = {
    code: 193721,
    name: "Noise-Canceling Speakers",
    price: 74.99
};
const saleProduct = currentProduct;
console.log(saleProduct);
```

Here's the output you'd see:

```
{code: 193721, name: "Noise-Canceling Speakers", price: 74.99}
```

Awesome! The `saleProduct` object appears to be a copy of the `currentProduct` object. However, what happens if you change a value in the copied object? Take a look:

```
saleProduct.price = 59.99;
console.log(currentProduct);
```

This code changes the `price` value in the copied object. Here's what you get when you display the original object:

```
{code: 193721, name: "Noise-Canceling Speakers", price: 59.99}
```

No, your eyes don't deceive you. Changing something in the copied object also changed the same thing in the original! Why? Because when you set saleProduct = currentProduct, you're pointing currentProduct at the same memory object as the one saleProduct points to. Change one object and the other object changes in the same way.

To get a true copy of an object, use the spread operator (bk03ch11/example06. html):

```
// Define the original object
let currentProduct = {
    code: 193721,
    name: "Noise-Canceling Speakers",
    price: 74.99
};

// Make a copy using the spread operator
const saleProduct = {...currentProduct};

// Change the price in the copied object
saleProduct.price = 59.99;

// Display the updated copy
console.log(saleProduct);

// Confirm that the original is unchanged
console.log(currentProduct);
```

Note, in particular, the following line:

```
const saleProduct = {...currentProduct};
```

The...currentProduct operand tells the browser, in effect, "Yoo-hoo, browser person! Please take all the property-value pairs in currentProduct and insert them here as separate property-value pairs. You're a dear!" In other words, the spread operator is expanding or "spreading out" the property-value pairs in the specified object. Since, in this case, those property-value pairs are expanded into an object literal, the result is a true copy of the original object.

Figure 11-4 shows that, indeed, the original object remains unchanged after the copied object was modified.

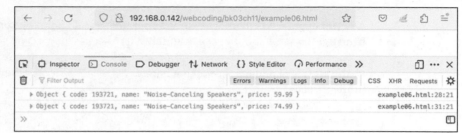

Merging objects

One common object-related operation is merging two or more objects into a single object. For example, suppose you have two user-related objects: one that holds the user's contact data and one that holds the user's shipping info. If you want to combine these into a single object, you could do something like this:

```
const userContact = {
    firstName: "Alan",
    lastName: "Milne",
    email: "aa@poohbear.com"
};

const userShipping = {
    street: "321 Main Street",
    city: "Toad Suck",
    state: "AR",
    zip: "12345"
};

const userInfo = {
    firstName: userContact.firstName,
    lastName: userContact.lastName,
    email: userContact.email,
    street: userShipping.street,
    city: userShipping.city,
    state: userShipping.state,
    zip: userShipping.zip
};
```

Yes, that gets the job done, but it seems like a lot of work to repeat all those property names when defining the merged object. Imagine if you wanted to merge four or five objects or objects with a few dozen properties. Forget it!

More JavaScript Goodies

A better approach is to use the spread operator, as I do here (bk03ch11/example07.
html):

```javascript
// Define the user's contact data
const userContact = {
    firstName: "Alan",
    lastName: "Milne",
    email: "aa@poohbear.com"
};

// Define the user's shipping data
const userShipping = {
    street: "321 Main Street",
    city: "Toad Suck",
    state: "AR",
    zip: "12345"
};

// Merge the objects using the spread operator
const userInfo = {
    ...userContact,
    ...userShipping
};

// Display the merged object
console.log(userInfo);
```

Figure 11-5 shows the merged object.

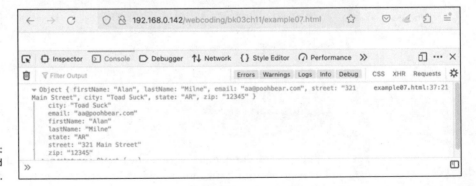

FIGURE 11-5:
The merged
object.

Using the spread operator with a string

When used with a string, the spread operator expands the individual characters in the string. That expansion makes it easy to populate an array with a string's characters. You'd normally populate an array with a string's letters using the split() method:

```
const str = "step on no pets";
const chars = str.split("");
// chars: ["s", "t", "e", "p", " ", "o", "n", " ", "n", "o",
   "p". "e", "t", "s"]
```

That works, but it's not obvious what the split() method is doing here. You can make this operation a little clearer and a little less verbose by using the spread operator:

```
const str = "step on no pets";
const chars = [...str];
// chars: ["s", "t", "e", "p", " ", "o", "n", " ", "n", "o",
   "p". "e", "t", "s"]
```

Here's an example (bk03ch11/example08.html) that uses the spread operator on a string as part of a function that tests whether the string is a palindrome:

```
// isPalindrome() checks whether the input string is a
   palindrome
function isPalindrome(testStr) {

    // Use the spread operator to create an array of the
   string's characters
    const chars = [...testStr];

    // Create a new array with the characters reversed
    const reversedChars = [...chars].reverse();

    // Check to see if the strings generated by the two arrays
   are identical
    return chars.join('') === reversedChars.join('');
}

// Define a string to test
const str = "step on no pets";
```

```
// Get the result
const result = isPalindrome(str);

// Display the result message
console.log(`"${str}" ${result ? "is" : "is not"} a
    palindrome.`);
```

Figure 11-6 shows the result message from this script.

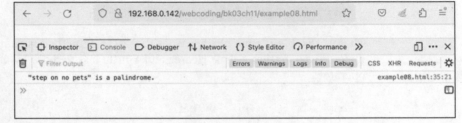

FIGURE 11-6:
Yep: "step on
no pets" is a
palindrome.

Condensing Arrays with the Rest Parameter

If you read the preceding section about the spread operator, which is represented by three dots (. . .), prepare to be, if not confused, then at the very least perplexed. Why? Because in this section you learn about something called the rest parameter, which is represented by — wait for it — three dots (. . .)! Why the JavaScript poohbahs decided to use the same symbol for two different operations is above my pay grade, but I thought I ought to at least warn you before proceeding. Okay, where were we?

Most of the time you'll know exactly how many arguments a function requires, but every now and then you'll need a bit more flexibility. That is, a function may take two arguments most of the time, but in certain situations your script may need to pass three, four, or even more arguments.

For example, here's a simple function that creates a DOM element (refer to Book 3, Chapter 6) and adds a single class to the element:

```
function createElement(tagName, className) {

    // Create the element
    const element = document.createElement(tagName);
```

```
    // Add the class
    element.classList.add(className);

    // Return the new element
    return element;
}

// Call the createElement() function
const div = createElement('div', 'container');

// Display the element's HTML
console.log(div.outerHTML);
```

Running this script displays the following output in the console:

```
<div class="container"></div>
```

That's all good, but it's easy to imagine scenarios where you might want to add two or three or even a dozen class names to the new element. How can you handle these scenarios? By applying the rest parameter (...) to the last function argument:

```
function myFunction(argA, argB, ...moreArgs) {
    JavaScript statements
}
```

Now consider the following function calls:

```
myFunction("eeny", "meeny");
myFunction("eeny", "meeny", "miney", "mo");
```

In the first call, the two passed values are stored as expected in the function's argA and argB parameters. In the second call the first two passed values are stored in the argA and argB parameters, but the next two are stored in the moreArgs parameter as an array:

```
// argA = "eeny"
// argB = "meeny"
// moreArgs = ["miney", "mo"]
```

The following code (bk03ch11/example09.html) creates a new DOM element and uses the rest parameter to handle adding any number of class names to the new element:

```javascript
function createElement(tagName, ...classNames) {

    // Create the element
    const element = document.createElement(tagName);

    // Loop through the classNames array to add the classes
    for (const className of classNames) {
        element.classList.add(className);
    }

    // Return the new element
    return element;
}

// Call the createElement() function
const div = createElement('div', 'container', 'grid',
    'dark-mode');

// Display the element's HTML
console.log(div.outerHTML);
```

Figure 11-7 shows the HTML code for the element created by this script.

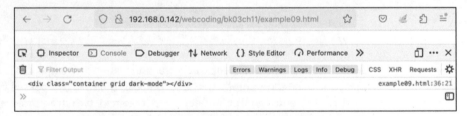

FIGURE 11-7:
Creating a DOM
element with
any number of
class names.

Exporting and Importing Code

As your web development projects expand, so does the footprint of your JavaScript code:

» The smallest projects have all the code between the <script> and </script> tags in an HTML file.

>> Small-to-medium projects move the JavaScript code to a separate .js file that is referenced in each of the project's HTML files:

```
<script src="code.js"></script>
```

>> Medium-to-large projects have the main JavaScript code in one file and then other code — such as common functions, shopping cart code, and site-wide utilities — in separate .js files that are referenced in each of the project's HTML files:

```
<script src="functions.js"></script>
<script src="shopping-cart.js"></script>
<script src="utilities.js"></script>
<script src="code.js"></script>
```

WARNING

The order of the script elements is important since the web browser parses these files in the order in which they appear. If, say, the utilities.js file requires code from the functions.js file, the <script> tag for the utilities.js file must appear later than the <script> tag for the functions.js file or you'll get an error.

The last technique of referencing every JavaScript file in every HTML file works fine, but it's often overkill. For example, what if a script in the current page requires only a single function from a particular .js file? Similarly, what if a .js file has a thousand lines of code, but your script needs to use the values of only two variables from that file?

If you find that you need only certain bits of code from some JavaScript files, consider turning those files into modules. A *module* is a standalone chunk of JavaScript that encapsulates specific logic or functionality. Modules offer many benefits, but the main one for our purposes is that you can export specific module items (such as functions or variables) and then import just what you need within either another JavaScript file or a <script> tag. The next two sections take you through the specifics of exporting and importing module code.

Exporting variables, functions, and other strangers

If you have a JavaScript file that contains code that you want to make available to your other scripts, turn that file into a module by exporting the items you want to make available.

Defining named exports

The most straightforward way to export an item is to add the `export` keyword to the beginning of the item's declaration. Here are some examples:

```
export let myVariable = 42;
export const PI = Math.PI;
export function areaOfCircle(radius) {
    return PI * Math.pow(radius, 2);
}
```

Alternatively, you can declare the variables and functions normally and then export them later as a list between braces ({ and }) after the `export` keyword (bk03ch11/example10.js):

```
let myVariable = 42;
const PI = Math.PI;
function areaOfCircle(radius) {
    return PI * Math.pow(radius, 2);
}
export { myVariable as yourVariable, PI, areaOfCircle };
```

Note in the first exported item the use of the `as` keyword to specify a different export name for (in this case) a variable. Why would you want to export an item under a different name? One reason would be to match a name already being used in your other code. Similarly, you might not be able to export the item under its original name because that name might conflict with an existing name in your other code.

REMEMBER

As I show in the "Importing what you've exported" section, when you define a named export, you must import the item using the same name as you used to export it.

Defining a default export

You can make a particular item a bit easier to import by setting up that item as a module's default export. Here's an example that sets up a function as a module's default export:

```
export default function ouncesToGrams(oz) {
    return oz * 28.3495;
}
```

This example uses a named function, but you can also use an anonymous function or an arrow function (refer to Book 3, Chapter 5).

You can also use the default export to export an expression rather than a function. Here's an example (bk03ch11/example10.js):

```
const date = new Date();
const days = ['Sunday', 'Monday', 'Tuesday', 'Wednesday',
   'Thursday', 'Friday', 'Saturday'];
export default days[date.getDay()];
```

This code creates a date, defines the days array with the days of the week, and then returns the current day of the week as the module's default export.

Importing what you've exported

The point of exporting a variable, a function, or an expression is to use that code elsewhere in your project. You use exported code by importing it into either another JavaScript file or a ‹script› tag. Either way, it's important that you tell the browser that you're working with a module and not a regular JavaScript file. You give the browser this info by adding type="module" to the script tag.

If the code that does the importing resides in a separate JavaScript file, your HTML file's ‹head› tag will need to include a reference to the export module that looks like this:

```
<script src="./module.js" type="module"></script>
```

(Note that the path ./module.js means "the module.js file that resides in the same directly as the file that contains this ‹script› tag." If the module resides in a subdirectory, you'll need to modify the path accordingly.)

If the code that does the importing resides in a ‹script› tag, you'll need to modify that tag as follows:

```
<script type="module">
    // JavaScript code goes here
</script>
```

With that out of the way, the next couple of sections provide the importing details.

Importing named exports

To import named exports, you use the following syntax:

```
import { list } from "module";
```

where *list* is a comma-separated list of the named exports you want to import. Note that you must import each item using the same name as you used when exporting the item. However, if you prefer to use a particular imported item under a different name, you can import it using the as keyword to create an alias. For example:

```
import { yourVariable as myVariable } from "./module.js"
```

where *module* is the path and filename of the JavaScript module that contains the exported code. An alias is useful when you need the imported item's name to match a name you're already using in the code that contains the import statement. Similarly, the original import name might conflict with an existing name in the code that contains the import statement, so you need to use an alias, instead.

Here's an example (bk03ch11/example11.html):

```
// Import the named exports from example10.js
import { yourVariable as myVariable, PI, areaOfCircle } from "./
    example10.js";

// Give them a whirl
console.log(`The area of a circle with radius ${myVariable} is
    ${areaOfCircle(myVariable)}`);
```

Importing a default export

Here's the syntax to import a module's default export:

```
import defaultExport from "module";
```

where:

>> *defaultExport* is the name you want to apply to the default export. Even if the export module defined a name for the default export, you can use any legit JavaScript name here.

>> *module* is the path and filename of the JavaScript module that contains the exported code.

Here's an example (bk03ch11/example11.html):

```
// Import the default export from example10.js
import dayOfTheWeek from "./example10.js";

// Display it
console.log(`The current day of the week is ${dayOfTheWeek}`);
```

4

Coding the Back End: PHP and MySQL

Contents at a Glance

IN THIS CHAPTER

» **Getting comfy with PHP**

» **Building PHP expressions**

» **Controlling PHP code**

» **Figuring out functions and objects**

» **Debugging PHP**

Chapter **1**

Learning PHP Coding Basics

In the end, what I think set PHP apart in the early days, and still does today, is that it always tries to find the shortest path to solving the Web problem . . . When you need something up and working by Friday so you don't have to spend all weekend leafing through 800-page manuals, PHP starts to look pretty good.

— RASMUS LERDORF, CREATOR OF PHP

You code the front end of a web project using tools such as HTML and CSS (see Book 2), and JavaScript (see Book 3). You can build awesome web pages using just those front-end tools, but if you want to build pages that are dynamic and applike, you need to bring in the back end and use it to harness the power of the web server.

For web projects, the back end most often means storing data in a MySQL database and accessing that data by using the PHP programming language. I cover all that in Chapters 2 and 3 of this minibook. For now, you need some background in PHP coding.

In this chapter, you explore PHP from a web developer's perspective, and by the time you're done you'll know everything you need to know about PHP variables, expressions, arrays, loops, functions, and objects. In short, you'll be ready to join the web coding big leagues by bringing together the front end and the back end to create truly spectacular and useful web pages and apps.

Understanding How PHP Scripts Work

PHP is a *server-side* programming language, which means that PHP code executes only on the web server, not in the web browser. Most web servers today come with a piece of software called a *PHP processor*, and it's the job of the PHP processor to run any PHP code sent its way. That PHP code can come in two different packages:

>> **As a pure PHP file:** This is a file on the web server, usually one with a filename that uses the .php extension. When I call this a "pure" PHP file, I mean the file contains nothing but PHP code. Such files are rarely loaded directly into the web browser. Instead, pure PHP files are usually called by JavaScript code, most often either to process form input or to ask for data from a MySQL database.

>> **As part of an HTML file:** This is a regular HTML file, but with one or more chunks of PHP code embedded in the file. On most web servers, this file requires the .php extension to enable the server to execute the PHP statements.

Whatever the package, the PHP code is processed as follows:

1. A web browser requests the PHP or HTML file.

2. When the web server sees that the file contains PHP code, it passes that code along to the PHP processor.

3. The PHP processor parses and executes the PHP code.

4. If the PHP code contains any statements that output text or HTML tags or both, the PHP processor returns that output to the web server.

5. The web server sends the output from Step 4 to the web browser.

REMEMBER

It's important to understand that, in the end, no PHP code is ever sent to the web browser. All the browser gets is the output of the PHP code. Yes, it's possible to run PHP scripts that don't output anything, but in web development the main job of most of your PHP code will be to return some data to the browser.

Learning the basic syntax of PHP scripts

You tell the web server that you want to run some PHP code by surrounding that code with the PHP tags:

```php
<?php
    Your PHP statements go here
?>
```

For example, PHP's basic output mechanism is the echo *output* command, where *output* is a string containing text and/or HTML tags:

```php
<?php
    echo "<h1>Hello PHP World!</h1>";
?>
```

REMEMBER

Note that the echo statement ends with a semicolon. All PHP statements require a semicolon at the end.

If you place just the preceding code in a .php file (check out bk04ch01/example01. php in this book's example files) and load that file into a web browser, you see the output shown in Figure 1-1.

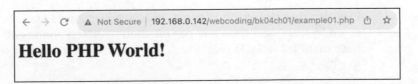

FIGURE 1-1: The output of PHP's echo command.

Alternatively, you can embed the PHP code in an HTML file, as shown in the following example (check out bk04ch01/example02.php):

```html
<!DOCTYPE html>
<html lang="en">
    <head>
        <meta charset="UTF-8">
        <title>Book 4, Chapter 1, Example 2</title>
    </head>
    <body>
        <p>
            Here's the output of the PHP script:
        </p>
```

```
    <?php
        echo "<h1>Hello PHP World!</h1>";
    ?>
    </body>
</html>
```

Figure 1-2 shows the result.

FIGURE 1-2:
You can also
embed PHP
output within an
HTML file.

Declaring PHP variables

As with JavaScript (see Book 3, Chapter 2), PHP uses variables for storing data to use in expressions and functions, and PHP supports the standard literal data types: integers (such as 5 or –17), floating-point numbers (such as 2.4 or 3.14159), strings (such as "Hello" or 'World'), and Booleans (TRUE or FALSE).

PHP variable names must begin with a dollar sign ($), followed by a letter or underscore, and then any combination of letters, numbers, or underscores. Note that PHP variable names are case-sensitive, so $str isn't the same variable as $STR.

You don't need any special keyword (such as JavaScript's let or const) to declare a variable. Instead, you declare a variable in PHP by assigning the variable a value:

```
$str = "Hello World!";
$interest_rate = 0.03;
$app_loaded = FALSE;
```

Building PHP expressions

When you build a PHP expression — that is, a collection of symbols, words, and numbers that performs a calculation and produces a result — you can use mostly the same operators as in JavaScript (see Book 3, Chapter 3):

>> **Arithmetic:** Addition (+), subtraction (–), multiplication (∗), division (/), modulus (%), and exponentiation (∗∗).

>> **Incrementing and decrementing:** Post-increment ($var++), pre-increment (++$var), post-decrement ($var−−), and pre-decrement (−−$var).

>> **Comparison:** Equal (=), not equal (!=), greater than (>), less than (<), greater than or equal (>=), less than or equal (<=), identity (===), and non-identity (!==). In PHP you can also use <> as the not equal operator.

>> **Logical:** And (&&), Or (||), and Not (!). In PHP you can also use and as the And operator and or as the Or operator.

Where PHP differs from JavaScript is with the string concatenation operator, which in PHP is the dot (.) symbol rather than JavaScript's plus (+) symbol. Here's an example (bk04ch01/example03.php):, and Figure 1-3 shows the result.

```php
<?php
    $str1 = "<h2>Concatenate ";
    $str2 = "Me!</h2>";
    echo $str1 . $str2;
?>
```

FIGURE 1-3:
In PHP, you use the dot (.) operator to concatenate two strings.

Outputting Text and Tags

Your back-end PHP scripts pass data to your web app's front end (HTML and JavaScript) not by using some complex communications link but simply by outputting the data. I talk about this in more detail in Book 4, Chapter 3, but for now let's look at the mechanisms PHP offers for outputting data.

PHP's simplest output tool is the print command:

```
print output;
```

where *output* is a string — which could be a string literal, string variable, string property value, or the string result of a function — that you want to output. You can include HTML tags in the output string.

```php
<?php
    print "<h1>Hello World!</h1>";
?>
```

To output more than one item, you need to use PHP's echo command:

```php
echo output;
```

where *output* is one or more strings — which could be string literals, string variables, string property values, or the string results of a function — that you want to output. If you include two or more output items, separate each one with a comma. You can include HTML tags in any of the output strings:

```php
<?php
    $str1 = "<h2>Concatenate ";
    $str2 = "Me!</h2>";
    echo $str1, $str2;
?>
```

Adding line breaks

If you use PHP to generate quite a lot of HTML and text for your page, you need to be careful how you structure the output. To see what I mean, first check out the following PHP code (bk04ch01/example04.php):

```php
<?php
    $str1 = "<div>What does PHP stand for?</div>";
    $str2 = "<div>It's a <i>recursive acronym</i>:</div>";
    $str3 = "<div>PHP: Hypertext Preprocessor</div>";
    echo $str1, $str2, $str3;
?>
```

This code declares three strings — all div elements with text — and uses echo to output them. Figure 1-4 shows two browser windows. In the upper window, you can see that the output from the preceding code looks fine. However, the lower window shows the source code for the page and, as you can see, all the output text and tags appear on a single line.

To make the source code text easier to read, you should add line breaks to your PHP output strings. You insert a line break using the *newline* character \n (which doesn't appear on the web page). Here's the revised code (with \n added to the end of the $str1 and $str2 variables; refer to bk04ch01/example05.php), and Figure 1-5 shows that the source code now appears on multiple lines:

```php
<?php
    $str1 = "<div>What does PHP stand for?</div>\n";
    $str2 = "<div>It's a <i>recursive acronym</i>:</div>\n";
    $str3 = "<div>PHP: Hypertext Preprocessor</div>";
    echo $str1, $str2, $str3;
?>
```

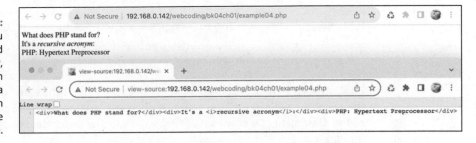

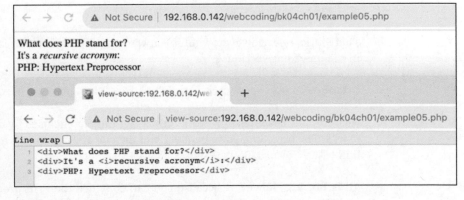

WARNING

The \n newline code only works in a string that uses double quotation marks. If you use single quotation marks, PHP outputs the characters \n instead of creating a newline. For example:

```php
echo 'Ready\nSet\nGo!';
```

The output of this statement is

```
Ready\nSet\nGo!
```

Mixing and escaping quotation marks

You can enclose PHP string literals in either double quotation marks or single quotation marks, but not both:

```
$order = "Double espresso";         // This is legal
$book = 'A Singular Man';            // So's this
$weather = 'Mixed precipitation";    // This is not legal
```

However, mixing quotation mark types is sometimes necessary. Consider this:

```
$tag = "<a href="https://wordspy.com">";
```

That statement will cough up an error because PHP thinks the string ends after the second double quotation mark, so it doesn't know what to do with the rest of the statement. To solve this problem, swap the outer double quotation marks for singles:

```
$tag = '<a href="https://wordspy.com/">';
```

That works fine. However, what if you want to add some line breaks, as I describe in the preceding section:

```
$tag = '<a href="https://wordspy.com/">\nWord Spy\n</a>';
```

Nice try, but newlines (\n) work only when they're enclosed by double quotation marks. The preceding statement will not include any line breaks and will show the link text as \nWord Spy\n. Sigh.

All is not lost, however, because you can convince the PHP processor to treat a quotation mark as a string literal (instead of a string delimiter), by preceding the quotation mark with a backslash (\). This process is known in the trade as *escaping* the quotation mark. For example, you can fix the preceding example by enclosing the entire string in double quotation marks (to get the newlines to work) and escaping the double quotation marks used for the ‹a› tag's href value:

```
$tag = "<a href=\"https://wordspy.com/\">\nWord Spy\n</a>";
```

Outputting variables in strings

One very useful feature of PHP strings is that you can insert a variable name into a string and the PHP processor will handily replace the variable name with its current value. Here's an example:

```php
<?php
    $title = "Inflatable Dartboard Landing Page";
    $tag = "<title>$title</title>";
    echo $tag;
?>
```

The output of this code is

```
<title>Inflatable Dartboard Landing Page</title>
```

Some folks call this *interpolating* the variable, but we'll have none of that here.

Alas, variable value substitution works only with strings enclosed by double quotation marks. If you use single quotation marks, PHP outputs the variable name instead of its value. For example, this

```php
<?php
    $title = "Inflatable Dartboard Landing Page";
    $tag = '<title>$title</title>';
    echo $tag;
?>
```

outputs this:

```
<title>$title</title>
```

Outputting long strings

If you have a long string to output, one way to do it would be to break up the string into multiple variables, add newlines at the end of each, if needed, and output each variable.

That works, but PHP offers a shortcut where you output everything as a single string but span the string across multiple lines. For example, I can take the final code from the "Adding line breaks" section and achieve the same result by rewriting it as follows (bk04ch01/example06.php):

```php
<?php
$str1 = "<div>What does PHP stand for?</div>
<div>It's a <i>recursive acronym</i>:</div>
<div>PHP: Hypertext Preprocessor</div>";
```

```
echo $str1;
?>
```

The implied newlines at the end of the second and third lines are written to the page, so the page source code will look the same as it does in Figure 1-5.

Outputting really long strings

For a super-long string, you can use PHP's *here document* (or *heredoc*) syntax:

```
<<<terminator
Super-long string goes here
terminator;
```

where `terminator` is a label that marks the beginning and end of the string. The label at the end must appear on a line by itself (except for the closing semicolon), with no whitespace before or after the label.

This syntax also supports variable names, so if you include a variable in the string, PHP will substitute the current value of that variable when it outputs the string.

Here's an example (bk04ch01/example07.html):

```
<?php
    $author = "Rasmus Lerdorf";
    $str = <<<END_OF_STRING
    <blockquote>
    In the end, what I think set PHP apart in the early
    days, and still does today, is that it always tries
    to find the shortest path to solving the Web
    problem. It does not try to be a general-purpose
    scripting language and anybody who's looking to
    solve a Web problem will usually find a very direct
    solution through PHP. Many of the alternatives that
    claim to solve the Web problem are just too complex.
    When you need something up and working by Friday so
    you don't have to spend all weekend leafing through
    800-page manuals, PHP starts to look pretty good.
    -$author
    </blockquote>
END_OF_STRING;
    echo $str;
?>
```

Note that I declared a variable named $author, and then I included that variable name in the string (on the second-to-last line of the string). PHP treats a heredoc string as though it was enclosed by double quotation marks, so it substitutes the variable value in the output. Figure 1-6 shows the result.

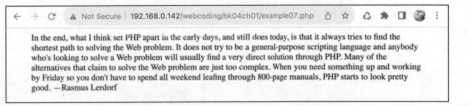

In the end, what I think set PHP apart in the early days, and still does today, is that it always tries to find the shortest path to solving the Web problem. It does not try to be a general-purpose scripting language and anybody who's looking to solve a Web problem will usually find a very direct solution through PHP. Many of the alternatives that claim to solve the Web problem are just too complex. When you need something up and working by Friday so you don't have to spend all weekend leafing through 800-page manuals, PHP starts to look pretty good. —Rasmus Lerdorf

Working with PHP Arrays

Let's take a quick look at arrays in PHP. I'm going to skip lightly over arrays here because I talk about them in detail in Book 3, Chapter 8.

Declaring arrays

PHP gives you a bunch of ways to declare and populate arrays. Probably the most straightforward method is to assign values to explicit index numbers:

```
$array_name[index] = value;
```

where:

>> $array_name is the name of the array variable.

>> index is the optional array index number you want to work with.

>> value is the value you want to assign to the array index number.

For example, the following statements assign string values to the first three elements (that is, the elements at array indexes 0, 1, and 2) of an array named $team_nicknames (bk04ch01/example08.php):

```
$team_nicknames[0] = 'Banana Slugs';
$team_nicknames[1] = 'Fighting Okra';
$team_nicknames[2] = 'Golden Flashes';
```

Note in the syntax that I said the *index* parameter was optional. If you leave it out, PHP assigns the index numbers automatically. So, as long as the $team_nicknames variable doesn't already contain elements, the following code is equivalent to the preceding code (bk04ch01/example09.php):

```
$team_nicknames[] = 'Banana Slugs';
$team_nicknames[] = 'Fighting Okra';
$team_nicknames[] = 'Golden Flashes';
```

To add multiple array values in a single statement, you can use PHP's array keyword:

```
$array_name = array(value1, value1, etc.);
```

where:

» $array_name is the name of the array variable.

» value1, value2, and so on are the values you want to assign to the array.

Here's an example (bk04ch01/example10.php):

```
<?php
    $team_nicknames = array('Banana Slugs', 'Fighting Okra',
  'Golden Flashes');
    echo $team_nicknames[0];
?>
```

The output of this code is

```
Banana Slugs
```

Giving associative arrays a look

Most PHP arrays use numeric index values, but in web development work it's often handy to work with string index values, which are called *keys*. An array that uses keys instead of a numeric index is called an *associative array* because you're associating each key with a value to create an array of key/value pairs.

Here's an example (bk04ch01/example11.php):

```php
<?php
    $team_nicknames['Santa Cruz'] = 'Banana Slugs';
    $team_nicknames['Delta State'] = 'Fighting Okra';
    $team_nicknames['Kent State'] = 'Golden Flashes';
    echo $team_nicknames['Delta State'];
?>
```

The output of this code is

```
Fighting Okra
```

To create an associative array using the array keyword, you assign each key/value pair using the => operator, as in this example (bk04ch01/example12.php):

```php
<?php
    $team_nicknames = array('Santa Cruz' => 'Banana Slugs',
    'Delta State' => 'Fighting Okra', 'Kent State' => 'Golden
    Flashes');
    echo $team_nicknames['Kent State'];
?>
```

The output of this code is

```
Golden Flashes
```

Outputting array values

You can use the echo or print keyword to output individual array values. However, what if you want to see all the values stored in an array? Rather than, say, looping through the array, PHP offers the print_r() function, which outputs the current value of a variable:

```
print_r($variable);
```

where $variable is the name of the variable you want to output.

If you use an array as the print_r() parameter, PHP outputs the contents of the array as key/value pairs. For example, the following code (bk04ch01/example12.php)

```
<pre>
<?php
    $team_nicknames = array('Banana Slugs', 'Fighting Okra',
  'Golden Flashes');
    print_r($team_nicknames);
?>
</pre>
```

outputs the following:

```
Array
(
    [0] => Banana Slugs
    [1] => Fighting Okra
    [2] => Golden Flashes
)
```

TIP

Note that I surrounded the PHP code with the <pre> tag to get the output on multiple lines rather than a single hard-to-read line.

Sorting arrays

If you need your array values sorted alphanumerically, PHP offers a handful of functions that will get the job done. The function you use depends on the type of sort you want (ascending or descending) and whether your array uses numeric indexes or string keys (that is, it's an associative array).

For numeric indexes, you can use the sort() function to sort the values in ascending order (0 to 9, then A to Z, then a to z), or the rsort() function to sort the values in descending order (z to a, then Z to A, then 9 to 0):

```
sort($array);
rsort($array);
```

where $array is the name of the array you want to sort.

Here's an example (bk04ch01/example14.php):

```
<pre>
<?php
    $oxymorons = array('Pretty ugly', 'Jumbo shrimp', 'Act
  naturally', 'Original copy');
    sort($oxymorons);
```

```
        print_r($oxymorons);
?>
</pre>
```

Here's the output:

```
Array
(
    [0] => Act naturally
    [1] => Jumbo shrimp
    [2] => Original copy
    [3] => Pretty ugly
)
```

For associative arrays, you can use the asort() function to sort the values in ascending order (0 to 9, then A to Z, then a to z), or the arsort() function to sort the values in descending order (z to a, then Z to A, then 9 to 0):

```
asort($array);
arsort($array);
```

where $array is the name of the associative array you want to sort.

Here's an example (bk04ch01/example15.php):

```
<pre>
<?php
    $team_nicknames = array('Santa Cruz' => 'Banana Slugs',
  'Delta State' => 'Fighting Okra', 'Kent State' => 'Golden
  Flashes');
    arsort($team_nicknames);
    print_r($team_nicknames);
?>
</pre>
```

Here's the output:

```
Array
(
    [Kent State] => Golden Flashes
    [Delta State] => Fighting Okra
    [Santa Cruz] => Banana Slugs
)
```

Looping through array values

PHP offers a special loop called `foreach()` that you can use to loop through an array's values. Here's the syntax:

```
foreach($array as $key => $value) {
    Loop statements go here
}
```

where:

» *$array* is the name of the array you want to loop through.

» *$key* is an optional variable name that PHP uses to store the key of the current array item.

» *$value* is a variable name that PHP uses to store the value of the current array item.

Here's an example (bk04ch01/example16.php):

```php
<?php
    $team_nicknames = array('Santa Cruz' => 'Banana Slugs',
    'Delta State' => 'Fighting Okra', 'Kent State' => 'Golden
    Flashes');
    foreach($team_nicknames as $school => $nickname) {
        echo "The team nickname for $school is $nickname.<br>";
    }
?>
```

Here's the output:

```
The team nickname for Santa Cruz is Banana Slugs.
The team nickname for Delta State is Fighting Okra.
The team nickname for Kent State is Golden Flashes.
```

Creating multidimensional arrays

A *multidimensional array* is one where two or more values are stored in each array element. In a one-dimensional array, the *value* is usually a string, number, or Boolean. Now imagine, instead, that *value* is an array literal. For a two-dimensional array, the general syntax for assigning an array to an array element looks like this:

```
arrayName[index] = Array(value1, value2);
```

As an example, say you want to store an array of background and foreground colors. Here's how you might declare and populate such an array (bk04ch01/example17.php):

```php
<?php
    $colorArray[0] = Array('white', 'black');
    $colorArray[1] = Array('aliceblue', 'midnightblue');
    $colorArray[2] = Array('honeydew', 'darkgreen');
    echo $colorArray[1][1];
?>
```

Here's the output:

```
midnightblue
```

Alternatively, you can declare and populate an associative array (bk04ch01/example18.php):

```php
<?php
    $colorArray['scheme1'] = Array('foreground' => 'white',
    'background' => 'black');
    $colorArray['scheme2'] = Array('foreground' => 'aliceblue',
    'background' => 'midnightblue');
    $colorArray['scheme3'] = Array('foreground' => 'honeydew',
    'background' => 'darkgreen');
    echo $colorArray['scheme2']['foreground'];
?>
```

Here's the output:

```
aliceblue
```

Controlling the Flow of Your PHP Code

I go through a detailed discussion of controlling code with decisions and loops in Book 3, Chapter 4. That chapter focuses on JavaScript code, but the structures for making decisions and looping are identical in both JavaScript and PHP. Therefore, I just quickly summarize the available statements here, and refer you to Book 3, Chapter 4 to fill in the details.

Making decisions with if()

You make simple true/false decisions in PHP using the `if()` statement:

```
if (expression) {
    statements-if-true
}
```

where:

>> *expression* is a comparison or logical expression that returns `true` or `false`.

>> *statements-if-true* is the statement or statements to run if *expression* returns `true`. If *expression* returns `false`, PHP skips over the statements.

Here's an example (bk04ch01/example19.php):

```
if ($original_amount !== 0) {
    $percent_increase = 100 * (($new_amount - $original_amount)
  / $original_amount);
}
```

To run one group of statements if the condition returns `true` and a different group if the result is `false`, use an `if()...else` statement:

```
if (expression) {
    statements-if-true
} else {
    statements-if-false
}
```

where:

>> *expression* is a comparison or logical expression that returns `true` or `false`.

>> *statements-if-true* is the block of statements you want PHP to run if *expression* returns `true`.

>> *statements-if-false* is the block of statements you want executed if *expression* returns `false`.

Here's an example (bk04ch01/example20.php):

```php
<?php
    if ($currentHour < 12) {
        $greeting = "Good morning!";
    } else {
        $greeting = "Good day!";
    }
    echo $greeting;
?>
```

A third syntax for the if()...else statement lets you string together as many logical tests as you need:

```php
if (expression1) {
    statements-if-expression1-true
} elseif (expression2) {
    statements-if-expression2-true
}
etc.
else {
    statements-if-false
}
```

REMEMBER

This syntax represents a rare instance where PHP and JavaScript control structures are different (however slightly): You use the keywords else if in JavaScript, but the single keyword elseif in PHP.

The following code shows a script that uses a nested if() statement (bk04ch01/example21.php):

```php
<?php
    if ($currentHour < 12) {
        $greeting = "Good morning!";
    } elseif ($currentHour < 18) {
        $greeting = "Good afternoon!";
    } else {
        $greeting = "Good evening!";
    }
    echo $greeting;
?>
```

Making decisions with switch()

When you need to make a whole bunch of tests (say, four or more), PHP offers the `switch()` statement. Here's the syntax:

```
switch(expression) {
    case case1:
        case1 statements
        break;
    case case2:
        case2 statements
        break;
    etc.
    default:
        default statements
}
```

where:

>> *expression* is an expression that is evaluated at the beginning of the structure. It must return a value (numeric, string, or Boolean).

>> *case1, case2,* and so on are the possible values for *expression*. PHP examines each case value to see whether one matches the result of *expression* and, if it does, executes the *statements* associated with that case.

>> break statement tells PHP to stop processing the rest of the `switch()` statement.

Here's an example (bk04ch01/example22.php):

```
switch($season) {
    case 'winter':
        $footwear = 'snowshoes';
        break;
    case 'spring':
        $footwear = 'galoshes';
        break;
    case 'summer':
        $footwear = 'flip-flops';
        break;
    case 'fall':
        $footwear = 'hiking boots';
        break;
}
```

Looping with while()

PHP's while() loop uses the following syntax:

```
while (expression) {
    statements
}
```

where:

>> *expression* is a comparison or logical expression that determines how many times the loop gets executed.

>> *statements* is the block of statements to execute each time through the loop.

Here's an example (bko4cho1/example23.php):

```php
<?php
    $counter = 1;
    while ($counter <= 12) {
        // Generate a random number between 1 and 100
        $randoms[$counter - 1] = rand(1, 100);
        $counter++;
    }
    print_r($randoms);
?>
```

Looping with for()

The structure of a PHP for() loop looks like this:

```
for ($counter = start; expression; $counter++) {
    statements
}
```

where:

>> *$counter* is a numeric variable used as a loop counter.

>> *start* is the initial value of $counter.

>> *expression* is a comparison or logical expression that determines the number of times through the loop.

>> $counter++ is the increment operator applied to the $counter variable.

>> *statements* are the statements to execute each time through the loop.

Here's an example (bk04ch01/example24.php):

```php
<?php
    for ($counter = 0; $counter < 12; $counter++) {
        // Generate a random number between 1 and 100
        $randoms[$counter] = rand(1, 100);
    }
    print_r($randoms);
?>
```

Looping with do. . .while()

PHP's do...while() loop uses the following syntax:

```
do {
    statements
}
while (expression);
```

where:

>> *statements* is the block of statements to execute each time through the loop.

>> *expression* is a comparison or logical expression that determines how many times PHP runs through the loop.

Here's an example (bk04ch01/example25.php):

```php
<?php
    $counter = 0;
    do {
        // Generate a random number between 1 and 100
        $randoms[$counter] = rand(1, 100);
        $counter++;
    }
    while ($counter < 12);
    print_r($randoms);
?>
```

Working with PHP Functions

I talk about functions until I'm blue in the face in Book 3, Chapter 5. PHP and JavaScript handle functions in the same way, so here I give you a quick overview from the PHP side of things.

The basic structure of a function looks like this:

```
function function_name(arguments) {
    statements
}
```

where:

>> `function` identifies the block of code that follows it as a function.

>> `function_name` is a unique name for the function.

>> `arguments` is one or more optional values that are passed to the function and that act as variables within the function.

>> `statements` is the code that performs the function's tasks or calculations.

Here's an example (bk04ch01/example26.php):

```
function display_header() {
    echo "<header>\n";
    echo "<img src=\"images/notw.png\" alt=\"News of the Word
logo\">\n";
    echo "<h1>News of the Word</h1>\n";
    echo "<h3>Language news you won't find anywhere else (for
good reason!)</h3>\n";
    echo "</header>";
}
```

To call the function, include in your script a statement consisting of the function name, followed by parentheses:

```
display_header();
```

Passing values to functions

An *argument* is a value that is sent — or *passed*, in programming terms — to the function. The argument acts just like a variable, and it automatically stores whatever value is sent. Here's an example (bk04ch01/example27.php):

```
display_header('notw.png');

function display_header($img_file) {
    echo "<header>\n";
    echo "<img src=\"images/$img_file\" alt=\"News of the Word
logo\">\n";
    echo "<h1>News of the Word</h1>\n";
    echo "<h3>Language news you won't find anywhere else (for
good reason!)</h3>\n";
    echo "</header>";
}
```

Returning a value from a function

If your function calculates a result, you can send that result back to the statement that called the function by using a return statement:

```
return result;
```

As an example, I constructed a function that calculates and then returns the tip on a restaurant bill (bk04ch01/example28.php):

```
$preTipTotal = 100.00;
$tipPercentage = 0.15;

function calculate_tip($preTip, $tipPercent) {
    $tipResult = $preTip * $tipPercent;
    return $tipResult;
}
$tipCost = calculate_tip($preTipTotal, $tipPercentage);
$totalBill = $preTipTotal + $tipCost;
echo "Your total bill is \$$totalBill";
```

Working with PHP Objects

I discuss objects from a JavaScript point of view in Book 3, Chapter 6, so here I just recall that an *object* is a programmable element that has two key characteristics:

>> You can make changes to the object's *properties*.

>> You can make the object perform a task by activating a *method* associated with the object.

I use objects extensively in Book 4, Chapter 3 when I talk about using PHP to access a MySQL database, so the next few sections provide some necessary background.

Rolling your own objects

Let's take a quick look at creating custom objects in PHP. In the object-oriented world, a *class* acts as a sort of object template. A cookie cutter provides a good analogy. The cookie cutter isn't a cookie, but when you use the cookie cutter, it creates a cookie that has a predefined shape. A class is the same way. It's not an object, but using it (or *instancing* it, to use the vernacular) creates an object that has the class characteristics. These characteristics are governed by the *members* of the class, which are its properties and methods.

Creating a custom class

You define a custom class by using the `class` keyword:

```
class Name {
    Class properties and methods go here
}
```

where *Name* is the name you want to assign to your class. Class names traditionally begin with an uppercase letter.

Here's an example:

```
class Invoice {
}
```

I'll use this class to create customer invoice objects (refer to (bk04ch01/example29.php).

Adding properties to the class

The next step is to define the class properties, which are PHP variables preceded by the `public` keyword, which makes them available to code outside the class. Let's add a few properties to the `Invoice` class:

```
class Invoice {
    public $customer_id;
    public $subtotal;
    public $tax_rate;
}
```

A bit later I show you how to create an object from a class. In most cases you want to initialize some or all of the properties when you create the object, and to do that you must add a special `__construct()` function to the class definition. Here's the general syntax:

```
public function __construct($Arg1, $Arg2, ...) {
    $this->prop1 = $Arg1;
    $this->prop2 = $Arg2;
    etc.
}
```

where:

>> *$Arg1* , *$Arg2*, and so on are the initial values of the object properties.

>> `$this->` refers to the object in which the code is running; the `->` character pair is called the *object operator* and you use it to access an object's properties and methods.

>> *prop1* , *prop2*, and so on are references to the class properties, minus the $.

To extend the example:

```
class Invoice {
    public $customer_id;
    public $subtotal;
    public $tax_rate;

    public function __construct($Customer_ID, $Subtotal,
    $Tax_Rate) {
        $this->customer_id = $Customer_ID;
```

```
        $this->subtotal = $Subtotal;
        $this->tax_rate = $Tax_Rate;
    }
}
```

Adding methods to the class

The last step in creating your custom class is to add one or more functions that will be used as the class methods. Here's the general syntax:

```
public function method() {
    Method code goes here
}
```

where *method* is the name of the method.

To complete our example class, add a method that calculates the invoice total and rounds it to two decimal places:

```
class Invoice {
    public $customer_id;
    public $subtotal;
    public $tax_rate;

    public function __construct($Customer_ID, $Subtotal,
  $Tax_Rate) {
        $this->customer_id = $Customer_ID;
        $this->subtotal = $Subtotal;
        $this->tax_rate = $Tax_Rate;
    }

    public function calculate_total() {
        $total = $this->subtotal * (1 + $this->tax_rate);
        return round($total, 2);
    }
}
```

Creating an object

Given a class — whether it's a built-in PHP class or a class you've created yourself — you can create an object from the class, which is known as an *instance* of the class. Here's the general format to use:

```
$object = new Class(value1, value2, ...);
```

where:

» $object is the variable name of the object.

» Class is the name of the class on which to base the object.

» value1, value2, and so on are the optional initial values you want to assign to the object's properties.

Here's a statement that creates an instance of the Invoice class from the previous section:

```
$inv = new Invoice('BONAP', 59.85, .07);
```

Working with object properties

You refer to an object property by using the object operator (->):

```
object->property
```

where:

» object is the object that has the property.

» property is the name of the property you want to work with.

Here's an example that creates an object instance and then references the object's customer_id property:

```
$inv = new Invoice('BONAP', 59.85, .07);
$current_customer = $inv->customer_id;
```

To change the value of a property, use the following generic syntax:

```
object->property = value;
```

where:

» *object* is the object that has the property.

» *property* is the name of the property you want to change.

» *value* is a literal value (such as a string or number) or an expression that returns the value to which you want to set the property.

Here's an example:

```
$inv->subtotal = 99.95;
```

Working with object methods

To run a method, you use the following syntax:

```
object->method(arg1, arg2, ...)
```

where:

» *object* is the object that has the method you want to work with.

» *method* is the name of the method you want to execute.

» *arg1* , *arg2*, and so on are the arguments required by the method, if any.

Here's an example:

```
$inv = new Invoice('BONAP', 59.85, .07);
$invoice_total = $inv->calculate_total();
```

IN THIS CHAPTER

» Learning about MySQL and what it can do

» Building MySQL databases and tables

» Getting your head around SQL

» Selecting data with queries

» Modifying data with queries

Chapter **2**

Building and Querying MySQL Databases

MySQL is a fast and powerful, yet easy-to-use, database system that offers just about anything a website would need in order to find and serve up data to browsers.

— ROBIN NIXON

One of the central themes of this book is that today's web is all about dynamic content. Sure, if you have (or your client has) just one or two web pages to show the world, the standard front-end web development tools — HTML, CSS, and JavaScript — are more than enough to get the job done. However, it's much more likely that a modern website will consist of dozens, perhaps even hundreds, of pages, with new content added regularly. Believe me, as the developer or administrator of such a site, you don't want to hand-code all those pages as static HTML and CSS. Life's too short!

Fortunately, you don't have to hand-assemble all those pages if you get the back end of the web development world doing the hard work for you. The key is the database software that stores your site info on the server, and that's what this chapter is all about. Here you discover the MySQL database program and learn all that it can do to help you build and maintain dynamic, robust, and fast websites of any size.

What Is MySQL?

In simplest terms, a *database* is a collection of information with some sort of underlying structure and organization. MySQL (pronounced "my ess-kew-ell," or sometimes "my sequel") is a *database management system* (DBMS) that runs on the server. This means MySQL will not only store the data you want to use as the source for some (or perhaps even all) of the data you want to display on your web page, but it will also supply you with the means to manage this data (by sorting, searching, extracting, and so on).

The official description of MySQL is that it's a *relational* database management system (RDBMS). The *relational* part means that you can set up relations between various parts of a database. For example, most businesses assign some sort of account number for each of their customers. So, a database of customer information would include a column for this account number (as well as the name, address, credit limit, and so on). Similarly, you could also include the account number column in a collection of accounts receivable invoices (along with the invoice date, amount, and so on). In this way, you can relate each invoice to the appropriate customer information. (So, for example, you could easily look up phone numbers and call those deadbeat customers whose invoices are more than 90 days past due!)

MySQL is a massive piece of software that can do incredibly complicated things. Fortunately, as web developers, we need to use only a small subset of MySQL's features, and we don't have to get into anything mind-blowingly complex. To get started on developing dynamic web pages, in fact, you need to know about only two pieces of the MySQL puzzle: tables and queries.

Tables: Containers for your data

In MySQL databases, you store your information in an object called a *table*. Tables are essentially a grid, where each vertical segment represents a *column* (a specific category of information) and each horizontal segment represents a *row* (a single record in the table).

Figure 2-1 shows a table of customer data. Note how the table includes separate columns for each logical grouping of the data (company name, contact name, and so on).

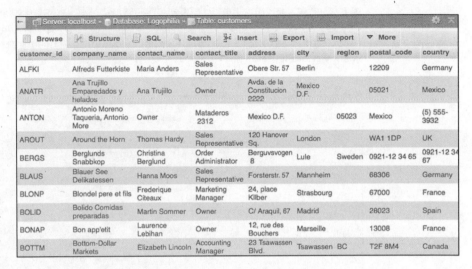

customer_id	company_name	contact_name	contact_title	address	city	region	postal_code	country
ALFKI	Alfreds Futterkiste	Maria Anders	Sales Representative	Obere Str. 57	Berlin		12209	Germany
ANATR	Ana Trujillo Emparedados y helados	Ana Trujillo	Owner	Avda. de la Constitucion 2222	Mexico D.F.		05021	Mexico
ANTON	Antonio Moreno Taqueria, Antonio More	Owner	Mataderos 2312	Mexico D.F.		05023	Mexico	(5) 555-3932
AROUT	Around the Horn	Thomas Hardy	Sales Representative	120 Hanover Sq.	London		WA1 1DP	UK
BERGS	Berglunds Snabbkop	Christina Berglund	Order Administrator	Berguvsvogen 8	Lule	Sweden	0921-12 34 65	0921-12 34 67
BLAUS	Blauer See Delikatessen	Hanna Moos	Sales Representative	Forsterstr. 57	Mannheim		68306	Germany
BLONP	Blondel pere et fils	Frederique Citeaux	Marketing Manager	24, place Kilber	Strasbourg		67000	France
BOLID	Bolido Comidas preparadas	Martin Sommer	Owner	C/ Araquil, 67	Madrid		28023	Spain
BONAP	Bon app'etit	Laurence Lebihan	Owner	12, rue des Bouchers	Marseille		13008	France
BOTTM	Bottom-Dollar Markets	Elizabeth Lincoln	Accounting Manager	23 Tsawassen Blvd.	Tsawassen	BC	T2F 8M4	Canada

FIGURE 2-1: In MySQL databases, tables store the raw data.

REMEMBER

In web development, you use MySQL tables to store the data that will appear in your pages. Getting that data from the server to the web page requires five steps:

1. On the web page, some JavaScript code launches a PHP script on the server.

2. That PHP script asks a MySQL database for the data required by the web page.

3. The PHP script configures the data into a format JavaScript can understand.

4. PHP sends the data back to the web page.

5. The JavaScript code accepts the data and displays it on the page.

I go through these steps in glorious detail in Book 4, Chapter 3 and in Book 6, Chapter 1.

Queries: Asking questions of your data

By far the most common concern expressed by new database users (and many old-timers, as well) is how to extract the information they need from all that data. What if, for example, you have a database of accounts receivable invoices and your boss wants a web page that tells them how many invoices are more than 150 days past due? You can't hand-code such a page because, for a large database, your page would be out of date before you were done. The better way would be to ask MySQL to do the work for you by creating another type of database object: a query.

Queries are, literally, questions you ask of your data. In this case, you could ask MySQL to display a list of all invoices more than 150 days past due.

Queries let you extract from one or more tables a subset of the data. For example, in a table of customer names and addresses, what if I wanted to see a list of firms that are located in France? No problem. I'd just set up a query that asks, in effect, "Which rows have `'France'` in the `country` column?" The answer to this question is shown in Figure 2-2.

FIGURE 2-2:
You use MySQL queries to extract a subset of the data from one or more tables.

customer_id	company_name	contact_name	contact_title	address	city	region	postal_code	country
BLONP	Blondel pere et fils	Frederique Citeaux	Marketing Manager	24, place Kllber	Strasbourg		67000	France
BONAP	Bon app'etit	Laurence Lebihan	Owner	12, rue des Bouchers	Marseille		13008	France
DUMON	Du monde entier	Janine Labrune	Owner	67, rue des Cinquante Otages	Nantes		44000	France
FRANR	France restauration	Carine Schmitt	Marketing Manager	54, rue Royale	Nantes		44000	France
LACOR	La corne d'abondance	Daniel Tonini	Sales Representative	67, avenue de l'Europe	Versailles		78000	France
LAMAI	La maison d'Asie	Annette Roulet	Sales Manager	1 rue Alsace-Lorraine	Toulouse		31000	France
SPECD	Sp?cialit?s du monde	Dominique Perrier	Marketing Manager	25, rue Lauriston	Paris		75016	France
VICTE	Victuailles en stock	Mary Saveley	Sales Agent	2, rue du Commerce	Lyon		69004	France
VINET	Vins et alcools Chevalier	Paul Henriot	Accounting Manager	59 rue de l'Abbaye	Reims		51100	France

The actual querying process is performed using a technology called Structured Query Language (or SQL, pronounced "ess-kew-ell"). In the five-step procedure I mention in the preceding section, the SQL portion takes place in Step 2.

Introducing phpMyAdmin

To work with MySQL — whether it's creating a database, importing or exporting data, adding a table, inserting and editing data, or testing SQL statements to use in your PHP code — almost all web hosts offer a web application called phpMy Admin. (It's an odd name, I know: It means, more or less, "PHP-based MySQL Administration.")

In the XAMPP web development environment that I discuss in Book 1, Chapter 2, you have two ways to get phpMyAdmin on the job (make sure you have the Apache web server running):

>> **Dashboard:** From the XAMPP Dashboard page (http://localhost/dashboard), click the phpMyAdmin link in the header.

>> **Direct:** Use a web browser to surf to http://localhost/phpmyadmin.

Figure 2-3 shows the default phpMyAdmin page.

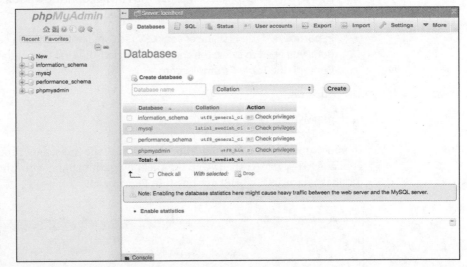

FIGURE 2-3:
From the XAMPP Dashboard, click phpMyAdmin to open the phpMyAdmin web app.

The navigation pane on the left shows the default databases that come with php-MyAdmin (don't mess with these!), while the tabs across the top — Databases, SQL, and so on — take you to different parts of the application.

Importing data into MySQL

Before I talk about building a database from scratch, let me first go through the procedure for getting some existing data into MySQL. phpMyAdmin supports several import formats, but you'll most likely want to use a comma-separated values (.csv) file, where the column data in each row is separated by commas. Another possibility is a SQL (.sql) file, which is a backup file for a MySQL database:

1. **In phpMyAdmin, click the Import tab.**

If you don't see the Import tab, click More, and then click Import.

2. **In the File to Import section, click Browse (Windows) or Choose File (Mac).**

Your operating system's file chooser dialog appears.

3. **Click the file that contains the data you want to import, and then click Open.**

4. **In the Format section, make sure the list shows the correct format for the file you chose.**

If you're importing a CSV file, the list should have CSV selected; if you're importing a SQL backup file, the list should have SQL selected.

5. **If you're importing a CSV file, use the Format-Specific Options section to tell phpMyAdmin the structure of the file.**

In particular, if the first line of your CSV file contains the column names of your data, you need to select the check box labeled The First Line of the File Contains the Table Column Names.

6. **Click Go.**

phpMyAdmin imports the data.

If you imported a CSV file, you should see the message Import has been successfully finished, and in the navigation pane you should see a new database named CSV_DB, as shown in Figure 2-4.

FIGURE 2-4:
Importing a CSV
file creates the
CSV_DB database.

Here are the steps to follow to rename the database and the table that contains the imported data:

1. **In the navigation pane, click CSV_DB.**

phpMyAdmin opens the database. Note that you now see a table named TBL_NAME, which contains the imported CSV data. I show you how to rename it beginning with Step 6.

2. **Click the Operations tab.**

If you don't see the Operations tab, click More and then click Operations.

3. **In the Rename Database To section, type the new database name in the text box provided.**

4. **Click Go.**

   phpMyAdmin asks you to confirm.

5. **Click OK.**

   phpMyAdmin changes the database name.

6. **In the navigation pane, click TBL_NAME.**

7. **Click the Operations tab.**

   If you don't see the Operations tab, click More and then click Operations.

8. **In the Rename Table To text box in the Table Options section, type the new table name.**

9. **Click Go.**

   phpMyAdmin changes the table name.

Backing up MySQL data

As you work with phpMyAdmin, you should run periodic backups to make sure your data is safe. Here are the steps to follow:

1. **In phpMyAdmin, click the Export tab.**

   If you don't see the Export tab, click More and then click Export.

2. **In the Format section, use the list to select SQL (although this is the default format).**

3. **Click Go.**

   phpMyAdmin exports the data, which your web browser then downloads to your computer.

Creating a MySQL Database and Its Tables

If you don't import your data, you need to create your own MySQL databases and populate them with the tables that will hold the data.

Creating a MySQL database

The first question you need to ask yourself is: Do I need just a single database or multiple databases? As a web developer, you'll almost always need multiple databases. Here's why:

>> You need a separate database for each website you build.

>> You need a separate database for each web app you build.

>> You need a separate database for each client you have.

If you are just building a single website or app and have no clients, one database is fine. But know that MySQL is ready and willing to accommodate almost any number of databases you care to throw at it.

Here are the steps to follow to create a database using phpMyAdmin:

1. **In the navigation pane, click New that appears at the top of the navigation tree.**

2. **In the Database Name text box in the Create Database section, type the name you want to use.**

3. **In the Collation list, select utf8_general_ci.**

Collation refers to how MySQL compares characters (for example, when sorting data). In this case, you're telling MySQL to use a standard, case-insensitive (for example, a equals A) collation on the UTF-8 character set.

4. **Click Create.**

phpMyAdmin creates the database for you.

Designing your table

You need to plan your table design before you create it. By asking yourself a few questions in advance, you can save yourself the trouble of redesigning your table later. For simple tables, you need to ask yourself three basic questions:

>> Does the table belong in the current database?

>> What type of data should I store in each table?

>> What columns should I use to store the data?

The next few sections examine these questions in more detail.

Does the table belong in the current database?

Each database you create should be set up for a specific purpose: a website, a web app, a client, and so on. Once you know the purpose of the database, you can decide if the table you want to create fits in with the database theme.

For example, if the purpose of the database is to store a client's data, it would be inappropriate to include a table that stores your personal blog posts. Similarly, it wouldn't make sense to include a table of a web app's user accounts in a database that belongs to an entirely different website.

What type of data should I store in each table?

The most important step in creating a table is determining the information you want it to contain. In theory, MySQL tables can be quite large: up to 4,096 columns and many millions (even billions) of rows. In practice, however, you should strive to keep your tables as small as possible. Doing so saves memory and makes managing the data easier. Ideally, you should aim to set up all your tables with only essential information.

Suppose you want to store user information in a database. You have to decide whether you want all your users in a single table or separate tables for each type of user. For example, a table of customers would include detailed information such as each person's first and last names, postal address, phone number, and payment preference. By contrast, a table of people who have opted-in to receive your newsletters might store each person's email address, the newsletters they want to receive, the subscription type (full or digest), and more. There's not a lot of overlap between these two types of customers, so it probably makes sense to create two separate tables.

When you've decided on the tables you want to use, you need to think about how much data you want to store in each table. In your customers table, for example, would you also want to include information on each person's site customizations, account creation date, date of last visit, and product preferences? This might all be crucial information for you, but you need to remember that the more data you store, the longer it will take to query and sort the data.

What columns should I use to store the data?

Now you're almost ready for action. The last thing you need to figure out is the specific columns to include in the database. For the most part, the columns are determined by the data itself. For example, a database of business contacts would certainly include columns for name, address, and phone number. But should you split the name into two columns — one for the first name and one for the last name? If you think you'll need to sort the table by last name, then, yes, you probably should. What about the address? You'll probably need individual columns for the street, city, state, and ZIP code.

Here are two general rules to follow when deciding how many columns to include in your tables:

>> Ask yourself whether you really need the data for a particular column (or if you might need it in the near future). For example, if you think your table of contact names might someday be used to create form letters, a column to record titles (Ms., Mr., Dr., and so on) would come in handy. When in doubt, err on the side of too many columns rather than too few.

>> Always split your data into the smallest columns that make sense. Splitting first and last names is common practice, but creating a separate column for, say, the phone number area code would probably be overkill.

REMEMBER

Don't sweat the design process too much. It's easy to make changes down the road (by adding or deleting columns), so you're never stuck with a bad design.

Deciding which column to use for a primary key

When you create a table, you need to decide which column to use as the primary key. The *primary key* is a column that uses a unique number or character sequence to identify each row in the table. Keys are used constantly in the real world. Your Social Security number is a key that identifies you in government records. Most machines and appliances have unique serial numbers. This book (like most books) has a 13-digit ISBN — International Standard Book Number (which you can see on the back cover).

Why are primary keys necessary? Well, for one thing, MySQL creates an *index* for the primary key column. You can perform searches on indexed data much more quickly than on regular data; therefore, many MySQL operations perform faster if a primary key is present. Keys also make it easy to find rows in a table because the key entries are unique (things such as last names and addresses can have multiple spellings, which makes them hard to find). Finally, once a table has a primary key, MySQL adds its data editing tools, which enable you to modify, copy, and delete table data.

You can configure the table so that MySQL sets and maintains the primary key for you, or you can do it yourself. Which one do you choose? Here are some guidelines:

>> If your data contains a number or character sequence that uniquely defines each row, you can set the key yourself. For example, invoices usually have unique numbers that are perfect for a primary key. Other columns that can serve as primary keys are employee IDs, customer account numbers, and purchase order numbers.

>> If your data has no such unique identifier, let MySQL create a key for you. MySQL will set up an AUTO_INCREMENT column that will automatically assign a unique number to each row (the first row will be 1, the second 2, and so on).

Relating tables

MySQL is a *relational* database system, which means that you can establish relationships between multiple tables. As an example, suppose you have a database that contains (at least) two tables:

>> **orders:** This table holds data on orders placed by your customers, including the customer name and the date of the order. It also includes an order_id column as the primary key, as shown in Figure 2-5.

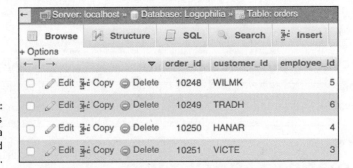

FIGURE 2-5:
The orders table includes a column named order_id.

>> **order_details:** This table holds data on the specific products that make up each order: the product name, the unit price, the quantity ordered. It also includes an order_id field, as shown in Figure 2-6.

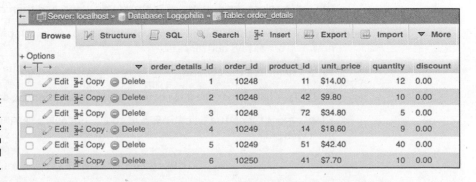

FIGURE 2-6:
The order_details table also includes a column named order_id.

Why not lump both tables into a single table? Well, that would mean that, for each product ordered, you'd have to include the name of the customer, the order date, and so on. If the customer purchased ten different products, this information would be repeated ten times. To avoid such waste, the data is kept in separate tables, and the two tables are *related* on the common column called order_id.

For example, notice in Figure 2-5 that the first row in the orders table has an order_id value of 10248. Now check out Figure 2-6, where you see that the first three rows of the order_details table also have an order_id value of 10248. This means that when you join these tables on the related order_id field, MySQL combines the data, as shown in Figure 2-7. For example, notice that the first three rows still have an order_id value of 10248, but they now also include the customer_id column from the orders table.

FIGURE 2-7: The order_ details and orders tables joined on the common column named order_id.

order_details_id	order_id	product_id	unit_price	quantity	discount	customer_id
1	10248	11	$14.00	12	0.00	WILMK
2	10248	42	$9.80	10	0.00	WILMK
3	10248	72	$34.80	5	0.00	WILMK
4	10249	14	$18.60	9	0.00	TRADH
5	10249	51	$42.40	40	0.00	TRADH
6	10250	41	$7.70	10	0.00	HANAR
7	10250	51	$42.40	35	0.15	HANAR

Creating a MySQL table

Here are the steps to follow to create a table in a MySQL database:

1. **In the navigation pane, click the database in which you want to add the table.**

2. **Click the Structure tab. In the Create New Table section, type a name for the table, select the number of columns you want, and then click Create.**

   If you're not sure how many columns you need, just make your best guess for now. You can always add more later on.

3. **Type a name for the column.**

4. **In the Type list, select the data type you want to use for the data.**

   There's a long list of data types to wade through, but only a few make sense in most web projects:

- **INT:** Stores an integer value between -2,147,483,648 and 2,147,483,648. For really small integer values, consider using either TINYINT (-128 to 127 or 0 to 255) or SMALLINT (-32,768 to 32,767 or 0 to 65,535).

- **VARCHAR:** Stores a variable-length string between 0 and 65,535 characters long. If you need to store super-long chunks of text, consider MEDIUMTEXT (up to 16,777,215 characters) instead.

- **DATE:** Stores a date and time value.

5. **If you selected VARCHAR in Step 4, you can use the Length/Values field to enter a maximum size for the column.**

6. **Use the Default list to specify a default value that MySQL will enter automatically into the column when you create a row.**

   If you want the current date and time in a DATE column, select CURRENT_TIMESTAMP. Otherwise, select As Defined, and then enter a value in the text box that appears.

7. **In the Collation list, select utf8_general_ci.**

8. **To allow MySQL to enter no value into the column, select the Null check box.**

   If you leave Null deselected, be sure you always specify a value for the column.

9. **If you want MySQL to index the column, use the Index list to select the type of index you want.**

   In most cases you should choose the all-purpose INDEX type; if the column values are all different, select the UNIQUE type; for a text-heavy field, select the FULLTEXT type.

   Don't index every column. Instead, you only need to index those columns that you'll be using for sorting and querying.

10. **Repeat Steps 3 through 9 until you've defined all your columns.**

11. **Click Save.**

Adding data to a table

Ideally, most of your table data will be inserted automatically, either by importing data or by having your page users fill in an HTML form (see Book 6, Chapters 2 and 3). If you do need to enter table data by hand, here's how it's done:

1. **In the navigation pane, click the table in which you want the data added.**

2. **Click the Insert tab.**

   phpMyAdmin displays empty text boxes for each column in the table.

3. **If you see two sets of text boxes, scroll down to the bottom of the Insert tab and change Continue Insertion with 2 Rows to Continue Insertion with 1 Row.**

4. **In the Value fields, add a value for each column.**

   If a column accepts null values (that is, if the column's Null check box is selected), it's okay to leave that column's Value field blank.

5. **If you want to add multiple rows, use the two lists near the bottom of the page to select Insert as New Row and then Insert Another New Row.**

6. **To insert the data, click Go.**

Creating a primary key

When you import a table, MySQL doesn't automatically create a primary key, so you need to follow these steps to create the primary key yourself:

1. **In the navigation pane, click the table you want to work with.**

2. **Click the Structure tab.**

3. **Select the check box that appears to the left of the column you want to use as the primary key.**

   Make sure you select a column that contains only unique values.

4. **Click Primary.**

   MySQL configures the column as the table's primary key.

What happens if none of your table's fields contain unique items? In that case, you need to create a column to use as the primary key. Here's how:

1. **In the navigation pane, click the table you want to work with.**

2. **Click the Structure tab.**

3. **Leave the Add 1 Columns as is, but select At Beginning of Table in the list, and then click Go.**

4. **Type a name for the primary key field.**

   If you're not sure what name to use, something like *table*_id would work, where *table* is the name of the table.

5. **Select the A_I (AUTO_INCREMENT) check box.**

   MySQL displays the Add Index dialog.

6. **Leave the default settings as they are, and then click Go.**

7. **Click Save.**

   MySQL adds the field and automatically populates it with unique integer values.

Querying MySQL Data

It's all well and good having a bunch of data hunkered down in a MySQL database, but as a web developer, your real concern is getting that data from the server to the web page. That complete journey is the subject of both Book 4, Chapter 3 and Book 6, Chapter 1, but I'm going to tackle the first leg of the trip here and show you how to specify the data that will eventually get sent to the page. The technique I show you is called *querying* the data, and the tool of choice is Structured Query Language, or SQL.

What is SQL?

SQL is a collection of commands that interrogate or modify — *query*, in the SQL vernacular — MySQL data in some way. SQL is huge, but as a web developer you really only need to know about four query types:

» **SELECT:** Returns a subset of a table's data

» **INSERT:** Adds a new row to a table

» **UPDATE:** Modifies a table's existing data

» **DELETE:** Removes one or more rows from a table

In the case of the SELECT, UPDATE, and DELETE query types, you target the specific rows you want to work with by specifying *criteria*, which are extra parameters that define one or more conditions the rows must meet. For example, you might want to run a SELECT query that returns only customers where the country column is equal to France. Similarly, you might want to run a DELETE query on only the items in the products table where the discontinued column has the value TRUE.

Creating a SELECT query

The most common type of query is the SELECT query that returns rows from one or more tables based on the columns you choose and the criteria you apply to those columns. It's called a *SELECT* query not only because you use it to select certain rows but also because it's based on the SQL language's SELECT statement. SELECT is the SQL "verb" that you'll see and work with most often, and it's used to create a subset based on the table, columns, criteria, and other clauses specified in the statement. Here's a simplified syntax for the SELECT verb:

```
SELECT select_columns
    FROM table_name
    WHERE criteria
    ORDER BY sort_columns [DESC]
```

where:

>> SELECT *select_columns* specifies the names of the columns you want in your subset. If you want all the columns, use * instead.

>> FROM *table_name* is the name of the table that contains the data.

>> WHERE *criteria* filters the data to give you only those rows that match the specified *criteria*.

>> ORDER BY *sort_columns* sorts the results in ascending order based on the data in the columns specified by *sort_columns* (separated by commas, if you have more than one). Use the optional DESC keyword to sort the rows in descending order.

The most basic SELECT query is one that returns all the rows from a table. For example, the following SELECT statement returns all the rows from the customers table:

```
SELECT *
    FROM customers
```

In the following example, only the company_name, city, and country columns are returned in the results:

```
SELECT company_name, city, country
    FROM customers
```

Here's another example that sorts the rows based on the values in the company_name column:

```
SELECT *
    FROM customers
    ORDER BY company_name
```

Understanding query criteria

The heart of any query is its *criteria,* which are a set of expressions that determine the rows included in the query results. All query expressions have the same general structure. They contain one or more *operands* — which can be literal values (such as 123 or "USA" or 2024–08–23), *identifiers* (names of MySQL objects, such as tables), or functions — separated by one or more *operators* — the symbols that combine the operands in some way, such as the plus sign (+) and the greater than sign (›).

Most criteria expressions are logical formulas that, when applied to each row in the table, return TRUE or FALSE. The subset contains only those rows for which the expression returns TRUE.

Comparison operators

You use comparison operators to compare field values to a literal, a function result, or a value in another field. Table 2-1 lists MySQL's comparison operators.

TABLE 2-1 **Comparison Operators for Criteria Expressions**

Operator	General Form	Matches Rows Where . . .
=	= *Value*	The column value is equal to *Value*
<>	<> *Value*	The column value is not equal to *Value*
>	> *Value*	The column value is greater than *Value*
>=	>= *Value*	The column value is greater than or equal to *Value*
<	< *Value*	The column value is less than *Value*
<=	<= *Value*	The column value is less than or equal to *Value*

For example, suppose you have a products table with a units_in_stock column. If you want a SELECT query to return just those products that are out of stock, you'd use the following SQL statement:

```
SELECT *
    FROM products
    WHERE units_in_stock = 0
```

The LIKE operator

If you need to allow for multiple spellings in a text column, or if you're not sure how to spell a word you want to use, the *wildcard characters* can help. There are two wildcards: The underscore (_) substitutes for a single character, and the percent sign (%) substitutes for a group of characters. You use them in combination with the LIKE operator, as shown in Table 2-2.

TABLE 2-2

The LIKE Operator for Criteria Expressions

Example	Matches Rows Where . . .
LIKE 'Re_d'	The column value is Reid, Read, reed, and so on
LIKE 'M_'	The column value is MA, MD, ME, and so on
LIKE 'R%'	The column value begins with R
LIKE '%office%'	The column value contains the word office
LIKE '2024-12-%'	The column value is any date in December 2024

The BETWEEN. . .AND operator

If you need to select rows where a column value lies between two other values, use the BETWEEN. . .AND operator. For example, suppose you want to see all the rows in the order_details table where the quantity value is between (and includes) 50 and 100. Here's a SELECT statement that does the job:

```
SELECT *
    FROM order_details
    WHERE quantity BETWEEN 50 AND 100
```

You can use this operator for numbers, dates, and even text.

The IN operator

You use the IN operator to match rows where the specified column value is one of a set of values. For example, suppose you want to return a subset of the customers table that contains only those rows where the region column equals NY, CA, TX, IN, or ME. Here's the SELECT statement to use:

```
SELECT *
    FROM customers
    WHERE region IN('NY','CA','TX','IN','ME')
```

The IS NULL operator

What do you do if you want to select rows where a certain column is empty? For example, a table of invoices might have a date_paid column where, if this column is empty, it means the invoice hasn't been paid yet. For these challenges, MySQL provides the IS NULL operator. Applying this operator to a column selects only those rows whereby the column is empty. Here's an example:

```
SELECT *
    FROM invoices
    WHERE date_paid IS NULL
```

To select rows when a particular column is *not* empty, use the IS NOT NULL operator.

Compound criteria and the logical operators

Sometimes a single expression just doesn't do the job. For more sophisticated needs, you can set up *compound criteria* where you enter either multiple expressions for the same column or multiple expressions for different columns. You use the logical operators to combine or modify expressions. Table 2-3 summarizes MySQL's logical operators.

TABLE 2-3 ## Logical Operators for Criteria Expressions

Operator	General Form	Matches Rows When . . .
AND	*Expr1* AND *Expr2*	Both *Expr1* and *Expr2* are TRUE
OR	*Expr1* OR *Expr2*	At least one of *Expr1* and *Expr2* is TRUE
NOT	NOT *Expr*	*Expr* is not TRUE
XOR	*Expr1* XOR *Expr2*	Only one of *Expr1* and *Expr2* is TRUE (XOR is short for *exclusive or*)

The AND and OR operators let you create compound criteria using a single expression. For example, suppose you want to match all the rows in your products table where the units_in_stock column is either 0 or greater than or equal to 100. The following SELECT statement does the job:

```
SELECT *
    FROM products
    WHERE units_in_stock = 0 OR units_in_stock >= 100
```

The NOT operator looks for rows that *don't* match a particular logical expression. In a table of customer data, for example, if you want to find all non-North American customers, you'd filter out the customers by using the country column, like so:

```
SELECT *
    FROM customers
    WHERE NOT country = 'USA' AND
          NOT country = 'Canada' AND
          NOT country 'Mexico'
```

Querying multiple tables

Although most of your MySQL queries will use just a single table, some of the most useful and powerful queries involve two (or more) tables. The type of multiple-table query you'll see and use most often is called an *inner join* because it joins two tables based on a common column.

To create an inner join on two tables, use the following version of the FROM clause:

```
FROM table1
    INNER JOIN table2
    ON table1.column = table2.column
```

Here, *table1* and *table2* are the names of the two tables you want to join, and *table1.column* and *table2.column* are the common columns in each table. Note that the column names don't have to be the same.

For example, suppose you have two tables: orders and order_details, and they each have a column named order_id that stores a value that is unique for each order. The following SELECT statement sets up an inner join on these tables:

```
SELECT *
    FROM orders
    INNER JOIN order_details
    ON orders.order_id = order_details.order_id
```

If you want only certain columns from both tables in the results, specify the column names after the SELECT command using the *table.column* syntax, as in this example:

```
SELECT orders.order_id, orders.customer_id, order_details.
    quantity
    FROM orders
    INNER JOIN order_details
    ON orders.order_id = order_details.order_id
```

INNER JOINS? OUTER JOINS? WHAT'S THE DIFFERENCE?

Besides inner joins, MySQL also supports a variation on the multiple-table query theme called an *outer join*. To understand the difference between these two join types, let's run through some examples using the sample data in the following table.

The novelties Table		The suppliers Table
name	**supplier**	**supplier**
Inflatable Dartboard	Facepalm LLC	Facepalm LLC
Banana Peel Welcome Mat	Facepalm LLC	RUSerious, Ltd.
Non-Reflective Mirror	Facepalm LLC	Silly Stuff, Inc.
Fireproof Firewood	Internal	Nov-L-T Industries
Donut Holes	Internal	
No-String Guitar	Internal	
Helium Paperweight	RUSerious, Ltd.	
Sandpaper Bathroom Tissue	RUSerious, Ltd.	
All-Stick Frying Pan	Silly Stuff, Inc.	
Water-Resistant Sponge	Silly Stuff, Inc.	

The novelties table has two columns: name and supplier, and the suppliers table has a single column: supplier. Here are three things to note about these tables:

- The two tables have the supplier column in common.

- The novelties table includes several rows that use Internal as the supplier value, but Internal is not listed in the suppliers table.

- The suppliers table includes one row — Nov-L-T Industries — that is not used anywhere in the novelties table.

(continued)

(continued)

An inner join only returns the overlapping data between two tables. To visualize this, consider the following Venn diagram.

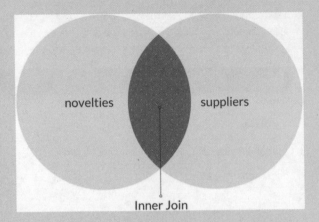

Here's a SELECT statement that runs an inner join on the novelties and suppliers tables:

```
SELECT novelties.name, suppliers.supplier
    FROM novelties
    INNER JOIN suppliers
    ON novelties.supplier = suppliers.supplier
```

Here are the results:

novelties.name	suppliers.supplier
Inflatable Dartboard	Facepalm LLC
Banana Peel Welcome Mat	Facepalm LLC
Non-Reflective Mirror	Facepalm LLC
Helium Paperweight	RUSerious, Ltd.
Sandpaper Bathroom Tissue	RUSerious, Ltd.
All-Stick Frying Pan	Silly Stuff, Inc.
Water-Resistant Sponge	Silly Stuff, Inc.

Note that from the novelties table we don't see any of the rows that had Internal as the supplier value because that value doesn't appear in the suppliers table.

Similarly, we don't see the Nov-L-T Industries supplier because that value doesn't appear in the `novelties` table.

However, suppose we want all the novelties to appear in the results. That's called a *left outer join*, and to see why, take a look at the following Venn diagram. This join includes all the `novelties` rows, plus the overlapping data from the `suppliers` table.

Left Outer Join

Here's a SELECT statement that runs a left outer join on the `novelties` and `suppliers` tables:

```
SELECT novelties.name, suppliers.supplier
    FROM novelties
    LEFT OUTER JOIN suppliers
    ON novelties.supplier = suppliers.supplier
```

Here are the results:

name	supplier
Inflatable Dartboard	Facepalm LLC
Banana Peel Welcome Mat	Facepalm LLC
Non-Reflective Mirror	Facepalm LLC
Fireproof Firewood	NULL
Donut Holes	NULL
No-String Guitar	NULL
Helium Paperweight	RUSerious, Ltd.

(continued)

(continued)

name	supplier
Sandpaper Bathroom Tissue	RUSerious, Ltd.
All-Stick Frying Pan	Silly Stuff, Inc.
Water-Resistant Sponge	Silly Stuff, Inc.

Note that for those novelties that don't have a corresponding `supplier` value in the suppliers table, MySQL returns NULL.

Finally, you might want all the suppliers to appear in the results. That's called a *right outer join,* and you can see why by taking a peek at the following Venn diagram. This join includes all the `suppliers` rows, plus the overlapping data from the `novelties` table.

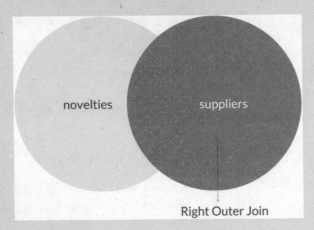

Right Outer Join

Here's a SELECT statement that runs a right outer join on the `novelties` and `suppliers` tables:

```
SELECT novelties.name, suppliers.supplier
    FROM novelties
    RIGHT OUTER JOIN suppliers
    ON novelties.supplier = suppliers.supplier
```

Here are the results:

name	supplier
Inflatable Dartboard	Facepalm LLC
Banana Peel Welcome Mat	Facepalm LLC

name	supplier
Non-Reflective Mirror	Facepalm LLC
NULL	Nov-L-T Industries
Helium Paperweight	RUSerious, Ltd.
Sandpaper Bathroom Tissue	RUSerious, Ltd.
All-Stick Frying Pan	Silly Stuff, Inc.
Water-Resistant Sponge	Silly Stuff, Inc.

Note that for those suppliers that don't have a corresponding supplier value in the novelties table, MySQL returns NULL.

Adding table data with an INSERT query

An INSERT query adds a new row to an existing table. In MySQL, you build an INSERT query using the INSERT verb:

```
INSERT
    INTO table (columns)
    VALUES (values)
```

where:

>> *table* is the name of the table into which you want the row appended.

>> *columns* is a comma-separated list of column names from *table*. The values you specify will be added to these columns.

>> *values* is a comma-separated list of values that you want to add. The order of these values must correspond with the order of the column names in the *columns* parameter.

For example, suppose we have a table named categories that includes three fields: category_id, category_name, and description. First, assume that category_id is the table's primary key and its value is generated automatically by an AUTO_INCREMENT function, which means you can ignore it when building your INSERT query. Therefore, you can use the following SQL statement to add a new row:

```
INSERT
    INTO categories (category_name, description)
    VALUES ('Breads', 'Multi-grain, rye, and other
deliciousness')
```

Modifying table data with an UPDATE query

An UPDATE query modifies the values in one or more columns and optionally restricts the scope of the updating to those rows that satisfy some criteria. In MySQL, you build an UPDATE query by using the UPDATE verb to construct a statement with the following syntax:

```
UPDATE table
    SET column1=value1,column2=value2,...
    WHERE criteria
```

where:

>> *table* is the table that contains the data you want to update.

>> *column1=value1,column2=value2*, and so on are the new values you want to assign to the specified columns.

>> *criteria* is the criteria that define which rows will be updated.

For example, suppose you have a products table and want to increase the values in the unit_price column by 5 percent for the Beverages category (category_id = 1). This is the same as multiplying the current unit_price values by 1.05, so the UPDATE statement looks like this:

```
UPDATE products
    SET unit_price = unit_price*1.05
    WHERE CategoryID = 1
```

Removing table data with a DELETE query

A DELETE query removes rows from a table and optionally restricts the scope of the deletion to those rows that satisfy some criteria. If you don't include criteria, MySQL deletes every row in the specified table.

In MySQL, you build a delete query by using the DELETE verb to construct a statement with the following syntax:

```
DELETE
    FROM table
    WHERE criteria
```

where:

» *table* is the table that contains the rows you want to delete.

» *criteria* is the criteria that defines which rows will be deleted.

For example, if you want to delete those rows in the products table where the supplier_id value is 1, you use the following SQL statement:

```
DELETE
    FROM products
    WHERE supplier_id = 1
```

IN THIS CHAPTER

» **Understanding web development's most enduring marriage**

» **Connecting to a MySQL database with PHP**

» **Using PHP to access MySQL data with a SELECT query**

» **Processing the SELECT query results**

» **Rendering server data to the browser**

» **Using PHP to run INSERT, UPDATE, and DELETE queries**

Chapter **3**

Using PHP to Access MySQL Data

PHP and MySQL work together to provide powerful, flexible components that can keep up with the expanding database driven development needs of virtually any organization, large or small.

— ISAAC DUNLAP

Run a Google search on the text `PHP MySQL "Match made in heaven"` and you'll get more than a few results. I'm not surprised one bit because it seems as though these two technologies were meant to be together; a case of love at first byte, as it were.

What's the secret of their success as a couple? First, it helps that they're both free (not the usual prerequisite for marriage success, I know), which ensures that they're both widely available and widely supported. Second, both PHP and MySQL reward a little bit of learning effort with a lot of flexibility and power right off the bat. Although both are complex, sophisticated pieces of technology, you need to learn only a few basics to take your web development skills to a whole new level.

I cover the first two parts of those basics in Chapters 1 and 2 of this minibook. In this chapter, I bring everything together by showing you how to combine PHP and MySQL to create the foundation you need to build truly dynamic and powerful web applications.

Understanding the Role of PHP and MySQL in Your Web App

Before getting to the trees of actual PHP code, I want to take a moment to look out over the forest of the server back end, so you're comfortable and familiar with the process. Specifically, I want to look at how PHP and MySQL team up to deliver the back-end portion of a web app. Rather than getting bogged down in an abstract discussion of what happens when a user requests a page that requires some data from the server, I'll use a concrete example.

The following steps take you through the back-end process that happens when a hypothetical web app to display this book's sample code gets a request for a specific example:

1. Someone requests the web page of a specific book sample page. Here's a for instance:

   ```
   https://example.com/example.php?book=4& chapter=1&
       example=2
   ```

   The PHP script file is example.php and the request data — known to the cognoscenti as a *query string* — is everything after the question mark (?): book=4&chapter=1&example=2. This string is requesting the second example from Book 4, Chapter 1.

2. The web server retrieves example.php and sends it to the PHP processor.

3. The PHP script parses the query string to determine which sample the user is requesting.

   For the query string shown in Step 1, the script would extract the book number as 4, the chapter number as 1, and the example number as 2.

4. The script connects to the database that stores the code samples.

5. The script uses the query string data to create and run a SELECT query that returns the sample code.

   The SELECT statement looks something like this:

   ```
   SELECT *
       FROM examples
       WHERE book_num=4 AND chapter_num=1 AND example_num=2
   ```

6. The script massages the SELECT results into a format readable by the browser.

   This format is usually just HTML, but another popular format is JSON (JavaScript Object Notation), which you learn about in Book 6, Chapter 1.

7. The web server sends the formatted data to the web browser, which displays the code sample.

The rest of this chapter expands on Steps 3 through 6.

Using PHP to Access MySQL Data

When used as the back end of a web app, PHP's main job is to interact with MySQL to retrieve the data requested by the app and then format that data so that it's usable by the app for display in the browser. To do all that, PHP runs through five steps:

1. Get the request parameters from the URL query string.

2. Connect to the MySQL database.

3. Create and run a SELECT query to extract the requested data.

4. Get the data ready to be sent to the browser.

5. Output the data for the web browser.

I talk about INSERT, UPDATE, and DELETE queries later in this chapter, but the next few sections take you through the details of this five-step procedure from the point of view of a SELECT query.

WARNING

In the sections that follow, I don't discuss security techniques for blocking malicious hacking attempts. That's a crucial topic, however, so I devote a big chunk of Book 7, Chapter 4 to the all-important details, which you should read before deploying any dynamic web apps.

Parsing the query string

Many PHP scripts don't require any information from the web app to get the data that the app needs. For example, if the script's job is to return every record from a table or to return a predetermined subset of a table, your app just needs to call the script.

However, it's more common for a web app to decide on-the-fly (say, based on user input or some other event) what data it requires, and in such cases it needs to let the server know what to send. To get your web app to request data from the web server, you send a query string to the server. You can send a query string using two different methods:

>> **GET:** Specifies the data by adding the query string to the URL of the request. This is the method I talk about in this chapter.

>> **POST:** Specifies the data by adding it to the HTTP header of the request. This method is associated with HTML forms and some AJAX requests, which I cover in Book 6.

In the GET case, the query string is a series of name-value pairs that use the following general form:

```
name1=value1&name2=value2&...
```

Here's an example:

```
book=4& chapter=1& example=2
```

In the case of a GET request, you build the request by taking the URL of the PHP script that will handle the request, adding a question mark (?) to designate the boundary between the script address and the query string, and then adding the query string itself. Here's an example:

```
https://example.com/example.php?book=4& chapter=1& example=2
```

Now your PHP script has something to work with, and you access the query string data by using PHP's $_GET variable, which is an associative array created from the query string's name-value pairs. Specifically, the array's keys are the query string's names, and the array's values are the corresponding query string values. For example, the preceding URL creates the following $_GET array:

```
$_GET['book'] => 4
$_GET['chapter'] => 1
$_GET['example'] => 2
```

However, it's good programming practice to not assume that the $_GET array is populated successfully every time. You should check each element of the array by using PHP's isset() function, which returns true if a variable exists and has a value other than null. Here's some PHP code that checks that each element of the preceding $_GET array exists and isn't null (check out bk04ch03/example01.php in this book's example files):

```php
if (isset($_GET['book'])) {
    $book_num = $_GET['book'];
} else {
    echo 'The "book" parameter is missing!<br>';
    echo 'We are done here, sorry.';
    exit(0);
}
if (isset($_GET['chapter'])) {
    $chapter_num = $_GET['chapter'];
} else {
    echo 'The "chapter" parameter is missing!<br>';
    echo 'Sorry it didn\'t work out.';
    exit(0);
}
if (isset($_GET['example'])) {
    $example_num = $_GET['example'];
} else {
    echo 'The "example" parameter is missing!<br>';
    echo 'You had <em>one</em> job!';
    exit(0);
}
echo 'Got the query string!<br>
    Book number: ' . $book_num . '<br>
    Chapter number: ' . $chapter_num . '<br>
    Example number: ' . $example_num . '<br>';
```

This code checks each element of the $_GET array:

» If the element exists and isn't null, the code assigns the array value to a variable.

» If the element either doesn't exist or is null, the code outputs a message specifying the missing parameter and then stops the code by running the exit(0) function. (The 0 means that you're terminating the script in the standard way.)

Connecting to the MySQL database

You give PHP access to MySQL through an object called MySQLi (short for *MySQL Improved*). You can actually bring PHP and MySQL together in several ways, but MySQLi is both modern and straightforward, so it's the one I cover in this book.

You connect to a MySQL database by creating a new MySQLi connection. Here's the general format to use:

```
$var = mysqli_connect(hostname, username, password, database);
```

where:

>> *$var* is the variable that stores the new MySQLi connection.

>> *hostname* is the name of the server running MySQL. If the server is on the same computer as your script (which is usually the case), you can use localhost as the *hostname*.

>> *username* is the account name of a user who has access to the MySQL database.

>> *password* is the password associated with the *username* account.

>> *database* is the name of the MySQL database.

Here's a script that sets up the connection parameters by using four variables, and then creates the new MySQLi connection (check out bk04ch03/example02.php):

```php
<?php
    $host = 'localhost';
    $user = 'root';
    $password = 'shhhhhhh';
    $database = 'examples';

    $connection = mysqli_connect($host, $user, $password,
  $database);
?>
```

However, you shouldn't connect to a database without also checking that the connection was successful. Fortunately, MySQLi makes this easy by setting two properties when an error occurs:

>> mysqli_connect_errno(): Returns the error number

>> mysqli_connect_error(): Returns the error message

The `mysqli_connect()` method returns `false` if the connection fails, so your code can use an `if()` test to check for failure and, in that case, return the values of `mysqli_connect_errno()` and `mysqli_connect_error()`(bk04ch03/example02.php):

```
if(!connection) {
    echo 'Connection Failed!
        Error #' . mysqli_connect_errno()
            . ': ' . mysqli_connect_error();
    exit(0);
}
```

If an error occurs, the code displays a message like the one shown in Figure 3-1 and then runs `exit(0)` to stop execution of the script.

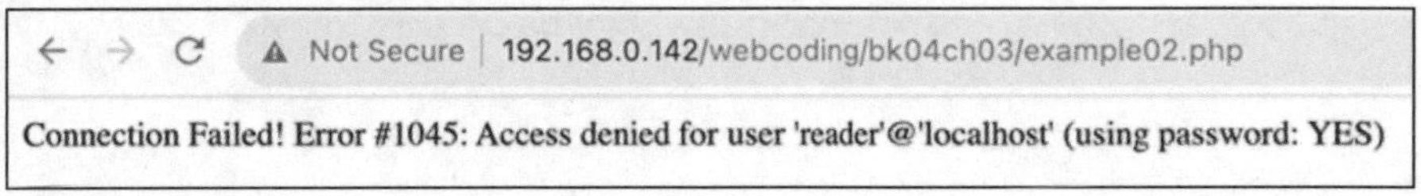

FIGURE 3-1:
An example of
an error number
and message
generated by the
MySQLi object.

← → C ⚠ Not Secure | 192.168.0.142/webcoding/bk04ch03/example02.php

Connection Failed! Error #1045: Access denied for user 'reader'@'localhost' (using password: YES)

Before moving on to querying the database, you need to add two quick house-keeping chores to your code. First, tell MySQLi to use the UTF-8 character set:

```
mysqli_set_charset($connection, 'utf8');
```

In the preceding statement, replace *$connection* with the name of your MySQLi connection variable.

Second, use the `mysqli_close()` method to close the database connection by adding the following statement at the end of your script (that is, just before the `?>` closing tag):

```
$mysqli_close($connection);
```

Again, remember to replace *$connection* with the name of your MySQLi connection variable.

Creating and running the SELECT query

To run a SELECT query on the database, you need to create a string variable to hold the SELECT statement and then use that string to run MySQLi's `mysqli_query()` method:

```
mysqli_query(connection, sql)
```

where:

>> *connection* is the MySQLi connection to the database.

>> *sql* is the SQL SELECT statement you want to use the query the database.

Here's an example (bk04ch03/example03.php):

```php
$sql = 'SELECT category_name, description
        FROM categories';
$result = mysqli_query($connection, $sql);

// Check for a query error
if (!$result) {
    echo 'Query Failed!
          Error: ' . mysqli_error($connection);
    exit(0);
}
```

The result of the query is stored in the $result variable. You might think that this variable now holds all the data, but that's not the case. Instead, $result is an object that contains information about the data, not the data itself. You make use of that information in the next section, but for now note that you can use the result object to check for an error in the query. That is, if $result is null, the query failed, so display the error message (using MySQLi's mysqli_error() method) and exit the script.

TIP

If you want to know how many rows the SELECT query returned, you can use the mysqli_num_rows() method on the result object:

```php
$total_rows = mysqli_num_rows($result);
```

Storing the query results in an array

The object returned by the mysqli_query() method is really just a pointer to the actual data, but you can use the object to retrieve the SELECT query's rows. You can do this in various ways, but I go the associative array route, which uses the MySQL's mysqli_fetch_all() method to return all the rows as an associative array:

```php
$array = $mysqli_fetch_all(result, MYSQLI_ASSOC);
```

where:

» $array is the name of the associative array you want to use to hold the query rows

» result is the result object returned by MySQLi's mysqli_query() method

REMEMBER

If you prefer to work with a numeric array, replace the MYSQLI_ASSOC constant with MYSQLI_NUM.

Note that the array is two dimensional, which makes sense because table data is two-dimensional (that is, it consists of one or more rows and one or more columns).

I'll make this more concrete by extending the example (bk04ch03/ example03.php):

```php
// Create a SELECT query
$sql = 'SELECT category_name, description
            FROM categories';

// Run the query
$result = mysqli_query($connection, $sql);

// Check for a query error
if (!$result) {
    echo 'Query Failed!
        Error: ' . mysqli_error($connection);
    exit(0);
}

// Get the query rows as an associative array
$rows = mysqli_fetch_all($result, MYSQLI_ASSOC);

// Get the total number of rows
$total_rows = mysqli_num_rows($result);

echo "Returned $total_rows categories:<br>";
```

Here, mysqli_fetch_all() stores the query result as an array named $rows. The code then uses mysqli__num_rows() to get the total number of rows in the array.

Looping through the query results

By storing the query results in an array, you make it easy to process the data by looping through the array using a `foreach()` loop (bk04ch03/example03.php):

```php
// Get the query rows as an associative array
$rows = mysqli_fetch_all($result, MYSQLI_ASSOC);

[skip some code]

// Loop through the rows
foreach($rows as $row) {
    echo $row['category_name'] . ': ' . $row['description'] .
  '<br>';
}
```

Here's what's happening in the `foreach()` loop:

>> Each item in the `$rows` array is referenced using the `$row` variable.

>> Each `$row` item is itself an associative array, where the key-value pairs are the column names and their values.

>> Because the keys of the `$row` array are the column names, the code can refer to the values using the `$row['column']` syntax.

Figure 3-2 shows the output of the script.

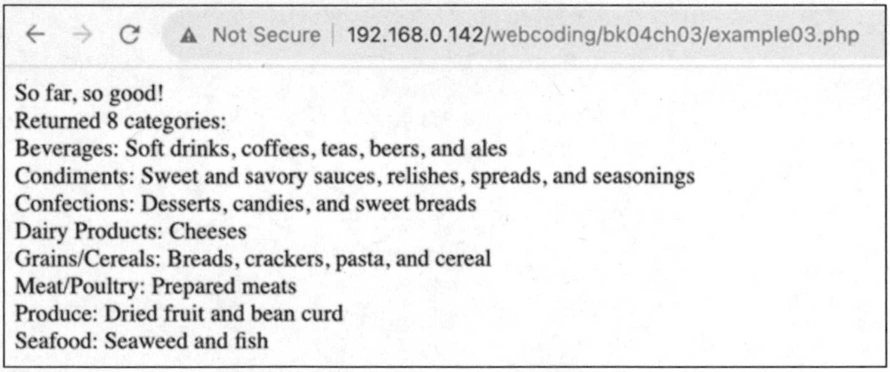

← → C   ⚠ Not Secure | 192.168.0.142/webcoding/bk04ch03/example03.php

So far, so good!
Returned 8 categories:
Beverages: Soft drinks, coffees, teas, beers, and ales
Condiments: Sweet and savory sauces, relishes, spreads, and seasonings
Confections: Desserts, candies, and sweet breads
Dairy Products: Cheeses
Grains/Cereals: Breads, crackers, pasta, and cereal
Meat/Poultry: Prepared meats
Produce: Dried fruit and bean curd
Seafood: Seaweed and fish

FIGURE 3-2:
The output of the PHP script.

Incorporating query string values in the query

I talk earlier in this chapter about how you can use $_GET to parse a URL's query string, so now I show you an example that uses a query string value in a SELECT query. First, here's the code (bk04ch03/example04.php):

```php
<?php
    // Parse the query string
    if (isset($_GET['category'])) {
        $category_num = $_GET['category'];
    } else {
        echo 'The "category" parameter is missing!<br>';
        echo 'We are done here, sorry. ';
        exit(0);
    }

    // Store the database connection parameters
    $host = 'localhost';
    $user = 'root';
    $password = 'shhhhhhh';
    $database = 'northwind;
    // Create a new MySQLi object with the database connection
parameters
    $connection = mysqli_connect($host, $user, $password,
$database);

    // Create a SELECT query
    // This is an INNER JOIN of the products and
    // categories tables, based on the category_id
    // value that was in the query string
    $sql = "SELECT products.product_name,
                   products.unit_price,
                   products.units_in_stock,
                   categories.category_name
            FROM products
            INNER JOIN categories
            ON products.category_id = categories.category_id
            WHERE products.category_id = $category_num";

    // Run the query
    $result = mysqli_query($connection, $sql);
```

```
    // Get the query rows as an associative array
    $rows = mysqli_fetch_all($result, MYSQLI_ASSOC);

    // Get the category name
    $category = $rows[0]['category_name'];
?>
```

First, note that to keep the code shorter, I removed the error-checking code. There's quite a bit going on here, so I'll go through it piece by piece:

>> The script resides in an HTML file, and you'd load the file using a URL that looks something like this:

```
https://example.com/example04.php?category=1
```

>> The first part of the script uses $_GET['category'] to get the category number from the query string, and that value is stored in the $category_num variable.

>> The script then builds a SQL SELECT statement, which is an inner join on the products and categories tables. The WHERE clause restricts the results to just those products that have the category value from the query string:

```
WHERE products.category_id = $category_num
```

>> The mysqli_query() method runs the SELECT query and stores the result in the $result object.

>> The mysqli_fetch _all() method fetches the data as an associative array that gets stored in the $rows object.

>> The category name is stored in a variable.

The final step is to render the fetched data to the web browser.

Rendering the data to the browser

Later in the book (see, in particular, Book 6), you learn how to use JavaScript to not only fetch data from the server by calling a PHP script, but also to write that data to the web page. However, in many cases it's faster and more straightforward to use PHP to write the data directly to the page. This is called *rendering* the data to the browser, and it's one of the most important and widely used PHP techniques for web developers.

The underlying idea is that within a .php file, you can intermingle both PHP code and HTML code. In most applications, this intermingling happens as follows:

1. Populate the file with your regular HTML code.

2. At the top of the file (that is, above the `<!DOCTYPE html>` tag), add a PHP block (that is, PHP code between `<?php` and `?>`) that performs all the actions required to get the page data from the server: connecting to the database; gathering the query string values; creating an SQL statement; running the query; and fetching the query data.

3. Within your HTML code, insert small PHP blocks (again, I'm talking about PHP code between `<?php` and `?>`) that perform the rendering of the data. These smaller blocks will usually do one or both of the following:

   - Insert some structural PHP code, such as the code that starts and ends a foreach loop.

   - Insert PHP code that writes data to the page, usually in the form echo *data*, where *data* is a reference (such as a variable name) to the data you want to write.

REMEMBER

If you're worried about web surfers having access to sensitive PHP code such as your database connection parameters, you can unfurrow your brow because all code in a PHP block is executed on the server and then stripped when the file is sent to the web browser.

I'll now demonstrate the intermingling of HTML and PHP using the file bk04ch03/example04.php in this book's example files. The top of example04.php looks like this:

```php
<?php
    // Parse the query string
    if (isset($_GET['category'])) {
        $category_num = $_GET['category'];
    } else {

The rest of the PHP code (refer to the previous section) goes
here.

    // Get the query rows as an associative array
    $rows = mysqli_fetch_all($result, MYSQLI_ASSOC);

    // Get the category name
    $category = $rows[0]['category_name'];
?>
<!DOCTYPE html>
```

The top of the file contains all the PHP code from the preceding section. The last line is the beginning of the HTML code, which continues as follows:

```html
<html lang="en">
<head>
    <meta charset="utf-8">
    <title>Products - <?php echo $category; ?></title>
    <style>
        .align-left {
            text-align: left;
        }
        .align-right {
            text-align: right;
            width: 75px;
        }
    </style>
</head>
```

In this code, you see the first PHP data rendering as part of the `<title>` tag:

```php
<?php echo $category; ?>
```

This code uses `echo` to output the value of the $category variable. So, for example, if the value of the $category variable is the string Beverages, the web browser will render the `<title>` tag as follows:

```html
<title>Products - Beverages</title>
```

A similar rendering happens at the top of the page body:

```html
<body>
    <h2><?php echo $category; ?></h2>
    <table>
    <tr>
    <th class="align-left">Product</th>
    <th class="align-right">Price</th>
    <th class="align-right">In Stock</th>
    </tr>
```

Again, the code uses `echo` to output the value of the $category variable, this time between the `<h2>` and `</h2>` tags. Note, as well, that the HTML then sets up the top part of a table. The rest of the table gets populated with a combination of PHP code and HTML tags:

```php
<?php
    // Loop through the rows
    foreach($rows as $row) {
?>
    <tr>
    <td><?php echo $row['product_name']; ?></td>
    <td class="align-right"><?php echo $row['unit_price'];
    ?></td>
    <td class="align-right"><?php echo $row['units_in_stock'];
    ?></td>
    </tr>
<?php
    }
?>
    </table>
```

No less than five PHP blocks are at work here:

» The first block sets up the beginning of a foreach loop to run through the associative array of data returned by the query.

» Between the first set of <td></td> tags, echo $row['product_name']; outputs the name of the current product.

» Between the second set of <td></td> tags, echo $row['unit_price']; outputs the unit price of the current product.

» Between the third set of <td></td> tags, echo $row['units_in_stock']; outputs the units in stock for the current product.

» The final PHP code block closes the foreach loop with the right brace (}).

The PHP file ends with the following code:

```php
<?php
    // That's it for now
    mysqli_close($connection);
?>

</body>
</html>
```

A final PHP block closes the database connection, and then the closing HTML tags appear. Figure 3-3 shows the resulting page.

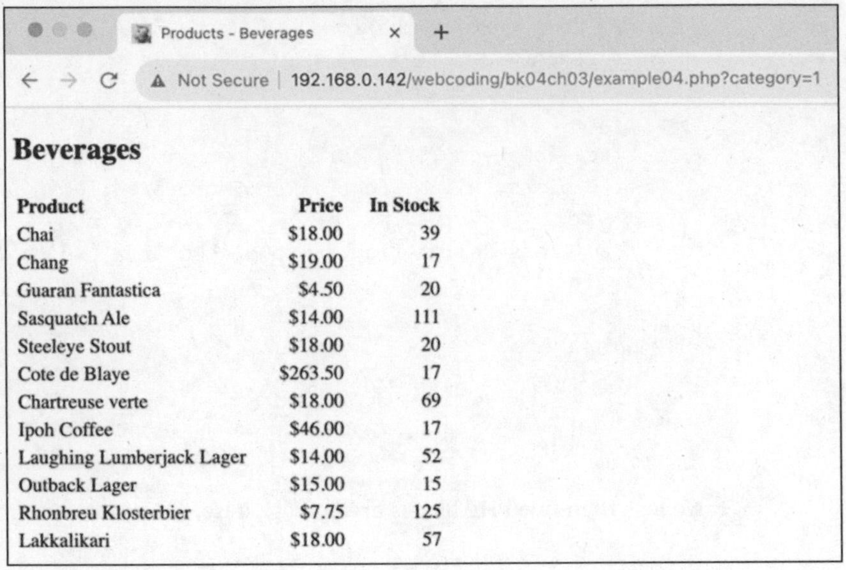
Products - Beverages
Not Secure | 192.168.0.142/webcoding/bk04ch03/example04.php?category=1
Beverages
Product Price In Stock
Chai $18.00 39
Chang $19.00 17
Guaran Fantastica $4.50 20
Sasquatch Ale $14.00 111
Steeleye Stout $18.00 20
Cote de Blaye $263.50 17
Chartreuse verte $18.00 69
Ipoh Coffee $46.00 17
Laughing Lumberjack Lager $14.00 52
Outback Lager $15.00 15
Rhonbreu Klosterbier $7.75 125
Lakkalikari $18.00 57

FIGURE 3-3: The output of the script, which lays out the query data in an HTML table.

Creating and Running Insert, Update, and Delete Queries

Performing INSERT, UPDATE, and DELETE queries in PHP is much simpler than performing SELECT queries because once your code has checked whether the query completed successfully, you're done. Here's an example that runs an INSERT query (bk04ch03/example05.php):

```
<?php

    // Store the database connection parameters
    $host = 'localhost';
    $user = 'root';
    $password = 'shhhhhhh';
    $database = 'northwind';
    // Create a new MySQLi object with the database connection
  parameters
    $connection = mysqli_connect($host, $user, $password,
  $database);
```

```php
    // Check for a connection error
    if(!$connection) {
        echo 'Connection Failed!
            Error #' . mysqli_connect_errno()
                . ': ' . mysqli_connect_error();
        exit(0);
    } else {
        echo 'So far, so good!';
    }

    // Create an INSERT query
    $sql = "INSERT
            INTO categories (category_name, description)
            VALUES ('Breads', 'Multi-grain, rye, and other
deliciousness')";

    // Run the query
    $result = mysqli_query($connection, $sql);

    // Check for a query error
    if (!$result) {
        echo 'Query Failed!
            Error: ' . mysqli_error($connection);
        exit(0);
    }
?>
```

When given an INSERT, UPDATE, or DELETE statement, MySQLi's mysqli_query() method returns true if the query executed successfully, or false if the query failed.

Separating Your MySQL Login Credentials

When you're building a web app or some other medium-to-large web project that requires a back end, you'll soon notice that your PHP scripts that access the project's MySQL data begin to multiply in a rabbitlike fashion. Before you know it, you've got 10 or 20 such scripts lying around. What do these scripts have in common? They all include the same code for connecting to the project's MySQL database. It's not a big deal to just copy and paste that code into each new script, but it can be a huge deal if one day you have to change your login credentials. For example, for security reasons you might decide to change the password. That means you now have to wade through every single one of your scripts and make that change. Annoying!

A better way to go is to make use of PHP's `require` statement, which enables you to insert the contents of a specified PHP file into the current PHP file:

```
require php_file;
```

where *php_file* is the path and filename of the PHP file you want to insert.

So, what you do is take your MySQL database credentials code and paste it into a separate PHP file:

```php
<?php
    $host = 'localhost';
    $user = 'root';
    $password = 'shhhhhhh';
    $database = 'northwind';
?>
```

Say this file is named `credentials.php`. If it resides in the same directory as your scripts, you'd replace the credentials code in your PHP scripts with the following statement:

```
require 'credentials.php';
```

If the credentials file resides in a subdirectory, you need to include the full path to the file:

```
require '/includes/credentials.php';
```

Note that if PHP can't find or load this file for some reason, the script will halt with an error.

5
Debugging Your Code

Contents at a Glance

Chapter **1**

Debugging CSS Code

CSS, like other languages, becomes easier to debug when you take time to learn a bit about its quirks. It also helps to become familiar with tools to help you both debug and prevent creating bugs in the first place.

— STEPHANIE ECKLES

CSS is awesome. With just a few rules, you can turn a drab, lifeless page into a work of art that is a pleasure to read and will have your visitors clamoring for more.

CSS is also a pain in the you-know-what. You add what appears to be a straight-forward rule to your CSS, save your work, refresh your browser and . . . *nothing changes!* Or maybe things change, but not in the way you expected. Cue the cartoon steam shooting out your ears.

Let me say at this point that although these kinds of frustrations are the stuff of legend in the CSS community, they do *not* mean, as some folks would have it, that CSS is illogical or stupid or broken. A large group of dedicated and smart people create the CSS standards and, believe me, these folks know what they're doing! It may be a tough pill to swallow, but the truth is that if your CSS seems to be behaving illogically or stupidly or brokenly, it means your code is to blame, not CSS itself.

That's okay, though, because there's a way out of every CSS jam. When you stumble upon a particularly ornery CSS problem, you can turn to your favorite browser's web development tools (which all the cool kids shorten to *dev tools*). These tools provide plenty of features to help you troubleshoot wonky CSS code, as you discover in this chapter.

In this chapter, I use the example page shown in Figure 1-1 which has a crowded top-left corner that I want to debug. (In the book's example files, check out bk05ch01/example01.html.)

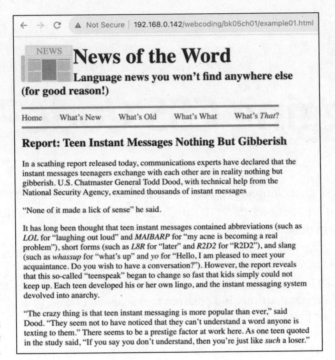

FIGURE 1-1: The web page that I'll debug.

Displaying the Web Development Tools

Most web developers debug their CSS using Google Chrome, so I focus on that browser in this chapter. But here's how you open the web development tools in not only Chrome but also the various flavors of Firefox, Microsoft Edge, and Safari:

>> **Chrome for Windows:** Click Customize, click the control Google Chrome icon (three vertical dots to the right of the address bar), and then choose More Tools⇨Developer Tools. Shortcut: Ctrl+Shift+I.

>> **Chrome for Mac:** Choose View↔Developer↔Developer Tools. Shortcut: Option+⌘+I.

>> **Firefox for Windows:** Click the open Application menu icon (three horizontal lines on the far right of the toolbar) and then choose More Tools ↔Web Developer Tools. Shortcut: Ctrl+Shift+I.

>> **Firefox for Mac:** Choose Tools↔Browser Tools↔Web Developer Tools. Shortcut: Option+⌘+I.

>> **Microsoft Edge:** Click the settings and more icon (three vertical dots to the right of the address bar), and then choose More Tools↔Developer Tools. Shortcut: Ctrl+Shift+I.

>> **Safari:** Choose Develop↔Show Web Inspector. Shortcut: Option+⌘+I. If the Develop menu isn't around, select Safari↔Settings, click the Advanced tab, and then select the Show Develop Menu in Menu Bar check box.

TIP

In all browser development tools, you can configure where the pane appears in relation to the browser window. In Chrome, click the customize icon (three verti-cal dots near the upper-right corner of the dev tools) and then click the dock to right, dock to bottom, or dock to left icon (see Figure 1-2). if you prefer a floating pane that you can move around, click the undock icon.

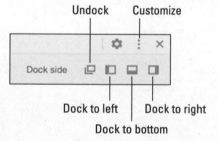

FIGURE 1-2:
Choose where the development tools pane appears in the browser window.

Inspecting an Element

If an element on the page doesn't look right or has gone awry in some other way, the most basic CSS debugging technique is to examine how the web browser has interpreted your CSS code. This is known as *inspecting* the element.

To begin your inspection of any element on a web page, use the following techniques:

>> If you don't already have your browser's web development tools open, right-click the element and then click Inspect (or, in Safari, Inspect Element).

This opens your browser's development tools, displays the Elements tab (it's called Inspector in Firefox), and highlights the element's HTML.

>> If your browser's web development tools are already open, click the Elements tab (the Inspector tab in Firefox), and then click the tag of the element you want to inspect.

>> If the web development tools are already open, click the select an element icon (labeled in Figure 1-3) and then click an element on the rendered page.

Figure 1-3 shows the page from Figure 1-1 with the header's img element selected.

...and the browser highlights the element and displays its dimensions

The selected element's style rules appear in the Styles pane

Hover over the element you want to inspect...

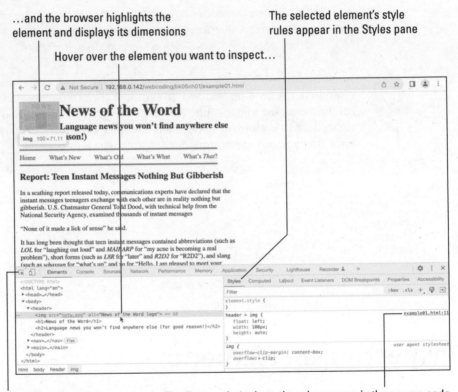

FIGURE 1-3:
Inspecting the img element.

Select an element

The line number where the rule appears in the source code

There are two things to note here:

>> The left side of the tab shows the page's HTML code as it was interpreted by the browser.

>> When you hover the mouse pointer over an element, the browser highlights the element in the rendered page and displays the element's dimensions.

Inspecting an element's styles

When you click an element in the HTML code, the Styles subtab on the right shows the style rules that have been applied to the element. (In some browsers, particularly Safari and Firefox, there's a separate Styles pane in the middle.) There are usually two or three types of style rules:

>> The style rules that you created. To the right of each rule, the browser displays the filename of the rule's source code and the line number where the rule appears in that file.

>> Rules from your CSS reset, if you're using one.

>> Rules where the location is user agent stylesheet, which means these are rules applied by the browser.

The order of the rules isn't random. On the contrary, the browser orders the rules by their relative importance — or *weight*, as CSS types call it — with the most important rules at the top. How does the browser decide which rules are more important than others? Ah, that's a topic I cover in Book 2, Chapter 2.

If the list of rules for an element is long, you can zero in on a particular rule by typing all or part of the rule's selector in the Filter text box. For example, if you type **header**, the browser filters the rules to include only those that have header somewhere in the selector.

When you're debugging your styles, one of the first things you should look for is a line through a style declaration. This line tells you one of two important things:

>> **The declaration has been overridden by another declaration elsewhere in the CSS.** For example, check out the Styles subtab in Figure 1-4. At the bottom, notice the line through the nav element's display: block declaration, which came from the user agent stylesheet. That declaration was overridden by the display: flex declaration that I added to the nav element in my CSS. (Refer to Book 2, Chapter 4 to learn about laying out page elements with Flexbox.)

>> **The declaration is wrong in some way.** If there's a line through the declaration and also a warning icon to its left, the web browser couldn't process the declaration, either because the browser doesn't support the property or value or because the property or value is invalid. For example, in the Styles subtab shown in Figure 1-5, one of the a element declarations has a line through it and a warning icon next to it. Why? Upon closer inspection, you can read that the property name is font-varaint, but it's supposed to be font-variant.

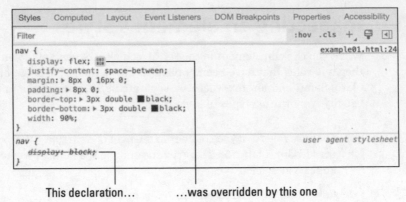

FIGURE 1-4:
A line through a
declaration
tells you it
has been
overridden
by another
declaration.

This declaration...   ...was overridden by this one

FIGURE 1-5:
The browser
displays a
warning icon and
a crossed-out
declaration for
unsupported or
invalid properties
or values.

A misspelled property name is the culprit here

Inspecting an element's box model

If the spacing within or around an element isn't what you were expecting, some kind of problem with the *box model* — that is, the element's padding, border, margin, width, or height — should be your first suspect. Click the element you want to inspect and then click the Computed tab.

The browser shows the element's box model abstractly as a series of concentric rectangles (check out Figure 1-6), where the innermost rectangle is the content box, and then successive rectangles represent the padding, the border, and finally the margin. The content box shows the width and height of the element, with each of the other rectangles showing the four values (top, right, bottom, and left) for the corresponding box model component.

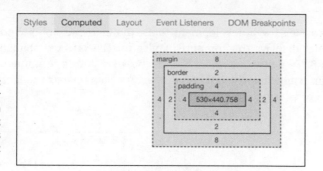

FIGURE 1-6:
The browser displays an element's box model as a series of concentric rectangles.

How does all this help for debugging? Viewing the values that the browser is using for padding and margin, in particular, can help you solve spacing problems. For example, back in Figure 1-1, note that the header image in the upper-left corner has no space around it. To understand why, I can inspect the img element. Lo and behold, as shown in the Figure 1-7, that element has *no* padding or margins (that is, the browser displays dashes instead of values), which explains why the image is being crowded by its web page neighbors.

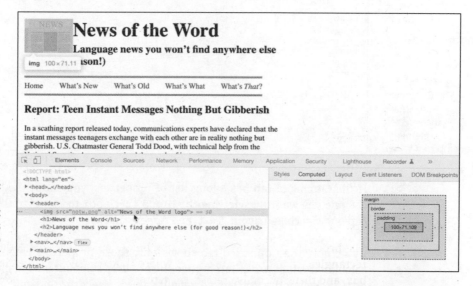

FIGURE 1-7:
The img element's box model tells us that it has no margin or padding set.

Inspecting an element's computed styles

An element's *computed styles* are the final property values calculated by the browser after weighing all available CSS rules (such as the default user agent styles, your CSS reset, and the styles you define). If an element isn't displaying the way you thought it would, its computed styles can at least tell you why the browser is rendering the element the way it is.

In the browser's web development tools, the Elements tab includes a Computed subtab that displays the computed styles for the selected element, as shown in Figure 1-8. To figure out where the web browser got its computed value, click the expansion triangle to the left of a property, which reveals the location of the rule the browser is using.

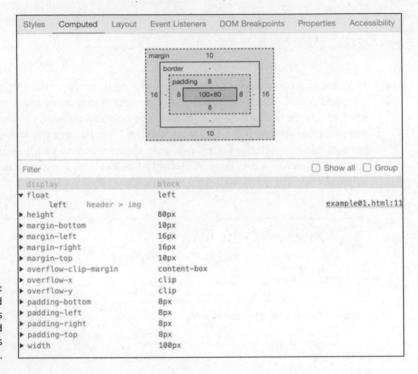

FIGURE 1-8:
The Computed
tab shows
the selected
element's
computed styles.

TIP If the Computed tab has a long list of properties, you can make it easier to find the one you want by selecting the Group check box to organize the properties by category (such as Layout, Text, and Appearance).

TIP By default, the Computed tab shows only those properties where the browser's calculated values are different than the browser's defaults. To inspect every property, including the unchanged default values, select the Show All check box.

Inspecting an element's layout

The final feature of the Elements tab that you might find useful for troubleshooting CSS is the Layout tab, which offers tools for visualizing layouts that use the following technologies:

>> **CSS Grid:** Enables you to add an overlay that shows the grid and its track numbers. You can also optionally view track sizes, named areas, and extended grid lines. Refer to Book 2, Chapter 4 to learn how to lay out a page using CSS Grid.

>> **Flexbox:** Enables you to add a simple overlay to help you visualize your flex container and its items. Refer to Book 2, Chapter 4 to learn how to lay out a page using Flexbox and how to use the overlay to inspect a flex layout.

Editing a Property Value

If the web development tools were just about inspecting CSS, they'd be useful, for sure, but hardly game changing. Fortunately, your browser's development tools enable you to not only view the current CSS but also *change it.* That is, you can make temporary, on-the-fly adjustments to just about any property value. As soon as you edit an existing property value, the browser automatically updates the rendered page to reflect the change.

Why is this a game-changer? Because normally to make a change, you'd have to go back to your HTML or CSS file, edit the CSS as needed, save your work, possibly upload the edited file, switch to your browser, and then refresh the page. And if the edit didn't give you the result you want and you decided to try something else, you'd need to go back to the CSS and reverse the change you just made.

That's a lot of work for what is, most of the time, a small adjustment to a property value. With the web development tools, you can make that change quickly and without messing with your original code. There's no muss and not even a little fuss.

Here's how it works:

1. **In the Elements tab of the browser development tools, click the element you want to modify.**

2. **On the Styles subtab, click the property value you want to edit.**

   The browser opens the value for editing.

3. **Edit the value.**

   You can edit the property value in the following ways:

   - *To replace the entire value:* Just type the new value. This works because when you first click the property value, the browser selects the entire entry, so your typing replaces that selection.

- *To select a new value from a list:* Press Delete to remove the current value, and then click the new value from the list the browser displays. Note that this technique works only for property values that accept a defined set of keywords as values.

- *To edit only part of the property value:* Click the value a second time to place an insertion point cursor inside the field; then make your edits.

- *To increment the current numeric value:* Press the up arrow key; to decrement the current numeric value, press the down arrow key.

4. **When you're done with your changes, press Enter or Return.**

For a box model property, you can also edit the values directly on the box model representation (refer to Figure 1-6) in the Computed tab. Here's how it works:

1. **In the Elements tab of the browser development tools, click the element you want to modify.**

2. **Click the Computed tab.**

3. **In the box model, double-click the value you want to edit.**

   In the content box, double-click either the width or the height to edit that value. Otherwise, in the padding, border, or margin rectangle, double-click the existing top, right, bottom, or left value.

   The browser opens the value for editing.

4. **Type the new value, and then press Enter or Return.**

Disabling a Declaration

A useful what–if question to ask yourself when you're debugging CSS is, "What if declaration A wasn't in rule B?" In other words, how would the browser render an element differently if that element's rule didn't include a particular declaration?

No need to go back to your CSS source code and comment out that declaration. Instead, your browser's web development environment makes it a snap to disable any rule that's not a default user agent stylesheet rule. Here's how:

1. **In the Elements tab of the browser development tools, click the element you want to modify.**

2. **On the Styles subtab, hover your mouse pointer over the rule that contains the declaration you want to disable.**

The browser displays a check box to the left of each declaration in the rule, as shown in Figure 1-9.

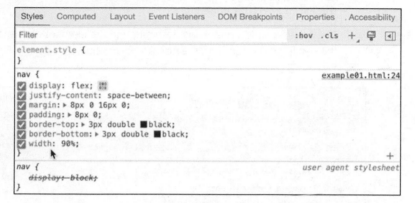

FIGURE 1-9:
Hovering the mouse pointer over a rule adds check boxes beside each declaration.

3. **Deselect the check box for the declaration you want to disable.**

The browser displays the effect of disabling the declaration. When you're ready to enable the declaration again, repeat Steps 1 and 2 and then select the check box.

Adding an Inline Declaration to an Element

Rather than have you disable an existing declaration, as I describe in the previous section, your CSS troubleshooting chores might require you to add a declaration to an element. Happily, as with disabling a declaration, you don't need to modify your existing CSS to add a declaration because you can perform this task within the convenient confines of the web development tools.

Here are the steps to follow to add a declaration:

1. **In the Elements tab of the browser development tools, click the element you want to modify.**

2. **On the Styles subtab, click the `element.style` rule (it's at the top of the list of styles, just below the Filter box).**

The browser creates an empty CSS declaration and places the cursor in the property field, just before the colon (:).

3. **Start typing the CSS property you want to use. In the list of properties that match what you've typed, click the property when it appears; then press Tab.**

The browser moves the cursor to the empty value field.

4. **Either type the property value you want to use or select the value from the list (if any) that appears.**

The browser adds a new inline declaration to the element's tag and updates the rendered element with the new property value, as shown in Figure 1-10.

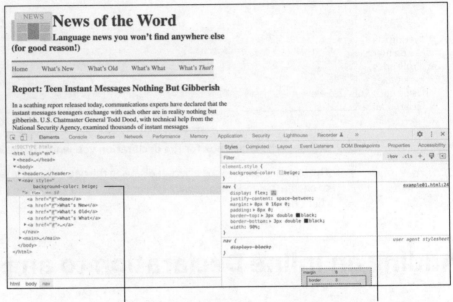

FIGURE 1-10:
You can add
new declarations
to an element.

...the browser adds a style attribute to the element

When you add a declaration here...

Adding an Element Declaration to the Inspector Stylesheet

As is shown in Figure 1-10, the browser adds a `style` attribute to the element's tag. That's fine, but inline styles create a lot of weight (in the CSS sense; refer to Book 2, Chapter 2's discussion of the cascade to learn more), which might not give you an accurate picture of things. A better method — that is, one that creates a bit less weight — is to add the new rule to a special stylesheet called the inspector stylesheet. The *inspector stylesheet* is a temporary set of styles that the browser uses only while you're inspecting elements. Any rules you add to the inspector stylesheet will override your own rules, which is what you want.

Here are the steps to follow to add a new rule to the inspector stylesheet:

1. **In the Elements tab of the browser development tools, click the element you want to modify.**

2. **On the Styles subtab toolbar, click the new style rule icon (labeled in Figure 1-11).**

   The browser starts a new rule using the element selector that has the highest importance. It also opens the selector field for editing.

3. **Modify the rule's selector as needed, and then press Tab.**

   The browser creates an empty CSS declaration and places the cursor in the property field, just before the colon (:).

4. **Start typing the CSS property you want to use. In the list of properties that match what you've typed, click the property when it appears, and then press Tab.**

   The browser moves the cursor to the empty value field.

5. **Either type the property value you want to use or select the value from the list (if any) that appears.**

   The browser adds the new rule to the inspector stylesheet and updates the rendered element with the new declaration, as shown in Figure 1-11.

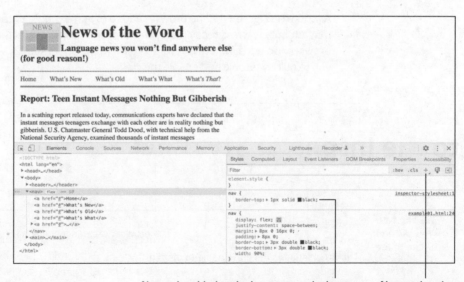

FIGURE 1-11: You can add new rules to the inspector stylesheet.

New rule added to the inspector stylesheet   New style rule

CHAPTER 1 **Debugging CSS Code**   533

TIP

You can edit the inspector stylesheet by clicking the `inspector-stylesheet` link that appears to the right of your new rule. After you have the inspector stylesheet open for editing, feel free to use any selector you want to add new rules, including class rules, which you can then add to the element, as I describe in the next section.

Adding a Class to an Element

Another useful what-if question to ask when debugging a recalcitrant element is, "What if I applied a class to that element?" That is, if a particular class is already defined somewhere in your CSS, would adding that class to the element — inserting the class name into the tag's `class` attribute — solve the problem? Good question!

To add an existing class — one where a rule that uses that class as the selector, which could be in your own CSS, a third-party CSS file, or the inspector stylesheet — to an element, follow these steps:

1. **In the Elements tab of the browser development tools, click the element you want to modify.**

2. **On the Styles subtab toolbar, click the .cls button.**

   The browser displays the Add New Class text box.

3. **Type the name of the class, and then press Enter or Return.**

   As shown in Figure 1-12, the browser adds a `class` attribute to the element (if that attribute wasn't already there) and adds the class name as the value. The browser also adds a check box for the class to the Styles subtab, which enables you to quickly disable and enable the class.

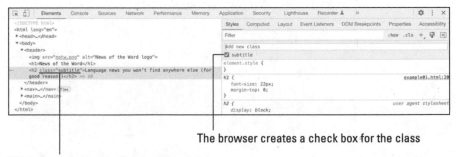

FIGURE 1-12:
You can add a class to the element.

The browser creates a check box for the class

The browser adds the class name to the tag

Simulating a Pseudo-Class State

In Book 2, Chapter 2, I briefly discuss pseudo-classes and how useful they are as selectors. Several pseudo-classes deal with user behavior, such as the user hovering the mouse pointer over an element, the user putting the focus on an element, and the user clicking a button.

One conundrum you may come across when debugging your CSS is that your pseudo-class rules don't show up in the Styles pane of your browser's web development tools. That's a pain because what if you want to try out new or modified values in your pseudo-class rules?

Fear not, dear debugger, because your web development tools have you covered with a feature that enables you to quickly toggle several element states on and off. When you toggle on a state such as hover, the browser adds your :hover pseudo-class rule to the Styles pane and you can play around with that rule as needed.

Click the element you want to work with. (For example, if you're following along using bk05ch01/example02.html, click any a element in the nav element.) Then, on the Styles subtab toolbar, click the :hov button. The browser displays the collection of check boxes shown in Figure 1-13. Each check box corresponds to a pseudo-class: :active, :hover, :focus, and so on. To simulate a particular state and therefore display whatever rule uses that pseudo-class as its selector, select the check box. Deselect the check box to deactivate the element state.

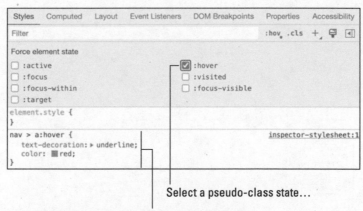

FIGURE 1-13:
You can simulate pseudo-class states such as :active and :hover.

Select a pseudo-class state...

...and the browser displays the pseudo-class rule

IN THIS CHAPTER

» Learning JavaScript's error types

» Debugging errors by using the Console window

» Setting breakpoints

» Watching variable and expression values

» Learning JavaScript's most common errors and error messages

Chapter **2**

Debugging JavaScript Code

Testing proves a programmer's failure. Debugging is the programmer's vindication.

— BORIS BEIZER

It usually doesn't take too long to get short scripts and functions up and running. However, as your code grows larger and more complex, errors inevitably creep in. In fact, it has been proven mathematically that any code beyond a minimum level of complexity will contain at least one error, and probably quite a lot more.

Many of the bugs that crawl into your code will consist of simple syntax problems that you can fix quickly, but others will be more subtle and harder to find. For the latter — whether the errors are incorrect values returned by functions or problems with the overall logic of a script — you need to be able to get inside your code to scope out what's wrong.

The good news is that JavaScript and modern web browsers offer a ton of top-notch debugging tools that can remove some of the burden of program problem solving. In this chapter, you delve into these tools to explore how they can help you find and fix most programming errors. You also investigate a number of tips and techniques that can go a long way in helping you avoid coding errors in the first place.

Understanding JavaScript's Error Types

When a problem occurs, the first thing you need to determine is what kind of error you're dealing with. The three basic error types are syntax errors, runtime errors, and logic errors.

Syntax errors

Syntax errors arise from misspelled or missing keywords or incorrect punctuation. JavaScript almost always catches these errors when you load the page (which is why syntax errors are also known as *load-time errors*). That is, as JavaScript reads the script's statements, it checks each one for syntax errors. If it finds an error, it stops processing the script and displays an error message. Here's an example statement (check out bk05ch02/example01.html in this book's example files) with a typical syntax error (can you spot it?). Figure 2-1 shows how the error is flagged in the Firefox Console window.

```
const pageFooter - document.querySelector("footer");
```

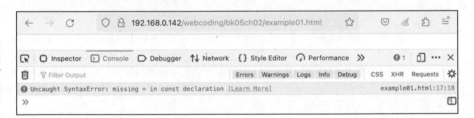

Runtime errors

Runtime errors occur during the execution of a script. They generally mean that JavaScript has stumbled upon a statement that it can't figure out. A runtime error might be caused by trying to use an uninitialized variable in an expression or by using a property or method with the wrong object.

If your script has statements that execute as the page loads, and no syntax errors have been found, JavaScript will attempt to run those statements. If it comes across a statement with a problem, it halts execution of the script and displays the error. If your script has one or more functions, JavaScript doesn't look for runtime errors in those functions until you call them.

Here's some code (check out bk05ch02/example02.html) in which I misspelled a variable name in the third line (pagefooter instead of pageFooter). Figure 2-2 shows the Chrome Console window displaying the runtime error that results.

```
const pageFooter = document.querySelector("footer");
const currDate = new Date();
pagefooter.innerHTML = "Copyright " + currDate.getFullYear() + "
    Logophilia Limited.";
```

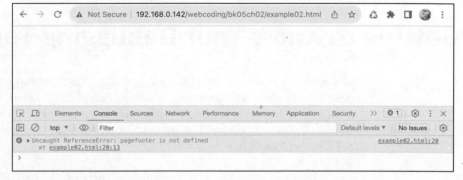

FIGURE 2-2:
The Chrome Console window displaying data about a typical runtime error.

Logic errors

If your code zigs instead of zags, the cause is usually a *logic error*, which is a flaw in the logic of your script. It might be a loop that never ends or a switch test that doesn't switch to anything.

Logic errors are the toughest to pin down because you don't get an error message to give you clues about what went wrong and where. What you usually need to do is set up *debugging code* that helps you monitor values and trace the execution of your program. I go through the most useful debugging techniques later in this chapter.

Getting to Know Your Debugging Tools

All major web browsers come with a sophisticated set of debugging tools that can make your life as a web developer much easier and much saner. Most web developers debug their scripts using Google Chrome, so I focus on that browser in this chapter. But in this section, I give you an overview of the tools available in all the major browsers and how to get at them.

Here's how you open the web development tools in Chrome, Firefox, Microsoft Edge, and Safari:

» **Chrome for Windows:** Click Customize, click the Control Google Chrome icon (three vertical dots to the right of the address bar), and then choose More Tools⇨Developer Tools. Shortcut: Ctrl+Shift+I.

» **Chrome for Mac:** Choose View⇨Developer⇨Developer Tools. Shortcut: Option+⌘+I.

» **Firefox for Windows:** Click the open Application menu icon (three horizontal lines on the far right of the toolbar), and then choose More Tools ⇨Web Developer Tools. Shortcut: Ctrl+Shift+I.

» **Firefox for Mac:** Choose Tools⇨Browser Tools⇨Web Developer Tools. Shortcut: Option+⌘+I.

>> **Microsoft Edge:** Click Settings, click the more icon (three vertical dots to the right of the address bar), and then choose More Tools⇨Developer Tools. Shortcut: Ctrl+Shift+I.

>> **Safari:** Click Develop⇨Show Web Inspector. Shortcut: Option+⌘+I. If you don't have the Develop menu, click Safari⇨Settings, click the Advanced tab, and then select the Show Develop Menu in Menu Bar check box.

These development tools vary in the features they offer, but each provides the same set of basic tools, which are the tools you'll use most often. These basic web development tools include the following:

>> **HTML viewer:** This tab (called Inspector in Firefox and Elements in the other browsers) shows the HTML source code used in the web page. When you hover the mouse pointer over a tag, the browser highlights the element in the displayed page and shows its width and height, as shown in Figure 2-3. When you click a tag, the browser shows the CSS styles applied with the tag, as well as the tag's box dimensions (again, refer to Figure 2-3).

The element's width and height   The selected element is highlighted on the page

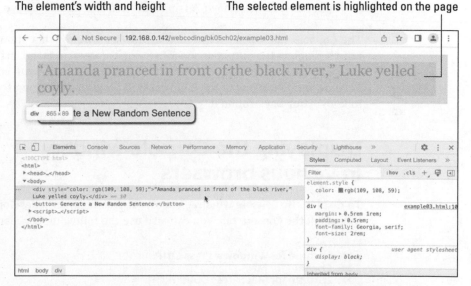

FIGURE 2-3:
The HTML viewer, such as Chrome's Elements tab, enables you to inspect each element's styles and box dimensions.

>> **Console:** This tab enables you to view error messages, log messages, test expressions, and execute statements. I cover the Console window in more detail in the next section.

>> **Debugging tool:** This tab (called Debugger in Firefox and Sources in the other browsers) enables you to pause code execution, step through your code,

watch the values of variables and properties, and much more. This is the most important JavaScript debugging tool, so I cover it in detail later in this chapter.

>> **Network:** This tab tells you how long it takes to load each file referenced by your web page. If you find that your page is slow to load, this tab can help you find the bottleneck.

>> **Web storage:** This tab (called Application in Chrome and Edge and Storage in Firefox and Safari) enables you to examine data stored in the browser using the Web Storage API, which I discuss in Book 3, Chapter 10.

Debugging with the Console Window

If your web page is behaving strangely — for example, the page is blank or missing elements — you should first check your HTML code to make sure it's correct. (Common HTML errors are not finishing a tag with a greater than sign — > — not including a closing tag, and missing a closing quotation mark for an attribute value.) If your HTML checks out, there's a good chance that your JavaScript code is wonky. How do you know? A trip to the Console window is your first step.

The Console window is an interactive browser window that shows warnings and errors, displays the output of console.log() statements, and enables you to execute expressions and statements without having to run your entire script. The Console window is one of the handiest web browser debugging tools, so you need to know your way around it.

Displaying the Console window in various browsers

To display the Console window, open your web browser's development tools and then click the Console tab. You can also use the following keyboard shortcuts:

>> **Chrome for Windows:** Press Ctrl+Shift+J.

>> **Chrome for Mac:** Press Option+⌘+J.

>> **Firefox for Windows:** Press Ctrl+Shift+K.

>> **Firefox for Mac:** Press Option+⌘+K.

>> **Microsoft Edge:** Press Ctrl+Shift+J.

>> **Safari:** Press Option+⌘+C.

Logging data to the Console window

You can use the `console.log()` method of the special `Console` object to print text and expression values in the Console window:

```
console.log(output)
```

where *output* is the expression you want to print in the Console window. The *output* expression can be a text string, a variable, an object property, a function result, or any combination of these.

You can also use the handy `console.table()` method to output the values of arrays or objects in an easy-to-read tabular format:

```
console.table(output)
```

where *output* is the array or object (as a variable or as a literal) you want to view in the Console window.

For debugging purposes, you most often use the Console window to keep an eye on the values of variables, object properties, and expressions. That is, when your code sets or changes the value of something, you insert a `console.log()` (or `console.table()`) statement that outputs the new value. When the script execution is complete, you can open the Console window and then check out the logged value or values.

Executing code in the Console window

One of the great features of the Console window is that it's interactive, which means that you can not only read messages generated by the browser or by your `console.log()` statements but also type code directly into the Console window. That is, you can use the Console window to execute expressions and statements. There are many uses for this feature:

>> You can try some experimental expressions or statements to determine their effect on the script.

>> When the script is paused, you can output the current value of a variable or property.

>> When the script is paused, you can change the value of a variable or property. For example, if you notice that a variable with a value of zero is about to be used as a divisor, you can change that variable to a nonzero value to avoid crashing the script.

>> When the script is paused, you can run a function or method to determine whether it operates as expected under the current conditions.

Each browser's Console tab includes a text box (usually marked by a > prompt) that you can use to enter your expressions or statements.

TIP

You can execute multiple statements in the Console window by separating each statement with a semicolon. For example, you can test a for... loop by entering a statement similar to the following:

```
for (let i=1; i < 10; i += 1){console.log(i**2); console.log(i**3);}
```

TIP

If you want to repeat an earlier code execution in the Console window, or if you want to run some code that's very similar to code you ran earlier, you can recall statements and expressions that you used in the current browser session. Press the up arrow key to scroll back through your previously executed code; press the down arrow key to scroll forward through your code.

Pausing Your Code

Pausing your code midstream lets you examine certain elements, such as the current values of variables and properties. It also lets you execute program code one statement at a time so that you can monitor the flow of the script.

When you pause your code, JavaScript enters *break mode*, which means that the browser displays its debugging tool and highlights the current statement (the one that JavaScript will execute next). Figure 2-4 shows a script in break mode in Chrome's debugger (the Sources tab).

Entering break mode

JavaScript gives you two ways to enter break mode:

>> By setting breakpoints

>> By using a debugger statement

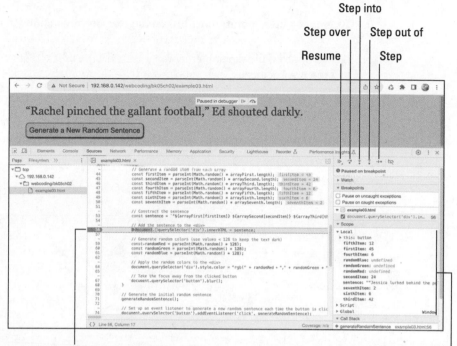

Step into

Step over   Step out of

Resume   Step

"Rachel pinched the gallant football," Ed shouted darkly.

[Generate a New Random Sentence]

The browser pauses on the current statement   The current values of the script's variables

Setting a breakpoint

If you know approximately where an error or a logic flaw is occurring, you can enter break mode at a specific statement in the script by setting a *breakpoint*. Here are the steps to set a breakpoint:

1. **Display your web browser's developer tools and switch to the debugging tool (such as the Sources tab in Chrome).**

2. **Open the file that contains the JavaScript code you want to debug.**

How you do this depends on the browser: In Chrome (and most browsers), you have two choices:

- In the left pane, click the HTML file (if your JavaScript code is in a `script` element in your HTML file) or the JavaScript (`.js`) file (if your code resides in an external JavaScript file).

- Press Ctrl+P (Windows) or ⌘+P (macOS) and then click the file in the list that appears.

3. **Locate the statement where you want to enter break mode.**

JavaScript will run every line of code up to but not including this statement.

4. **Click the line number to the left of the statement to set the breakpoint.**

To remove a breakpoint, most browsers give you three choices:

>> To disable a breakpoint temporarily, deselect the breakpoint's check box in the Breakpoints list.

>> To disable all your breakpoints temporarily, click the deactivate breakpoint icon (labeled in Figure 2-5). Click this icon again to reactivate all breakpoints.

>> To remove a breakpoint completely, click the statement's line number.

Deactivate breakpoints

FIGURE 2-5:
In the browser's debugging tool, click a line number to set a breakpoint on that statement.

Click a line number to set a breakpoint   Deselect to disable the breakpoint

Entering break mode using a debugger statement

When developing your web pages, you'll often test the robustness of a script by sending it various test values or by trying it out under different conditions. In many cases, you'll want to enter break mode to make sure things appear okay. You could set breakpoints at specific statements, but you lose them if you close the file. For something a little more permanent, you can include a debugger statement in a script. JavaScript automatically enters break mode whenever it encounters a debugger statement.

Here's a bit of code that includes a debugger statement (bk05ch02/example03.html):

```
// Add the sentence to the <div>
document.querySelector('div').innerHTML = sentence;

// Generate random colors (use values < 128 to keep the text dark)
const randomRed = parseInt(Math.random() * 128);
```

```
const randomGreen = parseInt(Math.random() * 128);
const randomBlue = parseInt(Math.random() * 128);
debugger;
```

Exiting break mode

To exit break mode, you can use either of the following methods in the browser's debugging tool:

>> Click the resume icon. Chrome's version of this icon is labeled in Figure 2-4.

>> Press the browser's Resume keyboard shortcut. In Chrome (and most browsers), either press F8 or press Ctrl+\ (Windows) or ⌘+\ (macOS).

Stepping Through Your Code

One of the most common (and most useful) debugging techniques is to step through the code one statement at a time. Doing so lets you get a feel for the program flow to make sure that things such as loops and function calls are executing properly. You can use four techniques:

>> Step one statement at a time

>> Step into some code

>> Step over some code

>> Step out of some code

Stepping one statement at a time

The most common way of stepping through your code is to step one statement at a time. In break mode, *stepping one statement at a time* means two things:

>> You execute the current statement and then pause on the next statement.

>> If the current statement to run is a function call, stepping takes you into the function and pauses at the function's first statement. You can then continue to step through the function until you execute the last statement, at which point the browser returns you to the statement after the function call.

To step through your code one statement at a time, set a breakpoint and then after your code is in break mode, do one of the following to step through a single statement:

» Click the step icon. (Refer to Figure 2-4 for Chrome's version of this icon.)

» Press the browser's step keyboard shortcut. In Chrome (and most browsers, except Firefox, which doesn't support step as of this writing; use the step into button, instead), press F9..

Keep stepping through until the script ends or until you're ready to resume normal execution (by clicking the resume icon).

Stepping into some code

In all the major browsers (except Firefox), *stepping into some code* is the same as stepping through the code one statement at a time. The difference comes when a statement executes asynchronously (that is, it performs its operation after some delay rather than right away).

To understand the difference, consider the following code (I added line numbers to the left; they're not part of the code; check out bk05ch02/example04.html):

```
1    setTimeout(() => {
2        console.log('Inside the setTimeout() block!');
3    }, 5000);
4    console.log('Outside the setTimeout) block!');
```

This code uses setTimeout() to execute an anonymous function after 5 seconds (5,000 milliseconds). Suppose you enter break mode at the setTimeout() statement (line 1). What happens if you use step versus step into here? Check it out:

» **Step:** Clicking the step icon doesn't take you to line 2, as you might expect. Instead, because setTimeout() is asynchronous, step essentially ignores the anonymous function and takes you directly to line 4.

» **Step into:** Clicking the step into icon *does* take you to line 2 but only after the specified delay (5 seconds, in this case). You can then step through the anonymous function as needed.

To step into your code, set a breakpoint and then do one of the following after your code is in break mode:

>> Click the step into icon. (Refer to Figure 2-4 for Chrome's version of this icon.)

>> Press the browser's step into keyboard shortcut. In Chrome (and most browsers), either press F11 or press Ctrl+; (Windows) or ⌘+; (macOS).

REMEMBER

My description of step into here doesn't apply (at least as I write this) to Firefox. Instead, the Firefox step into feature works like the step feature I describe in the preceding section.

Stepping over some code

Some statements call other functions. If you're not interested in stepping through a called function, you can step over it. *Stepping over a function* means that JavaScript executes the function normally and then resumes break mode at the next statement *after* the function call.

To step over a function, first either step through your code until you come to the function call you want to step over, or set a breakpoint on the function call and refresh the web page. When you're in break mode, you can step over the function using any of the following techniques:

>> Click the step over icon. (Refer to Figure 2-4 for Chrome's version of this icon.)

>> Press the browser's step over keyboard shortcut. In Chrome (and most browsers), either press F10 or press Ctrl+' (Windows) or ⌘+' (macOS).

Stepping out of some code

I'm always accidentally stepping into functions I'd rather step over. If the function is short, I just step through it until I'm back in the original code. If the function is long, however, I don't want to waste time stepping through every statement. Instead, I invoke the *step out feature* using any of these methods:

>> Click the step out icon. (Refer to Figure 2-4 for Chrome's version of this icon.)

>> Press the browser's step out keyboard shortcut. In Chrome (and most browsers), either press Shift+F11 or press Ctrl+Shift+; (Windows) or ⌘+Shift+; (macOS).

JavaScript executes the rest of the function and then reenters break mode at the first line after the function call.

Monitoring Script Values

Many runtime and logic errors are the result of (or, in some cases, can result in) variables or properties assuming unexpected values. If your script uses or changes these elements in several places, you'll need to enter break mode and monitor the values of these elements to figure out where things go awry. The browser developer tools offer three main ways to keep an eye on your script values:

>> View the current value of a single variable.

>> View the current values of all the variables in both the local and global scopes.

>> View the value of a custom expression or object property.

Viewing a single variable value

If you just want to eyeball the current value of a variable, the developer tools in Chrome (and all major browsers) make this straightforward:

1. **Enter break mode in the code that contains the variable you want to check.**

2. **If the script hasn't yet set the value of the variable, step through the code until you're past the statement that supplies the variable with a value.**

   If you're interested in how the variable's value changes during the script, step through the script until you're past any statement that changes the value.

3. **Hover the mouse pointer over the variable name.**

   The browser pops up a tooltip that displays the variable's current value. Figure 2-6 shows an example. Also note in Figure 2-6 that the dev tools display the current value of any variable immediately after any statement that sets or changes the variable value.

```
39
-     // This function generates the random sentence from the above arrays
41    function    erateRandomSentence() {
42          97
-     // Gene ate a random item from each array
44    const firstItem = parseInt(Math.random() * arrayFirst.length);   firstItem = 97
45    const secondItem = parseInt(Math.random() * arraySecond.length);  secondItem = 27
46    const thirdItem = parseInt(Math.random() * arrayThird.length);   thirdItem = 37
47    const fourthItem = parseInt(Math.random() * arrayFourth.length);  fourthItem = 87
48    const fifthItem = parseInt(Math.random() * arrayFifth.length);   fifthItem = 65
49    const sixthItem = parseInt(Math.random() * arraySixth.length);   sixthItem = 1
50    const seventhItem = parseInt(Math.random() * arraySeventh.length);  seventhItem = 0
51
-     // Construct the sentence
53    const sentence = "${arrayFirst[firstItem]} ${arraySecond[secondItem]} ${arrayThird[t
54
```

FIGURE 2-6:
In break mode, hover the mouse pointer over a variable name to display the variable's current value.

Tooltip

Current variable values also appear after the line that sets or changes the value

Viewing all variable values

Most of the values you'll want to monitor will be variables, which come in three flavors (or *scopes*):

>> **Block scope:** Variables declared in the current statement block and available only to that block

>> **Local scope:** Variables declared in the current function and available only to that function

>> **Global scope:** Variables declared outside any function or block, which makes them available to any script or function on the page

For more detailed coverage of variable scope, refer to Book 3, Chapter 5.

When you're in break mode, the Chrome debugging tool (like all major browser debuggers) displays a pane on the right that includes a section that shows the current values of all your declared variables (refer to Figure 2-7). In Chrome, the section is named Scope and includes several lists: Block (for block-scoped variables), Local (for local variables) and Script (for global variables). Confusingly, there's also a Global section that references just the Window object.

FIGURE 2-7:
In break mode, Chrome's Scope section shows the current values of the local and global variables.

Local variables of the generateRandomSentence() function

In Figure 2-7, note that some local variables show the value `undefined`. These variables are undefined because the script hasn't yet reached the point where the variables are assigned a value.

Adding a watch expression

Besides monitoring variable values, JavaScript also lets you monitor the results of any expression or the current value of an object property. To do this, you need to set up a *watch expression* that defines what you want to monitor. These watch expressions appear in a special section of the browser's debugging tools. Here's how to add a watch expression in Chrome (the steps in other major browsers are similar):

1. **Put your code into break mode.**

2. **Open the Watch section in the right pane.**

3. **Click the add watch expression icon (+).**

A blank text box appears.

4. **Type your expression in the text box, and then press Enter or Return.**

The browser adds the expression and then displays the current value of the expression to the right. Figure 2-8 shows an example.

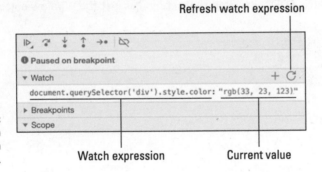

Refresh watch expression

Watch expression   Current value

FIGURE 2-8:
You can define a
watch expression
for your code.

You can use the following techniques to work with your watch expressions:

>> **Edit a watch expression.** Double-click the expression, edit it, and then press Enter or Return.

>> **Update the values of your watch expressions.** Click the refresh watch expression icon (labeled in Figure 2-8).

>> **Delete a watch expression.** Hover the mouse pointer over the watch expression you want to remove; then click the delete icon (X) that appears to the right of the expression.

More Debugging Strategies

Debugging your scripts can be a frustrating job, even for relatively small scripts. Here are a few tips to keep in mind when tracking down programming problems:

>> **Indent your code for readability.** JavaScript code is immeasurably more readable when you indent the code in each statement block. Readable code is that much easier to trace and decipher, so your debugging efforts have one less hurdle to negotiate. How far you indent is a matter of personal style, but two or four spaces is typical:

```
function myFunction() {
    Each statement in this function
    block is indented four spaces.
}
```

If you nest one block inside another, indent the nested block by another four spaces:

```
function myFunction() {
    Each statement in this function
    block is indented four spaces.
    for (const item of someArray) {
        Each statement in this nested for...of
        block is indented another four spaces.
    }
}
```

>> **Break down complex tasks.** Don't try to solve all your problems at once. If you have a large script or function that isn't working right, test it in small chunks to try to narrow down the problem.

>> **Break up long statements.** One of the most complicated aspects of script debugging is making sense out of long statements (especially expressions). The Console window can help (you can use it to print parts of the statement), but it's usually best to keep your statements as short as possible. After you get things working properly, you can often recombine statements for more efficient code.

>> **Comment out problem statements.** If a particular statement is giving you problems, you can temporarily deactivate it by placing two slashes (//) at the beginning of the line. The slashes tell JavaScript to treat the line as a comment. If you have a number of statements you want to skip, place /* at the beginning of the first statement and */ at the end of the last statement.

>> **Use comments to document your scripts.** Speaking of comments, it's a programming truism that good code — meaning (at least in part) code that uses clear variable and function names and a logical structure — should be self-explanatory. However, almost every piece of non-trivial code contains sections that, when you examine them later, aren't immediately obvious. For those section, it's another programming truism that you can never add enough explanatory comments. The more comments you add to complex and potentially obscure chunks of your code, the easier your scripts will be to debug.

The 10 Most Common JavaScript Errors

When you encounter a script problem, the first thing you should do is examine your code for the most common errors. To help you do that, here's a list of the ten most common errors made by both beginning and experienced programmers:

>> **JavaScript keywords as variable names:** Because JavaScript has many reserved words and keywords built into the language, it's common to accidentally use one of these words as a variable or function name. Double-check your names to make sure you're not using any reserved words, or the names of any objects, properties, or methods.

>> **Misspelled variables and other names:** Check your variable and function names to make sure you spell them consistently throughout the script. Also, check the spelling of the objects, properties, and methods you use.

>> **Misused uppercase and lowercase letters:** JavaScript is a *case-sensitive* language, which means it treats each letter differently depending on whether it's uppercase or lowercase. For example, consider the following two statements:

```
const firstName = "Millicent";
const message = "Welcome " + firstname;
```

The first statement declares a variable named firstName, but the second statement uses firstname. This code would generate the error firstname is not defined (or something similar, depending on the browser) because JavaScript thinks that firstname is a different (and uninitialized) variable.

>> **Mismatched quotation marks:** In any statement where you began a string literal with a quotation mark (" or '), always check to make sure that you included the corresponding closing quotation mark at the end of the string. Also, check whether you used one or more instances of the same quotation mark within the string. If so, either edit the string to use the proper escape sequence (\" or \') or switch to back ticks (`):

```
// Bad
const myString = "There are no "bad" programs.";

// Better
const myString = "There are no \"bad\" programs.";

// Best
const myString = `There are no "bad" programs.`;
```

TIP

» **Mismatched parentheses:** Examine your code for statements that contain a left parenthesis — (— and make sure there's a corresponding right parenthesis —). This rule applies also to square brackets — [and] — and braces — { and }.

For complex expressions that include three or more sets of parentheses, a quick match-up check is to count the number of left parentheses in the expression and then count the number of right parentheses. If these numbers don't match, you know you have a mismatch somewhere in the expression.

» **Missed parentheses after function names:** Speaking of parentheses, if your script calls a function or method that doesn't take any arguments, check that you included the parentheses — ( ) — after the name of the function or method:

```
function tryThis() {
    alert("Parentheses travel in pairs!");
}

// This won't work
tryThis;

// This will
tryThis();
```

» **Improper use of braces:** JavaScript uses braces to mark the start ({) and end (}) of statement blocks associated with functions, tests involving if and switch, and loops, including for...of, for, while, and do...while. It's easy to miss one or both braces in a block, and it's even easier to get the braces mixed up when nesting one test or loop inside another. Double-check your braces to make sure each block has both an opening and a closing brace.

TIP

One way to ensure that you don't miss any braces is to position them consistently throughout your script. For example, many people prefer to use the traditional style for brace positions:

```
keyword {
    statements
}
```

(Here, *keyword* means the statement — such as function or if — that defines the block.) If you prefer this style, use it all through your script so that you know exactly where to find each brace.

An easy way to ensure that you never forget a closing brace is to enter it immediately after entering the opening brace. That is, you type {, press Enter twice, and then type }.

Also, use indentation consistently for the statements within the block. Consistent indentation makes it much easier to view the braces, particularly when you have one block nested within another.

» **Using = or == instead of ===:** The identity operator (===) is one of the least intuitive JavaScript features because the assignment operator (=) feels so much more natural. The equality operator (==) can cause problems because it often converts the data types before making the comparison. Therefore, check all your comparison expressions to make sure you always use === instead of = or ==.

» **Conflicts between global variables and block or local variables:** A global variable is available throughout the entire page, even within blocks and functions. So, within a block or function, make sure that you don't declare and use a variable that has the same name as a global variable.

» **The use of a page element before it's loaded:** JavaScript runs through a page's HTML one line at a time and checks the syntax of each JavaScript statement as it comes to it. If your code refers to an element (such as a form field) that JavaScript hasn't come to yet, it will generate an error. Therefore, if your code deals with an element, always place the script after the element in the HTML file.

The 10 Most Common JavaScript Error Messages

To help you decipher the error messages that JavaScript throws your way, here's a list of the ten most common errors and what they mean:

» **Syntax error:** This load-time error means that JavaScript has detected improper syntax in a statement. The error message almost always tells you the line and character where the error occurs. For example, if you refer to the error message shown in Figure 2-1, note that to the right of the error message you see the following:

```
example01.html:17:18
```

This text means that the error occurs in the example01.html file, on line 17, at character position 18 (counting from the start of the statement).

» **Expected (or Missing (:** These messages mean that you forgot to include a left parenthesis:

```
function changeBackgroundColor newColor) {
```

If you forget a right parenthesis instead, you'll get Expected) or Missing):

```
function changeBackgroundColor (newColor{
```

» **Expected { or Missing { before function body:** These errors tell you that your code is missing the opening brace for a function:

```
function changeBackgroundColor (newColor)
    statements
}
```

If you're missing the closing brace instead, you'll get the errors Expected } or Missing } after function body.

» **Unexpected end of input or Missing } in compound statement:** These messages indicate that you forgot the closing brace in an if block or other compound statement:

```
if (currentHour < 12) {
    console.log("Good morning!");
} else {
    console.log("Good day!");
```

If you forget the opening brace, instead, you'll get a Syntax error message that points, confusingly, to the block's closing brace (which is the point where the browser first realizes that there's an error).

» **Missing ; or Missing ; after for-loop initializer|condition:** These errors mean that a for loop definition is missing a semicolon (;), either because you forgot the semicolon or because you used some other character (such as a comma):

```
for (let counter = 1; counter < 5, counter += 1) {
```

» **Unexpected identifier or Missing ; before statement:** These errors tell you that the preceding statement didn't end properly for some reason or that you've begun a new statement with an invalid value. In JavaScript, statements are supposed to end with a semicolon (;), but using a semicolon is optional. So, if JavaScript thinks you haven't finished a statement properly, it assumes that a semicolon is missing. For example, this can happen if you forget to include the opening /* to begin a multiple-line comment:

```
Start the comment (oops!)
Close the comment */
```

» **X is not defined:** This message most often refers to a variable named X that has not been declared or initialized and that you're trying to use in an expression. If that's the case, declare and initialize the variable. Another possible cause is a string literal that isn't enclosed in quotation marks. Finally, also check whether you misspelled the variable name:

```
const grossProfit = 100000;
const profitSharing = grossPrifit * profitSharingPercent;
```

» **X is not an object or X has no properties:** These messages mean that your code refers to an object that doesn't exist or to a property that doesn't belong to the specified object. Check whether you misspelled the object or property or, for the second case, that you're using the wrong object:

```
document.alert("Nope!")
```

» **Unterminated string constant or Unterminated string literal:** Both messages mean that you began a string literal with a quotation mark but forgot to include the closing quotation mark:

```
const greeting = "Welcome to my website!
```

» **A script on this page is causing [browser name] to run slowly. Do you want to abort the script? or Lengthy JavaScript still running. Continue?:** These errors tell you that your code has probably fallen into an infinite loop. You don't get any specific information about what's causing the problem, so you'll need to scour your code carefully for the possible cause.

IN THIS CHAPTER

» **Setting up PHP for debugging**

» **Examining the PHP error log**

» **Outputting variable values with echo and print**

» **Making good use of print_r()**

» **Getting to know var_dump()**

Chapter **3**

Debugging PHP Code

The most effective debugging tool is still careful thought, coupled with judiciously placed print statements.

— BRIAN KERNIGHAN

Debugging — the art, science, and (sometimes) magic of finding and correcting programming errors — is a vital part of all web development. Why? Because no one — not even the nerdiest and most experienced of coders — can write anything moderately complex without introducing an error (or, more likely, a half dozen errors). Programming just works that way. Don't ask me why because I really have no idea. It just does. So, when some code doesn't work the first time (or even the tenth time), it doesn't mean you're a lousy coder. It just means you're normal. Believe me, it happens to absolutely *everyone* who codes.

JavaScript code runs inside the browser, so debugging that code is (more or less) straightforward because, in a sense, the code runs right before your eyes. This lets you set up breakpoints, watches, and the other debugging tools that I talk about in Book 5, Chapter 2. PHP code, however, runs on the server, so it all happens backstage, as it were. By the time it gets to you (that is, to the browser), the code is done and all you see is the output. That makes PHP code harder to debug, but, thankfully, not impossible to debug. This chapter takes you through a few useful PHP debugging techniques.

Configuring php.ini for Debugging

Your first step in setting up PHP for debugging is the `php.ini` file, which is the PHP configuration file. In the XAMPP web development environment, which I discuss in Book 1, Chapter 2, here are the default locations of `php.ini`:

>> **Windows:** `C:\xampp\php\php.ini`

>> **Mac:** `/Applications/XAMPP/xamppfiles/etc/php.ini`

If you can't locate the file, make sure your Apache web server is running, open the XAMPP dashboard (`http://localhost/dashboard`), and click PHPInfo (or surf directly to `http://localhost/dashboard/phpinfo.php`). Look for the Loaded Configuration File setting, as shown in Figure 3-1.

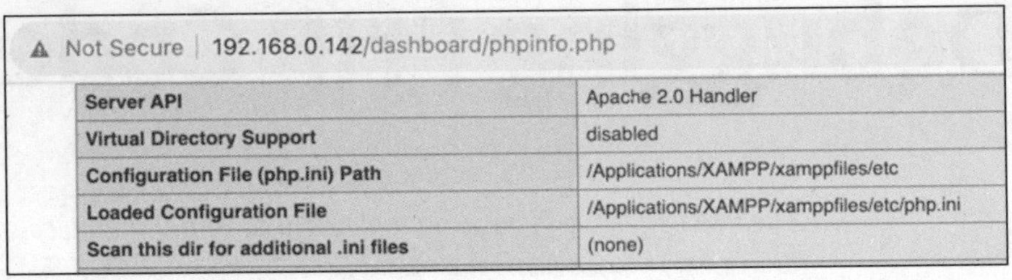

FIGURE 3-1:
Examine
the Loaded
Configuration
File setting to
determine the
location of php.i.

⚠ Not Secure	192.168.0.142/dashboard/phpinfo.php
Server API	Apache 2.0 Handler
Virtual Directory Support	disabled
Configuration File (php.ini) Path	/Applications/XAMPP/xamppfiles/etc
Loaded Configuration File	/Applications/XAMPP/xamppfiles/etc/php.ini
Scan this dir for additional .ini files	(none)

Open `php.ini` in your favorite text editor, and then modify the following settings (`php.ini` is a long document, so you should search for each setting to save time):

>> `display_errors`: Determines whether PHP outputs its error messages to the web browser. In a production environment, you want `display_errors` set to `Off` because you don't want site visitors seeing ugly PHP error messages. However, in a development environment, you definitely want `display_errors` set to `On` so you can see where your code went wrong:

```
display_errors=On
```

>> `error_reporting`: Specifies which types of errors PHP flags. The constant `E_ALL` flags all errors, and the constant `E_STRICT` flags code that doesn't meet recommended PHP standards. You don't need `E_STRICT` in a production environment, but it's useful in a development environment:

```
error_reporting=E_ALL | E_STRICT
```

REMEMBER

You need to restart the web server to put the new `php.ini` settings into effect. In the XAMPP dashboard, click Manage Servers, click Apache Web Server, and then click Restart.

With `display_errors` set to `On`, you'll now see error messages in the browser window. For example, take a look at the following statement (check out bk05ch03/example01.php in this book's example files):

```
display_header('notw.png';
```

Can you spot the error? Yep: The `display_header` function call is missing its closing parenthesis. Figure 3-2 shows how PHP flags this error. Note that the message includes not only the error but also the location of the file and, crucially, the line number of the statement that generated the error.

FIGURE 3-2:
A typical PHP error message, showing the error, file path and name, and line number.

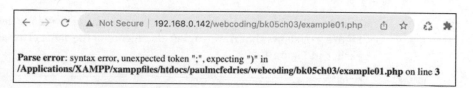

Accessing the PHP Error Log

Setting `display_errors` to `On` is very useful in your development environment, but the PHP default is to set `display_errors` to `Off` in a production environment. The `Off` setting prevents your visitors from seeing error messages, and it also boosts security because you don't want those visitors seeing sensitive information such as the location of your PHP script.

So, what happens when PHP generates an error with `display_errors` set to `Off`? It depends on the error, but in most cases you see either a blank web page or a server error message such as `500 - Internal server error`. Neither is particularly helpful, but all is not lost because PHP still records the error message to the PHP error log.

That's nice, but where is this error log stored on the server? That depends on the server, but you can find out by opening the `php.ini` file as I describe in the preceding section. You can also run the following script:

```php
<?php
    phpinfo();
?>
```

This code displays the PHP configuration data, which includes an `error_log` setting that tells you where the PHP error log is stored, as shown in Figure 3-3.

FIGURE 3-3:
The php.ini
file will tell you
the location
of your
PHP error log.

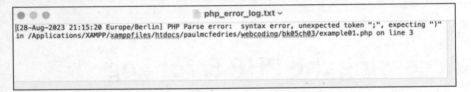

← → C ⚠ Not Secure | 192.168.0.142/dashboard/phpinfo.php	

Directive	Local Value
error_log	/Applications/XAMPP/xamppfiles/logs/php_error_log
error_log_mode	0644
error_prepend_string	no value

In some cases, you see just the name of a file — usually `error_log` — and that means the server generates the error log in the same directory as the PHP file that caused the error. So, if you store all your PHP scripts in a `php` subdirectory, your error log will appear in that subdirectory.

Double-click the error log to open it in your operating system's default text editor. Figure 3-4 shows that the error log also recorded the same error as the one shown earlier in Figure 3-2.

FIGURE 3-4:
The error
shown earlier
in Figure 3-2
was also
recorded in the
PHP error log.

```
● ● ●                            php_error_log.txt ⌄
[28-Aug-2023 21:15:20 Europe/Berlin] PHP Parse error:  syntax error, unexpected token ";", expecting ")"
in /Applications/XAMPP/xamppfiles/htdocs/paulmcfedries/webcoding/bk05ch03/example01.php on line 3
```

REMEMBER

Error messages appear in the error log with the oldest messages at the top, so you need to scroll to the bottom of the file to see the most recent error.

Outputting Variable Values

Since PHP code executes "over there" on the server instead of "in here" on the web browser, you can't set breakpoints or add watch expressions to monitor the values of PHP variables. However, you can do the next best thing by strategically using the PHP built-in statements that output the current value of whatever variable, expression, or function result you want to watch. PHP has tons of these statements, but the rest of this chapter introduces you to the ones you'll use most often.

TIP

Some sophisticated tools enable you to step through your PHP code and offer other debugging techniques. These tools are beyond the scope of this book. If you're interested, check out Xdebug (`https://xdebug.org/`), which works with popular code editors such as Visual Studio Code.

Debugging with echo statements

By far the most common PHP debugging technique is to add echo (or print) statements, which output the current value of whatever variable, expression, or function result you want to monitor.

For example, here's a loop that generates a dozen random numbers between 1 and 100. To watch the random values as they're generated, I included an echo statement within the loop (check out bk05ch03/example02.php):

```php
<?php
    for ($i = 0; $i < 12; $i++) {
        $randoms[$i] = rand(1, 100);
        echo "Random array value $i is $randoms[$i]<br>";
    }
?>
```

Figure 3-5 shows what the output looks like in the browser.

```
←  →  C   ⚠ Not Secure | 192.168.0.142/webcoding/bk05ch03/example02.php

Random array value 0 is 91
Random array value 1 is 68
Random array value 2 is 73
Random array value 3 is 43
Random array value 4 is 7
Random array value 5 is 62
Random array value 6 is 25
Random array value 7 is 24
Random array value 8 is 42
Random array value 9 is 99
Random array value 10 is 18
Random array value 11 is 7
```

FIGURE 3-5: Adding an echo statement outputs the expression to the browser window.

Another good use of echo statements for debugging is when your PHP code fails, but you don't get an error message. Now you have no idea where the problem lies, so what's a web developer to do? You can gradually narrow down where the error occurs by adding an echo statement to your code that outputs a message like

Debugging PHP Code

`Made it this far!`. If you see that message, you move the `echo` statement a little farther down the code, repeating this procedure until you don't see the message, meaning the code failed before getting to the `echo` statement.

Alternatively, you can sprinkle several `echo` statements throughout your code. You can either give each one a different output message, or you can take advantage of one of PHP's so-called *magic constants*: `__LINE__`. This constant tells you the current line of the code that's being executed, so you could add the following `echo` statement throughout your code:

```
echo 'Made it to line #' . __LINE__;
```

Debugging with print_r() statements

Another way to output the value of a variable is with the `print_r()` function, which outputs human-readable information about a specified variable:

```
print_r(variable, return)
```

where:

>> *variable* is the name of the variable you want to work with.

>> *return* is a Boolean value that, when set to `true`, returns the variable information rather than outputs it. (This feature enables you to, for example, store the output in another variable.) The default is `false`, which outputs the variable value.

If *variable* is a string or number, `print_r()` outputs the current value of the variable. If *variable* is an array, `print_r()` outputs the array keys and item values.

For example, in the preceding section, the code used an `echo` statement to output the current value of the array each time through the loop. As an alternative, you could wait until the loop completes and then run `print_r($randoms)` to output the entire array (bk05ch03/example03.php):

```
<pre>
<?php
    for ($i = 0; $i < 12; $i++) {
        $randoms[$i] = rand(1, 100);
    }
    print_r($randoms);
?>
</pre>
```

Note that I surrounded the PHP code with `<pre>` and `</pre>` tags, which display the array output on separate lines instead of a single line, as shown in Figure 3-6.

```
Array
(
    [0] => 99
    [1] => 82
    [2] => 94
    [3] => 24
    [4] => 52
    [5] => 92
    [6] => 25
    [7] => 61
    [8] => 34
    [9] => 99
    [10] => 99
    [11] => 42
)
```

FIGURE 3-6: Using print_r() to output the keys and values of an array.

Debugging with var_dump() statements

PHP features such as echo and print_r() make it easy to see values associated with variables and arrays, but sometimes your debugging efforts require a bit more information. For example, you might want to know the data type of a variable. You can get both the data type and the current value of a variable or expression by using PHP's var_dump() function:

```
var_dump(expression(s));
```

where *expression(s)* represents one or more variable names or expressions.

Here's an update to the random number generator that dumps the value of the $i variable each time through the loop and the value of the $randoms array after the loop (bk05ch03/example04.php):

```
<pre>
<?php
    for ($i = 0; $i < 12; $i++) {
        $randoms[$i] = rand(1, 100);
        var_dump($i);
    }
    var_dump($randoms);
?>
</pre>
```

Figure 3-7 shows an example of the output.

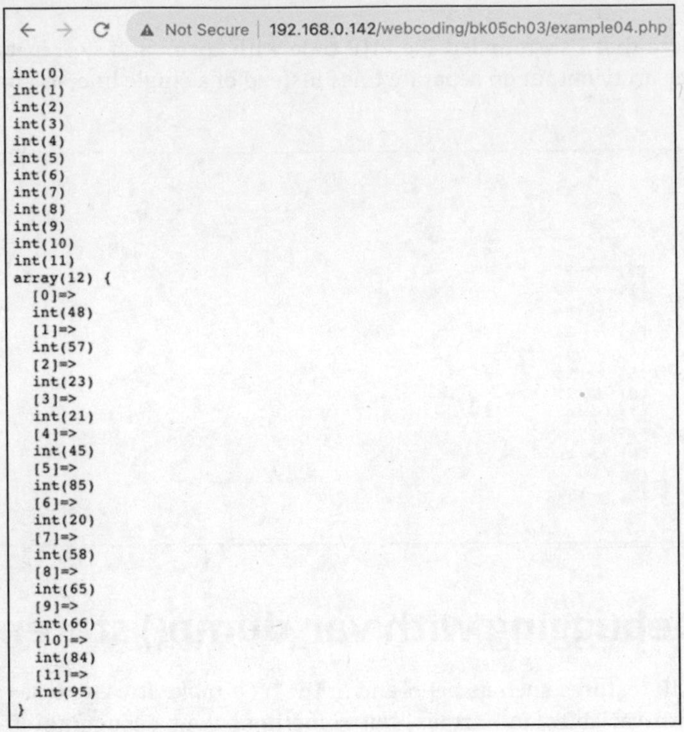
Not Secure
192.168.0.142/webcoding/bk05ch03/example04.php
int(0)
int(1)
int(2)
int(3)
int(4)
int(5)
int(6)
int(7)
int(8)
int(9)
int(10)
int(11)
array(12) {
[0]=>
int(48)
[1]=>
int(57)
[2]=>
int(23)
[3]=>
int(21)
[4]=>
int(45)
[5]=>
int(85)
[6]=>
int(20)
[7]=>
int(58)
[8]=>
int(65)
[9]=>
int(66)
[10]=>
int(84)
[11]=>
int(95)
}

FIGURE 3-7: Using var_dump() to output information about some variables.

6

Coding Dynamic and Static Web Pages

Contents at a Glance

Chapter **1**

Fetching Data with PHP, JavaScript, and JSON

The Fetch API is a game-changer for developers, giving them unparalleled flexibility . . . to easily and quickly make URL requests from your browser.

— DANIELLE ELLIS

When coding web pages, it feels like there's a great divide between the browser front end and the server back end. When you're working on the front end, you can use HTML tags, CSS properties, and JavaScript code to build, style, and animate your pages. When you're working on the back end, you can use MySQL and PHP code to define, access, and manipulate data. That all works, but front-end code without back-end data produces a lifeless page, whereas back-end data without front-end code produces useless information.

To create a truly dynamic web page, you need to cross this divide. You need to give your web page a mechanism to interact with the server to ask for and receive server data, and you need to give the server a mechanism to return that data in a format the page can understand and manipulate. In this chapter, you investigate two such mechanisms: asynchronous operations and the Fetch API for sending data back and forth between the web page and the server.

Getting Your Head Around Asynchronous Operations

When your web page code deals with only front-end operations, the web browser executes that code one statement after the other, in each case waiting for the current statement to complete before moving on to the next one. In programming parlance, this wait-for-a-task-to-complete-before-moving-to-the-next-task mode is described as *synchronous*.

However, synchronous operations become a problem when you start dealing with back-end tasks, such as asking a remote server to send some data. Why is that a problem? Because you don't know in advance how long a back-end task might take. Typically, front-end statements execute in milliseconds, but it might take a remote server multiple seconds to respond to a request for data. Performing such tasks synchronously means that your code must wait for the server operation to complete before continuing; the remainder of your code is said to be *blocked* by the server request. Blocked code will almost certainly lead to thumb-twiddling frustration on the part of your users.

Fortunately, you can keep your users happy and their thumbs constructively occupied by implementing some powerful techniques that prevent code blocking. The way modern JavaScript prevents such code blocking is by using asynchronous operations, where *asynchronous* describes an operation that runs separately in the background and therefore doesn't prevent the rest of the code from executing.

TECHNICAL STUFF

PROMISES, PROMISES

The technology underlying modern JavaScript asynchronous operations is the *promise*, which is an object returned by an asynchronous operation. The promise represents not only the current state of the operation but also the operation's eventual completion or failure. All practical asynchronous operations used in this book hide the creation of a Promise object, but you can create your own Promise objects using the Promise() constructor:

```
const promiseVar = new Promise((resolve, reject) => {
    // Asynchronous operation code goes here
```

```
            if (/* operation is successful */) {
                // Fulfill the promise
                resolve("Success!");
            } else {
                // Reject the promise
                reject("Failure!");
            }
        });
```

where:

- *promiseVar* is the name of the variable that holds the new Promise object.

- resolve is the function that runs when the asynchronous operation is successful.

- reject is the function that runs when the asynchronous operation fails.

You then handle the result of the promise using the Promise object's then( ) and catch( ) methods. You use then( ) to handle a fulfilled promise and catch( ) to handle a failed promise:

```
myPromise
    .then(result => {
        console.log("The promise was resolved with: ", result);
    })
    .catch(error => {
        console.log("The promise was rejected with: ", error);
    });
```

You can also chain together multiple promises. For a full example, see bk06ch01/ example01.html in this book's example files.

Again, the preceding code is the slightly older and slightly more verbose method of handling promises. As you see in this chapter, modern JavaScript takes a slightly different approach that hides most of these details.

Before getting to the JavaScript code that handles asynchronous operations, you need some example asynchronous code (refer to bk06ch01/example02.html):

```
// Converts a string asynchronously to uppercase after two
    seconds
function asynchronousUpperCase(str) {

    // Return a new Promise object
```

```
    return new Promise((resolve, reject) => {

        // Use setTimeout() to delay two seconds
        setTimeout(() => {

            // Check that a String object was passed
            if (typeof str === 'string') {

                // If so, resolve the promise and return the
    string as uppercase
                resolve(str.toUpperCase());
            } else {

                // If not, reject the promise and return an
    error message
                reject('Input is not a string');
            }
        }, 2000);
    });
}
```

The point of the asynchronousUpperCase() function is to convert the passed string value to uppercase letters. To make this function asynchronous, the code uses the setTimeout() method, which delays the conversion to uppercase by two seconds. The function handles the asynchronous nature of the operation by returning a Promise object that resolves if the passed parameter is a string and that fails if the passed parameter is not a string. (I explain JavaScript promises in the "Promises, promises" sidebar.)

Solving synchronous problems with async functions

JavaScript has several techniques for making operations asynchronous, but the method I use in this chapter (and throughout the rest of the book) is the *async function*, which is a named or anonymous function declaration preceded by the keyword async.

Here's the syntax for a named asynchronous function:

```
async function functionName() {
    // Asynchronous function code goes here
}
```

where *functionName* is the name of the asynchronous function.

Here's an example:

```
async function handleAsynchronous() {
    // Asynchronous function code goes here
}
```

For an anonymous asynchronous function, you can use either of the following:

```
async function() {
    // Asynchronous function code goes here
}
```

or:

```
async () => {
    // Asynchronous handling code goes here
}
```

Here's an example:

```
const form = document.querySelector('form');
form.addEventListener('submit', async function(event) {
    // Asynchronous form submission code goes here
}
```

WARNING

The async keyword was introduced in ECMAScript 2017 (ES8) and has excellent modern browser support. However, its relative newness means you can't use it if you need to support really old browsers, such as Internet Explorer 11 and earlier.

Using await to wait for an asynchronous operation to complete

Asynchronous operations are awesome, but they create a new problem that's sort of the opposite of the blocking problem described previously. When you eventually get the data from the server, you almost always have to process that data in some way: perform data conversions, write the data to existing HTML elements on the page, create elements for the data, and so on. In other words, in this case you *don't* want the browser to process these statements right away. What's needed here is a way to say something like, "Yo, wait until you get all the data from the server, and then perform the following tasks to process that data."

The way you convince the browser to hold off until an asynchronous operation is complete before processing the code that follows is by using the await operator:

```
const resultVar = await expression
```

where:

» *resultVar* is the name of the variable that stores the result of the asynchronous operation.

» *expression* is a reference to an object that runs an asynchronous operation. This is usually a call to a function that returns a Promise object. (See the "Promises, promises" sidebar to learn about promises.)

You almost always use the await operator in an async function. Here's an example (bk06ch01/example02.html):

```
async function handleAsynchronous() {

    // Perform the asynchronous operation and store the result
    const result = await asynchronousUpperCase('hello world');

    // Display the result
    console.log(`Result: ${result}`);
}

// Run it
handleAsynchronous();
```

The handleAsynchronous() function uses the await operator to call the asynchronousUpperCase() function with the hello world string. The return value of the asynchronous operation is stored in the result variable, which is then written to the Console window, as shown in Figure 1-1.

FIGURE 1-1:
The result of the asynchronous operation.

The await operator was introduced in ECMAScript 2017 (ES8) and has top-notch support in modern browsers. However, you can't use await if you need to support ancient browsers, such as Internet Explorer 11 and earlier.

Chaining multiple asynchronous operations

It's common to require multiple asynchronous operations, where each subsequent asynchronous operation must wait until the previous operation is complete. You can handle this kind of scenario by *chaining* multiple await expressions by running one after the other in the order you need them to execute. Here's an expanded example of converting multiple strings to uppercase by chaining the asynchronous function calls (bk06ch01/example03.html):

```
async function handleAsynchronous() {
    // Perform the first asynchronous operation and store the
    result
    const firstResult = await asynchronousUpperCase('hello');

    // Display the first result
    console.log(`First result: ${firstResult}`);

    // Perform the second asynchronous operation and store the
    result
    const secondResult = await asynchronousUpperCase('world');

    // Display the second result
    console.log(`Second result: ${secondResult}`);
}

// Run it
handleAsynchronous();
```

This code uses the await operator to run the asynchronousUpperCase() function twice, first with the string hello and second with the string world. Figure 1-2 shows the results that get displayed in the Console window.

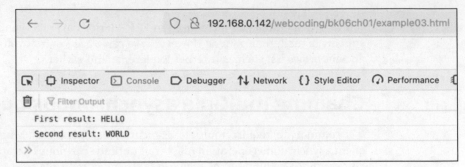

FIGURE 1-2:
The result of
the chained
asynchronous
operations.

Handling asynchronous rejection responses

In the code in the previous few sections, I assumed that the asynchronous operation would be successful. However, it's prudent to include code that handles an unsuccessful asynchronous operation. The way you do that in modern JavaScript is to use a try...catch statement:

```
try {
    Try statements
} catch {
    Catch statements
} finally {
    Finally statements
}
```

where:

» *Try statements* is a block of statements that JavaScript always executes at the beginning the try...catch construct.

» *Catch statements* is a block of statements that JavaScript executes only if an error occurs in the try block.

» *Finally statements* is a block of statements that JavaScript always executes before exiting the try...catch construct.

The try block is mandatory and the rest of the construct is either the catch block, the finally block, or both. However, almost all try...catch statements consist of a try block followed by a catch block.

For asynchronous operations, you handle successful results in the try block and failure results in the catch block. Here's an example (bk06ch01/example04.html):

```
async function handleAsynchronous() {
    // Handle successful asynchronous results
```

```
    try {
        // Perform the first asynchronous operation and store
the result
        const firstResult = await asynchronousUpperCase('h
ello');
        console.log(`First result: ${firstResult}`);

        // Perform the second asynchronous operation and store
the result
        const secondResult = await asynchronousUpperCase
('world');
        console.log(`Second result: ${secondResult}`);

        // Perform the third asynchronous operation and store
the result
        // Send a number instead of a string to raise an error
        const thirdResult = await asynchronousUpperCase(42);
        console.log(`Third result: ${thirdResult}`);

    // Handle failed asynchronous results
    } catch (error) {
        console.log(`An error occurred: ${error}`);
    }
}

// Run it
handleAsynchronous();
```

In the `try` block, the code chains together three asynchronous operations. The
first two pass the string `hello` and `world` to the asynchronous function and so
return successful results. The third call to the function passes the number 42,
which forces a failed asynchronous operation, the result of which is handled by
the `catch` block. Figure 1-3 shows the results.

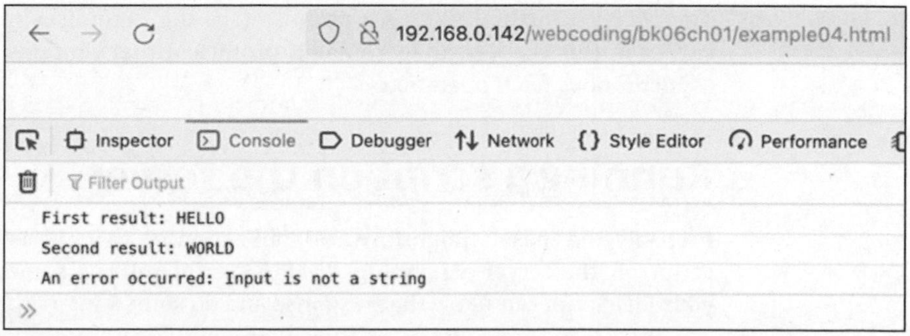

FIGURE 1-3:
The result of
three chained
asynchronous
operations, two
successes and
one failure.

Getting Remote Data Asynchronously with the Fetch API

Asynchronous operations shine when you use them to fetch data from a server and display that data on a web page. Doing this fetching asynchronously offers the following advantages:

>> **Non-blocking code:** The requested data is retrieved from the server in the background while the rest of your code runs.

>> **Data parsing and transformation:** One or more specified statements run only after the data has been completely received.

>> **Data updates without page reloads:** The requested data can affect only specified page elements while leaving the rest of the page as is.

In modern JavaScript, you fetch remote data by using, appropriately enough, the Fetch API, which I discuss over the next few sections.

Fetching data with the fetch() method

The workhorse of the Fetch API is the fetch() method, which you use to grab a resource from the network. Here's the simplified version of the fetch() syntax:

```
const responseVar = await fetch(resource);
```

where:

>> *responseVar* is the name of the variable that stores the response returned by the asynchronous fetch() operation.

>> *resource* is the URL of the resource you want to fetch.

The fetch() method returns a promise (see the "Promises, promises" sidebar, earlier in this chapter, to learn about promises) that contains the results of the asynchronous fetch operation.

Running a script on the server

Probably the most straightforward application of fetch() is to execute a PHP script on the server. Assuming the PHP script returns some sort of response, your JavaScript can parse that response and do something with it (such as display the response text in the Console window). To run a script on the server, call the `fetch()` function with the URL or path of the PHP file:

```
fetch(PHPFile)
```

where *PHPFile* is the name of the PHP file you want to execute on the server. If the file resides in a directory that's different than the current file's directory, you need to include the path.

For example, here's a simple PHP script (bk06ch01/example05.php):

```php
<?php
    header('Content-Type: application/text');
    header('Access-Control-Allow-Origin: *');

    echo 'Hello Fetch API World!';
?>
```

Now here's some JavaScript that uses `fetch()` to run the PHP script (bk06ch01/example05.html; note that this file includes `try...catch` error handling code not shown here):

```javascript
async function runServerScript() {

    // Run the PHP script
    const response = await fetch('example05.php');

    // Check that we got a good response
    if (response.ok) {

        // Parse the response as text
        const data = await response.text();

        // Write the response text to the Console
        console.log(data);
    }

// Run the async function
runServerScript();
```

The PHP script returns (via the `echo` statement) the message `Hello Fetch API World!`. The JavaScript parses that response with `response.text()`, and then outputs the message to the Console window, as shown in Figure 1-4.

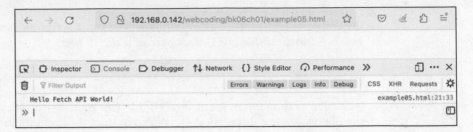

FIGURE 1-4:
The PHP script
response
displayed in the
Console window.

Updating an element with fetched data

One of the most common and most useful asynchronous techniques is to update just a single element on the page with data from the server. All the other elements on the page stay the same, so the user's experience isn't disrupted by a jarring and annoying page reload.

How you use this method depends on what you want to load and whether you want to run some code when the load is done. The next couple of sections take you through the possibilities.

Loading an HTML file

One common use of `fetch()` is to populate a page element with the contents of an HTML file. Here's the general syntax to use:

```
fetch(HTMLFile)
```

where *HTMLFile* is the name of the file that contains the HTML code you want loaded into the page element. If the file resides in a directory that's different than the current file's directory, you need to include the path info, as well.

For example, here's an `<h1>` tag that represents the entire contents of a file named `hellofetchworld.html` (bk06ch01/hellofetchworld.html):

```
<h1>Hello Fetch World!</h1>
```

Now consider the following HTML code (bk06ch01/example06.html; note that this file includes `try...catch` and other error handling code not shown here):

```
<body>
    <div id="target">
    </div>

    <script>
```

```
        // Set up an asynchronous function
        async function loadHTMLFile() {

            // Fetch the data asynchronously
            const response = await fetch('hellofetchworld.html');

            // Parse the response as text
            const data = await response.text();

            // Get a reference to the target element
            const target = document.getElementById('target');

            // Write the data to the target
            target.innerHTML = data;
        }

        // Run the async function
        loadHTMLFile();
    </script>
</body>
```

The `<body>` tag includes a `div` element that uses an `id` value of `target`. When the page is loaded, the script runs the following statement:

```
loadHTMLFile();
```

This statement calls the asynchronous function `loadHTMLFile()`, which uses `fetch()` to grab the contents of `hellofetchworld.html` from the server:

```
const response = await fetch('hellofetchworld.html');
```

Technically, what `fetch()` does is return a promise, so once the promise is resolved the code needs to parse the returned data. In this case, the data we want is HTML, which is just text, so we parse the data asynchronously using the `response` object's `text()` method:

```
const data = await response.text();
```

The script then gets a reference to the element that uses the `id` value of `target` (that is, the page's `<div>` tag) and then inserts the HTML data into that element:

```
target.innerHTML = data;
```

Figure 1-5 shows the result.

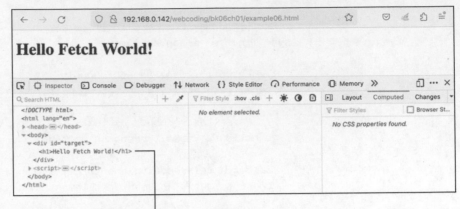

FIGURE 1-5:
Using JavaScript's
`fetch()`
method to load
the contents of
an HTML file into
a page element.

The h1 element from the external HTML file

WARNING

A built-in browser security restriction called the *same-origin policy* allows a script to access data from another file only if both files have the same *origin*, meaning the following must be the same for both:

>> **Protocol:** Usually, both files must use http or both must use https. If one file uses http and the other uses https, the fetch() call will fail.

>> **Host name:** The two files can't be on different subdomains. If one file uses mydomain.com and the other uses www.mydomain.com, the fetch() call will fail.

>> **Port number:** The two files must use the same port number. The standard HTTP port is 80, but if you call the script with, say, port 88 (that is, http://mydomain.com:88/), the fetch() call will fail.

Therefore, make sure that the HTML file you request has the same origin as the file that contains the fetch() statement.

Loading output from a PHP script

If you have a PHP script that uses echo or print to output HTML tags and text, you can use fetch() to insert that output into a page element. The general syntax is nearly identical to the one for loading an HTML file:

```
fetch(PHPFile)
```

where *PHPFile* is the name of the file that contains the PHP code. If the PHP file sits in a directory other than the current file's directory, include the path info.

For example, here's a PHP file named `get-server-time.php` (bk06ch01/ get-server-time.php):

```php
<?php
    $current_time = date('H:i:s');
    echo "The time on the server is $current_time.";
?>
```

The script gets the current time on the server and then outputs a message displaying the time. Now consider the following HTML code (bk06ch01/ example07.html):

```html
<body>
    <h2 id="target">
    </h2>
    <script>
        // Set up an asynchronous function
        async function displayCurrentTime() {

            // Fetch the data asynchronously
            const response = await fetch('get-server-time.php');

            // Parse the response as text
            const data = await response.text();

            // Get a reference to the target element
            const target = document.getElementById('target');

            // Write the data to the target
            target.innerHTML = data;
        }

        // Run the async function
        displayCurrentTime();
    </script>
</body>
```

The script used `fetch()` to call `get-server-time.php`, parses the response asynchronously with `response.text()`, and then loads the output into the `<h2>` tag, as shown in Figure 1-6.

WARNING

The same-origin policy that I mention earlier for HTML files is also in effect for PHP files. That is, the PHP script you request must have the same origin as the file that contains the `fetch()` statement.

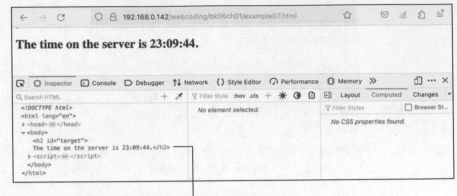

FIGURE 1-6:
Using the
`fetch()`
method to load
the output of a
PHP script into a
page element.

The output of the PHP script inserted into the h2 element

Learning more about GET and POST requests

REMEMBER

When you're working with Fetch API calls to the server, one of the decisions you must make is what request method to use: GET or POST. How on Earth are you supposed to do that? Fortunately, it mostly comes down to one thing: the length of the data. Since a GET request's data is tacked on the URL as a query string, the maximum length of that data is restricted by the maximum length of a URL. The actual limit depends on the browser and server, but the most common ceiling is 2,048 characters. Anything longer than that and the server might cough up a `414 Request URI Too Long` error. If you're sending longer data (such as a blog entry), use a POST request.

Another consideration is security. GET requests operate by adding a query string to the end of the URL, which is easily seen by the user (or someone snooping over the user's shoulder), so GET is the wrong choice when you're sending sensitive data, such as a password. By contrast, POST data is sent in the body of the request, which is secure as long as you're sending the request over an encrypted connection (that is, via HTTPS).

TIP

If you only ever send relatively small amounts of data to the server, you can certainly stick with using just GET requests. However, some developers use both, even when sending small amounts of data, as a way of making their code more readable:

>> Use a GET request when you want to retrieve data from the server without modifying the server data in any way.

>> Use a POST request when you want to modify — that is, add, update, or delete — server data.

Handling form POST requests in PHP

I cover handling GET requests in PHP code in Book 4, Chapter 3. Handling POST requests is similar when you're dealing with form data, so here I just take a quick look at how you handle them in PHP.

When you submit a FormData object as the POST request body (I show how this is done in Book 6, Chapter 2), you access the data by using PHP's $_POST variable, which is an associative array created from the form data.

For example, suppose your form has fields named book, chapter, and example, and these fields have the values 6, 1, and 2, respectively. Then this example creates the following $_POST array:

```
$_POST['book'] => 6
$_POST['chapter'] => 1
$_POST['example'] => 2
```

As with the $_GET array, your code should check that each of the expected elements of the $_POST array exists by using PHP's isset() function, which returns true if a variable exists and has a value other than null. Here's an example:

```
if (isset($_POST['book'])) {
    $book_num = $_POST['book'];
} else {
    echo 'The "book" parameter is missing!<br>';
    echo 'We are done here, sorry.';
    exit(0);
}
```

Handling object POST requests in PHP

Although you'll usually send form data with your POST requests, you can also send a JavaScript object, if that's how your data is stored.

First, to send object data to the server, you need to convert the object to a JSON string by using the stringify() method (refer to Book 3, Chapter 10). Here's an example:

```
myData = {
    name: Paul,
    email: pmcfedries@gmail.com
}
```

```
const response = await fetch('script.php', {
    method: 'POST',
    body: JSON.stringify(myData)
});
```

When you use this method, note that the sent data isn't accessible via the $_POST variable in PHP. Instead, you access the data as follows:

```
// Get the raw POST data
$rawData = file_get_contents("php://input");

// Decode the JSON string
$data = json_decode($rawData, true);

// Access the data
$name = $data["name"];
echo "<h1>Welcome, $name!</h1>";
```

This code uses php://input to access PHP's read-only data input stream, which contains the raw POST data. The script then uses json_decode() to convert the JSON string (stored in the $rawData variable) to an associative array. The script then uses the array to access the data.

Sending and retrieving data

Probably the most common remote data scenario is that you send some data to the server, a PHP script on the server uses that data to retrieve something, the PHP script returns the retrieved data, and then your front-end JavaScript displays the result.

For example, suppose you want to know the total value of the inventory (that is, the units in stock multiplied by the price of each unit) for a particular category. Here's a partial PHP script (bk06ch01/example08.php) that does the job:

```
// Get the raw POST data
$rawData = file_get_contents("php://input");

// Decode the JSON string
$data = json_decode($rawData, true);

// Access the data
$category_num = $data['category'];
```

```
// Create and run a SELECT query
$sql = "SELECT unit_price, units_in_stock
            FROM products
            WHERE category_id = $category_num";

// Run the query
$result = mysqli_query($connection, $sql);

// Get the query rows as an associative array
$rows = mysqli_fetch_all($result, MYSQLI_ASSOC);

$inventory_total = 0;

// Loop through the rows
foreach($rows as $row) {
    // Update the inventory total with price * units
    $inventory_total += (float) $row['unit_price'] * (float)
  $row['units_in_stock'];
}
echo $inventory_total;
```

This script (which has many parts not shown, such as the MySQL connection statements) takes a category value via POST and runs a SELECT query that returns the unit_price and units_in_stock for that category. The code then loops through the returned rows, adding to the inventory_total variable each time by multiplying unit_price and units_in_stock. The script finishes by echoing the final value of inventory_total.

Now consider the front-end code (bk06ch01/example08.html):

CSS:

```
div {
    color: green;
    font-size: 1.25rem;
}
.warning {
    color: red;
    font-weight: bold;
}
```

HTML:

```
<h1>Inventory Report</h1>
<div></div>
```

JavaScript:

```javascript
// Function to get the total inventory cost from the server
async function getInventoryTotal() {

    // Data to send via POST
    const postData = {
        category: 1
    }

    // Send the POST request
    const response = await fetch('example08.php', {
        method: 'POST',
        body: JSON.stringify(postData)
    });

    // Parse the response as text
    const inventoryTotal = await response.text();

    // Get a reference to the output div
    const outputDiv = document.querySelector('div');

    // Define the default message
    let msg = `The total inventory is \$${inventoryTotal}`;

    // Is the inventory total over $10,000?
    if (inventoryTotal >= 10000) {
        // If so, set up a warning message, instead
        msg = `WARNING! Total inventory is \$${inventoryTotal}`;
        outputDiv.classList.add('warning');
    }

    // Output the message
    outputDiv.innerHTML = msg;
}

// Run the function
getInventoryTotal();
```

The asynchronous `getInventoryPost()` function declares a JavaScript object that contains a category value. The function then uses `fetch()` to send a POST request with the JSON stringified object as the request body. The function stores the PHP output (that is, the `$inventory_total` value) in the `inventoryTotal` variable, sets up a default message, and checks to see if `inventoryTotal` is over `10000`. If it is, the code changes the message and adds the `warning` class to the `div` element. Finally, the code displays the message in the `div`. Figure 1-7 shows an example result.

FIGURE 1-7:
A warning message displayed by the `getInventory Total()` function.

Inventory Report

WARNING! Total inventory is $13083.41

Returning Fetch API Data as JSON Text

The real power of JSON becomes clear during Fetch API calls when you want to return to the web page a complex set of data, usually an array of database records. Sure, you can use your PHP code to loop through the array and output the data along with some HTML tags and text. However, most web apps don't want to merely display the data; they want to process the data in some way, and that means handling the data using an asynchronous function. We still have the rather large problem of getting the server data to the web page, but that's where JSON comes in. Because JSON data is just text, it's easy to transfer that data between the server and the web page.

Converting server data to the JSON format

You might be shaking in your boots imagining the complexity of the code required to convert an array of database records into the JSON format. Shake no more, because, amazingly, it takes but a single line of PHP code to do the job! PHP comes with a handy and powerful `json_encode()` function, which can take any value and automagically turn it into a JSON object. Here's the syntax:

```
json_encode(value, options)
```

where:

>> *value* is the value you want to convert to JSON. For most of your Fetch API calls, the value will be an array of MySQL table rows returned by the `mysqli_fetch_all()` method.

>> *options* is an optional series of constants, separated by the OR operator (|). These constants determine how the function encodes special characters such as quotation marks. Here are four you'll use most often:

- JSON_HEX_TAG: Encodes less than (<) and greater than (>) as \u003C and \u003E, respectively

- JSON_HEX_AMP: Encodes ampersands (&) as \u0026

- JSON_HEX_APOS: Encodes single quotation marks (') as \u0027

- JSON_HEX_QUOT: Encodes double quotation marks (") as \u0022

The usual procedure is to store the output of `json_encode()` in a variable, and then `echo` or `print` that variable. Here's an example (where it's assumed that the `$rows` variable contains an array of MySQL rows):

```
$JSON_data = json_encode($rows, JSON_HEX_APOS | JSON_HEX_QUOT);
echo $JSON_data;
```

Here's a longer example that assumes you've already used PHP to connect to a MySQL database, and the resulting MySQLi connection object is stored in the `$connection` variable (bk06ch01/example09.php):

```
// Create a SELECT query
$sql = "SELECT company_name, contact_name, contact_title,
   contact_email
            FROM suppliers";

// Run the query
$result = mysqli_query($connection, $sql);

// Get the query rows as an associative array
$rows = mysqli_fetch_all($result, MYSQLI_ASSOC);

// Convert the array to JSON
$JSON_data = json_encode($rows, JSON_HEX_APOS | JSON_HEX_QUOT);

// Output the JSON
echo $JSON_data;
```

Here's a partial listing of what gets stored in $JSON_data:

```
[
{
    "company_name": "Exotic Liquids",
    "contact_name": "Charlotte Cooper",
    "contact_title": "Purchasing Manager",
    "contact_email": "charlottecooper@exoticliquids.com"
}, {
    "company_name": "New Orleans Cajun Delights",
    "contact_name": "Shelley Burke",
    "contact_title": "Order Administrator",
    "contact_email": "shelleyburke@neworleanscajundelights.com"
}, {
    "company_name": "Grandma Kelly\u0027s Homestead",
    "contact_name": "Regina Murphy",
    "contact_title": "Sales Representative",
    "contact_email": "reginamurphy@grandmakellyshomestead.com"
},
etc.
]
```

Note that this is an array of JSON strings, each of which represents a row from the data returned by the MySQL SELECT query. Note, too, that I've formatted this with newlines and spaces to make it easier to read. The data stored in the variable doesn't contain whitespace.

Handling JSON data returned by the server

To process JSON data returned by a PHP script, use the Response interface's json() method to parse the returned data. Here's the syntax:

```
const data = await response.json();
```

where:

» *data* is the variable that will stored the parsed data.

» *response* is the variable that contains the Promise returned by the fetch() call to the PHP script.

Here's some code that processes the PHP output from the previous section (bk06ch01/example09.html):

HTML:

```
<h1>Supplier Contacts</h1>
<main></main>
```

JavaScript:

```
async function getSuppliers() {
    // Send the request
    const response = await fetch('example09.php');

    // Parse the JSON response
    const suppliers = await response.json();

    // Loop through the suppliers array
    for (let i = 0; i < suppliers.length; i += 1) {
        document.querySelector('main')
                .insertAdjacentHTML('beforeend',
`<section id="contact${i}"></section>`);
        document.querySelector(`#contact${i}`)
                .insertAdjacentHTML('beforeend', `<div>Company:
  ${suppliers[i].company_name}</div>`);
        document.querySelector(`#contact${i}`)
                .insertAdjacentHTML('beforeend',`<div>Contact:
  ${suppliers[i].contact_name}</div>`);
        document.querySelector(`#contact${i}`)
                .insertAdjacentHTML('beforeend',`<div>Title:
  ${suppliers[i].contact_title}</div>`);
        document.querySelector(`#contact${i}`)
                .insertAdjacentHTML('beforeend',`<div>Email:
  ${suppliers[i].contact_email}</div>`);
    }
}

// Run the function
getSuppliers();
```

The code fetches the suppliers' data and then loops through the array of suppliers' contacts:

>> A new ‹section› with an id set to `contact${i}` is appended to main.

>> A ‹div› tag for each of the four pieces of contact data (company_name, contact_name, contact_title, and contact_email) is appended to the new ‹section› tag.

Figure 1-8 shows part of the resulting page.

FIGURE 1-8: The asynchronous function loops through the JSON array, appending each object to the ‹main› tag.

IN THIS CHAPTER

» **Understanding web form basics**

» **Coding text boxes, check boxes, and radio buttons**

» **Programming lists, labels, and buttons**

» **Monitoring and triggering form events**

» **Submitting the form data**

Chapter **2**

Building and Processing Web Forms

From humble beginnings, forms in HTML5 are now tremendously flexible and powerful, providing natively much of the functionality that we as developers have been adding in with JavaScript over the years.

— PETER GASSTON

A dynamic web page is one that interacts with the user and responds in some way to that interaction. However, when I use the word *interaction* here, I don't mean (or I don't just mean) users scrolling through your content and clicking a link here and there. A dynamic web page solicits feedback from the user and then responds to that feedback in an appropriate way (whatever *appropriate* might mean in that context). Sure, you can pester your page visitors for info by tossing them a confirm or prompt box or two, but these are mere toys in the land of web interactivity. The real tools for soliciting feedback and then acting on it — that is, for making your pages truly dynamic — are web forms.

In this chapter, you explore all that web forms have to offer. After mastering the basics, you investigate the amazing new features offered by HTML web forms, unearth the power of form events, and learn how to dress up your form data and send it off to the web server. It's a veritable forms smorgasbord, so tuck in!

What Is a Web Form?

Most modern programs toss a dialog box in your face if they need to extract some information from you. For example, selecting a program's Print command most likely results in some kind of Print dialog box showing up. The purpose of this dialog box is to ask for info such as the number of copies you want, the pages you want to print, and the printer you want to use.

A *form* is essentially the web page equivalent of a dialog box. It's a page section populated with text boxes, lists, check boxes, command buttons, and other controls to get information from the user. For example, Figure 2-1 shows a form from my website. People can use this form to send me a message. The form includes a text box for the person's name, another for their email address, a larger text area for the message, and a command button to send the data to my server.

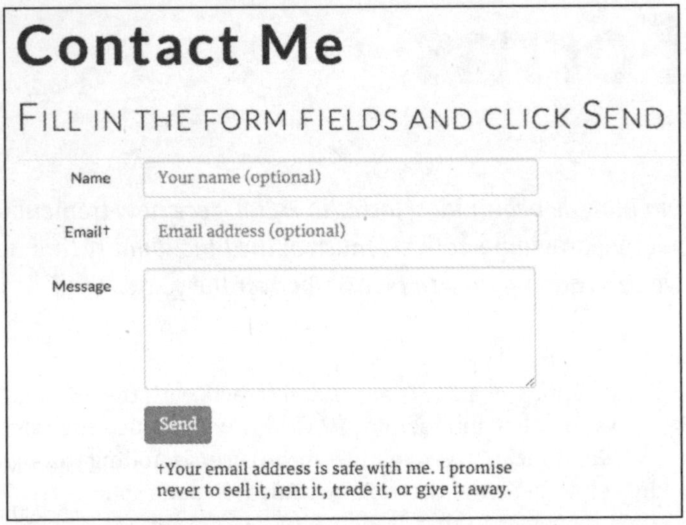

Contact Me

FILL IN THE FORM FIELDS AND CLICK SEND

Name — Your name (optional)

Email† — Email address (optional)

Message

Send

†Your email address is safe with me. I promise never to sell it, rent it, trade it, or give it away.

FIGURE 2-1:
A typical web form.

Contact forms are very common, but there are lots of other uses for forms:

>> If you put out a newsletter, you can use a form to sign up subscribers.

>> If your website includes pages with restricted access, you can use a form to get a person's username and password for verification.

>> If you have information in a database, you can use a form to have people specify what information they want to access.

>> If your site has a search feature, you can use a form to get the search text and offer options for filtering and sorting the search results.

Understanding How Web Forms Work

A web form is a little data-gathering machine. What kinds of data can it gather? You name it:

>> Text, from a single word up to a long post

>> Numbers, dates, and times

>> Which item is (or items are) selected in a list

>> Whether a check box is selected

>> Which one of a group of radio buttons is selected

What happens to that data after you've gathered it? The data can travel two roads: Server Street and Local Lane.

The Server Street route means that your web server gets in on the action. Here are the basic steps that occur:

1. The user clicks a button to submit the form.

2. Your JavaScript code gathers and readies the form data for sending.

3. The code uses a Fetch API call (refer to Book 6, Chapter 1) to send the form data to a PHP script on the server.

4. The PHP script extracts the form data.

5. PHP uses some or all of the form data to build and execute a MySQL query.

6. PHP outputs either the requested data or some kind of code that indicates the result of the operation.

7. Your JavaScript code processes the data returned by the server and updates the web page accordingly.

The Local Lane route doesn't get the web server involved at all:

1. The user changes the form data in some way.

2. Your JavaScript code detects the changed data.

3. The event handler for the changed form field updates the web page based on the changed data.

In this chapter, I show you how to build a form and then how to handle form events, which will enable you to stroll down Local Lane as much as you want. I also cover submitting data at the end of the chapter, which gives you everything you need to know for getting to Server Street.

Building an HTML Web Form

You build web forms with your bare hands using special HTML tags. The latest version of HTML includes many new form goodies, most of which now have great browser support, so I show you both the oldie-but-goodie and the latest-and-greatest in the form world over the next few sections.

Setting up the form

To get your form started, you wrap everything inside the ‹form› tag:

```
<form>
</form>
```

In this book, you create forms that either update the page locally or submit data to the server via the Fetch API. All that front-end interaction is controlled by JavaScript code, so you don't need any special attributes in the ‹form› tag.

However, I'd be remiss if I didn't mention the version of the ‹form› tag you need to use if you want your form data submitted directly to a script on the server:

```
<form action="script" method="method">
```

where:

>> *script* is the URL of the server script you want to use to process the form data.

>> *method* is the method you want to use to send the data: get or post. (I talk about the difference between these two methods in Book 6, Chapter 1.)

Here's an example:

```
<form
action="https://paulmcfedries.com/webcoding/bk06ch02/get-
   supplier-contacts.php"
method="post">
```

WARNING

If you're just using the form to add local interaction to the web page and you won't be submitting any form data to the server, technically you don't need the <form> tag. However, you should use one anyway most of the time because including the <form> tag enables the user to submit the form by pressing Enter or Return, and it also gets you a submit button (such as Go) in mobile browsers.

Adding a form button

Most forms include a button that users click when they've completed the form and want to initiate the form's underlying action. This action is known as *submitting* the form, and that term has traditionally meant sending the form data to a server-side script for processing. These days, however, and certainly in this book, *submitting* the form can also mean

» Updating something on the web page without sending anything to the server. For example, clicking a button might set the page's background color.

» Running a function that gathers the form data and uses a Fetch API call to send the data to the server and process what the server sends back. For example, if the form asks for the person's username and password, clicking the form button would launch the login process.

The old style of submitting a form is to use an <input> where the type attribute is set to submit:

```
<input type="submit" value="buttonText">
```

where *buttonText* is the text that appears on the button face.

For example:

```
<input type="submit" value="Submit Me!">
```

This style is rarely used in modern web development because it's a bit tricky to style such a button. For that reason, most web developers use the <button> tag, instead:

```
<button type="submit">buttonText</button>
```

where *buttonText* is the text that appears on the button face.

For example:

```
<button type="submit">Ship It</button>
```

TIP

For better looking buttons, use CSS to style the following (check out bk06ch02/ example01.html in this book's example files):

>> **Rounded corners:** To control the roundness of the button corners, use the border-radius property set to either a measurement (in, say, pixels) or a percentage. For example:

```
button {
    border-radius: 15px;
}
```

>> **Drop shadow:** To add a drop shadow to a button, apply the box-shadow *x* *y* *blur color* property, where *x* is the horizontal offset of the shadow, *y* is the vertical offset of the shadow, *blur* is the amount the shadow is blurred, and *color* is the shadow color. For example:

```
button {
    box-shadow: 3px 3px 5px gray;
}
```

Looking at the HTMLFormElement Object

A form element is an HTMLFormElement object that offers a few potentially useful properties (in each case, assume that *form* is a reference to a form element object):

>> *form*.action: The value of the form's action attribute

>> *form*.elements: Returns a collection (an HTMLFormControlsCollection object) of all the form's controls

>> *form*.length: The number of controls in the form

>> *form*.method: The value of the form's method attribute

>> *form*.name: The value of the form's name attribute

>> *form*.target: The value of the form's target attribute

Taking a Peek at the HTMLInputElement Object

Any form field that's based on the `input` element is an `HTMLInputElement` object that offers quite a few useful properties (in each case, assume that *input* is a reference to an `input` element object):

>> *input*.`form`: The form (an `HTMLFormElement` object) in which the element resides

>> *input*.`labels`: Returns a `NodeList` of the `label` elements associated with the element

>> *input*.`name`: The value of the element's name attribute

>> *input*.`type`: The element's type attribute

>> *input*.`value`: The current value of the element

>> *input*.`valueAsDate`: The current value of the element, interpreted as a date

>> *input*.`valueAsNumber`: The current value of the element, interpreted as a time value, and then as a number

Programming Text Fields

Text-based fields are the most commonly used form elements, and most of them use the `<input>` tag:

```
<input id="textId" type="textType" name="textName"
    value="textValue" placeholder="textPrompt">
```

where:

>> *textId* is a unique identifier for the text field.

>> *textType* is the kind of text field you want to use in your form.

>> *textName* is the name you assign to the field. If you'll be submitting the form data via the Fetch API, you must include a name value for each field.

>> *textValue* is the initial value of the field, if any.

>> *textPrompt* is text that appears temporarily in the field when the page first loads and is used to prompt the user about the required input. The placeholder text disappears as soon as the user starts typing in the field.

Here's a list of the available text-based types you can use for the `type` attribute:

>> `text`: Displays a text box into which the user types a line of text. Add the `size` attribute to specify the width of the field, in characters (the default is 20). Here's an example:

```
<input type="text" name="company" size="50">
```

>> `number`: Displays a text box into which the user types a numeric value. Most browsers add a spin box that enables the user to increment or decrement the number by clicking the up or down arrow, respectively. Check out this example:

```
<input type="number" name="points" value="100">
```

I should also mention the `range` type, which displays a slider control that enables the user to click and drag to choose a numeric value between a specified minimum and maximum:

```
<input type="range" name="transparency" min="0" max="100"
    value="100">
```

>> `email`: Displays a text box into which the user types an email address. Add the `multiple` attribute to allow the user to type two or more addresses, separated by commas. Add the `size` attribute to specify the width of the field, in characters. An example for you:

```
<input type="email" name="user-email" placeholder="you@
    yourdomain.com">
```

>> `url`: Displays a text box into which the user types a URL. Add the `size` attribute to specify the width of the field, in characters. Here's a for instance:

```
<input type="url" name="homepage" placeholder="e.g.,
    http://domain.com/">
```

>> `tel`: Displays a text box into which the user types a telephone number. Use the `size` attribute to specify the width of the field, in characters. Here's an example:

```
<input type="tel" name="mobile" placeholder="(xxx)
    xxx-xxxx">
```

» `time`: Displays a text box into which the user types a time, usually hours and minutes. For example:

```
<input type="time" name="start-time">
```

» `password`: Displays a text box into which the user types a password. The typed characters appear as dots (•). Add the `autocomplete` attribute to specify whether the user's browser or password management software can automatically enter the password. Set the attribute to `current-password` to allow password autocompletion or to `off` to disallow autocompletion. Need an example? Done:

```
<input type="password" name="userpassword"
    autocomplete="current-password">
```

» `search`: Displays a text box into which the user types a search term. Add the `size` attribute to specify the width of the field, in characters. Why, yes, I do have an example:

```
<input type="search" name="q" placeholder="Type a
    search term">
```

» `hidden`: Adds an input field to the form but doesn't display the field to the user. That sounds weird, I know, but it's a handy way to store a value that you want to include in the submit, but you don't want the user to see or modify on the page. Here's an example:

```
<input id="userSession" name="user-session" type="hidden"
    value="jwr274">
```

REMEMBER

Some ancient browsers don't get special text fields such as `email` and `time`, but you can still use them in your pages because those clueless browsers will ignore the `type` attribute and just display a standard `text` field.

That was a lot of text-related fields, but we're not done yet! You need to know about two others:

» `<textarea>`: Displays a text box into which the user can type multiple lines of text. Add the `rows` attribute to specify how many lines of text are displayed. If you want default text to appear in the text box, add the text between the `<textarea>` and `</textarea>` tags. Here's an example:

```
<textarea name="message" rows="5">
Default text goes here.
</textarea>
```

» `<label>`: Associates a label with a form field. You can use a label in two ways. In the first method, you surround the form field with `<label>` and `</label>` tags, and insert the label text before or after the field, like so:

```
<label>
Email:
<input type="email" name="user-email" placeholder="you@
  yourdomain.com">
</label>
```

In the second method, you add an `id` value to the field tag, set the `<label>` tag's `for` attribute to the same value, and insert the label text between the `<label>` and `</label>` tags, as I've done here:

```
<label for="useremail">Email:</label>
<input id="useremail" type="email" name="user-email"
  placeholder="you@yourdomain.com">
```

Figure 2-2 demonstrates each of these text fields (refer to bk06ch02/example02.html).

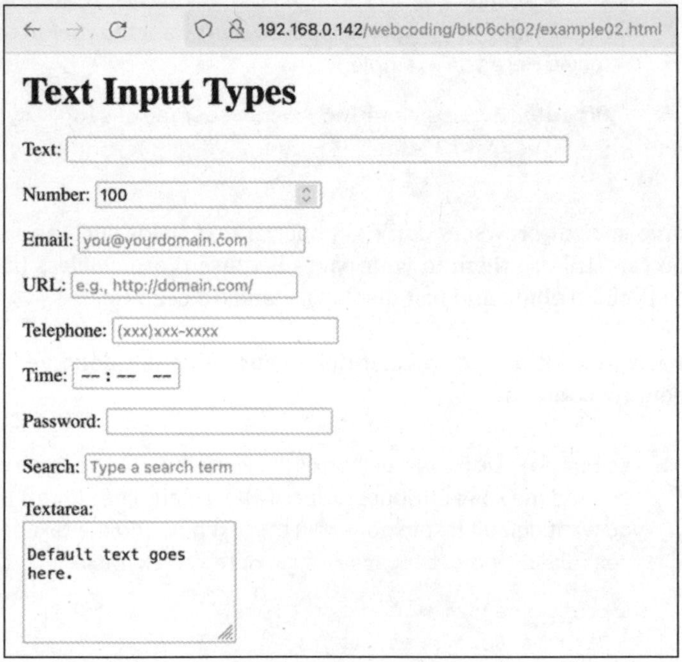

FIGURE 2-2:
The various text input types you can use in your forms.

Referencing text fields by field type

One common form-scripting technique is to run an operation on every field of the same type. For example, you may want to apply a style to all the URL fields. Here's the JavaScript selector to use to select all `input` elements of a given type:

```
document.querySelectorAll('input[type=fieldType]')
```

where `fieldType` is the `type` attribute value you want to select, such as `text` or `url`.

Here's an example where the JavaScript returns the set of all `input` elements that use the type `url` (bk06ch02/example03.html):

HTML:

```
<label for="url1">
    Site 1:
</label>
<input id="url1" type="url" name="url1" value="https://">

<label for="url2">
    Site 2:
</label>
<input id="url2" type="url" name="url2" value="https://">

<label for="url3">
    Site 3:
</label>
<input id="url3" type="url" name="url3" value="https://">
```

JavaScript:

```
const urlFields = document.querySelectorAll('input[type=url]');
console.log(urlFields);
```

Getting a text field value

Your script can get the current value of any text field by using one of the field object's value-related properties:

```
field.value
field.valueAsDate
field.valueAsNumber
```

where *field* is a reference to the form field object you want to work with.

Here's an example (check out bk06ch02/example04.html):

HTML:

```
<label for="search-field">
    Search the site:
</label>
<input id="search-field" name="q" type="search">
```

JavaScript:

```
const searchString = document.getElementById('search-field').value;
console.log(searchString);
```

Setting a text field value

To change a text field value, assign the new string to the field object's value property:

```
field.value = value;
```

where:

>> *field* is a reference to the form field object you want to work with.

>> *value* is the string you want to assign to the text field.

Here's an example (bk06ch02/example05.html):

HTML:

```
<label for="homepage-field">
    Type your homepage address:
</label>
<input id="homepage-field" name="homepage" type="url"
  value="HTTPS://PAULMCFEDRIES.COM/"">
```

JavaScript:

```
const homepageField = document.getElementById('homepage-field');
const homepageURL = homepageField.value;
homepageField.value = homepageURL.toLowerCase();
```

The HTML code defines an input element of type url where the default value is in all-uppercase letters. The JavaScript code grabs a URL, converts it to all-lowercase characters, and then returns it to the same url field. As shown in Figure 2-3, the text box now displays all-lowercase letters.

```
←  →  C          ○  &  192.168.0.142/webcoding/bk06ch02/example05.html
```

Type your homepage address:

```
https://paulmcfedries.com/
```

Coding Check Boxes

You use a check box in a web form to toggle a setting on (that is, the check box is selected) and off (the check box is deselected). You create a check box by including in your form the following version of the <input> tag:

```
<input id="checkId" type="checkbox" name="checkName"
    value="checkValue" [checked]>
```

where:

» *checkId* is a unique identifier for the check box.

» *checkName* is the name you want to assign to the check box.

» *checkValue* is the value you want to assign to the check box. Note that this is a hidden value that your script can access when the form is submitted; the user never encounters it.

» checked (optional) means the check box is initially selected.

REMEMBER

One strange thing about a check box field is that it's included in the form submission only if it's selected. If the check box is deselected, it's not included in the submission.

Referencing check boxes

If your code needs to reference all the check boxes in a page, use the following selector (bk06ch02/example06.html):

```
document.querySelectorAll('input[type=checkbox]')
```

If you just want the check boxes from a particular form, use a descendant or child selector on the form's id value:

```
document.querySelectorAll('#formid input[type=checkbox]')
```

or:

```
document.querySelectorAll('#formid > input[type=checkbox]')
```

Getting the check box state

You have to be a bit careful when discussing the "value" of a check box. If it's the value attribute you want to work with, getting this is no different than getting the value property of a text field by using the checkbox object's value property.

However, you're more likely to be interested in whether a check box is selected or deselected. This is called the check box *state*. In that case, you need to examine the checkbox object's checked property instead:

```
checkbox.checked
```

where *checkbox* is a reference to the checkbox object you want to work with.

The checked property returns true if the check box is selected, or false if the check box is deselected.

Here's an example (bk06ch02/example07.html):

HTML:

```
<label>
    <input id="autosave" type="checkbox" name="autosave">
    Autosave this project
</label>
```

JavaScript:

```
const autoSaveCheckBox = document.querySelector('#autosave');
if (autoSaveCheckBox.checked) {
    console.log(`${autoSaveCheckBox.name} is checked`);
} else {
    console.log(`${autoSaveCheckBox.name} is unchecked`);
}
```

The JavaScript code stores a reference to the checkbox object in the autoSave CheckBox variable. Then an if statement examines the object's checked property and displays a different message in the console depending on whether checked returns true or false.

Setting the check box state

To set a check box field to either the selected or deselected state, assign a Boolean expression to the checked property:

```
checkbox.checked = Boolean;
```

where:

>> *checkbox* is a reference to the checkbox object you want to work with.

>> *Boolean* is the Boolean value or expression you want to assign to the checkbox object. Use true to select the checkbox object; use false to deselect the checkbox object.

For example, suppose you have a form with a large number of check boxes and you want to set up that form so that the user can select at most three check boxes. Here's some code that does the job (bk06ch02/example08.html):

```
document.querySelector('form').addEventListener('click',
  event => {

    // Make sure a checkbox was clicked
    if (event.target.type === 'checkbox') {

        // Get the total number of selected checkboxes
        const totalSelected = document.querySelectorAll('input
[type=checkbox]:checked').length;

        // Are there more than three selected checkboxes?
        if (totalSelected > 3) {

            // If so, deselect the checkbox that was just
  clicked
            event.target.checked = false;
        }
    }
});
```

This event handler runs when anything inside the `form` element is clicked, passing a reference to the click event as the parameter `event`. Then the code uses the `:checked` selector to return the set of all `checkbox` elements that have the `checked` attribute, and the `length` property tells you how many are in the set. An `if` test checks whether more than three are now selected. If that's true, the code deselects the check box that was just clicked.

Dealing with Radio Buttons

If you want to offer your users a collection of related options, only one of which can be selected at a time, radio buttons are the way to go. Form radio buttons congregate in groups of two or more where only one button in the group can be selected at any time. If the user clicks another button in that group, it becomes selected and the previously selected button becomes deselected.

You create a radio button using the following variation of the `<input>` tag:

```
<input id="radioId" type="radio" name="radioGroup"
    value="radioValue" [checked]>
```

where:

>> *radioId* is a unique identifier for the radio button.

>> *radioGroup* is the name you want to assign to the group of radio buttons. All the radio buttons that use the same name value belong to that group.

>> *radioValue* is the value you want to assign to the radio button. If this radio button is selected when the form is submitted, this is the value that's included in the submission.

>> checked (optional) means the radio button is initially selected.

Referencing radio buttons

If your code needs to work with all the radio buttons in a page, use this JavaScript selector:

```
document.querySelectorAll('input[type=radio]')
```

If you want the radio buttons from a particular form, use a descendant or child selector on the form's id value:

```
document.querySelectorAll('#formid input[type=radio]')
```

or:

```
document.querySelectorAll('#formid > input[type=radio]')
```

If you require just the radio buttons from a particular group, use the following JavaScript selector, where *radioGroup* is the common name of the group:

```
document.querySelectorAll('input[name=radioGroup]')
```

Getting a radio button state

If your code needs to know whether a particular radio button is selected or deselected, you need to determine the radio button *state*. You do that by examining the radio button's checked attribute, like so:

```
radio.checked
```

where *radio* is a reference to the radio button object you want to work with.

The checked attribute returns true if the radio button is selected, or false if the button is deselected.

For example, consider the following HTML (bk06ch02/example09.html):

```
<form>
    <fieldset>
        <legend>
            Select a delivery method
        </legend>
        <label>
            <input type="radio" id="carrier-pigeon"
  name="delivery" value="pigeon" checked>Carrier pigeon
        </label>
        <label>
            <input type="radio" id="pony-express"
  name="delivery" value="pony">Pony express
        </label>
```

```
        <label>
              <input type="radio" id="snail-mail" name="delivery"
    value="postal">Snail mail
          </label>
          <label>
              <input type="radio" id="some-punk" name="delivery"
    value="bikecourier">Some punk on a bike
          </label>
      </fieldset>
</form>
```

The following statement stores the state of the radio button with the id value of pony-express:

```
const ponySelected = document.querySelector('#pony-express').
    checked;
```

However, it's more likely that your code will want to know which radio button in a group is selected. You can do that by applying the :checked selector to the group and then getting the value property of the returned object:

```
const deliveryMethod = document.querySelector('input
    [name=delivery]:checked').value;
```

TIP

To get the text of the label associated with a radio button, use the input element's labels property to get a reference to the label element, and then use the innerText property to get the label text:

```
document.querySelector('input[name=delivery]:checked').
    labels[0].innerTextinnerText);
```

Setting the radio button state

To set a radio button field to either the selected or deselected state, assign a Boolean expression to the checked attribute:

```
radio.checked = Boolean;
```

where:

>> *radio* is a reference to the radio button object you want to change.

>> *Boolean* is the Boolean value or expression you want to assign to the radio button object. Use true to select the radio button; use false to deselect the radio button object.

For example, in the HTML code from the preceding section, the initial state of the form group had the first radio button selected. You can reset the group by selecting that button. You could get a reference to the id of the first radio button, but what if later you change (or someone else changes) the order of the radio buttons? A safer way is to get a reference to the first radio button in the group, whatever it may be, and then select that element. Here's some code that does this (bk06ch02/example10.html):

```
const firstRadioButton = document.querySelectorAll('input[name=
   delivery]')[0];
firstRadioButton.checked = true;
```

This code uses querySelectorAll() to return a NodeList collection of all the radio buttons in the delivery group; next it uses [0] to reference just the first element in the collection. Then that element's checked property is set to true.

Programming Selection Lists

Selection lists are common sights in HTML forms because they enable the web developer to display a relatively large number of choices in a compact control that most users know how to operate.

To create the list container, you use the ‹select› tag:

```
<select id="selectId" name="selectName" size="selectSize"
   [multiple]>
```

where:

>> *selectId* is a unique identifier for the selection list.

>> *selectName* is the name you want to assign to the selection list.

>> *selectSize* is the optional number of rows in the selection list box that are visible. If you omit this value, the browser displays the list as a drop-down box.

>> multiple (optional) means the user is allowed to select multiple options in the list.

For each item in the list, you add an <option> tag between the <select> and </select> tags:

```
<option value="optionValue" [selected]>
```

where:

>> *optionValue* is the value you want to assign to the list option.

>> selected (optional) means the list option is initially selected.

Checking out the HTMLSelectElement object

A selection list is an HTMLSelectElement object that offers quite a few useful properties (in each case, assume that *select* is a reference to a selection list object):

>> *select*.form: The form (an HTMLFormElement object) in which the selection list resides.

>> *select*.length: The number of option elements in the selection list.

>> *select*.multiple: A Boolean value that returns true if the selection list includes the multiple attribute and false otherwise.

>> *select*.name: The value of the selection list's name attribute.

>> *select*.options: The option elements (an HTMLOptionsCollection object) contained in the selection list.

>> *select*.selectedIndex: The index of the first selected option element (index values begin at 0 for the first option element). This property returns –1 if no option elements are selected.

>> *select*.selectedOptions: The option elements (an HTMLCollection object) that are currently selected in the selection list.

>> *select*.type: The selection list type, which is select–one for a regular list or select–multiple for a list with the multiple attribute applied.

>> *select*.value: The value property of the first selected option element. If no option element is selected, this property returns the empty string.

Checking out the HTMLOptionElement object

Each option element in a selection list is an HTMLOptionElement object. Here are a few useful HTMLOptionElement properties to bear in mind (in each case, assume that *option* is a reference to an option element object):

>> *option*.defaultSelected: A Boolean value that returns true if the option element included the selected attribute by default and false otherwise

>> *option*.form: The form (an HTMLFormElement object) in which the option element resides

>> *option*.index: The index of the option element within the selection list (index values begin at 0 for the first option element)

>> *option*.selected: A Boolean value that returns true if the option element is currently selected and false otherwise

>> *option*.text: The text content of the option element

>> *option*.value: The value of the value attribute of the option element

Referencing selection list options

If your code needs to work with all the options in a selection list, use the selection list object's options property (bk06ch02/example11.html) :

```
document.querySelector(list).options
```

where *list* is a selector that specifies the select element you want to work with.

To work with a particular option in a list, use JavaScript's square brackets operator ([]) to specify the index of the option's position in the list (bk06ch02/example11.html):

```
document.querySelector(list).options[n]
```

where:

>> *list* is a selector that specifies the select element you want to work with.

>> *n* is the index of the option in the returned NodeList collection (where 0 is the first option, 1 is the second option, and so on).

To get the option's text (that is, the text that appears in the list), use the option object's text property :

```
document.querySelector(list).options[2].text
```

Getting the selected list option

If your code needs to know whether a particular option in a selection list is selected or deselected, examine the option's selected property, like so:

```
option.selected
```

where *option* is a reference to the option object you want to work with.

The selected attribute returns true if the option is selected or false if the option is deselected.

For example, consider the following selection list:

```
<select id="hair-color" name="hair-color">
    <option value="black">Black</option>
    <option value="blonde">Blonde</option>
    <option value="brunette" selected>Brunette</option>
    <option value="red">Red</option>
    <option value="neon">Something neon</option>
    <option value="none">None</option>
</select>
```

The following JavaScript statement stores the state of the first item in the selection list:

```
let black = document.querySelector('#hair-color').options[0].
    selected;
```

However, you'll more likely want to know which option in the selection list is selected. You do that via the list's selectedOptions property:

```
const hairColor = document.querySelector('#hair-color').
    selectedOptions[0];
```

This isn't a multiselect list, so specifying selectedOptions[0] returns the selected option element. In this example, your code could use hairColor.text to get the text of the selected option.

If the list includes the `multiple` attribute, the `selectedOptions` property may return an `HTMLCollection` object that contains multiple elements. Your code needs to allow for that by, say, looping through the collection (bk06ch02/example12.html):

HTML:

```html
<select id="hair-products" name="hair-products" size="5"
  multiple>
    <option value="gel" selected>Gel</option>
    <option value="grecian-formula" selected>Grecian Formula
  </option>
    <option value="mousse">Mousse</option>
    <option value="peroxide">Peroxide</option>
    <option value="shoe-black">Shoe black</option>
</select>
```

JavaScript:

```javascript
const selectedHairProducts = document.querySelector('#hair-
  products').selectedOptions;
for (const hairProduct of selectedHairProducts) {
    console.log(hairProduct.text);
}
```

Changing the selected option

To set a selection list option to either the selected or deselected state, assign a Boolean expression to the option object's `selected` property:

```
option.selected = Boolean;
```

where:

>> *option* is a reference to the `option` element you want to modify.

>> *Boolean* is the Boolean value or expression you want to assign to the option object. Use `true` to select the option; use `false` to deselect the option.

Using the HTML code from the preceding section, the following statement selects the third option in the list:

```javascript
document.querySelector('#hair-products').options[2].selected =
  true;
```

If the initial state of a multiple-selection list had no items selected, you may want to reset the list by deselecting all the options. You can do that by setting the selection list object's `selectedIndex` property to –1:

```
document.querySelector('#hair-products').selectedIndex = -1;
```

Handling and Triggering Form Events

With all the clicking, typing, tabbing, and dragging that goes on, web forms are veritable event factories. Fortunately, you can let most of these events pass you by. But a few events will come in handy, both in running code when the event occurs and in triggering the events yourself.

Most form events are clicks, so you can handle them by setting `click` event handlers using JavaScript's `addEventListener()` method (which I covered in Book 3, Chapter 7). Here's an example (bk06ch02/example13.html):

HTML:

```
<form>
    <label for="user">Username:</label>
    <input id="user" type="text" name="username">
    <label for="pwd">Password:</label>
    <input id="pwd" type="password" name="password">
</form>
```

JavaScript:

```
document.querySelector('form').addEventListener('click', () => {
    console.log('Thanks for clicking the form!');
});
```

This example listens for clicks on the entire `form` element, but you can also create `click` event handlers for buttons, `input` elements, check boxes, radio buttons, and more.

Setting the focus

One simple feature that can improve the user experience on your form pages is to set the focus on the first form field when your page loads. Setting the focus saves the user from having to make that annoying click inside the first field.

To get this done, run JavaScript's `focus()` method on the element that you want to have the focus at startup:

```
field.focus()
```

where `field` is a reference to the form field that should have the focus.

Here's an example that sets the focus on the text field with `id` equal to `user` at startup (bk06ch02/example14.html):

HTML:

```html
<form>
    <label for="user">Username:</label>
    <input id="user" type="text" name="username">
    <label for="pwd">Password:</label>
    <input id="pwd" type="password" name="password">
</form>
```

JavaScript:

```javascript
document.querySelector('#user').focus();
```

Monitoring the focus event

Rather than setting the focus, you may want to monitor when a particular field gets the focus (for example, by the user clicking or tabbing into the field). You can do that by setting up a `focus` event handler on the field:

```javascript
field.addEventListener('focus', () => {
    Focus code goes here
});
```

where `field` is a reference to the form field you want to monitor for the `focus` event.

Here's an example (bk06ch02/example15.html):

```javascript
document.querySelector('#user').addEventListener('focus',
    () => {
    console.log('The username field has the focus!');
});
```

Monitoring the blur event

The opposite of setting the focus on an element is *blurring* an element, which removes the focus from the element. You blur an element by running the `blur()` method on the element, which causes it to lose focus:

```
field.blur()
```

where `field` is a reference to the form field you no longer want to have the focus.

However, rather than blurring an element, you're more likely to want to run some code when a particular element is blurred (for example, by the user clicking or tabbing out of the field). You can monitor for a particular blurred element by setting up a `blur()` event handler:

```
field.addEventListener('blur', () => {
    Blur code goes here
});
```

where `field` is a reference to the form field you want to monitor for the `blur` event.

Here's an example (bk06ch02/example16.html):

```
document.querySelector('#user').addEventListener('blur', () => {
    console.log('The username field no longer has the focus!');
});
```

Listening for element changes

One of the most useful form events is the `change` event, which fires when the value or state of a field is modified. When this event fires depends on the element type:

>> For a `textarea` element and the various text-related `input` elements, the change event fires when the element loses the focus.

>> For check boxes, radio buttons, selection lists, and pickers, the change event fires as soon as the user clicks the element to modify the selection or value.

You listen for a field's change events by setting up a `change()` event handler:

```
field.addEventListener('change', () => {
    Change code goes here
});
```

where *field* is a reference to the form field you want to monitor for the change event.

Here's an example (bk06ch02/example17.html):

HTML:

```
<label for="bgcolor">Select a background color</label>
<input id="bgcolor" type="color" name="bg-color"
  value="#ffffff">
```

JavaScript:

```
document.querySelector('#bgcolor').addEventListener('change',
  (event) => {
    const backgroundColor = event.target.value;
    document.body.bgColor = backgroundColor;
});
```

The HTML code sets up a color picker. The JavaScript code applies the change event handler to the color picker. When the change event fires on the picker, the code stores the new color value in the backgroundColor variable by referencing event.target.value, where event.target refers to the element to which the event listener is bound (the color picker, in this case). The code then applies that color to the body element's bgColor property.

REMEMBER

Note that I used the regular anonymous function syntax instead of the arrow function syntax for the event handler. I did that because inside an arrow function, this always refers to the parent of the object we're listening on (that parent is the Window object in this example). When you need this to refer to the object you're listening on, use the regular anonymous function syntax.

Creating Keyboard Shortcuts for Form Controls

A web page is very much a click- (or tap-) friendly medium, but that doesn't mean you can't build some keyboard support into your interface. For example, adding the tabindex="0" attribute to any HTML tag automatically makes that element "tabbable" (meaning that a user can set the focus on that element by tapping the tab key one or more times).

Another good example is a button that you feature on most or all of your pages. In that case, you can set up a keyboard shortcut that enables a user to execute the button by pressing a key or key combination.

You define a keyboard shortcut for a web page by setting up an event handler for the document object's keydown event (which fires when the user presses, but hasn't yet released, a key). Depending on the type of shortcut, you may also be able to define the shortcut using the document object's keyup event (which fires when the user releases a pressed key). Your event handler needs to look for two kinds of keys:

>> **Special keys:** The Alt, Ctrl (Control on a Mac), Shift, and Meta (that is, ⌘ on a Mac) keys. When the user presses a special key, the KeyboardEvent object sets one of the following properties to true: altKey (for Alt), ctrlKey (for Ctrl or Control), shiftKey (for Shift), or metaKey (for ⌘).

>> **Any other key:** The letters, numbers, and symbols on a typical keyboard. In this case, the pressed key is returned as the KeyboardEvent object's key property.

Here's an example (bk06ch02/example18.html):

HTML:

```
<button type="button">
    Run Me!
</button>
<p>
    Keyboard shortcut: Ctrl+Shift+B
</p>
```

JavaScript:

```
// Add a listener for the button's 'click' event
document
    .querySelector('button')
    .addEventListener('click',
    (e) => {
        // Change the button text
        e.target.innerText = 'Thanks!';

        // Reset the button after 3 seconds
        setTimeout(() => document
```

```
            .querySelector('button').innerText = 'Run Me!',
            3000);
    }
);

// Add a listener for the 'keydown' event
document
    .addEventListener('keydown',
    function(e) {
        // Check whether Ctrl+Shift+B are all pressed
        if(e.ctrlKey && e.shiftKey && e.key === 'B') {
            // If so, trigger the button's 'click' event
            document.querySelector('button').click();
        }
    }
);
```

The HTML code creates a simple button. The JavaScript code sets up an event handler for the button's `click` event, which changes the button text, and then uses `setTimeout()` to change the text back after three seconds. The code also sets up a `keydown` event handler that checks whether the Ctrl, Shift, and B keys were pressed at the same time. If so, the code invokes the button's `click()` method, which fires the `click` event and triggers the `click` event handler.

Submitting the Form

There's one form event that I didn't cover in the preceding section, and it's a big-gie: the `submit` event, which fires when the form data is to be sent to the server. Here's the general syntax:

```
form.addEventListener('submit', (e) => {
    Submit code goes here
});
```

where:

➤ *form* is a reference to the form you want to monitor for the `submit` event.

➤ e is the argument that represents the event object.

You'll rarely, if ever, allow the `submit` event to occur directly. Instead, you'll want to intercept the `submit` so that you can gather the data and then send it to the server yourself using a Fetch API call. Handling the submit event yourself gives you much more control over both what is sent to the server and how what is sent back from the server is processed.

Triggering the submit event

Here's a list of the various ways that the submit event gets triggered:

» When the user clicks a button or input element that resides in a <form> tag and has its type attribute set to submit

» When the user clicks a button element that resides in a <form> tag and has no type attribute

» When the user presses Enter or Return while a form element has the focus, and either a button or input element resides in the <form> tag and has its type attribute set to submit, or a button element resides in the <form> tag and has no type attribute

» When your code runs the submit() method on a form:

```
form.submit();
```

where form is a reference to the form you want to submit

Preventing the default form submission

You control the form submission yourself by sending the data to the server with a Fetch API call. The submit event doesn't know that, however, and it will try to submit the form data anyway. That's a no-no, so you need to prevent the default form submission by using the event object's preventDefault() method:

```
myForm.submit(function(e) {
    e.preventDefault();
});
```

Preparing the data for submission

Before you can submit your form data, you need to convert it to a format that your server's PHP script can work with. This conversion always begins by gathering the data from the form's field into a FormData object:

```
new FormData(form)
```

where *form* is a reference to the form that has the data you want to gather.

If you'll be submitting the data by using the POST request method, you don't need to do anything else to the resulting FormData object. If you'll be using the GET request method, however, then extra step is needed because the GET format requires a string of *name=value* pairs, separated by ampersands (&). To convert your form data to this format, use JavaScript's URLSearchParams()constructor:

```
new URLSearchParams(formData).toString()
```

where *formData* is a reference to the FormData object that has the data you want to submit via GET.

For example (bk06ch02/example19.html):

```
const form = document.querySelector('form');
const formData = new FormData(form);
const queryParams = new URLSearchParams(formData).toString();
```

The queryParams variable now holds a string of *name=value* pairs, which (as I discuss in the next section) you can tack on to the end of the URL you send to the server using fetch().

Submitting the form data

Now you're almost ready to submit the data. As an example, here's some HTML code for a form and div that I'll use to output the form results:

```
<form>
    <div>
        <label for="first">First name:</label>
        <input id="first" type="text" name="firstname">
    </div>
    <div>
        <label for="last">Last name:</label>
        <input id="last" type="text" name="lastname">
    </div>
    <div>
        <label for="nick">Nickname:</label>
        <input id="nick" type="text" name="nickname">
    </div>
    <button type="submit" onclick="submitForm(event)">Submit
</button>
```

```
        </form>

<div class="output">
</div>
```

First, here's the general JavaScript code that submits the form via the Fetch API using the GET request method:

```
fetch(`url?${queryParams}`)
```

where:

» *url* is the full URL of the PHP script that will process the GET request.

» *queryParams* is a reference to a string that contains the *name=value* pairs created from your form data.

Here's an asynchronous function (bk06ch02/example20.html) that submits the data using a GET request and processes the result (which just echoes back the form data, as shown in Figure 2-4):

```
async function submitForm(event) {
    // Prevent the default form submission
    event.preventDefault();

    // Get a reference to the form
    const form = document.querySelector('form');

    // Gather the form data
    const formData = new FormData(form);

    // Create the query string to add to the fetch() URL
    const queryParams = new URLSearchParams(formData).
toString();

    // Submit the data as a GET request using query parameters
    const response = await fetch(`http://localhost/php/echo-
form-fields-get.php?${queryParams}`);
```

```
    // Parse the data asynchronously
    const data = await response.text();

    // Get a reference to the target element
    const target = document.querySelector('.output');

    // Write the data to the target
    target.innerHTML = data;
}
```

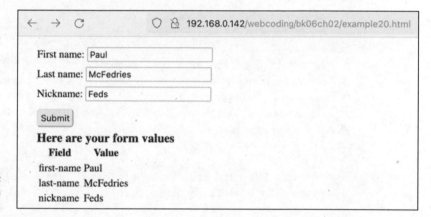

FIGURE 2-4:
An example form
submission.

REMEMBER

To make the code in this section easier to understand, I removed all the error-handling statements. Refer to the example files to get the full code for both scripts.

Here's the general JavaScript code that submits the form via the Fetch API using the POST request method:

```
fetch('url', {
    method: 'POST',
    body: formData
});
```

where:

>> *url* is the full URL of the PHP script that will process the POST request.

>> *formData* is a reference to a FormData object that holds the form data.

Here's an asynchronous function (bk06ch02/example21.html) that submits the data using a POST request and processes the result:

```javascript
async function submitForm(event) {

    // Prevent the default form submission
    event.preventDefault();

    // Get a reference to the form
    const form = document.querySelector('form');

    // Gather the form data
    const formData = new FormData(form);

    // Submit the data as a POST request
    const response = await fetch('http://localhost/php/echo-
form-fields-post.php', {
        method: 'POST',
        body: formData
    });

    // Parse the data asynchronously
    const data = await response.text();

    // Get a reference to the target element
    const target = document.querySelector('.output');

    // Write the data to the target
    target.innerHTML = data;
}
```

WARNING

We're missing one very important stop on our road to dynamic web pages: We haven't validated the form data! Form validation is so important, in fact, that I devote an entire chapter to it: Book 6, Chapter 3. Don't miss it!

Chapter **3**

Validating Form Data

Garbage in, garbage out. Or rather more felicitously: The tree of nonsense is watered with error, and from its branches swing the pumpkins of disaster.

— NICK HARKAWAY

In the old computing axiom of *garbage in, garbage out* (*GIGO*), or if in your genes or heart you're British, *rubbish in, rubbish out* (yes, *RIRO*), lies a cautionary tale. If the data that goes into a system is inaccurate, incomplete, incompatible, or in some other way invalid, the information that comes out of that system will be outdated, outlandish, outrageous, or just outright wrong. What does this have to do with you as a web developer? Plenty, because it's your job to make sure that the data the user enters into a form is accurate, complete, and compatible with your system.

In a word, you have to make sure the data is valid. If that sounds like a lot of work, I have some happy news for you: HTML has data validation baked in, so you can just piggyback on the hard work of some real nerds. In this chapter, you explore these HTML validation techniques. Ah, but your work isn't over yet, friend. You also have to validate the same data once again on the server. Crazy? Like a fox. But there's more good news on the server side of things, because PHP has a few ready-to-run tools that take most of the pain out of validation. In this chapter, you also dive deep into those tools. Sleeves rolled up? Then let's begin.

Validating Form Data in the Browser

Before JavaScript came along, web servers would spend inordinate amounts of processing time checking the data submitted from a form and, all too often, returning the data back to the user to fill in an empty field or fix some invalid entry. Someone eventually realized that machines costing tens of thousands of dollars (which was the cost of the average server machine when the web was in swaddling clothes) ought to have better things to do with their time than chastising users for not entering their email address correctly (or whatever). Wouldn't it make infinitely more sense for the validation of a form's data to first occur in the browser *before* the form was even submitted?

The answer to that is an unqualified "Duh!" And once JavaScript took hold with its browser-based scripting, using it to do form validation on the browser became the new language's most important and useful feature. Alas, data validation is a complex business, so it didn't take long for everyone's JavaScript validation code to run to hundreds or even thousands of lines. Plus, there was no standardization, meaning that every web project had to create its own validation code from scratch, pretty much guaranteeing it wouldn't work like any other web project's validation code. Isn't there a better way?

Give me another "Duh!" Perhaps that's why the big brains in charge of making HTML more useful decided to do something about the situation. Several types of form validation are part of HTML, which means now you can get the web browser to handle your validation chores, with little or no JavaScript.

WARNING

HTML validation has huge browser support, so no major worries there. However, a tiny minority of older browsers will still scoff at your browser validation efforts. Not to worry, though: You'll get them on the server side!

Making a form field mandatory

It's common for a form to contain at least one field that the user must fill in. For example, if your form is for a login, you certainly need both the username and password fields to be *mandatory*, meaning you want to set up the form so that the submission won't go through unless both fields are filled in.

Here are a few things you can do to encourage users to fill in mandatory fields:

> » Make it clear which fields are mandatory. Many sites place an asterisk before or after a field and include a note such as Fields marked with * are required at the top of the form.

>> For a radio button group, always set up your form so that one of the `<input>` tags includes the `checked` attribute. This ensures that one option will always be selected.

>> For a selection list, make sure that one of the `<option>` tags includes the `selected` attribute.

Outside these techniques, you can make any field mandatory by adding the `required` attribute to the form field tag. Here's an example (check out bk06ch03/example01.html in this book's example files):

```
<form>
    <div>
        <label for="fave-beatle">Favorite Beatle:</label>
        <input id="fave-beatle" type="text" required>
        <button type="submit">Submit</button>
    </div>
</form>
```

The `<input>` tag has the `required` attribute. If you leave this field blank and try to submit the form, the browser prevents the submission and displays a message telling you to fill in the field. This message is slightly different, depending on the web browser. Figure 3-1 shows the message that Chrome displays.

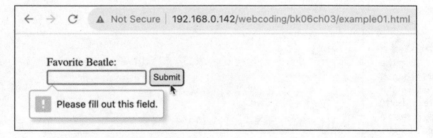

FIGURE 3-1: Add the required attribute to a form field to ensure that the field gets filled in.

Restricting the length of a text field

Another useful built-in HTML validation technique is setting restrictions on the length of the value entered in a text field. For example, you might want a password value to have a minimum length, and you might want a username to have a maximum length. Easier done than said:

>> To add a minimum length restriction, set the `minlength` attribute to the least number of characters the user must enter.

» To add a maximum length restriction, set the maxlength attribute to the most number of characters the user can enter.

Take a look at an example (check out bk06ch03/example02.html):

```
<form>
    <div>
        <label for="acct-handle">Account handle (6-12 chars):
    </label>
        <input id="acct-handle"
               type="text"
               placeholder="Enter 6-12 characters"
               minlength="6"
               maxlength="12">
        <button type="submit">Submit</button>
    </div>
</form>
```

The <input> tag asks for a value no less than 6 and no more than 12 characters long. If the user enters a value shorter or longer and tries to submit the form, the browser prevents the submission and displays a message asking for more or fewer characters. Figure 3-2 shows the version of the message that Firefox displays.

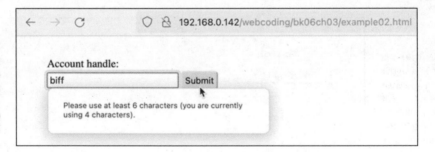

Setting maximum and minimum values on a numeric field

HTML can also validate a numeric field based on a specified minimum or maximum value for the field. Here are the attributes to use:

» min: To add a minimum value restriction, set the min attribute to the smallest allowable value the user can enter.

>> max: To add a maximum value restriction, set the max attribute to the largest allowable value the user can enter.

Here's an example (bk06ch03/example03.html):

```
<form>
    <div>
        <label for="loan-term">Loan term (years):</label>
        <input id="loan-term"
               type="number"
               placeholder="3-25"
               min="3"
               max="25">
        <button type="submit">Submit</button>
    </div>
</form>
```

The number <input> tag asks for a value between 3 and 25. If the user enters a value outside this range and tries to submit the form, the browser prevents the submission and displays a message to reenter a value that's either less than or equal to the maximum (as shown in Figure 3-3) or greater than or equal to the minimum.

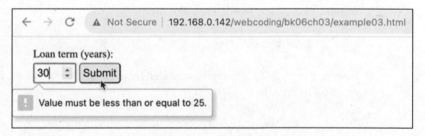

Validating email fields

Generic field validation attributes such as required, minlength, and max are useful, but some form fields need a more targeted validation technique. In a field that accepts an email address, for example, any entered value should look something like username@domain. If that sounds like a daunting challenge, you're right, it is. Fortunately, that challenge has already been taken up by some of the best coders on the planet. The result? Built-in HTML validation for email addresses. And when I say "built-in," I mean built-in, because once you specify type="email" in the <input> tag, modern web browsers will automatically validate the field input to make sure it looks like an email address when the form is submitted, as shown in Figure 3-4 (refer to bk06ch03/example04.html).

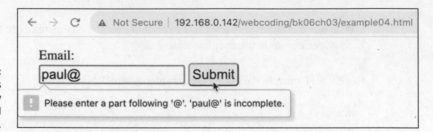

FIGURE 3-4:
Modern browsers
automatically
validate email
fields.

Making field values conform to a pattern

One of the most powerful and flexible HTML validation techniques is *pattern matching,* where you specify a pattern of letters, numbers, and other symbols that the field input must match. You add pattern matching validation to a text, email, url, tel, search, or password field by adding the pattern attribute:

```
pattern="regular_expression"
```

where *regular_expression* is a type of expression called a *regular expression* that uses special symbols to define the pattern you want to apply to the field.

For example, suppose you want to set up a pattern for a ten-digit North American telephone number that includes dashes, such as 555-123-4567 or 888-987-6543. In a regular expression, the symbol \d represents any digit from 0 to 9, so your regular expression would look like this:

```
\d\d\d-\d\d\d-\d\d\d\d
```

Here's the regular expression added to a telephone number field (bk06ch03/example05.html):

```
<input id="user-phone"
       type="tel"
       pattern="\d\d\d-\d\d\d-\d\d\d\d"
       placeholder="e.g., 123-456-7890"
       title="Enter a 10-digit number in the format
   123-456-7890">
```

TIP

It's a good idea to add the title attribute and use it to describe the pattern you want to user to enter. Also, you can find all kinds of useful, ready-made patterns at the HTML5 Pattern site: www.html5pattern.com.

HTML5 is the version of HTML that included most of the validation features that I talk about in this section (plus lots of other useful features, such as the semantic sectioning tags from Book 2, Chapter 1). The name *HTML5* was put out to pasture a few years ago, and now HTML has no versions, just an ever-changing specification called the HTML Living Standard (https://html.spec.whatwg.org).

Table 3-1 summarizes the most useful regular expression symbols to use with the `pattern` attribute. See "Regular Expressions Reference," at the end of this chapter, for a more detailed look at this powerful tool.

TABLE 3-1   **The Most Useful Regular Expression Symbols**

Symbol	Matches
\d	Any digit from 0 through 9
\D	Any character that is not a digit from 0 through 9
.	Any character
\s	Any whitespace character, such as the space, tab (\t), newline (\n), and carriage return (\r)
\S	Any non-whitespace character
[ ]	Whatever characters are listed between the square brackets
[c1–c2]	Anything in the range of letters or digits from c1 to c2
[^]	Everything except whatever characters are listed between the square brackets
[^c1–c2]	Everything except the characters in the range of letters or digits from c1 to c2
?	If the character preceding it appears just once or not at all
*	If the character preceding it is missing or if it appears one or more times
+	If the character preceding it appears one or more times
{n}	If the character preceding it appears exactly n times
{n,}	If the character preceding it appears at least n times
{n,m}	If the character preceding it appears at least n times and no more than m times
p1	p2	Pattern p1 or pattern p2

From this table, you can see that an alternative way to write the 10-digit telephone regular expression would be the following:

```
[0-9]{3}-[0-9]{3}-[0-9]{4}
```

Styling invalid fields

One useful thing you can do as a web developer is make it obvious for the user when a form field contains invalid data. Sure, the browser will display its little tooltip to alert the user when they submit the form, but that tooltip stays onscreen for only a few seconds. It would be better to style the invalid field in some way, so the user always knows it needs fixing.

One straightforward way to do that is to take advantage of the CSS :invalid pseudo-selector, which enables you to apply a CSS rule to any invalid field. For example, here's a rule that adds a red highlight around any <input> tag that is invalid:

```css
input:invalid {
    border-color: rgba(255, 0, 0, .5);
    box-shadow: 0 0 10px 2px rgba(255, 0, 0, .8);
}
```

The problem, however, is that the web browser checks for invalid fields as soon as it loads the page. So, for example, if you have fields with the required attribute that are initially empty when the page loads, the browser will flag those as invalid and apply the invalid styling. Your users will be saying, "Gimme a break, I just got here!"

One way to work around this problem is to display an initial message (such as required) beside each required field, and then replace that message with something positive (such as a check mark) when the field is filled in.

Here's some code that does that (bk06ch03/example06.html):

HTML:

```html
<form>
    <div>
        <label for="user-name">Name:</label>
        <input id="user-name"
                type="text"
```

```
                    placeholder="Optional"
                    required>
            <span></span>
        </div>
        <div>
            <label for="user-email">Email:</label>
            <input id="user-email"
                    type="email"
                    placeholder="e.g., you@domain.com"
                    required>
            <span></span>
        </div>
        <button type="submit">Submit</button>
    </form>
```

CSS:

```
input:invalid+span::after {
    content: ' (required) ';
    color: red;
}
input:valid+span::after {
    content: '\2713';
    color: green;
}
```

Note in the HTML code that both fields have the `required` attribute and both fields also have an empty `span` element right after them. Those `span` elements are where you'll put your messages, and that's what the CSS code is doing:

>> The first CSS rule looks for any invalid `input` field, and then uses the adjacent sibling selector (+) to select the `span` that comes immediately after the field. The `::after` pseudo-element adds the content (`required`) to the `span` and colors it red.

>> The second CSS rule is similar, except that it looks for any valid `input` field, and then adds a green check mark (given by Unicode character 2713) to the `span`.

Figure 3-5 shows these rules in action, where the Name field is valid and the Email field is invalid.

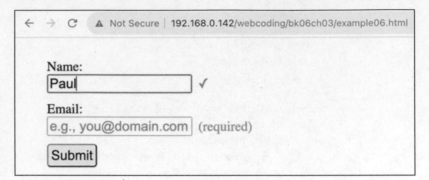

FIGURE 3-5:
The CSS rules
add a green
check mark to
valid fields, and
the red text
(required) to
invalid fields.

Another approach is to use JavaScript to listen for the invalid event firing on any input element. The invalid event fires when the user tries to submit the form and one or more fields contain invalid data. In your event handler, you could then apply a predefined class to the invalid field. Here's some code that does just that (bk06ch03/example07.html):

HTML:

```
<form>
    <div>
        <label for="user-name">Name:</label>
        <input id="user-name"
               type="text"
               placeholder="Your name"
               required>
    </div>
    <div>
        <label for="user-email">Email:</label>
        <input id="user-email"
               type="email"
               placeholder="e.g., you@domain.com"
               required>
    </div>
    <button type="submit">Submit</button>
</form>
```

CSS:

```
.error {
    border-color: rgba(255, 0, 0, .5);
    box-shadow: 0 0 10px 2px rgba(255, 0, 0, .8);
}
```

```
input:valid {
    border-color: lightgray;
    box-shadow: none;
}
```

JavaScript:

```
const inputs = document.querySelectorAll('input');
for (const input of inputs) {
    input.addEventListener('invalid', () => {
        input.classList.add('error');
    });
}
```

The HTML code is the same as in the preceding example, minus the extra `<span>` tags. The CSS code defines a rule for the error class that uses border-color and box-shadow to add a red-tinged highlight to an element. The input:valid selector removes the border and box shadow when the field becomes valid. The JavaScript code loops through all the input elements and adds to each an event listener for the invalid event. When that event fires, the event handler adds the error class to the input element.

Validating Form Data on the Server

You might have looked at the title of this section and cried, "The server! But we just went through validating form data in the browser! Surely we don't have to validate on the server, as well!?" First of all, calm down. Second, yep, it would be nice if we lived in a world where validating form data in the web browser was good enough. Alas, that Shangri-La doesn't exist. The problem, you see, is that a few folks are still surfing with very old web browsers that don't support either `<input>` tag types, such as number, email, and date, or browser-based validation. It's also possible that someone might, innocently or maliciously, bypass your form and send data directly to the server (say, by using a URL query string).

Either way, you can't be certain that the data that shows up on the server's doorstep has been validated, so it's up to your server script to ensure that the data is legit before processing it. Happily, as you see in the next few sections, PHP is loaded with features that make validating data straightforward and painless.

Checking for required fields

If one or more fields in your form are mandatory, you can check those fields on the server by using PHP's `empty()` function:

```
empty(expression)
```

where *expression* is the literal, variable, expression, or function result that you want to test.

The `empty()` function returns FALSE if the expression exists and has a non-empty, non-zero value; it returns TRUE otherwise.

I'll go through a complete example that shows one way to handle validation errors on the server. First, here's some HTML (bk06ch03/example08.html):

```html
<form>
    <div>
        <label for="user-name">Name</label>
        <input id="user-name"
               type="text"
               name="user-name">
    </div>
    <div>
        <label for="user-email">Email</label>
        <input id="user-email"
               type="email"
               name="user-email">
    </div>
    <button type="submit" onclick="submitForm()">Submit</button>
</form>
<article class="output"></article>
```

The form has two text fields, and there's also an `<article>` tag that you'll use a bit later to output the server results.

On the server, I created a PHP file named `validate-required-fields.php`:

```php
<?php
    header('Content-Type: application/json');
    header('Access-Control-Allow-Origin: *');

    // Store the default status
    $server_results['status'] = 'success';
```

```php
    // Check the user-name field
    if(isset($_GET['user-name'])) {
        $user_name = $_GET['user-name'];
        // Is it empty?
        if(empty($user_name)) {
            // If so, update the status and add an error message
for the field
            $server_results['status'] = 'error';
            $server_results['user-name'] = 'Missing user name';
        }
    }
    // Check the user-email field
    if(isset($_GET['user-email'])) {
        $user_email = $_GET['user-email'];
        // Is it empty?
        if(empty($user_email)) {
            // If so, update the status and add an error message
for the field
            $server_results['status'] = 'error';
            $server_results['user-email'] = 'Missing email
address';
        }
    }
    // If status is still "success", add the success message
    if($server_results['status'] === 'success') {
        $message = "Success! Thanks for submitting the form,
$user_name.";
        $server_results['message'] = $message;
    }
    // Create and then output the JSON data
    $JSON_data = json_encode($server_results, JSON_HEX_APOS |
JSON_HEX_QUOT);
    echo $JSON_data;
?>
```

This script uses the $server_results associative array to store the data that gets sent back to the browser. At first the array's status key is set to success. Then the script checks the user-name field from the $_GET array: If the field is empty, the array's status key is set to error and an array item is added that sets an error message for the field. The same process is then used for the user-email field. If after those checks the array's status key is still set to success (meaning there were no validation errors), the array is updated with a success message. Finally, the array is converted to JSON and outputted.

A successful submission outputs JSON that looks like this:

```
{
    "status": "success",
    "message": "Success! Thanks for submitting the form, Paul."
}
```

An unsuccessful submission outputs JSON that looks like this:

```
{
    "status": "error",
    "user-name": "Missing user name",
    "user-email": "Missing email address"
}
```

Back on the client, the form element's submit event handler converts and submits the form data, and then processes the result (bk06ch03/example08.html):

```
async function submitForm(event) {

    event.preventDefault();

    // Get a reference to the form
    const form = document.querySelector('form');

    // Gather the form data
    const formData = new FormData(form);

    // Create the query string
    const queryParams = new URLSearchParams(formData).
    toString();

    // Submit the data as a GET request
    const response = await fetch(`http://localhost/php/validate-
    required-fields.php?${queryParams}`);

    // Parse the data asynchronously
    const data = await response.json();

    // Get a reference to the output element, then display it
    const output = document.querySelector('.output');
    output.style.display = 'block';

    // Check the validation status
    if(data.status === 'success') {
```

```
            // Output the success result
            output.innerHTML = data.message;
    } else {
            // Output the validation error(s)
            let outputString = '<section>Whoops! There were
errors:</section>';
        for (const key in data) {
            if (data.hasOwnProperty(key)) {
                if (key != 'status') {
                    // Get the label text
                    const label = document.querySelector(`label
[for=${key}]`).innerText;
                    outputString += `<section>Error in ${label}
field: ${data[key]}</section>`;
                }
            }
        }
        // Output the error result
        output.innerHTML = outputString;
    }
}
```

The asynchronous function gathers the form data, creates a query string from
that data, and uses fetch() to submit the data using a GET request. The function
then uses response.json() to parse the JSON returned by the server. After setting
up the output element, the function checks the value of data.status: If it equals
success, the script's success message is displayed. Otherwise, the for() loop
adds each error message to the output element. Figure 3-6 shows an example.

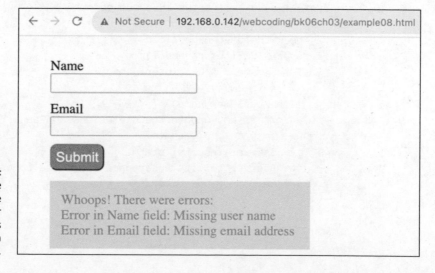

FIGURE 3-6:
Some
example
validation error
messages
returned from
the server script.

Validating text data

Besides validating that a text field exists, you might also want to perform two other validation checks on a text field:

» **The field contains alphabetic characters only:** To ensure that the field contains only lowercase or uppercase letters, use the ctype_ alpha() function:

```
ctype_alpha(text)
```

where *text* is your form field's text data. The ctype_alpha() function returns TRUE if the field contains only letters or FALSE otherwise.

» **The field length is greater than or equal to some minimum value, less than or equal to some maximum value, or both.** To check the length of the field, use the strlen() function:

```
strlen(text)
```

where *text* is your form field's text data. The strlen() function returns the number of characters in the field.

Here's some PHP code that performs these checks on a form field called user-name (and bk06ch03/example09.html gives this script a whirl):

```php
<?php
    header('Content-Type: application/json');
    header('Access-Control-Allow-Origin: *');

    // Store the default status
    $server_results['status'] = 'success';

    // Check the user-name field
    if(isset($_GET['user-name'])) {
        $user_name = $_GET['user-name'];
        // Is it empty?
        if(empty($user_name)) {
            // If so, update the status and add an error message
    for the field
            $server_results['status'] = 'error';
            $server_results['user-name'] = 'Missing user name';
        } else {
```

```php
            // Does it contain non-alphabetic characters?
            if(!ctype_alpha($user_name)){
                // If so, update the status and add an error
message for the field
                $server_results['status'] = 'error';
                $server_results['user-name'] = 'User name must
be text';
            } else {
                // Does the user name contains less than 3 or
more than 12 characters?
                if(strlen($user_name) < 3 || strlen($user_name)
> 12) {
                    // If so, update the status and add an error
message for the field
                    $server_results['status'] = 'error';
                    $server_results['user-name'] = 'User name
must be 3 to 12 characters long';
                }
            }
        }
    }
    // If status is still "success", add the success message
    if($server_results['status'] === 'success') {
        $message = "Success! Thanks for submitting the form,
$user_name.";
        $server_results['message'] = $message;
    }
    // Create and then output the JSON data
    $JSON_data = json_encode($server_results, JSON_HEX_APOS |
JSON_HEX_QUOT);
    echo $JSON_data;
?>
```

Validating a field based on the data type

If you want to ensure the value of a field is a particular data type, PHP offers a powerful function called filter_var() that can help:

```php
filter_var(var, filter, options)
```

where:

>> *var* is the variable, expression, or function result you want to check.

>> *filter* is an optional constant value that determines the data type you want to check. Here are some useful filters:

- FILTER_VALIDATE_BOOLEAN: Checks for a Boolean value

- FILTER_VALIDATE_EMAIL: Checks for a valid email address

- FILTER_VALIDATE_FLOAT: Checks for a floating-point value

- FILTER_VALIDATE_INT: Checks for an integer value

- FILTER_VALIDATE_URL: Checks for a valid URL

>> *options* is an optional array that sets one or more options for the *filter*. For example, FILTER_VALIDATE_INT accepts the options min_range and max_range, which set the minimum and maximum allowable integers. Here's the setup for a minimum of 0 and a maximum of 100:

```
array('options' => array('min_range' => 0,
    'max_range' => 100))
```

The filter_var() function returns the data if it's valid according to the specified filter; if the data isn't valid, the function returns FALSE (or NULL, if you're using FILTER_VALIDATE_BOOLEAN).

Here's an example script (validate-integer-fields.php) that checks for integer values within an allowable range (bk06ch03/example10.html calls this script):

```php
<?php
    header('Content-Type: application/json');
    header('Access-Control-Allow-Origin: *');

    // Store the default status
    $server_results['status'] = 'success';

    // Check the user-age field
    if(isset($_GET['user-age'])) {
        $user_age = $_GET['user-age'];
        // Is it empty?
        if(empty($user_age)) {
            // Add an error message for the field
            $server_results['status'] = 'error';
            $server_results['user-age'] = 'Missing age value';
        } else {
```

```php
            // Is the field not an integer?
            if(!filter_var($user_age, FILTER_VALIDATE_INT)){
                // Add an error message for the field
                $server_results['status'] = 'error';
                $server_results['user-age'] = 'Age must be an
integer';
            } else {
                // Is the age not between 14 and 114?
                $options = array('options' => array('min_range'
=> 14, 'max_range' => 114));
                if(!filter_var($user_age, FILTER_VALIDATE_INT,
$options)) {
                    // Add an error message for the field
                    $server_results['status'] = 'error';
                    $server_results['user-age'] = 'Age must be
between 14 and 114';
                }
            }
        }
    }
    // If status is "success", add the success message
    if($server_results['status'] === 'success') {
        $message = "Success! You don't look a day over " .
intval($user_age - 1) . ".";
        $server_results['message'] = $message;
    }
    // Create and then output the JSON data
    $JSON_data = json_encode($server_results, JSON_HEX_APOS |
JSON_HEX_QUOT);
    echo $JSON_data;
?>
```

The script uses filter_var($user_age, FILTER_VALIDATE_INT) twice: first without and then with the *options* parameter. The first instance just checks for an integer value, whereas the second checks for an integer between 14 and 114. The integer check is redundant here, but I added both so you could get a feel for how filter_var() works.

Validating against a pattern

If you want to use a regular expression to validate a field value, PHP says "No problem!" by offering you the preg_match() function. Here's the simplified syntax:

```
preg_match(pattern, string)
```

where:

>> *pattern* is the regular expression, which you enter as a string. Note, too, that the regular expression must be surrounded by slashes (/).

>> *string* is the string (such as a form field value) that you want to match against the regular expression.

The `preg_match()` function returns `TRUE` if `string` matches `pattern`, and `FALSE` otherwise.

For example, suppose you want to check an account number to ensure that it uses the pattern AA-12345 — that is, two uppercase letters, a hyphen, and then five numbers. Assuming that the value is stored in a variable named `$account_number`, here's a `preg_match()` function that will validate the variable (refer to validate-with-pattern.php and bk06ch03/example11.html in this book's example files):

```
preg_match('/[A-Z]{2}-[0-9]{5}/', $account_number)
```

Regular Expressions Reference

TECHNICAL STUFF

You can validate form data using regular expressions either in the web browser by adding a `pattern` attribute to the field or on the server by using PHP's `preg_match()` function. To help you get the most out of these powerful techniques, the rest of this chapter takes you through some examples that show you how to use the regular expression symbols. In the examples that follow, remember to surround the regular expression with slashes (/) when you use it in the `preg_match()` function; you don't need the slashes when you use the regular expression as a `pattern` attribute value.

Here are the symbols you can use in your regular expressions:

>> \d: Matches any digit from 0 through 9:

Regular Expression	String	Match?
\d\d\d	"123"	Yes
\d\d\d\d	"123"	No
\d\d\d	"12C"	No
\d\d\d-\d\d\d-\d\d\d\d	"123-555-6789"	Yes

» \D: Matches any character that's not a digit from 0 through 9:

Regular Expression	String	Match?
\D\D\D	"AB!"	Yes
\D\D\D	"A1B"	No
\D-\D\D\D\D	"A-BCDE"	Yes

» \w: Matches any character that's a letter, a digit, or an underscore (_):

Regular Expression	String	Match?
\w\w\w	"F1"	Yes
\w\w\w	"F+1"	No
A\w\	"A"	Yes
A\w\	"A!"	No

» \W: Matches any character that's not a letter, a digit, or an underscore (_):

Regular Expression	String	Match?
\W\W\W\W	"<!--"	Yes
\W\W\W	"<a>"	No
1\W\	"10"	No
1\W\	"1!"	Yes

» . (dot): Matches any character that's not a newline:

Regular Expression	String	Match?
. . . .	"ABCD"	Yes
. . . .	"123"	No
A. .	"A@B"	Yes

» \s: Matches any whitespace character, such as the space, tab (\t), newline (\n), and carriage return (\r):

Regular Expression	String	Match?
\d\d\d\s\d\d\d\d	"123 4567"	Yes
\d\d\d\s\d\d\d\d	"123–4567"	No
\d\d\d\s\d\d\d\d	"123 4567"	No

» \S: Matches any non-whitespace character:

Regular Expression	String	Match?
\d\d\d\S\d\d\d\d	"123 4567"	No
\d\d\d\S\d\d\d\d	"123–4567"	Yes
A\SB	"A+B"	Yes

» []: Matches whatever characters are listed between the square brackets. The [] symbol also accepts a range of letters or digits or both:

Regular Expression	String	Match?
[+–]\d\d\d	"+123"	Yes
[+–]\d\d\d	"$123"	No
[2468]–A	"2-A"	Yes
[2468]–A	"1-A"	No
[(]\d\d\d[)]\d\d\d–\d\d\d\d	"(123)555-6789"	Yes
[A–Z]\d\d\d	"A123"	Yes
[A–Z]\d\d\d	"a123"	No
[A–Za–z]\d\d\d	"a123"	Yes
[0–5]A	"3A"	Yes
[0–5]A	"6A"	No
[0–59]A	"9A"	Yes

REMEMBER

Remember that the range [0–59] matches the digits 0 to 5 or 9 and *not* the range 0 to 59.

» [^] : Matches everything but whatever characters are listed between the square brackets. As with the [] symbol, you can use letter or digit ranges.

Regular Expression	String	Match?
[^+−]\d\d\d	"+123"	No
[^+−]\d\d\d	"123"	Yes
[^2468]−A	"2-A"	No
[^2468]−A	"1-A"	Yes
[^A−Z]\d\d\d	"A123"	No
[^A−Z]\d\d\d	"a123"	Yes
[^A−Za−z]\d\d\d	"#123"	Yes
[^0−5]A	"3A"	No
[^0−5]A	"6A"	Yes
[^0−59]A	"9A"	No

» \b: Matches one or more characters if they appear on a word boundary (that is, at the beginning or the end of a word). If you place \b before the characters, it matches if they appear at the beginning of a word; if you place \b after the characters, it matches if they appear at the end of a word.

Regular Expression	String	Match?
\bode	"odeon"	Yes
\bode	"code"	No
ode\b	"code"	Yes
ode\b	"odeon"	No
\bode\b	"ode"	Yes

>> \B: Matches one or more characters if they don't appear on a word boundary (the beginning or the end of a word). If you place \B before the characters, it matches if they don't appear at the beginning of a word; if you place \B after the characters, it matches if they don't appear at the end of a word.

Regular Expression	String	Match?
\Bode	"odeon"	No
\Bode	"code"	Yes
ode\B	"code"	No
ode\B	"odeon"	Yes
\Bode\B	"code"	No
\Bode\B	"coder"	Yes

>> ?: Matches if the character preceding it appears just once or not at all:

Regular Expression	String	Match?
e-?mail	"email"	Yes
e-?mail	"e-mail"	Yes
e-?mail	"e--mail"	No
e-?mail	"e:mail"	No

>> *: Matches if the character preceding it is missing or if it appears one or more times:

Regular Expression	String	Match?
e-*mail	"email"	Yes
e-*mail	"e-mail"	Yes
e-*mail	"e--mail"	Yes
e-*mail	"e:mail"	No

>> +: Matches if the character preceding it appears one or more times:

Regular Expression	String	Match?
e-+mail	"email"	No
e-+mail	"e-mail"	Yes
e-+mail	"e--mail"	Yes
e-+mail	"e:mail"	No

>> {n}: Matches if the character preceding it appears exactly n times:

Regular Expression	String	Match?
lo{2}p	"loop"	Yes
lo{2}p	"lop"	No
\d{5}	"12345"	Yes
\d{5}-\d{4}	"12345-6789"	Yes

>> {n, }: Matches if the character preceding it appears at least n times:

Regular Expression	String	Match?
lo{2,}p	"loop"	Yes
lo{2,}p	"lop"	No
lo{2,}p	"looop"	Yes
\d{5,}	"12345"	Yes
\d{5,}	"123456"	Yes
\d{5,}	"1234"	No

» {n,m}: Matches if the character preceding it appears at least *n* times and no more than *m* times:

Regular Expression	String	Match?
lo{1,2}p	"loop"	Yes
lo{1,2}p	"lop"	Yes
lo{1,2}p	"looop"	No
\d{1,5}	"12345"	Yes
\d{1,5}	"123456"	No
\d{1,5}	"1234"	Yes

» ^: Matches if the characters that come after it appear at the beginning of the string:

Regular Expression	String	Match?
^Java	"JavaScript"	Yes
^Java	"HotJava"	No
^[^+-]?\d\d\d	"123"	Yes
^[^+-]?\d\d\d	"+123"	No

» $: Matches if the characters that come before it appear at the end of the string:

Regular Expression	String	Match?
Java$	"JavaScript"	No
Java$	"HotJava"	Yes
\d\d\.\d%$	"12.3%"	Yes
\d\d\.\d%$	"12.30%"	No

TIP

If you need to include one of the characters from a regular expression symbol as a literal in your expression, escape the character by preceding it with a backslash (\). For example, suppose you want to see if a string ends with .com. The following regular expression won't work because the dot (.) symbol represents any character except a newline:

```
.com$
```

To force the regular expression to match only a literal dot, escape the dot, like this:

```
\.com$
```

» |: Place this symbol between two patterns, and the regular expression matches if the string matches one pattern or the other. (Don't confuse this symbol with JavaScript's OR operator: ||.)

Regular Expression	String	Match?
^(\d{5}|\d{5}-\d{4})$	"12345"	Yes
^(\d{5}|\d{5}-\d{4})$	"12345-6789"	Yes
^(\d{5}|\d{5}-\d{4})$	"123456789"	No

REMEMBER

The preceding examples use parentheses to group the two patterns together. With regular expressions, you can use parentheses to group items and set precedence, just as you can with JavaScript expressions. A regular expression of the form ^(*pattern*)$ means that the pattern defines the entire string, not just some of the characters in the string.

Chapter **4**

Coding Static Web Pages

With static HTML, [the] story is pretty simple. You. . .write the code (including your content). Then, once it's on the server, it's always like that. There's no background processing going on — your site is always right there in its finished form.

— BRIAN JACKSON

O ne of the unfortunate hallmarks of web coding and development over the past dozen years or so is an ever-increasing level of complexity for the developer. New web coding frameworks get released alarmingly frequently, with each new "solution" boasting a learning curve even steeper than the previous one. (A *framework*, just so you know, is a set of tools and resources for building and managing websites.) A solid framework is probably a necessity when you're building an enterprise-level site, but do you need one for small or even medium-sized projects?

My answer to that question is a resounding "No!" Precisely zero frameworks are used in this book. (This edition even removed the jQuery code from the previous edition because modern JavaScript no longer needs jQuery.) My belief is that when web development uses nothing but pure HTML, CSS, JavaScript, and PHP, web development is easier to learn and a joy to master. Appreciating the inherent simplicity of using these languages in their pure state has been one of the main goals of this book.

In this chapter, you double-down on that simplicity by exploring the purest kind of website: one that consists of nothing but static HTML, CSS, and JavaScript files.

Static? Dynamic? What Am I Even Talking About?

Before diving into the code, I should take a second to make sure you're comfortable with this chapter's basic dichotomy: static versus dynamic.

First, a *dynamic web page* is one where some of the page content resides in a web server database and where that content can change after the page has been deployed. Why would page content change? Quite a few reasons:

>> If new data gets added to the server database, the web page content changes to reflect that new data.

>> If existing data gets modified on the server database, the web page content changes to reflect that modification.

>> If the user requests different data (say, by submitting a form), the web page content changes to reflect that request.

Dynamic web pages are flexible, but they can be a little on the slow side because the page is relying on a server connection and a database query for at least some of its content. Dynamic web pages can also be user-unfriendly because, especially when using Fetch API POST requests to fetch data, the URL doesn't change, so the user can't bookmark what might appear to be a "new" page or navigate a history of page changes.

To help solve these and other problems, a *static web page* is one where the complete page content is written to an HTML file and that file doesn't change unless you, as the developer, make changes directly to the file and then deploy your changes. With no server connection or database queries in sight, static web pages load blazingly fast and are always bookmarkable and navigable by users.

Building Your Own Static Site Generator

The traditional way of building a static website is to code the HTML files manually, link to whatever images, CSS, and JavaScript the page requires, and then deploy everything to the server. If you need to tweak the content or code, you fire up your trusty editor, make the changes, and then redeploy the file.

This method works fine for the smallest websites, but as your site grows, the inefficiencies become all the more glaring. For example, if you have a navigation bar on each page, adding or changing a link is no big deal for a few pages, but it's a huge timesuck for a few dozen pages. Similarly, if you decide to redesign your site, propagating the new design to more than a handful of pages is no one's idea of a good time.

That's why, once your site grows beyond even just a few pages, you should consider setting up your own *static site generator* (often shortened to *SSG*), which is a server app that consists of the following components:

>> A data structure (such as an array or a MySQL database) that contains the content unique to each page: title, subtitle, text and HTML tags, and so on

>> PHP files that contain the common components of all your pages, such as the page header and footer

>> An HTML file that serves as a template for all your pages

>> A PHP script that brings the above three components together to create each HTML file for your website

The script in that last point is the heart of your SSG, so here's a closer look at how the script works its static magic:

1. If the page content is in a database, connect to the database, use a query to return the data, and then store the data in an array.

2. Set up a loop to iterate through each page in the array. For each page, do the following:

   a. Create an output buffer.

   b. Include your page template in the output buffer.

   c. Write all the buffered content to an HTML file.

At the end of the loop, you'll have a shiny, new set of HTML files, which you can then deploy to the web. (Not sure what a "buffer" is? No worries: All will be revealed shortly.)

Using GitHub to Store Your Static Site Files

Once you've generated your static site files, it's certainly possible to use FTP or a similar technology to upload those files to a web host of your choice. The only downside to this approach is that when you generate new files or revise existing files, you must manually keep track of what's new and changed and then upload those changes as needed. Similarly, if you rename a file or delete a file, you must log in to your server to propagate those changes to the server versions of the files.

That's no great burden, for sure, but in this chapter I'm going to show you a method where you can automate much of the uploading and deployment of your site. The secret is to use GitHub (`https://github.com`) to store your static files. GitHub is an online service for storing and managing the code for programming projects. GitHub is a vast and exceedingly complex tool that's used by programming teams all over the world. Fortunately, for the purposes of your static site projects, you can ignore 99 percent of GitHub's features. Instead, you'll use GitHub to make two things easier for these projects:

>> Use a few simple GitHub commands to quickly and easily upload any changes you make to your static files (including file additions, changes, renames, and deletions).

>> Deploy your static site using a web host that automatically checks your GitHub storage for changes. When the host detects a change — such as a new, changed, renamed, or deleted file — the host redeploys your static site right away.

Best of all, the most popular tools that deploy from your GitHub account offer free web hosting for all but the largest of sites. And since GitHub also offers a free plan, you can deploy almost any static website for exactly zero dollars. Sweet!

Getting started with GitHub

Before getting to the specifics of using GitHub to store your static site files, you need to perform a few housekeeping chores: setting up your GitHub account, generating a personal access token, and installing the Git software. The next three sections provide the details.

Setting up an account

Your first task is to set up a GitHub account, which you can do by navigating to `https://github.com` and then clicking Sign Up. You enter your email address, a password, and a username, and then, after a security check or two, you're good to go. When you get to the point in the process where you're asked to choose a plan, be sure to click Continue for Free.

Generating a personal access token

You'll be accessing your GitHub stuff remotely, so you won't be surprised to hear that there's a tightly guarded security barrier that your GitHub-related commands have to pass through. The method that GitHub uses to prevent unauthorized folks from also being able to pass through that barrier is the *personal access token,* which is a string of 40 random characters. The next item on your GitHub setup to-do list is to generate a personal access code for your static website project. Here's how it's done:

1. **Use your favorite web browser to navigate to** `https://github.com`.

2. **Sign in to your GitHub account, if you're not signed in automatically.**

   GitHub takes you to your Dashboard page.

3. **Click your account avatar in the upper-right corner, and then click Settings.**

4. **At the bottom of the left sidebar, click Developer Settings.**

5. **Select Personal Access Tokens⇨Tokens (Classic).**

6. **Select Generate New Token⇨Generate New Token (Classic).**

   The New Personal Access Token (Classic) page appears.

7. **In the Note text box, name the token.**

8. **In the Expiration list, select when your token expires.**

   When your token expires, you'll need to generate a new one if you still need access. So, you have a couple of ways to go here:

   - If you need access to GitHub for only a certain amount of time (for example, once you've deployed your site, you won't be making any changes to it), set the expiration time to an interval that takes you just beyond the time you need.

   - If you need access to GitHub indefinitely (for example, you expect to make regular changes to your site even after you deploy it), choose whatever expiration interval you're comfortable with. GitHub will send you an email when your token is about to expire, and it's relatively easy to regenerate an existing token.

You might be sorely tempted to choose No Expiration to avoid the hassle of regenerating your token. However, if you choose to give your token no expiration date and it is compromised, you've just given the attacker eternal access to your stuff. It's not worth it.

The rest of the page presents a dishearteningly long list of check boxes that you use to specify what actions can be performed using this token.

9. **To keep things simple, select only the Repo check box, as shown in Figure 4-1.**

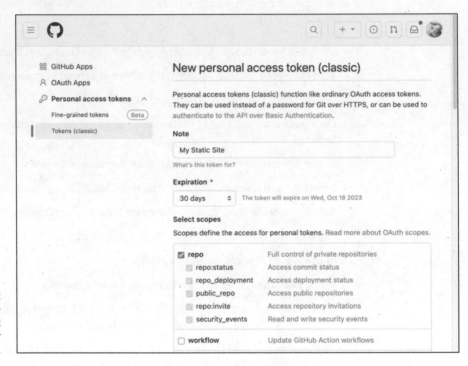

FIGURE 4-1: Select only the Repo check box to make your life easier.

10. **Scroll down to the bottom of the page and then click Generate Token.**

GitHub generates your new token and then displays it, as shown in Figure 4-2.

This is the only time that GitHub will show you the token, so be sure to complete the next two steps to store your token somewhere safe.

11. **Click the copy icon (labeled in Figure 4-2) to the right of your token.**

12. **Paste the token into a file so that you always have a copy of it nearby.**

Make sure the text file isn't stored in a folder that other people can access.

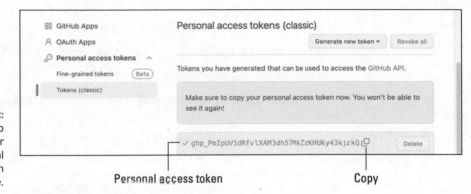

Personal access token   Copy

Installing Git

Your only other startup task is to download the Git software to your computer:

» **Git for Windows:** Head to https://git-scm.com/download/win and download the 32-bit or 64-bit version of Git. (To learn your system type, select Start➪Settings, click System, click About, and then read the System Type text, which will say something like 64-bit operating system.) Run the downloaded file to install Git. (The installer asks a ton of questions, but you're fine leaving the default options selected throughout the install procedure.)

» **Git for macOS:** Install Homebrew from https://brew.sh/. Then open Terminal, type **brew install git**, and then press Return to install Git.

Setting up a GitHub repository for your project

A GitHub storage location is called a *repository* (often shortened to *repo*) and you typically set up one repository for each of your static website projects. Here are the steps to follow to create a new repository on the GitHub website:

1. **Use your closest web browser to navigate to** https://github.com.

2. **Sign in to your GitHub account, if you're not signed in automatically.**

   GitHub takes you to your Dashboard page.

3. **Start a new repo using one of the following methods:**

   ● If you see the Create Your First Project sidebar, click the Create Repository button.

- If you see the Top Repositories sidebar, click New.

- Click Create New (+) in the GitHub toolbar, and then click New Repository.

  You end up at the Create a New Repository page.

4. **In the repository name text box, type the name you want to use for your repo.**

   Your name can be any combination of letters, numbers, hyphens (-), underscores (_), and periods (.). As you type your repo name, GitHub checks to make sure you haven't already used the name in your account and, as shown in Figure 4-3, tells you the name is available if you haven't.

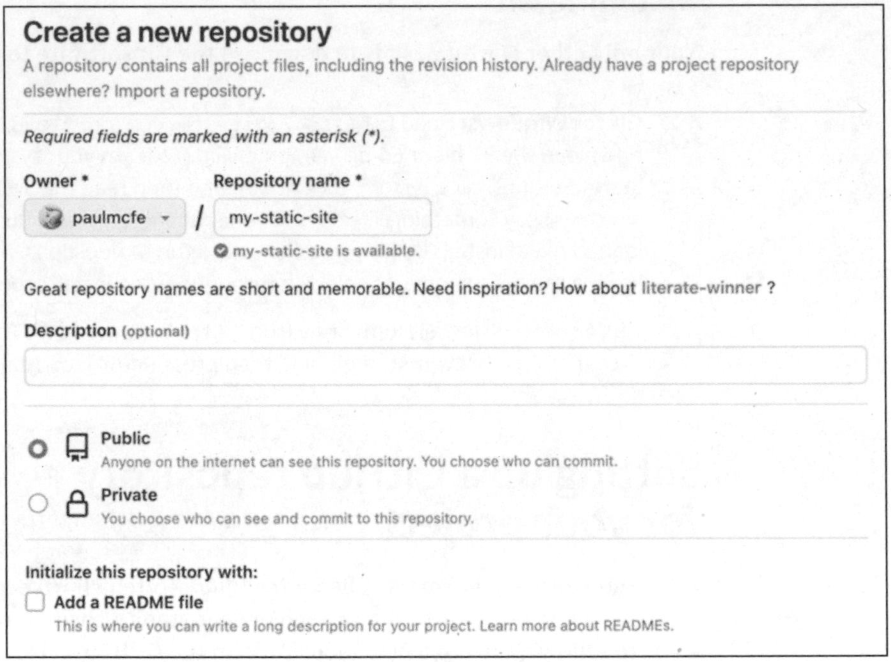

Create a new repository

A repository contains all project files, including the revision history. Already have a project repository elsewhere? Import a repository.

Required fields are marked with an asterisk (*).

Owner *   **Repository name ***

🐙 paulmcfe ▾ / my-static-site

✅ my-static-site is available.

Great repository names are short and memorable. Need inspiration? How about literate-winner ?

Description (optional)

⠀

○ 🖥 **Public**
Anyone on the internet can see this repository. You choose who can commit.

○ 🔒 **Private**
You choose who can see and commit to this repository.

Initialize this repository with:

☐ **Add a README file**
This is where you can write a long description for your project. Learn more about READMEs.

FIGURE 4-3:
GitHub checks to make sure you haven't already used the name for another repo.

5. **Choose who can access your repo:**

   - *Public:* Anyone with internet access can view your repo's files.

   - *Private:* Only you can see your repo.

   Later you learn how to deploy your repository to GitHub Pages. If you're using a GitHub free account, you must set your repository's visibility to public. (If you want to deploy a private repo, upgrade to a GitHub Pro account.)

6. **Ignore the other repo options and click Create Repository.**

   GitHub creates a new repo for you.

After GitHub creates the repo, it drops you off at the repo's home page, which will look something like the one shown in Figure 4-4. Later, once you've uploaded your static site files, a list of those files will appear here.

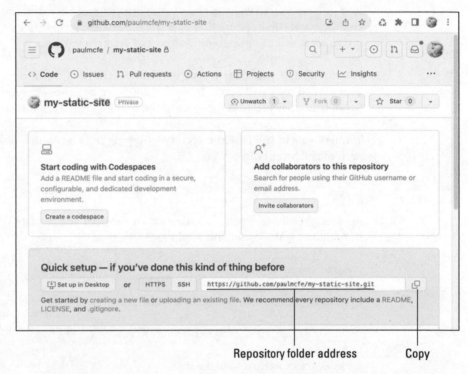

FIGURE 4-4:
The repo home
page includes
the all-important
address of
the repository
folder (.git).

You don't need worry about too much here, with the important exception of the location of the repository folder, which is the .git URL pointed out in Figure 4-4. You're going to need this address when you clone the repo in the next section.

Cloning the GitHub repository to your computer

Once you've created a repo on GitHub, you're ready to make a local copy of the repo on your computer. In GitHub lingo, making a local copy is called *cloning* the repo.

To get started, first open your computer's command-line app:

>> **Windows 11:** Press Win+S to start a search, type **terminal**, and then click the Terminal app in the search results. (Alternatively, type **cmd** and then click the Command Prompt app.)

>> **macOS:** Click the Spotlight icon in the menu bar, type **terminal**, and then click the Terminal app in the search results.

With the command line in front of you, your first task is to navigate to the directory into which you want to clone your GitHub repo. Note that the cloning process creates a new subdirectory that uses the repo name, so in this step you're navigating to what will be the parent directory of your cloned repo.

For example, if you clone a repo named `my-static-site` into `c:\xampp\htdocs`, your cloned repo will reside in the `c:\xampp\htdocs\my-static-site` directory. So, in this case, you first navigate to the `c:\xampp\htdocs` directory.

You navigate to the parent directory by typing the `cd` command, a space, and the path of the parent directory:

```
cd path-to-parent-directory
```

Replace `path-to-parent-directory` with the path you want to use. For example, in Windows 11 the command might look like this:

```
cd c:\xampp\htdocs
```

In macOS, the command might look like this:

```
cd /Applications/XAMPP/xamppfiles/htdocs
```

Press Enter or Return to make it so.

With that done, clone the repo by running the `git clone` command, followed by Enter or Return:

```
git clone repository-folder-url.git
```

Replace `repository-folder-url.git` with the URL of your repo folder, as pointed out earlier in Figure 4-4. Here's an example:

```
git clone https://github.com/paulmcfe/my-static-site.git
```

TIP

One easy way to avoid typos is to click the copy icon to the right of the URL (refer to Figure 4-4). At the command line, type **git clone**, type a space, then paste the copied URL.

You'll be prompted to authenticate your GitHub credentials. There are two possibilities here:

> **» You see the Connect to GitHub dialog box:** Click the Token tab, paste your personal access token into the text box (as shown in Figure 4-5), then click Sign In.

FIGURE 4-5:
In the
Connect to
GitHub
dialog box, use
the Token tab
to paste your
personal
access code.

> **» You see a command line prompt for your username:** Type your GitHub username and press Enter or Return. Now you'll be prompted for your password. However, instead of entering your GitHub password here, you need to paste your personal access token. If, after pasting the token, you don't see the token (or even dots representing the token), that's fine: Just press Enter or Return to continue and all will be well.

Either way, if you see a warning along the lines of You appear to have cloned an empty repository, nod your head knowingly and move on with your life.

Once your repo is cloned, navigate to the repo directory with the following command:

```
cd repo-name
```

Replace `repo-name` with the name of your repo.

Staging, committing, and pushing changes to the repository

Your cloned repository is empty now, but you'll soon be adding lots of static files to the directory, editing exiting files, and renaming and deleting files. You need to regularly send all your changes to the remote repository on GitHub. That's a three-step process:

1. *Stage* the changes by telling Git which file or files you want to send:

   ```
   git add .
   ```

2. *Commit* the changes by confirming that you want to send them:

   ```
   git commit -m "Commit message"
   ```

   Replace *Commit message* with a short message describing the changes you made (such as "Updated page title" or "Generated static pages").

3. *Push* the changes by sending them to the remote repo:

   ```
   git push origin main
   ```

   This command tells Git to update the remote repository (designated by origin) with the committed changes from the local repository (designated by main).

Forging Your HTML Template File

I mention earlier that if you were to just cobble together all your static HTML files by hand, a serious time commitment is required when you need to make a significant change to the files. And the more files you have, the more onerous the job.

One of the major timesaving features of getting PHP to generate your static files is that you can regenerate your entire site in seconds flat if you set everything up right. The key to this apparent miracle is that you manually build just a single HTML file, called a *template.* Your PHP script uses that template to build all your other static HTML files. Later, when you want to make a change to your site, you change only the template and then run your PHP script to regenerate all the files based on that changed template. And just like that, you're done!

Here's a template file (refer to bk06ch04/template.php in this chapter's example files) that I'll use as an example:

```
<!doctype html>
<html lang="en">
    <head>
        <meta charset="utf-8">
        <title><?php echo $page['title']; ?></title>
        <link href="styles.css" rel="stylesheet">
    </head>

<body>
        <header>
            <h1>My Static Site</h1>
            <p class="subtitle">"Look, ma, no server!"</p>
        </header>
        <nav>
            <?php include "nav.html" ?>
        </nav>
        <main>
            <article>
                <h2><?php echo $page['title']; ?></h2>
                <h3><?php echo $page['subtitle']; ?></h3>
                <p>
                    <?php echo $page['content']; ?>
                </p>
                <p>
                    Next page: <?php echo $next_page; ?>
                </p>
            </article>
        </main>
        <footer>
            &copy; <?php echo date("Y"); ?> Paul McFedries
        </footer>
    </body>
</html>
```

The first thing to note about this file is that it mostly consists of HTML tags and text. These are the tags and text common to all the site pages.

The nav section contains the following:

```
<?php include "nav.html" ?>
```

This is PHP code to insert the text and code from a file named nav.html. The key here is PHP's include statement:

```
include file;
```

where *file* is the path and name of the file with the code and text you want to include. If the template file and the include file reside in the same directory, you don't need to include the path.

REMEMBER

You have to use the `include` statement only if your static website requires multiple templates. If your site needs just one template file, you might as well just plop the tags and text from the other file directly into the template.

Finally, the template file also includes several instructions to insert the current contents of PHP variables, expressions, and data structures. For example, both the `title` element and the `h2` element include the following:

```
<?php echo $page['title']; ?>
```

As you see a bit later, the PHP script that acts as the static site generator includes an associative array named $page that includes an item named `title` that stores the title of the page currently being generated. The preceding statement uses `echo` to write the current value of `$page['title']`' to the page.

Similarly, the following statement writes the current value of the $next_page variable to the page:

```
<?php echo $next_page; ?>
```

And, in the `footer` element, the following statement writes the current year to the page:

```
<?php echo date("Y"); ?>
```

Using PHP to Generate the Static Pages

Once you've set up your template as I describe in the preceding section, you're ready to code your static site generator in PHP. The assumption with any SSG is that the information unique to each page resides in a data structure somewhere on your server. The basic idea behind any SSG is that you gather all that page data into an array, loop through the array, and within each iteration of the loop you use the current array data to generate that page.

Access the unique page data

The unique page data will almost always reside in a MySQL database. Your SSG would connect to that database, query the database to return the unique page data, and then store the result in an array. However, for this example, I simplify things by using an array of associative arrays, each of which contains the unique page data:

```php
<?php

// Put the unique page data into an array of arrays
$pages = [
    [
        'filename' => 'index.html',
        'title'    => 'Home Page',
        'subtitle' => 'The Home Page Subtitle',
        'content'  => 'This is the content for the home page.'
    ],    [
        'filename' => 'page1.html',
        'title'    => 'Page 1',
        'subtitle' => 'The Page 1 Subtitle',
        'content'  => 'This is the content for Page 1.'
    ],
    [
        'filename' => 'page2.html',
        'title'    => 'Page 2',
        'subtitle' => 'The Page 2 Subtitle',
        'content'  => 'This is the content for Page 2.'
    ],
    [
        'filename' => 'page3.html',
        'title'    => 'Page 3',
        'subtitle' => 'The Page 3 Subtitle',
        'content'  => 'This is the content for Page 3.'
    ]
];
```

Building the rest of the static site generator

The secret sauce of any PHP static site generator is the `ob_start()` function. This function turns on *output buffering*, which means that all PHP output goes to a buffer (essentially a memory location). In particular, anything you `echo`, `print`, or `include` goes into this buffer. Crucially, any file you `include` into the buffer takes on the current scope of the PHP script, so any PHP variables or data structures in that scope get resolved in the included file. So, for the purposes of the SSG, including the template file in the buffer enables that file to access the $pages array as well as any in-scope variables.

Here's the code that loops through the $pages array:

```php
// Set up some variables
$total_pages = count($pages);
$current_page = 1;

// Loop through each page and generate the static HTML file
foreach ($pages as $page) {

    // Start buffering the output
    ob_start();

    // Create the link to the next page
    if ($current_page === $total_pages) {
        $current_page = 1;
        $next_page = '<a href="' . $pages[0]['filename'] . '">'
. $pages[0]['title'] . '</a>';
    } else {
        $next_page = '<a href="' . $pages[$current_page]
['filename'] . '">' . $pages[$current_page]['title'] . '</a>';
    }

    // Include the template file
    include 'template.php';

    // Save the buffered content
    $htmlContent = ob_get_clean();

    // Save the content to the static HTML file
    file_put_contents($page['filename'], $htmlContent);

    echo "Static file " . $page['filename'] . " generated!\r\n";

    // Increment the current page number
    $current_page++;
}
?>
```

After declaring a couple of variables that the code later uses to construct the link to the next page, a foreach loop iterates through the $pages array, with the current page represented as $page. The code runs ob_start() to begin output buffering, and constructs the link to the next page, which gets stored in the $next_page variable. The generator then includes the template.php file to add it to the buffer.

At this point, the script is done outputting stuff to the buffer, so the buffer content is stored as follows:

```
$htmlContent = ob_get_clean();
```

The `ob_get_clean()` function returns the content of the buffer (which gets stored in the $htmlContent variable), and then cleans out the buffer. Next the SSG outputs the content to the static HTML file:

```
file_put_contents($page['filename'], $htmlContent);
```

The `file_put_contents()` function puts what's stored in the $htmlContent variable into the file given by $page['filename'].

Generating the static files

Before you generate your website's static files, make sure all of the following are in the repository folder that Git created earlier when you cloned your GitHub repository:

>> Your HTML template file

>> Your support files (images, CSS files, and so on)

>> Your PHP static site generator file

You can now run the static site generator as follows:

>> **Windows 11:** In Terminal or Command Prompt, navigate to the repository folder, and then run the following command:

```
C:\xampp\php\php ssg
```

>> **macOS:** In Terminal, navigate to the repository folder, and then run the following command:

```
/Applications/xampp/xamppfiles/bin/php ssg
```

In both cases, replace *ssg* with the name of your static site generator file. Also, modify the path if you installed XAMPP in a folder other than the default. When you run the file, you'll see an output similar to the one shown in Figure 4-6.

FIGURE 4-6:
The output of
the static site
generator.

```
● ● ●                          🗀 my-static-site — -zsh — 107×24
paul@Pauls-MacBook-Pro my-static-site % /Applications/xampp/xampppfiles/bin/php generate-static-site.php
Static file index.html generated!
Static file page1.html generated!
Static file page2.html generated!
Static file page3.html generated!
paul@Pauls-MacBook-Pro my-static-site %
```

Pushing your files to GitHub

REMEMBER

Once your static site generator has done its job, it's time to get your files on GitHub. As a refresher, here are the three commands you need to run from the repository folder (pressing Enter or Return after each):

```
git add .
git commit —m "Uploading static files"
git push origin main
```

Repeat as needed each time you make changes to any of your files or each time you regenerate your static pages. (It's a best practice to modify the `commit` message to reflect the change or changes you made.)

With that done, you're ready to deploy your static website.

Deploying Your Static Website

Once you've used your PHP static site generator script to build your static web pages and once you've pushed all your static site files to GitHub, aren't you done? After all, the files are now online, right? True, but a GitHub repository doesn't have the capability of serving your files to web browsers. No, for your static pages to form a true website, you need to deploy them to a web host.

As I mention earlier, it's certainly possible to use FTP to upload your static site files to any web host. However, in this chapter I introduce you to GitHub repositories because you can configure certain web hosts to automatically deploy your website from a specified GitHub repository. Once you have such a web host configured, every time you push changes to your GitHub repository, the web host automatically redeploys your website and your changes are online lickety-split (usually in less than a minute).

Happily, one of the companies that offers such hosting is GitHub itself, which is the easiest route because you've already got a GitHub account set up and you don't have to leave GitHub to configure the deployment. If you're using a GitHub free account, your repository must have public visibility. To deploy a private repository, you need to upgrade to GitHub Pro.

If your repository is currently private, you can switch it to public by displaying the repository on GitHub, clicking Settings (the one in the toolbar, to the right of the Insights command), scrolling down to the bottom of the page (to the ominously named Danger Zone section), clicking Change Visibility, and then clicking Change to Public. Follow the confirmations and other prompts that appear.

I provide the instructions for deploying your static site repository to GitHub Pages, but of course you're free to look elsewhere for hosting. Two free web hosts that can deploy directly from a GitHub repository are Cloudflare Pages (https://pages.cloudflare.com/) and Netlify (https://netlify.com/).

GitHub Pages comes with a few restrictions, but the only ones that matter to you are that your website size can't be larger than 1GB and you get a monthly bandwidth cap of 100GB. (*Bandwidth* is the amount of data per month that your site transfers to web browsers.) These generous caps won't be a problem for your site.

Follow these steps to deploy your repo to GitHub Pages:

1. **Navigate to** https://github.com **and sign in, if you're not signed in already.**

2. **Click the repository you want to deploy.**

   If you don't see the repo in the left sidebar, click Show More to display more repos.

3. **In the repository toolbar, click Settings.**

4. **In the sidebar, click Pages.**

   The repo's GitHub Pages page appears.

5. **In the Branch section, click the drop-down list that currently says None and then click main to select that branch, as shown in Figure 4-7.**

   GitHub adds a Select Folder list, but you can ignore it.

6. **Click Save.**

   GitHub deploys your repo.

Refresh the page and you should now see a message that says Your site is live at *URL*, where *URL* is the address of the Pages site. Figure 4-8 shows an example. Click Visit Site to give your newly deployed static site a test drive.

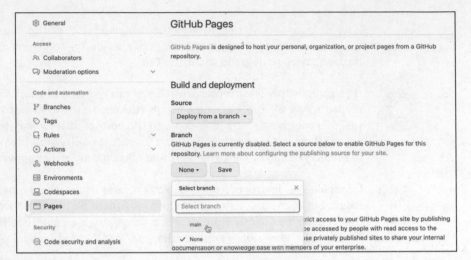

FIGURE 4-7:
Select your repo's
main branch for
the deployment.

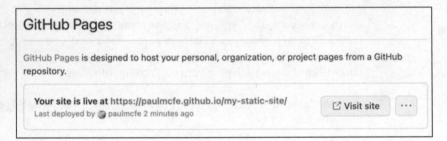

FIGURE 4-8:
Refresh the
page to see the
address of your
repo's Pages
deployment.

TIP

The URL of your GitHub Pages site is `https://username.github.io/repo/`, where `username` is your GitHub username and `repo` is the name of the repo you deployed. However, if you have your own domain name, you can use that name with your deployed site instead. Follow Steps 1 through 4 in the preceding list to display your repo's GitHub Pages page, type your domain in the Custom Domain text box, and then click Save. Follow the instructions that appear for verifying that you own the domain.

7

Building
Web Apps

Contents at a Glance

IN THIS CHAPTER

» Learning about web apps

» Figuring out your app's functionality

» Determining your app's data requirements

» Planning your app's workflow

» Visualizing your app's interface

Chapter **1**

Planning a Web App

What you can do, or dream you can, begin it,

Boldness has genius, power, and magic in it.

— JOHANN WOLFGANG VON GOETHE

There are many reasons to get and stay interested in web coding and development. Here are a just a few: the challenge of learning something new; the confidence that comes from figuring out hard or complex problems; the satisfactions that inhere from getting code to work; the desire to get a job in web development; the feeling that you're operating right at the leading edge of the modern world. These are all great and motivating reasons to code for the web, but there's another reason to dive deep into CSS and JavaScript and all the rest: as an outlet for your creative side.

Sure, anybody who learns a bit of HTML and a few CSS properties can put up pages of information, but as a full-stack web developer who also knows JavaScript, MySQL, and PHP, you have all the tools you need to create bold and beautiful apps for the web. That's where the real creativity lies: having a vision of something cool, interesting, and fun and then using code to realize that vision for other people to see and use. This minibook helps you unleash the right side of your brain and make your creative vision a reality by showing you a few crucial upgrades to your web coding and development skills and know-how. First up: the all-important planning process.

What Is a Web App?

If you go to the web home for a company called Alphabet (https://abc.xyz), you get a general introduction to the company, plus some information for investors, news releases, links to corporate documents such as the company bylaws, and so on. But Alphabet is also the parent company for some of the web's most iconic spots:

>> **Google** (www.google.com): Search the web.

>> **Gmail** (https://mail.google.com): Send and receive email messages.

>> **Google Maps** (https://maps.google.com): Locate and get directions to places using maps.

>> **YouTube** (www.youtube.com): Play and upload videos.

What's the difference between the parent Alphabet site and these other sites? Lots, of course, but I think two differences are most important:

>> Each of the other sites is focused on a single task or topic: searching, emailing, maps, or videos.

>> Each of the other sites offers an interface that enables the user to operate the site in some way. For example, Google has a simple search form, whereas Gmail looks like an email inbox and offers commands such as Compose and Reply.

REMEMBER

In other words, the Alphabet home is a basic website that's really just a collection of documents you can navigate, whereas the likes of Google, Gmail, Google Maps, and YouTube are more like the applications you use on your computer. They are, in short, *web apps*, because although they reside on the web and are built using web technologies such as HTML, CSS, JavaScript, MySQL, and PHP, they enable you to perform tasks and create things just like a computer application does.

Fortunately, you don't have to have an idea for the next YouTube or Gmail to get started coding web apps. (Although, hey, if you do, I say go for it!) Web apps can be anything you want, as long as they enable you or your users to do something. If that something happens to be fun, creative, interesting, or useful, congratulations: You've made the world a better place.

Planning Your Web App: The Basics

If you're like me, when you come up with an exciting idea for a web app, the first thing you want to do is open your trusty text editor and start bashing out some code. That's a satisfying way to go, but believe me, that satisfaction dissipates fast when you're forced to go back and redo a bunch of code or restructure your database because, in your haste, you took a wrong turn and ended up at a dead end or too far from your goal.

I plea, then, for just a bit of restraint so that you can spend the first hour or two of your project thinking about what you want to build and laying out the steps required to get there. Think of it like planning a car trip. You know your destination, but it's unlikely you'll want to just get in the car and start driving in the general direction of your goal. You need to plan your route, load up with supplies such as gas, water, and food, gather tools such as a GPS, and so on. To figure out the web-development equivalents of such things, it helps to ask yourself five questions:

REMEMBER

>> What is my app's functionality?

>> What are my app's data requirements?

>> How will my app work?

>> How many pages will my app require?

>> What will my app's pages look like?

The next few sections go through these questions both in a general way and more specifically with an app idea called FootPower!, which is a simple app for logging and viewing three foot-propelled activities: walking, running, and cycling.

What is my app's functionality?

The first stage in planning any web app is understanding what you want the app to do. You can break this down into two categories:

>> **User functions:** These are the tasks that users performs when they operate whatever controls your app provides. The standard four tasks are given by the unfortunately named CRUD acronym: creating, reading, updating, and deleting.

>> **App functions:** These are tasks that your app performs outside the interface controls. Examples are creating user accounts, signing users in and out, handling forgotten passwords, and backing up data.

For FootPower!, here's a list of the user functions I'd implement:

>> Creating new activities, each of which records activity details such as the type of activity and the activity date, distance, and duration

>> Viewing previous activities, with the capability to filter the activities by date and type

>> Editing an existing activity

>> Deleting an activity

Here are the app functions I'd implement:

>> Creating users

>> Verifying new users by sending a verification email

>> Signing existing users in and out

>> Maintaining users' app settings

>> Handling forgotten passwords

>> Deleting user accounts

What are my app's data requirements?

Web apps don't necessarily have to use a back end. If your web app is a calculator, for example, you'd need to present only the front-end interface to the user; no back-end database or Fetch API calls are required. But if your app requires persistent data — which might be data you supply or data created by each user — you need to store that data in a MySQL database and use Fetch API calls to transfer that data between the browser and the server.

REMEMBER

Before you load up phpMyAdmin, however, you need to sit down and figure out what you want to store in your database. Web app data generally falls into three categories:

>> **User data:** If your app has user accounts, you need to store account data such as the username or email address, the password, profile settings, and site preferences.

>> **User-generated data:** If your app enables users to create things, you need to save that data so that it can be restored to users the next time they sign in.

>> **App data:** If your app presents data to users, you need to store that data in MySQL. You might also want to store behind-the-app-scenes data such as analytics and visitor statistics.

For an app such as FootPower!, the data requirements would fall into two segments:

>> The app would have user accounts, so the app would need a MySQL table to store each account's email address, password, verification status, and a few site preferences.

>> Users would be recording their foot-propelled movements, so the app would need two tables to store this data:

- Each user would create a log of their activities, so the app would need a table to record the data for each of these logs, basically just a unique log ID, the ID of the user who owns the log, and the date the log was created.

- Within each user's log would be the activities themselves, which the app would store in a separate table that includes a unique ID for each activity, the user's log ID, and fields for each chunk of activity data: type, date, distance, and duration.

How will my app work?

REMEMBER

Once you know what you want your app to do and what data your app requires, you're ready to tackle how your app works. This is called the app's *workflow*, and it covers at a high level what the app does and the order in which it does those things. A simple flowchart is usually the way to go here: Just map out what happens from the time users type in your app URL to the time they leave the page.

Figure 1-1 shows the workflow I envision for the FootPower! app.

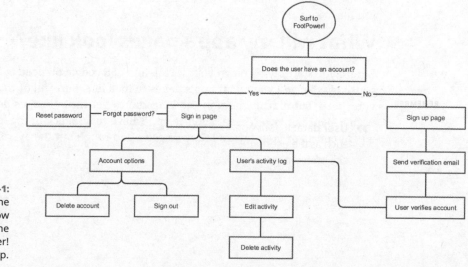

FIGURE 1-1: The workflow for the FootPower! app.

How many pages will my app require?

Your app's workflow should tell you fairly specifically how many pages your app needs. Most web apps are focused on a single set of related tasks, so your users will spend most of their time on the page that provides the app's main interface, usually the home page. However, your app will need other pages to handle tasks such as registering users, signing in users, and displaying account options. Record every page you need; this information will act as an overall to-do list for the front end.

Here's a potential list of pages for the FootPower! app:

>> The home page, which would require two versions:

- The unregistered or signed-out version of the home page, which would serve as a kind of ad for the app

- The signed-in version, which would show the user's activity log and enable log-based tasks such as creating, filtering, editing, and deleting activities

>> A page that enables new users to register

>> A page letting new users know that a verification email has been sent

>> A sign-in page

>> A page that enables the user to edit and delete activities

>> A password reset page

>> An account options page

>> An account delete page

What will my app's pages look like?

Before you start laying down your HTML and CSS code, you need to have a decent sense of what you want your app's pages to look like. Sure, all of that might be in your head, but it really pays in the long run to get those images down on paper with a sketch or two. These sketches don't have to be fancy in the least. Just take a pen, pencil, or your favorite Crayola color and rough out the overall structure.

Simple forms (such as those for signing in or resetting a password) don't require much effort, but for more elaborate pages, such as your app's home page, you need to flesh out the design a bit: header, navigation, main content, sidebar, footer, and so on.

Figure 1-2 shows an example sketch for the FootPower! app's home page.

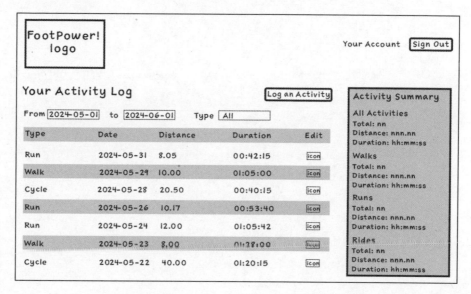

FIGURE 1-2:
A sketch of the home page for the FootPower! app.

With your web app plan in place, you're ready to start coding the app. In the next chapter, you learn how to make your web app's layout responsive.

IN THIS CHAPTER

» **Using Flexbox, Grid, and viewport units for fluid layouts**

» **Using media, container, and user preference queries for adaptive layouts**

» **Making your page typography responsive**

» **Delivering images responsively**

» **Getting to know the mobile-first approach to layout**

Chapter **2**

Making a Web App Responsive

The web's greatest strength, I believe, is often seen as a limitation, as a defect. It is the nature of the web to be flexible, and it should be our role as designers and developers to embrace this flexibility and produce pages which, by being flexible, are accessible to all.

— JOHN ALLSOP

A web app is something like the online equivalent of a desktop program, but that doesn't mean you should build your web app to look good and work properly only on desktop-sized screens. Why not? For the simple reason that your app's visitors will be using a wide range of device sizes, from PCs with gigantic displays several feet wide, all the way down to smartphones with screens just a few inches wide. On the modern web, one size definitely does not fit all, so you need to plan your app so that its *user experience* (*UX*, to the cognoscenti) — that is, what visitors see and interact with — is positive for everyone.

In this chapter, you investigate the rich world of responsive web design, which enables your web app to work well and look good on everything from a smartphone to smart TV. You learn how to use Flexbox or Grid or both to make your layouts fluid with just a few properties; how to use queries to make your layouts adaptive; and how to deliver images with responsiveness in mind. You also dive into the biggest trend in web app layout: the mobile-first approach.

Defining a Responsive Layout

To make your web app look good and operate well on any size screen, you need to plan your app with responsiveness in mind. A *responsive* web app is one that changes its layout, styling, and often also its content to ensure that the app works on whatever screen size or device type the reader is using.

To understand why you need to code responsively from the start of your web app, consider the two main nonresponsive layouts you could otherwise use:

>> **Fixed width:** A layout in which the width of the content is set to a fixed size. In this case, if the fixed width is greater than the width of the screen, most of the time the user must scroll horizontally to get to all the content, as shown in Figure 2-1 (check out bk07ch02/example01.html in this book's example files).

FIGURE 2-1:
When a web app has a fixed width, users with small screens must scroll horizontally to get to all the content.

>> **No width:** A layout in which the content has no set width. You may think that having no width would enable the text and images to wrap nicely on a small screen, and you'd be right. However, the problem is on larger screens, where your text lines expand to fill the browser width. As shown in Figure 2-2 (check out bk07ch02/example02.html), those lines can become ridiculously long, to the point where scanning the lines becomes just about impossible.

You could describe both of these scenarios as "don't-care" layouts, because neither one concerns itself with what device or screen size is being used. If you don't want to be a "don't-care" developer, you need to build "care" into your web apps right from the start. How do you do that? By taking all (not some, *all*) of the following into account with each line of code you write:

>> **Device type:** These days, people who surf to your app may be using a phone, tablet, notebook computer, desktop computer, or any of the various smart devices now available: TV, watch, refrigerator, lawn mower, and so on. All these devices have different screen sizes, and your goal should be to design your app so that it looks good and works well on every screen size.

>> **Browser window size:** Not every computer user who visits your app will do so with their browser window maximized. Some people prefer a relatively small window; others choose to use their operating system's split-screen feature; still others may dynamically resize the browser window depending on your app content. The point is that you can't design your app with the idea that your visitors will use only a few common viewport sizes.

>> **Screen orientation:** Smartphone and tablet users can easily switch their devices from portrait to landscape orientation, and some swivel (or rotating) monitors can also make the same switch. Your app needs to gracefully handle the change from one orientation to another without breaking a sweat.

>> **User zoom level:** Some folks navigate the web with their browser's zoom level cranked up. That is, instead of the default 100 percent zoom level, some

people use 125, 150, or even 200 percent. Your app should still be readable and usable even at these higher magnifications.

>> **User default font size:** Rather than (or sometimes in addition to) raising the zoom level, some people amp up the default font size from 16px to 20px, 24px, 32px, or even higher. Your app should not only honor that change (by not styling your font sizes using an absolute unit, such as pixels) but also look okay and work properly at these higher font sizes.

>> **User preferences:** Many of the people who visit your app will have customized their operating system to use settings such as dark mode, high-contrast colors, and reduced motion in animation effects. Your app should acknowledge these preferences by checking for them and implementing the necessary CSS when a preference is detected.

>> **Device and network performance:** Lots of people traipse the web using underpowered devices, slow network connections, and limited bandwidth. Your app shouldn't leave these people behind by burdening them with unnecessary data or features.

TIP

You can use your browser's dev tools to simulate slower network speeds. In Chrome (most other browsers are similar), open the dev tools (for example, by right-clicking the web page and then clicking Inspect), click the Network tab, click the Throttling list (it says No Throttling, by default), and then select a network speed: Fast 3G, Slow 3G, or even Offline. You can also click Add to create a custom throttling profile. To simulate a slower device CPU, click the Performance tab, click the capture settings icon (gear), and then use the CPU list to select a slowdown option (4x Slowdown or 6x Slowdown). You can now reload your app to test its performance with these simulated slowdowns in place.

A responsive web app is one that successfully handles all these different scenarios. That might sound like a daunting task, but modern CSS is powerful enough that you can get all or most of the way to your responsive goal by adopting one of the following approaches:

>> **Fluid layout:** A layout that adjusts smoothly in response to small changes in the browser environment, such as a changing viewport size

>> **Adaptive layout:** A layout that adjusts only when certain predefined criteria are met, such as the viewport width crossing a specified threshold

REMEMBER

Note that these are not either/or choices. Relatively simple apps may use only fluid or only adaptive techniques, but more complex apps may combine elements of both techniques.

The next two sections explain fluid and adaptive layouts in more detail.

Going with the Flow: Fluid Layouts

The early days of responsive design were all about desktop versus mobile users, to the point where CSS designers were required to build *two* entirely separate sites: one site that worked fine on desktops and another site that was optimized for mobile users.

That strategy was madness, for sure, but there remains a lingering odor of the desktop/mobile dyad in modern web development circles, where it's common to use responsive techniques (usually media queries; check out the section "Querying Your Way to Responsiveness: Adaptive Layouts," later in this chapter) to make sure an app looks good on mobile device screens and in browser windows maximized on desktop monitors, but that's it. However, I guarantee that a large percentage of your users will visit your app using a browser window that's in between those sizes.

To ensure that your app looks good and works the way it should no matter what size browser window the user has, or even when the user changes the window size on the fly, you need to build your app using fluid-layout techniques. What is a fluid layout, anyway? It's a big subject, but for this section's purposes, I can narrow it to the following:

>> Block-level elements naturally fill the space available.

>> Block-level elements expand as the viewport expands and shrink as the viewport shrinks.

>> Block-level elements wrap onto multiple rows (or columns) naturally as the viewport gets smaller.

>> Large text (not body text) expands and contracts along with the viewport.

>> Image sizes expand and contract along with the viewport.

In the ideal fluid layout, you use CSS to give the web browser a few guidelines about how you want your layout to work, but then you leave it up to the browser to figure out the rest.

How Flexbox makes an app fluid

The best strategy you can use to create a fluid layout is to deploy Flexbox for one-dimensional layouts and CSS Grid for two-dimensional layouts. I discuss CSS Grid in the next section. Here I focus on the inherent responsiveness of Flexbox-based layouts. (Check out Book 2, Chapter 4 for all the Flexbox details.)

First, you can get flex items to naturally fill the space available in the flex container *and* expand and contract along with the viewport by adding a single declaration to each flex item:

```
flex: 1;
```

This is equivalent to setting the following three declarations:

```
flex-grow: 1;
flex-shrink: 1;
flex-basis: 0;
```

flex-grow: 1 enables the items to expand along the primary axis as the viewport size changes; flex-shrink: 1 enables the items to contract along the primary axis as the viewport size changes; and flex-basis: 0 sets no restriction on the size of the items (except for not shrinking any smaller than the minimum content size).

If all your flex items have similar content and similar box model properties (padding, and so on), setting flex: 1 on each item means you end up with equal-size columns (if you're using flex-direction: row) or rows (if you're using flex-direction: column).

Setting flex: 1 on all flex items means you're not particular about the item sizes in the main axis direction (such as width for flex-direction: row). However, for many layouts, you'll want some control over item sizes, such as setting minimum widths for an article element and an aside element. If these elements normally lay out side by side, you'll have an overflow problem when the viewport width shrinks below the combined minimum widths of the two elements. To fix that problem fluidly, tell the browser to wrap the flex items when there isn't enough room to display them side by side:

```
flex-wrap: wrap;
```

For example, check out the following code (bk07ch02/example03.html):

HTML (abbreviated version):

```
<header>
    ...
</header>
<nav>
    ...
</nav>
```

```
<main>
    <article>
        <h2>
            Irate Grammarians Will See <em>You</em> in Court,
    Mister!
        </h2>
        <p>
            KALAMAZOO, Michigan—A group of disgruntled
    grammarians calling themselves "Mad, We Are, As Hell" has
    filed a number of civil lawsuits over the past few weeks.
    The targets of these suits are writers, raconteurs, and
    professional man-in-the-street interviewees who, they claim,
    are inveterate violators of the rules of grammar.
        </p>
        etc.
    </article>
    <aside>
        <h3>Related Stories</h3>
        <p>
            It's Official: Teen Instant Messages Nothing But
    Gibberish
        </p>
        etc.
    </aside>
</main>
```

CSS:

```
body {
    max-width: 60rem;
}
main {
    display: flex;
    flex-wrap: wrap;
}
article {
    flex: 3;
    min-width: 22rem;
}
aside {
    flex: 1;
    min-width: 16rem;
}
```

This `main` element is a two-column flex container: an `article` element on the left and an `aside` element on the right. The `body` element has a maximum width of `60rem` that's inherited by the `main` element, so by setting `flex: 3` on the `article` element and `flex: 1` on the `aside` element, these columns take up the full width of the container, as shown in the desktop screen in Figure 2-3.

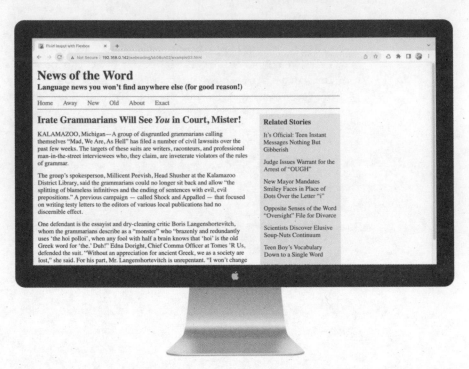

FIGURE 2-3:
The web app as it appears in a desktop browser viewport.

The code also sets minimum widths on the `article` element (`22rem`) and the `aside` element (`16rem`), so when the browser viewport width drops below `38rem` (the combined minimum widths of the two elements), the `main` element's `flex-wrap: wrap` declaration kicks in, and the `aside` element wraps, so now you have a single-column layout, as shown in Figure 2-4.

How CSS Grid makes an app fluid

Depending on your app content, CSS Grid can be a great choice for turning a static layout into a fluid one. (Check out Book 2, Chapter 4 to learn how CSS Grid works.) Grid has many options for building in responsiveness, but the following three techniques will get you there in most cases:

>> Use `fr` units to allow grid items to fill the available space in the grid container.

FIGURE 2-4:
In a smaller
viewport, the
`main` element
becomes a single
column (left)
because the
`aside` element
has wrapped
(right).

>> Let the browser do some of the work for you by specifying only a column template or a row template (not both).

>> In your template, use the `auto-fit` keyword to let the browser perform the column-width or row-height calculations automatically.

For example, the following declaration tells the browser to automatically fit the container width with equal-sized (`1fr`) columns that are no less than `15rem` wide:

```
grid-template-columns: repeat(auto-fit, minmax(15rem, 1fr));
```

Here's an example that puts this declaration to work (bk07ch02/example04.html):

HTML (abbreviated):

```
<header>
    <h1>The Vibrant Edges of Language</h1>
    <p class="subtitle">In which our intrepid writers let loose
  with talk of word play in all its forms</p>
</header>
<main>
```

```
    <p>
    We have a deep-rooted delight in the comic effect of words
in English, and not just in advertising jingles but at the
highest level of endeavor. <br>—BILL BRYSON, <i>The Mother
Tongue</i>, 1990
    </p><p>
    etc.
</main>
```

CSS:

```
main {
    display: grid;
    grid-template-columns: repeat(auto-fit, minmax(15rem, 1fr));
    gap: 2rem;
}
main > p:nth-child(even) {
    background: hsl(208deg 50% 80%);
}
```

On a larger screen, the main element is a four-column grid, as shown in Figure 2-5.

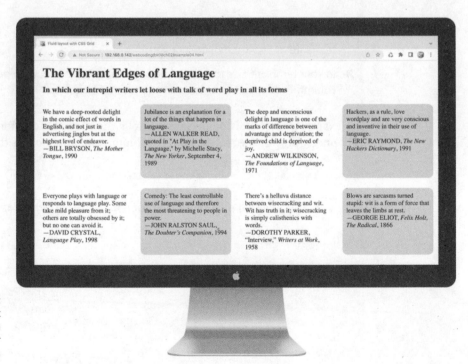

FIGURE 2-5:
The grid layout
as it appears in a
desktop browser
viewport.

Reduce the width of the viewport a bit and the layout automatically switches to a three-column grid, as shown in Figure 2-6.

FIGURE 2-6:
The grid layout as it appears in a tablet viewport.

Reduce the viewport width even more and eventually the layout automatically switches to a two-column layout, and then a single-column layout, as shown in Figure 2-7.

Taking advantage of viewport units

One of the easiest ways to build fluidity into your layouts is to use the viewport units that I mention in Book 2, Chapter 2. Here they are again, in Table 2-1.

I should also mention a few new viewport units that have been available in most major browsers for a little while but don't yet have universal support. These viewport units were created to handle the inconvenient fact that most mobile browsers hide their user interface (UI) features (such as the toolbar and address/search bar) when you scroll down the page, and then show those features when you scroll back up. This means you're really dealing with three viewports:

>> **Small viewport:** The viewport available when the browser UI is shown. This viewport is small because the browser UI takes up a portion of the screen.

FIGURE 2-7:
The grid layout
as it appears in
a smartphone
viewport.

TABLE 2-1

CSS Viewport Measurement Units

Unit	Name	Measured Relative to
vw	viewport width	1/100 of the viewport width
vh	viewport height	1/100 of the viewport height
vmin	viewport minimum	1/100 of the viewport's smaller dimension
vmax	viewport maximum	1/100 of the viewport's larger dimension

» **Large viewport:** The viewport available when the browser UI is hidden. This viewport is large because the browser UI no longer takes up a portion of the screen.

» **Dynamic viewport:** The browser viewport currently displayed, which could be small or large depending on the user's scrolling behavior.

Given these viewports, Table 2-2 lists the new units that are based on these sizes.

TABLE 2-2 **New CSS Viewport Measurement Units**

Unit	Name	Measured Relative to
svw	small viewport width	1/100 of the small viewport width
svh	small viewport height	1/100 of the small viewport height
svmin	small viewport minimum	1/100 of the small viewport's smaller dimension
svmax	small viewport maximum	1/100 of the small viewport's larger dimension
lvw	large viewport width	1/100 of the large viewport width
lvh	large viewport height	1/100 of the large viewport height
lvmin	large viewport minimum	1/100 of the large viewport's smaller dimension
lvmax	large viewport maximum	1/100 of the large viewport's larger dimension
dvw	dynamic viewport width	1/100 of the dynamic viewport width
dvh	dynamic viewport height	1/100 of the dynamic viewport height
dvmin	dynamic viewport minimum	1/100 of the dynamic viewport's smaller dimension
dmax	dynamic viewport maximum	1/100 of the dynamic viewport's larger dimension

TIP

As I write this, these new viewport units have just over 90 percent browser support. To keep an eye on this support level, use the following Can I Use page: https://caniuse.com/viewport-unit-variants.

The advantage of viewport units is that they automatically scale along with the changing viewport size, so they're fluid by default. If the user changes the size of the browser window or rotates their device to a different orientation, a property that uses a viewport-based unit will automatically scale to match the new viewport width or height.

For example, if you're using a grid layout and you've set gaps with the row-gap and column-gap properties, you may want those gaps to grow and shrink along with the viewport. Here's one way to accomplish this (bk07ch02/example05.html):

```
column-gap: 2vw;
row-gap: 2vh;
```

Making typography fluid

Although many developers use viewport units for features such as grid gaps, padding, margins, and even element widths and heights, by far the most common use case for viewport units is fluid typography. That is, by setting your font-size properties to values that use viewport units, your type will scale along with the viewport size.

Note that this doesn't mean doing something like this:

```
font-size: 1.5vmax;
```

The problem is that this isn't an accessible approach because it overrides the user's custom font size setting. A better way to go is to combine a rem unit (for accessibility) and a viewport unit (for fluidity) by using the CSS calc() function.

The calc() function takes two or more literal values or expressions, performs one or more arithmetic operations on those values, and then returns the result of that calculation, which is then assigned to whatever property you're working with. Here's the syntax:

```
property: calc(expression);
```

where:

>> *property* is the CSS property to which you want to assign the calc() result.

>> *expression* is two or more CSS measurement values — called the *operands* of the expression — with each pair interspersed with a symbol — known as an *operator* — that defines the type of calculation to perform:

  • *operand*: This is usually a literal value such as 50px or 10rem, but it can also be an expression or even another calc() function. You can mix measurement units.

  • *operator*: The calc() function supports four operations: addition (which uses the + operator), subtraction (–), multiplication (∗), and division (/). If you use multiple operators in the expression, note that multiplication and division are normally performed before addition and subtraction. You can force calc() to perform a particular operation first by putting parentheses () around the operation.

Here are a few calc() functions with some example expressions:

```
calc(50vw + 10px)
calc(100vh - 5rem)
```

```
calc(10% * 3)
calc(100% / 8)
calc(100vw - (5rem + 10px))
```

In the last example, `calc()` performs the addition `5rem + 10px` first because it's in parentheses, and then `calc()` performs the subtraction.

For fluid font sizes, you'd use `calc()` as in this example:

```
font-size: calc(0.75rem + 1vmax);
```

A calculation like this is suitable for regular text. For headings, you'll need to experiment a bit to figure out what suits your app. For example, an `h1` element might use the following declaration:

```
font-size: calc(1.75rem + 2vmax);
```

Introducing your best fluid friend: clamp()

The problem with using viewport units for font sizes is that you lose some control over the final value of whatever property you're working with. That's by design, of course, because part of the value proposition for a fluid layout is to cede some control to the browser and let it do more of the responsive heavy lifting.

However, viewport-based font sizes, although they can look fine at intermediate screen sizes, can become unreadably small at the smallest viewport widths and comically large when faced with the largest viewports. Fortunately, you can turn to the powerful `clamp()` function to set minimum and maximum values for your fluid calculations:

```
property: clamp(min, expression, max);
```

where:

>> *property* is the CSS property to which you want to assign the `clamp()` result.

>> *min* is the lowest value that can be assigned to *property*.

>> *expression* is the preferred value that you want assigned to *property*. This can be a literal value, an expression, or a CSS function, such as `calc()`.

>> *max* is the highest value that can be assigned to *property*.

The idea behind clamp() is that the browser evaluates the *expression* parameter and then assigns a value to the property as follows:

» If the *expression* value is between *min* and *max*, the browser uses the *expression* result as the property value.

» If the *expression* value is less than *min*, the browser uses *min* as the property value.

» If the *expression* value is greater than *max*, the browser uses *max* as the property value.

For example, if the smallest size you want for your regular text is 1.25rem and the largest size is 1.75rem, the following clamp() function will do the job (bk07ch02/example06.html):

```
font-size: clamp(1.25rem, 0.75rem + 1vmax, 1.75rem);
```

Querying Your Way to Responsiveness: Adaptive Layouts

In Book 3, Chapter 4, I talk about controlling JavaScript using if...else statements, where a script runs one block of code if a specified expression is true and a different block of code if that expression is false.

CSS has something similar called a *query*, where you test for a particular condition and, if that condition is true, the browser applies one or more styles. If the condition is false, the browser just skips over those styles. (So, a query is like a JavaScript if statement without the else part.)

CSS offers quite a few query types, but for your purposes here, you can consider just the following three:

» **Media query:** A query that interrogates some aspect of the screen, usually the viewport width

» **Container query:** A query that examines some feature of a parent or ancestor element, such as the element's width or orientation

» **User preference query:** A special type of media query that checks whether the user has declared a preference for a particular feature, such as dark mode

In each case, the point is to use the query to create an *adaptive layout*, which is a layout that changes depending on the result of the query. In each case, you can specify a declaration block that the browser applies if the query is true. This makes adaptive layouts more powerful than fluid layouts because you can apply just about any CSS rule you want when a query is true:

>> You can hide a displayed element or show a hidden element.

>> You can modify an existing layout, such as changing a three-column grid to a one- or two-column grid.

>> You can switch to a different layout type, such as from Grid to Flexbox.

>> If you're using Flexbox, you can change the order of the elements.

>> You can modify any CSS property, such as font-size, width, and margin.

The next three sections take you through the specifics of each query type.

Interrogating the screen with media queries

By far the most common type of adaptive layout uses a CSS feature called a *media query*, which is the @media keyword, an expression that evaluates to either true or false, and a code block consisting of one or more style rules. (Since the media query starts with @, the at symbol, this type of CSS mega-rule is called an *at-rule*.) The expression interrogates some feature of the viewport, usually its width. If that expression is true for the current device, the browser applies the media query's style rules; if the expression is false, the browser ignores the media query's rules. Here's the syntax:

```
@media (expression) {
    declarations
}
```

where:

>> *expression* is a property-value pair that the browser uses to test the current device viewport.

>> *declarations* are the style declarations that the browser applies if *expression* is true.

There are lots of different possibilities for *expression*, but the vast majority of media queries test for a viewport width that's either less than or equal to some value or greater than or equal to some value.

To test for a viewport width that's greater than or equal to some value, use the `min-width` property:

```
@media (min-width: value) {
    declarations
}
```

where *value* is a length value using any of the standard CSS measurement units.

To test for a viewport width that's less than or equal to some value, use the `max-width` property:

```
@media (max-width: value) {
    declarations
}
```

where *value* is a length value using any of the standard CSS measurement units.

Here's an example (bk07ch02/example07.html):

HTML:

```
<header>
    <img src="images/notw.png" alt="News of the Word logo"
  class="site-logo">
    <h1>News of the Word</h1>
    <p class="subtitle">Language news you won't find anywhere
  else (for good reason!)</p>
</header>
```

CSS:

```
@media (max-width: 40rem) {
    .site-logo {
        display: none;
    }
}
```

This media query looks for a viewport width of 40rem or less. When that's true, the rule inside the media query block runs, which sets the display property to none for the header image (which uses the class site-logo). As shown in Figure 2-8, the logo appears in a tablet-sized viewport but doesn't appear in the smartphone-sized viewport shown in Figure 2-9.

FIGURE 2-8:
The header logo appears in a tablet-sized viewport.

FIGURE 2-9:
On a smartphone-sized viewport, the media query expression is true, so the header logo is hidden.

RANGE SYNTAX FOR MEDIA QUERIES

Coming soon to a stylesheet near you: *range syntax* for media queries. Range syntax enables you to use comparison operators (check out Book 3, Chapter 3) such as less than (<) and greater than or equal (>=) along with properties such as width to build your media query expressions. For example, the range syntax equivalent for the media query example looks like this:

```
@media (40rem <= width <= 60rem) {
    declarations
}
```

Monitor the Can I Use page https://caniuse.com/css-media-range-syntax to learn when there's enough browser support to use range syntax in your web projects.

TIP

You can specify multiple expressions in your media queries. For example, if you separate expressions with the keyword and, the browser applies the style rules only if all the expressions are true:

```
@media (expression1) and (expression2) {
    declarations
}
```

Similarly, if you separate expressions with the keyword or, the browser applies the style rules if one or more of the expressions are true:

```
@media (expression1) or (expression2) {
    declarations
}
```

For example, if you wanted to target viewport sizes between 40rem and 60rem, you'd do this:

```
@media (min-width: 40rem) and (max-width: 60rem) {
    declarations
}
```

Laying out trees instead of forests with container queries

The media queries that I talk about in the preceding section have been a staple of CSS layout since at least 2009 and are even supported by Internet Explorer 9 and later. The chief advantage of media queries over the fluid techniques I talk about earlier (check out "Going with the Flow: Fluid Layouts") is that when a media query expression is true, you can write very specific style rules for the browser to apply to one or more elements.

But media queries, although still useful and relevant, are starting to show their age a bit for two reasons:

>> Media queries almost always interrogate the size of the entire viewport.

>> Modern web design is focused on the idea of the *component*, which is a standalone collection of elements, particularly one that gets reused in different contexts.

For example, a component for a product might have a photo of the product, a header with the product name, some body text describing the product, and some action buttons related to the product. Here are some example contexts where this component may get used:

>> On the product landing app, this component may take up most of the viewport.

>> On the site home app, the product may be featured with a large card.

>> On the product catalog app, the component may be a medium-sized card.

>> In the site's navigation sidebar, the component may be a small card, perhaps without the image.

These different contexts require different layouts for the component. Media queries don't work well in this scenario because they examine only the size of the whole viewport, and in each of the preceding contexts, the viewport size may not change.

So, it's no wonder the entire CSS community is abuzz with excitement over a new adaptive layout technology called *container queries*. These queries enable you to examine the width (and a few other properties) of a parent element (the container that gives these queries their name) and then apply style rules to the child and descendant elements whenever that width (or whatever) meets your specified criteria.

So, for example, assuming that your product component is wrapped in a parent element, such as a div, a container query would examine, say, the width of that div and apply different styles to the child and descendant elements — the image, heading, text, and links — depending on the result.

As I write this, container queries have only recently become supported by all major browsers, so they're not quite ready for production use. However, there's a good chance container queries will have near-universal support (say, over 90 percent) by the time you read this, so check out the following Can I Use page to find out where things stand: https://caniuse.com/css-container-queries.

Setting up the query container

To work with container queries, you first set up an element as the query container. This will be the parent or ancestor of the child or descendant elements you want to style. To set up an element as a query container, use the container-type property:

```
element {
    container-type: value;
}
```

where:

» *element* is the parent or ancestor of the elements you want to style.

» *value* specifies the dimension or dimensions to use in the container query. Use inline-size if in your container query you want to interrogate only the container's width (assuming a horizontal inline direction). Use size instead if you want to interrogate width or height or both in your container query.

Here's an example (bk07ch02/example08.html) that sets up the default layout for a product card:

HTML:

```
<div class="card-container">
    <div class="card-wrapper">
        <img class="card-image" src="images/inflatable-
dartboard.png" alt="Inflatable dartboard product photo">
        <div>
            <h3 class="card-title">Inflatable Dartboard</h3>
            <p class="card-description">
                Yes, it's the world-famous inflatable dartboard!
No hassle setup! Comes with an easy-to-use inflation tube.
Just take a deep breath and blow. And blow. Keep going.
Anyway, within a few hours, you'll be ready to play darts. Now
only $1,999! Patch kit sold separately.
            </p>
```

```
            <div class="card-actions">
                <button class="card-button learn-more">Learn
more</button>
                <button class="card-button add-to-cart">Add to
cart</button>
            </div>
        </div>
    </div>
</div>
```

CSS:

```
.card-container {
    container-type: inline-size;
}
.card-wrapper {
    display: grid;
    gap: 1.5rem;
    grid-template-columns: auto auto;
    grid-template-rows: auto;
}
.card-image {
    min-width: auto;
    height: auto;
    object-fit: cover;
    object-position: center;
    overflow: hidden;
}
.card-title {
    text-align: left;
}
.card-actions {
    display: flex;
    gap: 1rem;
    justify-content: flex-start;
}
```

Of particular interest is the parent div with class card-container. That div is styled in the CSS as a query container:

```
.card-container {
    container-type: inline-size;
}
```

Figure 2-10 shows the default card.

FIGURE 2-10:
A product card in
its default layout.

TIP

If you want to have multiple query containers on your app, you need to name each container by adding the `container-name` property to the container element:

```
element {
    container-type: value;
    container-name: name;
}
```

Querying the container

With your query container set up, you're ready to query it using the `@container` at-rule:

```
@container (expression) {
    declarations
}
```

where:

>> *expression* is an expression that the browser uses to test some property of the container, such as its width.

>> *declarations* are the style declarations that the browser applies if *expression* is true.

For example, here's a container query for the product card from the preceding section that applies its style rules when the container's width is less than 25rem:

```
@container (width < 25rem) {
    .card-wrapper {
        align-items: center;
```

```
        display: block;
        padding: 1rem;
    }
    .card-image {
        display: none;
    }
    .card-title {
        margin-top: 0;
    }
}
```

Figure 2-11 shows the resulting card when its container is less than 25rem wide.

Inflatable Dartboard

Yes, it's the world-famous inflatable dartboard! No hassle setup! Comes with an easy-to-use inflation tube. Just take a deep breath and blow. And blow. Keep going. Anyway, within a few hours, you'll be ready to play darts. Now only $1,999! Patch kit sold separately.

LEARN MORE   ADD TO CART

FIGURE 2-11: The product card layout when the parent element is less than 25rem wide.

As with media queries, you can also use multiple expressions in your container queries. Separate expressions with and to apply the rules only when every expression is true; separate expressions with or to apply the rules only when at least one of the expressions is true.

Here's a container query for the product card from the preceding section that applies its style rules when the container's width is greater than 25rem and less than 35rem:

```
@container (width > 25rem) and (width < 35rem) {
    .card-wrapper {
        grid-template-columns: auto;
        grid-template-rows: auto auto;
    }
}
```

```
    .card-image {
      width: 100%;
      height: 10rem;
    }
    .card-title {
        text-align: center;
    }
    .card-actions {
        justify-content: center;
    }
  }
```

Figure 2-12 shows the resulting card layout when the container is between 25rem and 35rem wide.

Inflatable Dartboard

Yes, it's the world-famous inflatable dartboard! No hassle setup! Comes with an easy-to-use inflation tube. Just take a deep breath and blow. And blow. Keep going. Anyway, within a few hours, you'll be ready to play darts. Now only $1,999! Patch kit sold separately.

LEARN MORE   ADD TO CART

FIGURE 2-12: The product card layout when the parent element is between 25rem and 35rem wide.

Working with container query units

After you've set up an element as a query container, you're free to size that element's children and descendants using *container query units*, which are measurement units that are relative to the dimensions of the query container. Table 2-3 lists the available container query units you can use.

TABLE 2-3

CSS Container Query Measurement Units

Unit	Name	Measured Relative to
cqw	container width	1/100 of the container width
cqh	container height	1/100 of the container height
cqmin	container minimum	1/100 of the container's smaller dimension
cqmax	container maximum	1/100 of the container's larger dimension

Respecting your visitors with user preference queries

Through their operating system's settings, users can express certain preferences related to how their device looks and operates. For example, many people choose to use either a light color scheme or a dark color scheme, as shown in Figure 2-13.

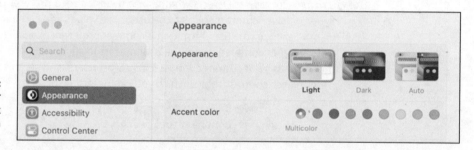

FIGURE 2-13: Choosing either a light or a dark color scheme in macOS.

You can use a CSS media query to detect some of these user preferences and style your app accordingly. Here's the general syntax:

```
@media (preference: value) {
    declarations
}
```

where:

» *preference* is a keyword that specifies which preference you're detecting.

» *value* is the preference setting your query is looking for.

» *declarations* are the style declarations that the browser applies if *preference* matches *value*.

Although more preferences are in the offing, for now you can detect three. Here are the associated keywords and values:

» prefers-color-scheme: Detects whether the user has set a preference for the color scheme. The two values you can query are dark or light. The usual procedure here is to set up your app assuming the light color scheme, and then use something like the following to apply darker colors if the dark color scheme preference is detected:

```
@media (prefers-color-scheme: dark) {
    /* Dark color scheme colors go here */
}
```

TIP

If you use the hsl() function for your colors, one easy way to convert a light color to a dark variant is to subtract the lightness value from 100 while keeping the hue and saturation values the same. For example, if the light color is hsl(180deg 50% 80%), the corresponding dark mode color will be hsl(180deg 50% 20%).

» prefers-contrast: Detects whether the user has set a preference for higher or lower contrast colors to be used. The values you can query are no-preference (the user hasn't set a contrast preference), more (the user prefers higher contrast), less (the user prefers lower contrast), or custom (the user has set a custom contrast level). Most users who set this preference prefer higher-contrast colors, which you can detect as follows:

```
@media (prefers-contrast: more) {
    /* Higher-contrast colors go here */
}
```

» prefers-reduced-motion: Detects whether the user has set a preference for a reduced level of animation effects and similar nonessential motion on the screen. The values you can query are no-preference (the user hasn't set a reduced motion preference) or reduced (the user prefers reduced motion). Here's a media query that detects whether the user prefers reduced motion and, if so, sets all animations to their minimums:

```
@media (prefers-reduced-motion: reduce) {
    *,
    ::after,
    ::before {
        animation-duration: 0.01ms;
        animation-iteration-count: 1;
        transition-duration: 0.01ms;
        scroll-behavior: auto;
    }
}
```

You can use the browser dev tools to test these preferences without having to toggle them in your operating system's settings app. In Chrome, open the dev tools, click the customize and control dev tools icon (three vertical dots near the upper-right corner of the dev tools pane), choose More Tools ⇨ Rendering, and then use the controls that emulate each user preference.

TIP

Working with Images Responsively

When planning a web app, you always need to consider the effect of images, both on your design and on your users.

Making images responsive

On the design side, you need to ensure that your images scale responsively, depending on the screen width or height. For example, if the user's screen is 1,024 pixels wide, an image that's 800 pixels wide will fit with no problem, but that same image will overflow a 400-pixel-wide screen. You create responsive images with the following CSS rule:

```
image {
    max-width: 100%;
    height: auto;
}
```

REMEMBER

Here, image is a selector that references the image or images you want to be responsive. Setting max-width: 100% enables the image width to scale smaller or larger as the viewport (or the image's container) changes size, but also mandates that the image can't scale larger than its original width. Setting height: auto cajoles the browser into maintaining the image's original aspect ratio by calculating the height automatically based on the image's current width.

TIP

Occasionally, you'll want the image height instead of its width to be responsive. To do that, you use the following variation on the preceding rule:

```
image {
    max-height: 100%;
    width: auto;
}
```

Delivering images responsively

On the user side, delivering images that are far larger than the screen size can be a major problem. Sure, you can make the images responsive, but you're still sending a file that's larger than necessary down the tubes, which won't be appreciated by mobile surfers using slow connections with limited data plans.

Instead, you need to deliver to the user a version of the image file that's appropriately sized for the device screen. For example, you might deliver the full-size image to desktop users, a medium-sized version to tablet folks, and a small-sized version to smartphone users. That sounds like a complex bit of business, but HTML lets you handle everything from the comfort of the `<img>` tag. The secret? The `sizes` and `srcset` attributes.

The `sizes` attribute is a collection of *expression-width* pairs:

>> The *expression* part specifies a screen feature, such as a minimum or maximum width, surrounded by parentheses.

>> The *width* part specifies how wide you want the image displayed on screens that match the expression.

For example, to specify that on screens up to 600 pixels wide, you want an image displayed with a width of 90vw, you'd use the following expression-width pair:

```
(max-width: 600px) 90vw
```

A typical `sizes` attribute is a collection of expression-width pairs, separated by commas. Here's the general syntax to use:

```
sizes="(expression1) width1,
       (expression2) width2,
       etc.,
       widthN"
```

Note that the last item doesn't specify an expression. This syntax tells the web browser that the specified width applies to any screen that doesn't match any of the expressions.

Here's an example:

```
sizes="(max-width: 600px) 90vw,
       (max-width: 1000px) 60vw,
       30vw"
```

The srcset attribute is a comma-separated list of image file locations, each followed by the image width and letter w. Here's the general syntax:

```
srcset="location1 width1w,
        location2 width2w,
        etc.">
```

This syntax gives the browser a choice of image sizes, and it picks the best one based on the current device screen dimensions and the preferred widths you specify in the sizes attribute. Here's a full example:

```
<img src="images/img-small.jpg" alt=""
     sizes="(max-width: 600px) 90vw,
            (max-width: 1000px) 60vw,
            30vw"
     srcset="images/img-small.jpg 450w,
             images/img-medium.jpg 900w,
             images/img-large.jpg 1350w">
```

Figure 2-14 shows how the browser serves up different images for different screen sizes (bk07ch02/example09.html).

The sizes and srcset attributes don't always work the way you might expect. For example, if the browser finds that, say, the large version of the image is already stored in its cache, it will usually decide that it's faster and easier on the bandwidth to just grab the image from the cache and scale it instead of going back to the server to download a more appropriately sized file for the current screen.

FIGURE 2-14:
With the `<img>` tag's `sizes` and `srcset` attributes on the job, the browser serves up different versions of the image for different screen sizes.

Exploring the Principles of Mobile-First Development

If you've been hanging around the web for a while, you probably remember the days when you'd surf to a site using a small screen such as a smartphone or similar portable device, and instead of getting the regular version of the site, you'd get the mobile version. In rare cases, this alternate version would be optimized for mobile viewing and navigation, but more likely it was just a poor facsimile of the regular site with a few font changes and all the interesting and useful features removed.

From the web developer's viewpoint, the poor quality of those mobile sites isn't all that surprising. After all, who wants to build and maintain two versions of the same site? Fortunately, the days of requiring an entirely different site to support mobile users are long gone. Yes, using responsive web design enables you to create a single site that looks and works great on everything from a wall-mounted display to a handheld device. But in modern web development, there's a strong case to be made that all web apps should be built from the ground up as though they were going to be displayed only on mobile devices. In the rest of this chapter, you explore the principles and techniques behind this mobile-first approach to web development.

Embracing mobile-first web development

As I discuss earlier in this chapter, when you develop a web app to look good and work well on a desktop-sized screen, you can employ a number of responsive tricks to make that same code look good and work well on a mobile device screen:

>> Set up a Flexbox or Grid layout that automatically adjusts to any size screen.

>> Use viewport units, particularly with font sizes.

>> Use media queries to remove elements when the screen width falls below a specified threshold.

REMEMBER

That third technique — the one where you remove stuff that doesn't fit on a smaller screen — is known in the web coding trade as *regressive enhancement* (*RE*). RE has ruled the web development world for many years, but lately there's been a backlash against it. Here's why:

>> RE relegates mobile screens to second-class web citizenship.

>> RE leads to undisciplined development because coders and designers inevitably stuff a desktop-sized screen with content, widgets, and all the web bells and whistles.

What's the solution? You've probably guessed it by now: *progressive enhancement,* which means starting with content that fits on the smallest screen size that you need to support and then adding components as the screen gets bigger. When the original content represents what's essential about your app and the base screen width is optimized for mobile devices — especially today's most popular smartphones — you've got yourself a *mobile-first* approach to web development.

Let me be honest right off the top: Mobile-first web development is daunting because if you're used to having the giant canvas of a desktop screen to play with, starting instead with a screen that's a mere 360 or 400 pixels across can feel claustrophobic. However, I can assure you that it seems that way only because of the natural tendency to wonder how you're possibly going to shoehorn your massive app into such a tiny space. Mobile-first thinking takes the opposite approach by ignoring (at least at the beginning) large screens and focusing instead on what works best for mobile screens, which after all, represent the majority of your app visitors. Thinking the mobile-first way isn't hard; it just means keeping a few key design principles in mind.

Mobile first means content first

One of the biggest advantages of taking a mobile-first approach to web development is that it forces you to prioritize. That is, a mobile-first design means that you include in the initial layout only those app elements that are essential to the user's experience of the app. This essential-stuff-only idea is partly a response to having a smaller screen size in which to display that stuff, but it's also a necessity for many mobile users who are surfing with sluggish internet connections and limited data plans. It's your job — no, scratch that, it's your *duty* — as a conscientious web developer to make sure that those users aren't served anything superfluous, frivolous, or in any other way nonessential.

That's all well and good, I hear you thinking, but define *superfluous* and *frivolous.* Good point. The problem, of course, is that one web developer's skippable appetizer is another's essential meat and potatoes. Only you can decide between what's inconsequential and what's vital, depending on your app goals and your potential audience.

So, the first step toward a mobile-first design is to decide what's most important in the following content categories:

>> **Text:** Decide what words are essential to get your app's message across. Usability expert Steve Krug tells web designers to "Get rid of half the words on each page, then get rid of half of what's left." For a mobile-first app, you may need to halve the words once again. Be ruthless. Does the user really need that message from the CEO or your About Us text? Probably not.

>> **Images:** Decide what images are essential for the user, or whether images are needed at all. The problem with images is that, although everyone likes a bit of eye candy, that sweetness comes at the cost of screen real estate and bandwidth. If you really do need to include an image or two in your mobile-first page, at least serve up smaller images to your mobile visitors. To learn how to do that, check out "Working with Images Responsively," earlier in this chapter.

>> **Navigation:** All users need to be able to navigate your site, but the recent trend is to create gigantic menus that include links to every section and app on the site. Decide which of those links are truly important for navigation and just include those in your mobile first layout.

>> **Widgets:** Modern web apps are festooned with widgets for social media, content scrollers, photo light boxes, automatic video playback, and, of course, advertising. Mobile users want content first, so consider ditching the widgets altogether. If there's a widget you really want to include and you're sure it won't put an excessive burden on either the app's load time or the user's bandwidth, push the widget to the bottom of the page.

Pick a testing width that makes sense for your site

REMEMBER

For most websites, testing a mobile-first layout should begin with the smallest devices, which these days means smartphones with screens that are 360 pixels wide. However, you don't necessarily have to begin your testing with a width as small as 360px. If you have access to your site analytics, they should tell you what devices your visitors use. If you find that all or most of your mobile users are on devices that are at least 400 pixels wide, that's the initial width you should test for your mobile-first layout.

Get your content to scale with the device

For your mobile-first approach to be successful, it's paramount that you configure each app on your site to scale horizontally with the width of the device screen. You do that by adding the following ‹meta› tag to the head section of each app:

TIP

```
<meta name="viewport" content="width=device-width,
    initial-scale=1.0">
```

This instructs the web browser to do two things:

>> Set the initial width of the page content to the width of the device screen.

>> Set the initial zoom level of the app to 1.0, which means that the page is neither zoomed in nor zoomed out.

Build your CSS the mobile-first way

When you're ready to start coding the CSS for your app, understand that the style definitions and rules that you write will be your app defaults — that is, these are the styles the browser will display on all devices, unless you've defined one or more media queries (or container queries) to override these defaults. You shouldn't have to write any special rules as long as you follow a few basic tenets of responsive web design:

REMEMBER

>> Use the viewport units for measures such as width and padding.

>> Use the rem units for font sizes.

>> Make all your images responsive.

>> Use Grid or Flexbox for the app layout. If you're using Flexbox, be sure to apply flex-wrap: wrap to any flex container.

It's also important to make sure that your mobile-first layout renders the content just as you want it to appear on the mobile screen. This means avoiding any tricks such as using the Flexbox order property to mess around with the order of the app elements.

Finally, and perhaps most important, be sure to hide any unnecessary content by styling that content with display: none.

In the end, your mobile-first CSS should be the very model of simplicity and economy.

Choose a non-mobile breakpoint that makes sense for your content

Your mobile-first CSS code probably includes several elements that you've hidden with display: none. I assume you want to show those elements eventually (otherwise, you'd have deleted them), so you need to decide when you want them shown. Specifically, you need to decide what the minimum screen width is that will show your content successfully.

Note that I didn't say that you should decide when to show your hidden content based on the width of a target device. For example, for years developers considered a screen to be wide enough when it was at least as wide as an iPad screen in portrait mode, which for the longest time was 768 pixels. Fair enough, but today Apple offers five iPad models, each with a different screen width.

TIP

Devices change constantly, and it's a fool's game to try to keep up with them. Forget all that. Instead, decide what minimum width is best for your app when the hidden content is made visible. How can you do that? Here's one easy way:

1. **Load your app into the Chrome web browser.**

2. **Display Chrome's developer tools.**

Press either Ctrl+Shift+I (Windows) or ⌘+Shift+I (Mac).

3. **Use your mouse to adjust the size of the browser window:**

- If the developer tools are below or undocked from the browser viewport, drag the right or left edge of the browser window.

- If the developer tools are docked to the right or left of the browser viewport, drag the vertical bar that separates the developer tools from the viewport.

4. **Read the current viewport dimensions, which Chrome displays in the upper-right corner of the viewport.**

The dimensions appear as width x height, in pixels.

5. **Narrow the window to your mobile-first testing width (such as 360px).**

6. **Increase the width and, as you do, watch how your layout changes.**

In particular, watch for the width where the content first looks the way you want it to appear in larger screens. Make a note of that width.

REMEMBER

The width where your full content looks good is the basis for a CSS media query breakpoint that you'll use to display the elements hidden in the mobile-first layout. For example, say that your mobile-first layout hides the aside element and that you found that your full content looks right at a width of 742px. You then can set up the following media query (using 750px for a round number):

```
@media (min-width: 750px) {
    aside {
        display: block;
    }
}
```

This media query tells the browser that when the screen width is 750px or more, display the aside element.

IN THIS CHAPTER

» **Understanding the case for accessibility on the web**

» **Learning how people with disabilities surf the web**

» **Structuring your pages for accessibility**

» **Making images and other web page media accessible**

» **Choosing accessible colors**

» **Validating your page accessibility**

Chapter **3**

Making a Web App Accessible

The power of the Web is in its universality. Access by everyone regardless of disability is an essential aspect.

— TIM BERNERS-LEE

f you're lucky enough to have good eyesight, adequate hearing, decent motor skills, and a brain that does its job well (most of the time, anyway), it's easy to lull yourself into thinking that *everyone* who visits your web app will have had the same luck in life. Falling into that trap means you'll build your app thinking that if it looks good and works well for you, it will also look good and work well for all your visitors.

In this chapter, I explain why, no matter how good a hand you've drawn in life, it's thoughtful, ethical, and smart to remember that there are lots of people — I'm talking a *billion* people worldwide — who've been given tougher cards to play in the form of some kind of significant disability. In this chapter, I hope to convince you that your web apps, no matter how simple, are simply not done until you've made them accessible to everyone, regardless of their abilities. In this chapter, I show you that configuring your web apps to make them accessible to every visitor is not only the right thing to do but also an easy thing to do.

Why You Need to Make Your Apps Accessible

If you were opening a brick-and-mortar retail operation, it's very unlikely that you'd design your storefront with barbed wire blocking the door! Sure, certain agile or freakishly long-legged people might still be able to enter your store by leaping or stepping over the barbed wire, but why on earth would you design things to prevent everyone else from entering? You wouldn't, of course, because that level of inaccessibility is obviously counter productive and, well, silly.

When you design a web app that looks good and works well only for people with able eyes and ears and sufficient control over their limbs and mind, you're essentially blocking access to your app with the digital equivalent of barbed wire.

Accessibility is a right

The United Nations Convention on the Rights of Persons with Disabilities requires stakeholders to take measures to "promote access for persons with disabilities to new information and communications technologies and systems, including the Internet." In other words, access to the web is nothing less than a *fundamental human right*.

When planning a web app, the thoughtful developer remains aware at all times that the people who visit and use the app come with different abilities. When planning a web app, the ethical developer understands that even though every person is different, they all have an equal right to use the app. When you give everyone equal access to your web app, you're making your app *accessible.*

Accessibility, then, is not only a right but also the right thing to do.

REMEMBER

In online discussions and essays, accessibility is often shortened to *a11y*: that is, the letter *a*, followed by the number *11*, and then the letter *y*. Why 11? Because that's how many letters there are between the *a* and *y* in *accessibility*. Also, *a11y* looks like the word *ally*, which underlines the idea that anyone who implements accessibility features is an ally to the people with disabilities.

Accessibility brings other benefits

I'm sure that all the incentive you need to make your web apps accessible to all comers is that doing so is morally and ethically correct. However, making your apps accessible does bring other benefits.

For example, an app built with accessibility in mind is also a search-engine-friendly app, meaning that your accessible app will rank higher in search results than a similar, nonaccessible app.

An accessible app also provides benefits for non-disabled groups, such as people who surf with images turned off or who have to deal with extremely slow internet speeds.

Finally, it's easy to make a business case for going accessible:

>> **Accessibility gives you instant access to a big market:** According to the World Health Organization, about 1.3 billion people have some form of significant disability, and it's estimated that those billion-plus people wield a spending power in excess of six trillion dollars. That's a lot of zeroes! If you want to sell things on your site, why exclude such a huge chunk of the market?

>> **Accessibility may also be the legally required thing to do:** In many jurisdictions, it's now illegal for commercial websites to be inaccessible. Most countries have policies in place that require businesses to offer equal access to all. If your business website has global reach, failing to make the site accessible subjects your company to huge legal risk.

>> **Accessibility makes you look good:** Making your business apps accessible to all creates goodwill, puts a shine on your brand, and makes you part of the solution, not part of the problem.

REMEMBER

Whatever motivates you to make your apps accessible is awesome. However, making any web app one hundred percent accessible to one hundred percent of your visitors, while perhaps a noble and worthy goal, is impossible, as upcoming pages explain.

Understanding Web Accessibility

Isn't it a burden to have to add features to your apps to make them accessible? Nope, not even close. As long as you build your apps with equal access in mind from the get-go, incorporating accessible features takes little effort on your part.

As you see later in this chapter, web accessibility isn't hard or onerous to implement. Or, I should say, it's not hard or onerous to implement *if* you understand who requires accessible features and why they require them, and what types of assistive technologies are used by people with disabilities. The next couple of sections tell you everything you need to know.

Understanding who needs accessibility

One of the main complaints about web innovation these days is that web developers are building apps and services that solve only the developers' own problems. Food-delivery, groceries-to-your-door, and pet-sitting services are just a few of the many examples. The problem here is thinking that if I have a problem that needs to be solved, everybody else in the world must also want that problem solved. More broadly, these apps are examples of a web developer assuming that everyone who uses a site is basically just like the developer.

To really *get* accessibility, the first step is to understand deeply one simple fact:

> Your users are not you.

In particular, an alarmingly high portion (estimates range from 5 to 20 percent) of the people who visit your site live with some form of disability to a varying degree.

REMEMBER

ACCESSIBILITY ISN'T ABOUT ONLY PEOPLE WITH DISABILITIES

Although the focus of your accessibility efforts should be on accommodating users with disabilities as best you can, it's important to remember that your accessibility tweaks also help a wide range of other users, including the following:

- Users who surf the web using nonstandard devices, such as smart TVs, smart watches, and game consoles. These devices often either lack mouse support or offer only a rudimentary capability to move and click a pointer. So, in that sense, users of these devices have many of the same challenges as people with motor disabilities.

- Users with slow internet connections, restrictive bandwidth caps, or low-power computers may surf the web with images turned off, which makes sites load faster and uses less bandwidth. So, these users are similar to people with visual impairments in that they rely on your descriptions of your app images.

- Users who surf the web using mobile devices such as smartphones and tablets usually don't have access to a mouse. Therefore, site features that rely on, say, hovering a mouse pointer over a page object won't work for those users, which makes them similar to people who don't have the ability to use a mouse.

With these users in mind, you can see that accessibility can be defined in the broadest sense as making your website functional for as many people as possible.

What types of disability am I talking about? Planning for accessibility means taking the following conditions into account:

» **Visual:** Includes full or partial blindness, color-blindness, and reduced vision

» **Auditory:** Includes full or partial deafness, difficulty hearing, the inability to hear sounds at certain frequencies, and tinnitus

» **Motor:** Includes the inability to use a pointing device such as a mouse, restricted movement, lack of fine motor control, excessive trembling or shaking, and slow reflexes or response times

» **Cognitive:** Includes learning disabilities, focusing problems, impaired memory, and extreme distractibility

In each case, the disability may have been something present at birth or could have come about through disease or trauma. However, it's also important to remember that one or more of these disabilities may be the result of simply getting older. Folks who are no longer spring chickens (or even summer chickens, for that matter) could have reduced visual acuity, partial or complete deafness, reduced motor control, and mild to significant cognitive impairment. And because the planet's population (with just a few exceptions) is rapidly getting older, the number of people surfing the web with some form of disability is only going to grow.

Learning about assistive technologies for web surfing

Knowing that many people who visit your apps will have some type of disability doesn't do you much good unless you also know how that disability changes their web experience. How does a person with limited eyesight "read" a web app? How does someone who can't control a mouse "click" a link?

The answer to these and similar questions is that most people with disabilities use some form of software or hardware tool to help them surf to, read, navigate, and interact with a web app. These tools fall under the rubric of *assistive technology*

(AT), and knowing the tools that users with disabilities turn to is crucial in helping you design your web apps to be accessible.

Assistive technologies for visual disabilities

People with limited eyesight use a variety of AT to make screen elements easier to see:

» **Screen magnifier:** A hardware device or software utility that magnifies a portion of the screen. Windows offers the Magnifier program; macOS, iOS, and iPadOS have the Zoom feature; and Android has the Magnification setting.

» **The web browser's Zoom feature:** All the major web browsers offer a Zoom command that magnifies the entire page.

» **Custom browser text size:** All major browsers enable the user to set a custom text size.

For users who are blind or nearly blind, a screen reader is the AT of choice. A *screen reader* is a software program that reads aloud whatever text appears on a web page, including the following:

» Headings

» Page text

» Link text

» Descriptions of images and other media

Third-party screen readers are available, but all operating systems have built-in screen readers, including Narrator for Windows and VoiceOver for macOS. Having free access to the powerful screen reader in your operating system is great news because it means you can crank it up and try surfing the web with it to get a feel for how it works.

Assistive technologies for auditory disabilities

People with poor hearing often use special headphones or hearing aids to boost sound input. For people who are deaf or nearly deaf, however, you can make a couple of accommodations:

» If your app has video content, the video should include the capability to turn on captions.

» If your app has audio content, provide a link to a transcript of the audio.

Assistive technologies for motor disabilities

Some people with profound motor disabilities can surf the web (or use any computer function) only with a head-pointer device. However, for most people with a motor disability, the major problem is that they lack sufficient control to operate a mouse or trackpad. Instead, they rely on the keyboard to interact with web apps, so your apps need to be navigable via keyboard input. See "Making Your Apps Keyboard-Friendly," later in this chapter.

Assistive technologies for cognitive disabilities

Some people with certain types of cognitive impairment use software tools to help them focus on the task at hand. You can also set up your web apps to help people focus and to avoid unnecessary confusion:

» Don't add bling to your apps just for the sake of being flashy. Keep your app design as simple as possible.

» Keep your navigation and layout consistent across all your pages.

» Provide clear and simple instructions for tasks such as filling out forms.

» Wherever possible, stick to web conventions such as underlined link text.

Making Your App Structure Accessible

By far the easiest way to get a big jump on making your web apps accessible is by baking accessibility into the HTML structure itself. Does this mean jumping through a bunch of new hoops and learning a lot of new tags and attributes? Nope. Quite the opposite: It really means using headings and semantic sectioning elements just the way I talk about using them earlier in the book (see Book 2, Chapter 1).

Using headings hierarchically

Users of screen readers often get a feel for a page by navigating through its headings. To assist such users, you should first ensure that each heading makes sense when read aloud and accurately describes the contents of the section to follow. You should also use headings in a way that honors their built-in hierarchy:

» **Use only one** h1 **element per page:** That h1 element should be the page title.

» **Use** h2 **for headings:** For all the main headings on your page, use the h2 element.

>> **Use** h3 **for subheadings, and so on:** Inside each h2 element, the main subheadings should be h3 elements. Similarly, within an h3 the main sub-subheadings should be h4 elements; within an h4 the main sub-sub-subheadings should be h5 elements, and within an h5 the main sub-sub-sub-subheadings should be h6 elements.

>> **Don't skip headings:** Don't go from, say, an h2 to an h4 just because you feel like it or prefer the look of the text (see the next item).

>> **Don't use headings for decorative purposes:** Don't use a heading just because you need something bold or because you like the size of that heading's text. That's what CSS is for.

Using semantic sectioning elements

You certainly could build your app with nothing but styled div elements (and an alarming number of web coders do exactly that!), but the result is not only messy and unstructured but also an accessibility nightmare. Why? Because a screen reader or other assistive tech has nothing to grab onto, so to speak. Sure, it will still speak (or whatever) the page content, but there will be no context.

Fortunately, it doesn't take you any longer to build your app using the semantic sectioning elements — such as header, nav, main, article, and footer — that I talk about in Book 2 Chapter 1. This approach not only provides welcome structure to the page layout but also gives you accessibility for free because these so-called *landmarks* help assistive tech make sense of the page and screen readers will include the underlying semantic meaning as part of the readout.

For example, when a screen reader comes across a nav element, it will usually say "navigation," and when it comes across a header element, it will usually say "banner."

Making Text Accessible

Almost all web apps are mostly text, so if you can make your text accessible, you've gone a long way towards making your app accessible. Here are a few pointers to bear in mind:

>> **Don't use absolute measurement units for text sizes:** One of the first things someone with poor eyesight might do before surfing the web is customize their browser with a larger default text size. If you then style your

text with an absolute measurement unit such as pixels, you override that larger default size. You have suddenly become extremely unpopular with that person and with everyone else who has taken the trouble to adjust their browser's text. Accessible text starts with text sizes that use a relative measurement unit, such as em or rem.

» **Make sure the text is readable:** Don't size your text ridiculously small, and make sure there's sufficient contrast between the text color and the background color (see "Ensuring Sufficient Color Contrast," later in this chapter).

» **Make link text descriptive.** For each link on your page, the link text should describe what lies on the other side of the link. Screen readers speak link text aloud, so if your link just says "Click" or "Click here," you're not telling your visitor anything useful about where the link goes.

Do this:

```
<a href="kumquats.html">Learn more about kumquats</a>
```

Don't do this:

```
To learn more about kumquats, <a href="kumquats.html">click
    here</a>
```

» **Don't hide text if you don't have to:** It's possible to use CSS or JavaScript to temporarily hide text that doesn't need to be displayed at the moment. For example, you can create tabs where the content of one tab is visible and the content of the other tabs is not. The standard way of making some text not visible is to hide it, but that plays havoc with screen readers, which don't see the hidden text. So, if you can help it, never hide your page text.

Making Media Accessible

Web page text is inherently accessibility-friendly because screen readers speak it aloud by default. With a bit of care, you can make your text easier to read for people with less than perfect eyesight. Unfortunately, that friendliness doesn't apply to web page media, including images, videos, and audio snippets. These elements are harder to make accessible, but there's still plenty you can do to make sure that all your visitors can enjoy your page media elements (or at least know what they're missing).

Specifying alt text for images

To help visually impaired users or users who are surfing with images turned off, you can use the `<img>` tag's `alt` attribute to provide a description for each significant image on your page. For the visually impaired, a screen reader reads aloud the value of every `<img>` tag's `alt` attribute, so important or structural images should include a brief description as the `alt` value:

```
<img src="instagram.png" alt="Icon for link to Instagram">
```

Here are some notes on writing useful `alt` text:

» Keep it short. Longwinded descriptions are rarely needed or useful.

» Say directly what the image represents.

» Include meaningful details from the image. Here, *meaningful* means relevant to the context of the page or surrounding text.

» Don't repeat any info that's already in the surrounding text.

» You don't need to add an `alt` value for purely decorative images, but you must include the `alt` tag (set to an empty string: `alt=""`) or your HTML code won't validate.

Making other media accessible

Compared to images, video and audio content take a bit more work to make them accessible, which essentially means doing one of the following:

» **Audio content:** Auditorily impaired users can't hear content delivered via the `audio` element. You can support these users by making a transcript of the audio available.

» **Video content:** Visually impaired users can't see content delivered via the `video` element, while auditorily impaired users can't hear the `video` element's audio track. For the former, you can create an audio description track that provides a narration of what's happening in the video. For the latter, a transcript of the video's audio track should be made available and your video should have closed captions or subtitles that appear while the video is playing.

One way of making captions or subtitles appear while a video is playing is to create a Web Video Text Tracks (WebVTT) file, which is a text file that contains time cues and text to display during those cues.

TIP

The building of a WebVTT text file is straightforward, but it's beyond the scope of this book. Fortunately, an excellent description of the format is on the Mozilla Developer Network at `https://developer.mozilla.org/en-US/docs/Web/API/WebVTT_API`.

Once you have your WebVTT file (which uses the `.vtt` extension), you then use the `track` element to let the browser know the file is available for a `video` element:

```
<track kind="type" src="filename">
```

where:

>> *type* is the type of track. For *value*, you can use any of the following keywords: `subtitles` (this is the default), `captions`, `descriptions` (descriptions of the video content), or `chapters` (chapter titles only).

>> *filename* is the filename (and path, if the file resides in a directory other than the one that stores the HTML file) of the WebVTT file.

You insert the `<track>` tag between the `<video>` and `</video>` tags, like so:

```
<video
    src="/media/videos/kumquats.mp4"
    controls
    <track
        kind="captions"
        src="/media/cc/kumquats-captions.vtt">
</video>
```

Buffing Up Your App Accessibility Semantics

Whenever you're wearing your "accessibility" hat, one of the key questions you need to ask yourself for each element on your app is, "What might an assistive technology need to know about this element?" That is, what information do you need to provide so that a screen reader or similar AT can determine the purpose of the element?

In other words, you want to make the *meaning* of each element clear, and the info you provide about the meaning of each element is referred to as *accessibility semantics*. Over the next few sections, I talk about a few ways that you can enhance the accessibility semantics of your apps.

Adding form field labels

In Book 6, Chapter 2, I talk about the `label` element, which you can use to associate a text label or caption with a form field. You can use two methods:

>> **Implicit label:** Surround the form field with `<label>` and `</label>` tags, and insert the label text either before or after the field. Here's an example:

```
<label>
    Favorite vegetable:
    <input type="text">
</label>
```

>> **Explicit label:** Insert an `id` value into the field tag, set the `<label>` tag's `for` attribute to the same value, and insert the label text between the `<label>` and `</label>` tags. Here's a for instance:

```
<label for="fave-veg">Favorite vegetable:</label>
<input id="fave-veg" type="text">
```

Adding the `<label>` tag provides two accessibility wins:

>> It enables the user to select the field by also clicking the label. This approach increases the target area for clicking, which helps users with unsteady hands.

>> The label text is now associated with the field, which means a screen reader will read out the label text when the user selects the field.

Be sure to add a label for every `<input>` tag, as well as each `<select>` and `<textarea>` tag.

Understanding ARIA roles, state, and properties

The World Wide Web Consortium is home to the Web Accessibility Initiative (WAI), which aims to make the web an accessible place for everyone. One of the key WAI technologies is Accessible Rich Internet Applications (ARIA), is a collection of roles, states, and properties designed to bring accessibility semantics to every element of your web app's user interface:

>> **ARIA role:** A keyword that defines what type of user interface control a page element represents. For example, if you've coded a div element to look and work like a command button, that element's role is button. You assign a role to an element using the role attribute, like so:

```
<div role="button">Apply Changes</div>
```

>> **ARIA property:** A value that describes some aspect of the user interface control. For example, if you want to include placeholder text in an editable div element, you can let assistive technologies know about the placeholder by adding the aria-placeholder attribute:

```
<div
    contenteditable
    role="textbox"
    aria-placeholder="user@domain.com">
</div>
```

>> **ARIA state:** A keyboard or value that specifies the current condition of the user interface control. For example, if your web application uses a div element as an on/off switch but that element is currently disabled, you can signal that disabled state to assistive technologies by setting the aria-disabled attribute to true:

```
<div role="switch" aria-disabled="true"></div>
```

The three main categories of ARIA roles are

>> Landmark roles

>> Section structure roles

>> Widget roles

REMEMBER

I talk about the roles in each of these categories in the next few sections. However, it's important to understand that you don't need to use ARIA roles if you use semantic HTML elements because those elements have implicit roles that are understood by assistive technologies. For example, the button element has an implicit button role, so there's no need to include role="button" in the <button> tag. See https://developer.mozilla.org/en-US/docs/Web/Accessibility/ARIA/Roles/ for a satisfyingly complete look at the ARIA roles.

Landmark ARIA roles

Landmark ARIA roles identify major structural elements of the app, and assistive technologies use these landmarks to enable the user to navigate quickly through the major sections of a app. Table 3-1 lists the landmark roles and their corresponding HTML semantic elements.

TABLE 3-1   ## Landmark ARIA Roles

ARIA Role	HTML Semantic Element
banner	header
complementary	aside
contentinfo	footer
form	form
main	main
navigation	nav
region	section
search	N/A

The search role doesn't have an equivalent HTML element, but most of the time you'll use it within a form element, like this:

```
<form role="search">
    Your search controls go here
</form>
```

WARNING

The point of landmark roles (and their corresponding HTML sectioning elements) is to give assistive tech a forest-instead-of-the-trees view of the page. Therefore, don't overuse landmark roles or you run the risk of your page appearing to be nothing but trees!

Section structure ARIA roles

Section structure ARIA roles identify sections of page content with a specific purpose. Most section structure ARIA roles have a semantic HTML equivalent, but a few don't, and I list those in Table 3-2.

Table 3-3 lists the section structure ARIA roles that have semantic HTML equivalents. In each case, it's best to use the semantic HTML elements instead of the ARIA roles.

Widget ARIA roles

Widget ARIA roles identify interactive user interface elements. Table 3-4 lists those widget ARIA roles that don't have semantic HTML equivalents.

TABLE 3-2   **Section Structure Roles without HTML Equivalents**

ARIA Role	Description
feed	Identifies a scrollable list of items where new items are added as the user scrolls to the bottom of the list
math	Identifies a mathematical expression
none (or presentation)	Hides an element's implicit ARIA role from assistive technologies
note	Identifies a section with content that is ancillary to the main app topic
toolbar	Identifies a section with controls that are meant to be used as a toolbar
tooltip	Identifies text that appears when the user hovers the mouse pointer over an element or gives the element focus via the keyboard

TABLE 3-3   **Section Structure Roles with HTML Equivalents**

ARIA Role	HTML Semantic Element
article	article
cell	td
definition	dfn
figure	figure
heading	h1 through h6
img	img or picture
list	ol or ul
listitem	li
meter	meter
row	tr
rowgroup	tbody, thead, or tfoot
rowheader	th
table	table
term	dfn or dt

Making a Web App Accessible

TABLE 3-4 **Widget Roles without HTML Equivalents**

ARIA Role	Identifies
combobox	An input control that enables the user to either type a value or select a value from a list
menu	A control that enables the user to select an item from a list of choices
menubar	A control that contains a set of menu widgets
scrollbar	A app object that controls vertical or horizontal scrolling within a viewing region
searchbox	A text box control used specifically to input text for a search operation
slider	An input control that enables the user to choose from a range of values
spinbutton	An input control that enables the user to increment or decrement a value
switch	An input control that the user can alternate between the on and off state
tab	A control that, when selected, displays its associated tabpanel widget
tablist	A control that contains a set of tab widgets
tabpanel	A control that contains the content of the currently selected tab widget
tree	A widget that enables the user to select one or more items from a hierarchical set
treegrid	A tabular version of a tree widget
treeitem	An item in a tree widget

There are also a few widget ARIA roles that have semantic HTML equivalents, as I outline in Table 3-5. In each case, it's best to use the semantic HTML elements instead of the ARIA roles because all modern assistive technologies understand the semantic HTML elements and adding ARIA roles could create confusion for the user.

TABLE 3-5 **Widget Roles with HTML Equivalents**

ARIA Role	HTML Semantic Element
button	button
checkbox	input type="checkbox"
link	a
option	option
progressbar	progress
radio	input type="radio"
textbox	input type="text"

Differentiating semantic app elements of the same type

One problem you run into when trying to accommodate screen readers in your code is when you have multiple semantic page elements of the same type. For example, your app might have two nav elements: one in the page header, another in the page article, as shown here:

```
<header>
    <nav>
        <h3>Site Navigation</h3>
        Site navigation code goes here
    </nav>
</header>

<main>
    <article>
        <nav>
            <h3>Article Navigation</h3>
            Article navigation code goes here
        </nav>
    </article>
</main>
```

How can a screen reader user find out what each nav element does? One option is to navigate through the elements to see what each one contains, a time-consuming and burdensome process. A better way is to add an id attribute to the h3 element within each nav element, and then use the aria-labelledby attribute in the nav element to specify the id of the associated heading. Here's the updated example:

```
<header>
    <nav aria-labelledby="site-navigation">
        <h3 id="site-navigation">Site Navigation</h3>
        Site navigation code goes here
    </nav>
</header>

<main>
    <article>
        <nav aria-labelledby="article-navigation">
            <h3 id="article-navigation">Article Navigation</h3>
            Article navigation code goes here
        </nav>
    </article>
</main>
```

For example, within the header element, the `<h3>` tag now has an id attribute with the site-navigation value. In the nav element, the aria-labelledby attribute is also given the site-navigation value. This tells the screen reader that the Site Navigation text describes this particular nav element.

What if your user interface doesn't have a handy h3 (or whatever) element to act as the label? No problemo. You can use the aria-label attribute directly in the tag you want to label:

```
<header>
    <nav aria-label="Site Navigation">
        Site navigation code goes here
    </nav>
</header>

<main>
    <article>
        <nav aria-label="Article Navigation">
            Article navigation code goes here
        </nav>
    </article>
</main>
```

Making Your Apps Keyboard-Friendly

Many users with disabilities lack the dexterity or the ability to use a mouse or other pointing device. Many of those users navigate and interact with web apps using the keyboard, so it's vital that your web apps be keyboard-friendly.

Out of the box, HTML offers the following keyboard support:

>> Form controls and links are navigable via the keyboard.

>> All other HTML elements are *not* navigable via the keyboard.

>> Pressing Tab moves the focus forward from the current element to the next navigable element, where *forward* refers to the direction that the elements appear in the HTML source code.

>> Pressing Shift+Tab moves the focus backward from the current element to the previous navigable element, where *backward* refers to the reverse direction that the elements appear in the HTML source code.

>> For navigable elements that have multiple components — such as a group of radio buttons or a selection list — once the user places the focus on the element, the user can navigate the components inside the element by pressing the arrow keys.

>> Pressing the spacebar selects the current element. When a button element has the focus, for example, pressing the spacebar is the same as clicking the button; when a check box has the focus, pressing the spacebar toggles the check box between the selected (checked) and nonselected (unchecked) state.

The order in which the app elements receive the focus as you press Tab is called — no surprises here— the *tab order*. What *is* surprising is that the tab order isn't set in stone, meaning that you can both add elements to it and remove elements from it. The next two sections provide the details.

TIP

Another way you can ramp up the keyboard friendliness of your web app is to assign shortcut keys to user interface controls. Defining keyboard shortcuts falls under the spell of JavaScript and I cover that technique in Book 6, Chapter 2.

Adding an element to the tab order

If you stick with native HTML elements, there's probably nothing extra you need do for accessible keyboard access. However, what if you have, say, a div or span element that you want to be accessible by pressing Tab or Shift+Tab? That's no problem because all that's required is plopping tabindex="0" into the tag, like this:

```
<div role="tablist" tabindex="0">
```

When the web browser sees tabindex="0" inside a tag, it automatically adds that element to the tab order, so users will be able to navigate to the element using Tab or Shift+Tab. How awesome is *that*?

Removing an element from the tab order

Every once in a while, you might end up with a navigable page element that you *don't* want in the tab order. For example, if an element is disabled, there's no point in users navigating to it using Tab or Shift+Tab.

To remove an element from the tab order, insert `tabindex="-1"` into the element's tag, like so:

```
<button tabindex="-1">
    Can't touch this
</button>
```

When the web browser stumbles upon `tabindex="-1"` inside a tag, it removes that element from the tab order, so users pressing Tab or Shift+Tab will skip right over it.

Ensuring Sufficient Color Contrast

Some people — even some people with decent eyesight — have trouble reading web page text if there isn't sufficient contrast between the color of the text and the color of the background. For example, it's distressingly common these days to see either light gray text on a slightly lighter gray background (see Figure 3-1, left) or dark gray text on a slightly darker gray background (see Figure 3-1, right). Some web designers think this is cool, but the rest of us might use some saltier language to describe it.

The examples in Figure 3-1 are admittedly a bit extreme, but you shouldn't assume that just because you can easily read your text, everyone will have just as easy a time. Lots of people with either a visual impairment or aging eyes have trouble reading text that appears insufficiently darker or lighter than the background.

FIGURE 3-1:
Light text on a light background (left) and dark text on a dark background (right).

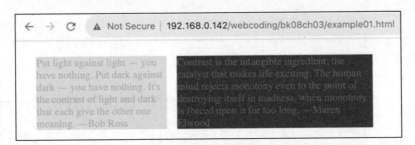

So, how do you know when the foreground and background colors you've chosen have enough color contrast? You can turn to a measurement called the *contrast ratio*, which compares the hue and luminance (brightness) of one color with the hue and luminance of another. The result is a number greater than or equal to one with the following properties:

>> The lower the number, the lower the contrast between the two colors.

>> The higher the number, the greater the contrast between the two colors.

>> A contrast ratio of 1 means the two colors are the same (or close enough to being the same).

Okay, so what is *sufficient* color contrast? The world's web accessibility gurus have decreed that a contrast ratio of 4.5 or higher is what you need to shoot for. Happily, you don't have to worry about calculating contrast ratios yourself. Instead, you can use an online tool called WebAIM (Web Accessibility In Mind) Contrast Checker, which is available at `https://webaim.org/resources/contrastchecker/`. In both the Foreground Color and Background Color boxes, either enter an RGB hex color code or click the color swatch to choose a color. Instantly, the app spits out the contrast ratio (see Figure 3-2).

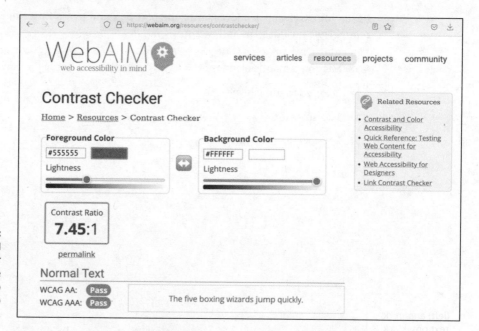

FIGURE 3-2: Use the WebAIM Contrast Checker to find out the contrast ratio between any two colors.

Validating the Accessibility of an App

Keeping track of all the accessibility tweaks I discuss in this chapter might seem daunting. What if you miss something? That's a legit concern, but the web can help. Once your app is on the web, you can check its accessibility by heading over to the Web Accessibility Evaluation Tool (WAVE) at `http://wave.webaim.org`, shown in Figure 3-3.

Paste your web app's address into the text box and press Enter or Return to see a report that includes the following:

>> Missing semantic elements

>> Skipped heading levels

>> Too-small text

>> Too-low color contrast ratios

IN THIS CHAPTER

» Getting familiar with security issues

» Sanitizing data coming into the server

» Sanitizing data going out from the server

» Securing file uploads and user passwords

» Setting up secure directories and sessions

Chapter **4**

Securing a Web App

"I saw the head of the company on CNN or something. He said nobody could get into their network. Their security systems were foolproof. I wanted to see if that was true." "Were they?" "As a matter of fact, yeah, they were foolproof. The problem is that you don't have to protect yourself against fools. You have to protect yourself against people like me."

— JEFFERY DEAVER

Like it or not (and I suspect not), we live in a world populated by a small but determined band of miscreants who spend all their time, energy, and intellect trying to deface, destroy, or exploit web apps just like the ones you want to build. And make no mistake: If you put an unprotected web app online, sooner or later (almost certainly sooner) it will be found by one or more (almost certainly more) of these evildoers and bad things will inevitably ensue.

So, grab yourself a marker and a piece of paper, write the word *SECURITY* in big, bold letters, and tape the paper to your cat's forehead as a constant reminder that building a web app really means building a *secure* web app. And I don't mean building your app and then bolting on some security features at the very end — no, you need to bake in the security goodness right from the start.

Fortunately, if you implement multiple lines of defense — a strategy sometimes called *defense in depth* — you can inoculate your app against all but the most determined attacks. In this chapter, you dive deep into the all-important world of web app security. You learn what dangers your web apps might encounter and how to keep an innocent web app safe in the face of those dangers.

Web App Security: Nutshell Version

As important as web app security is, you might be surprised to hear that I can summarize it with just two axioms:

REMEMBER

>> **Never trust data sent to the server.** For example, if you have a form with a text field, an attacker can insert a specially constructed text string that forces MySQL to perform unwanted actions, such as deleting data. Alternatively, it's possible for an attacker to submit data to the server without using your form at all.

>> **Always control data sent from the server.** When you send data back to the web page, you need to be sure that you're not sending anything dangerous. For example, if an attacker uses a form's text field to submit a `<script>` tag with malicious JavaScript code, and you then redisplay the form's values without checking them, that script will execute. Similarly, if you use the server to store sensitive data such as sign-in passwords and private information, you need to install safeguards so that this data doesn't fall into the wrong hands.

The following section takes you through the most common security problems.

Understanding the Dangers

It often seems that there are almost as many security exploits as there are low-lifes trying to compromise our apps. However, the most common security dangers fall into four main categories: SQL injection, cross-site scripting, insecure file uploads, and unauthorized access.

SQL injection

WARNING

Probably the most common exploit, *SQL injection* involves inserting some malicious code into an ordinary SQL command, such as a SELECT or DELETE statement. Consider the following sign-in form:

```
<form>
    <label for="username">User name:</label>
    <input id="username" type="text" name="user">
    <label for="password">Password:</label>
    <input id="password" type="password" name="pass">
</form>
```

When this form is submitted, a PHP script to sign in the user might look, in part, like this:

```
<?php
    $user = $_POST['user'];
    $pass = $_POST['pass'];
    $sql = "SELECT *
            FROM users
            WHERE username='$user' AND password='$pass'";
?>
```

That works fine as long as the user types a legit username and password, but what happens if some scoundrel types admin' # in the user field and nothing in the password field? Here's the resulting value of the $sql variable:

```
SELECT * FROM users WHERE username='admin' #' AND password=''
```

The key here is the hash symbol (#), which marks the beginning of a comment in an SQL command, meaning that the rest of the line is ignored. (MySQL also uses -- to mark the start of a comment.) That is, the actual SQL command that gets processed is this:

```
SELECT * FROM users WHERE username='admin'
```

Congratulations, some criminal has just signed in as the administrator!

As another example, suppose your web app has a button that, when clicked, deletes an item from the current user's data. Your Fetch API call might pass along a user-id and an item-id, meaning that your PHP script would do something like the following to remove the specified item:

```
<?php
    $user_id = $_POST['user-id'];
    $item_id = $_POST['item-id'];
    $sql = "DELETE
            FROM items
            WHERE userid='$user_id' AND itemid='$item_id'";
?>
```

Looks fine from here, but suppose some fiend passes the following as the user-id value: whatever' OR 1=1 #. Assuming the item-id value is blank, here's the resulting $sql variable value:

```
DELETE FROM items WHERE userid='whatever' OR 1=1 #' AND
   itemid=''
```

Taking the comment symbol (#) into account, the actual command looks like this:

```
DELETE FROM items WHERE userid='whatever' OR 1=1
```

The 1=1 part always returns TRUE, so the result is that the command deletes everything from the items table!

Cross-site scripting (XSS)

WARNING

Cross-site scripting (usually shortened to *XSS*) is a way of surreptitiously forcing an innocent user to launch an attacker's malicious script. This happens most often when the malefactor uses a phishing email or similar ruse to trick the user into visiting a page that spoofs a form used on a legitimate site.

For example, suppose the form asks the user to enter their credit card number and password. If this were a normal form submission and the user entered either the wrong credit card number of the wrong password, the PHP script on the server might redisplay the form to ask the user to try again:

```php
<?php
    $cc = $_POST['credit-card'];
    $pw = $_POST['password'];

    // Code that checks these inputs goes here

    // If one or both inputs are invalid:
    echo '<input type="text" name="credit-card" value="' .
  $cc . '">';
    echo '<input type="password" name="password">';
?>
```

Note, in particular, that this "helpful" script redisplays the credit card value (stored in the $cc variable) in the text field. Imagine, then, that our attacker's spoofed form actually sends the following text instead of the credit card number:

```
"><script>alert('Ha ha!');</script><a href="
```

Here's the resulting HTML (which I tidied up a bit so you can see what's going on):

```
<input type="text" name="credit-card" value="">
<script>
    alert('Ha ha!');
</script>
<a href="">
<input type="password" name="password" value="">
```

What happens here? That's right: The JavaScript code between the `<script>` and `</script>` tags executes and, believe me, in the real world it's unlikely to just display an innocuous alert box.

Insecure file uploads

WARNING

If your web app allows users to upload files — for example, you might want to allow each user to upload a small image to use as a profile avatar —you open a new can of security worms because a malicious user can

>> Upload huge files, which tax the server's resources.

>> Upload a nasty script instead of, say, an image.

>> Overwrite existing server files.

Unauthorized access

WARNING

If your web app requires users to sign in with a username (or email address) and password, keeping those passwords secure is of paramount importance. Otherwise, an unauthorized interloper could sign in as a legitimate user and destroy or tamper with that user's data, post messages or other content under that user's name, and even delete the user's account.

Sanitizing Incoming Data

Defending your web app begins with *sanitizing* any data sent to the server. The five main ways to sanitize data are converting, filtering, data type checking, whitelisting, and using prepared statements.

Converting incoming data

Converting incoming data means encoding the input's potentially dangerous characters to harmless equivalents. The most useful PHP function for this is `htmlspecialchars()`, which takes a string input and converts the following special characters to an HTML entity code or an HTML character code:

Character	Name	Is converted to
<	less than	<
>	greater than	>
"	double quote	"
'	single quote	'
&	ampersand	&

Here's an example (bk07ch04/example01.html):

HTML:

```
<form>
    <label for="message">Send me a message:</label><br>
    <textarea id="message" name="message">
        <script>
            alert("Take that!")
        </script>
    </textarea><br>
    <button>Submit</button>
</form>

<label for="output">Output:</label><br>
<div id="output">
</div>
```

JavaScript (with error-checking code removed for clarity):

```
// Get a reference to the form
const form = document.querySelector('form');

// Listen for the submit event
form.addEventListener('submit', async (event) => {
```

```
    // Prevent the default form submission
    event.preventDefault();

    // Get the form data
    const formData = new FormData(form);

    // Ship it via fetch() POST
    const response = await fetch('http://localhost/webcoding/
bk07ch04/example01.php', {
        method: 'POST',
        body: formData
    });

    // Get the sanitized string
    const data = await response.text();

    // Output the (no longer dangerous) string
    document.querySelector('#output').innerText = data;
});
```

Here's the PHP code (bk07ch04/example01.php; I removed the error-checking code for clarity):

```
<?php
    header('Content-Type: application/html');
    header('Access-Control-Allow-Origin: *');

    $msg = $_POST['message'];

    // Convert the string to harmless characters
    echo htmlspecialchars($msg);
?>
```

In the HTML form, note the text in the `textarea` element:

```
<script>
    alert("Take that!")
</script>
```

Yikes! Not to worry, though, because the PHP script sanitizes it to harmless text, as shown below the Output: label in Figure 4-1.

TIP

A similar PHP function is `htmlentities()`, which takes a string input and converts any special characters (not just the five listed previously) to either an HTML entity code, if one exists, or to an HTML character code.

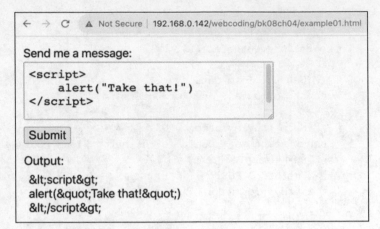

Filtering incoming data

Filtering incoming data means removing unwanted characters from an input. This step is useful for security — for example, by stripping dangerous characters from, say, an email field — but it's useful also for sanitizing incoming data. For example, if your app expects a particular input to be an integer, it's helpful to strip any characters that aren't digits or the characters plus (+) and minus (−).

To filter incoming data, use PHP's `filter_input()` function and specify one or more of the function's sanitizing filters:

```
filter_input(input_type, input, filter)
```

where:

>> *input_type* is a constant that specifies the type of input. Use INPUT_GET for GET requests; use INPUT_POST for POST requests.

>> *input* is the input value you want to sanitize.

>> *filter* is a constant that determines the characters you want to remove from *input*. Here are some useful filters:

  ● FILTER_SANITIZE_EMAIL: Removes all characters except letters, numbers, and the following: !#$%&'*+−?^_`{|}~@.[]

  ● FILTER_SANITIZE_NUMBER_FLOAT: Removes all characters except numbers, decimal point (.), thousands separator (,), scientific notation (e and E), plus (+), and minus (−). To allow decimals, add the FILTER_FLAG_ALLOW_FRACTION flag; to allow the thousands separator, add the FILTER_FLAG_ALLOW_THOUSAND flag; to allow scientific notation, add the FILTER_FLAG_ALLOW_SCIENTIFIC flag. Note that, of these last three flags, you can use only one at a time.

- FILTER_SANITIZE_NUMBER_INT: Removes all characters except numbers, plus (+), and minus (–).

- FILTER_SANITIZE_SPECIAL_CHARS: HTML-encodes less than (<), greater than (>), single quote ('), double quote ("), ampersand (&), and control characters such as tab, line feed, and carriage return.

- FILTER_SANITIZE_URL: Removes all characters except letters, numbers, and the following: $-_.+!*'(),{}|\\^~[]`<>#%";/?:@&=

Here's an example (bk07ch04/example02.html):

HTML:

```
<form>
    <fieldset>
        <legend>Submit your score:</legend>
        <label for="name">Name:</label>
        <input type="text" id="name" name="name"
  value="<script>alert('Here comes trouble!')
  </script>"><br>
        <label for="email">Email:</label>
        <input type="text" id="email" name="email"
  value="<script>alert('Uh oh!')</script>"><br>
        <label for="age">Age:</label>
        <input type="text" id="age" name="age" value="#42#"><br>
        <label for="score">Score:</label>
        <input type="text" id="score" name="score"
  value="1,024.5"><br>
        <button>Submit</button>
    </fieldset>
</form>
<p>
<label for="output">Output:</label>
<div id="output">
</div>
```

JavaScript (with error-checking code removed for clarity):

```
// Get a reference to the form
const form = document.querySelector('form');

// Listen for the submit event
form.addEventListener('submit', async (event) => {
```

```
    // Prevent the default form submission
    event.preventDefault();

    // Get the form data
    const formData = new FormData(form);

    // Ship it via fetch() POST
    const response = await fetch('http://localhost/webcoding/
bk07ch04/example02.php', {
        method: 'POST',
        body: formData
    });

    // Get the filtered data
    const data = await response.json();

    // Output the data
    const output = document.querySelector('#output');
    for (let key in data) {
        if (data.hasOwnProperty(key)) {
            output.insertAdjacentHTML('beforeend', '<div>');
            output.insertAdjacentText('beforeend', `${key}:
${data[key]}`);
            output.insertAdjacentHTML('beforeend', '<\div>');
        }
    }
});
```

The form contains four text fields used to gather the user's name, email address, age, and score (which might be a rating or similar value). (Note that, in a production form, you'd use HTML's built-in field types: `email` for the email field and `number` for the age and score fields.) Note that the default values I assigned to each field are either dangerous (the `script` elements in the name and email fields) or contain extra characters (the # characters in the age field) or unwanted characters (the comma in the score field).

Here's the PHP script called by the `fetch()` function (bk07ch04/example02.php; I removed the error-checking code for clarity):

```
<?php
    header('Content-Type: application/json');
    header('Access-Control-Allow-Origin: *');
```

```php
    // Filter the name field
    $name = filter_input(INPUT_POST, 'name',
FILTER_SANITIZE_SPECIAL_CHARS);

    // Filter the email field
    $email = filter_input(INPUT_POST, 'email',
FILTER_SANITIZE_EMAIL);

    // Filter the age field
    $age = filter_input(INPUT_POST, 'age',
FILTER_SANITIZE_NUMBER_INT);

    // Filter the score field
    $score = filter_input(INPUT_POST, 'score', FILTER_SANITIZE_
NUMBER_FLOAT, FILTER_FLAG_ALLOW_FRACTION);

    // Put the filtered data into an array
    $form_data = array('name' => $name,
                       'email' => $email,
                       'age' => $age,
                       'score' => $score);

    // Convert the array to JSON
    $JSON_data = json_encode($form_data, JSON_HEX_APOS |
JSON_HEX_QUOT);

    // Output the JSON
    echo $JSON_data;
?>
```

The JavaScript code grabs the returned JSON data, loops through the resulting object, and displays the filtered values, as shown in Figure 4-2.

Checking the data type of incoming data

Data type checking means testing the data type of the input to ensure that it matches what's expected. PHP calls this *character type checking*, and it offers the following functions:

>> ctype_alnum(*input*): Returns TRUE if *input* contains only letters or numbers or both

>> ctype_alpha(*input*): Returns TRUE if *input* contains only letters

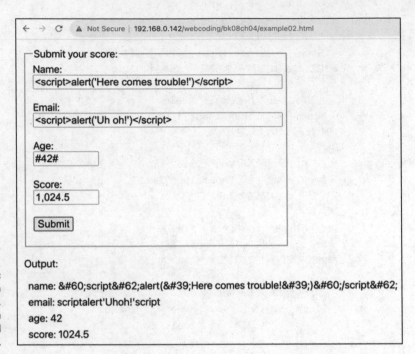

FIGURE 4-2:
When this form
is submitted,
the Output area
shows the filtered
form values.

» `ctype_digit(input)`: Returns TRUE if *input* contains only numbers

» `ctype_lower(input)`: Returns TRUE if *input* contains only lowercase letters

» `ctype_upper(input)`: Returns TRUE if *input* contains only uppercase letters

Here's an example (bk07ch04/example03.html):

HTML:

```
<form>
    <fieldset>
        <legend>Dad Joke Generator</legend>
        <label for="joke-number">Joke # (1-50):</label>
        <input type="text" id="joke-number" name="joke-number"
  value="#42"><br>
        <button>Submit</button>
    </fieldset>
</form>
<p>
<label for="output">Joke:</label>
<div id="output">
</div>
```

JavaScript (with error-checking code removed for clarity):

```javascript
// Get a reference to the form
const form = document.querySelector('form');

// Listen for the submit event
form.addEventListener('submit', async (event) => {

    // Prevent the default form submission
    event.preventDefault();

    // Get the form data
    const formData = new FormData(form);

    // Ship it via fetch() POST
    const response = await fetch('http://localhost/webcoding/
bk07ch04/example03.php', {
        method: 'POST',
        body: formData
    });

    // Get the data
    const data = await response.text();

    // Output the data
    const output = document.querySelector('#output');
    output.textContent = data;
});
```

The form contains a single text field where the user inputs a number between 1 and 50, each of which corresponds to a different Dad joke on the server. The default value is #42, which isn't a number.

Here's the PHP script called by the fetch() function (bk07ch04/example03.php; I removed the error-checking code for clarity):

```php
<?php
    header('Content-Type: application/text');
    header('Access-Control-Allow-Origin: *');

    // Make sure we have the joke-number input
    if (isset($_POST['joke-number'])) {
        // Make sure the joke number input is numeric
        if (!ctype_digit($_POST['joke-number'])) {
            // If not, alert the user
```

```
            echo 'The joke must be a number!<br>';
            echo 'Please try again.';
            exit(0);
        }
    }

    // Store the joke number, subtracting 1 to allow for the
0-based array
    $dad_joke_num = $_POST['joke-number'] - 1;

    // Here come the jokes
    $dad_jokes = [
        "Time flies like an arrow; fruit flies like a banana.",
        "I used to be a baker because I kneaded dough.",
        "I used to play piano by ear, but now I use my hands.",
        "Why was the broom late? It over swept.",
        "I'm reading a book about anti-gravity. It's impossible
    to put down!",
etc.
    ];

    // Output the joke as text
    echo $dad_jokes[$dad_joke_num];
?>
```

The PHP script uses `ctype_digit()` to check whether the input value is numeric. If it isn't, the script returns a message to the user, as shown in Figure 4-3; otherwise, the script returns the requested joke as text.

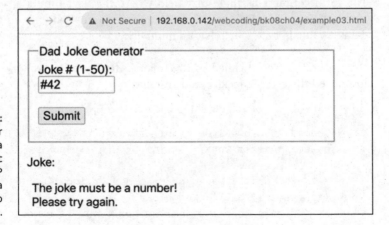

FIGURE 4-3: If the user submits a non-numeric value, the PHP script returns a message to try again.

Whitelisting incoming data

Whitelisting means allowing only certain values in an input. For example, suppose the input is an account number of the form 12–3456, that is, two numbers, a hyphen (–), and then four numbers. You can't use `ctype_digit()` on this value directly because of the hyphen, but you can temporarily remove the hyphen and then check the resulting value:

```
$acct_num = $_POST['account-number'];
$allowed = '-';
$new_input = str_replace($allowed, '', $acct_num);
if(ctype_digit($new_input) === false) {
    exit(0);
}
```

This code uses the `str_replace()` function to replace hyphens with the empty string (which removes them) and then runs `ctype_digit()` on the result.

TIP

If your input has multiple acceptable characters, you can whitelist them all by setting the `$allowed` variable to an array:

```
$allowed = array(',', '.', '$');
```

Using prepared statements

As I show earlier in this chapter, the nastiness that is SQL injection works by tricking an innocent SQL statement into running malevolent code. You can (and should) try to prevent that by sanitizing your form inputs, but MySQL also offers a powerful technique that gives you exquisite control over the type of data that gets included in an SQL statement. The technique is called *prepared statements* (or sometimes *parameterized statements* or *parameterized queries*), and it means you no longer send an SQL statement directly to the database server. Instead, the query now proceeds in three separate stages:

1. The preparation stage.

This stage involves running an SQL-like statement through MySQLi's `mysqli_ prepare ()` method. Most importantly, you replace each external value (that is, each value received from a web form) with a question mark (?), which acts as a placeholder for the value. The statement you've thus prepared acts as a kind of template that MySQLi will use to run the query.

2. The binding stage.

This stage involves using MySQLi's `mysqli_stmt_bind_param()` method to define each external value as a parameter, and then bind that parameter to the prepared statement. Specifically, MySQLi replaces each ? placeholder with a parameter. The binding specifies a data type (such as a string or integer) for each parameter.

3. The execution stage.

The final stage runs MySQLi's `mysqli_stmt_execute()` method on the prepared statement. This hands off the running of the SQL command to the server, which uses the combination of the prepared statement template and the bound parameters to run the SQL operation.

Because the server knows what data types to accept for the external values, it can't run injected SQL code as actual code. Instead, it treats the injection as text (or whatever data type you specify), and the SQL operation runs in complete safety.

Here's an example (bk07ch04/example04.html):

HTML:

```
<form>
    <fieldset>
        <legend>Customer Orders By Employee</legend>
        <label for="customer">Customer:</label>
        <select id="customer" name="customer">
            <option value="ALFKI">Alfreds Futterkiste</option>
            <option value="ANATR">Ana Trujillo Emparedados y
helados</option>
            <option value="ANTON">Antonio Moreno Taqueria
    </option>
etc.
        </select>
        <label for="employee">Employee:</label>
        <select id="employee" name="employee">
            <option value="5">Steven Buchanan</option>
            <option value="8">Laura Callahan</option>
            <option value="1">Nancy Davolio</option>
            <option value="9">Anne Dodsworth</option>
            <option value="2">Andrew Fuller</option>
            <option value="7">Robert King</option>
            <option value="3">Janet Leverling</option>
            <option value="4">Margaret Peacock</option>
            <option value="6">Michael Suyama</option>
```

```
        </select><br>
        <button>Submit</button>
    </fieldset>
</form>
<p>
<label for="output">Orders:</label>
<div id="output">
</div>
```

JavaScript (with error-checking code removed for clarity):

```
// Get a reference to the form
const form = document.querySelector('form');

// Listen for the submit event
form.addEventListener('submit', async (event) => {

    // Prevent the default form submission
    event.preventDefault();

    // Get the form data
    const formData = new FormData(form);

    // Ship it via fetch() POST
    const response = await fetch('http://localhost/webcoding/
bk07ch04/example04.php', {
        method: 'POST',
        body: formData
    });

    // Get the data
    const data = await response.json();

    // Get a reference to the output element and then clear it
    const output = document.querySelector('#output');
    output.innerHTML = '';

    // Check for no data returned
    if (data.length === 0) {
        output.innerText = "No orders returned. Please try again
with a different customer and/or employee."
    }

    // Iterate the returned array of orders
    data.forEach((orderData, index) => {
```

```
      // Insert a section element to hold the order data
      output.insertAdjacentHTML('beforeend',
`<section id="order-${index}">`);

      // Get a reference to the new section element
      let order = document.querySelector(`#order-${index}`);

      // Iterate the object contained in the current array
item (orderData)
      for (let key in orderData) {
          // Insert a div element to hold the order data
          order.insertAdjacentHTML('beforeend', '<div>');
          order.insertAdjacentText('beforeend', `${key}:
${orderData[key]}`);
          order.insertAdjacentHTML('beforeend', '<\div>');
      }
      output.insertAdjacentHTML('beforeend', '</section>');
  });
});
```

The HTML sets up two selection lists: one for customers and one for employees. The idea behind this form is to query the database to return all customer orders placed by a particular employee. The JavaScript gathers the form data, submits it to the server using the Fetch API, and then processes the result, which is an array of objects, where each object contains the order data.

The fetch() method calls example04.php, which contains the following code (bk07ch01/example04.php; I removed some of the error-checking code for clarity):

```
<?php
    header('Content-Type: application/json');
    header('Access-Control-Allow-Origin: *');

    // Make sure we have the customer input
    if (isset($_POST['customer'])) {
        // Make sure the customer input is alpha
        if (!ctype_alpha($_POST['customer'])) {
            // If not, alert the user
            echo 'The customer must be only letters!<br>';
            echo 'Please try again.';
            exit(0);
        }
    }
```

```php
    // Filter and store the customer code
    $customer = filter_input(INPUT_POST, 'customer',
FILTER_SANITIZE_SPECIAL_CHARS);

    // Make sure we have the employee input
    if (isset($_POST['employee'])) {
        // Make sure the employee input is numeric
        if (!ctype_digit($_POST['employee'])) {
            // If not, alert the user
            echo 'The employee must be a number!<br>';
            echo 'Please try again.';
            exit(0);
        }
    }
    // Filter and store the employee code
    $employee = filter_input(INPUT_POST, 'employee',
FILTER_SANITIZE_NUMBER_INT);

    // Store the database connection parameters
    $host = 'localhost';
    $user = 'root';
    $password = '';
    $database = 'northwind';

    // Create a new MySQLi object with the database connection
parameters
    $connection = mysqli_connect($host, $user, $password,
$database);

    // Declare a string for the query template
    // Use ? to add a placeholder for each external value
    $sql = "SELECT *
            FROM orders
            INNER JOIN customers
            ON orders.customer_id = customers.customer_id
            WHERE orders.customer_id = ?
            AND orders.employee_id = ?";

    // Prepare the statement template
    $stmt = mysqli_prepare($connection, $sql);

    // Bind the parameters (one string, one integer)
    mysqli_stmt_bind_param($stmt, "si", $customer, $employee);
```

```
        // Execute the prepared statement
        mysqli_stmt_execute($stmt);

        // Get the results
        $result = mysqli_stmt_get_result($stmt);

        // Get the query rows as an associative array
        $rows = mysqli_fetch_all($result, MYSQLI_ASSOC);

        // That's it for now
        mysqli_close($connection);

        // Convert the array to JSON
        $JSON_data = json_encode($rows, JSON_HEX_APOS |
    JSON_HEX_QUOT);

        // Output the JSON
        echo $JSON_data;
    ?>
```

The code checks and sanitizes the POST input and stores the data in two variables: $customer and $employee. The code then declares the string $sql to the SQL text, but with ? placeholders used instead of the external values. The code runs the mysqli_prepare ($connection, $sql) method to create the prepared statement, which is stored in the $stmt variable. Now the code runs mysqli_stmt_bind_param() to bind the external values:

```
mysqli_stmt_bind_param(statement, types, parameter(s))
```

where:

>> *statement* is a reference to the prepared statement.

>> *types* is a string that specifies, in order, the data type of each parameter. The four possible values are s (string), i (integer), d (double; that is, a floating-point value), and b (blob; that is, a binary object, such as an image).

>> *parameter(s)* is one or more parameters you want to bind. If you have multiple parameters, separate them with commas.

The code runs the mysqli_stmt_execute($stmt) method to run the prepared statement, and then uses mysqli_stmt_get_result($stmt) to get the result of the SQL operation. The code stores the query rows in the $rows associative array, which is then converted to JSON (see the next section to learn about the json_encode() function) and outputted. Figure 4-4 shows an example output.

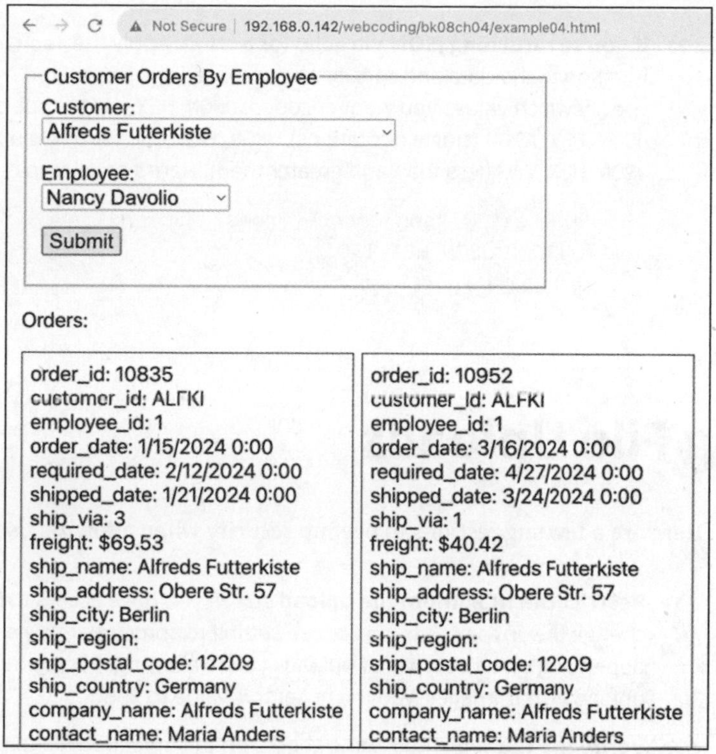

FIGURE 4-4:
A database query
rendered safe by
using prepared
statements.

Escaping Outgoing Data

Before you send data back to the web page, you need to ensure that you're not sending back anything that could produce unexpected or even malicious results. That means converting problematic characters such as ampersand (&), less than (<), greater than (>), and double quotation mark (") to HTML entities or character codes. This is called *escaping* the data.

How you do this depends on how you're returning the data:

>> **If you're returning strings via** echo **(or** print**):** Apply the htmlentities() function to each string that might contain data that needs to be escaped:

```
echo htmlentities($user_bio);
```

>> **If you're returning JSON via** `echo` (**or** `print`): Apply the `json_encode()` function to the data and specify one or more flags (separated by |) that specify which values you want encoded: JSON_HEX_AMP (ampersands), JSON_HEX_APOS (single quotations), JSON_HEX_QUOT (double quotations), or JSON_HEX_TAG (less than and greater than). Here's an example:

```
$JSON_text = json_encode($rows, JSON_HEX_APOS | JSON_HEX_
    QUOT | JSON_HEX_TAG);
echo $JSON_text;
```

Securing File Uploads

Here are a few suggestions to beef up security when allowing users to upload files:

>> **Restrict the maximum file upload size.** If you have access to `php.ini`, change the `upload_max_filesize` setting to some relatively small value, depending on what types of uploads you're allowing. For example, if users can upload avatar images, you might set this value to 2MB.

>> **Verify the file type.** Run some checks on the uploaded file to make sure its file type conforms to what your web app is expecting. For example, check the file extension to make sure it matches the type (or types) of file you allow. If you're expecting a binary file such as an image, run PHP's `is_binary()` function on the uploaded file; if this function returns FALSE, you can reject the upload because it might be a script (which is text).

>> **Use PHP's FTP functions to handle the upload.** If you have access to an FTP server, PHP's built-in FTP functions are a secure way to handle the file upload:

- `ftp_connect()`: Sets up a connection to the FTP server
- `ftp_login()`: Sends your login credentials to the FTP server
- `ftp_put()`: Transfers a file from the user's PC to the server
- `ftp_close()`: Disconnects from the FTP server

Securing Passwords

If your web app has registered users who must sign in with a password, it's essential that you do everything you can to enable users to create strong passwords and to store those passwords on the server is a secure way.

REMEMBER

Letting users create strong passwords means following these guidelines:

>> Don't place any restrictions on the character types (lowercase letters, upper-case letters, numbers, and symbols) that can be used to build a password.

>> Do require that users form their passwords using at least one character from three or, ideally, all four character types.

>> Don't set a maximum length on the password. Longer passwords are always more secure than shorter ones.

>> Do set a minimum length on the password. Eight characters is probably reasonable.

Here are some suggestions for storing and handling passwords securely:

>> **Don't transfer passwords in a URL query string.** Query strings are visible in the browser window and get added to the server logs, so any passwords are exposed.

>> **Don't store passwords in plain text.** If you do, and your system gets compromised, the attacker will have an easy time wreaking havoc on your users' accounts.

>> **Do store passwords encrypted.** You encrypt each password using a *hash*, which is a function that scrambles the password by performing a mathematical function that's easy to run but extremely difficult to reverse. PHP makes it easy to hash a password by offering the password_hash( ) function.

>> **Do salt your passwords.** A *salt* is random data added to the password before it gets hashed, which makes it even harder to decrypt. Salting is handled automatically by the password_hash( ) function.

>> **Do allow users to change their passwords.** It's good (though seldom followed) practice to change your password regularly, so you should offer this capability to your users.

>> **Don't send a password over email.** Email is sent as plain text, so it's easy for a malicious user to intercept the password.

Here's an example (bk07ch04/example05.html):

```
<form>
    <fieldset>
        <legend>Create Account:</legend>
        <label for="email">Email:</label>
        <input type="email" id="email" name="email" value="user@
example.com"><br>
```

```
        <label for="password">Password:</label>
        <input type="password" id="password"
  name="password"><br>
        <button>Create Account</button>
    </fieldset>
</form>
<p>
<label for="output">Output:</label>
<div id="output">
</div>
```

JavaScript (with error-checking code removed for clarity):

```
// Get a reference to the form
const form = document.querySelector('form');

// Listen for the submit event
form.addEventListener('submit', async (event) => {

    // Prevent the default form submission
    event.preventDefault();

    // Get the form data
    const formData = new FormData(form);

    // Ship it via fetch() POST
    const response = await fetch('http://localhost/webcoding/
  bk07ch04/example05.php', {
        method: 'POST',
        body: formData
    });

    // Get the data
    const data = await response.text();

    // Output the data
    const output = document.querySelector('#output');
    output.innerHTML = data;
});
```

The HTML code sets up a form with two fields to create a user account: one for the user's email address and another for the user's password. In the JavaScript, the fetch() method calls example05.php, which contains the following code (bk07ch01/example05.php; I removed some of the error-checking code for clarity):

```php
<?php
    header('Content-Type: application/text');
    header('Access-Control-Allow-Origin: *');

    // Filter and store the email address
    $email = filter_input(INPUT_POST, 'email',
FILTER_SANITIZE_EMAIL);

    // Store the trimmed password without filtering it
    $password = trim($_POST['password']);

    // Hash the password
    $hashedPassword = password_hash($password,
PASSWORD_DEFAULT);

    // This is where you'd store the credentials in your
database.
    // For now, just output the credentials
    echo "Email: $email<br>Hashed password: $hashedPassword";
?>
```

The PHP code sanitizes the email input, trims the password to remove any extra spaces, and then hashes the password. Note, however, that the password isn't filtered because we don't want to change the password. This approach doesn't create a security problem because we store only the hashed version of the password and would never send the raw password to the browser.

From here, the script would normally connect to a MySQL database and store the credentials. In the example script, I just send the credentials (the email address and hashed password) back to the browser, as shown in Figure 4-5.

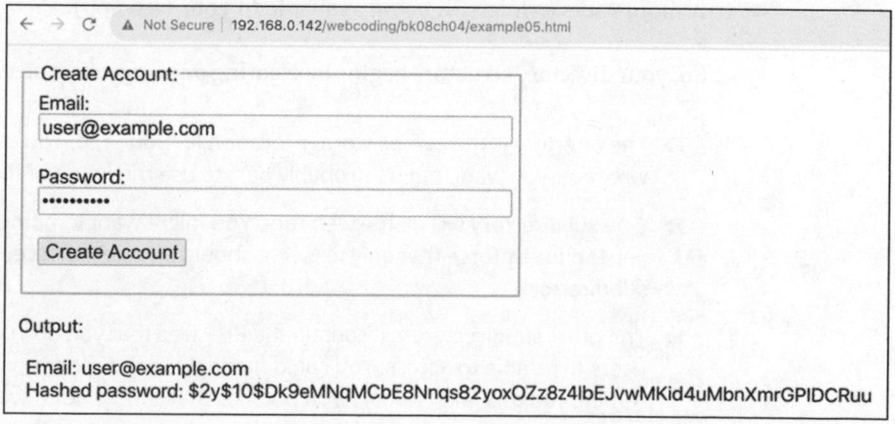

FIGURE 4-5: An example of a hashed password.

Setting Up a Secure Directory Structure

Your web app back-end work usually begins by setting up some directories and subdirectories to store your app's files. Doing this at the start offers two benefits:

REMEMBER

>> **Organization:** Even a small app can end up with quite a few files, from PHP scripts to HTML code to external CSS and JavaScript files. If you add your directories on-the-fly as they're needed, it's a certainty they'll end up a bit of a mess, with files scattered hither and thither (as my grandmother used to say). It's better to come up with a sensible directory structure now and stick with it throughout the development cycle.

>> **Security:** A smart back-end developer divides their files between those that users need to view and operate the web app and those that only do work behind the scenes. The former should be accessible to the public, but it's best to configure things so that the latter aren't accessible to anyone but you.

Okay, I hear you saying, "Organization I can get on board with, but what's all this about security?" Good question. The answer follows.

WARNING

When your app is on the web, it's stored in a directory that the web server makes publicly available to anyone who comes along. This public accessibility means that it's at least technically possible for someone to gain direct access to the files stored in that directory. That access isn't a big thing for your HTML, CSS, and JavaScript files, which anyone can easily view. However, it's a huge deal for your PHP files, which can contain sensitive information such as your database credentials.

REMEMBER

To see how you prevent such unauthorized access, you need to understand that every web app has a top-level directory, which is known as either the *web root* or the *document root.* The web root is the directory that the server makes accessible to the public, which means that anything outside the web root is inaccessible to remote users (while still being available to your web app).

So, your directory structure begins by creating one directory and two subdirectories:

>> The directory is the overall storage location for your app. You can name this whatever you want, but it's probably best to use the name of the app.

>> One subdirectory will be the web root. You might want to name your web root `public` to reinforce that only files that should be publicly accessible go in this subdirectory.

>> The other subdirectory will contain the PHP files that you don't want remote users to be able to access. You could name this subdirectory `private` to remind you that this is where you put files that should not have public access.

Defining PHP constants

It's a rare web app that doesn't have one or more variables that are used through-out the back-end code but whose value must never change. For example, when you're managing server data, your PHP files are constantly logging into the MySQL database, which requires credentials such as a username and password. That username and password are the same throughout your code, but your code will fail if, somehow, these values get changed.

REMEMBER

A variable that never changes value sounds almost like an oxymoron, so perhaps that's why programmers of yore came up with the idea of the *constant*, a special kind of variable that, once defined with a value, can't be changed. You set up a constant in PHP by using the `define()` function:

```
define(name, value)
```

where:

>> *name* is the name of the constant. By convention, constant names are all uppercase and don't begin with a dollar sign ($).

>> *value* is the value of the constant. The value must be an integer, floating point number, string, or Boolean.

Here's an example:

```
define("GREETING", "Hello Constant World!")
```

It's good web app practice to gather all your constants and put them in a separate file, which you can then include in any other PHP file that requires one or more of the constants. (I talk about how you include a PHP file in another PHP file in the next section.) Here's an example PHP file that defines some database credentials for an app:

```php
<?php
    define('HOST', 'localhost');
    define('USER', 'root');
    define('PASSWORD', '');
    define('DATABASE', 'northwind');
?>
```

You could name this file `constants.php` and add it to the app's `private` directory.

Including code from another PHP file

Most web apps are multi-page affairs, which means your app consists of multiple PHP files, each of which performs a specific task, such as creating data, retrieving data, or logging in a user. Depending on the structure of your app, each of these PHP files will include some or all of the following:

>> Constants used throughout the project

>> Database login credentials

>> Database connection code

>> Classes, functions, and other code used on each page

>> Common interface elements such as the header, app navigation, sidebar, and footer

You don't want to copy and paste all this code into each PHP file because if the code changes, you have to update every instance of the code. Instead, place each chunk of common code in its own PHP file and save those files in a subdirectory. Earlier in this chapter, I explain that you should create two common subdirectories for such files, one in the public directory and one in the private directory.

To get a common file's code into another PHP file, you could use PHP's include statement (refer to Book 6, Chapter 4). However, when it comes to including code knickknacks such as constants, classes, functions, and database connection code, it's vital that such things are included only once. To ensure that a file gets included only once, use PHP's include_once statement:

```
include_once file;
```

where *file* is the path and name of the file with the code you want to include.

For example, earlier I showed a file named constants.php, stored in an app's private subdirectory. To include that file in another file located in the same directory, you'd use the following statement:

```
include_once 'constants.php';
```

Alternatively, to include that file in another file located in the web root directory, you'd use the following statement:

```
include_once '../private/constants.php';
```

The double dots (..) stand for "go up one directory," so here they take the script up to the app's filesystem root, and from there the statement adds the path to constants.php.

Understanding PHP Sessions

One of the biggest web app challenges is keeping track of certain bits of information as the user moves from page to page within the app. For example, when someone first surfs to the app's home page, your PHP code might store the current date and time in a variable, with the goal of, say, tracking how long that person spends using the app. A worthy goal, to be sure, but when the user moves on to another page in the app, your saved date and time gets destroyed.

Similarly, suppose the user's first name is stored in the database and you use the first name to personalize each page. Does that mean every time the user accesses a different page in your app, your code must query the database just to get the name?

REMEMBER

The first scenario is ineffective and the second is inefficient, so is there a better way? You bet there is: PHP sessions. In the PHP world, a *session* is the period that users spend interacting with a web app, no matter how many different app pages they navigate.

Starting a PHP session

You start a session by invoking the session_start() function:

```
session_start();
```

Once you've done that, the session remains active until the user closes the browser window. Your web server also specifies a maximum lifetime for a session, usually 1,440 seconds (24 minutes). You can check this by running echo phpinfo() and looking for the session.gc_maxlifetime value. You can work around this time-out in one of two ways:

» By adding the session_start() function to each page, which refreshes the session

» By running PHP's session_status() function, which returns the constant PHP_SESSION_NONE if the user doesn't have a current session

How does a session help you keep track of information about a user? By offering an array called $_SESSION, which you can populate with whatever values you want to track:

```
$_SESSION['start_time'] = time();
$_SESSION['user_first_name'] = 'Biff';
$_SESSION['logged_in'] = 1;
```

Securing a PHP session

A PHP session is a vital link between your users and your app because it enables you to store data that makes each user's experience easier, more efficient, and more seamless. However, because sessions are such a powerful tool, the world's dark-side hackers have come up with a number of ingenious ways to hijack user sessions and thereby gain access to session data.

A full tutorial on protecting your users from would-be session-stealers would require an entire book, but there's a relatively simple technique you can use to thwart all but the most tenacious villains. The technique involves a value called a *token*, which is a random collection of numbers and letters, usually 32 characters long. How does a token serve to keep a session secure? It's a three-step process:

1. When the session begins, generate a new token and store it in the $_SESSION array.

2. In each form used by your web app, include a hidden input field (that is, an <input> tag where the type attribute is set to hidden) and set the value of that field to the session's token value.

3. In your PHP script that processes the form data, compare the value of the form's hidden field with the token value stored in the $_SESSION array. If they're identical, it means the form submission is secure (that is, the form was submitted by the session user) and you can safely proceed. If they're different, however, it almost certainly means that an attacker was trying to pull a fast one and your code should stop processing the form data.

REMEMBER

You can create some random data in PHP in a bunch of ways, but a good one for our purposes is openssl_random_pseudo_bytes():

```
openssl_random_pseudo_bytes(length)
```

where *length* is an integer that specifies the number of random bytes you want returned.

The openssl_random_pseudo_bytes() function returns a string of random bytes, but byte values aren't much good to us. We need to convert the binary string to a hexadecimal string, and that's the job of PHP's bin2hex() function:

```
bin2hex(str)
```

where *str* is the binary string you want to convert.

For example, 16 bytes will convert to 32 hex characters, so you can use something like the following expression to generate a token:

```
bin2hex(openssl_random_pseudo_bytes(16));
```

This creates a value similar to the following:

```
387f90ce4b3d8f9bd7e4b38068c9fce3
```

For your session, you store the result in the $_SESSION array, like so:

```
$_SESSION['token'] = bin2hex(openssl_random_pseudo_bytes(16));
```

It's also good practice to generate a fresh token after a certain period of time has elapsed, say 15 minutes. To handle this, when the session starts you use the $_SESSION array to store the current time plus the expiration time:

```
$_SESSION['token_expires'] = time() + 900;
```

PHP's time() function returns the number of seconds since January 1, 1970, so adding 900 sets the expiration time to 15 minutes in the future. Your web app would then use each session refresh to check whether the token has expired:

```
if (time() > $_SESSION['token_expires']){
    $_SESSION['token'] =
bin2hex(openssl_random_pseudo_bytes(16));
    $_SESSION['token_expires'] = time() + 900;
}
```

Creating a Back-End Initialization File

When performing any task, a typical web app must first run through a number of back-end chores, including the following:

>> Setting the error reporting level

>> Starting a session for the current user, if one hasn't been started already

>> Creating a token for the session

>> Including common files, such as a file of constants used throughout the app

>> Connecting to the database, if the app uses server data

You can cram some or all of these chores into a back-end initialization file that you store in your web app's `private` directory. Here's an example (bk07ch04/ example06.php):

```php
<?php
    // Make sure we see all the errors and warnings
    error_reporting(E_ALL | E_STRICT);

    // Start a session
    session_start();

    // Have we not created a token for this session,
    // or has the token expired?
    if (!isset($_SESSION['token']) ||  time() > $_SESSION
['token_expires']){
        $_SESSION['token'] = bin2hex(openssl_random_
pseudo_bytes(16));
        $_SESSION['token_expires'] = time() + 900;
    }

    // Include the app constants
    include_once 'constants.php';

    // Connect to the database
    $mysqli = mysqli_connect(HOST, USER, PASSWORD, DATABASE);

    // Check for an error
    if(!$mysqli) {
        echo 'Connection Failed!
```

```
                    Error #' . mysqli_connect_errno()
                        . ': ' . mysqli_connect_error();
        exit(0);
    }
?>
```

This code cranks up the error reporting to 11 for the purposes of debugging, starts a new session, creates a session token (if needed), includes the constants file (which contains the database credentials), and then connects to the database and creates a MySQLi object.

To use this file, place the following PHP code at the top of all your web page files:

```
<?php
    include_once '../private/initialization.php';
?>
```

WARNING

You want to use error_reporting(E_ALL | E_STRICT) when you're developing your web app because you want the PHP processor to let you know when something's amiss, either as an error (E_ALL) or as non-standard PHP code (E_STRICT). However, you certainly don't want your app's users to see these errors or warnings, so when you're ready for your web app to go live, edit initialization.php to follow this statement:

```
error_reporting(E_ALL | E_STRICT)
```

with these statements:

```
ini_set('display_errors', 0);
ini_set('log_errors', 1);
ini_set('error_log', '../private/logs/error_log');
```

These statements configure PHP to not display errors onscreen but to log them to a file, the name and path of which is specified in the final statement.

Securing a Web App

Index

Symbols

A

JavaScript, 273–303
  anonymous functions, 286–290
  arrow functions, 290–292
  calling, 275–280
  defined, 274
  function scope, 297–298
  interval, 294–295
  overview, 273–274
  passing values to, 280–285
  placing, 275–276
  recursive functions, 299–303
  returning values from, 285–286
  structure of, 274–275
  timeout, 292–294
  variable scope, 295–299
PHP, 465–466
  overview, 465
  passing values to, 466
  returning value from, 466

G

Gasston, Peter, 595
Gates, Bill, 349
Geertz, Clifford, 423
generic fonts, 96–97
GET requests, 504–505, 584
getAttribute() method, 337
getDate() method, 398
getDay() method, 398
getFullYear() method, 398, 404
getHours() method, 398
getItem() method, 421
getMilliseconds() method, 398
getMinutes() method, 398
getMonth() method, 398–399
getSeconds() method, 398
getTime() method, 398, 408
GIF (Graphics Interchange Format) images, 74
GIT software, installing, 663
GitHub
  committing to changes, 668
  personal access token, 661–663

pushing changes, 668
pushing files to, 674–676
repository for book, 5
staging changes, 668
storing static web pages in, 660–668
  cloning repository, 665–667
  committing to changes, 668
  installing GIT software, 663
  personal access token, 661–663
  pushing changes, 668
  setting up account, 660–661
  setting up repository, 663–665
  staging changes, 668
global scope, JavaScript variables, 298–299
Gmail, 680
GoDaddy, 42
Goethe, Johann Wolfgang von, 23, 679
Google, 680
Google Fonts, 97
Google Maps, 680
Graphics Interchange Format (GIF) images, 74
greater than (>) operator, 229, 231, 243
greater than or equal (>=) operator, 229, 232, 243
grid containers, 171
grid gaps, 172–173
grid items
  aligning, 176–177
  assigning, 173–176
grid template, 171–172

H

<h1> to <h6> tags, 65–66
Harkaway, Nick, 629
:has pseudo-class, 113
Haverbeke, Marijn, 203
head property, 317
<head> tag, 58
<header> tag, 77–78
here document (heredoc) syntax, 452
hexadecimal integer values, 212
hierarchies, DOM, 315–316
Homebrew, 663

N

O

object (–›) operator, 470

object methods, 310–311

object POST requests, 585–586

objects

converting JSON string to JavaScript object, 418–419

document object model, 306–315

customizing, 311–314

defined, 306–307

object methods, 310–311

properties, 307–310

web APIs, 314–315

JavaScript, 429–432

PHP, 467–471

adding methods to class, 469

adding properties to class, 468–469

creating, 470

custom class, 467

methods, 471

properties, 470–471

online resources

accessibility

WAVE, 745

WebAIM Contrast Checker, 745

Alphabet, 680

Gmail, 680

Google, 680

Google Maps, 680

YouTube, 680

Apache Friends, 26, 31

Can I Use

container queries support levels, 708

range syntax support levels, 706

viewport unit support levels, 699

Cloudflare Pages, 675

CSS selector specificity calculator, 100

domain name services, 42

GoDaddy, 42

Register.com, 42

example used in book, 4–5

Flexbox, 165

FTP services, 49

CuteFTP, 49

Cyberduck, 49

FileZilla, 49

Transmit, 49

Git, 663

GitHub

accounts, 663

creating repositories, 660

repository for book, 5

Google Fonts, 97

Homebrew, 663

HTML Living Standard, 635

JSONLint, 416

Mozilla

ARIA roles, 737

Developer Network, 708

Netlify, 675

text editors, 37

Brackets, 37

Notepad++, 37

Nova, 37, 49

Sublime Text, 37

Visual Studio Code, 37

Web Dev Workshop, 100

web hosting providers, 45

CNET Web Hosting Solutions, 45

PC Magazine Web Site Hosting Services Revi, 45

Review Hell, 45

Review Signal Web Hosting Reviews, 45

WebDev Workshop, 5

XAMPP

Dashboard, 477

for OS X, 31

for Windows, 26

Xdebug, 563

operands, JavaScript, 218

operating systems

Unix systems

case-sensitive, 48

defined, 43

Windows systems

defined, 43

XAMPP for, 25–31

operators

-- (decrement) operator, 219, 223–224, 243

– (negation) operator, 219, 243

– (subtraction) operator, 219, 222, 243

! (NOT) logical operator, 238–240, 243

!= (inequality) operator, 229, 231, 243

!== (strict inequality) operator, 229, 235, 243

% (modulus) operator, 219, 225–226, 243

%= assignment operator, 220

&& (AND) logical operator, 238, 240–243, 252

* (multiplication) operator, 219, 224, 243

*= assignment operator, 220

. (property access) operator, 308

/ (division) operator, 104–105, 219, 224–225, 243

/= assignment operator, 220

?: (ternary) operator, 236–237, 243

^= assignment operator, 220

|| (OR) logical operator, 238, 239–243, 252

+ (addition) operator, 219, 220, 243

+ (concatenation) operator, 243

+ operator, 410–411

++ (increment) operator, 219, 220–222, 243

+= assignment operator, 220, 226

< (less than) operator, 229, 231–232, 243

< comparison operator, 489

<= (less than or equal) operator, 229, 232–233, 243

<= comparison operator, 489

<> comparison operator, 489

–= assignment operator, 220, 226

= comparison operator, 489

== (equality) operator, 229, 230, 243

=== (strict equality) operator, 229, 234, 243

> (greater than) operator, 229, 231, 243

> comparison operator, 489

>= (greater than or equal) operator, 229, 232, 243

>= comparison operator, 489

addition (+) operator, 219, 220, 243

BETWEEN...AND operator, 490

IS NULL operator, 491

LIKE operator, 490

NOT logical operator, 491

IN operator, 490

OR logical operator, 491

XOR logical operator, 491

OR (||) logical operator, 238–243, 252

OR logical operator, 491

ordered lists, 72–73

outer joins, MySQL, 493–497

outputting PHP data, 447–453

    adding line breaks, 448–449

    long strings, 451–453

    overview, 447–448

    quotation marks, 450

    variables in strings, 450–451

P

<p> tag, 16–17, 61

p1|p2 regular expression symbol, 635

padding, CSS box model, 128–129

page elements

    JavaScript, 556

    updating with fetched data, 580–584

page layout, CSS

    CSS box model, 134–136

    CSS Grid, 170–180

        aligning grid items, 176–177

        assigning grid items, 173–176

        grid container, 171

        grid gaps, 172–173

        grid template, 171–172

        laying out content columns with, 177–180

        overview, 170

    Flexbox, 152–170

        aligning flex items along primary axis, 156

        aligning flex items along secondary axis, 157–158

        centering elements, 158–160

        configuring flex items to grow, 161–163

        configuring flex items to shrink, 164–166

        flex container, 153–156

        laying out content columns with, 166–170

        navigation bar, 160–161

        overview, 152–153

    macro level, 152

    micro level, 152

    overview, 151–152

parameterized statements/queries, MySQL, 761–767

parent elements, 103

Y

About the Author

Paul McFedries is the president of Logophilia Limited, a technical writing company, and has worked with computers large and small since 1975. While now primarily a writer, Paul has worked as a programmer, consultant, database developer, and website developer. He has written more than 100 books that have sold over four million copies worldwide. Paul invites everyone to drop by his personal website at `https://paulmcfedries.com`, or to follow him on X (@paulmcf) or Facebook (`www.facebook.com/PaulMcFedries/`).

Dedication

I dedicated the first edition of this book to my recently deceased mother. If I was to then dedicate this second edition of the book to my recently passed father, I know what you'd say: "For crying out loud, man, stop working on this book!" I hear you, but I'm going to dedicate this edition to my dad anyway, who lived to the ripe old age of 95 and was relatively healthy and sharp even at that advanced age. Dad, you were an excellent role model right to the end! This one's for you.

Author's Acknowledgments

If we're ever at the same cocktail party and you overhear me saying something like "I wrote a book," I hereby give you permission to wag your finger at me and say "Tsk, tsk." Why the scolding? Because although I did write this book's text and take its screenshots, those represent only a part of what constitutes a "book." The rest of it is brought to you by the dedication and professionalism of Wiley's editing, graphics, and production teams, who toiled long and hard to turn my text and images into an actual book.

I offer my heartfelt thanks to everyone at Wiley who made this book possible, but I'd like to extend some special thank-you's to the folks I worked with directly: executive editor Steve Hayes, project manager and copy editor Susan Pink, proofreader Debbye Butler, and technical editor Guy-Hart Davis. I'd also like to give a big shout-out to my agent, Carole Jelen, for helping to make this project possible.

Publisher's Acknowledgments

Managing Editor: Sofia Malik
Copy Editor: Susan Pink
Project Editor: Susan Pink
Technical Editor: Guy Hart-Davis

Proofreader: Debbye Butler
Production Editor: Saikarthick Kumarasamy
Cover Image: © Weiquan Lin/Getty Images

Leverage the power

Dummies is the global leader in the reference category and one of the most trusted and highly regarded brands in the world. No longer just focused on books, customers now have access to the dummies content they need in the format they want. Together we'll craft a solution that engages your customers, stands out from the competition, and helps you meet your goals.

Advertising & Sponsorships

Connect with an engaged audience on a powerful multimedia site, and position your message alongside expert how-to content. Dummies.com is a one-stop shop for free, online information and know-how curated by a team of experts.

- Targeted ads
- Video
- Email Marketing
- Microsites
- Sweepstakes sponsorship

20 MILLION PAGE VIEWS EVERY SINGLE MONTH

15 MILLION UNIQUE VISITORS PER MONTH

43% OF ALL VISITORS ACCESS THE SITE VIA THEIR MOBILE DEVICES

700,000 NEWSLETTER SUBSCRIPTIONS TO THE INBOXES OF

300,000 UNIQUE INDIVIDUALS EVERY WEEK

# of dummies

Custom Publishing

Reach a global audience in any language by creating a solution that will differentiate you from competitors, amplify your message, and encourage customers to make a buying decision.

- Apps
- Books
- eBooks
- Video
- Audio
- Webinars

Brand Licensing & Content

Leverage the strength of the world's most popular reference brand to reach new audiences and channels of distribution.

For more information, visit **dummies.com/biz**

PERSONAL ENRICHMENT

Staying Sharp
9781119187790
USA $26.00
CAN $31.99
UK £19.99

Facebook
9781119179030
USA $21.99
CAN $25.99
UK £16.99

Guitar
9781119293354
USA $24.99
CAN $29.99
UK £17.99

Investing
9781119293347
USA $22.99
CAN $27.99
UK £16.99

Beekeeping
9781119310068
USA $22.99
CAN $27.99
UK £16.99

Digital Photography
9781119235606
USA $24.99
CAN $29.99
UK £17.99

Meditation
9781119251163
USA $24.99
CAN $29.99
UK £17.99

Pregnancy
9781119235491
USA $26.99
CAN $31.99
UK £19.99

Samsung Galaxy S7
9781119279952
USA $24.99
CAN $29.99
UK £17.99

iPhone
9781119283133
USA $24.99
CAN $29.99
UK £17.99

Crocheting
9781119287117
USA $24.99
CAN $29.99
UK £16.99

Nutrition
9781119130246
USA $22.99
CAN $27.99
UK £16.99

PROFESSIONAL DEVELOPMENT

Windows 10
9781119311041
USA $24.99
CAN $29.99
UK £17.99

AutoCAD
9781119255796
USA $39.99
CAN $47.99
UK £27.99

Excel 2016
9781119293439
USA $26.99
CAN $31.99
UK £19.99

QuickBooks 2017
9781119281467
USA $26.99
CAN $31.99
UK £19.99

macOS Sierra
9781119280651
USA $29.99
CAN $35.99
UK £21.99

LinkedIn
9781119251132
USA $24.99
CAN $29.99
UK £17.99

Windows 10
9781119310563
USA $34.00
CAN $41.99
UK £24.99

SharePoint 2016
9781119181705
USA $29.99
CAN $35.99
UK £21.99

Fundamental Analysis
9781119263593
USA $26.99
CAN $31.99
UK £19.99

Networking
9781119257769
USA $29.99
CAN $35.99
UK £21.99

Office 2016
9781119293477
USA $26.99
CAN $31.99
UK £19.99

Office 365
9781119265313
USA $24.99
CAN $29.99
UK £17.99

Salesforce.com
9781119239314
USA $29.99
CAN $35.99
UK £21.99

Coding
9781119293323
USA $29.99
CAN $35.99
UK £21.99

dummies.com

dummies®
A Wiley Brand